001313474   HDQ

D0090574

DATE DUE			
MAR 8 01			
APR 27 01			
MAY 14 01			
JUN 2 01			
JUN 23 01			
DEC 26 01			

01/01

JACKSON COUNTY
Library Services

HEADQUARTERS
413 West Main Street
Medford, Oregon 97501

ALSO BY MERYLE SECREST

Between Me and Life: A Biography of Romaine Brooks
Being Bernard Berenson
Kenneth Clark: A Biography
Salvador Dalí

Frank Lloyd Wright

Frank Lloyd Wright

by

MERYLE SECREST

New York   Alfred A. Knopf   1993

JACKSON COUNTY LIBRARY SERVICES
MEDFORD OREGON 97501

THIS IS A BORZOI BOOK
PUBLISHED BY ALFRED A. KNOPF, INC.

Copyright © 1992 by Meryle Secrest Beveridge
All rights reserved under International and Pan-American Copyright
Conventions. Published in the United States by Alfred A. Knopf,
Inc., New York, and simultaneously in Canada by Random House
of Canada Limited, Toronto. Distributed by Random House, Inc.,
New York.

Grateful acknowledgment is made for permission to quote from
the letters of Frank Lloyd Wright, © the Frank Lloyd Wright Foundation 1992, and courtesy of the Frank Lloyd Wright Archives; to
Sophia Mumford for permission to quote from the letters of the late
Lewis Mumford; to Robert, Oliver and Nicholas Gillham for permission to quote from "The Valley of the God-Almighty Joneses"
by Maginel Wright Barney; to the Milwaukee Journal for permission
to quote from "The Romance of Miriam Wright"; to Aimee Humphreys for permission to quote from an unpublished memoir by her
mother, Babette Eddleston; to Alan Crawford, for permission to quote
from his unpublished letter; to Mosette Broderick, executor of the
estate, for permission to quote from an unpublished letter by Henry-
Russell Hitchcock; to Felicity Ashbee, for permission to quote from
the letters and journals of C. R. and Janet Ashbee; to Carter H.
Manny, Jr., for permission to quote from his unpublished letter; to
Eric Lloyd Wright, president of Unity Chapel, Inc., for permission
to quote from "Trilogy" and "Heritage" and the unpublished letters
of his father, Frank Lloyd Wright, Jr.; to Mrs. Howard J. Barnett
for permission to quote from "The Lloyd Letters and Memorial Book";
and to the Frank Lloyd Wright Foundation for permission to quote
from Olgivanna Lloyd Wright's letter to Mrs. Andrew Porter.

ISBN 0-394-56436-7
LC 92-53168

Manufactured in the United States of America
Published September 9, 1992
Reprinted Three Times
Fifth Printing, January 1993

JACKSON COUNTY LIBRARY SERVICES
MEDFORD OREGON 97501

In memory of my father,
ALBERT EDWARD DOMAN (1904–1983)
who wanted to be an architect

Whoso would be a man must be a nonconformist.

—RALPH WALDO EMERSON

Contents

Contents

Acknowledgments

This book's scope has been greatly enlarged by the new availability of the archive of photographs, drawings, letters, books and other materials assembled by Frank Lloyd Wright and inherited by members of his Memorial Foundation.

Until recently this largest single source of information about the architect's life was, largely for practical reasons having to do with the size of the archive and the cost of maintaining a research facility, limited to specialists working in well-defined areas.

As the result of a grant from the Getty Foundation, the total archive of over one hundred thousand letters, documents and other materials has been placed on microfiche and completely indexed. It is now available for study at the Getty Center Archives for the History of Art and the Humanities in Santa Monica, California, which has a first-class research facility, as well as at the Frank Lloyd Wright Memorial Foundation in Scottsdale, Arizona. Even though three volumes of the architect's letters are now in print, the size of the archive has meant that only highlights of the correspondence could be touched upon, leaving the vast majority unexplored until now.

The collection, believed to be the largest of its kind assembled by an architect in modern times, begins in 1886 with a handwritten letter by Wright, then an apprentice architect aged nineteen, to his uncle, Jenkin Lloyd Jones, and ends shortly before his death in 1959. The archive is more complete after 1925, when Wright began to keep carbons of all his letters, than it is before that date, when he often wrote letters in longhand and kept no copies or, at best, retained only a draft of a letter, much amended and incomplete. Correspondence concerning his early architectural practice has also been lost, perhaps as a result of the many fires at Taliesin over the decades. Similarly, there are no letters to or from Wright's father, William Carey Wright, or his side of the family. The archive does include a large group of letters from his mother and sisters, and letters from Lloyd Jones family members who played important roles in his life. There are several letters to him from his second wife, Miriam Noel Wright, but none by his first wife, Catherine, and only one or two by his third wife, Olgivanna.

Wright was not only a dedicated letter keeper but also a talented letter writer, with a lifelong preference for paper rather than a telephone as a satisfying outlet for self-expression. Consequently his dispatches—on occasion, brickbats—paint a broad and vivid portrait of his thoughts and feelings over the decades. They also reveal the way he set about realizing his goals, demonstrating enormous resourcefulness and considerable advance planning. The tone was so idiosyncratic and singular that, paradoxically, it became predictable. One of the bons mots ascribed to Wright's principal secretary, Eugene Masselink, was that he could write as good a Wright letter as Wright himself. Be that as it may, the existence of this lively, opinionated and self-revelatory archive is the kind of treasure a biographer rarely encounters, as good a substitute for having known someone personally as could be hoped for.

I am indebted to Dr. Nicholas Olsberg, then director of the Getty Center Archives for the History of Art, Gene Waddell, associate archivist, and their staff, for making my stay at Santa Monica and work in the archives so delightful and in offering me every kind of courtesy and help. I am equally grateful for the many courtesies extended me by Bruce Brooks Pfeiffer, archivist of the Frank Lloyd Wright Memorial Foundation in Scottsdale. I particularly want to express my appreciation and thanks for the many hours spent on my behalf by Richard Carney, chief executive officer and managing trustee, who not only gave me numerous interviews but made introductions, wrote letters, offered suggestions and more than once treated me to the famous Taliesin hospitality. I would like to express my great gratitude to the Foundation for its generosity in granting me copyright permissions and for refraining from asking any conditions in return for this remarkable privilege. I am enormously indebted to it. I want especially to record my debt to the late William Wesley Peters, chairman of the board of trustees and raconteur par excellence, for his inimitable descriptions of the Fellowship's early days. I also wish to thank other members of the Taliesin Foundation who kindly allowed themselves to be interviewed: Cornelia Brierly, Tony Puttnam, Charles and Minerva Montooth, Joe Fabris, Dr. Joseph Rorke, Kenneth Burton

Lockhart, Susan Jacobs Lockhart, Heloise Crista, Kay Rattenbury, E. Thomas Casey, Effi Bantzer Casey and the former development director, Elaine Freed.

Members of Frank Lloyd Wright's family have been just as generous with their time, granting interviews followed up by lengthy telephone discussions and letters, as well as giving me access to private family papers and photographs. I am most of all appreciative of the many kindnesses extended to me by Wright's son, David Samuel Wright, and his wife, Gladys, who is the family archivist and ultimate authority on these matters. They invited me to their home, showed me their archives and provided me with important materials. I am also indebted to Iovanna Lloyd Wright, who readily granted me interviews and spoke to me at length about her childhood and young womanhood. I wish to thank Mrs. Robert Llewellyn Wright, who also gave me interviews and went through her photographic and other files on my behalf with patience and good humor. I am especially grateful to Franklin Wright Porter and his charming wife, Mary, who were my hosts for a fascinating weekend spent in long conversations and a lengthy perusal of their own extensive files on his uncle's life; to Elizabeth Wright Ingraham, who also entertained me regally and patiently answered my endless questions; to Mr. and Mrs. Eric Lloyd Wright, for their invaluable insights and for making available copies of Wright's letters to Frank Lloyd Wright, Jr.; to Rupert Pole, another grandson, for his generous help and many kindnesses; to Jenkin Lloyd Jones, son of Richard Lloyd Jones, who stepped in with vital help at a crucial moment; to his sister, Florence L. J. ("Bisser") Barnett, who was equally indulgent about my demands upon her time and help; to her daughter, Heidi Kiser; and to Mrs. Stuart Natof, daughter of Frances Lloyd Wright Caroë, who gave me important insights into her mother's life.

I am also indebted to those men and women who knew Wright and whose memories stretched back many decades, including John H. Howe and Lu Sparks Howe, who have taken endless trouble on my behalf and read my manuscript at an early stage; to Edgar Tafel, another early apprentice, for his kindly encouragement and helpful suggestions; to yet another charter apprentice, Elizabeth Kassler, for her unique reminiscences and her extraordinary hospitality and many kindnesses; and to Wright's old friends in Spring Green, including Robert Graves, Herbert and Eloise Fritz, Frances and Cary Caraway, who were equally generous with their time and help. I am especially grateful to Mr. and Mrs. Robert Graves, who invariably found a place for me to stay in Spring Green, sometimes on very short notice. I want to give my special thanks to the author Svetlana Alliluyeva, the second Mrs. William Wesley Peters, with whom I spent several days and who was unstintingly generous with her time and help. If her memories play a minor part in the story, it is only because her appearance at Taliesin postdates the chronological scope of this book. I would be remiss if I did not acknowledge the extraordinarily generous attitude of other specialists in Wright's oeuvre, such as the biographer Robert Twombly, who gave me cordial advice and much encouragement; to William Allin Storrer, author of the definitive catalogue of Wright's works; to Robert L. Sweeney, author of another indispensable guide, an annotated bibliography; to Prof. Thomas S. Hines, an early investigator of the maze of Wright's life; to Jonathan Lipman, author of an authoritative study of Wright's Johnson Wax buildings, who listened to my ideas with endless patience and gave constructive criticisms; and to Kathryn Smith, author of essays on Fallingwater, the Imperial Hotel, Hollyhock House and many other landmark studies, who gave me the benefit of her meticulous expertise. I wish to record my special thanks to my former colleague at the *Washington Post*, Wolf von Eckardt, who encouraged me at an early stage and gave me valuable advice about what to look for; to another dear friend, Sarah Booth Conroy, the *Washington Post's* columnist and astute observer of the Taliesin scene; and to Arthur Colt Holden, who treated me to some wonderful reminiscences and a delightful weekend in the Connecticut countryside. I also want to thank Frederick Gutheim, the distinguished architectural historian and scholar, for his patient and generous help at every stage and for listening to my ideas with humor and insights.

Invaluable help was given by those who were also willing to be interviewed, including Maria and Lynn A. Arbeen; Mrs. Russell Bletzer, niece of Wright's first wife, Catherine, who gave me important information; Mosette Broderick, executor of the Henry-Russell Hitchcock estate; Mrs. Joseph Brody and Mrs. Joy Corson, former residents of the Cheney House; Bill Calvert; Norma Noel Cawthon; Mr. and Mrs. Ralph Chalk of Blaenralltddu, Dyfed, Wales; Celia Clevenger; Mrs. Maurice J. Costello; Isabelle Doyle; Rod Duell; Jack Dunbar; Babette Eddleston, who provided me with a copy of her delightful memoir; Scott Elliott; Mrs. Charles Farnsley; Richard L. Feigen; Michael Findlay; Professor Kristine Ottesen Garrigan; Richard P. Goldman; Professor Thomas E. Graham; Professor Robert Gutman; Thomas

Heath; David W. Hicks, Jr.; Virginia Kazor, curator of Hollyhock House; Sandra Wilcoxon, Donald Kalec and Meg Klinkow of the Frank Lloyd Wright Home and Studio; Mrs. Joseph F. Johnston; Anthony Jones; Lydia Kaim; Eleanor Tobin Kenney; Doris Murray Kuhns; Lawrence C. Lemmon; Professor Marya Czarnecka-Lilien; Garnett McCoy of the Archives of American Art; Elizabeth McKee; Randall L. Makinson; Rev. and Mrs. Aubrey J. Martin; Ben Masselink; Peter and Mary Matthews; Mrs. Ernest Meyer; Karl E. Meyer; Margaret M. Mills, executive director of the American Academy and Institute of Arts and Letters; Mya Moran; Mrs. Lewis Mumford; Jan Furey Muntz; Virginia Nix; Elizabeth Gordon; John O'Hern, resident curator, Darwin D. Martin residence; Verna Ross Orndorff; Mimi Perloff; Prof. Pat Pinnell; Loren B. Pope; Prof. Jack Quinan; Henry Hope Reed; Mr. and Mrs. O. P. Reed, Jr.; Hope Rogers; Nathaniel Sample; Frank Sanchis of the National Trust for Historic Preservation; William H. Short, F.A.I.A.; Louise Averill Svendsen; Jo Tartt; Lisa Suter Taylor, director of the Cooper-Hewitt Museum; Felicia Van Veen, former director of the American Academy and Institute of Arts and Letters; Marcus Weston; Dr. F. Joseph Whelan; Richard Wolford; Jean Kennedy Wolford; Dr. Harry Wood; and Helmut Ziehe.

I also wish to thank those who proffered help, sent me clippings, books, photographs, reminiscences, articles, and made themselves available in endless ways: Henry Allen; Dr. Anthony Alofsin; James Atlas; Felicity Ashbee; Carolyn Backlund; Barbara Ballinger; Loretta Barrett; Helen J. Bass; Marc C. Bellassai; Elizabeth Bennett; Prof. Barry Bergdoll; Prof. Curtis Besinger; Paul Bierman-Lytle; A. G. Blackmore; Barbara Branden; James Breslin; Prof. H. Allen Brooks; Sylvia Burack; Elsie Carper; Anthony Carroll; Mrs. William Cass; Mr. and Mrs. Leslie Cheek, Jr.; Emmett D. Chisum; Victor Cohn; Chuck Conconi; Henry F. S. Cooper; Alan Crawford; Dr. George Crile, Jr.; Nancy Davis; Mitchell H. Dazey; Marian A. Despres; Prof. Leonard Eaton; Ross Edman; Dr. Harvey Einbinder; Bob Eisenhardt; Anne Ellis; Cynthia Fokakis; Phil H. Feddersen; Ann ffolliott; Jeannette Fields; Benjamin Forgey; the late Peter Fuller; Rev. Neil W. Gerdes; Neil Giffe; Jackie Glidden; Rev. P. B. Godfrey; Herman Gordon; Pedro Guerrero; Peter Gubin; Frances Benn Hall; Dr. Donald Hallmark; Dr. Michael A. Halls; Mary Jane Hamilton; David A. Hanks; Georgiana Hansen; Lily Harmon; Kay Henriksen; Prof. Mark Heyman; Joseph Holland; Thomas Howarth; John Patrick Hunter, associate editor of the *Madison Capital Times*; William Jerousek; Prof. Ellen

Johnson; Philip Johnson; Lewis Kachur; Prof. Vladimir Karfik; Dr. and Mrs. Louis Kaufman; the late Edgar Kaufmann, Jr.; Mr. and Mrs. Al Koch; the late David Lloyd Kreeger; Phyllis Lambert, director, Centre Canadien d'Architecture; David P. Lanferman; Esther M. Lloyd Jones; Ruth Lloyd Jones Leader; Jean Battey Lewis; Dr. E. James Lieberman; Dr. Vera Leikina-Svirskaya; Ron Larson; Lee Lescaze; Sherry Gillette Lewis; Serge Logan; Mrs. Mary Lutyens; Richard MacCormac, R.I.B.A.; the late Prof. Esther McCoy; Jerry and Nan McCoy; Carter Manny, Jr.; Grant Carpenter Manson; Luis Marden; William Marlin; R. Russell Maylone; Julia Meech-Pekarik; Prof. Narciso G. Menocal; Corinna Metcalf; R. Craig Miller; Waler Mocak; Prof. William Morgan; Jan Morris; Dorothy T. Mueller; the late Noverre Musson; Vincent Newton; Kenneth M. Nishimoto; Dr. Francis V. O'Connor; Leo Orso; Mrs. Dudley Owen; Peter Palumbo; Andrew Patrick; W. E. Pelegrino; Dr. and Mrs. Joseph Perloff; Mrs. Melva Phillips; Kathleen M. Raab; Proctor K. Raab; Mrs. Robert Richman; Rona Roob; Ruth A. Ruege; Richard W. Sackett; Helga Sandburg; Nils M. Schweizer, F.A.I.A.; Anita Shower; Gordon Sinykin of LaFollette and Sinykin Law Offices; Roy Slade, president, Cranbrook Academy of Art; Joan Shockey; Dale Smirl; Jeanne F. Smith; Mrs. Kenneth Paul Snoke; Prof. Paul Sprague; Gavin Stamp; Phil Stern; Audrey Stevenson; Mrs. Alexander Stoller; Diana Strazdes; Seán Sweeney; Roy R. Thomas; Anne Thompson; Prof. Franklin K. Toker; Mary C. Ternes; Harriet Tyson; John Vinci; Gretchen Wagner; William B. Walker, chief librarian, Thomas J. Watson Library, Metropolitan Museum of Art; Phyllis Wexler; Mary Lou White; David Wigdor; Burke Wilkinson; Michael Wilson; Marion V. Winters; Wim de Wit; Dr. Philip Zabriskie; and Madame Olivier Ziegel.

Among those universities, newspaper archives, private galleries, historical societies, libraries, museums and like institutions that have made material available for this study I wish to extend a special word of gratitude to Dr. Harold L. Miller and the staff of the State Historical Society of Wisconsin for giving me access to that institution's archive, with its major collection of materials about Wright's life and times. I would also like to thank Shonnie Finnegan, archivist of the State University of New York at Buffalo for her many kindnesses while I was studying her archive's important collection of letters between W. E. and Darwin D. Martin and Frank Lloyd Wright. I would also like to thank Margaret J. Kimball, manuscript librarian at Stanford University, whose institution also owns part of this collection, for coming to my aid at a crucial moment.

Other institutions that have permitted me to study in their archives, answered queries, sent material and helped in various ways are the Albright-Knox Art Gallery, the Allentown Art Museum, the American Academy and Institute of Arts and Letters, the American Institute of Architects Library, Andover-Harvard Theological Library, the Architectural Association (London) Library, the *Architectural Record*, the *Architectural Review*, the Archives of American Art, the Arizona Biltmore Hotel, the Art Institute of Chicago, the Arts Club of Chicago, the Avery Architectural Library (Columbia University), the Beinecke Rare Book and Manuscript Library (Yale), the Buffalo and Erie County Historical Society, the Carnegie Institute, the *Chicago Tribune* Library, the Chicago Historical Society, the Cooper-Hewitt Museum, Cornell University Libraries, the Courtauld Institute, the Cranbrook Academy of Art, the Dana-Thomas House, the Circuit Court of Dane County (Wisconsin), the Elvehjm Museum of Art, Fallingwater, the Fine Art Society, Florida Southern College, Leslie Hindman Auctioneers, Hirshl and Adler Modern Galleries, the Frank Lloyd Wright Home and Studio, the *Home News* of Spring Green, the Houghton Library (Harvard), the Houston Public Library, the Humanities Research Center (University of Texas), S. C. Johnson and Company, the Kelmscott Galleries, the *Madison Capital Times* Library, the Martin Luther King Library, the Los Angeles Public Library, the Library of Congress, Meadville/Lombard Theological School, the Metropolitan Museum of Art, the Meyer May House, the *Milwaukee Journal* Library, the Milwaukee Public Library, the *Minneapolis Star and Tribune* Library, the Museum of Modern Art, the National Building Museum Archives, the National Gallery of Art Library, the National Portrait Gallery, the National Trust for Historic Preservation, the Nederlands Documentatiecentrum voor de Bouwkunst, the New York Public Library, Northwestern University Library, Oak Park Public Library, Princeton University Library, the Max Protetch Gallery, the Royal Institute of British Architects, the Schindler House, Southern Illinois University, the State Historical Society of Iowa, Temple Hoyne Buell Center for the Study of American Architecture at Columbia University, the University of California at Los Angeles, the University of California at Santa Barbara, the University of Chicago Library, the University of Illinois at Urbana-Champaign Library, the Kenneth Spencer Research Library (University of Kansas), the University of Leicester Library, the University of Oregon Library, the University of Rochester Library, the University of Wales Press, the University of Wyoming American Heritage Center, Wayne State University Archives of Labor and Urban

Affairs, the University of Wisconsin (Platteville) Library, the *Washington Post* Library and Photo Department, and the University of Wyoming Library.

As I have discovered in the past, tackling some biographical subjects is rather like taking a firm grip on a fistful of nettles. This book, as I hope I have made clear, has been an unqualified joy to write, not just because I have been in the stimulating company of one of the world's great architects, but also because so many of his friends and specialists in his work went out of their way to help. I must also mention A. Douglas Jones, retired professor of architecture at Bristol University, twelve miles from my birthplace, whom I have not met but who took a benevolent interest in my work from the start. He and his son, David, a gifted photographer, made two trips to Wales to take pictures, on my behalf, of scenes I had hastily documented myself and with far less expertise. Several of them appear in this book, along with my warm thanks and deep appreciation. My researchers, Gene Gerard, Jennifer Baumann and Robin Weindruch, went out of their way to track down elusive materials and did so with tenacious zeal. This book would not have been written had it not been for my agent, Murray Pollinger, who would not let me give up hope, and upon whose sage advice I entirely rely. I am delighted that Robert A. Gottlieb took a kindly interest in my project before he left Alfred A. Knopf for *The New Yorker*. Victoria A. Wilson, my editor, has stimulated and encouraged me in what Bernard Berenson termed a "life enhancing" spirit, and Carmen Callil of Chatto and Windus has given me the benefit of her talent, energy and editorial intelligence. As for the work itself, paraphrasing Somerset Maugham, there are three rules for writing biography but, unfortunately, no one knows what they are. So, while I have sobbed and struggled, my husband, Thomas G. Beveridge, has performed the inestimable service of listening. "And if my selfe have leave to see, I need not their light, having thee."

Frank Lloyd Wright

i

Bedd Taliesin:
Taliesin's Grave

Fate has smashed these wonderful walls,
This broken city, has crumbled the work
Of giants. The roofs are gutted, the towers
Fallen, the gates ripped off, frost
In the mortar, everything moulded, gaping,
Collapsed.

"The Ruin"
Poems from the Old English

In a quiet family graveyard adjoining a field of Wisconsin corn, a tombstone marks the spot where Frank Lloyd Wright, architect, was buried in the spring of 1959. The grave is empty.

All around it are the neatly tended graves of his grandparents, his uncles and aunts, his mother, his sons and daughters, his comrades and their dead. A stone marks the grave of Richard Lloyd Jones, "Ein Tad," founder of the clan, the grand old man who was born in Wales before the turn of the nineteenth century. There is an identical marker for his wife, Mary Thomas, "Mallie," known as "Ein Mam," mother of eleven children and grandmother, when she died in 1870, of the three-year-old named Frank Wright. All around these pioneer immigrants lie their children: Thomas, John, Margaret, Mary, James, Enos, Nell and Jen, whom everyone called "the Aunts," and "Our Jenkin," the son who became a famous Unitarian minister in Chicago.

There is even a memorial for "Nanny," the little girl who died at the age of three as they made their way across the United States. The grave of Frank Wright's mother, Hannah, or Anna, as she preferred to be called, is also well marked. ("She loved the truth and sought it.") There are the graves of her two daughters, Maginel and Jane, of her grandchildren (most of Frank's children by his first wife, Catherine: John, Catherine, Frances and Robert Llewellyn). There is even a grave for Wright's murdered lover, a single stone under an immense evergreen, tilted and covered with moss. As for the grave of the architect, it is more prominent than any of the others. A semicircle of flowers, neatly tended, surrounds a planting of shrubbery, a single marking stone and the words "Love of an idea is love of God." One might almost suspect a tacit agreement to continue treating this particular spot as if Wright's grave had never been opened and his mortal remains removed.

Two stone pillars support a gate, and a path leads directly to the main entrance of the chapel beside the graveyard, hardly discernible beneath the penumbral shade of a heavy porch. Few come here nowadays, and perhaps no one remembers what happened to the fence, or wall, or whether there was a fence. No boundaries define the chapel's grounds. There is only a faint smell of mold; piles of wet clippings are left to decompose in matted clumps on the grass.

Whenever one goes there, Unity Chapel always appears to be in shadow. The impression is perhaps attributable to the generous overhanging roof, which tends to dwarf the modest windows of the one-floor building, or perhaps to the matte texture of the wine-red shingled exterior, which seems to soak up and absorb light. Or perhaps the stands of motionless fir trees, with their ragged, entwining shapes, were planted by Uncle Thomas Lloyd Jones so as to deflect the sun's rays at any hour of day. Some stubborn trompe l'oeil factor is at work here, for Unity Chapel, standing as it does beside a road on open ground in the Helena Valley (usually known as "The Valley") in Iowa County near Spring Green, surrounded by fields, ought to be instantly identifiable. Nevertheless its features are as blurred and indistinct as those in a painting by René Magritte in which, despite a sky of azure blue, buildings huddle in darkness on a deserted street.

The valley to which Frank Lloyd Wright's grandparents came and settled is inside the "Driftless Area" of Wisconsin, so called because it was protected, by hills to the north, from the great Wisconsin Ice Sheet, which swept south from the Arctic during the glacial epoch.

As a result, the vast plains and spectacular gorges left behind by the dwindling ice sheets are not characteristic of this particular landscape. Instead, there are the pianissimo charms of winding roads, closely linked hills and narrow valleys reminiscent of the tidy, neat little island from which the Lloyd Joneses had come. By the time they arrived in The Valley, many other Welsh, Cornish and Irish immigrants were already in the area, attracted by the fertile soils and "mineral" (galena, or lead ore) that had been found at Mineral Point in 1827. Some of the world's best hard-rock miners, the Cornish copper and tin workers, brought with them a knowledge of stone-cutting and masonry that they put to use in building new cottages not very far from The Valley. There were Welsh settlements all about: in Spring Green, Arena, Barneveld, Ridgeway, Dodgeville, Madison and Baraboo, to name a few. One of the first chapels, Peniel, in Pecatonica, near The Valley, was built in 1850. In the middle 1850s there were more Welsh, Scots and English in Milwaukee than Germans.

What must have also looked familiar and reassuring to the early Welsh settlers in The Valley were the outcroppings of natural limestone on the crests of the hills. "[T]hey assume configurations of great mystery and variety, astonishingly similar to rude stone monuments found in Celtic Britain. Menhirs, or freestanding stones, stand as sentinels on the hillsides; cromlechs, or balanced stones, appear in the valley floors, and rock outcroppings on the crests of hills open to form caves, becoming natural dolmens or ritual mounds." There were prairie grasses growing on open land, poplars and willows in the rich bottomland, and a forest of elm, maple, basswood, walnut, birch and hazel on the upper slopes. As Wright was to recall, "[H]e went through the moist woods that in their shade were treasuring the rainfall for the sloping fields below or to feed the clear springs in the ravines, wending his way along the ridges of the hills gay with Indian-pinks or shooting-stars, across wide meadows carpeted thick with tall grass on which the flowers seemed to float." Two decades after the family had settled in The Valley, Anna's boy had found, as Mircea Eliade wrote, that "the place is never 'chosen' by man; it is merely discovered by him; . . . the sacred place in some way reveals itself."

For years before the chapel was built, the land on which it stands was a gathering place for birthday parties, weddings, funerals and Unitarian Grove meetings. Jenkin Lloyd Jones, the son who became a minister, might give the "Gospel for To-day," a professor from a church in Minneapolis might speak on "True Radicalism," and the editor of the magazine *Unity* might lecture about "Cups of Cold Water." Teams of horses would arrive until fifty or more were tethered under the trees. Soon all manner of prose tracts were being passed out, along with a hundred hymn books. "[T]he great canvas from the hay-ricks became a Tabernacle for the day; ferns drooped and tall flowers glowed to make it beautiful; and at the open sides the meadow, the stream, the golden slopes and the hills beyond became church walls and frescoes." Then enormously long pine-board tables would be set up, and each family would unload hampers filled to the brim with sumptuous offerings. In his autobiography Wright recalled with the nostalgia of an indomitable appetite all that wholesome, substantial country fare: the roasted, stuffed chickens, the boiled hams, the hard-boiled eggs, the cucumbers you peeled and ate like bananas, the doughnuts smothered in sugar, the apple and pumpkin pies, the cakes and cookies of every scrumptious variety. All this was well washed down with milk (if you were young) and coffee (if you were old enough). There were no hampers of beer, wine or the like for the Temperance Joneses.

Open-air meetings, however, would never be enough. As the Welsh in America used to say, "The first thing a Frenchman does in a new country is to build a trading post, an American builds a city, a German builds a beer hall, and a Welshman builds a church." And, although he does not mention it in his autobiography, Wright, a mere adolescent at that stage, was ambitiously determined to build a chapel for his family himself. In the summer of 1885, when it became clear that Richard Lloyd Jones, at age eighty-six, was failing ("The near world was growing dim and distant to his eyes; but the Welsh village that he left forty years . . . ago lay bright and clear as in the sunlight"), Uncle Jenkin began to organize a building campaign. The family planned to build a modest three-room church with a tiny kitchen in one corner, to hold two hundred souls at the maximum, something homelike and pretty that would not disfigure the hills with "another stiff church-box" and that could be erected for $1,000 to $1,200.

Wright had just turned eighteen, was enrolled in the school of engineering at the University of Wisconsin in Madison, the state capital, some fifty miles away, and was apprenticed to an engineer specializing in heating, ventilation, sewers and drains. At once he sent off his sketches for the new building. "I have simply made them in pencil on a peice [*sic*] of old paper but the idea is my own and I have copied from nothing," he wrote. "Any changes which you may think proper or anything to be taken off if you will let me know I will make it satisfy you. . . . Wise & I have figured it up & it can be built for 10 or 12 hundred." He signed himself, "Aff. your nephew, F. Wright." Uncle Jenkin preferred the experienced pencil of his favorite architect, J. Lyman Silsbee, whom he had already engaged to build a new church, All Souls, for his Chicago parish. But F. Wright, young, eager, willing to learn, was allowed to help oversee construction of Unity Chapel. Once completed, the "cottage-church," as it was called, was a much-simplified version of the picturesque shingle style in which Silsbee specialized. Exterior shingles were a mottled brown, and the roof was dark red. Its two main rooms were an "audience room" to hear the sermons, with four rocking chairs thoughtfully provided for the older folk, and a "parlor" beyond to seat an overflow crowd, the two rooms separated only by a heavy curtain. It was said that the "boy architect" in the family had designed the interior decor. The ceilings were calcimined, one in terra-cotta and the other in olive green, colors that Wright much favored in later years. John H. Howe, who was his chief draftsman for almost thirty years, said, "He always claimed that the ceiling, which is designed in squares, was his own invention." If true, this would have been Frank Lloyd Wright's first architectural undertaking.

The chapel was opened in the summer of 1886, a few months after the death of Richard Lloyd Jones. It was dedicated to "Freedom, Fellowship and Character in Religion." Henry M. Simmons gave the dedication address. Then Jenkin Lloyd Jones, speaking first in Welsh, then in English, recalled that, in his days at Meadville School, some eighteen years before, he had organized his first church in the school-house nearby and had preached his first sermon there. Now at last he was speaking in their own church-home, and dedicating it to "the Truth which maketh free, to the Righteousness which maketh clean the heart . . . to the sanctity of home ties, to the honoring of our country, to an ever-growing Christianity, and to thanksgiving to the Father and his worship."

After that, Wright recalled the long summer Sundays when he and his cousins would get up early to collect great armfuls of branches, grasses, ferns and wildflowers and transform the severely plain interior into a conservatory. He would sit in his city clothes watching his uncles and aunts, their hair now gray, rocking quietly in a circle around the pulpit. The windows would be wide open, and so would the doors. Uncle Jenkin would be reaching a climactic moment and his audience would be in tears, something that always puzzled him: "they weep most when everything is best!" he wrote. Then they would be singing a familiar Welsh hymn with the brave words "step by step since time began we see the steady gain of man." Wright would look out of the windows, imagining the words swelling out across The Valley, reaching over the hills into the distance. He thought of battles to come, of victory and exaltation, while the old people around him wept again, perhaps from *hiraeth*, or longing.

To the visitor nowadays Unity Chapel is simply a melancholic stop on the compulsory tour of buildings and places in and around this verdant, still-unspoiled valley that mark the stages in Frank Lloyd Wright's life. As a boy he worked in and wandered over his uncles' farms; as a man, he built Taliesin, a grand—the grandest—house in The Valley, one that overlooked all of his land and theirs. To see the chapel as a relic is, however, to miss its importance in the life of the Lloyd Joneses and, also, in Wright's life. When he was born in 1867, his mother's family had been in the United States just twenty-three years (they arrived in New York in December 1844), and his mother had been born in Wales. Like so many other Welsh families, the Lloyd Joneses shared a fierce attachment to *yr hen wlad* (the old country) and to one another. What they wanted was not so much to join forces with the New World as make another version of the one they had left—one that was better, truer, more their own. Building their chapel had a particular meaning for them all. In the bad old years when the Welsh had been persecuted for worshipping outside the established church by the hated English, to be a freethinker, a Nonconformist, came to mean not only religious freedom but also political self-assertion. Every time a Welshman managed to worship as his conscience decreed—"Truth Against the World" was the Lloyd Jones motto—he furthered his country's cause of nationhood and independence. He had defied authority and triumphed. One might therefore make the fairly safe assumption that, in building Unity Chapel, the Lloyd Joneses were not only erecting a memorial to Richard Lloyd Jones, to their religious freedoms and to the blood links that united them, but asserting their right to be, not Americans, but Welsh.

* * *

Some scholars believe that Taliesin (or Taliessin), a Welsh bard of mythical stature, lived and wrote in the sixth century. This is contradicted by an equally reputable view that he lived in the Middle Ages. If one subscribes to the former view, one argues that this poet-hero was alluding to events of measureless antiquity in his celebrated verses, many of which record great battles. In any event it is agreed that Taliesin's poems were not written down until the thirteenth century and that they are allusive and difficult. Over the centuries, his heroic or mythical status has achieved formidable proportions. To the Welsh nowadays, it is said, Taliesin appears as "a characteristic hero figure of Celtic myth, the poet-prophet who enjoys a complex relationship with a sequence of levels of existence of which the physical world that surrounds and sustains us is only one numinous manifestation. . . . Taliesin carries with him something of the powers of the gods and spirits of the shape-shifting Celtic pantheon." Even his name is symbolic; it means "shining brow," and in later years Wright would offer this as an explanation for choosing it to adorn the house he had built on the side of a hill, thereby finessing the more relevant question, i.e., whether some association was intended between himself and the poet-prophet in question. It is certainly possible to perceive, in the siting of his famous home, now a vast, gently decaying complex of buildings, a Celtic reverence for the sacredness of place. When one also considers that the first version of Taliesin—constantly rebuilt, revised and expanded, the result of the artist's restless imagination as well as successive calamities—began in 1911, one begins to discern the qualities that set its creator apart from his contemporaries. To properly appreciate his contribution one should compare him with, for instance, John Wood the Elder and John Wood the Younger, who, in the eighteenth century, designed a harmonious succession of terraces for the gently rolling hills surrounding the English city of Bath. Like the Woods, Wright had grasped the importance of inserting his deft network of house, studio and farm buildings into the side of the hill, rather than imposing it on the landscape. He, too, sensed the effects to be gained from the contrast between a sophisticated architectural style and a gentle, pastoral setting. In common with the Woods, Wright had a vision of Arcadia, of man living in harmony with nature.

This chef d'oeuvre, this dream incarnate, this quintessential statement of the goals toward which Wright labored all his life, was designed, he later explained, after a study of those local outcroppings of rock that looked to be in such harmony with the dark red cedars

and white birches surrounding them. So he engaged teams of neighboring farmers to haul loads of native stone from a quarry on a hill a
mile away, and up his beloved hillside. "The stone went down for
pavements of terraces and courts. Stone was sent along the slopes into
great walls. Stone stepped up like ledges on to the hill and flung long
arms in any direction that brought the house to the ground. . . .

"Finally it was not so easy to tell where pavement and walls left
off, and ground began. . . . A clump of fine oaks that grew on the
hilltop stood untouched on one side above [a] court. A great curved
stone-walled seat inclosed [*sic*] the space just beneath them, and stone
pavement stepped down to a spring or fountain that welled up into
a pool at the center of the circle.

"But in the constitution of the whole—in the way the walls rose
from the plan and the spaces were roofed over—was the chief interest.
It was all supremely natural. The rooms went up into the roof, tentlike,
and were ribbanded overhead with marking strips of waxed soft wood.
The house was set so sun came through the openings into every room
some time during the day. Walls opened everywhere to views as the
windows swung out above the tree tops. . . ."

Nowadays this most innovative of dwellings has an ancient, fortresslike aspect. This seems partly due to the extraordinary size and
weight of the vast roof at Taliesin, which appears to have assumed
the functions usually associated with walls. It is sheltering, all-
enveloping, impregnable. The impression is furthered by the flights
of stone steps, worn and covered with lichen, and the low doors tucked
inconspicuously into the sides of thick stone façades. The feeling that
one has stumbled upon an ancient castle intensifies as one discovers
that this seldom-used building is inhabited by thousands of swifts.
They shoot across one's path, soar up into the branches and spiral
around the massive chimneys making a characteristic, curious chit-
tering sound as if repelling the casual visitor. And, although Taliesin
has been rebuilt repeatedly, it is now sliding into decay. The stones
making up the foundation are tilting. The plaster is crumbling. The
floors have shifted. The stonework is obscured by decades of dirt and
lichen. Mold is eating away at the old beams. Windows no longer fit
their frames. Latches are sprung, toilets do not flush, and, everywhere,
the birds are nesting in the chimneys.

Taliesin may have been "supremely natural," as its creator claimed,
but it is artful. Walking through the suite of rooms that made up
the private quarters of the architect and his family makes the visitor

realize that it is impossible to fully appreciate his achievement except by experiencing it. One then sees the intricacy of the overall concept: the way the low entrance hall gives one a glimpse of bright spaces beyond, the way the living room ceiling soars upward, the way banks of windows reveal panoramic views over The Valley and the way interior spaces are cunningly divided into nooks and crannies that tempt one to curl up with a book or engage in an intimate conversation. And, for all its complexity, this suite of rooms has an overall coherence. There are the same uses of stone, plaster, stucco, heavy wooden dark beams, low benches, built-in shelves, cabinets, oriental carpets, gold leaf wall coverings, Japanese screens, oriental pottery, porcelain and objets d'art of all descriptions; the same soft tans, bronzes, leaf greens and the omnipresent Taliesin reds. "It is now as though the mind itself at times were some kind of recording film in endless reel, to go on perfecting and projecting pictures endlessly, seldom if ever the same," Wright wrote. "But the scene and scheme may show itself from infinitely varying angles as the point of view changes if [the] informing principle, the *impulse* living in it all, stays in place." So one sits in the living room, watching shadows move across the floor, and the stream he dammed under the windows to make a lake is vastly still. Inside the room, there is a kind of concentrated silence that makes the sound of a bird and nearby voices seem to come from a great distance. "Again, Taliesin!" he also wrote. "Three times built, twice destroyed, yet a place of great repose. When I am away from it, like some rubber band stretched out but ready to snap back immediately the pull is relaxed. . . . I get back to it happy to be there again."

Although Frank Lloyd Wright had reached the advanced age of ninety-one when he died in the spring of 1959, his uncluttered spirit, zest and appetite for life seemed indomitable. Richard Carney, now managing trustee and treasurer of the Frank Lloyd Wright Memorial Foundation, said, "There was absolutely nothing to lead you to suspect he'd get ill." Kay Rattenbury, another member of the Fellowship, recalled that, that Saturday, the group went on a picnic at Taliesin West, the architect's estate outside Scottsdale, a suburb of Phoenix, Arizona, where he spent his winters. Wright was looking a little pale but seemed fine. That night he was ill with stomach pains. "We thought it was the flu," Carney said. When he did not improve, Wright's doctor decided he should go to St. Joseph's Hospital in

Phoenix for tests. There, doctors discovered, and operated to remove, an intestinal obstruction. No evidence of any malignancy was found, and Wright was recovering well. Two days after the operation, on Wednesday, April 8, doctors said that he was holding his own for a man of his age. His condition was described as "satisfactory."

His third wife, Olgivanna, was staying at the hospital, where an impromptu bed had been made for her in a solarium. She sat beside her husband for two days as he lay in an oxygen tent, and visited him for the last time early on the morning of Thursday, April 9, at about 1 A.M. Then she went to bed. Night nurse Jessie Boganno of Glendale, Arizona, was with him at the moment of death. "He just sighed—and died," she said.

Wesley Peters, Wright's son-in-law, the late chairman of the board of trustees of the Frank Lloyd Wright Memorial Foundation, said, "I was in the hospital with Gene Masselink [Wright's personal secretary] and Dr. Joseph Rorke [his private physician] when Mr. Wright died. They came in and got Dr. Rorke. He went in and tried to do some heart resuscitation—in those days they didn't have a cardiac team—but it was no use." Peters, Carney and another member of the Fellowship, Kenneth Burton Lockhart, immediately made plans to transport Wright back to Spring Green for burial at Unity Chapel. "I was driving the pickup truck with the coffin in the back," Peters said. "We drove continuously, 1,800 miles, for twenty-eight hours." The suddenness of the event stunned them. "Nobody thought he was going to die." Another former apprentice, Elizabeth Kassler, who revisited Scottsdale after Wright's death, explained, "No room is so empty as the one in which you are expecting someone to arrive—at any moment—and they don't appear."

Wright's body was laid in a metal-clad coffin on a cloth of Cherokee-red velvet, the color he always chose. His coffin was placed in front of the great stone fireplace in Taliesin and filled with flowers; green sprigs had been placed in his hands. Then, at five o'clock on Sunday, April 12, just as the sun was setting, the old bell in Unity Chapel began to toll and kept on ringing. One of Wright's sons by his first marriage, Robert Llewellyn Wright, a Washington attorney, helped to carry the coffin down the steps to a waiting wagon, draped in more red velvet and covered with flowers. As the cameras clicked, Peters and Masselink began the drive to the chapel a half-mile away, pulled by a handsome pair of black Percheron horses named Bird and Chat, which had been lent by a neighbor. Olgivanna, Iovanna (Wright's seventh and last child) and other relatives and close friends followed on foot.

Rev. Max D. Gaebler of Madison's Unitarian Church, where Wright was a member, read the familiar Psalm 121, "I will lift up mine eyes unto the hills . . . ," and then an extract from "Self-Reliance" by Ralph Waldo Emerson: "Whoso would be a man must be a nonconformist. . . . Nothing is at last sacred but the integrity of your own mind." As the coffin was lowered, Mrs. Wright sobbed and made the sign of the cross. The minister read two final selections from the Book of Job, ending with, "Thou shalt come to thy grave in a full age, like as a shock of corn cometh in his season."

As soon as the news of Wright's death was announced, it was stated that the grave in which his body was to be placed would be a temporary one. Apprentices of the Taliesin Fellowship, those who had worked beside him, set up on end a large stone found in the quarry behind Taliesin, to mark the burial spot. A semicircle of the flowers Wright favored—daisies, the common tiger lilies of southern Wisconsin, peonies and the like—had been planted, but this was all by the way.

His apprentices knew that the architect had been working for the past year and a half on a new chapel that would adjoin Unity Chapel, to serve as his memorial and final resting place. Design work on the building was almost complete in the fall of 1958, and color drawings were made. Wright was putting the finishing touches on his "Unity Temple," as he called it, as recently as two weeks before his death on April 9. Howe said, "He was so pleased with his design for a Christian Science Church in Bolinas, California [never built], that he wanted something like it for himself." His own was to have been high and square, each wall measuring thirty feet in length. He had designed stone piers interspersed by strips of glass for the walls, and a central skylight. The interior was without decoration, save for a stone fireplace. A row of stone sarcophagi, flush with the ground and facing south, would line one wall. The temple would serve for contemplation and meditation and would house not only his mortal remains but also those of his wife Olgivanna, their daughter, Iovanna, and members of the Taliesin Fellowship.

Preliminary work had already begun. The footing was squared out, and blocks of stone to be used for the new chapel were hauled in from the Rock Springs Quarry, some twelve miles distant, and set up, ready for work, in neat piles. It is claimed that one can still see the outline on the ground marking the spot that Wright had chosen. "The stone was all piled there but Mr. Wright didn't feel any urgency to get started," Howe recalled. "It was just there for the stonemasons to deal with on their off-hours. He probably thought he was going to live forever." There could have been a further reason for Wright's uncharacteristic reluctance to begin a new project. Perhaps anticipating family opposition, he had not let it be known that he planned to tear down the first Unity Chapel, by then seldom used and deteriorating. Arguments about its historical importance in his architectural oeuvre would not have swayed him. Howe said, "He never liked his early buildings, and he couldn't wait to get them down. He never looked back. He always used to say, 'If you take care of the present, the past and future will take care of themselves.' "

Robert Graves, who was landscape architect at Taliesin during the last four years of Wright's life, whose land in The Valley now adjoins the Taliesin estate, and who owns the farm that once belonged to Wright's favorite uncle, James, recalled that Wright asked him to oversee the planting of an allée of trees to complement the new building. The plantings were designed so as to link visually the Taliesin estate, on one side of Route 23, the main road running through The Valley, and Unity Chapel opposite, on a side road.

"I got a price on 150 twelve- to fourteen-foot evergreens and informed him—he was in Arizona at the time—that I needed the money in advance. He sent me back a terse note, 'I am not accustomed to buying a pig in a poke,' but he did send a check. I got all the material ready, and when he returned, we spent three days in his car staking and planting a whole row of trees and shrubs along Route 23 to link the two properties. As it happens, the configuration of the road has been changed since, and what we did is no longer so obvious. But it was clear to me that Mr. Wright had given much thought to exactly how he intended to be buried. I remember that, when we had finished the planting, Mr. Wright turned to me and said, 'Taliesin is now finished,' and I was overwhelmed. It seemed a terrible thing for him to say."

Almost the first announcement from Wright's bereaved followers was that they intended to carry on his work. Among their first acts would be the fireproofing of a vault to house his precious drawings. The second would be to build the memorial chapel he had designed, and to move his remains there. Work, however, did not start, and those who lived in Spring Green began to realize that the Fellowship had shifted its emphasis from Wisconsin to Arizona. Robert Graves said, "Mrs. Wright set up a skeleton staff of two or three people, but for a couple of years after Mr. Wright's death we did not see her or the Fellowship." Others said that this was because Mrs. Wright felt far happier at Taliesin West, where she and her husband had spent their winters for decades, than she ever had in Wisconsin. So no one brought up the subject of the chapel, "because Mrs. Wright seemed quite content with the present grave," Howe explained. "A little bench was placed beside it where she could go to be contemplative, but she seldom went there."

Then, on March 1, 1985, Olgivanna Wright died in Scottsdale. Although she had been in poor health for the past year and a half, her death, like that of her husband, took everyone by surprise. The only person with her was Wright's former physician, Dr. Rorke. He called a meeting of the Fellowship to tell them that Mrs. Wright's dying wish was that she, her late husband and her daughter by her first marriage, the late Mrs. Wesley Peters, should all be cremated and removed to Scottsdale. The plan was to build a garden dedicated to all three and immure their ashes there. The wish was not stated in her will and appeared, to some members of the Fellowship, to have been a last-minute whim, and an ill-considered one at that. However, according to a former member, "The group had been totally emasculated over the years, and anything coming from Mrs. Wright had the aura of Holy Writ." In other words, save for the idea of exhuming and cremating Svetlana Peters, which was quietly dropped, there was no question in anyone's mind that Mrs. Wright's last wish would be honored. The only problem was exactly how this was to be accomplished. Anticipating some opposition, members of the Fellowship moved secretly and with dispatch. Wright's body was exhumed and cremated in Madison before John Hunter, associate editor of the local paper, the *Madison Capital Times*, learned about it. "A coroner's authority was required," he said, "and the man had been pledged to secrecy, but he did confirm that this was true." Hunter published the article, and there was an outcry.

"Oh, yes, that damn business," said Elizabeth Wright Ingraham, daughter of Wright's son John, an architect in her own right, and chairman of Unity Chapel, Inc., a family corporation established to restore the chapel and tend the burial grounds. She explained that her organization had had little power to refuse, since the necessary legal papers had been signed by Iovanna, Wright's only child by his third wife, Olgivanna, but Ingraham thought the chapel custodian appointed for the cemetery should have been notified. "I tried to sit on the fence, but I thought it was a gross miscalculation. One can say, 'Who cares where the body is?' but the actual act of taking a body out of a coffin is ghoulish. I asked the mortician, 'I suppose he's just bones, after twenty-six years?' and he said, 'Oh, no, he's marvelously intact.' I couldn't hear any more.

"I truly believe Olgivanna felt my grandfather was actually down there, and Iovanna certainly did. She told me, 'Daddy gets cold up there in Wisconsin.' And you know, when Olgivanna told you to do something, you did it."

Jack Howe, by then practicing architecture in Burnsville, Minnesota, was horrified, calling the exhumation an act of vandalism. He said, "The sneaky way it was done was particularly bad. They left the cemetery a mess, did not resod or level the ground, just threw some soil in the grave and replaced the stone marker. I was very angry when I saw it. . . . I think moving the body was inexcusable, even if Olgivanna did request it."

"My husband thought it was a desecration," said Betty Wright, wife of the late Robert Llewellyn Wright, the son who had helped carry his father's body to his grave. "After he was quoted in the newspapers, he had a telegram from Iovanna, who wrote, 'The heritage of Taliesin is not for the likes of you.'" This was a particularly low blow because everyone knew that Robert Llewellyn, along with Wright's other children by his first wife, had been disinherited years before, when Wright had established a nonprofit foundation, leaving all his worldly goods to those who would carry on his work. His will read, in part, "Having otherwise disposed of all my worldly goods I give and bequeath my love unto each of my beloved children . . . as a token of my affection for them."

The person most upset, however, was Wright's son David. He called the act "grave robbing." Mrs. Wright had wanted her husband's ashes beside her own for purely selfish reasons. "She'd be nobody without him," he said. Gladys Wright added that, when she went to Mrs. Wright's funeral, "No one approached me and told me they were going to do this."

To those less immediately involved, there was a symbolic significance in the removal of Wright's remains that transcended sentimental considerations. Such an act, wrote Karl E. Meyer, a native of Wisconsin, was the equivalent of "uprooting Jefferson from Monticello for reburial in Beverly Hills." No one could seriously argue that Wright really belonged in Arizona, given his origins, given all that he had written about The Valley, given the love and care he had lavished on Taliesin year after year, given the fact that he had rebuilt it and had always returned, and given that he had written, "I still feel myself as much a part of it as the trees and birds . . . and the red barns." To remove Wright from his Wisconsin roots impoverished them all. Other natives of the state agreed. At the end of April the Wisconsin house approved a resolution protesting the body's removal and asking for the return of his ashes; the senate concurred two weeks later. The state representative for the district that includes The Valley explained, in a letter to Peters, "Much more than ashes have been taken from Wisconsin—the citizens of the state have lost one evidence of our history, spirit and genius."

Wesley Peters was astonished and upset by the strength of the opposition. "Nobody here thought there would be such a violent feeling about it," he said. "But I don't think Mr. Wright would have felt otherwise about it. If it was what Mrs. Wright wished, I think he would have wanted it done." Richard Carney added, "Mrs. Wright didn't actually specify this in her will, but she had been talking about it for several years. We should have done it sooner. She was always saying, 'When we go to Wisconsin, I am going to see about it.' There was always the desire to establish a burial ground at Taliesin West. Legally it is very complex, but you can have ashes there." To him, it was a simple matter: "If Mrs. Wright said that is the burying ground, we have to come here." Peters, who had driven day and night to get his beloved master back to Wisconsin, and then moved with alacrity to return him to Arizona, had the air of a man torn by conflicting loyalties who was being roundly condemned for trying to do what was expected of him. When he was asked why he had moved Wright in the first place, he looked at a loss for explanations. He said, "We didn't think of anything else at the time."

When Wright's ashes were transported to Arizona it was announced that they would be moved to their final resting place within six months. A wall was to be built surrounding the memorial garden, and the remains of both Wrights would be immured within it. This was not done for several years. Richard Carney said that the original plans had been "too elaborate," and had been redrawn. In the interim, the ashes of both Wrights were "in storage," and there was speculation in some

quarters that Wright's remains might be quietly transferred back to
Wisconsin. Others thought this most unlikely. During this period,
all that could be said for certain was that his mortal remains were in
limbo, as a result, it would seem, of the conflicting loyalties, resentments and antagonisms that had followed him and made him, some
thirty years after his death, still a subject of controversy. One wanted
to agree with another granddaughter, the late Anne Baxter, the actress,
that ". . . he may be laughing for all we know, because his spirit is
much bigger than his bones." As for the chapel he wanted as a memorial to himself, more than three decades later most people seemed to
have brushed the fact aside. If there were a particular significance to
the curious coincidence that Wright's architectural career began, and
ended, with the same preoccupation—a chapel for the identical plot
of ground in The Valley—it went unrecorded.

2

The Black Spot

*Fate has opened
A single port: memory.*
"The Wanderer"
Poems from the Old English

Rev. Jenkin Lloyd Jones, "Our Jenkin," never forgot Black Week. That mesmerizing preacher loved to reminisce about his Lincolnesque childhood in a log cabin, some time after his parents, Richard and Mallie Lloyd Jones, had emigrated to the new country. Such was the power of his personality that however clichéd and repetitive his reminiscences—and it must be admitted that the famous preacher tended to become tiresome about his childhood as he grew older— his ability to rivet his listeners' attention never palled. Perhaps the message he had to give was embellished by that special form of delivery, known as *hwyl*, that is unique to Welsh preachers. This chanting style of preaching involves an ability to deliver certain passages of particular poignancy almost as if they were being sung. The successful practi- tioner of *hwyl* would begin in a minor key, mounting by calculated effects to a triumphant climax in a major chord, one beautifully calculated to inspire his listeners with a passionate, not to say fervently religious, response. One would not be surprised to find Rev. Jenkin Lloyd Jones a master of this difficult and delicate technique; he cer- tainly was aware that no story is more powerful than the one about the little boy who begins life in a log cabin. And so he remembered: pulling a cow out of the marsh, clearing the forests with oxen, "working on the road" with a gang of boys and men, the picnics, the deep snows and Black Week.

One day gentlemen in black coats assembled in the Wisconsin Welsh community in which he and his family were then living. These men, farmers from the surrounding hills, met each day at the primitive chapel the community had built over the hill, appearing for meals at the Lloyd Jones log-house, as Jenkin called it, the largest home thereabouts. That such generous hospitality was being offered to these anonymous, somewhat sinister figures, made a great impression on Jenkin once he understood the reason for their visits. They were about to condemn his parents of heresy.

In order to properly appreciate the predictability of this charge, made against two perfectly moral and upright people, a digression is necessary. The reasons involve an understanding of the traditions the parents had inherited through their own forebears, beliefs sustained in the context of a past in which radical religious thought, political rebellion, emerging nationalism and the rediscovery of an ancient culture were intricately intertwined. As far back as one cares to look in the family background of Richard and Mallie, one finds educators and preachers, literate men and women prepared to challenge authority of any kind, and particularly the established church. They must have been Dissenters—Nonconformists—from the earliest days. As Jan Morris points out in *The Matter of Wales*, although Protestantism was established there by the eighteenth century, Methodism would transform it.

"The growth of Nonconformism . . . , its tentative and daring beginnings, its phenomenal spread, its tremendous eruption of faith, hope and sacrifice, left an effect upon the country like the passing of a hurricane. . . . The Methodist Revival, *Y Diwygiad*, hurled everything topsy-turvy, demolishing the social structure, transforming the culture, shifting the self-image and the reputation of the people, and eventually giving rise to a great convulsion of power that was truly a revolution." Hard on the heels of the Methodists came representatives of other Protestant denominations just as committed to freedom of thought and as prepared to be attacked by mobs, ducked in ponds and forbidden to assemble.

"So severe were the punishments meted out to those who gathered together to worship outside the Church that they met secretly . . .

in dingles in the hills, in barns, or in the homes of sympathisers who were prepared to take the risk of sheltering them," wrote Anthony Jones in a history of the early Welsh chapels. One finds in the story of the Lloyd Joneses a consistent, stubborn insistence on their renegade opinions and a melancholic pride in being persecuted for them. As far back as 1696 one can find in their family a personage like Thomas David Rees, a farmer of some means, who was prepared to be disowned by his Church as long as he could worship according to his conscience. He founded the first Baptist congregation in Cardiganshire on a farm he owned in the parish of Llandysul, the very same parish from which the Lloyd Jones family would emigrate a century and a half later. His grandson, Jenkin Jones (c. 1700–1742), was even more radical and newfangled in his beliefs, since he was an Arminian. That is to say, he was a follower of Jacobus Arminius (1560–1609), a Dutch theologian who partially denied the divinity of Christ. Jenkin Jones, already a Nonconformist, had joined a group of even more liberal thinkers who were questioning the divinity of Christ and the Calvinists' belief in predestination, and were placing their emphasis upon the importance of free will and human intervention. Some, called Socinians after Fausto Sozzini (1539–1604), even argued that the Holy Trinity was a fallacious concept. There was no Father, Son and Holy Ghost, but simply One God, and Christianity was one of many paths toward enlightenment. That such beliefs had been advanced since the sixteenth century did not seem to help much. Other Welsh Nonconformists— Calvinistic Methodists, Baptists and Congregationalists—considered Arminians like Jenkin Jones to be dangerous when not positively heretical. Jones was barred from entering the pulpit of his own Independent church at Pantycreuddyn, and obliged to build a chapel on land he owned near Llwynrhydowen, four miles from Llandysul. There, he began to preach his "peculiar sentiments" with such fire that he terrified his listeners. Some thought these were the kind of beliefs one might expect of thieves and ruffians, since he dared to preach that everyone might enter heaven. Still others denounced his doctrine as a kind of poison that, if not immediately stamped out, would corrupt the country.

One discovers that the forefathers of Frank Lloyd Wright were tenacious fighters, with a way of surmounting seemingly impossible odds. While still in his twenties, Rev. Jenkin Jones managed to convert enough parishioners to earn the distinction of having established the first Arminian congregation in Wales. He built a second chapel at Llwynrhydowen and, before he died at a relatively early age, had the satisfaction of seeing a third Arminian church established in a nearby village, and of knowing that he had influenced several other ministers to follow his precepts. His nephew, David Lloyd, who succeeded him, was so successful at expanding the congregation that the chapel would no longer hold all the eager listeners. He was obliged to preach in the open air, sometimes to audiences of three thousand.

That tiny Arminian, later Unitarian, congregation, founded a few miles from the village of Llandysul early in the eighteenth century, is the proper starting point from which to consider the emigration of Richard and Mallie Lloyd Jones a century and a half later. A tradition had been established, and the family heritage inextricably linked, with men who fought for their right to think as they chose, no matter how heretical their notions, a trait that was to have some significance in the life of Frank Lloyd Wright. No one ever accused the Lloyd Joneses of deserting their principles. Viewed from the perspective of their own history and the imperatives of their age, they were even admirably conformist. Inside their corner of old Cardiganshire, now West Dyfed, everyone felt as they did. Rev. Jenkin Jones had so successfully convinced his congregations of the rightness of his doctrines that their area became, forever afterward, synonymous with a certain kind of Unitarian intractability. When a Calvinistic Methodist, Rev. Daniel Rowland, living a few miles to the north of Llandysul, attempted to convert these Unitarian congregations later in the eighteenth century, his words were in vain. Rev. Aubrey J. Martin, now retired as minister of the congregation that Jones had founded, explained, "The Methodists called our district the Black Spot of Socinianism because of their failure to convert us. To call someone a Socinian still has a sting to it." Within the walls of their faith, the Unitarians of Cardiganshire were united, clan-minded, tenaciously believing. Such unity had a defensive aspect: such absolute conviction of rightness was a psychological necessity since beyond their borders they were ostracized. To other Nonconformists they were a blight on the movement, an ineradicable stain. They were called "people without hope" and "utterly damned."

From the careful description Jenkin Lloyd Jones gives of Black Week, one concludes that Richard and Mallie were as much outcasts in Wisconsin as they had been in Cardiganshire. However, the point is also made that they had been invited to join the church from which they were now being expelled. In the early days, when settlements

*Capel Bryn Bach, where Frank Lloyd Wright's uncle Jenkin Jones preached
the first Unitarian sermon in 1726*

Llwynrhydowen chapel, now derelict

were tiny and to be Welsh, with the same language and background, mattered most, new immigrants usually agreed to disagree and worship together in what were called "union churches." An authority on the life of Jenkin Lloyd Jones, Prof. Thomas E. Graham, observed, "It didn't seem to matter to them if a church were more 'orthodox' than they were. They attended whatever was at hand, and associated with any Christians who did not reject them." However, Richard had insisted that he and his wife be allowed to retain the "precious faith which was the dearest thing they had carried with them over the seas," Jenkin wrote, "the heretical faith of the Socinians."

No doubt as the church grew, doctrinal differences began to assert themselves and members argued about such issues as baptism, the organization of the church and a host of other divisive issues. Most Nonconformists—Calvinistic Methodists, Baptists and Congregationalists—accepted the fundamental tenets of Calvinism rather than those of Arminianism and Socinianism. This made being a Unitarian as lonely a business in Wisconsin as it had been in Wales. The visiting men in black coats discovered a "canker of heresy" at the heart of the backwoods church, where Richard Lloyd Jones, it was charged, was "leading the young astray" at Bible class and Sunday school.

Mallie Lloyd Jones was all for withdrawing from the church, to spare everyone the embarrassment of her family's being thrown out; hers was "a nature keenly susceptible to spiritual suffering," her son explained. His father defended himself so successfully that the men in black coats were at a loss. Unable to prove their point, they then brought charges against the minister who had invited the Lloyd Joneses to become members. At that critical stage, Richard Lloyd Jones voluntarily left the church rather than have the minister be made the scapegoat. The Lloyd Joneses as a clan had the good fortune to live in interesting times, at a moment when demands for religious freedom and political reforms became almost synonymous. One sees the Lloyd Joneses and their distinguished forebears as uncommonly representative of an ancient people who had been defeated but never conquered, who had lived for centuries with their backs to the sea.

The very name of Wales is not Welsh, and for a reason. The Welsh call themselves *Cymry* (companions, comrades), their land *Cymru* and their language *Cymraeg*. The words *Welsh* and *Wales* were coined by the Teutonic invaders who fought to take over Britain in the centuries after the Roman withdrawal; the derivation is from *Walas* (strangers).

The Celts, by then well entrenched, had been strangers themselves centuries before. They, too, had migrated to the British Isles. One group is believed to have come from northern Europe, supposedly accounting for the tall, large-limbed Welshmen one finds in north Wales. As for the small, dark, stocky Welsh of the south, these are believed to be descended from a second wave of immigrants originating in the Iberian Peninsula. Each had colonized Britain by the third and fourth centuries before Christ, and all over Britain the language that was spoken now survives only in fragments: as Breton, as Scottish and Irish Gaelic and as modern Welsh, a language of poetry, legend and myth. The new invaders, the Romans, arriving in about A.D. 50, gradually pushed the Celts back to the farthest corners of Britain: to Cornwall in the southwestern tip, to the Highlands of Scotland, and to the mountainous peninsula of modern Wales, bordered on all sides by the Irish Sea. Finally the Welsh, too, were overrun.

Celtic society was structured around family relationships, and even distant ones were identified and cultivated. Women in those early days enjoyed more rights and privileges than did their Roman counterparts, and a child belonged to his mother's side of the family rather than to his father's. This bond was strengthened by the practice of sending a youngster to live with his mother's family for a considerable period. The Celts were imaginative and lavish hosts and great givers of presents as well, although their code was so precise and elaborate one wonders whether it were motivated as much by social one-upmanship as kindness of heart. Clans were grouped into tribes and surprisingly well governed. The ancient legal code of Wales, derived from Celtic law, was remarkably advanced and equable for its time. Marriage was regarded as an agreement rather than a sacrament, and could be ended by mutual consent. Illegitimate children's rights were as well protected as those of lawful ones. In civil matters, the provisions of a contract had more weight than legislation, and criminal laws were aimed at monetary compensation and "reconciliation rather than revenge: the intention was to re-establish social harmony, and the more terrible penalties of English law, the torturings, the gibbetings, the disembowelments, were unknown in independent Wales—even public whippings entered the country only with the Tudors."

The heritage of Celtic art, poetry and literature is legendary. Welsh folk stories and poems in particular appear to have survived the centuries with their Celtic roots still recognizable even though they were not committed to paper until medieval times. "Another detectably Celtic trait is a certain sense of the dream of things, a conviction that some other state of being exists, invisible but sensible, outside our own windows. To patriots of mystic tendency this is the truest manifestation of the Welsh identity: . . . it can be traced soberly enough to the animism of Celtic thought, which found the divine in every leaf and tree, which knew the spirits of the running streams, and believed the next world, like the last, to be with us all the time."

In Gaul, the Druids supposedly believed the oak tree to have mystical powers and ate acorns and mistletoe to improve their powers of divination. In Ireland, the walnut and rowan trees were sacred. In Wales, the talisman was the apple tree, and a Welshman's favorite meal used to be pork with applesauce. Celts were notorious for their alcoholic intake, which supposedly accounted for their mercurial temperaments. In fact the tendency to fly off the handle at a moment's notice was considered a particular characteristic of the Celts. Today, observers believe they see "the same volatile mixture of flamboyance, wild courage and easy discouragement that the Roman writers reported among the Gallic tribes. The love of music, poetry and provocative conversation, are still readily apparent among the Welsh . . . and from their day until our own the learned man and the artist have been honoured in Welsh society as among few other peoples of the West."

In 1282, the Norman king of England overthrew the last and most powerful of the Welsh ruling families. Welsh self-government, the right to their own enlightened legal code, was extinguished, and with it a distinctive way of life. If this was the dominant mood, there were also some stubborn minor themes. The Welsh might be in political limbo, but they still had a language worth preserving and a rich cultural heritage; they had wonderful poets and authors, and they were still distinctively Welsh, despite the contaminating effects of English manners, mores and laws. To cherish their culture was the one thing they could still be proud of; it was "a type of cultural nationalism. . . ."

David Lloyd, the preacher who had attracted crowds of thousands to hear his sermons at Llandysul, was Richard Lloyd Jones's grandfather. It would seem that he was descended from a distinguished family, the Lloyds of Castell-hywel. One family memoir notes that, in the old days, the Lloyds had "enjoyed the title and privileges of nobility, but . . . for want of due reservation in the Articles of Union between Wales and England, lost their hereditary rank. . . ." If it

The children of Richard and Mallie Lloyd Jones, 1882. Back row, from left: Enos, Jennie, Jenkin, Mary and John. Front row, from left: James, Nell, Anna, Margaret and Thomas

The stone cottage of Blaenralltddu, in which the first five children of Richard and Mallie Lloyd Jones were born. Near the right-hand corner of the building is a plaque commemorating the birthplace of Jenkin Lloyd Jones.

An early Lloyd Jones farmhouse in The Valley near Spring Green,
Wisconsin

St. Tysul's, the parish church at Llandysul

had not been for the English rulers, in other words, the Lloyds would still be somebody. As it was, their name retained great cachet, and sometime after David Lloyd's daughter Margaret married John Enoch Jones, a young man of lesser status, the unhyphenated Lloyd Jones family name begins to appear. Their son Richard, a black-haired, handsome, vigorous-looking man of six-feet-two, may not have composed poems in Greek as his grandfather did, but he was a fine lay preacher, made hats part-time and was a tenant farmer on twenty-three acres in the parish of Llanwenog, with a yoke of oxen, some dairy cattle and a herd of sheep. There he and his wife, Mallie, began raising a brood of what would become eleven children (four more would be born in the United States): Thomas, born in 1830; John, 1832; Margaret, 1835; Mary, 1836,* Hannah (later, Anna), 1838,* Nanny, 1840; and Jenkin, 1843.

Blaenralltddu, the old house (two bedrooms and a loft) in which Richard and Mallie Lloyd Jones lived, stands at the end of a dirt track off the road just outside Llandysul, now graced with a plaque identifying it as the birthplace of the famous Jenkin Lloyd Jones. Its nearest town, with a single climbing main street, is unremarkable except for a lovely old church with a Norman tower and painted arches dating from the reign of Henry III. In the wall of the choir vestry is an inscribed stone bearing a Latin memorial to Velloria, daughter of the old chieftain Brohomalgus; here, Richard's grandfather, Jenkin Jones, founder of the first Arminian congregation in Wales, is buried. But the area is full of churches and chapels with Lloyd Jones associations, many of them in partial ruins and with cousins and more distant relatives by the dozens buried in graveyards all around, at Pantydefaid and Llwynrhydowen. And Llandysul is one of the main centers of the Welsh wool industry, strategically situated on the banks of the Teifi where, in the old days, the river's boisterous waters drove the old waterwheels and where the mills still produce tweeds, flannels and some famous tapestries. Lampeter, a few miles east, is a charming small town, eerily quiet on Sunday mornings, where a retired minister out walking his dog might stop and chat with a stranger as if they had known each other for years. Then there is Pumpsaint and its pretty cottages, often built of flinty stone, the woodwork painted in primary reds and yellows, or stuccoed and washed in palest creams and yellows. The countryside around is steeply sloped, with patches of woodland threaded with clear streams and dotted here and there with small, whitewashed cottages, its scale intimate. It has the air of having been inhabited by meticulously neat, proud and possessive farmers for centuries. Life in this region, on what are called "hill-land" farms, may seem idyllic and unspoiled, but it has never been easy. The soil is thin, more suitable for raising sheep and dairy cattle than for growing crops, requiring backbreaking work and long hours for meager results. In that inhospitable countryside, whole communities might depend on supplementing their earnings by whatever could be gained from the use of common lands—peat for their fireplaces, perhaps, or extra grazing for their cattle. Unfortunately, English law allowed landowners to add to their acreage by making a claim on common land. Permission was as good as automatic, and between 1760 and 1820, over two thousand individual Enclosure Acts were passed, affecting land all over the British Isles. Small farmers and "squatters"—families who had built makeshift cottages on this so-called derelict land—found themselves evicted without ceremony, and a vast increase in rural poverty was the result.

> They hang the man and flog the woman
> That steals the goose from off the common
> But leave the greater criminal loose
> That steals the common from the goose.

A ruling class of thirty to forty families effectively monopolized the Welsh parliamentary seats in the House of Commons and the local patronage that went with them; the lesser gentry filled the benches. These magistrates were often in the position of judging cases in which their own interests were involved. In any event, they were drawn from the privileged classes, making biased verdicts commonplace. Adding to the general sense of alienation was the fact that trials were conducted in English. It all lent fuel to the belief that, as Oliver Goldsmith observed, "laws grind the poor and the rich men grind the law." There were many other grievances: tithes, extortionate rents, evictions, the general hostility of landlords, gamekeepers and officialdom, the unfairness of life—and the high price of bread. People were ready to strike out blindly, and found an easy target.

Before the advent of canals and railways, roads in remote areas were little more than horse trails. Much of the economic backwardness and isolation of Wales was attributed to the difficulty of getting in or out, and once travelers began to use carts and coaches rather than packhorses, the need for better roads became urgent. The custom grew up of making landowners responsible for building and maintaining roads through their properties and of allowing them to charge fees, i.e., tolls. This rough-and-ready system worked reasonably well for centuries, but by the 1830s there were many abuses. A traveler might have to pay three or four tolls in the course of a single journey. Market towns were often bristling with tollgates. Small farmers were particularly penalized, since they made constant trips to haul limestone, their only fertilizer, back and forth along the roads to their fields, in a period when harvests were poor. Individual payments were modest, but, collectively, they added their mite to the burden the small farmer carried: "The tolls . . . were an everyday, inescapable metaphor for the condition of their lives."

In some parts of rural Wales there was a custom, on certain nights of the year, of lighting bonfires and organizing torchlight processions led by men dressed as women. This arcane tradition may have been the inspiration for what has been called "the strangest series of riots that has occurred in our time." Beginning in the summer of 1839 and reaching a peak some four years later, in 1843, bands of horsemen roamed the countryside after dark dressed in skirts and shawls, their faces blackened. They called themselves the Maids of Rebecca—no one really knows why—and their targets were the hated tollgates. In a surprise attack they would set the thatched roofs alight and then attack the keeper when he or she came running out. The raid was usually over in seconds. By the time an alarm was out, the raiders had vanished into the hills. They were disciplined, they acted with stealth and suddenness, and they were desperate.

There were tollgates all over Wales, but the area in which these protests took place, in Cardigan and Carmarthen, is by an odd coincidence the part of Wales in which Richard and Mallie Lloyd Jones lived, the Black Spot of Unitarianism. The fact that the Lloyd Jones family left during the Rebecca Riots has not been remarked upon in family histories, but there is a close connection between the two dates. The riots began in earnest in March 1843, and the Lloyd Joneses decided to emigrate six months later, in September of that year. It may be just a coincidence, but the Lloyd Joneses could hardly have been unaware that terrorists had the countryside in an uproar, because raids were happening all around them. One of the first gates to be attacked was in the parish of Conwil Elfed on the road to Llandysul from Carmarthen in the south. Another attack took place in the same area two months later, and then a tollgate in Llandysul itself was destroyed. Shortly after that, in June 1843, after another gate, this one four miles outside the village of Llandysul, had been burned down, a mob of two to three thousand rioters was there to celebrate. Several hundred of them marched on Llandysul, their target the gate that had been pulled down and just restored. The rioters seized the four special constables guarding the gate and forced the men to help them tear it down again. By the middle of June, hardly a gate anywhere around Llandysul was left standing.

It is clear that no able-bodied man in Llandysul—a small village of perhaps a thousand souls—could have remained unaware or uninvolved. From the very beginning the rioters had depended upon door-to-door collections, and no family dared refuse. It was more than a local farmer's life was worth to be absent from their secret meetings. All this was happening at a time when a Welshman might be sentenced to death for rioting over the high price of food. The fact that Llandysul, situated on the border between Cardiganshire and Carmarthenshire, was even more a center of protest than Conwil Elfed, where the riots began, makes it likely that Richard Lloyd Jones was probably an active rioter himself. Over a century later, his hatred of the immensely wealthy squire Charles Lloyd, from whom he rented his land, was still common knowledge—that gentleman having driven roughshod over his fields and crops whenever he felt like it—so he would have needed little urging. And if he were looking for a biblical precedent, he might have received it from one of the local leaders of the riots, Thomas Emlyn Thomas, a Unitarian minister from the nearby village of Cribyn; it was known that dissenting ministers commonly "provided their hearers with scriptural justification for their action, even if they did not actually incite them to violence."

From the start the Maids of Rebecca had much more than the high cost of tolls on their minds; they were rebelling against the whole structure of society. In their pointed use of that despised language, Welsh, and in their emphasis on Welsh manners and mores, they were demonstrating their common cause with the rise of nationalism, which had become a major movement, in admiration of the French and American revolutions. Welsh societies in London, the Gwyneddigion, provided the intellectual basis for a revival of interest in ancient Welsh manuscripts, in history, language, literature and the law. One man in particular, a marvelously flamboyant figure named Iolo Morgannwg, is responsible for having revived the idea of the ancient (perhaps tenth century) national festival of the Eisteddfod. Morgannwg's revived version, a contest of music and poetry, began in

1850. He then invented a *Gorsedd*, or Order of Bards of the Island of Britain, in imitation of the bardic assemblies of former days. "With revolution coming hard on the heels of revolution, and a Tom Paine in every parish asserting that men could start the world all over again, they were swept by the multiple millenarianisms of the age of revolution. . . ."

The Rebecca Riots, and the upheaval they caused, were probably the main reason why Richard and Mallie left. They were fleeing from something, but also toward a dream that had bewitched the Welsh for half a century: that of a national home for the Welsh people on the American frontier. Since the Middle Ages a legend had circulated that a medieval Welsh prince, Madoc ab Owain Gwynedd, had sailed across the Atlantic in about A.D. 1170 and somehow landed in America. His descendants were now Welsh-speaking American Indians, whom some explorers claimed to have met.

The idea caused a sensation. Missionaries proclaimed their eagerness to find and convert the lost brothers. One Welsh explorer, John Evans, went looking for them (incidentally providing his future president, Thomas Jefferson, another American of Welsh descent, with the most accurate map then extant of the upper Missouri River Valley), and Welshmen at home, like William Jones (b. 1729), became authorities on the Land of Freedom. Jones, a self-taught, accomplished poet and musician, skilled antiquarian, amateur astronomer and physicist, brought the powers of his formidable personality to bear on organizing stock companies to promote emigration. The history of the Welsh-speaking people, he concluded, was one long struggle against English oppression. Their only hope "lay in the New World alongside the Lost Brothers."

No one ever found the Madoc Indians of course, but this hardly mattered since the romantic possibility "reinforced a sense of identity, added something to the flavor of an Israel to be created in the wilderness. The Madoc myth ran as an insistent descant to the Welsh diaspora of the 1780s; John Evans was slogging his way up the Missouri in quest of the Madoc Indians even as projectors were scouring the American frontier for the site of a *Gwladfa* or National Home; . . . They were building a *Kingdom of Wales*, as many a Welsh applicant for American citizenship told the clerks in Philadelphia." They also had a very clear idea of just what that new kingdom would be: exactly like the old one, but better and fairer. The free farmer, a minister wrote, would live on his own property, "and on his hearth the song of the harp and the company of the Welsh language. . . . There shall be there a chapel and school and a meeting house, and the old tongue as the means of worship and business, learning and government."

In the autumn of 1843 Mallie was pregnant again, which would have explained why the Lloyd Joneses waited a year before taking their momentous step. When the new baby arrived in the middle of November, it was named Jenkin, in honor of Richard's younger brother, who was already in the New World. His sister Rachel, her husband, Rees Beynon, and children and his sister Nell, with ten children, were all settled near one another in Wisconsin. Jenkin, a bachelor, had set sail a year before and, like his sisters before him, journeyed from one Welsh settlement to the next as he worked his way west in search of employment. He had visited Welsh communities in Utica and Steuben, New York, seen the slate quarries and coal mines of Pennsylvania where other Welshmen, with their special expertise, were in demand, traveling ever farther west across the Great Lakes to Galena and Mineral Point, that center of lead mining twenty miles or so to the south of the Lloyd Joneses' eventual home, The Valley. Jenkin's journey was typical of that made by other Welshmen, who had been warned not to remain in the East, where land was expensive and not so productive. There was plenty of good land to be had at fair prices in Illinois, Iowa and Wisconsin, and early Welsh settlers to Wisconsin were ecstatic about the quality of soil and gave glowing reports on their crop yields. Jenkin had passed through some wonderful wooded countryside on his way toward Mineral Point, and although clearing would be hard work, he thought it would be worth the effort. He urged them to join him.

Getting there, however, would be a nightmare. In the 1840s, most Welsh families emigrated from the port of Liverpool on sailing vessels, the new steam-powered and iron ships being considered useful only for river and coastal traffic. Richard and Mallie actually left for the New World from the back of their house. A long dirt track led over the hills for ten miles to the town of New Quay. They went in two hay wains, with the help of two cousins, sailing from that Welsh coastal town up the coast to Liverpool, and from there across the Atlantic. The length of the trip varied tremendously—from twenty days to six weeks—and although food was provided, travelers were advised to bring their own. Some endured terrifying crossings. Rev. John Jenkins, who preached in Wisconsin in the 1850s, spent three months on his crossing in 1841: "We had very stormy weather, and we were blown out of the Bay of Biscay and the Azore Islands; yes, we were nearly taken to Bermuda, and then back until we were in sight of New London. For eight days we were living on one biscuit a day along with a little water. Seven were buried at sea, and one may well imagine that we had a pretty bad look to us by the time we got to New York."

The Lloyd Joneses, crossing in the autumn of 1844, were almost as unlucky. The ship was small and uncomfortable and ran into heavy gales. The mainmast was carried away and the boat was forced to return to Liverpool, where they lived on board for two weeks while the necessary repairs were made. On the second voyage out, the boat took another battering. The sails were in shreds and the hull was leaking badly by the time they reached New York six weeks later. It was early December 1844.

Frank Lloyd Wright was almost ludicrously inept when it came to handling money, and it is instructive to see how soon this theme appears in the family history. The Lloyd Joneses are invariably prepared to trust a charming scoundrel, no matter how often they are warned to be on their guard. And when Welsh immigrants arrived at the New York docks, they received solemn warnings because, speaking little or no English, they were at the mercy of the first fast-talking stranger who came along. That was the trap, and Richard Lloyd Jones fell into it. He took the services of a Welsh-speaking "runner" to handle his baggage, allowed the man to escort them all to a seedy hotel and then to a money changer who unscrupulously fleeced him. Within seconds, the runner had disappeared, and Richard was left alone in a strange city, speaking no English, with a handful of useless foreign coins in his pocket and only the vaguest idea of where his hotel was.

That first scare was bad enough, but the family faced further hardships and real tragedy before they reached their Wisconsin destination a thousand miles farther west. Stuck for the winter in Utica because the lakes and canals were frozen, they set off dangerously early in the spring of 1845. The combined stresses were too much for the three-year-old Nanny. As they made their way by wagon from Utica to Rome, where they planned to pick up a canalboat, Nanny fell ill with a cold that rapidly became a high fever. The third morning on the road, she died in her mother's arms. They all stopped there and then, hollowing out a shallow grave in the bank by the roadside, which they lined with grass. As they were digging the grave, a group of canalboat men passed them, leading their mules to the boats in Rome. One called out, "Come on, Dick, that ain't Wisconsin, this ain't no picnic," misreading the signals. Mallie burst into a storm of weeping.

They traveled onward to Oconomowoc and thence to Ixonia, a neighboring Welsh settlement six miles from Watertown, where Jenkin, Rachel and Nell and their families had settled. Margaret, Richard's mother, wrote to tell one of his brothers, in 1852, "They are settled within a quarter of a mile to Rachel and are doing exceedingly well. So that I have from 30 to 40 between children and grandchildren in America living all in the same neighborhood. . . ." They had survived, but to say they were prospering would be an overstatement. Immigrant farmers of means usually bought established farms with buildings, cleared land and soil that had demonstrated its worth. Those less fortunate bought virgin land from the government, available in forty-acre parcels at the bargain price of $1.25 an acre. In making their choices, Richard and Jenkin repeated the error many of their countrymen would make, instinctively favoring a terrain that resembled the one they had left and that, in this case, presented identical disadvantages, with a few new ones thrown in. Not only was the land they chose stony and far less fertile than other land available, but it was heavily wooded, involving mammoth clearing problems. Newcomers, another immigrant wrote, would find "a country consisting of dreary forests, interspersed with settlements on the rudest scale, that the roads are generally in very bad condition, and, above all, that *everyone* must work hard with his own hands." They made a further mistake in buying some low-lying lands bordering their treed hillsides thinking that they would be "well-watered." That turned out to be truer than they knew. In summers the fields turned into marshes, fertile breeding grounds for mosquitoes, placing every new arrival in danger of contracting malaria. Brother Jenkin would die of what was then called "fever and ague."

It took the combined efforts of Jenkin and Richard, with the help of Thomas, now fifteen, John, thirteen, and no doubt Margaret and Mary as well, to clear the first lands and plant their first crops. Despite these handicaps and the birth of Elinor in 1845 (Jane, James and Enos were to follow in 1848, 1850 and 1853), Richard's farm prospered. In 1846 he bought his first two forty-acre parcels. He owned 110 acres when he left Ixonia, which he sold for the handsome price of $3,500.

The Lloyd Jones children would grow up having learned all about pioneer farming, and such domestic necessities as spinning, weaving, baking, dipping candles, churning butter and the like would have been essential skills as well. They would also need to know how to drill a well, dig out a root cellar, construct a fireplace and build a Dutch oven. In short, someone had to learn everything about building a house: that role fell to the eldest son, Thomas. His son would write, "he chose to be a builder," but given the battle for survival in which they were all engaged, it seems plausible that this choice was made for him. As soon as he could, Thomas trained as a carpenter, "and by intense application obtained a sufficient insight in geometry and advanced mathematics, which when applied to his architectural work placed him much in advance of the usual country carpenter." By the time Thomas was ready to marry, he had built himself a two-story house, and was accomplished enough to be in demand, building homes, schools and churches and the like throughout the countryside. Maginel Wright Barney, Frank Lloyd Wright's younger sister, recalled that her uncle was "slighter than the rest, and his hair and beard were neatly trimmed. I seem to remember him as rather gray all over. I can see him now slipping quietly along like a shadow through the lane of maples that led to his home. . . ."

In March 1856, ten years after they arrived in Ixonia, Richard and Mallie sold the farm. His brother Jenkin, who had bought land adjoining theirs, had died in the interim and a dispute arose between Richard and his sisters over its ownership (settled in Richard's favor). There is no doubt that the constant fear of malaria, the ever-growing family and the disappointing crop yields would have been persuasive reasons to move. There is also the possibility, raised by Jenkin's memoir of Black Week, that Richard and Mallie were, by then, estranged from their neighbors. One notes that, having arrived in The Valley, Richard and his children never ran the risk of joining another congregation, preferring to worship collectively in the open air. The trauma of Black Week would add a special urgency to Richard's dearest wish, the chapel of his own that he would not live to see finished. Everything that had happened would reinforce their Welsh clannishness, the impression they gave outsiders that they were enough unto themselves. If their area—at one time, they collectively held 1,800 acres—came to be known as "The Valley of the God-Almighty Joneses," there are some good reasons why.

To the north of Mineral Point, where brother Jenkin had stayed, were the villages of Dodgeville and Spring Green, the fertile Helena

Valley bordered on the north by the Wisconsin River, and several established Welsh settlements. In the settlement of Helena itself, on the southern banks of the Wisconsin River, a stopping place for men who floated the rafts of logs downstream to mills at St. Louis, a successful business for the making of lead shot had been established at Tower Hill. All this made the Helena Valley in Iowa County an up-and-coming place, but there were good enough reasons for wanting to remain in a countryside of such rich valleys, woods, streams and hills, and where there was plenty of government land available. The Lloyd Jones family worked farms for a few years before settling in The Valley on their own land in April 1864. For a time they lived just outside the village of Spring Green, then lived for a couple of years (1862–64) in Bear Creek, a rental farm near Lone Rock, also on the north bank of the Wisconsin River, a move that was to have some consequences in the life of their daughter Anna. Once finally installed on their own property in The Valley, however, they stayed. Richard and Mallie's homestead, the biggest and best they would own, is no longer standing. Their granddaughter Maginel remembered it as surrounded by "a picket fence twined with morning-glories and bean vines, its posts covered with shiny milk pails washed and drying in the sun." Aunt Mary's fourteen-room farmhouse survived her, but was struck by lightning and burned to the ground in the early 1940s. Uncle Enos's house was demolished. However, Uncle John's old farmhouse looks much as it did. Aunt Margaret's gambrel-roofed red cottage is still to be seen, as is Uncle Thomas's old house. Uncle James's home, on a bend of the road just past Unity Chapel, now much altered, still surveys "a lovely view of plowed fields striped in spring with tender green and later with green and yellow bands, lying like ribbons over the bones of the hills." Uncle Thomas built most of them, and a Welsh stonemason named Timothy carved the mantels of their fireplaces with mistletoe, holly and the family symbol, /|\ ,"Truth Against the World." The new land, with its homesteads, its fields and pastures, its streams with trout so tame they would feed from your hand, was the fulfillment of a dream for Richard and Mallie— the dream of "the free farmer on his own property, and on his hearth the song of the harp and the company of the Welsh language. . . ."

It was a moment of utter perfection in the lives of Richard and Mallie but it came very late. Mallie, "Ein Mam," who had borne eleven children, who had cooked, canned, washed, cleaned, dyed, ironed, knitted, spun, mended, made clothes, tended the garden, and no doubt harvested, chopped wood, carried fodder, fed and watered sheep, horses, pigs, cows and chickens as well, was worn out. She lived just five more years, dying in 1870 at the age of sixty-two or sixty-three. Her children remembered her as gentle and devoted, clairvoyant—she once had a vision in which she correctly saw her son Jenkin as wounded when he was fighting in the Civil War—a person who loved to tell about the old days in Wales and knew all the old fairy tales. To the end of her days, she spoke only Welsh.

As for that old radical, Richard, there is a photograph taken of him in 1883, two years before he died, surrounded by all his children, their husbands and wives, and his grandchildren, with an empty chair beside him where "Ein Mam" would have sat. He has a stick lying across his knees, his elbows rest negligently on the carved walnut arms of his great armchair, and he has the fixed gaze of a man for whom the word compromise had long since ceased to have a meaning. Growing deaf, forgetful, baffled, he staggered on, saying little, his voice, the wonderfully deep and rolling voice of the born preacher, still surprisingly resonant. That last summer he weeded the vegetables in the kitchen garden against the doctor's orders. "Perhaps he remembered all the springs he had spent uprooting those ageless trees, and something compelled him to enact a sad parody of his past strength one more time." So he bent, pulling plants at random, the weeds along with the young seedlings, and the aunts and uncles held their tongues.

The uncles were a handsome group. They resembled their father, being strongly built, with wide cheekbones and even features, shocks of dark curly hair and enormous beards, and James, at six-foot-two, was as tall as Richard had been. Maginel wrote, "To me they seemed gigantic beings who would toss me up for a kiss and I would shrink as my face was embedded in beard. Sometimes it would be damp with rain or fog, and then it was rather like kissing a swamp. The Uncles, as I've said, had a Biblical, apostolic look and once when four of them were driving through Madison in an open carriage someone yelled from the sidewalk: 'Hey, where's the other eight?' "

Young Jenkin, as has been noted, went off to fight in the Civil War—he and his family were united in opposition to slavery and passionate admirers of Lincoln—and, once the war was over, went to college in Meadville, Pennsylvania, following the example of his distinguished forebears and eponym. Uncle Thomas, making his mark as a country architect, could turn his hand at anything, whether it was the design of a new way to keep milk cool, which was much imitated, or the complete blueprints for a big new schoolhouse, which he would build for his clever sisters some years later. Uncle James, the tallest and most handsome, was set on his ambition to be a farmer; because there was not enough money for Uncle Enos to continue in college, he would do likewise. Uncle John, like Uncle Thomas, had always worked; as a mere child in Wales he had tended sheep. Among the stories Mallie told were of setting out to visit little John and Thomas as they sat on the mountainside, taking along something good to eat and warm clothes as well as her knitting. For his part, John remembered reciting the hymns his mother had taught him, as he sat there alone, in an effort to keep awake. Uncle John became the family miller and ground wheat for everyone for miles around. Maginel can remember seeing him at the door of his mill, "a spectral figure whitened with flour from head to foot."

She also recalled that when a piece of steel from a broken tool lodged in his hand, John refused to have it removed, shrugging off everyone's concern. Eventually his hand had to be amputated, but by then a cancer had started that would kill him. He would never allow painkillers because "they would blur my mind."

This stoicism was much admired among the Lloyd Joneses. Like all farm children, the boys were men by the ages of ten or eleven, expected to work long hours, to take on heavy responsibilities and to deal alone, somehow, with whatever emergency arose. Uncle James, riding old Kate in the early spring of 1862 when he was just twelve, was sent out to round up the work animals. Crossing a field he discovered a fine frozen pond and, although he might have known better, urged his horse to try the ice. The ice held, but the horse slipped, James fell, and Kate landed on his leg, breaking it. "Somehow he managed to haul himself back aboard the horse and get home, faint with pain." That would have been admired too.

They had acquired an admirable fixity of purpose from having watched their parents struggle and surmount fearful odds. From Richard they would have learned the stance of the radical: a combination of prickly willingness to be insulted, belligerent readiness to strike back against real and imagined wrongs and, perhaps, far below the surface, an underdog's awful fear that he is as worthless as the rest of the world believes. In short, they were true descendants of Rev. Jenkin Jones, founder of the first Arminian church in Llandysul, proud of their religion, pious and moralistic, as fiercely willing to defend that as anything else, but also passionately partisan where other oppressed minorities were concerned: slaves in the South, or the broken, pathetic Indians they encountered. As young men they struggled manfully to become self-sufficient. Because they had learned to work so hard and long, "add tired to tired," as Frank Lloyd Wright never ceased to exhort others, they had great physical stamina. They were incredibly brave, and they all had disastrous accidents at one time or another, making it difficult to know how much to ascribe to a too-obsessive determination to succeed, how much to recklessness and fatigue and how much to sheer bad luck. As a young carpenter, Uncle Thomas set up in business with a young friend, had built his own shop and seemed well on his way. But one time he was in too much of a hurry to dry out some lumber and stacked it too close to the heating pipe. The shop was carelessly left unattended, some board ends and shavings in front of the stove caught on fire, and the whole building went up in smoke. Of course, he and his partner had no insurance.

The biography of Enos, the youngest son, written by his son Chester, makes frequent references to accidents caused because one of the brothers was left alone with the sheep when an older one should have been there to help guard against wolves, and then the wolves descended, or other brothers thought it would be a lark to ride their horses into the river, and Enos almost drowned. And so the reminiscences go on. It is an odd coincidence that every Lloyd Jones brother but one, the preacher Jenkin, suffered a serious setback at some period or another of his life. In the spring of 1879, when he was forty-nine, Thomas fell from the second floor of a building, breaking two ribs and puncturing a lung, an injury from which he never fully recovered and which helped impoverish him. John's bad hand handicapped him for years. Enos had his share of childhood accidents, and was taken out of college when the family ran out of money. James, everyone's favorite and fond hope, was perhaps the most accident-prone of all. At least one other serious accident when he was young is recorded (he dropped an axe on his foot), and the circumstances of his death would bring them all down with him, but that is the subject for a later chapter. It is at least possible that Richard, in particular, was authoritarian and demanding, and that pressure to succeed was unwearying. In that case, a spectacular accident—totally outside conscious control—was the only way a driven Lloyd Jones son, or daughter, might lighten the load without recriminations. At that point they might decently retire from battle, but if they did not, there was only one end in sight. Did she remember, Frank Lloyd Wright asked his sister, Maginel, one day, "you told me once, when I was reaching so high, that someday I would pull something down that would destroy me."

As one would expect, James was also a stern taskmaster, a fact his nephew Frank would remember all his life. This trait was much leavened by James's innate kindliness and generosity. His brothers were the same. They tried to be loving parents, always thinking of the next present, no matter how modest, and they loved picnics, usually initiated by Uncle Thomas. Enos remembered many family gatherings, bonfires, tramps through the woods and skating parties, fun at Hallowe'en and April Fools' Day and wonderful molasses taffy and cakes and cookies and pies. They all loved music, books and poetry. Thomas's son recalled that his father could make sense out of Shakespeare's most baffling passages, which he loved to read aloud on the long winter evenings, as he did Longfellow. In the spring of 1862, when Jenkin was fighting in the Civil War and it was believed that a generous supply of onions would prevent scurvy, the cause of Jenkin's comrades became the Lloyd Jones cause. The whole family planted enough onions for a regiment and bent their backs all summer long, weeding and hoeing to ensure a big crop. Months later the family was still receiving letters of thanks. The favorite was, "Your onions brought tears to my eyes."

"Tall, wise, protective, they seemed almost as immortal and invincible as gods," Maginel wrote of her uncles. "They were knowledge and authority and strength. They would be there always, and no harm could come to them—would dare to come to them. Or that is how it seemed to us."

As for the girls in the family, Jane (often called Jennie) was hauntingly beautiful when she was young. The other four tended to have long, thin, sensible faces, rather than high-cheekboned ones, and a spartan look about them. Three of them became teachers: Jennie, Elinor (called Nell) and Hannah (Anna); Margaret and Mary got married. The Lloyd Jones children still traced their ancestry—one recalls that there were ministers and educators on both sides—back through their paternal grandmother to the aristocratic Lloyd family. A remnant of the old Celtic emphasis on the superior claims of the mother's clan can be seen in some of the Lloyd Jones daughters when one considers that two of those who married achieved the feat of folding their husbands into their family circle, rather than vice versa. Maginel Wright Barney, one of the few sources of lore about the women in the family, believed that non-Welsh husbands or wives were never quite accepted. "It was a disadvantage . . . something not quite right; just as it was not quite right for Aunt Mary to have married a Scot, or my mother to have married a New Englander."

Aunt-Mary-who-married-the-Scot seems to have been the jolliest one. Aunt Margaret, four years Anna's senior, the first girl in the family, is generally described as the peacemaker. Nell and Jennie, who never married, becoming known to everyone as the Aunts, built Hillside, their unique boarding school, in The Valley. Jennie was everyone's favorite. Nell seemed to be sterner, sadder, less approachable. She had fallen in love with a handsome young man, and they were engaged to marry. Then she contracted smallpox. Her face became deeply scarred, and her hair went white. Her fiancé came to visit her, was appalled, and never returned. It was, by chance, the summer of the onions, when she was just seventeen.

" 'Aunt Nell, how did you bear it?' " Maginel asked. " 'What did you *do*?'

"She gave me a grim little smile. 'I hoed onions my dear,' she said. 'I just hoed onions all summer long.' "

The Lloyd Jones girls, then, were expected to face disaster with the same stoicism as the boys, and they must have worked just as hard, or harder. That their epoch would have treated them as less important people than their brothers is too obvious to need emphasis. Nevertheless, they were not as downtrodden as their relatives in Wales, as Maginel discovered when she eventually went to visit a distant Welsh cousin in Landysul and witnessed the manner in which he bullied his wife and daughters. One would also expect them, as members of a large family, to have grown up with little individual attention. Jane wrote a revealing reminiscence that supports this thesis. Her greatest joy as a child was the summer she was kept at home to help her mother while the others went to school. One does not find a hint of reproach that she was losing out on the fun of being with her playmates, and not even a twinge of self-pity at the hard work involved. She was deliriously happy because she had been singled out as the favored one—she had her mother all to herself. It must have been the first and last time that this ever happened to her.

Children who are inadequately nurtured are said to idealize their parents, and this certainly seems to have happened with the girls in the Lloyd Jones family. Maternal love is the theme of Jane's reminiscence; it almost seems to have been the highest possible good. Mother lived for her children, and, as a reward, they idealized her. She was guardian of the hearth and home, she transmitted the cultural values, she kept the family together, and, as we have seen, the children belonged most of all to her. She was literally their first teacher in the early pioneer years, and since teaching and mothering were so closely allied—perhaps even synonymous in the minds of "Ein Mam's" daughters—one is not surprised to find that three out of five became teachers.

By the time Nell and Jennie were old enough to go to academy and college, the family could afford to help with the cost of their education. They soon held important teaching positions. Before they established their own school, Aunt Nell was head of the history department in the River Falls State Normal School in Wisconsin, while Aunt Jennie had become director of kindergarten training schools in St. Paul, Minnesota. Anna, who was seven years older than Nell and ten years older than Jennie, was just as interested in teaching, but not so fortunate in her training. She learned the way many young women could enter the profession in those days, i.e., she went from being a promising pupil in an elementary school to an assistant teacher. From that time onward, she taught herself. "Education obsessed her," her daughter wrote, "and she would teach anyone who showed even the vaguest desire to learn. She did not wait for pupils to seek her out: she went to them, willingly." One must not forget that Anna's first language was Welsh, and although she learned to pen her letters to copperplate perfection, and her grammar was punctiliously correct, she never mastered spelling and would cheerfully write out a word phonetically, leading to some curiously original constructions.

As Maginel described her, Anna was tall (five-foot-eight) and handsome, with large brown eyes, a wide forehead and a mass of curly hair that she pulled to the back of her head, where it fell in ringlets in what was called "a waterfall." She never changed her hairstyle when it went out of style, just as she never wore corsets even when wasp waists were all the rage, and although she loved color, she would not wear it. One sees her in early photographs, her hair parted dead center and pulled back severely from her face, wearing a prim white collar and a cameo brooch.

Anna is often described as self-reliant, an idea much reinforced by her daughter's description of her as a fine horsewoman, out in all weather, a soldier's cape with hood and brass buttons slung over her shoulders. "I like to imagine my mother, bare-headed, curly haired,

*Wright's mother,
Anna Lloyd Jones*

*The Lloyd Jones family, 1883, taken shortly before the death of Richard
Lloyd Jones (center, with stick between his legs). The empty chair beside him
was placed in memory of his late wife, Mallie. From left, back row: Enos
holding baby Chester, James holding baby Scott, John, Nettie, Thomas B.
Jones, Margaret, Thomas, Esther, William Carey Wright, Anna, James
Philip and Mary. Middle row, from left: Elinor holding baby Agnes,
Laura holding baby Maud, J. Richard holding Gwen, Orren, Ellen, Ed-
ward, M. Helen, Jane, her niece Jane standing behind her, Elsie, Mar-
garet and Anna Nell. Front row, from left: Thomas, Mary, Jenkin,
Charles, Richard, Frank with Maginel on his lap, Susan with Mary
Lloyd at her feet and Jenkin with Richard at his feet*

sitting straight in the saddle, her beautiful intelligent eyes appreciating
all they saw, and a strand of traveler's joy, pulled from a hedgerow,
wreathed around the pommel." Anna was a second mother to her
younger brothers and sisters—Enos recalls how hard she tried to teach
him to read and write—and Maginel remembered that "by the time
she was fifteen she had acted as assistant to the midwife in half a dozen
family births." Perhaps it was not unusual for a girl in a pioneer
society to assist at her own mother's lyings-in (if this is the correct
inference), but it presents a picture of someone who did not have
much of a childhood, an impression reinforced by her comment in old
age (to her son) that she had felt hemmed in all her life by circumstance.

From an early account, which gives an excellent insight into Anna's
character and, more particularly, from letters she wrote to her son
that have recently been made available for study, Anna emerges as
impulsive, erratic, headstrong and completely at the mercy of some
very uncomfortable and conflicting emotions. To begin with, she
believed with her sisters that she should be a model of maternal love
and all the tender virtues, yet be stoical, self-sufficient, ride like a
man and scorn feminine accoutrements. As a Lloyd, she should strive
all her life to be worthy of that exalted name, and make others aware
of her claim to superior social status while remaining proud of her
humble farm origins. As a Lloyd Jones, and heir to a long tradition
of religious radicalism, it was her obligation to fight against discrimination and bigotry, showing others the way by being better, truer
and braver than they were—more like Lincoln, more like Jesus, even.
In old age she was still talking about the cultivation of moral attributes,
using a garden as her hackneyed metaphor. Such pious moralizing and
easy sentimentality came naturally to Victorians, but it is evident that
Anna literally believed she should live up to her Bunyanesque ideals.
But the situation was more complicated still, since, being a Lloyd
Jones, a high premium was placed on combativeness, on prevailing
against impossible odds: "Truth Against the World." Yet if she were
to live up to her own perfectionistic standards, there was no room for
anger and retaliation, since it was her Christian duty to suppress
rancorous thoughts. Someone who is attempting to live up to such
exacting standards of behavior may, sooner or later, despair of continually striving to "do better," and, indeed, Anna enraged was a
reckless and obstinate fighter. Proud of her minority status, tenacious
in her loyalties, emotionally unpredictable, torn by conflicting sets of
obligations, aloof and stubborn, Anna was not an easy person to
understand or ignore.

Anna was sentimental about the past. She wrote about the travails her family had undergone in the early days and reminded her son of the role faith had played in sustaining them during those difficult times. She was equally sentimental about The Valley, where she had lived since the age of fourteen and which was the setting for her fondest memories. To The Valley had been transferred all of an uprooted child's longing to feel again the security of a loved and familiar landscape. For Anna it was a holy place; it was "consecrated ground."

Her children have described Anna's sensitive love for nature, and it is one of her most marked characteristics. Such an awareness, she wrote, came from "Ein Mam," who taught them the traditional lore about plants, animals and flowers, linking those thoughts with ideas of religion. It was an old-fashioned idea of education now thought, she wrote in 1919, to be modern and novel. At will she could lie down, close her eyes, and see The Valley in all its splendor. She wrote of the first heralds of spring, the clumps of bright color underfoot, the boughs unveiling their first shoots, the return of migrant birds, and all those beloved and heartening demonstrations of life's rebirth that made her feel, then at least, that there was something to hope for. The Welsh concept of nature as one's fortress in adversity, and a salve to the soul, is evident here. She believed, in common with Juvenal, that "Nature and wisdom always say the same," and exhorted her son to study the natural world, to estimable effect. She might then link concepts of Truth, Beauty, Simplicity and Nature with the idea of a home, the perfect home, or just a single wonderful room, something that would have had a poignant symbolism for someone who might never have had a room of her own as a child. After one move into new quarters, and after the movers had placed a table in just the right corner of her bay window, she wrote feelingly about the reassurance of such familiar objects and how she felt restored to life almost, as if her room and her very existence were one and the same. But perhaps her most telling comment to her son, often repeated, was the high and almost sacred importance she placed upon the role of architect. There was no distinction to be made between her brother Jenkin's role as a preacher for the Truth and the edifices her son was building.

Here, then, is an emotionally troubled but intelligent, responsive, and gifted woman who might have made her mark, had she been given the educational opportunity, but who would stand back while her younger sisters received these advantages, leaving her own promise largely unfulfilled. This must account for the theme of melancholy and regret one finds in Maginel's conclusion: "She . . . had always seemed to yearn for some elusive thing, something that refused to take shape, to come forward into the consciousness and make itself known."

Anna did not marry until she was twenty-seven or twenty-eight, which would have been considered late, and nothing is known about her life as a young woman. The only safe guess is that she never taught too far from home, and would have returned to the family hearth each weekend, if not each evening. If they were teaching far from their homes, rural teachers customarily lodged with their pupils' families, the length of stay depending on the number of children enrolled in school. So it is conceivable, as is asserted in one account, that Anna met her future husband, William Carey Wright, when she went to board with him and his three children while his first wife, Permelia, was alive. The oldest child by that marriage, Charles William, could have been ready for school by then. One has to believe, however, that Anna's stay was brief, since the most reliable account of that period, written by one of William's children, makes no mention of her presence. Further, no documentation to support this has ever been found, according to Mary Jane Hamilton, a Wisconsin scholar and expert on the early history of the Lloyd Jones family.

What is known is that Permelia Holcomb Wright and Anna Lloyd Jones had relatives in common. The Lloyd Joneses' move to Bear Creek, outside Lone Rock, made them near neighbors of a family named Thomas. Permelia Wright was related to the Thomases through her mother; Anna was also related to the same branch of Thomases through her mother. There is yet another way William Wright and Anna Lloyd Jones might have met: he was superintendent of the school district in which she worked.

The Lloyd Jones family was building in The Valley, and living in Bear Creek in 1863, the year Permelia died in childbirth. Elizabeth Amelia, almost three, George Irving, five, and Charles William, seven, were put in the care of their maternal grandmother.

The date of Anna and William's marriage is variously given as 1865 or 1866 (the most authoritative being August 17, 1866), and it is possible that there might have been some connection between the move of Richard and Mallie Lloyd Jones to The Valley and the marriage of their daughter Anna. One by one, the children were leaving. Jenkin had gone off to the Civil War and then to college, and the Aunts, Nell and Jennie, were set in the direction of teaching careers. Thomas was living in the house he had built for his wife of three years. John was about to get married, Margaret had already married, and of the first five, those children born in Wales, only Mary and Anna remained unmarried. Mallie Lloyd Jones was still in her fifties but, as has been noted, did not have long to live. "Ein Mam" may have wanted to see Anna settled in a home of her own. For his part, William Wright was newly bereft and in need of a mother for his children without delay. The added factor of Anna's Thomas connections, making her almost a relative of Permelia's, could have made a favorable impression on William.

What would certainly have been important to Anna was her future husband's pedigree, and this, he could claim, was more distinguished than her own. True, he was not Welsh, but it is said that his ancestor, a seventeenth century English noblewoman named Mabel Harlakenden, could trace her lineage back to William the Conqueror and even to Cardie the Saxon, A.D. 512. William Wright's father, David, was a Baptist minister, and he himself studied medicine and law before establishing himself as an organist and teacher of the pianoforte. When Anna met him, he was studying for the ministry.

It is thought that William Wright married Anna strictly for practical reasons and that, for her part, the marriage offered a last chance to escape spinsterhood. No one has considered the possibility that Anna might have been head over heels in love, though this could have been the simple truth. Over and over again one finds evidence that William was one of life's darlings: he never met a single person who did not like him. Arriving in Lone Rock in 1859, where he set up as a lawyer, although he never had a degree, he was appointed commissioner of the Richland County Circuit Court within a year. When he announced his candidacy for county school superintendent, a local newspaper editor wrote enthusiastically, "Probably no better man could be selected. His friends speak very highly of him." He was a mesmerizing lecturer. He gave the eulogy for Abraham Lincoln in Lone Rock in April 1865, and it was reported that he made "an appropriate and eloquent address which . . . was highly praised by all who heard it." If he gave concerts on the pianoforte, or recitals— he had a fine bass voice—these would be the best anyone had ever heard. When he wrote waltzes, polkas and gavottes in the popular, sentimental taste of the day, publishers magically appeared. When he tried his hand at business in a new town, he was certain to be described as up-and-coming, an asset to the community. It seems he had only to appear in order to be snapped up, made much of and offered tempting opportunities. Such a man, one would think, could not help succeeding. And yet no sooner had he arrived and conquered than he would mysteriously depart, sometimes within the year. Conventional accounts draw a polite veil over the likely reason for this pattern of striking success and collapse of hopes, which does, however, point to a defect of character that would not be immediately apparent. To Anna this divinely talented, literate, accomplished and alluring man must have seemed like a phenomenon, her tutelary escort to a wider and more wonderful world. He must have seemed to have all the attributes she felt herself to lack; and from envy to adoration is a short step.

William Wright was fourteen years Anna's senior, and by 1883, standing in the back row of a family photograph, he, at fifty-eight years old, with white hair and beard, looks to be much older and bears an uncanny resemblance to Richard Lloyd Jones, identically bearded, in the front row. Pictures of him as a younger man show him to have been most handsome, with a broad forehead, finely formed features and a natty bow tie—he always was a jaunty dresser. One can imagine the objections of Richard and Mallie to an American of English stock, born and raised in New England, rather than a proper Welshman, although these might have been merely a matter of form. Anna could quickly point to her future husband's polish, culture and pronounced musical gifts, always a mitigating factor for the Lloyd Joneses. She could talk about the stir he made when he eulogized their hero, President Lincoln. She could dwell on the fact that he had recently been ordained a minister. Even if he were a Baptist, which certainly was a drawback, he had been "called" to preach, another persuasive argument. At any rate, they were married. In May 1867, William and Anna moved from Lone Rock to Richland Center, where he would oversee construction of the Central Baptist Society's new building. One month later, on June 8, Anna gave birth to Frank Lincoln Wright.

3

The Shining Brow

Yet through his flight he could understand the twittering of the birds
in the coppice, the thoughts of the little snakes darting from the brushwood,
and the stir of life in the hidden centers of the ground.

—THOMAS S. JONES, JR.
Taliesin

If Frank Lloyd Wright had wanted to be thought of as a chosen one, a savior, he could not have chosen a better mate than his third wife, Olgivanna. In the books and articles she wrote after his death, Olgivanna Lloyd Wright painted an exalted portrait of her beloved. "He can weave himself like a cobra around the mountain range and he can rear like a flying Pegasus ready to take off to the highest pinnacle" is a characteristic example. So it is not surprising to find her writing, with respect to the day he was born, that "he told me that he had made his entrance into the world on a stormy night and described it to me as though he had witnessed the prophetic initiation. 'The wind rose over the earth forcing trees low to the ground. Lightning ignited the clouds, and thunder struck like a great fury.' 'Yours was a prophetic birth,' his mother told him."

Nor could he have improved on his mother, Anna Lloyd Jones Wright, whose fiercely partisan love for her son is almost a legend. On his twentieth birthday, June 8, 1887, Anna rose early as she had the day he was born. He arrived at eight a.m. and she greeted him with rapture, she wrote; but then, the sanctity of Mother Love and the marvel and wonder of babies were subjects of which Anna never tired. Her son was her Prince, and whether she actually told him that his birth had been prophesied hardly needs to be proved. Given Anna Wright's convictions, tirelessly repeated, it is perfectly possible that, by adulthood if not before, Frank Lloyd Wright saw himself as pre-destined. It is also logical that he would look for metaphors in the rich tradition of fairy tales and pagan Celtic myths that had been handed on to him by Anna, believing as she did in the children's story hour, through her own mother. She would have told him about the sacred places in Wales connected by tradition to supernatural events: "Until recently, firm belief kept alive stories of the *Telwyth Teg*, or the fairy folk, whose kingdom is a place of great poetic power. This is because the Heaven World of the Celts was not situated in some inhuman region of space, but was here on earth."

The name Wright would choose for his home, Taliesin, betrays the force of this early indoctrination since Taliesin is not only an actual historical personage but also a poet-savior, magician, spinner of rid-dles, seer and supernatural being. Taliesin's story is cited in Joseph Campbell's *The Hero with a Thousand Faces* as one more example of a legendary figure who, being made privy to supernatural knowledge, is destined to die and be reborn. In his original incarnation, Taliesin was Gwion Bach, a village boy who found himself charged by the goddess Caridwen (linked with crop fertility and also poetry and letters) to stir a vast kettle in which she was concocting a magical brew that would confer inspiration. By accident, three drops of the boiling liquid splashed on his finger and when, to stop the burning, he licked off the liquid, he suddenly "foresaw everything that was to come." What he also saw was that Caridwen meant to kill him. He fled, changing his shape in an effort to outwit her, but she was even faster and eventually caught and ate him. "And, as the story says, she bore him nine months, and when she was delivered of him, she could not find it in her heart to kill him, by reason of his beauty. So she wrapped him in a leathern bag, and cast him into the sea to the mercy of God, on the twenty-ninth day of April." His bag washed up into a fish trap, where it was discovered next morning by Elphin, son of a wealthy landowner, and his men. On finding a beautiful baby boy, Elphin's men said, "Behold a radiant brow [*taliesin*]!" "Taliesin be he called," said Elphin. Elphin was at first disappointed with his catch, but was reassured by the magical child, already able to talk in rhyme, who explained, "Primary chief bard am I to Elphin/ And my original country is the region of the summer stars;/ Idno and Heinin called me Merddin,/ At length every king will call me Taliesin."

One can see how attractive this figure, with his seer's wand and magician's cape, would have seemed to Wright, born as he was into a Welsh family of radical thinkers, outcasts beyond their own small circle but privately convinced of their special, even exalted status. Such an identification with a miraculous and priestlike being can be seen as an immature attempt to compensate for an ignominious beginning and a felt lack of advantages. That his parents were poverty-stricken is evident from his mother's letters. For someone so exquisitely sensitive to the *genius loci* and with such a gift for celebrating it, Wright was laconic to the point of taciturnity about his birthplace, and discouraged anyone who inquired about it, even his sister Maginel. After his death, an abandoned bungalow in Richland Center that was scheduled for demolition briefly made the papers when it was said that, according to local tradition, it had been Wright's birthplace. It was in a ruinous state, with tilting floors and no doors, but a case for its preservation was hard to make since it was clear that, architecturally speaking, there was nothing to save.

As has been noted, William and Anna had moved to the county seat of Richland Center a month before the birth of their first child where, as his daughter Elizabeth Wright Heller wrote, William had been "called to preach," as well as oversee construction of the new Central Baptist Society Building. In short, Anna was caring not only for a new baby but also for Lizzie, six, George Irving, eight, and Charles William, ten.

William Carey Wright made an immediately favorable impression in Richland Center as preacher and musician—his first local concert was given in aid of the church building fund—and, predictably, was flatteringly reviewed by the local paper. But Richland Center was a disappointment, and despite the "donation parties" organized to bring in some extra funds for the Wright household, and to help feed four children (with another on the way), William was chronically short of funds. So before long he was planning to move to McGregor, Iowa, on the Mississippi River. They arrived in March 1869, just one month, perhaps by another coincidence, before the birth of Mary Jane, later known as Jennie. Again, Wright preached; he was given the post of temporary pastor for the Baptist Church, and tried to make some

*Purported to be the birthplace of Frank Lloyd Wright in
Richland Center, Wisconsin*

money as a businessman: he bought a part interest in the music
department of a general store. Wherever he went, Wright demonstrated his dazzling gift for attracting the friendship of prominent
local men and women, not to mention the town's newspaper editors.
The flattering notices began, "Our city has reason to be glad that so
valuable a gentleman has been added to its religious, musical and
social lists," wrote the *McGregor Times*. His listeners came to "expect
something original, practical and unhackneyed from Mr. Wright,"
the same newspaper commented. "He is a plain speaker and for that
we like him." Another triumph, and another disappointment. Two
years after their arrival, the Wrights again packed up and left. They
were taken in by Anna's family at Hillside (Lizzie was sent to stay
with her Grandmother Holcomb), while William prepared for his next
move to Pawtucket, Rhode Island, where he had been "called to
preach" at the High Street Baptist Church. It might have seemed like
a promotion, but, as has been observed, only someone as impractical

as William Carey Wright could have thought so. The original church
had burned down three years before. Arriving in December 1871, the
Reverend Mr. Wright faced the enormous task of raising funds to
rebuild his church and also clear up his congregation's past debts.

Anna, facing her third move in five years of marriage, with five
children in her charge, settled the family in nearby Central Falls,
where, for the first year, they were obliged to live on the first and
third floors of a house, surely one of the most unpleasant living arrangements that can be imagined. The situation improved slightly
during their second year, Lizzie noted, when they had a whole house
to themselves. William tackled his new role with his customary energy
and zest. For three years he worked tirelessly, and although he did
not succeed in rescuing the church (after he left, the property was sold
to the town as a high school), no one thought him to blame. The
task had been too difficult for any mortal, and the minister had been
"earnest, unwearied, successful, as far as circumstances permitted."
His public appearances were, as usual, closely followed by the local
newspapers and always favorably received. When not fund raising,
William could be found making political speeches or lecturing on
temperance, one of his favorite subjects, or talking about ancient
Egypt, another specialty. The local Baptist societies snapped him up,
and his congregation doted on him. They rallied around in a good-
natured, clumsy way to meet the family's pressing needs when the
church, as often happened, could not pay his salary, arriving at the
house with casseroles and some dollar bills as well. These "donation
parties" were humorously recounted in the usual social columns. Two
years later, William and Anna conceded defeat. Again, to judge from
their actions, they left before they seemed to have anywhere else to
go. He did not take up a new post until September 1874, but they
left Pawtucket in December 1873. They waited out the intervening
months at the home of his father, Rev. David Wright, in Essex,
Connecticut. Then they moved once more, this time to Weymouth,
Massachusetts, in the environs of Boston, where William had been
"called to preach" at the First Baptist Church.

William's predictable pattern of easy success followed by stunning
disappointment makes only one conclusion evident: that he was wildly
impractical about money. Even his daughter Lizzie, who adored him
and defended his actions, wrote that "he had no financial sense whatever." Her explanation implied that her father was too rarefied a being
to be concerned with such worldly matters. One guesses that this was

probably quite true, and that William saw himself as someone of rare intellectual endowments and accomplishments: as a silver-tongued preacher, an irresistible singer and instrumentalist, an exemplary teacher and model citizen. He was showering his gifts on his community, and that was the end of his responsibility to life. The attitude seems familiar and reminds one, as Oliver Goldsmith wrote in his life of that eighteenth century arbiter of manners at Bath, Beau Nash, of "those young men who, by youth and too much money, are taught to look on extravagance as a virtue." Living beyond one's income was proof of breeding, and so William Carey Wright, consistently charming, exhorting and dazzling, pursued the life of a gentleman and a scholar with a fine disdain for his tradesmen's bills. Those with such a glowing conviction of others' obligations often have the happy knack of convincing society that it does, indeed, owe them a living, at least for a while. The one to be pitied is the partner, expected to forgive and forgive again, when there is nothing in the pantry and no money to buy shoes. She, at least, cannot support the delusion of grandeur, but neither can she voice her disapproval very freely when everyone else believes her husband to be so charming, so cultivated and so gifted—and when she also wishes secretly that the mirage of position were a reality. Behind closed doors her reproaches can be predicted, along with the kind of defense William would be expected to make. Besides, he was capable of fits of generosity, with a devilish willingness to clean out his pockets if, by some chance, there was money in them. When Lizzie got married, William helped her fiancé pick out a lavish wedding gift: a Story and Camp organ. He even paid for the freight, his daughter noted with satisfaction. William never suspected that he might be playing a role in his own downfall. His daughter recalled that, as an old man, her father gloomily reviewed his past and concluded that he had never had a chance.

If one accepts the possibility that money—how to get it and spend it—was one of the enduring battles raging between Anna and William, it becomes easier to see why the marriage failed. Anna would not have minded the hard work (after all, she was a farmer's daughter), but she would have minded the fact that life never seemed to get any easier. She, with three of her husband's children to take care of, would have resented his cavalier attitude toward feeding and clothing them. She would have been disappointed that she, with some social status in the community as the pastor's wife, did not have the house to go with it. She once told her daughter Jennie that she had lived for years in the hope that she might one day be able to indulge in her love for beautiful objects. Against all the odds, she had made sure the children would not suffer. In old age her thoughts returned to the endless household work it had taken to bring up children and make them look tidy on no money at all. Of all the crosses she had to bear, cooking was perhaps the worst. She never had managed to like it. As for the times when they would have to pack up and leave, swallow their pride and beg their relatives for a roof over their heads, these were the unkindest of all. When Frank was apparently snubbed by a relative and complained about it to his mother, Anna replied that this was nothing new. She had suffered from the same treatment when she had been bundled off to her father's one summer because they were penniless. Anna did not reproach her relatives who, she implied, were justified. The person who had let them down was Frank's father.

Money can often be a substitute for love, and perhaps it became such a central issue because Anna felt that William did not love her, or did not love her enough. She had, after all, grown up in constant competition with her brothers and sisters for her parents' attention. She had, after all, married someone she might have expected to be paternal, someone much more outwardly self-assured, certainly more accomplished, than she was, someone she hoped would lift her to a higher social and intellectual plane. So he had disappointed her on this score. Furthermore, she apparently discovered very soon that William's heart still belonged, if not to Permelia, then certainly to Permelia's children and especially to Elizabeth. Elizabeth Wright Heller's memoir of her childhood paints a classic portrait of a hateful, vengeful, almost demonic stepmother, and one gains the impression that Anna was competing with her stepchildren for their father's attention as a child among children, while using an adult's unfair advantage. When Anna went for her, Lizzie would run to hide behind her father, and Anna would have to stop, like a child caught misbehaving. Lizzie casually observed that her stepmother was actually jealous of her. Anna's fierce absorption in her firstborn begins to take on another aspect if one places it within the framework of her particular emotional dilemma: she was just one more in the crowd fighting a losing battle for love. Her husband might prefer his little girl (and, after all, those children belonged to the Holcomb family, not the Lloyd Joneses, if one accepts her Welsh reasoning), but her baby boy, and later her girls, were hers alone. Anna turned on Frank the full force of her starved emotional needs, and if there was a considerable element of primitive vindictiveness involved, and if she could get even with William by attacking Elizabeth and adoring Frank, so much the better. William had failed her in the most crucial way a husband can fail a wife. He had withheld the undivided love that was her due, and so he owed her money.

Frank Lloyd Wright always explained that his choice of profession had been decided for him by his mother before he was born. The good-natured way in which he seemed to imply that he had never had any alternative was, no doubt, perfectly true. But to believe that the choice of architecture was frivolously made would be to misunderstand Anna Lloyd Wright and her priorities as the pioneering daughter of Welsh immigrants. Her brothers had obediently made their own wishes sub-servient to the group's needs. Thomas, the firstborn, had painstakingly evolved from backwoods carpenter to a man who could design and build a house. At the time of Frank's birth, he was thirty-seven years old and in demand all over The Valley. That he might have served as an exemplary model is obvious; as Anna's eldest brother, his im-portance would have been second only to "Ein Tad's." What the family needed now was someone to build a church for them, the religious radicals and outcasts, in their adopted Valley. Erecting a building consecrated to their beliefs was their goal and passion in the years when Frank was growing up and "Ein Tad" was still alive. There is reason to doubt whether the wood engravings of English cathedrals that Wright describes in his autobiography could have been hanging around his crib as early as he thought they were. The point at issue here surely is that this is what Wright thought he remembered. From Frank's earliest moments Anna had successfully managed to fix his gaze on the future work she had planned for him. Wright wrote in his autobiography, "The boy, she said, was to build beautiful buildings . . . she intended him to be an Architect." That he should capitalize the word also reflects her influence. "I had grown up from childhood with the idea that there was nothing quite so sacrosanct, so high, so sacred as an architect, a builder," he said in later years. Behind that belief was Anna's central philosophy, as summed up in her favorite quotation from Shakespeare, "And this our life, exempt from public haunt/ Finds tongues in trees, books in the running brooks/ Sermons in stones, and good in everything." For "good in everything," Anna would have substituted the word God. "And I say they are just alike;

only Jenkin preached; Frank builds." So, to prepare her son for his elevated future role, Anna, believing in prenatal influences, tried to keep her thoughts on a higher plane. But she was also an experienced teacher, and the actual prospect of having a child could well have plunged her into her first real study of child development. Entirely self-educated, with no formal training to bias her responses, she was very receptive to new ideas. The summer of Frank's birth, her sister Nell, twenty-two, would have been finishing her studies, and sister Jennie, at nineteen, would have been starting her own. It seems possible, even likely, that whatever Nell and Jennie were learning at this impressionable stage would have been handed on to Anna; Jennie, after all, would become a director in charge of training teachers in kindergarten methods. When she came to write about their mother, Jennie observed, "When . . . I took up the study of early child development as voiced by Froebel and others, I was astonished to find how very familiar the philosophy seemed. . . ." So the link is a direct one through Jane Lloyd Jones to Anna Lloyd Wright and the teachings of the great Friedrich Froebel, a pioneer in the field of early child development and inventor of the kindergarten.

The early life of Friedrich Wilhelm August Froebel, born in the small German principality of Schwarzburg-Rudolstadt, Germany, late in the eighteenth century, has certain parallels with that of Anna Lloyd Wright and her sisters. He, too, was the child of a pastor (in his case, a Lutheran), and if the Lloyd Jones girls saw little of their mother, he saw nothing at all, since his died when he was nine months old. Like them, he idealized her, "creating in his imagination an ideal mother who is the central figure in one of his most famous books, *Mother Songs and Games*, where she is virtually canonized as a saint," his biographer wrote. He was a solitary boy and spent much time, as they did, in direct contemplation of nature. He, too, felt he had gained an insight into the essential unity of things through such daily exposure. Like Froebel, Anna believed education must provide the child with an awareness of the natural law, so as to "develop the powers of reason and convey a sense of the harmony and order of God: 'God's works reflect the logic of his spirit and human education cannot do anything better than imitate the logic of nature.' " Anna's dictum that "education [was] the direct manifestation of God," as her son described it, would seem directly derived from Froebel; his belief in the "Divine Principle of Unity" would have had an irresistible appeal for her. As her son wrote of the Lloyd Joneses, "UNITY was their

Pupils of the seventh and eighth grades of the Second Ward School, Madison, 1880–81: Frank Lloyd Wright, age thirteen, last row at top right, wearing a neckline bow and a belted jacket

watchword, the sign and symbol that thrilled them, the UNITY of all things!" In his Rousseauian belief in the essential goodness of the human spirit, and his emphasis on nature and spirit as manifestations of an ultimate reality, Froebel was rebelling against the whole concept of education as it was then taught. Children were not, as they were being treated, inert lumps of clay to be imprinted with a teacher's stamp, but potentially creative, productive beings whose active wills should be encouraged, whose latent abilities studied and whose physical development carefully fostered. One dared not wait until school age, Froebel reasoned. One had to begin at the age of three or before; one had to educate the mother so that she, too, worked toward her child's harmonious unfolding. One started with the right clothes, the proper diet, the right influences, the correct games and exercises, and plenty of healthy, spontaneous contact with the natural world. Froebel's games and exercises—called "gifts"—are the area of his teachings most often mentioned in a discussion of Wright's development as an architect. Wright was already nine years old before he was introduced to these kindergarten training aids, the first textbook in English having been published two years before (in 1874). The main issue, however, should be how soon Anna was introduced to Froebel's ideas and how extensive his influence was. It seems likely that from Wright's earliest childhood she followed his precepts to the letter, and that a great deal of the successful nurturing of Wright's genius is due to the enlightened teachings of Friedrich Froebel.

"At length every king will call me Taliesin. . . ." It is perfectly true that a broad high forehead was one of Wright's most telling physical characteristics. Apart from this distinctive feature, one would not have called him handsome at any age. His face was too long and thin, his chin tended to recede, his nose was too prominent, and his mouth, full-lipped when he was young, pulled into a thin sharp line as he aged. He resembled his emphatically featured mother more than he did his debonair father or his Welsh uncles, with their even features, square cheekbones and impudent eyes.

Conventions of the day ensured that no expression might animate the early portraits that have survived of Wright as a child and adolescent, and so evidence of the allure of his personality—the mercurial shifts of mood, the avid interest in ideas, the impudent wit and fierce enthusiasms—comes later. One sees only a look of earnest—one would have said, high-minded—purpose and some hint of the forcefulness of his character by the directness of his gaze.

He was blessed all his life with a superb physical constitution. Contrary to some beliefs, Wright was perfectly capable of telling a story against himself, and liked to talk about the time when he thought he was really ill and needed a gallbladder operation. He sought the advice of G. I. Gurdjieff, philosopher and mystic, spiritual advisor to Olgivanna Wright, whom she also consulted about physical ailments. After a searching look at Wright's eyes, Gurdjieff invited the couple to dinner. He had prepared the most indigestible meal Wright had ever seen in his life. A succession of hot dishes (presumably curries) was followed by a salad tossed with mysterious ingredients and washed down with a large glass of Armagnac. Believing that he was in for it either way, Wright obediently swallowed the lot. That night he felt absolutely terrible. "Well I guess that settles it!" he told Olgivanna. "You're a widow now!" He finally managed to sleep and, in the morning, what had been "burned out" of him was the notion that there was anything wrong with his digestion. Credit for that enduring vitality can be given to Froebel if Anna had, indeed, learned anything from him, since her attitude toward nutrition was a model of enlightened thinking. There never was any nonsense about pies, cakes and store candies, or even fancy sauces and similar culinary elaborations. The stern emphasis was always on quality food and plenty of it, in its plainest possible guise: healthful stews, brown breads, unsweetened fruits, unadorned meats and the inclusion of the skins of fruits and vegetables for their sun-baked, life-giving qualities. She would have learned about the medicinal value of herbs from her mother, and certainly put more faith in natural remedies than store-bought ones. Elizabeth Wright Heller, who has almost nothing good to say about her stepmother, did concede that when she was ill with "inflammatory rheumatism," presumably rheumatoid arthritis, Anna gave her a series of water treatments that eased her pain when nothing else helped, and nursed her selflessly until she recovered. In her memoir Lizzie was willing to give Anna credit where it was due. Anna's valuable legacy to her son was a lifelong preference for simple, healthful dishes and a trust in the body's own recuperative powers. He knew it, although he could not resist reproaching her with these beliefs occasionally. "Bringing up your children on graham bread, porridge and religion, are you?" he would retort, and try to make it sting.

As for Wright's upbringing, it is always assumed that he was a mama's boy and that this pampering is responsible for certain shortcomings of character. As is usual with such conclusions there is a partial truth to the observation. One of his students wondered, in later years, how "Mr. Wright," as he was always called, could have lived even for a day without a wife. He never made his own bed, picked up his clothes or washed his socks. Shirts remained wherever he dropped them, and if there were no clean ones, he would just wear a dirty one again.

If being wholeheartedly for her child, encouraging him and giving him daily signs of her devotion, was spoiling him, then Anna indulged Frank to good effect. Her conviction that he was destined for greatness gave him, without a doubt, the fortitude he needed once he was launched into his precarious profession, the determination to do well and the air of assurance that caused closefisted businessmen to part with large sums without a murmur.

Her partisanship, however, contained an element that was less constructive. It reinforced her son's belief that the feelings of others need not be taken into account, and discouraged any tendency to empathize.

It also helped foster a feeling of guilt and challenged his innate sense of fairness. An incident from childhood, which he relates in his autobiography, illustrates this. He and his parents were spending a spring and summer in The Valley staying with his grandfather (this was probably 1878, when Frank was turning eleven). As he was playing in the fields with his cousins, none of whom he knew well, he got the idea that it would be great fun to have a party that evening. The more he imagined it, the more real it became. It is conceivable, though he does not mention it, that the party was his attempt to gain stature in the eyes of these cousins. At any rate he described the party in such vivid detail—the presents, the feast and the games—that he had them all convinced, and was half convinced himself.

His cousins went home to get dressed, and he returned to the house, saying nothing. Evening came and the boys, all washed and brushed up, appeared at the door in their best clothes. To her son's great relief, Anna took in the situation at a glance. She made molasses candy, gave them popcorn and ginger cookies, persuaded her husband to play "Pop Goes the Weasel" on his violin and even found presents of a sort for the guests. In short, sensing his need to make an impression, she entered wholeheartedly into the game. Her ability to empathize was admirable. However, she ruined the effect by what happened next. She asked him, "Why did you want to fool your cousins, Frank?" He started talking fast. Of course he had no intention of doing any such thing. They had spoiled it all by believing him. They should never have shown up expecting a party: the technique commonly known as blaming the victim. And Anna, instead of pointing out gently what was happening, allowed Frank to talk his way out of it. He wrote, "And Mother understood. Nobody else."

What is interesting about this episode are the questions it raises as one sees Wright frantically trying to exonerate himself. As the French have it, *Qui s'excuse, s'accuse*, and the fear of being blamed runs parallel, in the Lloyd Jones family, with an image of God the Father that is much closer to the avenging God of the Old Testament than the forgiving God of the New. He makes this clear in the first pages of his autobiography, when he describes his terror of his grandfather, mixed up in his mind with the prophet Isaiah: "Isaiah's awful Lord smote the poor multitudes with a mighty continuous smite, never taking away the gory, dreadful hand outstretched to smite more. . . ." Terrible punishments awaited the wrongdoer unless he could somehow argue his way free. By the age of ten, Wright was already a master. That, however, meant he must forever live with the uncomfortable feeling that he was getting away with something. One of Wright's less amiable traits was his talent for bamboozling others and getting the better of them. That would give rise to severe self-reproach as he weighed his own actions and found himself wanting. "Now that I am actually embarked," he wrote to his sister Jennie in 1905, as he left for his first trip to Japan, "I feel like an escaped convict, as though I had taken something which didn't belong to me and was trying to get away with it."

In short, Wright was in an emotional double bind: too frightened of the consequences to confess his wrongdoing, and too influenced by overly stringent standards of personal conduct to avoid the reproaches of a censorious conscience. His solution was to refine his techniques of avoiding the issues, and if he learned to be unscrupulous, and blame others for his own shortcomings, then he would worry about it later. In short, he was the victim of an upbringing that was erratic as well as arbitrary, sometimes believed to be the most difficult for any child to surmount. His parents' attitudes veered between being too lax and too rigid and coercive. Although Frank seldom experienced the rough side of Anna's tongue, he could not have avoided knowing that she, when aroused, could be a frightening figure, as Lizzie had learned to her cost. That was one more reason for keeping Anna placated and charmed, so that he would never be subjected to similar treatment.

One sees similarly contradictory traits of behavior in what can be discerned about the complex personality of William Carey Wright. One has seen how this model of bonhomie, learning and accomplishment, who began every new start with renewed hope and easy successes, always seemed to snatch failure from the jaws of victory. There was a strain of pessimism that underlay the sunny surface. In future years he would give his first family—Charles, George and Elizabeth—the uncritical love and support he withheld in some measure from Jennie and Maginel, and, it seems clear, denied his son Frank. While doing justice to his father as a musician and intellectual, Frank called him "irascible." Taking piano lessons was an ordeal: "His knuckles were rapped by the lead pencil in the impatient hand that would sometimes force the boy's hand into position at practice time. . . ." Resentful of Anna's preferential treatment, perhaps sensing the flaw in her handling of her son, William tried to overcompensate by not letting Frank get away with anything. In one famous episode, Frank describes the ordeal of pumping the bellows of the organ his father played in church and the agony of being forced to keep pumping, even when his arms felt as if they would fall off. He wrote, curiously in the third person, "The boy worked away for dear life to keep air in the bellows, knowing only too well what would happen to him should he give out." The inference was that he would be "taken to the woodshed," although, if one believes Lizzie, that did not happen often enough. And when Anna saw William rolling up his sleeves and heading for Frank, she would, like the tactician she was, pick a fight with Jennie so as to divert her husband's attention because "she knew Father thought more of Jennie than he did of Frank," Lizzie wrote. Lizzie was already shrewdly aware of the manipulative moves of adults, and no doubt Frank learned once more that unscrupulous behavior was perfectly acceptable in the right cause.

Another famous incident from Wright's autobiography describes his introduction to farm life—when he was sent to stay on Uncle James's farm in The Valley—and the backbreaking work involved. While one believes that farm work was just as arduous as Wright described it, the main reason for its detailed description would seem to be to arouse the reader's sympathy for the small victim. He, hardly more than a child, was actually being worked until he dropped, if one can believe him, under the unrelenting gaze of the adults. Whenever he protested, they simply told him to "add tired to tired" (that maxim he quoted so approvingly in later years). What appeared to make an indelible impression on him was that no matter how much he tried to wriggle his way out of the work, they would not let him get away. The first time he escaped he was discovered and treated with kindness by his Uncle Enos, and persuaded to return. The second time, Uncle James found him, and perhaps he was not so forgiving, because once inside the farm gate, his nephew disappeared once more. All night, he lay in a haystack, listening to the calls of his uncle and aunt and feeling triumphant. "An eye for an eye, and tooth for a tooth," he exulted. It was "worthy of Isaiah." It was a temporary victory since he was back at work the next day. For once he had lost, or had he? That summer, whenever he could slip away, he would sit and daydream. Then Uncle James would call again, "Frank! Frank! Come back!"—and he would know he had won. It is a very interesting episode since it demonstrates the solution he would choose, all his life, when faced with what seemed to be an intolerable situation. It also betrays a certain need for vindictive triumph that, as an adult, would reinforce his determination to win, whatever the cost.

On the surface, then, adults in the Lloyd Jones and Wright branches of Frank Lloyd Wright's family tree tried to hold themselves and their offspring to exacting standards of morality. Obedience was stressed, but beneath the façade, these same grown-ups schemed and connived, hitting back when they were hurt, manipulating others, getting even, denying their true motives, showing themselves to be inconsistent and emotionally immature. As heirs to minority status, proud of their radical tradition and centuries of guerrilla resistance they, by accident or design, seemed to be training their children to be rebels. The memoirs of Elizabeth Heller and Frank Lloyd Wright both suggest this. Anna Lloyd Wright would fly at Elizabeth in a rage and, one gets the impression, use her as a substitute for the real target of her wrath. Once that pattern was clear, William sent his daughter to live with relatives and, during her years of transition from child to adolescent, Lizzie's feelings underwent a transformation from stark terror to a determination to get even. This transformation of attitude was helped by her discovery that at least one of Anna's daughters was not in the least scared of her mother, but talked back to her. Lizzie recalled that on one occasion when Anna was complaining unfairly about her husband, Jennie sharply reprimanded her. To Lizzie's astonishment, nothing happened. Pretty soon Lizzie was bold enough to try the same tactic. One day, Anna observed her stepdaughter outside the house talking to a group of her school friends and wanted to know what they had been talking about. Anna was sure she was being criticized behind her back. Lizzie piped up boldly that Anna was about the last subject she ever wanted to bring up, and her stepmother, for once, could not think of a thing to say.

There are similar parallels in the relationship between William Carey Wright and his son. That emotionally distant, demanding, secretly jealous parent presented essentially the same conundrum to his son that Anna Lloyd Wright had presented to her stepdaughter, and was offering a similar indoctrination. As a small child, Frank looked up to the formidable figure of his father in the Weymouth, Massachusetts, pulpit, from his seat below, in the front row of the church, with mingled respect and fear. But one Sunday morning, when the family was walking to church and Frank was seven years old, his father discovered he had forgotten to put on a necktie. He ran back to get one, but the key to the house would not work, and he had to break through a window. Finally William Wright reappeared, wearing a necktie at last but with a bleeding finger. The discovery that, behind the august façade, was a flustered human being had an effect on Frank, young as he was. He explained, "I looked up at him and . . . saw him differently. . . . And do you know he didn't seem at all formidable after that." By the time Frank had become an adolescent, he, too, saw his relationship with his father as a battle of wills, one he intended to win. Just before his father left home, he took Frank into the stable to be "thrashed." Wright wrote, ". . . the young rebel got his father down on the floor, held him there until his father promised to let him alone." He later explained to his mother that his father was to blame for thinking he could still use physical punishment on his son. What William Wright had to say was not recorded, but the main point was that he had allowed his son to prevail. Defiance, in other words, had been rewarded.

The incident directly parallels the period when Wright, himself the father of adolescent sons, dealt with rebellion in an identical manner. He describes an occasion when Lloyd and John decided to soak him with a garden hose, on the front lawn, in full view of a group of neighbors. Despite his angry shouts they refused to stop. Wright finally "charged" them, soaking wet, while his neighbors roared. Authority, Wright noted ruefully, was "getting a bad break." Another lesson in outwitting the pendragon was being handed on, as no doubt it had been for centuries. It is significant that in describing the moment when he wrestled with and defeated his father, Frank Lloyd Wright called himself "the young rebel."

"All art constantly aspires towards the condition of music. . . ." He was proud of his father and particularly of his musical talent. Both he and Maginel have a similar memory of their father in the midst of composing a particular waltz, rondo, galop or polka, scurrying from his desk to piano and back again, his pen held crosswise in his mouth and ink on his whiskers. Maginel recalled him singing "Rocked in the Cradle of the Deep," accompanying himself, with his white head thrown back. Frank remembered the evenings when, as he hovered between sleeping and waking, he heard his father playing the piano into the small hours, dreamily memorizing great stretches of Bach's preludes and Beethoven's symphonies, those great cathedrals of sound. He took up the piano eagerly and had learned many of Mendelssohn's "Songs Without Words" by heart by the time he was an adolescent, as well as Beethoven's Minuet in G. By his own account he would have to be prevented from showing off at every opportunity. What he remembered best were evenings when Jennie, equally eager, would play and he and his friends would sing Gilbert and Sullivan—all the rage at the time—while Mother, with Maginel on her lap, made an appreciative audience and Father's study door was open to "let in the fun." Those evenings, he wrote, "were no concerts. They were happy riots. No one could tell where laughter left off and singing began." His descriptions put one in mind of analyses of painting by Walter Pater (1839–1894), who was, with the great English art critic and writer John Ruskin, and with A. W. N. Pugin, an early-nineteenth-century British reformer, one of the leading theoreticians of the Aesthetic Movement in the arts, architecture and interior decor that was in vogue in the post–Civil War years when Wright was growing up. For Wright, music would become an integral part of a room, essential to his concept of harmonious living. Pater, too, seemed to conclude that the work of the artist Giorgione had reached particularly sublime heights for its ability to suggest that his scenes were filled with music, whether he was depicting a pastoral glade, a pool in which people were fishing or a moment "in the twilight, as one passes through an unfamiliar room." And Wright's comment "Living seemed a kind of listening to him—then" exactly mirrors Pater's "Life itself is conceived as a sort of listening."

The sensibility that Emerson said "distinguishes the stick of timber of the wood-cutter from the tree of the poet" is at work in Wright's reminiscences about his life on Uncle James's farm. Wright was never too exhausted or thirsty to miss, in the midst of taking a draft of cool water, the sound of a meadowlark. He was alert to the "world of daylight gold" that Pater, too, saw woven through every facet of the Italian landscape, even the blackest cypress. Wright delighted in "night shadows so wonderfully blue," in the "dark sprays of slender metallic straight lines," in "catkins cutting circles," "milkweed blossoming to scatter its snowy fleece on every breeze" and even such humble and ignored sights as a patch of dead weeds glinting against a background of snow. His lyrical passages, self-conscious as they are, do give a vivid testimony to the fact that very little ever escaped his gaze. In fact, he had an extraordinary visual memory, and it is doubtful whether he ever forgot anything he saw. If, as he described his responses, he intended to explain the lessons he was learning from nature, then he had fastened on the first imperative, as Pater saw it, i.e., to experience the sensuous element of art. As for Mr. Emerson, whom "one's mother, father, aunts and uncles were always quoting," Maginel wrote, he believed that "such is . . . the plastic power of the human eye, that the primary forms, as the sky, the mountain, the tree, the animal, give us a delight *in and for themselves.* . . ." Such raw material then had to be transformed by what Pater called "the informing, artistic spirit." The subject matter of a poem, or the content of a painting and the circumstances that had brought them both about, must be considered secondary to the "form, the spirit of the handling," Pater believed. This aspect "should become an end in itself, should penetrate every part of the matter." It was the final goal toward which all art was striving. One senses that Wright was groping toward a similar conclusion when he wrote that an architect needed to understand "the secret that gave *character* to the trees."

Wright's descriptions of his Valley, which run like a leitmotif through his autobiography, to him an inexhaustible source of delight and the fulcrum of his artistic sensibility, have a quality of painted idylls, like those Giorgionesque landscapes depicting an enchanted, Arcadian world. Even at the age of sixty, when he was writing these memoirs, he still knew where the rare white and purple lady slippers grew, where one could catch sleek frogs, where one could find the homes of skunks and snakes, the quicksand in the streams and the secret nests of swallows. He had roamed over every inch of the shallow, sloping hillside on which he would build his house; The Valley had become, as Pater had written, "a country of the pure reason or half-imaginative memory." Wright gives another indication of the role this landscape, and art generally, would come to play in his emotional life by occasionally hinting at the feelings they evoked. Even while he was pumping the organ for his father, and in acute pain, he was still capable of forgetting what he was doing and becoming transported with delight by a particularly affecting passage. Similarly, he never could look at the splash of red made by a lily against the green of a verdant pasture without being moved, he wrote. He had experienced that frisson of discovery that marks a true aesthete.

Maginel Lloyd Wright (christened Margaret Ellen, shortened to Maggie Nell and thence the name she always used) has an early memory of the long parlor, the main living room in the house in Madison, Wisconsin, to which her family moved in 1879. She made a point of describing it in her memoir, obviously much impressed by its restraint and refinement: gleaming maple hardwood floors, sheer white curtains, geraniums in pots on the windowsill, tasteful arrangements of branches and dried leaves in vases, oriental carpets in brilliant colors on a white ground, and unusual folding chairs upholstered in red-and-white and green-and-white carpeting, with wool fringes on the arms and seats. Her brother remembered other rooms similarly furnished with Indian rugs, cream-colored net curtains, a few good engravings framed with narrow bands of maple, and books everywhere.

Even though no photographs have survived, the unadorned curtains and Indian and oriental rugs serve to distinguish these rooms at once from those interiors one associates with the period: clashing colors and patterns on oversize furniture and a clutter of fans, pottery, paintings, antimacassars, cushions and miscellaneous objets d'art so claustrophobic as to still bring a reaction when one looks at faded photographs. Maginel, who would become known for her delicate drawings and paintings, sensed instinctively that her mother had achieved a triumph in that house, given the small-town atmosphere in which they were living and the general level of public taste. How that transformation was achieved is not known, but one notes that the rooms in question were created a few years after Anna had visited the great Philadelphia Centennial Exposition of the summer of 1876. Wright has written that his mother's visit to the exhibition (whether he went himself is not known) introduced her, and then himself, to the Froebel games and exercises, or "gifts." Ambitious to have her son become an architect, she would also have paid close attention to the new ideas from Europe being advanced at that famous exhibition by means of the Aesthetic Movement. These ideas were adopted at once in the decade that followed, from the mid-1870s to the mid-1880s. New societies and clubs formed to bring standards of taste to bear on the appalling objects then being produced by the Industrial Revolution. The idea that the words *artistic* and *tasteful* ought to be associated with china, glass, serving dishes, wall tiles, teaspoons and clocks, not to mention wallpaper and carpets, was one whose time had come. The exhibition also served to introduce a newly moneyed class to the possibilities of not just Chinese and Japanese designs but also such exotica as Egyptian, Moorish and Indian. The evidence of the objects in the Madison home, as well as Wright's comment that his mother was following the then "modern" vogue for refinement, speaks for itself. Whether by accident or design, the rooms Anna created could not have been better suited to sharpen the artistic awareness of her future architect.

The house in Madison where they were to live for the next several years, the first they were ever to own, made a similar impression on Frank Lloyd Wright. He goes into some detail about the property on the corner of Gorham and Livingston streets, which was very close to Lake Mendota, one of the four beautiful lakes around which the town had grown. Madison was any Wisconsin village on a somewhat larger scale, Wright wrote, but the fact that it was the state's capital, had a dome of Michelangelesque appearance and was the seat of the state university gave it a cachet somewhat out of the ordinary.

The Wright family had pursued its usual bumpy course before arriving at the Madison homestead. William Wright's period in Weymouth, Massachusetts, had been somewhat atypical in that he managed to stay there for three years. There his last child, Maginel, was born in the early summer of 1877. By October he and his family were back in Wisconsin and spending another stay of some months with Anna's Lloyd Jones relatives. Anna's brother Jenkin, ordained in 1870, was already an influential Unitarian minister, the missionary secretary of the Western Union Conference, and perhaps his growing influence in the church and the chronically impoverished state of the Wrights had something to do with William Wright's decision; at any rate, he left the Baptist Church and became a Unitarian. He soon became pastor of the Liberal (Unitarian) Church in the hamlet of Wyoming near The Valley, and was also made secretary of the Wisconsin Conference of Unitarians and Independent Societies.

As usual, William Wright's Madison beginnings were as promising as all the others had been. "As a lecturer, Mr. Wright is one of the best," a local paper observed, "and none should fail to hear him." With his customary zest, William had also opened a Conservatory of Music above "some kind of store" on Pinckney Street and was trying to make it succeed. But Wright was getting older (he was then fifty-five), and the disappointments of the marriage must have been taking their toll. His son Frank nowhere mentions his father's three children by his first marriage, and the omission was certainly deliberate, but it is fair to say that by the Madison years, those of Frank's most complete childhood memories, these three children were gone. Charles William, "wild over machinery," according to his sister Lizzie, had become apprenticed to a machinist when they were still living in Pawtucket. He would follow his father into the ministry. The second son, George Irving, left to study law; he would eventually become a judge. By 1874 Lizzie had been removed from the scene and sent to stay with her Holcomb relatives. That left Frank, Jane and Maginel, who was so fragile as a baby she had to be carried around on a pillow for months. The move to Madison, much closer to the beloved Valley, brought them into the Lloyd Jones sphere of influence and those particularly active men and women, Jenkin, James, Enos and the Aunts, Jennie and Nell. One believes that as Anna's disenchantment with her marriage became acute, she would have been bound to turn toward the people she could count on. Frank remembers Uncle James arriving at their Madison home one day with a wagon and a cow tied to the back. He had brought the animal all that distance just so that "Anna's children might have good fresh milk."

What Maginel and Frank remembered best about the Madison house was his bedroom, the door of which displayed a large sign on which was written from top to bottom:

SANCTUM SANCTORUM

with an additional (KEEP OUT) below.

The room, up under the roof of the story-and-a-half house, was long and low, with sloping sides and dormer windows. It must have been cold in winter and suffocatingly warm in summer, but what Maginel remembered was its distinctive smell. The Sanctum's uniqueness had to do with a mixture of printer's ink, oil paints, shellac and turpentine. Frank had installed a printing press, a scroll saw for making wall brackets, blocks of paper, numerous colored inks, pencils and oils—his first makeshift studio. He had painted some wall plaques, one depicting a "startled-looking" robin and nest of eggs, another a painting of an apple tree in blossom against a blue sky. During the school year he went to the old Second Ward Grammar School on Gorham Street, and was admitted to the old Madison High School in the mid-1880s. Thomas S. Hines, Jr., in the first study of Wright's Madison years, established that the architect had poor to average grades in most of his subjects—algebra, rhetoric, botany and physics—during the 1884–85 school year. There is no evidence that he ever graduated.

When one considers that he had by then attended schools in Weymouth, Massachusetts, and, conceivably, Essex, Connecticut, and The Valley as well, before continuing in an elementary school in Madison, one can understand why his academic career was undistinguished. Moving from town to town was unsettling, and so much emotional energy would have been needed to cope with a whole new set of circumstances and personalities that one could predict the result: "aloneness, shyness, isolation and solitariness." And, indeed, he was "afraid of people," he wrote. "The fearful unknown to him—people." So he played piano and viola, painted his earthenware churns, worked on his printing press and read *Hans Brinker,* Jules Verne's *Michael Strogoff, Hector Servadac,* Goethe's Wilhelm Meister novels and tattered thrillers from the Nickel Library. His contact with other young males seems to have been limited to those occasions when he would attempt to dazzle them with imaginary parties or, as he also recalled, would bring down the contents of his parents' attic onto the sidewalk and proceed to give everything away. That lavish gifts and ostentatious spending became connected, in his mind, with ways to impress, make himself feel important, is contained in another incident in which he described buying stocks of candy for a group of older boys and, at their urging, telling the storekeeper to "charge it to the Town Pump." When he discovered how easy it was, he kept trotting back for more free candy, that is, until the end of the month when his father received the bill.

He had found one close friend, a boy even more of an outsider than he obviously felt he was. Frank, then about fourteen, was coming home from school one autumn day shortly after they had moved to Madison when he encountered a group of boys tormenting a cripple, a boy who had lost both legs to polio. They had thrown his crutches out of reach and were attempting to bury him in a pile of leaves from which he periodically emerged spluttering and crying. Frank got up his courage and drove the other boys off. Then he gave the cripple, Robie Lamp, his crutches and helped him up onto his feet. When he got home, indignant and close to tears, and described the incident to his mother, she readily agreed to allow him to bring Robie home. After that, Maginel observed, Robie spent almost as much time at their house as he did at his own.

It was Robie with whom Frank shared his printing press, and it was their joint idea to form their own printing company and talk the wealthy father of another boy into advancing them two hundred dollars, a princely sum in those days, so that they could buy a larger press and more type. It was Robie to whom Frank told all his secrets, who helped him build his kites with incredible tails, with whom he designed his waterwheels, who sketched with him and studied music with him at his father's academy. (Robie took up the violin.) Their friendship went on into adulthood, and Frank designed a small, square brick house in Madison especially suited to Robie's physical needs, with its own roof garden. Frank's indignation, when aroused, would forever be marshaled to defend society's underdogs, the impoverished and downtrodden. Although his relationship with his sister Jane was uneasy—they were too close in age for it to be otherwise—Maginel, who was ten years his junior, was another matter. He would toss her up in the air, defend her in arguments and comfort her in thunderstorms, which she hated. He was her wonderful, laughing, protective big brother. At about this time he became entranced by the *Arabian Nights*, those tales in Arabic that had been translated into French almost two centuries before and were being rediscovered because of new translations into English: a nine-volume edition appeared during the years 1882–84. No doubt he relished the tales of Ali Baba and Sinbad the Sailor, but it was Aladdin who held his interest, Aladdin, that clever, resourceful boy who triumphed over every obstacle because he had a magical lamp.

Secret dreams of glory perhaps helped to compensate for his life's dreary reality and times when, required to recite before the whole class, he would be in an agony of embarrassment and apprehension. Those excruciating moments of adolescence were so vivid that when he came to write his memoir he complained they had prevented him from becoming a self-confident speaker, quite forgetting the progress he had made in that direction during the intervening years.

On one occasion in particular, his mother made the choice of his recitation, a typical Victorian monologue that began, "Oh, sir, I am a poor widow with children." It was short enough and seemed to fit the bill. But he could not bring himself to learn it. He kept putting that off, "as though he sensed some evil in it," he wrote. He finally managed to become word-perfect at his mother's urging, but when the time to deliver the monologue came he could not get beyond the first sentence. The whole thing suddenly struck him as ridiculous. Each time he began, he trailed away, until his classmates roared with laughter and he slunk back to his seat in acute mortification. Later that day, in the school yard, boys ran after him shouting, "Oh, sir, I am a widow with children. . . ."

What Frank sensed but could not put into words was that he was somehow being made a pawn at a moment of crisis in his mother's life. In the autumn of 1881 his father's father, Rev. David Wright, who had married his parents, took a candle upstairs in his home in Essex, Connecticut, sat down and wrote a farewell letter to each of his three sons. Then he went to bed and quietly died. He had reached the great age of ninety-three. Perhaps his letter to his son William contained the news that William's inheritance would be a life insurance policy. Perhaps William and Anna already knew that the money was coming one day; in any event, it was heaven sent since it appeared to have been enough to pay off the debt on their Madison home and provide for some improvements as well.

Two years later, in about February 1883, Anna stopped sharing her husband's bed. She took the room over the sitting room that was the warmer one, leaving him with the coldest room, he complained. When he repeatedly asked for the return of his marital rights, she said she no longer loved him, and hated the very ground he walked on. It seems fairly obvious that Anna saw this as the moment to force her husband out of her life, by any means, however unscrupulous, as his complaint to the Circuit Court of Dane County subsequently demonstrated.

She neglected her duties as a wife, he testified. Many times his bed went unmade even though he paid a hired girl to do such tasks. Anna ignored his wishes and comfort in respect to meals and obliged him to do his own mending, "because when I requested her to do anything it was often neglected" or badly done and thrown in his face or on the floor. He did concede that he might have made a mistake in asking some of her relatives whether there were any insanity in the family. "I did not suppose this was ever to be spoken of," he said primly, but "it was communicated to her and she complained of it. . . ."

In effect, Anna began her campaign sometime after her husband had inherited his money, and kept it up until he finally left and filed for divorce in the summer of 1884, about a year and a half later. Her resolve, however, went in fits and starts—periods at home were followed by so-called trips when she seems to have been wrestling with the idea of moving out herself. In August 1883, she made a visit to friends, and he went to see her in an effort to reconcile, but was rebuffed.

Then Anna's brothers paid a call. They are not identified, but one can assume they probably included Jenkin, James and Enos. If William would agree to leave, and make over the house to Anna, they would do the rest, they said. In other words, they would take the financial responsibility off his hands if he would do what she wanted. William agreed. He moved out with a few sticks of furniture, his clothes, books, papers and musical instruments, and renewed his ties with his first family, leaving Jennie, Maginel and Frank with the inescapable conclusion that their only relatives were the Lloyd Joneses. The split this created led to complete loss of contact between the two sides of Frank Lloyd Wright's family and a kind of tacit agreement by everyone not to mention the other family and certainly not with approval. There is no evidence that Frank Lloyd Wright ever saw his father again, and he did not attend his father's funeral in Lone Rock in 1904.

Leaving a wife and children without any means of support, even if her brothers did plan to take over, would make any man uncomfortable, let alone a minister of the cloth, unless he could convince himself that he had been very badly treated indeed. Forcing a husband out, even when the marriage had been unhappy for years, was another guarantee of a guilty conscience unless a wife could somehow make herself believe that he had deserted her. Even so, Anna and her daughters knew that she faced social disapproval, perhaps ostracism, as a divorced woman in the 1880s. Therefore Anna and William each fought to save face and, in a way, both won. The court decreed that Anna had "left" William because she had moved out of his bed, and she could honestly counter that he had walked out of the door. Behind the self-justifications, it is clear that William was relieved. He had remained married for the sake of his new family but at the cost of losing his first, which meant even more to him. He would soon be sixty and, no doubt, was tired out by emotional problems he could not solve. He testified that he tried to provide for Anna and the children to the best of his ability, and gave her the bulk of his income (one remembers that, in those days, a wife had only the money her husband cared to provide) and that this was never enough. In his view, she was extravagant; she angrily resisted his charges. The actual break seems to have been precipitated by one last quarrel over money, the fifty dollars left from his inheritance after all the bills were paid. She wanted him to give that to her; he wanted to keep it for "a rainy day." It was inconceivable to him that she would want the last penny he had; it was inconceivable to her that he would refuse. The wrangling reinforces one's suspicion that something else entirely was at stake here, a suspicion that is confirmed by an incident Maginel related. She stated that after her father had left home, he met her one afternoon coming home from kindergarten. He looked at her shabby clothes— she was wearing a pair of scuffed slippers—took her into town and bought her a new pair of shoes and a hat. When she got back home wearing these objects, Anna calmly stuffed them into the old wood range in the kitchen and burned them. Maginel thought she understood. The problem was that the clothes were cheap and eye-catching, rather than sober and in good taste. This was only one element of the story, because Anna then took her daughter back to town and bought her "the finest pair of little French kid shoes she could find." It would have been Anna's Celtic tradition that one gave with an open hand, because tawdry gifts demeaned the recipient. The larger issue, here, however, had to do with William and the way in which he had failed her.

The day her father left, when Maginel was seven, Anna closed the door and took her into the living room, where a coal fire flickered behind the isinglass window of the stove. Anna took out the old wine-colored wallet she carried, opened it and showed Maginel a fifty-cent piece. "This," she said, "is all the money I have in the world."

Maginel's memoirs, and those of her brother, make the break look dramatic and final. If one can believe William's testimony, and it is plausible, this was not the case. He said that he went to see his wife afterward, and wrote three letters asking for a reconciliation before concluding that the cause was hopeless. One wonders whether Frank's laconic account masks a fear that his mother's love for him had been the cause of the rift. "She lived much in him," he wrote revealingly, speaking of himself. Perhaps this was why "the father never loved the son at any time." They had been rivals for Anna's love, and Frank had won. It was because of him that the divorce had happened. If this was what he really thought, it would explain the perfunctory tone of the memoir. He has more to say about the aftermath of the divorce: the social disgrace they all felt, though they did not understand why, and the effect it had on him, making him shyer, more sensitive, more distrustful. It was "one more handicap."

Maginel, too, felt uncomfortable. When she went to visit the family of four spinsters who lived next door, they badgered her with questions about her father. "Where's your father, dear?" they would ask, gently but relentlessly. "Tell us about your father." Maginel asked her mother what she should answer. Anna replied without hesitation, "Say he's dead."

4

Aladdin

Old as man's moral life is this urge to grow.
—FRANK LLOYD WRIGHT
An Autobiography

Family stories about William Carey Wright frequently illustrate his happy ability to tackle a new craft or profession and quickly excel. The year he left home he was studying Sanskrit. No doubt he mastered that language as effortlessly as, it was said, he had mastered the art and craft of violin making and the teaching of musical instruments. The story is told that he came home one day and announced to Anna that he was about to teach the guitar. Anna protested, "You don't know how!" He answered, "I'll learn."

One finds the same kind of sunny self-assurance in his son Frank. When it came to one's work, one had infinite options, and proficiency could always be acquired. In fairness to both men, they were prepared to work tirelessly to bring that about. Frank's sense of vocation, instilled by his mother, his amazing reserves of energy and the charming first impression he invariably made were important assets. If he already thought of himself as a superhero, the Aladdin with magical powers that he describes in his autobiography, it was a distinct advantage, contributing greatly to the allure of his personality.

He was now eighteen and the head of his family. Anna's firstborn would be expected to set an example and establish himself in a profession as fast as possible. Early independence was, in short, encouraged and fostered. If he were secretly afraid of others and emotionally insecure in close relationships, then he had that in common with most adolescents. If he knew little about his own inner life and misinterpreted the little he did know, then he was typical of most American men of his generation.

One finds him, in those summers of his adolescence, up with the lark on Sunday mornings, gathering flowers for church and, later, looking dreamily out of the open window and imagining the triumphs to come. Nature had given him less height and bulk than he would have preferred, had such decisions been up to him, but he made up for it by always presenting what Italians call a *bella figura*. His father had set him an early example; so did Anna. He hints, in his autobiography, that the grown-ups decided that all that poetry, music and painting were making him too effete and foppish, and this led to the decision to toughen him up on Uncle James's farm. Toughened he certainly became, but the masculine indoctrination had no effect on his choice of clothes, which, by the time he was middle-aged, would become positively bizarre. When he was barely twenty his mother was already begging him not to make a sartorial exhibition of himself. The idea of a stovepipe hat and a cane—such attire would give people the wrong idea. He should present himself as a person of substance, not a dandy—advice that was certainly ignored.

At about this time he changed his middle name from Lincoln to Lloyd. The Welsh family to which Frank Lloyd Wright belonged shared a casual attitude toward the picking up and dropping of names and nicknames. As has been noted, Hannah became Anna, Mary Thomas was Mallie, Jane was Jen or Jennie, and even Uncle Jenkin was usually known as Jenk. One might also change one's name to telegraph disapproval. Enos Lloyd Jones had originally been named for his uncle Enoch, but then the grown-ups had a falling out and he became Enos. Wright's sister Jane christened her son after her brother, but then the latter did something outrageous and Jane decreed that Frank would become Franklin ever after, and he did. It is a safe guess that the substitute of Lloyd for Lincoln was similarly motivated, but it also is a clear indication of the direction of Wright's sympathies. He also adopted the Lloyd Jones family motto. He chose to describe the symbol ⁄⁀\, Truth Against the World, picturesquely, as being immensely old and Celtic. As Jan Morris has established, it was nothing of the kind, but had been invented early in the nineteenth

Frank Lloyd Wright, age twenty

century by Iolo Morgannwg, that Welshman who did more than almost anyone else to revive an interest in the Welsh heritage. Morgannwg's organization of bards, or *Gorsedd*, needed a bardic symbol and so Morgannwg created **/|**, with the explanation "And God vocalizing his name said **/|**, and with the Word all the world sprang into being, singing in an ecstasy of joy **/|**, and repeating the name of the Deity." The quotation reads in full:

VOICE AGAINST RESOUNDING VOICE
TRUTH AGAINST THE WORLD
GOD AND ALL GOODNESS,

which the Lloyd Jones clan abbreviated to that manifesto most appropriate for a family of rebels and outcasts.

Wright believed himself destined for greatness, but there was a dark side to the inner image, if one accepts the hypothesis that the early relationship between mother and child is pivotal. Anna's fiercely partisan love has obscured the fact that she was making some weighty demands upon her son, but her letters provide the clear evidence. Over and over again she presents Lincoln, and Christ himself, as examples that Frank must emulate. But, since she utterly believed in her son, she knew he was capable of such superhuman achievements. She added revealingly that, had she been born with the same advantages, there would have been nothing she could not do—clear evidence that she had transferred to Frank her unfulfilled ambitions. There was, in other words, an even more fundamental reason for his fear of being blamed and his inner conviction of being a confidence artist, a trickster, all surface and no substance, and that was the suspicion that he was not lovable for who he was but only for the person Anna wanted him to be. Since, by way of compensation, he had so many pressing reasons to think of himself as a perfect being, any awareness of his human imperfection was likely to shake the very foundations of his life. At such moments he would show evidence of what has been called "the flight forward," an unconscious courting of catastrophe and ruin, one calculated to stop him in his tracks as spectacularly as possible, *but one that would always look like an accident.* By blaming the vengeful hand of fate, he could excuse his own conduct and protect himself from his overly severe conscience and a secret conviction of worthlessness. In his autobiography he describes an occasion when, as an adolescent on Uncle James's farm, he was judged to be "a man," old enough to be left alone in a field. He was given a team of horses hitched to a row of planks that, when dragged across the harrowed field, would smooth out the rows in preparation for planting corn. He was riding one of the planks when it jumped up unexpectedly, having hit an obstacle, throwing him forward onto the breeching of his pair of horses. The animals continued to trot, and he hung there helplessly, aware that if he fell the "plankers" would go over him. He was rescued by a hired man before he was seriously hurt.

"In action," he wrote, "there is release from anguish of mind." What photographs there are of the young Wright give an indication of an almost painful eagerness. He looks like a man poised to spring to his feet the second the shutter has clicked; there is nothing calm or relaxed about him. That tireless determination to succeed is evident in the chronicle of his life in the years following his father's departure. Anna may have looked mournfully at the single coin left in her old wine-colored wallet, but one guesses that, to her son, poverty was a minor detail, not worth a moment's concern. He immediately enrolled as a special student at the University of Wisconsin, taking courses in French, mathematics, English composition and engineering. With his mother's help, he obtained a part-time job with a professor of civil engineering at the university, Allan D. Conover, and was paid thirty-five dollars a month. As a junior draftsman he played a modest role during construction of the university's Science Hall, a large, neo-Richardsonian structure for which Conover was building supervisor. As has been noted, the moment he knew his family was building the chapel he proposed himself as architect and convinced himself that he, or at least his Uncle Jenkin, was fully qualified.

Normally, the role of builder-architect would have gone to Thomas, Anna's eldest brother. But Thomas's fall from the second floor of the new home he was building for his family in the spring of 1879 turned him into a semi-invalid. By 1885, he had been obliged to give up much of his construction work and was attempting to recoup his losses by selling timber from a tract of land that he had bought in tandem with his brother James. He continued to advise, instruct and supervise to some extent, but his incapacity had effectively left the field open for the next architect in the family. Seeing his opportunity, Frank jumped in.

University records show that Wright attended classes for two semesters, from January to December 1886. By early 1887 he was gone—out of school and in Chicago, where he had found a job in the office of J. Lyman Silsbee, the architect Jenkin Lloyd Jones commissioned to build the family chapel, as well as All Souls Unitarian Church for his Chicago congregation. Exactly when Wright went to Chicago is the kind of question that tantalizes scholars, but the best guess is that he was working for Silsbee by February 1887, since his Aunt Nell was writing in early March to ask how he liked it there; shortly after that, he published a drawing of Silsbee's completed Unity Chapel. No one believes that Wright's account of his hiring at Silsbee's, in which he slipped in through the back door, not letting his identity be known, can possibly be true. He was very much on the scene during construction of the family chapel and must have met someone from Silsbee's office then, if not the architect himself. The chapel opened in the summer of 1886, and, a few months later, he was employed by its architect and making a drawing of that building for a magazine. He might not have wanted Uncle Jenk to know he had left school and taken that job, but that is another matter.

The most puzzling issue is why Wright should be at pains to present himself as a struggling outsider, hired on merit alone, with no strings pulled by anyone. The account he gave was published in 1932, when he was in his sixties and, one believes, bent on fashioning a legend. By then he was unwilling to concede that he had ever been helped, or that anyone whose ideas predated his own could possibly have influenced him. He came from nowhere and out of nothing, a full-fledged genius; to have admitted to less would have threatened his grandiose inner image of Aladdin, the boy with a magical lamp. However, one guesses that the nineteen-year-old who had just landed a job in Chicago was thanking his lucky stars that he, through his influential uncle, had been given such a painless introduction to a powerful Chicago architect and such an open sesame to his chosen career.

One can make another reasonable guess at the possible motive for his sudden departure from Madison after just one year in school. He had joined the university's Association of Engineers and Phi Delta Theta, a social fraternity. Somehow, he was finding money for tuition, clothes, books, social events and monthly fraternity dues at a time when his mother, with no income of her own, was most certainly being supported by her brothers and seems to have been taking in lodgers as well. That first or second Christmas on their own, possibly the Christmas of 1886–87, brother James helped out in another practical way. His wife was making an extended visit to relatives in California, and the decision was made to bring Anna and Maginel under his roof—Jane had begun her teaching career—where Anna could act as housekeeper and, incidentally, save on her own heating bills. Frank was sent to board with neighbors. That Christmas an avalanche of expensive gifts arrived from Frank, including a Shetland shawl and a photograph album for his mother and, for Maginel, an adorable crocheted basket containing a bouquet of skeins of brightly colored yarns, tied into the shape of flowers and scented with sachet, the most beautiful gift she had ever received. Maginel was in an ecstasy of delight; Anna wanted to know where Frank had found the money. That was easy; he had sold a number of his mother's most valuable books. He also wrote that he had pawned his father's and his favorite calfbound copy of Plutarch's *Parallel Lives* and a valuable set of Gibbon's *The History of the Decline and Fall of the Roman Empire*, as well as a mink collar of his mother's. All of this was justified in pursuit of his determination to become an architect.

Once he had arrived, at least three of Anna's letters in the spring and summer of 1887 are concerned with the debts he left behind in Madison. In May 1887, when he was not yet twenty, she was referring to his debts and urging him not to spend any more money. Sometime later, she wrote to remind him that she was expecting some money so as to cover part of the bills he had left behind. There is a hint that he had concealed from her the extent of the problem, but she was confident that he would make good on his promises. Still later, she was harping on the theme of how to pay his Madison debts. It was high time he learned to manage money wisely. She was almost at her wit's end. One day, when she went to pay Jennie's bill in a local store, she was handed another bill for Frank, seven dollars for some "dancing gaiters." The shock was almost too much to take. Finally, in September, she was begging him to settle up on the problems he had left behind, reminding him that she had gone to work (not explained in her letters) to help pay off his bills and that only ten days remained on the loan he had taken out from the bank. It was now a question of his good name and hers as well; he could not let her down. If it had been William's role to spend money with gentlemanly unconcern and his wife's to fret and nag and agonize over unpaid bills, then that destructive pattern was being repeated with a vengeance by her son. His awful determination to live beyond his means, which he would attempt to turn into a virtue by saying that one should pursue the luxuries and let the necessities take care of themselves, his lifelong spendthrift habits, which would have such disastrous consequences, had become firmly entrenched before he was twenty. Anna, while fussing, fretting, exhorting and begging, allowed him to continue believing that he could get away with it. Anna paid up.

Uncle Jenkin had been opposed to Frank's abandoning his studies, not out of sheer perversity but, one suspects, because of genuine concern about his nephew's chances for a secure future. The role the remarkable Jenkin Lloyd Jones would play in Wright's life has been ignored, but family letters have established that he, now with a wife and two children of his own and actively engaged in what would become an international career, had taken over considerable financial and emotional responsibility for William's children. He had arranged William's transfer from the Baptist faith to Unitarianism, the main purpose of which seems to have been a desperate last-ditch attempt to save the family from bankruptcy. He watched William roll from job to job for twenty years, and saw him walk away from his marriage without a backward glance at his family. Jenkin must have come to some dour conclusions about William, in light of the emphasis he, and all the Lloyd Joneses, placed on self-discipline, integrity, altruism and endurance—all the sterling virtues William appeared to lack. Seeing Frank abandon his studies to try his luck in a new city must have sounded ominously familiar. Lloyd Joneses did not slither away at the first sign of trouble; they stood up and fought like men. Like the other males in his family, Jenkin might have seen his function in Frank's life as corrective. If he could make Frank toe the straight and narrow, he might be able to counteract William's example and lessen the effect of Anna's leniencies. But even if this were not a valid concern, he, like Anna and the rest of the family, placed an almost mystical emphasis on the importance of an education. Even when all hopes of college had been dashed, Anna still urged Frank to go on reading and studying, if only to make Uncle Jenkin happy. He would not regret it, she wrote.

Whenever an uncompromising stance was taken by an authoritative figure, Frank, characteristically, became automatically opposed as a matter of principle, whatever the merits of the argument; and he would always slip through every net. But it would be a mistake to assume that because he was now swinging a cane and running up some hefty debts, the only example he was emulating came from his foot-loose, spendthrift, engaging, emotionally elusive father. By being the man he was, "Uncle Jenk" provided Frank with a positive example of just what a bold and militant radical can accomplish when his or her reformist zeal is channeled into constructive directions. A distinguished family history of battling against odds for liberty, justice, fairness and truth had left its distinct mark on Jenkin's character. He had, while still an adolescent, served in the Civil War, an experience that made him an ardent pacifist and admirer of Lincoln. After graduating from the Unitarian seminary in Meadville, Pennsylvania, he worked for several years as a pastor and missionary in Illinois and Wisconsin, where his exceptional gifts as an orator, his energy, endurance, idealism and ability to reach his audiences, were quickly recognized. He revitalized a Unitarian church that was about to close, created a Sunday school program, invented a "Unity Club" and helped start a Unitarian newspaper. He was soon given larger responsibilities, becoming, by 1881, the equivalent of a bishop for a Unitarian constituency that extended from western New York to the Rocky Mountains. Some three years before, in 1878, he had demonstrated his ability to tackle a challenge of this dimension by traveling almost twelve thousand miles as he gave 184 speeches, taking night trains, cattle and freight trains, and bedding down between connections on depot floors.

Working with Jane Addams, Susan B. Anthony, Edward Everett Hale, Booker T. Washington, William Jennings Bryan and a host of others, he espoused every progressive liberal position from prohibition, racial justice, education, women's rights, poverty relief and political reform to pacifism and the humane treatment of animals. One would have to compare him with General William Booth, founder of the Salvation Army, for his wide-ranging concerns and the persuasive influence of his personality. Although he was based in Chicago, Unity Chapel and its Valley were always his spiritual home, and he was constantly being called upon to bring the crowds into its two small rooms. When Maginel knew him, he was a handsome man of middle height and commanding presence, with a snow-white beard. "Once he asked a small boy, 'Do you know who I am, my little man?' and the child replied promptly, 'Oh yes, sir, Santa Claus.' " Like many admirable people, Jenkin Lloyd Jones was not an easy person at close quarters, and could be stiff-necked and uncompromising. But he did have a wry sense of humor. In an attempt to bring World War I to an end, Rev. Jenkin Lloyd Jones sailed on the Ford Peace Ship with other American pacifists. On his return to New York, he was met at the pier by Robert Moses, a relative by marriage, who asked what he had accomplished. "Uncle Jenk stroked his white whiskers reflectively and replied, 'We made a deep impression in the neutral countries.' " Jenkin stood for something admirable: for the continuity of the un-shaken Lloyd Jones belief in personal integrity, universal liberty and their faith in a Divine Providence. A great many of Jenkin Lloyd Jones's beliefs, which were the topics of debate around the dinner table when Frank Lloyd Wright was an adolescent, would find their echoes in that architect's own speeches in later years. He spent many an evening at the parsonage, meeting some important and influential people: "Dr. Thomas, Rabbi Hirsh, Jane Addams, Mangasarian and others," he wrote. He added simply, "I enjoyed listening."

Listening: that was something he did well. His eager, retentive mind missed little, and perhaps because he felt the lack of formal schooling keenly—the fact that he lied about it all his life indicates that he did—and because he had such sterling examples all around him of self-educated men, he prospered. He had the very rare gift of knowing what he needed to learn at any particular moment and seeking out that knowledge. Then, too, life itself offered its lessons. One of the most harrowing came while he was still in Madison, working in Conover's office. The city was then building a wing onto its state capitol. The architect, a certain Mr. Jones, had laid the foundations well. Huge concrete piers in the basement had been built to support columns of cast iron. It was a very safe foundation, so secure, in fact, that the builder thought he could economize with barrows of broken brick and stone. All the walls and floors had been built, and the interior was pretty well completed when, one day, the whole wing collapsed. Wright was passing by when it happened. He heard the terrible roar, saw a cloud of dust "rising high into the summer air," heard the screams and saw the mangled bodies being extracted from the wreckage. He stood there, sickened, "clinging to the iron fence" and watching for hours, and dreamed of the haunting tragedy for days. Perhaps the fact that the architect's name was Jones (though they were not related) gave particular poignance to the terrible lesson he learned that day. In any event, not one Wright building ever collapsed, and at least one of them was notorious for the trouble it caused when the wreckers tried to pull it down.

That ability to make the best possible use of every opportunity to learn never flagged. When he was in his sixties and lecturing in New York before World War II, one of the men in the audience was Arthur Holden, an architect who would eventually act as his liaison, facilitating construction of the Guggenheim Museum. At question time, Holden asked how long it had been since Wright had read Alexis de Tocqueville's book *Democracy in America*, and mentioned a particular passage. As it happened, Wright had never heard of Tocqueville, but when they met again some months later, Holden learned that Wright had immediately gone out and bought the book, and could cite the particular passage almost by heart. Perhaps he no longer believed that education was salvation, but he seemed to be taking no chances.

He had another gift that was almost as valuable. When one considers that, as an adolescent, he had beguiled a wealthy friend's father out of two hundred dollars, it is clear that he had already learned the value of ingratiating himself with important people, and that he had taken his lessons from a master. Thanks to Uncle Jenkin, he had superb opportunities; thanks to his father, he knew how to seize the initiative, and his secret sense of being permanently handicapped (because he lacked fortune or formal training and was at a shameful disadvantage socially) would always spur him onward. In the future his attitude toward others, while it contained genuine appreciation, liking and even love, would be tempered by a shrewd assessment of that person's potential usefulness. As he wrote of his cousins, while he loved them he also "beguiled them, showed off for them, used them, fooled them. . . ." And, for those inevitable moments of doubt and discouragement, he had his mother. In later years he wrote, "You seem very wonderfully optimistic . . . and your words always give me a new strength—or rouse what I have latent in me to the work at hand."

Joseph Lyman Silsbee (1845–1913), a fashionable architect for the nouveaux riches, in whose office Wright worked for about a year, was a minister's son, which may have explained his fondness for hiring the same: besides Wright, there were three others in the office. The fact that Wright had New England parentage probably also helped, since Silsbee had been born in Salem, Massachusetts, educated at Harvard and had practiced on the East Coast before moving to Chicago. He was also a Unitarian. He would have been in his early forties when he hired Wright, and had perfected a gift for spotting young talent. Two of his other draftsmen, George Washington Maher and George Grant Elmslie, would also have distinguished careers; Elmslie succeeded Wright as chief designer at Adler and Sullivan when the latter left to establish his own practice. That year, 1887, the situation in Silsbee's office, it has been noted, was analogous to that in the Berlin office of Peter Behrens, some three decades later, when Mies van der Rohe, Walter Gropius and Le Corbusier were all on the staff. In any event, it was the best possible start for Wright even though Silsbee, whom he described as tall, aristocratic and wearing gold eyeglasses with a long gold chain dangling from his nose, seemed unimpressed by the newcomer's "experience" and offered him tracer's wages of eight dollars a week, take it or leave it. Wright not only took it, but leapt at the opportunity to make friends with the draftsman who had helped hire him, Cecil Corwin, one of the minister's sons. With his idiosyncratic combination of genuine liking and unabashed guile, Wright wangled an invitation to dinner, then a room in Corwin's house, and even borrowed money, explaining that he needed it to send to his mother. It was ten dollars, more than a week's wages. Corwin handed it over without a word. It would be repaid, Wright promised, two dollars at a time. He noted that a "characteristic" pattern had begun.

All Souls' Unitarian Church, which was receiving its finishing touches when Wright went to Silsbee's office, was a curious structure for which only a few faded photographs and drawings survive. It markedly resembled a Queen Anne house, which was what Uncle Jenk wanted. When he had persuaded Silsbee to move to Chicago and build his church some two years earlier, Uncle Jenk had been most approving of Silsbee's ability to create a "homey" look. If not particularly ecclesiastical in tone, Silsbee's designs were very much an outcome of the Aesthetic Movement, which had been introduced at the Philadelphia Centennial Exposition a decade earlier. One of the first styles to reflect the new aesthetic, Queen Anne had been invented by the British architect Richard Norman Shaw. It was intended as a nationalistic revival of the vernacular, and something of a repudiation of the Gothic Revival style then in vogue in England and the United States. Unfortunately, the style had little to do with the reign of Queen Anne in the early eighteenth century, but owed more to interpretations of the Elizabethan and Jacobean eras that had gone before. A Queen Anne house's identifying characteristic was a steeply pitched roof of irregular outlines, usually with a dominant gable facing front, but there were many other characteristics, including the use of half-timbering, spindlework, classical columns, patterned masonry and the like. Intricate and eclectic though these houses might be, they still looked like models of restraint and refinement when contrasted with the ostentatious muddle presented by the average High Victorian Gothic house then in fashion. At the very least, the style represented a genuine effort to bring a cohesive artistic philosophy to bear on an epoch of almost stupefying taste, to marry house to landscape, to apply unifying principles of design and to explore neglected architectural periods. Leading American architects quickly joined the movement and began a study of their own colonial heritage, forging a path toward what they all felt to be the ultimate goal, a uniquely American architecture. This was essential because, as the *American Architect* commented in 1876, the year of the exposition, "our domestic life is a type by itself."

On the East Coast, Henry Hobson Richardson, one of the giants of the new movement, made his own experiments in Queen Anne and Romanesque Revival buildings. He also helped launch a style that would be the height of fashion for the final two decades of the nineteenth century, the Shingle Style. Like Queen Anne, this was also an eclectic but quintessentially American mélange of many different elements, united by the use of wooden shingles for walls and roof. It was, in the 1880s, becoming the fashion for the educated and well-to-do, and Richardson was in great demand, as well as very much admired by his contemporaries in Chicago as well as the East Coast. His masterpiece, the Marshall Field Wholesale Store, had just been built when Wright arrived there, and two mansions were under construction on the North and South sides. Silsbee, in his modest, conventional way, was one of Richardson's most devoted admirers, having followed his lead through the same experimentation in styles: from Queen Anne, Romanesque and Colonial Revival to the up-to-date Shingle Style. In fact, Silsbee is given credit for introducing a mature version of that style to Chicago. Wright's transition, from a home in Madison decorated according to the principles of "art for art's sake" —that phrase popularized by the prophet of the Aesthetic Movement, Oscar Wilde—to the office of a well-established architect practicing what the movement preached, therefore seemed perfectly natural, if not inevitable.

Most famous men like to mention how little money they once earned, but Wright, seemingly indifferent to such petty concerns by the time he wrote his reminiscences, makes a painstaking point of it. He started at eight dollars a week; in a few months, that had been raised to twelve dollars, but he was not satisfied. George Washington Maher had just been hired at eighteen dollars, so Wright did not see why he should not be paid as much, even though Maher was more experienced. He was better than Maher. One sees, in these rationalizations, a sense of grievance that must have sorely tried the patience of his employer. When he wanted to be raised from twelve dollars to fifteen dollars a matter of months after he had been hired for eight dollars, Silsbee refused and Wright walked out. He found another job for the wage he wanted, eighteen dollars. Exactly how long he stayed away is not known, but the interval must have been short, and he was soon back in the old office at the salary he had vowed to get.

His account omits the probable cause of all this jockeying for money, one that is revealed in Anna's letters. He had left debts, and she was penniless—here is the reason behind the frantic determination to earn, and this has to be why, decades later, he could still feel indignation at the agony of pushing up his weekly wage by such painfully small increments. He was being driven by two imperatives: first, the need to dress in style, see and be seen, go to concerts, lectures and meetings, join clubs, buy theater tickets and books, visit "cozy restaurants," as he put it, and act like a young man-about-town, as he had seen his father do. But second, there had to be money left over to pay his debts and support his mother. He, as head of the family, was serious about that, and as soon as his salary stood at eighteen dollars he brought Anna and Maginel to Chicago, no doubt on the assumption that one establishment cost less than two. Uncle Jenkin was another presence looming in his life at that time, and All Souls, with its dozens of cultural events, its library and even a kindergarten, was a constant symbol of that man's achievements. Frank would have to prove himself, as Anna often reminded him. Uncle Jenkin might be his friend, but he did not approve of the direction Frank's life was taking.

When Wright went to Silsbee's office the architect was designing Edgewater, a high-class subdivision in Chicago, and the young draftsman spent hours watching the master at work. Using a soft black pencil, Silsbee would invent marvelous façades composed of "gable, turret and hip, with broad porches quietly domestic," Wright wrote. He described those swift, freely drawn pencil strokes as reminding him of "standing corn in the field waving in the breeze." Later he called it the gift of making pictures, drawing a correct distinction between the two-dimensional, or picturesque, approach to architecture and the emphasis on its spatial and sculptural qualities, which he thought more important. At the time, however, Silsbee's mastery of drawing mesmerized him and he set about learning to do likewise.

He may already have been contemplating his next move. He wrote that the new Chicago Auditorium was being built (1887–89), and the newspapers were full of articles about the architectural firm of Adler and Sullivan. He wondered how he could have missed that name when he was looking for work.

The books Wright studied in his search for mastery of drawing, ornamentation and design were, logically enough, works that reflected the central concepts of the Aesthetic Movement. He went first to *The Grammar of Ornament*, by Owen Jones, published in London some thirty years before. Following the lead of the British architects Augustus Welby Northmore Pugin and Henry Cole, as well as the writings of John Ruskin, Jones formulated the thirty-seven propositions that were needed to introduce aesthetic, i.e., artistic, concepts into contemporary design. In common with Pugin and Ruskin, Jones believed that the creative act must be true and good in order to be truly beautiful. The architect who would aspire to greatness must, in other words, be morally pure.

The second principle of the theoreticians, one also advanced by Jones, was that nature must be the inspiration. The student must study the structural forms found in nature and teach himself how to conventionalize, or abstract, his designs from them. Those stylized images must adhere to an exacting standard. While suggesting the natural forms that were their inspiration, the designs must also have an exact relationship to the object they decorated so that they enhanced, and did not detract, from it. Nature as inspiration was, of course, another familiar theme for the young architect. To study nature, learn from her, extracting her secrets, finding "tongues in trees" and "books in the running brooks": Wright could hardly have avoided the lesson, coming as it did with a single voice from so many directions. It is clear, however, that it was one he was particularly fitted to take to heart. Although he came to reject and deride Renaissance architecture, his character had been formed by the Renaissance ideal of man as a noble player on life's stage; in the concept that "there is an all-embracing destiny that gives high meaning to the course of a man's life. . . . In his deep sense of personal destiny, in his faith in the power of an 'organic Divinity' in the world, in his strong feelings about the relation of man to Nature, Wright revealed his complete devotion to that . . . image. . . ."

The Grammar of Ornament espoused the further point that what made the ornamental designs of previous periods so unique was that they somehow reflected the needs and values of their times. It was an idea that freed students of the Aesthetic Movement to return to first principles, looking for clues, not by imitating past styles, but "by understanding the organic and natural laws that created them." In short, Jones provided the theoretical framework that Wright would put to such good use as he mastered the task of transforming the structural forms found in nature into the alchemy of his art.

Wherever the student looked, whether to *The Grammar of Ornament* or to *Les Discours* and the *Dictionnaire raisonné* of Eugène Viollet-le-Duc, a French contributor to the Arts and Crafts Movement who stressed the principles of design and whose work he also studied, he would have heard the same refrain. He set about imprinting these ideas on his mind by the time-honored method of the apprentice, that is, by imitation. He bought a packet of one hundred sheets of onionskin tracing paper and went to work on the designs of Owen Jones, incidentally gaining practice in the art of exact observation, which was to become an important asset. After he had used every sheet in the packet, working evenings and Sunday mornings, he "needed exercise to straighten up. . . ."

Wright worked in Silsbee's office for less than a year, and it is hard to accept his claim that, by the end of this period, he could match Silsbee in freehand drawing and even rival the artistry of a Louis Sullivan, as Wright suggests in his autobiography. The drawings published during this period, 1887–88, in *The Inland Architect and News Record*, argue for the reverse. One would expect a student's first work to have a tentative quality, but his seems more timid than most. His renderings of Unity Chapel, the family church Silsbee designed, along with two of his own designs, one for a Unitarian chapel (never built) and another for his aunts' new school, have a stilted, agonized-over feeling, the work of someone in terror of putting a mark in the wrong place, and are certainly not the work of an instinctive artist who boldly puts down his lines, knowing exactly where they have to go to achieve the desired effect. Wright's drawings are conventional, stiff and quite lifeless.

As a result, scholars have questioned the date of the drawing Wright published in *Genius and the Mobocracy*, his biography of Sullivan, which he states he drew in 1887 or 1888 and which got him the job. Those experienced in dating an artist's work cannot accept that this masterly and impressionistic study for a house in La Grange, Illinois, the work of a confident and skilled delineator, could possibly have been executed so early. The drawing disqualifies itself on stylistic grounds also, being closer to the advanced and integrated designs of the late 1890s than the Silsbee-influenced Queen Anne and Shingle styles Wright was using in 1887–88. It stretches credulity to believe that Wright, who was able to draw and design with such skill at that period, would, once he had joined Sullivan's firm, go back to publishing more drawings in the same labored, clumsy, student's hand.

Wright came close to a confession of the truth in the same book, *Genius and the Mobocracy*, when he wrote, "Never having been a painter I had never drawn more than a little 'free-hand.' " It was a fault in him that he lacked the natural gift to emulate his master in designing ornamentation based on flowing, curvilinear forms abstracted from nature; whenever he felt himself on the defensive about this point, lacking such an essential talent, his first instinct was to deny the shortcoming and try to prove the reverse. But in fact, he eventually gave up the unequal struggle and forged his own style with a T square and triangle, creating those severe geometrical patterns based on the straight line and the rectangle that were to make him famous.

Whatever signs of promise Silsbee and Sullivan saw in Wright, his superior skill with a pencil was unlikely to have been among them. What they appreciated, no doubt, were qualities Wright would have taken for granted: an acute visual memory, an innate grasp of form, a quick mind, a ready wit and a charming eagerness to learn. No one could have stopped Wright from becoming a success, because he refused to be discouraged. Rebuffed by Uncle Jenk when he tried to design his family's chapel, he bounced back with new proposals a few months later, offering to design buildings for his aunts' new school. This time he was more kindly received.

The Hillside Home School, established in The Valley in 1886, was one more testimonial to the energy and initiative of the Lloyd Jones immigrants, not to mention their liberal, reformist and humanitarian views. The school had been conceived of by Nell and Jane, always called the Aunts, on the death of their father, Richard Lloyd Jones; as unmarried daughters, they had inherited his farm and homestead. By then, Nell was forty-one years old and Jane was thirty-eight. Both had made the transition to the more polished manners and mores of the city and must have looked like exotic beings to the country folk of The Valley. Both held themselves in the stylish swanlike manner, their waistlines corseted, wearing the ruffled trains and bustles, the silks and satins, that were all the rage in the 1880s. In short, they were women of some consequence in the world, but they had lost none of their Lloyd Jones idealism and pursued the latest notions on child development, including those of Froebel. It must have been their dream to start a school, and inheriting the farm and some money gave them the opportunity. There was a ready supply of children, sons and daughters of their brothers and sisters, growing up in The Valley.

From the first, the Aunts took children of all ages, from kindergarten through high school, providing a boarding school with a farm attached where each child, as a matter of course, had his own plot and knew each cow and horse by name. Nature walks were similarly stressed, and there were all manner of picnics and sports, including horseback riding, football and golf. Food was home-grown, and since the school was meant to be a home as well, such "homey" activities as sleigh rides, skating parties and theatricals were frequent. There were dances every weekend presided over by a dancing master from Madison who would arrive wearing tails and smelling of cloves and ballet slippers, an artificial rosebud in his lapel. It was one of the first coeducational schools, and its concept, that boys should learn the womanly arts, was most controversial, but there are photographs of boys stitching seams and darning socks to prove it.

As soon as Unity Chapel opened, the Aunts used it as a temporary school while they built larger quarters. They had decided to move their parents' cottage across the road and put their new building on its hillside site. Uncle Thomas was summoned to oversee the move, and a local contractor was hired to make the alterations and additions. As for their young nephew, by early March 1887 he had already been to Hillside to look the ground over, as Aunt Nell's letter establishes. The letter contains detailed instructions about floor plans—whether for the original Home Cottage or for the new building on the old site is not clear, but in any event she simply asked her young nephew to make a few sketches. She added that some of her friends were contributing their architectural notions. The nephew seems to have cut them all out fast. His resulting designs were evidently derived from those of Silsbee, and one of his authorized biographies more or less acknowledges that this architect played the largest role. Wright dismissed this first attempt as "amateurish."

Anna acted as matron of one of the dormitories the first year Hillside Home School was opened, and Maginel went to school there. Anna was somehow keeping the bills paid, and her son's great ambition, to become an architect, was already becoming a reality; by early 1888 he was working for Adler and Sullivan, one of Chicago's largest firms. It must have seemed, to his mother, that she stood in real danger of losing him. She "worried about where he was living and what he was eating"; so Anna sold her house, and she and Maginel took the tedious, clattering train ride to Chicago. There was another reason why Anna may have thought the moment ripe to join Frank: he was in love.

Catherine Lee Tobin, often called "Kitty," was sixteen years old when they first met. Wright described her as "gay-spirited, sunny-haired," and with "a frank, handsome countenance," but this hardly does justice to her appearance when she was turning from girlhood to young womanhood. With her exquisite oval forehead, widely spaced eyes, straight nose and firm chin, she resembled the statuesque creatures inhabiting the imaginary world of the Victorian neoclassical painter Lord Leighton of Stretton. She could have posed for any of the three flowerlike figures in his *Garden of the Hesperides* (1892) or for the portraits of the clear-browed, dignified graces in *The Days*, by the American painter Thomas Dewing, painted in that year of 1887. She personified the emerging American type that would be celebrated in the World's Columbian Exposition in Chicago in 1893, that is to say, tall, with well-formed limbs, radiating good health, vigorous and suitably virginal, yet at some level aware of her budding sexuality. She was, in sum, "the girl" any aesthete would immediately recognize, and she must have resembled uncannily that "intimate fairy princess" about whom Wright had dreamed two or three years before, who was somewhere, preparing herself for their union, who would inspire him to great deeds and "unquenchable triumphs."

These phrases point to his attitude toward women, one that remained remarkably consistent. The ideal woman, in his imagination, would have a grave, stately kind of beauty. Her hair might be glorious, as Catherine's was, a shining mass of red and gold, but it should be sedately, if not severely, dressed and kept close to the head. She should be elegantly slim and tolerably well educated and well bred. She should be interested in the arts and the finer things of life, active in her community, abstemious in her habits and careful with money. She should have views of her own, even aspirations, but none that would conflict with her major role of muse, inspiration, selfless helpmate and so on.

Given his generation, it is almost axiomatic that Wright would look for a girl willing to live through him. However, the dictates of convention are less important in this case than his narcissistic need

Unity Chapel, Wright's first architectural experience

The Old Home building at Hillside

Aunt Jennie

Aunt Nell

Catherine L. Wright with Marion Mahony

Catherine L. Wright as a young mother

for total and unconditional adoration from his nearest and dearest. And in Catherine he had found a girl apparently prepared to devote herself to these needs. To her children, she would be their all-in-all, and they the light of her existence; to her husband, she would be his emotional prop, support, uncritical encouragement, his "better half." She may have seemed to him to be charmingly unambitious and unfocused, the quintessence of feminine passivity, and there is an indication, during the two-year period they were obliged to wait before they could marry, that Catherine began to droop and sigh as convincingly as any princess locked up in an ivory tower. According to Jung, such a woman could well become the devoted and selfless companion of a man consumed by high ambition and the development of great talents; she might have valuable abilities of her own, but since she would be unaware of them, she would be likely to project, i.e., ascribe, them to her husband. The result would be to send him soaring "as if on a magic carpet to the highest summits of achievement." If Wright's narcissism led him more or less consciously to surround himself with those who would uncritically adore, it also guaranteed that he could have no real awareness of their needs, since they existed to serve him. And it is a safe guess that Catherine was far too immature to have any concept of the unequal bargain she was making. So the stage was set for future conflict, but none of that could have been predicted at the start. Wright was alone in a big city without his habitual emotional support and must have felt bereft. Within weeks of joining Silsbee's office, he was looking for consolation, and found it.

Were you the one, his sister Jane asked him in a letter in the spring of 1887, who took Jean Hand to a freshman party? Jean told a mutual friend that her date had been a Mr. Wright, and he was the "stiffest, horridest thing she ever met. . . ." Jane was in a teasing mood, and he had made no secret of the fact that girls terrified him, or so he said. However, he was an easy mark for some girls, if one can judge from a letter of his mother's, after he had moved to Chicago, asking if he still wrote to "Belle." What he apparently liked about Uncle Jenk's church were the opportunities for meeting attractive girls, especially when they "took him in hand," as he put it. He had already noticed Kitty in church and had been attracted to her some time before their unorthodox introduction. Both were attending a fancy dress party, costumed as characters out of Victor Hugo's *Les Misérables*, when she, not looking where she was going, collided with him on the dance floor. They bumped foreheads and fell in a heap. As Dickens wrote, "The ceremony of introduction, under such circumstances, was very soon performed," and from that moment on they were inseparable.

Catherine was the oldest of four. She had twin brothers, Charlie and Robert, aged twelve, and Arthur, a charming seven-year-old. The Tobins were a prosperous and socially respectable family of Unitarians living on Chicago's fashionable South Side. Flora Parish Tobin came from a family of merchandisers—her husband, Samuel Clark Tobin, was a wholesale salesman—and she had been a brilliant young teacher when they married, the first woman principal in the Chicago public school system. She had glorious red hair, usually wore a cameo with a lace fichu collar, was brisk, well organized and something of a disciplinarian. The future son-in-law correctly perceived that Samuel Clark Tobin, affable, emotional and outgoing, was content to be "managed" by his extremely capable wife. Samuel Tobin's great joy was his daughter, Kitty. As the only girl in a family of four, she was the center of attention, and such loving approval made her full of fun and good humor. She talked nonstop. She was devoted to her church and its pastor and was a confirmed nonsmoker and teetotaler. She was sensible. As soon as she discovered that Frank was helplessly bad with money, she resolved to help him manage it better. She was, her niece remembered, the greatest fun in the world, which did not prevent her from having decided opinions, ones she firmly voiced at the least provocation. Aunt Kitty, the niece recalled, made her think of a saying in the Tobin family, "Often in error but seldom in doubt." That contentiousness was to have some consequences as she matured. But for the moment, she was young, terribly anxious to please, and it is clear she adored Frank.

Wright's predilection for girls of superior social status has been remarked upon, and there is no doubt that his parents' divorce had given him a sense of his own inadequacy in this respect. But once in Chicago, such family skeletons were easier to keep hidden. In Chicago, he was Jenkin Lloyd Jones's nephew, therefore a prominent young Unitarian and quite a catch, with or without a fortune. So the argument that Wright married only to better himself socially cannot be taken too far. Neither can his own account, written after he was married to someone else, be completely relied upon. Catherine may, as he implies, have swept him off his feet, but on the other hand, one doubts whether anyone ever persuaded Wright to do something he positively would not do.

There is also the matter of his mother's opposition, which would have deflected anyone less determined. Anna had, from the first, feared his roving eye. In one letter written just after he left Madison, she strenuously urged him not to trifle with the feelings of girls while, in the same sentence, forbidding him to take any particular girl seriously. If she hoped to tie him in knots emotionally, her hopes were soon dashed. As soon as she learned of his new friendship, she launched an attack, but this led to an even more vigorous counterassault from her son. She switched tactics in the next round, telling him that she had burned his letter, that her feelings were hurt past repair, and that one day he would know what he had done. She was not trying to prevent him from having friends, not at all. She merely was exhorting him "to the dignity of a true gentleman." This impenetrable phrase must have baffled her son, but he could not have missed the point: that Anna was determined to remove Kitty from his life.

Whenever Anna felt threatened, she was prepared to use any weapon, and in this case she had several. Kitty presented no real challenge; Anna was an old hand at unnerving adolescent girls. Frank was another matter. Her letter showed she knew that she could not take the direct approach much further. But there were other possibilities. In his autobiography, Wright reconstructed at some length the conversation he had with Cecil Corwin when the latter tried to argue him out of "getting serious" with Kitty. They were both just children, Corwin said. Frank ought to get some experience of women, become a man of the world. Corwin's arguments sounded so suspiciously adult that Wright soon guessed their origin. When he challenged his mother about that, she did not have the grace to apologize. She was maddeningly cool, even condescending. Anna was an absolute master of this kind of thrust and parry, and it seemed at first as if she had won, because she had also tackled Mrs. Tobin and obtained her agreement to send Catherine away for three months. But she had seriously antagonized her son, as his account reveals. He was rightly offended, and the more cleverly his mother played her cards, the more tenderly he began to think of the lovely and absent Catherine, the first girl, he told Corwin, he had felt "at home" with.

At length Catherine returned. His autobiography relates that their friendship became more intimate, more ardent and more committed. Catherine reached her eighteenth birthday on March 25, 1889, and Frank was within a week of becoming twenty-two when, on June 1, 1889, they were married. It rained the whole day. Samuel Clark Tobin burst into tears. At the right psychological moment, Anna fainted.

5

Lieber Meister

Life as it flows is so much time wasted, and nothing can ever be recovered or truly possessed save under the form of eternity, which is also the form of art.

—GEORGE SANTAYANA

John Dos Passos has left a vivid description of the city Wright found when he went to live in Chicago: "[C]rossing and recrossing the bridges over the Chicago river in the jingle and clatter of traffic, the rattle of vans and loaded wagons and the stamping of big dray-horses and the hooting of towboats with barges and the rumbling whistle of lake steamers waiting for the draw, he thought of the great continent stretching a thousand miles east and south and north, two thousand miles west. . . ."

When Wright arrived, the city that was to play a pivotal role in his career as an architect was, for all practical purposes, only half a century old. Up to the 1830s, Chicago had been little more than a fort surrounded by a few farmhouses containing a population of fewer than two hundred. Although it was situated at the head of Lake Michigan, it was blocked by a sandbar half a mile long, making it inaccessible for months of the year. But its potential importance as a marketplace for commerce for the West and Middle West was obvious, and once the federal government had built a canal and eliminated the

need for portage, its future was secure. As early as 1848 it had become
an important port. By 1887, eight hundred thousand people lived
there, and by 1893, when Wright set up an independent practice,
the population had grown to a million. Cyrus McCormick began the
manufacture of his famous reaping machine there, George Pullman
designed and built the first railway sleeping car, and great names of
the stockyards and steel mills were established: Armour, Swift, Libby,
Hutchinson and Morris. By the 1860s city streets had been lifted out
of the mud, sometimes several feet above their old levels, and paved.

All that energy and money brought about a spectacular building
boom, and those architects not engaged in designing factories, offices,
churches and stores were erecting palaces for the new millionaires. To
add to the city's assets, from an architect's point of view, its famous
calamity had taken place: a fire in 1871 that broke out in the lumber
district and that, when it was finally contained twenty-seven hours
later, had destroyed some seventeen thousand buildings and left one
hundred thousand homeless. Reconstruction began immediately, and
Chicago risen from the ashes was richer, more energetic and more
progressive than ever. Electric lights took the place of the old gas
lamps, cable cars replaced the horse-drawn vehicles; the city became
a hub for the nation's railways, and in 1881 received its first telephone.
But perhaps the most spectacular developments of all were taking
place in architecture, as the demand for a fireproof building that would
also make profitable use of small lots brought about the invention of
the structural iron skeleton and the first skyscrapers.

One of the talented architects to be attracted by these stunning
opportunities was Louis Sullivan. This towering figure, a prophet of
modern American architecture, grew up in Boston, where he witnessed
the construction of some of Henry Hobson Richardson's finest works,
the Brattle Square and Trinity churches, firsthand. He studied at the
Massachusetts Institute of Technology and in Paris with Émile Vau-
dremer, a leading figure of the École des Beaux-Arts, but immediately
rejected the French academic tradition, considering it basically flawed.
He was much more influenced, according to the architectural historian
Henry-Russell Hitchcock, by Frank Furness, a Philadelphian for whom
he briefly worked, creator of some Victorian Gothic buildings Hitchcock called "wildly original." Sullivan then made his way west for
some firsthand instruction in what was then called "Chicago construction." There he worked in the office of William Le Baron Jenny, an
architect-engineer and leading figure in the design of the structural

Louis Sullivan, age forty-four, 1900

iron skeleton, along with the invention of a floating foundation that would answer the acute problems caused by Chicago's muddy soils. Sullivan then joined the firm of Dankmar Adler as chief designer in 1880. He was just twenty-four years old, but his remarkable gifts were already evident; three years later he had been made a partner. When Wright joined Adler and Sullivan, the man who would become his *"Lieber Meister"* was about to make a great breakthrough with the design, in 1890, of the Wainwright Building in St. Louis. Wright was there at the moment when Sullivan, who had been out for a walk in search of ideas, burst into the office and finished the sketch in a matter of minutes. Wright wrote, "I was perfectly aware of what had happened. This was Louis Sullivan's greatest moment—his greatest effort. The 'skyscraper' as a new thing under the sun, an entity with . . . beauty all its own, was born."

Not only was Sullivan a master of the new form; he was a theoretician of equal importance. He wrote widely about architecture, coining the famous phrase "form follows function," which would become the cornerstone of the new aesthetic, or anti-aesthetic, since it was based on the belief that architectural considerations should be strictly util-itarian ones. Norris Kelly Smith has argued that this was a meaning Sullivan never intended, pointing out that Sullivan's text gives bio-logical, or organic, forms as examples, not mechanical ones. In the natural world, the interrelationship of forms and functions stood for "relationships between the immaterial and the material, between the subjective and the objective—between the Infinite Spirit and the finite mind. . . ." Lewis Mumford, another distinguished architectural his-torian, thought, "The rigorists placed the mechanical functions of a building above its human functions; they neglected the feelings, the sentiments, and the interests of the person who was to occupy it. Instead of regarding engineering as a foundation for form, they treated it as an end." Nor did Sullivan, in his famous dictum, ever imply that ornamentation should be eliminated. In fact, his buildings became famous for his distinctive use of flowing patterns, their intricate and intertwining arabesques based on natural forms in the manner of Art Nouveau. These additions were to be used with discrimination and have a direct relationship with the object being decorated, the dictum espoused by Owen Jones in *The Grammar of Ornament*. But Sullivan took the idea farther when he wrote that architecture ought to express the spirit of a building's function by the harmony of its form, and become that conjunction between the material and immaterial that one found in nature. A waterworks, for instance, should not simply be an efficient pumping machine; its design should also convey the abstract qualities, the very essence of flowing water. In short, Sullivan's philosophy had more to do with the Aesthetic Movement than with modernism, and he was still less a proselytizer for a return to Greek and Roman classical forms. His designs and writings "monumentalized themes of central concern to the aesthetic architect." They also influ-enced Wright, as he wrote in his biography of his old mentor, *Genius and the Mobocracy*, published in 1949. It was an inspiration to watch Sullivan modeling and transforming his vision of an ideal into a reality, his "own soul's philosophy incarnate." Sullivan's belief in pure form "as integral rhythmic movement was what made him a lyric poet."

If Sullivan, by then thirty-two years old, was the artist-in-residence, his partner, Dankmar Adler, in his forties when Wright arrived, was very much the practical mind, author of numerous articles on foun-dations, structural systems, vertical transportation, lighting, venti-lation, acoustics and the nuts and bolts of the business. Wright recalled that Adler's "bushy brows . . . almost hid a pair of piercing grey eyes.

His square grey beard and squarish head seemed square with the building and his personal solidity was a guarantee that out of all that confusion would issue the beauty of order." That team of efficient visionary and engineer-manager, two men with such expansive ideas who built so well, was an immediate success. During one eight-year period (1887–95) the firm received almost ninety commissions: everything from theaters and tombs to opera houses. After 1891 they could afford to move into a brand-new office tower and rent two floors. The cause of the move had just been unveiled: a vast new building they had designed, the Auditorium Building. The main part of the complex was 10 stories high, contained 63,350 square feet of space and combined a 400-room hotel with space for 136 offices and shops. It also contained a monumental, 17-story tower that, in addition to the offices just mentioned, enclosed a 400-seat theater and the largest permanent concert hall built to that date. (It seated 4,000.) Sullivan's biographer wrote, "No wonder Chicago, as easily impressed by size as beauty, reeled at the achievement. . . ."

The Auditorium Building, generally recognized as a triumph of engineering for Adler and another feather in Sullivan's artistic cap, took four years to design and build (1886–90). Almost from the moment he arrived, Wright and the other young draftsmen in the office were taken up with the day-to-day details of designing and constructing the largest building in Chicago: invaluable practical experience. It was his good luck to be part of a rapidly expanding office; in such situations, being senior by a few months can make a difference, and Sullivan soon singled out Wright for the delicate work of faithfully transforming his own sketches for the building's actual structure, and its decorative details, into finished working drawings. Wright liked to say he had been the pencil in Sullivan's hand. He also claimed to have added some flourishes to the building himself. The night the building opened, Adelina Patti sang, and Benjamin Harrison, president of the United States, was in the audience. Wright noted, "The enthusiasm now evoked was contagious and we all floated upon it like small ships in a grand pageant."

There seems to have been nothing haphazard or fortuitous about the choices Wright was making in those first years after he arrived in Chicago. After talking his way into a job with the one architect to whom he already had an introduction, he was quick to isolate his next target, the firm most in the news in 1887–88. One hesitates to call him an opportunist, since no one could have risen so rapidly, even with Wright's confidence and charm, without exceptional promise. What he had to offer impressed everyone, but the fact that he made so few superfluous moves, and accomplished so much so soon, argues for a wonderfully shrewd and calculating nature.

So one should look for the reason in his choice of Oak Park as his future home. Although Oak Park, ten miles to the west, resisted incorporation, it was essentially a suburb of Chicago and growing just as rapidly—its population of four thousand in 1889 would double in ten years—and was proclaiming, "We have reclaimed the wilderness. . . ." Its new arrivals were the families of the Chicago stockbrokers, insurance executives, bankers, investors, department store magnates, manufacturers and the like who commuted each morning from the Oak Park railway station. The question often raised, why these prosperous and conservative men should become Wright's clients, has to be seen in the context of what was happening in their city at that time. These were the men making expansive decisions, gambling money on the radical use of new materials, erecting that astonishing new invention, the skyscraper, which would become imitated all over the United States.

Wright would soon become a father, and Oak Park had an excellent reputation for its schools. He loved culture, and Oak Park's citizens were enthusiastic readers of great literature, participators in amateur theatricals and indefatigable givers of the musicale. They had formed all sorts of trios and quartets and, by 1902, had built their own opera house, seating over a thousand. The town managed to support the venture for a few years before tacitly conceding that the gesture was too grand even for Oak Park. So Wright's rather sardonic comment that his town was known as "Saint's Rest," because it had so many churches, is not meant to be taken too seriously, in light of his own intensely religious background and church-focused life at the time. What might seem stuffy, straitlaced and claustrophobic about the lives of Oak Park's citizens, with their big white houses on broad, leafy avenues was, after Spring Green and Madison, comfortable and reassuring to Wright and his family. They moved in.

Wright had found a choice corner lot in the center of town, one side facing toward the main boulevard of Chicago Avenue and the other running along Forest Avenue, then only recently paved. It had once belonged to a landscape gardener, who had planted it with all manner of lilacs, snowballs and spireas, and in the spring it was vivid with white and blue violets, lilies of the valley and wild ginger. A

Drawing of the Chandler cottage, Tuxedo Park, New York, 1885–86, by architect Bruce Price

Frank Lloyd Wright's house, Oak Park, taken in 1965, showing, at left, the adjoining studio

white clapboard house, with scalloped eaves and a wooden teardrop at each corner, had recently been built on the Chicago Avenue side. On the Forest Avenue side, an old-fashioned barn still stood, vertically boarded and battened, with an interesting rusty color. Wright, in a more or less conscious echo of William Morris, wrote in 1932 that he had preferred the rustic picturesqueness of the barn to the contrived picturesqueness of the house. But neighbors were indignant that a barn had been left standing on "the best street in town," he wrote revealingly.

If it were the prize location, Wright wanted it. He had been working for Adler and Sullivan for a year when he married Catherine, and he and his mother had agreed on a plan to buy the house and lot with money realized from the sale of her Madison house. However, this was not enough, and her son needed a lump sum for his share.

Wright's habit of borrowing from people who liked him was so unvarying that one can safely infer that Sullivan soon liked him very much, since he advanced the money. In return, Wright allowed him to hold the mortgage and offered to bind himself to a five-year contract; this, at sixty dollars a week, was also generous; Adler said it made him the highest-paid draftsman in Chicago. It has been suggested that Sullivan's interest in Wright was sexual, but there is no question that Wright's interest in Sullivan was strictly practical. It was almost a quid pro quo: if you like me, then lend me money—a kind of cheerful expectation, based on Anna's repeated capitulations and easy conquests like Corwin, that someone would always appear to assume his responsibilities; and his confident charm of manner must have been irresistible to certain people. For Wright, Sullivan was a poet, philosopher and beau idéal, which would not have prevented him from thinking about what Sullivan could do for him. But the situation was more complex than that, in the intricate web of expectations Wright would weave around those who belonged to him: they always had his unpredictable but enduring fealty. He and his sister Jane fought all their lives—they were too close in age, too opinionated, for it to be otherwise—which never prevented them from defending each other against the rest of the world when necessary. Wright's young male friends tended to be in the mold of Robie Lamp, Cecil Corwin and George Grant Elmslie, i.e., quiet, unassuming, devoted, sterling characters who needed championing. When they first met, Sullivan was too much the celebrated architect to be seen in this light, although in later years, when the situation was reversed, Wright eventually published a biography the main point of which seemed to be that Sullivan was a genius and his detractors less than rabble. So when some in Adler and Sullivan's office began to resent Wright's favored position and looked as if they were spoiling for a fight, Wright decided that he needed lessons in boxing. Then he fought two battles with three of his rivals who took the precaution of bringing knives. By his own account he was twice victorious, though badly cut in one fight, with multiple stab wounds. Also by his account, he fought with no holds barred. He was certainly defending his privileged position, and he relished the chance to get even, but since most of his adversaries were men Adler had hired, Wright conceivably thought he was defending Sullivan's honor, Sullivan's choices and Sullivan's ideals. It would then be a point of pride never to mention what had happened.

When Frank and Kitty got married, they lived with Anna for some months while waiting for their new house to be built: a smallish, two-bedrooms-plus-studio house with a large front veranda and back porch, positioned well back from Chicago Avenue, its main rooms facing west and south. Construction began in late August 1889 and was probably completed just before the birth of their first child, Frank Lloyd Wright, Jr., on March 31, 1890. For most of her stay with Anna, Kitty was heavily pregnant and also depressed and miserable to find her mother-in-law still antagonistic. "Poor Kitty," Maginel wrote, "she didn't deserve so forcible an adversary as my mother." Their happiest times were spent in Kitty's room, sewing pincushions, needle books, pen wipers and the like from the sample books of pretty fabrics Kitty's father had given her. That is, until they overheard a stray comment from Anna to Jane or vice versa about the amateurish nature of their efforts, which would send them running to Kitty's room to collapse in tears. There is a family story that whenever she heard Anna coming, Kitty would hide in a closet.

The situation improved somewhat when Kitty and Frank moved into their own house, which their neighbors considered charming and original. There is an early photograph taken on the steps of their home shortly after it was built. A handsome oriental rug has been spread out in front of the door. The beautiful Catherine, seated in the center, holds up her Titian-haired baby. Uncle Jenk is standing to the left; sister Jane, wearing a striped blazer, flourishes a tennis racket; sister Maginel, in the background, has both hands on her brother's shoulders; Anna, all in black, leans toward the camera with a too-knowing smile; and Frank, his hair fractionally longer than the fashion, sporting a mustache and wearing the well-tailored clothes of a young gentleman, shows off his profile. Maginel recalled vividly the day Lloyd was born, Kitty's agonized groans and then the moment when there were "tears on my brother's white face as he ran across the garden to tell his mother of the birth of his firstborn."

The opening of the Auditorium Building late in 1889 and the move to new offices signaled a new stage in Wright's rapid advance at Adler and Sullivan. Years later, he published a diagram demonstrating that his had been the most important office, since it was right beside Sullivan's, more important even than Adler's or the office held by Paul Mueller, a young German engineer who handled all the mechanical details and worked directly under Adler. (Wright actually shared his office with Elmslie but omitted that fact.) As chief designer, Wright was in charge of a staff of thirty draftsmen and therefore in an excellent position to see how an architectural firm was structured. Being the person he was, he at once saw the point, or what Henry Hobson Richardson called the first rule of architecture, "Get the job." Most architectural firms of the day, he wrote, were composed of a successful senior partner whose name lent luster to the enterprise, then a man in the back room who did the real work and, third, someone with the right social connections, seen in all the right places, who knew where the next commission was coming from. In future years Wright would encompass all of these functions in his own tireless personality. But he never forgot the first rule of architecture.

In the days following the success of the Auditorium Building there was a new mood in the office, a new display of earnest concentration and an afterglow that lingered because it was such a feather in one's cap to be working for Adler and Sullivan in any capacity at all. Eventually the firm settled into something like a routine as projects for loft buildings, skyscrapers, hotels, factories, theaters and opera houses came through in a steady stream.

Adler and Sullivan built very few private houses. The firm's wealth was based on the commissions it obtained—a percentage of total costs—for its large-scale designs. Yet the quick-witted Wright seemed curiously blind to this lucrative fact. Almost from the first, the kinds of structures he wanted to build were houses. Since he chose this path despite the dictates of good sense, one must assume that the house had a particular and overriding significance for him. As a young man he already had a fully formed vision of the kind of house he wanted. His later work would evolve far from this original realization, but in all essential ways he remained faithful to its concepts. One finds, in this precocious need to create an environment, an ambiance, some clues to his preoccupations. In common with other aesthetes—Bernard Berenson and Kenneth Clark, to name two—Wright seemed incapable of any kind of work until he had created a harmonious atmosphere for himself. Wherever he was, all work stopped until he had built, or rebuilt, the room, changed the decor, moved the furniture, positioned his own talismanic images around him and found everything to his satisfaction.

The reasons are hard to find, but a reading of his autobiography provides some clues. Houses of his period were cut up, cluttered, claustrophobic; they buzzed and hummed at him. He longed for opened spaces, serene vistas and "ineffable harmonies." A house must be welcoming and encourage a feeling of well-being. It should be "intensely human." It should be a natural house. It should be a part of nature and encompass it; the two should be seamlessly linked. It should give one a feeling of unity, a sense that its parts were essential components of a larger whole. It should "crown the exuberance of life." Its roof should be low, wide and snug, a broad shelter. It should exude peace and serenity; one should be able to rest there and feel at home.

In retrospect, Wright seemed to have been most at home when he was abroad. He later described his year of exile in Fiesole in the most lyric terms. He imagined himself returning home one perfect evening, entering "the small solid door framed in the solid white blank wall," to find a wood fire burning and a delicious dinner waiting. Or, he and his love might be walking in the garden, admiring its pool and bower of yellow roses, with a small stone table set for two. It was "the house of houses." In other words, perfection to him was an entirely domestic scene, the felicity of two people in love, surrounded by beauty, in a hidden paradise. A home should be secretive and hold within it an ideal marriage, the one his mother never had. So perhaps a great deal of Wright's hopes and expectations were bound up with his mother's failed relationship. He would build anew, create a more perfect life to compensate them both for past unhappiness. He would put down his roots, just as that group of exiles, the Lloyd Joneses, had done as they attempted to create a better Wales, one more true to the ancestral dream image, in their Wisconsin valley.

There were, perhaps, further inferences to be drawn. The fact that Wright always talked about the nine wood engravings of Gothic cathedrals his mother supposedly hung around his crib may have a bearing here, as one recalls that Uncle Jenkin wanted Silsbee for an architect because his designs looked homey. To that devout Unitarian, as to his family, the church had always been their refuge, their one true home and the link between church and home can be traced back through Protestant thought. It "implies not only that there is something home-like about the church, but also that there is something church-like about the home," Norris Kelly Smith wrote. As this writer sees it, the problem Wright was wrestling with was "that of redefining and reaffirming the significance" of family life at a time when family life itself was disintegrating. That Wright thought the home must somehow be a bastion for morality is evident, given his comment that the American house "lied about everything." It was vulgar, wickedly extravagant, a nationwide waste, "a moral, social, aesthetic excrement." Commodity and delight, a serene sense of comfort and well-being, a close contact with nature, a homey feeling—all these attributes would take one only so far if, at the end, all that were expressed did not satisfy Wright's Puritan conscience. The first argument he and Kitty had came as they returned from their honeymoon. She objected to his plans to inscribe "mottoes" around their house, and he just as heatedly insisted. What he wanted were daily exhortations, reminders of right manners, right morals, right reflections upon the nature of things. Despite her, he managed to have "Truth Is Life!" carved over the fireplace in their first living room. Then he wondered whether it should have been "Life Is Truth!"

Once Wright discovered that Sullivan was not interested in houses and had eagerly offered himself, he was given several commissions to play with by his indulgent *Lieber Meister.* Sullivan even trusted Wright with two houses for himself, one a cottage in Ocean Springs, Mississippi, and the second a row house on Lake Avenue in Chicago, in which he lived for several years before relinquishing it to his brother Arthur. These and other designs were certainly in the manner of Sullivan, and the fact that Wright was chosen as designer must have meant that Sullivan had seen the gift that made Wright so exceptional: his precocious and almost uncanny ability to grasp a style. He perceived it and imitated it, but he often did more: at his best, he could cut through to its essence, interpreting it with a surer eye and a finer discrimination than anyone else. That versatile and fastidious eye was maturing rapidly as Wright designed his first houses in the Queen Anne and Shingle styles he had studied under Silsbee, as well as the

A seldom-seen view of the entrance hall of the William H. Winslow house with the living room beyond

Detail of the main façade of the William H. Winslow house, River Forest, Illinois

Charlotte Dickson Wainwright tomb, Bellefontaine Cemetery, St. Louis, Missouri, built in 1892 by Louis Sullivan

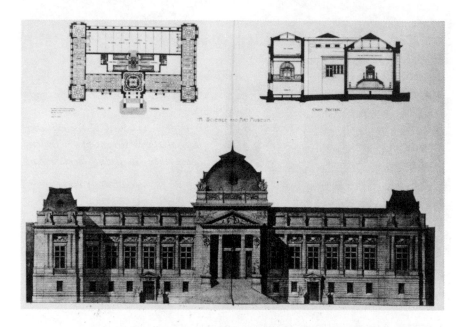

A Science and Art Museum prizewinning design by
Charles Rennie Mackintosh

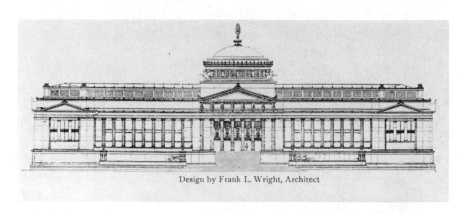

Design by Frank L. Wright, Architect

Frank Lloyd Wright's design for the Milwaukee Public Library competition

Sullivanesque. After all, those were the kinds of houses then in demand, and Wright, who intended to set up his own practice, knew the first principle of architecture.

Specialists in Wright's work have, in recent years, advanced the notion that his early designs were often derived from specific works by other architects. The Yale architectural historian Vincent Scully believes, for instance, that the house Wright designed for himself in 1889 was closely modeled on two houses built by another architect, Bruce Price, in Tuxedo Park, New York, three or four years before (1885–86). Professor Scully has published photographs to show the similarities between Wright's façade and that of Price's Kent house. Many of Wright's decorative designs are clearly modeled on those of Sullivan, particularly those for his Harlan and Winslow houses of 1892 and 1894. A mere amateur at the game of architectural connoisseurship can see the links between the façade of the tomb Sullivan designed in 1892 and the front of Wright's Winslow house, built two years later. Sullivan's massive entry portal is framed by a running frieze that forms squares on each side of it. Place windows in those blank spaces and one has the front door and adjoining windows of the Winslow house. The architectural historian Patrick Pinnell, also of Yale, believes that many other early designs are derived from house plans published by McKim, Mead and White, the famous New York architectural firm, notably Wright's Blossom house of 1892 and his design for an early client, Henry Cooper, the house with the controversial drawing date, which was never built. The dean of American architectural historians, Henry-Russell Hitchcock, whose study, *On the Nature of Materials*, is one of the standard texts on Wright, has seen clear resemblances between Wright's first important design for Adler and Sullivan, the James Charnley house of 1891, and another McKim, Mead and White design, a New York town house, built seven years before.

Yet another distinguished architectural historian, Professor H. Allen Brooks, has pointed out the parallels between one of Wright's best-known designs, that for a small "Prairie Town" house, first published in the *Ladies' Home Journal* of 1901, and a design for a house by Robert C. Spencer published earlier that year. (Professor Brooks concluded that since Wright's designs were so much better realized than Spencer's, the latter's work probably acted as a catalyst, helping him to achieve a synthesis.) Perhaps the most striking example of a direct steal, if it can be so termed, is the design Wright submitted in a competition for a new public library and museum in Milwaukee in 1893. (He did not win.) His drawing almost literally reproduces, point for point, that of another talented young architect, Charles Rennie Mackintosh. Mackintosh, then just a student, won a medal for his museum, and his drawing was published in the *British Architect* in 1890—some three years before. But the point hardly needs further elaboration since Wright himself conceded it, albeit sotto voce. Referring to these early experiments, he wrote, "I suppose I stole them." It gave him, he added, a most uneasy conscience.

These examples illustrate an aspect of architectural practice well known at the time, one that persists to this day. Any first-rate architect's office carried, as a matter of course, copies of the latest professional magazines from New York, London and elsewhere. Knowing what was being built, or about to be built, was part of every architect's stock-in-trade, particularly if he could anticipate that moment when the wave might sweep him up with it. Far from being blind to other influences, as he claimed, one gains the distinct impression that Wright was influenced, all his life, by everything he ever saw, however much the original idea might be transmuted and transformed by the alchemy of his imagination. He may well have been in the position analogous to that of someone with a powerful musical memory, that is to say, haunted by images, if not actually hounded by them, until he had exhausted all their possibilities. He, too, would be the victim of similar borrowings, and quite soon, to judge from the suburbs of Oak Park and River Forest in Chicago, where it is sometimes difficult to identify Wright's houses from their many imitations.

A further factor to consider is that Wright was never satisfied. Almost as soon as he had finished one design, he could see its flaws and invariably added, subtracted, simplified or elaborated upon it. Nowadays scholars have the baffling task of deciding how to restore those buildings on which he had the freest hand, i.e., his own home and studio at Oak Park and at Taliesin in Spring Green, since the master had remodeled, enlarged and obliterated with such gay abandon. At what point should they decide the house was "finished," since he never had? Wright lacked the slightest sentimental interest in a concept he had outgrown. As his associate John H. Howe has said, "He couldn't wait to tear it down." Denied this option with respect to some of his amateurish early efforts, still stubbornly standing, Wright could at least obfuscate and camouflage. As he also said, "Doctors bury their mistakes; architects have to cover them with vines."

Wright left Adler and Sullivan to go into private practice in the early summer of 1893. As he explained later, the reason for the break centered on the fact that, during the previous two or three years, he had been in private practice after hours. "Moonlighting," as it was called, was a common practice for young draftsmen ambitious to make a name for themselves, so common that Wright's five-year contract with the firm specifically ruled it out. A year before Wright signed it, in 1888, the Illinois State Association of Architects had met to consider the problem, which was thought to have reached epidemic proportions. It was even suggested that any architect who knowingly employed a moonlighting draftsman should be expelled. By the time he left, he and Kitty had two boys—Frank Lloyd Wright, Jr., always called Lloyd, then aged three, baby John, about seven months old— and were expecting their third child, daughter Catherine, who would be born early in 1894. So Wright, as potential father of three, could be expected to be looking for more money, given his habitual readiness to spend and more and more reasons for doing so. His commissions for Adler and Sullivan had dried up by 1892, so he quietly took off in his own direction, designing a total of six moonlighting houses. Three of them were houses near Sullivan's Chicago home. This had obvious perils, so Wright took the precaution of persuading his friend Corwin to announce publicly that he was their architect. But, some months later, the ruse was discovered, and Wright, with a year still to go on his contract, was dismissed. In other words, according to Wright's account, though he had admittedly violated the terms of his contract with Sullivan, his start in independent practice was involuntary. It came about because Adler and Sullivan kicked him out.

No doubt, all of this was true so far as it went. Sullivan would have felt justifiably enraged, after all his efforts on Wright's behalf, the sums of money lent, the opportunities given and the handsome salary he was paying every week. The fact that Wright then set up an office with Corwin, who had also worked for the firm, would have given Sullivan further cause for indignation. As Sullivan's biographer put it, "They [Wright and Corwin] also shared the knowledge that they had offended the one man who had inspired them most." However, there is a fair possibility that Sullivan had a more pressing reason to believe that his protégé, perhaps the one he counted on most to carry his standard forward, had let him down.

As has been noted, Sullivan had, from the start of his architectural career, rejected the training he had received in academic design from the École des Beaux-Arts, that is to say, the "academic discipline in

architecture embodied in imitated Renaissance and classical forms,"
as Hitchcock has described it. Sullivan's position did not change even
though a fashionable revival of that tradition was in the air. Eastern
architects of the mid-1880s, led by the firm of McKim, Mead and
White, were beginning to turn to the Renaissance for their inspiration.
They were following the example of the British architect Norman
Shaw, who had launched the Queen Anne style and was now championing a return to academic precepts. Shaw was, by general agreement, the most internationally influential architect of his time, setting
styles from the late 1860s until the outbreak of World War I. According to Hitchcock, McKim, Mead and White soon outstripped
Shaw in their elegant interpretations of the academic revival and, in
particular, in their design for the H. A. C. Taylor house of 1885 in
Newport, Rhode Island. Their success with this particular design,
in other words, set a new mood.

The evidence is that Wright began to venture in this direction
almost as soon as he started working for Sullivan. One of the great
surprises of the house he designed for himself in 1889, which, as has
been noted, was modeled on the Queen Anne designs of Bruce Price,
is the frieze one encounters as soon as one enters the front door. The
bas-relief, which depicts the eternal battle between evenly matched
forces, the war of the gods, is taken from the altar of Pergamum,
c. 200 B.C. Wright also makes use of dentil moldings in his living
room. These Greek-derived details are unmistakable early signs of the
direction of his thought.

Two years later, in 1891, his first great breakthrough came about
with a design for Adler and Sullivan, the James Charnley house in
Chicago. This "urban palazzo," as Hitchcock termed it, described by
Smith as the "work of a man of fastidious taste," with its severe,
uncompromising façade, its symmetrically placed windows and Italianate balcony, is considered more than just an adaptation of Sullivan's
large designs scaled down to domestic proportions; it is a classical
design of almost precocious restraint, clarity and refinement.

If Charnley's house was Wright's first great triumph, designed when
he was just twenty-four years old, a second came just a year later,
with a moonlighting commission for another client, George Blossom.
This large, handsome, symmetrical house, with its Palladian window
motifs and its interior rooms linked at the axes by arches, is seen by
Hitchcock as "a personal application of academic discipline" to ideas
inherited from Richardson and the Queen Anne style. It is also cited

as proof that Wright could have been one of the great academic architects. Wright's design for the Milwaukee Library and Museum competition, submitted late in 1893, is similarly derived. The third major breakthrough, the William Winslow house in River Forest, Wright's first commission after he left Sullivan, is yet another demonstration of his early mastery of classical form. Hitchcock cited the "serene horizontality of the design; the dignity, as urbane as that of the Charnley house, and the axial organization of the plan about the central chimney" in support of his assertion that, with the Winslow house, Wright had become the ablest academic designer in Chicago. (The house has since been named by the American Institute of Architects as one of seventeen Wright houses worthy to be retained as examples of his art.)

Since, in years to come, Wright would be considered a radical thinker in architecture, if not in most other areas of life, it seems anomalous, to say the least, that his first successes came within a highly conservative and stylized tradition. The reason, according to one theorist, has to do with the Froebel kindergarten training and, specifically, the exercises, or "games," that Anna brought home from the Philadelphia Centennial Exposition of 1876. Froebel's geometric blocks were designed to train children to make abstract patterns. These seemed simple, but were actually composed of many interlocking parts, the kind of training that seems heaven-sent for a future architect. Richard MacCormac, the British architect, further explained in a lecture to the Royal Society of Arts, that Wright's early houses shared a common trait, that of an overall unity "which Wright called simplicity achieved by reduction. . . . Like the Froebel exercises the house plans generally consist of interpenetrating squares and cruciforms which accommodate all the complexities of a domestic programme as it has previously developed in the suburban shingle style." This rigorous early training had, in other words, particularly suited Wright to understand the discipline of late eighteenth century French classicism and to adapt it in fresh new ways.

Hitchcock dated Wright's great period of classical design to 1892–93, that is to say, in the final year of his employment with Sullivan. Although he continued to experiment with other styles, Wright, in other words, had triumphed with a style that, however much it trembled on the verge of being high fashion, was absolutely inimical to his mentor, who could have seen well enough where his pupil was heading. If Wright disliked talking about his Queen Anne period and preferred to say as little as possible, he was completely silent about his early mastery of academic design. In fact, he did not have a single good word to say about the subject, and to ask him about the Renaissance was to guarantee a diatribe about that phenomenon as a "false dawn" and the death of architecture.

The event that actually precipitated the break between Wright and Sullivan was, in all likelihood, the great Chicago World's Fair of 1893. Almost as soon as it was decided that the booming city should be the site for this World's Columbian Exposition, architects were summoned to carry out the preliminary plan drafted by the famous landscape architects Frederick Law Olmsted and Henry Sargent Codman. They had decreed a group of harmonious buildings forming a court around a large lagoon. In Chicago, Adler and Sullivan was one of two prominent architectural firms; the other was that of Daniel H. Burnham and John Root. The plum position of coordinating the plans for the fair went to the latter. Very early in 1891 Burnham and Root, for whatever reason, selected its first group of five architects and architectural firms, all from the East Coast; among them was the firm of McKim, Mead and White. The decision came down in due course that the design of all the chief buildings would be Renaissance. Only then was a second group, of five Chicago firms, chosen. Among that group was the firm of Adler and Sullivan.

Although Wright was already experimenting, he did not make ambitious use of the new style until his Charnley house of 1891. By then he would have known which way the wind was blowing at the World's Fair. Perhaps he already thought, correctly as it turned out, that this imprimatur by the World's Fair would be bound to lead to a surge of interest in neoclassicism. As Sigfried Giedion wrote in *Space, Time and Architecture*, "Public, artists and literary people believed themselves to be witnessing a splendid rebirth of the great traditions of past ages," and only a few American voices were raised against this "seduction of public taste." Louis Sullivan's was one of them. He thought that "the damage wrought to this country by the Chicago World's Fair will last half a century." His own design of the Transportation Building received mixed reviews, being criticized for its lack of neoclassicism, and, according to Giedion, it marked the start of his decline in popularity as an architect.

If Wright's sympathies were now perfectly clear to Sullivan, and if his defection added, in years to come, to the latter's feelings of bitterness and betrayal, to Wright the situation must have seemed quite straightforward. When he joined Adler and Sullivan, the firm was approaching the height of its power and influence; by 1893, the fact that Sullivan had been denied an influential voice in planning for the fair could only mean that his star was on the decline. In the flush of his first enthusiasm for the new style, Wright might have seen himself as part of a vigorous new wave and Sullivan as a theoretician whose best days were behind him. Or perhaps it was necessary, even inevitable, that Wright should take the style seriously, since his livelihood depended upon it. The break was bound to come, and it was probably a relief to Wright to have Sullivan initiate it, given that the pupil's feelings were likely to be most uncomfortable. Wright's silence was broken only once, and one can gather something from his comment, made years later, that "this world's-fair wave of pseudo 'classic' now an 'ism, swept over and swept us all under."

In any case Wright's adherence to the new movement was destined to be brief. Sometime after the fair, perhaps in the spring of 1894, the Wrights were invited to meet Daniel Burnham, chief organizer of the fair and new president of the American Institute of Architects, by their mutual friend Edward C. Waller. Waller's house was directly opposite the new house Wright had just built for Winslow. Burnham had seen it and had pronounced it "a gentleman's house from grade to coping."

What Wright did not know was that Burnham had been in contact with Charles F. McKim, whose own design for the World's Fair had been based on the Villa Medici in Rome, about the latter's great ambition, i.e., to found an American Academy in Rome to solidify American interest in the classical tradition. McKim wrote to Burnham early in April 1894 to tell him that the "atelier" in Rome was close to being established, and to ask for Burnham's help in setting up some Chicago fellowships. It seems possible that Burnham's meeting with Wright took place soon afterward (Wright gives no date), since he had come to make Wright a generous proposal, all expenses paid: four years at the École des Beaux-Arts, a further two years in Rome at the new atelier and then a job in his office when he returned. Wright recreates the conversation that followed, always an indication of the importance he attached to an incident, and the attempt to set him on a course that, although he does not say so, he would have eagerly pursued just a year before. But by then Wright's instinct, which was unerring, had correctly seen that it was a false direction and would lead to a dead end. His refusal was nevertheless courageous, in light of his phenomenal successes to that date. He must have thought he had an even more fruitful avenue to pursue, and indeed he did.

6

Sermons in Stones

The law which it has been my effort chiefly to illustrate is the dependence of all noble design, in any kind, on the sculpture or painting of Organic Form.

—JOHN RUSKIN
The Two Paths

Frank Lloyd Wright's favorite occupation on a Sunday afternoon was to rearrange the furniture in his Oak Park house, and photographs of some of these experiments still exist, though they are seldom reproduced. They show that during his first six years there his living room, for instance, was filled with an eclectic assortment of furniture, bought at auctions, often grouped asymmetrically, so as to draw focus to one of the room's corners. There was a comfortable window seat, its bench well upholstered, equipped with plenty of cushions in contrasting colors and textures, an array of oriental area rugs, animal skins, large and luxuriant ferns, reproductions of Italian Renaissance paintings and other objects, shelves full of china and bric-a-brac and draped shawls and curtains—all of which demonstrated the continuing influence of the Aesthetic Movement on his taste.

Six years later Wright had redesigned his dining room, and the transformation was marked. Gone were the bric-a-brac, the textile patterns and the genteel effects of artistically draped shawls and cur-

Frank Lloyd Wright's living room as it was furnished before 1895

The Oak Park living room after construction was completed, 1889

*Earliest-known photograph of the newly remodeled dining room in Oak
Park, 1896–97, showing Ashbee-influenced chairs*

The fireplace inglenook in the Oak Park living room

tains, and in their place was a severely simplified decor emphasizing the horizontal, by means of wooden moldings running around the room, and the vertical, with much-elongated chairbacks composed of slats of wood that were his own design. The oak floor, finished in golden brown, was bare, and the only decorative elements in the room came from the leaded-glass windows in a pattern abstracted from a flower, a perforated wooden screen in the ceiling that provided diffused light, and vases of flowers. By 1895, in other words, Wright's taste had evolved from the consciously artistic toward a concept that was unified, pared down, bold and uncompromising.

The year of 1895 is the earliest date one can give to this clear evidence of a departure in his philosophy, but certain themes can be discerned from fragments of his lectures of the year before, in which he is already railing against mindless decoration and the fondness of most housewives—this would be a lifelong theme—for dark and dingy places in which to store a clutter of objects that no one would ever use. He exhorted his listeners to build with an overall concept and a single unifying theme in mind in their choices of everything from materials to the designs of windows, roofs, doors and furnishings, to make the work "honest, true to itself. . . ." Consistency and order, the elimination of extraneous detail, a return to natural forms, respect for materials and unity of design: it sounded like the manifesto of a new order and it was. Like the Aesthetic Movement, its predecessor, the Arts and Crafts Movement as it evolved in Britain in the 1880s was a reaction against a century of mass production and the havoc it had wrought, and a revival of the concept of medieval guilds and handcrafted objects of lasting beauty and utility. These goals had been shared by the Aesthetic Movement's artists and architects, with the aim of simply reasserting an aesthetic of beauty and the value of self-expression. William Morris, acknowledged leader of the Arts and Crafts Movement, ultimately came to reject what he considered the limited philosophy of art for art's sake and devoted himself to the cause of social reform. He was, in this respect, a true follower of the man he admired and whose energies were also focused, at the end of his life, on the whole problem of laissez-faire economics and the ills it generated: the art critic and writer John Ruskin. So there was a strong political agendum in the Arts and Crafts Movement, but this seems to have interested the young Wright far less than other aspects of its credo, which was as idealistic and wide-ranging as Ruskin's writings. As Alan Crawford, biographer of C. R. Ashbee, another leader of the movement, wrote, "Ask any Arts and Crafts man to give an account of his work and he would talk not only about techniques and materials, but also about the status of the decorative arts, the uses of wealth, the Industrial Revolution, work, nature, the home, honesty, simplicity and the Middle Ages."

One can see why a member of the Lloyd Jones family would leap enthusiastically into a movement that offered him such an inviting platform; having acquired a taste for pontificating, Wright would go on doing so for the rest of his days. As Robert Stein wrote in *John Ruskin and Aesthetic Thought in America, 1840–1900,* Ruskin's beliefs had been widely debated since the mid-nineteenth century and, by the time he died, he was one of England's four most famous living authors, on a par with Scott and Dickens. While Wright was still an adolescent, he had been given Ruskin's first book on architecture, *The Seven Lamps of Architecture,* and had read its sequel, *The Stones of Venice,* the book Carlyle praised as "a sermon in stones."

Ruskin's main thesis, that right emotion, true feeling and lofty thought were all included in concepts of what was beautiful, that, as Thoreau would write, "the perception of beauty is a moral test," was seized upon by Unitarians as they advanced their belief that man was a part of nature, not separate from it, and as they sought to teach a moral response to beauty based on an awareness of nature. If Ruskin thought that the pinnacle of architecture had been reached with the Gothic, then the Lloyd Joneses, and Anna among them, would also believe (hence the prints of cathedrals) that these great medieval edifices summed up all that an ennobled vision of art could achieve. Like Ruskin, Wright would come to declare that the Renaissance (since it represented a return to a heathen tradition) exemplified everything that was degenerate about architecture. Like Ruskin, Wright would wrestle with the secret that gave "character" to the trees, even the way in which architecture ought to be inspired by nature, since Ruskin "corrected the romantic misapprehension that Gothic was *derived* from the forms of nature, but at the same time he judged the *created* art of the Gothic by reference to the forms of nature. . . ." Anna's belief that architecture was a high and noble calling seems directly derived from Ruskin's dictum that architecture had an obligation to improve society, even that beauty existed in order "to convey the absolute values upon which a sound society must rest." As for Wright, the belief that the practice of true architecture ennobled its practitioner and set him apart from the common herd, would lead to some disastrous miscalculations in years to come. But, as he made common cause with the Arts and Crafts Movement, he set himself the daunting task of reflecting truth, beauty and moral feeling in his own work. Wright probably never realized the extent to which Ruskin's teachings had influenced him, but he clearly, perhaps inadvertently, demonstrated it. One of the terms most associated with his name is "organic architecture." He proselytized all his life for an architecture governed by the inner forces of nature and never realized, perhaps, that the term came directly from Ruskin.

Today, the idea that an architect has an obligation to encompass the values of an ideal society in his work has been unfashionable for decades. But when Wright first began independent practice in Chicago, he was just one of a number of architects, most of them younger men with reputations unmade, who saw the possibilities offered by the new movement, which was as much Romantic as it was reformist and revivalist. The emphasis by British architects on the cottage and small manor house presented new possibilities for architects struggling to find an alternative to vulgar ostentation: those French chateaux, Italian palazzi and even the beaux-arts classicism in vogue with the newly rich. In championing a return to humbler styles notable for their beauty of fitness of purpose, young American architects could talk about a need for an architecture that was untainted by foreign influences, that was home-grown, a quintessentially American architecture that they all, in one way or another, were competing to invent. If city houses, lined up in a row on their rectangular lots, were ugly and inconvenient, they would build beautifully and conveniently; if houses of the rich were a soulless pastiche of fashionable styles, they would espouse a return to truer, more basic dwellings imbued with all the sympathetic qualities of place that these lacked. The fact that the Arts and Crafts Movement—advocating a set of principles, not a style—took hold so quickly in Chicago is an indication of how well its goals were suited to these peculiarly American circumstances.

The English architect Philip Webb's design for William Morris's own home, the Red House (1859–60) is considered the prototype for the Arts and Crafts concept of the smaller, or artistic, house. That early experiment would be an inspiration for a new generation of architects, among them C. F. A. Voysey, who started practicing in the early 1880s, and then for M. H. Baillie Scott, Charles Rennie Mackintosh, C. R. Ashbee, C. Harrison Townsend, Sir Edwin Lutyens and many others. Their work, Hitchcock wrote, "seemed to breathe

the creative air in which Wright worked from the beginning of his independent practice." For Arts and Crafts architects, the fireplace was "a vital functional and symbolic feature: the 'hearth' to warm the home at the centre of home life, flame as the soul of the house," an old-fashioned and essentially Romantic view that they all espoused. The concept of the inglenook (a recessed fireplace with built-in benches on each side), another antiquated notion, had been revived by Shaw in the 1860s and was still in use by Arts and Crafts architects half a century later. For these designers, renouncing ostentation meant a return to semi-austerity: plain, unadorned walls (Voysey even argued against wallpaper), simple oak furniture and a solitary vase of flowers as the only ornamentation. Arts and Crafts architects were meticulous about building well—no short cuts were tolerated—and about "truth to materials," i.e., using brick, stone, wood and the like so as to enhance their unique qualities. They took enormous pains to fit their buildings harmoniously into the landscape, achieving in their best work an inextricable melding of one with the other. Voysey, one of the most influential members of the group, laid great stress on the enclosing and protective character of roofs. His hipped, pitched roofs swept almost to the ground, symbolizing spiritual as well as physical shelter. As Ernest Newton told the Architectural Association in London in 1891, "Belief in the sacredness of home-life is still left to us, and is itself a religion, pure and easy to believe. It requires no elaborate creeds, its worship is the simplest, its discipline the gentlest and its rewards are peace and contentment."

Like many seemingly chameleonlike personalities, Wright had a hidden aspect that showed him to be remarkably consistent and tenacious, particularly where some strongly held beliefs were concerned. One of his major themes, that of Unity, or "the whole titanic struggle to make things one in which he remained engaged," as Vincent Scully wrote, remains true of Wright, whether one sees this struggle from a purely aesthetic standpoint, or in terms of his quasi-mystical Celtic beliefs, or as stemming from the joint influence of his radical Unitarian background and Emersonian-Ruskinian ideals, or as the outward sign that he was seeking to resolve an inner conviction of being fragmented, incomplete, torn by conflicts and far from whole.

    That possibility is supported by a study of creativity, *The Dynamics of Creation*, by Anthony Storr, which explores some of the reasons why certain gifted men and women become creative artists while others with equal abilities do not. Storr's thesis is that the drive to create is often fueled by just such an awareness of inner fragmentation. "Creativity is one mode adopted by gifted people of coming to terms with, or finding symbolic solutions for, the internal tensions and dissociations from which all human beings suffer in varying degree," and in fact some tests of creative individuals show that they exhibit more psychopathological traits than the average. However, such studies also show as many strengths as weaknesses. To begin with, strongly creative people are much more independent-minded than their peers, finding it much less necessary to conform to generally accepted norms. They tend to be skeptical, even rebellious, and remarkably forceful advocates for their own views. The most creative of those among a group of architects "were primarily concerned with meeting an inner artistic standard of excellence which they discovered within themselves."

Very creative men are aesthetically sensitive to a degree often labeled, in Western society, as "feminine," Storr writes, and are able to make contact with the intuitive and irrational side of themselves, the wellspring of their dreams, visions and poetic fantasies. Along with an appreciation for design and form goes a preference for complexity, asymmetry and incompleteness, rather than whatever is simple, straightforward and completed; in fact, the idea of a problem to resolve seems to be essential since it acts as a stimulus to their creativity. They are intensely motivated, endlessly curious people, with a breadth of interests; great talkers, impulsive and expansive by nature. They have the ability to work over long periods toward complex goals with great tenacity of purpose. This inner strength has been remarked on down through the centuries. Hogarth, for instance, observed, "I know of no such thing as genius, genius is nothing but labour and diligence." In short, Storr's conclusion, that great gifts, unresolved emotional needs and determination are all involved, is important in helping to understand Wright's creativity and the search for self-knowledge in which he, as a creator, was ultimately involved.

Linking the real with the ideal, making symbolic representations of reality: one returns again to the concept of the home as sacred, which, one believes, had the largest single influence on Wright's decision to join the Arts and Crafts Movement. On the subject of his own work, what Wright had to say is far less self-revelatory than the symbols he chose, and the simpler they are, the more hidden meanings they can often be found to contain. One can therefore attach some importance to the symbol Wright designed for himself once he had set up as an independent architect and carved his name on a stone plaque beside his door. It was a square inside which was a cross inside a circle: the Celtic, or Iona, cross. Such antiquities, known for their great beauty and elaboration, were often used as markers, not only in the churchyard but also to proclaim the center of the village green and marketplace. On occasion they were used to mark boundaries or as totems to guide the traveler, and it is interesting to speculate that Wright may have employed his symbol with this in mind. One also wonders how much the circle could have had to do with the reconciliation of opposites already discussed, could in some sense have been a mandala, expressing the ultimate goal, to bring about a new center for the personality. For Wright, the cross inside a circle may also have been one more declaration of his mystical Celtic view of life, the sacred center of the cosmos, the infinite spirit and finite mind. He may have been referring here to yet another compelling psychic need, which was to see beyond outward forms and reach their spiritual essences, along with that magical and metaphysical moment when matter and spirit became one.

Christmas was the best time. Daughter Catherine (later, Catherine Wright Baxter) remembered the huge tree that would be set up in the enormous playroom that Wright built onto the house the year after she was born, in 1895, to prepare for the arrival of their fourth child, David Samuel. Rather than add on new bedrooms, Wright decided to transform the studio he had been using on the second floor into a dormitory, split in half so that baby Catherine could have one side and his sons, Lloyd, John and David, the other. Then he added a handsome playroom, using a trick he would employ over and over again: one went through a long, narrow, low-ceilinged corridor and into a room that seemed, because of the height of its glorious barrel-vaulted ceiling with a skylight in the center, to be far larger than it actually was. The entrance into a long, wide room, after the claustrophobia of the tunnel, gave one a feeling of expansiveness and release. The floor was bare of furniture, the walls were made of brick (Wright's first such use for interior walls), and there was an upper gallery that was ideal for puppet shows and other diversions, protected by a wooden balustrade and embellished with a copy of the *Winged Victory*, one of Wright's favorite statues. But there were also some low bay windows,

The children's playroom, showing the fireplace mural and barrel-vaulted ceiling

The cross that Wright adopted for his architectural practice

Example of a Welsh Celtic cross

just the right height for small children, cozy window seats and plenty of toy bins. The living room was kept for guests, the library was for reading, and the dining room was used only for meals. But the heart of the house, the room in which the children spent their early years, was this vast playroom, with its inviting spaces and its capacious fireplace crackling with five-foot logs.

The playroom belonged to the children, but not exclusively. Kitty's brother, Arthur Colson Tobin, had many memories of Sunday afternoons and evenings when there would be a roaring fire going and his sister and her husband would entertain their friends, perhaps with an oyster bake. There was Richard Bach, a sculptor of some reputation; Lorado Taft, then a young man; Max Bendix, concertmaster of the Chicago Symphony; and J. Freeman, an old violin expert for Lyon and Healy's store; and any number of other figures from the literary, musical and architectural worlds. The lawyer Clarence Darrow, whose friendship would be so valuable to Wright in years to come, was often there.

Arthur recalled one Sunday evening when an Italian expert in mosaics, Orlando Giannini, first came to visit the playroom and decided then and there that the half-circular space on the plaster wall above the fireplace was the perfect spot for a mural. So he improvised a scaffold and began to sketch. He drew and painted for many succeeding Sundays until he had completed his theme, doubtless one his host had suggested, "The Fisherman and the Genii" from the *Arabian Nights*. Exactly whose design it was is unclear. Tobin's memoir implies that it was Giannini's, while Wright called it "his first design in straight-line pattern," but in any event, Tobin retained a vivid memory of the artist on his ladder while the party went on all around him, and the host, who was so good at putting guests at their ease, and got on with everyone, improvised at the piano. "The house," Maginel wrote, "was filled with noise and laughter. . . ."

The playroom was where Frank kept his beloved player piano, and at night, sleeping in her mother's house around the corner, Maginel would be kept awake listening to the "rolling cadences and thundering majestic chords of Bach or Beethoven issuing across the garden from Frank's house . . . every night until two or three in the morning. He couldn't leave it alone, and he would experiment, moderating tempo and tone to bring out the expression called for. . . . He loved to show off his mastery of certain passages so that they sounded as if they were really being played by a virtuoso."

Wright never learned to read music, but he had such a fine musical ear that it hardly mattered. Whenever he came into a room he would sit down and ripple off his version of the "Old Kent Road," the music hall song that became a kind of signature tune. He insisted that his children learn to play something, although Robert Llewellyn, who took mandolin lessons (an instrument, he later decided, good only for glee clubs and fado singers), wondered how serious his father really had been about their musical education. John played the violin, David had a flute, Catherine played the piano and sang, and Lloyd became a fine cellist. Wright's love of the classics is so well known that his weakness for Gilbert and Sullivan, as well as Victorian music hall ballads, has been obscured, as has his love for vaudeville and what Llewellyn called "nut comics."

Both Llewellyn and John emphasized the gift their father had for charming anyone out of a bad mood, including a guest. "If they came downcast," John wrote, "Papa would roguishly laugh them out of it. He was an epic of wit and merriment that gave our home the feeling of a jolly carnival." He was a practical joker as well. John recalled the times when, seated beside his father at meals, he would see him swing an arm over his head. If John ducked, his father would pretend to be scratching his neck, but if John missed the maneuvre his father would "pop" him. John also told the story, perhaps apocryphal, about a burglary one night (Wright never carried keys and refused to lock doors). Wright turned on the lights so that the burglar could see better, then asked why "so handsome a fellow didn't get out and work in the light where he could be seen and appreciated." In short, he had that charm that was William Carey Wright's most priceless legacy, along with a sense of humor that was his strength and sometimes his defense. Llewellyn commented, "He had a lifelong habit of covering miserable situations with a bright smile."

Lloyd wrote about his father's passion for oriental rugs. He, his father and John would open up great bales of dirty rugs bought at auction and scrub them with soap and water until their colors glowed. Soon there were Japanese prints as well, which Lloyd helped unwrap, unbook, clean and mount, providing his first aesthetic experience and inspiring a love of Japanese art that had a lifelong influence on his own career as architect and landscape designer. Their father was adorable; he was the life of the party; he was a great tease; he introduced them to music, poetry, art; he had a love of nature and a Welsh belief in spirits, "gnomes and undines," and yet. One senses a note of sadness in these reminiscences. Wright was never unreservedly theirs—because he worked so hard, or because he was not quite fatherly enough, or because he loved them but could not show his feelings, or because his architectural creations were his real children. Perhaps there was an element of truth in all of these explanations; perhaps he could only be at his best with those who had no demands to make. One of the apprentices at Taliesin, years later, admired Wright's way with children. "He'd take my daughter by the thumb and lead her through the strawberry patch, giving her as many as she could eat."

Father teased and played with and indulged his children, worked mysteriously late at night and yawned on holiday mornings, but Mother was always there. Mother lived for her children and was their disciplinarian when necessary, since Father never punished them. She picked up the theme of Froebel and had the playroom floor marked out in an arrangement of circles and squares derived from his ideas. Here she ran a kindergarten class to teach his precepts to her children and to the rest of the neighborhood as well. Jeanne T. Bletzer, one of her nieces, recalled that her Aunt Kitty would come and keep house when her parents—her father was Arthur, the youngest—were away. Kitty was, in many ways, very indulgent. She would let Jeanne play by the hour with her glorious red hair, taking it down and putting it back up again. She had given each of the children a "fairy book" of blank pages, and each night, when they were asleep, she would add a poem or an illustration to the pages and tuck it under their pillows, to be discovered in the morning. She had, Mrs. Bletzer thought, "a childlike quality." She could also be impossible. Jeanne's sister, Eleanor Tobin Kenney, recalled that one time their father had been making wine in the basement, and while Aunt Kitty was in charge, all the corks popped and the bottles overflowed. Aunt Kitty, being the stern teetotaler that she was, pretended to have heard nothing at all, and Eleanor, aged eleven, was left to clean up the mess.

Aunt Kitty could also be thoughtless—she took Jeanne out on a streetcar ride one day when she had whooping cough—and there is some indication that she played favorites, making her sons feel more cherished than her daughters. Kitty was a teetotaler and had a terrific sweet tooth; she would not have coffee in the house and thought Coca-Cola was a drug, because it had "cocaine" in it. Contrary to some belief, she was not simply a compliant wife, although she was an adoring one. She was a woman of decided views ("She talked faster than she listened," her niece said) and was always ready to argue a point. Her son David recalled, "As a family we got along very well, but we were all opinionated and hard on each other. A lot of criticisms. But we were united against the outside world. Fights? Oh, yes, there were plenty of those. I remember after Dad put us in the dormitory, there was a seven-foot partition dividing the girls' side from the boys', and when our sisters were having slumber parties we would throw a pillow over the partition. It took some skill." Jeanne recalled interminable wranglings at her parents' dinner table when her father, whose views differed sharply from his sister's, would say warningly, "Now, Kitty!" and she would retort, "Now, Arthur!" Jeanne thought that however much Kitty loved Frank, she would not suffer in martyrish silence. "If he was doing something wrong, she'd tell him so."

Kitty, then, was a "woman of spirit," as she would have been described, but she certainly indulged her husband to a degree that would be considered heroic in today's world. After her first battle with him over the matter of mottoes to be emblazoned above doors, one she won (with the exception of the prominent statement over the fireplace), she seems to have relinquished any role in deciding what rooms should be built, what furnishings bought—one notes that Wright always decided on those—even how they should be placed. She tolerated the removal of draperies from windows, the covering of apertures said to be of such symbolic importance to women, confining herself to the areas of their life that he had left as her domain, i.e., running the household and bringing up their children. (One notes that they always had a cook and cleaning help.) She was the lady of the house, but it belonged to him, and as his passion for unity of design—first seen with the dining room of 1895—grew in conviction, she let him make these choices without demur. Perhaps most revealing of her willingness to play Eliza to his Pygmalion—and there was a young autocrat beneath the veneer of charm—was the fact that she even wore the clothes he had designed. (They were always in neutrals, presumably so as not to detract from the decor.) Willing abdication of independence can go no further, but one finds additional proof of Kitty's compliance in the fact that she lived in misery with Anna while waiting for their house to be built and for Lloyd's birth; tolerated the uproar again when she was pregnant with David in 1895; and, in 1898, with four small children and Frances Barbara on the way, she somehow kept the household going while Frank knocked down walls and ripped out doors again, so as to add on a large studio for his growing practice. Throughout it all, she steadfastly affirmed her husband's greatness.

Wright's family in a pivotal year, 1904. From far left: the architect, Mrs. Samuel Tobin holding the infant Llewellyn, John on the wall, Catherine in front, Frances behind her, Maginel with young David in front of her, Catherine in profile in the background and Lloyd as an adolescent

As child bride, Kitty had been no match for her calculating mother-in-law. One of the most difficult aspects of marriage for Kitty must have been living next door to the one person who (as everyone knew) would always try to drive a wedge between her son and any woman perceived as a rival. At least Kitty had her own parents nearby. Her children loved their grandmother Tobin (called Blue Gramma because Lloyd was color-blind and thought, as a child, her red hair was blue), whose house was a well-ordered refuge always stocked with first-class food, and who was such a force in their lives. She was on quite another plane from her ineffectual, kindly, card-playing husband, who could not manage without her and died soon after she did. Flora Tobin never lost her temper, she was always calm, and she somehow organized everyone without making them feel controlled. It was a remarkable show of skill, one that Llewellyn never forgot.

For Kitty and Frank, there were the obligatory trips to spend their vacations in Spring Green on one of the Lloyd Jones farms where, as any of Wright's sons would have joked, you only worked twice as hard as you did the rest of the year, and you sat on porches in the evenings listening to Uncle Enos plan his musicales and lectures to pay for the new piano in the chapel. Or you went to Unity Chapel with Uncle John (who fretted about the condition of the coffins), so that he could show you the new plantings and declare, "Now you will see that the little spot is dearer than ever." Or you might have listened to Uncle Thomas's complaining about his woodlot, the one he bought with Uncle James after he broke two ribs and punctured a lung, but which never paid for itself. Uncle James, that intrepid farmer, father of eight, who was superintendent of his sisters' farm at Hillside, who had been treasurer of the town of Wyoming and also its chairman, was always ready to buy land and had vastly increased his holdings. Letters from James to Jenkin indicate that he was also chronically short of money to pay taxes and other expenses. What the letters do not mention, since it went without saying, is that his relatives had cosigned on his mortgages. Most farm families expected that, since land, farm machinery, buildings and livestock were heavy investments. Such purchases were usually made when money was cheap and food prices high, and the more ambitious the farmer was, the more debts he was likely to carry. But one never knew when the prices might fall. Outwardly prosperous, James was facing an uncertain future— but so were the Aunts, who had signed over and over again for their favorite brother.

If the Lloyd Joneses were, by and large, feckless when it came to money, there were a few members prudent to the point of miserliness. Anna was one, and Jenkin was another. A study of the way he hoarded his tiny army wages during the Civil War demonstrates his ability to hold on to a dollar, which soon made him prosperous and the target of frequent appeals for money from his brothers and sisters. He had never yearned to farm, but he wanted his own piece of ground in the Helena Valley and soon saw his opportunity. His father had settled there partly because of Helena, that small settlement on the south bank of the Wisconsin River that grew up around the lead-shot business at Tower Hill (where, from a tower, molten lead was dropped into water below to form perfectly rounded shots). With the coming of the railroad, which bypassed Helena in favor of Spring Green on the other side of the river, and the decline of its one industry, Helena sank into decay. By 1889 it had been abandoned, and Jenkin bought Tower Hill at a tax sale for sixty dollars. He then set up the Tower Hill School of Religion and Ethics as a summer Unitarian encampment, built a summer cottage, Westhope, for his family and, with his usual herculean energy, had soon attracted crowds to hear lectures by leading American writers, scientists, politicians and ministers.

Jenkin, of course, was one of the chief draws. He had a limitless fund of topics, many centering on farm themes. One of his most celebrated sermons took as its theme the building of a barn and the work of their favorite stonemason, David Timothy, who had come

Jenkin Lloyd Jones and his wife on the
Henry Ford Peace Expedition to Europe, 1915–16

from their area of Wales (where he had built the beautiful new chapel of Llwynrhydowen) and had stayed to build Unity Chapel and Hillside Home School, carving the family motto of "Truth Against the World" over doorways and fireplaces. When he died, his funeral took place in Unity Chapel, and Jenkin eulogized him as "a barn-builder, a cellar-maker, a shaper of stone walls, a builder of houses for men to dwell in. . . ." Another favorite theme of Jenkin's was the great benefit of the machine to mankind and, in particular, the American reaper, since it made possible the feeding of multitudes.

Jenkin Lloyd Jones, who loomed so large in his nephew's life where philosophy and ideals were concerned, whose friendships on the national and international scene would give him such an unparalleled opportunity to meet influential men, whose wealthy Chicago friends could be counted on to find work for an up-and-coming architect, was always a problem for Wright. One sees, to a certain extent, the same antagonisms among all the Lloyd Jones males, those strong-willed, energetic and highly competitive people who never could manage to like one another's concepts, no matter how stubbornly they would fight for those same ideas on the outside. There would always be a clash of wills, in this case accentuated by the fact that Jenkin may have doubted that Frank was as experienced as he claimed, and distrusted his nephew's glib sales patter. If this were so, Frank had not learned the lessons of Unity Chapel when, in 1894, hearing that Uncle Jenk planned to build once again, he pressed his services upon his uncle. "How about the plans for the new building?" he wrote to Uncle Jenk in the early summer of 1894. "Am I to get a chance with the rest of the boys, or is it an open and shut walkaway for Silsbee [*sic*]." Jenkin did not have Silsbee in mind, but was not at all sure he wanted Frank either. What he did want, according to Professor Thomas E. Graham, "was to be his own architect. He kept trying to find people who would rubber-stamp what he wanted to do." That was not going to be Frank Lloyd Wright, and only deliberate delusion on both sides could have led to the decision to let Frank try his hand. Jenkin's concept was, even in this day and age, unusual. Not only did he want a larger building to house his growing congregation, not only did he no longer wish it to be "homey," much less decorated with spires, steeples and stained glass, but he also did not want it to look anything like a church. At about this time, Jenkin Lloyd Jones severed the connection between his congregation and the American Unitarian Association. It became just "All Souls' Church," and its pulpit was open to anyone, from the pope to a Brahman priest or a captain of the Salvation Army. His goal, to build a seven-day-a-week institution that would minister to the whole person, now seemed a reality. The Abraham Lincoln Center (named for his hero) would contain a sanctuary, a gymnasium, classrooms, meeting rooms and a library as well as residents' quarters. Since its function had become that of a social service agency, its founder wanted no nonsense about the way it should look. His nephew designed an office building, a Sullivanesque rectangle several stories high, that was a model of function and rectitude.

Uncle Jenk should have found it "a four-square building for a four-square gospel," as he put it, but he did not. He niggled and nagged and kept asking for revisions, made Wright collaborate with another architect (Dwight H. Perkins, who had just built a successful church) and even made his nephew submit his design to a New York architect for criticism. Wright suffered the indignity with remarkable

Romeo and Juliet windmill

restraint—the process seems to have taken three or four years—even writing contritely, "I should never think of lecturing, or being deliberately impertinent to you." He also tried to exercise that persuasive gift for which he became so rightly celebrated. "I *know* and *would stake my life* that you will like it when you know it," he wrote earnestly. Jenkin was not to be won over, and by the time the building was dedicated in 1905, Wright had long since left the project. It was one of the few battles he did not win.

Jenkin's caution—his nephew would have used another word—was equally apparent in the matter of the windmill the Aunts wanted built to complete their new water system beside the reservoir on top of the hill above the Hillside Home School. The Aunts were all for letting

Frank design something new, and the uncles, led by Jenkin, all for putting up something sensible, steel and cheap. The sisters prevailed, and Frank produced a sixty-foot wooden tower of a most radical and unusual design, an interlocking octagon and diamond (hence the name, the Romeo and Juliet windmill). It was to stand on a stone-and-concrete base, reinforced horizontally by a wooden platform every ten feet and clad in shingles, to match the building he had constructed for the Aunts a decade before. Nell and Jane thought it delightful. The uncles were sure it would fall down. The Aunts won again, and since, as Wright eventually wrote, their wonderful old stonemason was building the foundation, he knew that the tower would withstand any storm. One of the charming passages in Wright's autobiography describes the long vigil of the uncles as, one by one, growing old and going to their graves, they watched from their doorways whenever the wind came up to see the windmill fall, as they knew it must. Wright knew exactly what they would say. "Well, there it is—down at last! We thought so!" It was standing when he wrote those words in 1932, and is standing yet.

Wright's Lincoln Center project was one of the few occasions in which he willingly collaborated with other architects. But during the early years, before he had arrived at that synthesis of ideals and forms that would set him apart from his peers, he was involved in several quasi-partnerships and informal associations with a group of extremely promising young men making their names in the rapidly developing city. His first move after leaving Sullivan was to set up an office in the Schiller Building with his friend Cecil Corwin. Then he learned that a group of architects was taking an office in common in Steinway Hall, a new eleven-story office and theater building that Dwight H. Perkins, his collaborator for the Lincoln Center, had designed. Perkins and his friends Myron Hunt and George W. Maher were moving in together, presumably to save on costs, and had set up a joint outer office, with separate quarters within. It seemed like an ideal arrangement for Wright and Corwin, who moved in, though Corwin would soon leave, having decided he was in the wrong profession.

Wright already knew Maher, whom he had met when they both worked for Silsbee. Maher had left in 1888 to set up his own practice at the age of twenty-three, providing an example that would not have been lost on Wright, particularly since Maher was also making something of a name for himself as a theoretician. His particular interest was how to make a house look substantial, and he lectured frequently on ways to increase the effect of massiveness and solidity in design. Hunt, another gifted young architect who eventually moved to Southern California, was a year younger than Wright. Robert Spencer, who was two years older, was yet another. He would also take his cue from Voysey and Scott, "reinterpreting and simplifying architecture from the medieval past." Wright retained an office at Steinway Hall, even after he had built a studio onto his house and had attempted several partnerships with other young architects after Corwin, before deciding to take Sullivan's advice and "keep his office in his hat." The members of the Steinway Hall group are now considered the founders of the New School of the Midwest, or Prairie school, attesting to the way in which these men exchanged ideas. Wright acknowledged the value of that association in 1908 when he wrote, "How I longed for companionship until I began to know the younger men and how welcome was Robert Spencer, and then Myron Hunt, and Dwight Perkins. . . . Inspiring days they were, I am sure, for us all."

Wright had five commissions the first year of his independence, an enviable start for a young man. From then until 1900 his yearly total went from a low of two to a high of nine. The course, though bumpy, showed a steady advance, and as the jobs came in he added to his staff. By the time Charles E. White, Jr., a young and ambitious architect from the hills of Vermont, joined Wright's studio in 1903, Wright was employing seven people. Numerous young men continually came and went, whether painters, designers, sculptors or architects in training. But those who had the longest associations with him were Marion Mahony, a gifted designer of tables, chairs, murals and mosaics, renowned for her renderings (many of which were later exhibited as by Wright); Walter Burley Griffin, whom she later married, at that time general practical man and writer of specifications; Barry Byrne, a young novice who quickly gained in expertise; William E. Drummond, another valuable assistant; Isabel Roberts, secretary, who also worked on ornamental glass and for whom Wright would design one of his best houses; and John Van Bergen, later architect of many Oak Park houses. George Willis, one of Wright's youngest and most promising draftsmen, had already left by the time White arrived, following Hunt to Los Angeles—but by then, they were all jumping from job to job around the country.

As White had noticed, Frank Wright seemed to get many new commissions. Comments by some of his early clients show that they were often moved to hire him as architect not because of his buildings, which were considered bizarre by some of Chicago's staider citizens, but in spite of them. He was too delightful for words, according to an enthusiastic letter written by W. E. Martin to his younger brother, Darwin D. Martin, the man who would become Wright's lifelong patron and private Croesus. "A *splendid* type of manhood. He is not a *freak*—not a 'crank'—highly educated and polished, but *no dude*— a straightforward business-like man—with high ideals." He was, W. E. Martin concluded, "one of nature's *noblemen*." Another client, Arthur Heurtley, who in 1902 had commissioned one of Wright's most famous houses in Oak Park and also a cottage in northern Michigan, was, six years after construction, just as enthusiastic as Martin had been. Heurtley wrote to a German architect that Wright was one of the most remarkable men he had ever met. Not only was he a fine musician with a pronounced artistic sense in everything he did, but his character was impeccable, without a flaw. The man's work, in short, reflected the qualities of its creator, and he was proud to call that man his friend.

Wright's gift for making a charming impression was just one of the attributes he used to such advantage during his Oak Park years. He seemed to have infinite spare time for writing speeches, usually embellished with many crossings-out and balloons and often in several versions, setting out his ideas about architecture at leisurely length. He looked for opportunities to exhibit his renderings and models, and showed almost every year at the Chicago Architectural Club, beginning after his first year of practice. For that event, the invitation he designed included a photograph of a winged cherub holding some stalks of goldenrod that turned out to be his red-headed son John. He was eager to lecture, not just about architecture. Returning from Japan after a three-month stay in 1905, he proceeded to give a talk on its art, and then he and Catherine held a "Japanese social" at their home. She was also doing some lecturing of her own, and kept their social contacts alive through her activities with the Oak Park women's club.

By 1900 Wright's opinions on a number of topics were considered newsworthy enough to warrant prominence. If he had intended to live out his life in the columns of newspapers, he could not have acted any more effectively than he did in those first years, as he went about joining clubs, starting new ones, cultivating friendships, giving parties, advancing causes and, again and again, courting the press, just as his father had done. It is a measure of his success that, by July 1913, he had become a life member of the Press Club of Chicago.

One of his earliest triumphs was the not inconsiderable feat of persuading a magazine editor not just to write about his work but to let him hand-pick the writer—indeed, he would come to expect it. An early example of this is given by White, who noted, when he first arrived in Wright's studio late in 1903, that Wright had chosen Russell Sturgis, a noted but elderly architectural critic, to prepare an article about his work for the *Architectural Record*. But after meeting him, Wright decided that Sturgis did not "understand" the studio's work and intended to look for a younger man.

Although Wright's appetite for whatever might further his career was gargantuan, it was not limitless. White noted, early in 1905, "For the past three months it has been almost impossible to get [Wright] to give any attention to us. As he expresses it he 'has no appetite for work,' and I think the reason is that he has taken no period of complete rest . . . in several years. . . ." Wright left the next day for Japan and returned with his energy and enthusiasm restored. To be in a severe slump did not happen often since he had the rare gift of being able to relax, take trips to the theater, give parties, spend time at the piano, or go riding on his favorite black horse, Kano, in the woods and fields of the adjoining countryside (what would become the suburb of River Forest). He needed those periods of furious movement to compensate for long hours spent hunched over a drawing board, making precise calculations and diagrams. Riding Kano at a gallop was succeeded by equally headlong bursts of speed in his new, four-cylinder Stoddard Dayton sportscar, one of the first three cars in Oak Park, custom-made to his specifications with a yellow exterior, brown seats and brass trimmings. The citizens of Oak Park called it the "Yellow Devil." It could do sixty miles an hour, and Wright would clamber into it, in a linen duster and goggles, and roar through the streets of Oak Park with his long hair streaming in the breeze, often accompanied by some charming friend. Since the Chicago speed limit was twenty-five miles an hour, he paid plenty of speeding tickets.

This hard-working, clean-living, upright citizen of Oak Park had one failing, one that might have been expected, and that is revealed in Charles White's comment that if you worked for him, you had to be willing to "hang on by the teeth" and get paid whenever your employer happened to think of it. Wright wanted handmade cars and thoroughbred horses and beautiful surroundings; he needed to cut a *bella figura*, and so he spent too much. His checks were returned by the bank marked N.S.F., his bills for the butcher, baker, grocer and building supplier went unpaid for months, and though he confessed that this wildly improvident spending gave him anxious moments, he seemed unable to stop. Beyond the human need to impress, appear to be someone to reckon with and an aesthete's love of beautiful objects (convincing himself that because he was one of "nature's noblemen," he deserved them); behind all the rationalizations lay the scars of his long battles with Anna. And so, at night, the secret knowledge of heavy debts nagged at him like a remorseless conscience; it was "pricking him sharply, from underneath. . . ." He gave the clue to his hidden feelings when he wrote, "I suppose it is just a question as to how much punishment one can stand. . . ." The more frantically Anna tried to urge him to reform (as she had tried, and failed, to do with William), the more determined her son became to prove her wrong. And since she vacillated between punitiveness and overindulgence—he knew that if he resisted long enough, she would solve his problems—he learned nothing, except to endure the anxiety and wait out the reproaches, pleas and verbal "punishment" from his nearest and dearest and from his own conscience, as the price to be paid. So much, he also learned, depended on how cleverly one could flatter, fool and cajole people into forgetting. That marvelous ability was highly refined by the time his son Llewellyn was twelve years old. In an unpublished memoir, Llewellyn recalled visiting his father in Chicago and seeing him charm a determined creditor so thoroughly that the man left laughing at his jokes. Wright told his son he had just had an object lesson in how to avoid paying a bill. Or, if an arm of the law were involved, such as the sheriff who appeared one day to collect on unpaid bills for the children's playroom, and the matter simply could not be evaded, Wright's panache could be counted on to win a partial reprieve. In this case, the sheriff stayed until next morning, when Wright scraped together the eighty-five dollars owed by getting another advance on his salary. Then there were times when the saintly forbearance of a particular creditor would appeal to Wright's better nature, and he would contritely make good. When all else failed, and his back was to the wall, Wright would go on the attack, blaming everyone (banks, moneylenders, unscrupulous creditors) for his predicament, and he was a dangerous adversary. It was never a good idea to try to coerce or shame him into making good, although Kitty may have tried. He writes that, one day little Catherine, dirty and chewing gum, appeared in his studio just as he was trying to impress a very fashionable client. She stuck out a dirty little hand and said that Mama wanted money. A dime! Just a dime. And he had to confess that he did not have even a dime in his pocket. It was a great joke, and eventually Mama appeared to take her insistent daughter away, having proved her point.

There were disasters that would be self-inflicted (though they might not seem so to the person involved), and there were genuine catastrophes that struck at random; Wright was to have more than his share of both. Along with the consequences of extravagance, the theme of conflagration is almost a leitmotif of his life: "But I was on the smoking roofs, feet burned, lungs seared, hair and eyebrows gone, thunder rolling as the lightning flashed over the lurid scene. . . ." If, as his son John wrote, Wright believed that the righteous God of Isaiah had struck him down with a merciless hand and if, at such moments, he saw himself as a character out of the Old Testament, then he might have been forgiven. In retrospect it is difficult not to see the Iroquois fire of 1903 as an omen, the precursor of another, greater and more terrible blaze that would leave his life in ruins.

It all started innocently enough. Wright had bought tickets for a matinee performance of *Mr. Blue Beard Jr.*, a Christmas play for children at the Iroquois Theater in Chicago. David had typhoid fever, so Mama, as usual, was homebound, but Lloyd, aged thirteen, and John, aged eleven, were allowed to attend in the company of Blue Gramma. On December 30, 1903, they sat in third row center. A cousin, Rosalind Parish, a pretty twenty-year-old, was up in the balcony with a group of Wisconsin college girls. The "Christmas extravaganza," as it was called, was one of the biggest events of the year. That particular matinee, every one of the 1,800 seats was filled, mostly with parents and children. All went well until an octet began to sing "In the Pale Moonlight." Then, according to a newspaper report, a calcium light on a six-foot stand on the stage exploded, setting a tinseled backdrop alight. Flames, sparks and burning draperies began to drop onto the stage, and in a second the whole stage was on fire. The play's star, a comedian named Eddy Foy, rushed out, half in costume and half out of it, pleading for calm and asking that the asbestos safety curtain, which would have contained the fire, be dropped. As luck would have it, the curtain stuck halfway down.

One of the eyewitnesses, a professional ballplayer in an upper box, saw the fire's start and realized that fast action was called for. He ran down to an exit, but the usher refused to open the doors. The ballplayer threw him to one side and forced the locked doors open. By then there was a panicked crowd behind him. He was pushed against a second set of iron doors that were also locked. He managed to break that lock and freed up one of the exits. It was the same story at all the other exits from the theater; at one, a policeman actually tried to repel the crowd. In their panic, those behind forced those trapped by locked doors into a pyramid. More than six hundred men, women and children died, including Rosalind Parish—no one in the balcony escaped alive.

Back in the third row center, Blue Gramma, showing her famous presence of mind, stood up, removing the long hatpins from her hat, held them high over her head, and inched John, Lloyd and herself toward the nearest exit. John was forced away from her by the crowd and pinned against a column. "I began to feel faint and suffocated, it was almost impossible for me to stay on my feet. I worked my way around the corner of the column feeling as though I were being cut in two. Suddenly, carried as I had been many times in the strong current of the Wisconsin River, I found myself in the street." Blue Gramma had disappeared, and so had Lloyd. "No battlefield ever disclosed a more fearful scene," one journalist wrote. The bodies of women and children who had jumped, or been thrown, from windows were lying in the street; others were being carried out of the theater, and doctors were attending the wounded and dying. Suddenly, John caught sight of his father in the crowd. "He didn't talk, he just reached out and held me." Then Blue Gramma appeared. She had become separated from Lloyd as well, but he had fought his way free and was at home. John wrote, "I shall always remember the expression on Dad's face when he learned that we, all three, were safe and unharmed."

It has been suggested that the activities at Jane Addams's Hull House, a center for Arts and Crafts ideas in Chicago, played a role in calling Wright's attention to the movement. Wright refers to Hull House in his autobiography and would have known about events there through his uncle and also his wife, who was developing her interest in social issues. However, in those first years after Hull House was established in 1889, Jane Addams appears to have been more absorbed with the pressing issues of poverty, unemployment, sweat shops, child labor, truancy and lack of sanitation than with the arts and crafts. One concludes, from her reminiscences, that she did not turn her attention to these subjects much before 1895 or 1896, and by then Wright's interest was well established.

It seems more likely that the galvanizing event in his life may have been the publication in 1893, the year he left Sullivan, of a new magazine called the *Studio*, which first brought the ideas of the Arts and Crafts Movement to a wide audience. One does not know that he read the early issues, but it seems plausible, given his interest in trends, being published and his contacts with other young architects with similar enthusiasms. George Grant Elmslie, who stayed with Adler and Sullivan, reported that while the firm's office received the *British Architect*, it was seldom read, but the *Studio* and its American version, *International Studio*, were pounced upon. One can also deduce something from the fact that when, three years later, an American magazine was formed to promote the same concepts, Wright's hand was quickly evident. A year later he became one of the founding members of the Chicago society dedicated to the Arts and Crafts.

Wright's early acceptance of the Arts and Crafts Movement led to an architectural philosophy that was formative. As he must have seen, its architects had found the way to make a practical application of those ideals of truth, beauty and moral feeling that he espoused. They were doing so in fresh and novel ways, and because large goals rather than a particular style were at issue, he was given the scope he needed to develop his distinctive talent and demonstrate the extent of his creativity and versatility, those attributes that were so much admired in the movement. The emphasis on studying the qualities that made a particular landscape unique was another gift from the Arts and Crafts theoreticians to Wright and his fellow architects, helping them focus on the way to achieve an architecture uniquely suited to its Illinois setting. The Arts and Crafts Movement was a manifesto, a set of principles, but because British architects were the precursors, by the late 1890s such architects as Voysey, Baillie Scott, Lutyens and Ashbee were a decade ahead of the Americans in the task of translating high ideals into actual bricks and mortar. As has been noted, the principle of a completely unified concept, from chimney trim to placemats, had been one of the ideas that immediately captivated Wright in designing the dining room and furnishings of his house; his ability to unify every detail of his architecture would become one of his major accomplishments. The idea was daring and novel for Chicago, but it had already been demonstrated with some success by Arts and Crafts architects and there were, also, many historical precedents. In the eighteenth century, one thinks of the designs by the British architect Robert Adam at Kedleston for everything from murals to plate warmers, and in the nineteenth, of the town houses and room furnishings designed by such Art Nouveau innovators as Victor Horta. That Wright should start with a dining room is particularly interesting since it was one of the rooms Arts and Crafts architects deemed most important. "In common with most nineteenth- and twentieth-century conservative reform movements, Arts and Crafts designers believed that industrialism had shattered the family, bringing rootlessness and a loss of tradition: hence, emphasis centered on the family and hearth," Richard Guy Wilson wrote. Wright's design, with its severely high-backed chairs and uncompromisingly formal air, had an ecclesiastical look, which was very much in harmony with the movement's emphasis upon the ceremonial, or ritualistic, aspect of breaking bread.

Wright's designs in 1889 for his own living room gave it an inglenook fireplace, the symbolic way of stressing the importance of the hearth that he would use again and again in his early designs. In fact, the massive central chimney deep in the center of the house became an unvarying feature of his Prairie-school houses. Echoing the Arts and Crafts belief that the fireplace was the primeval center, almost the high altar of the house, he would write, "The big fireplace in the house . . . became now a place for a real fire. A real fireplace at that time was extraordinary. There were mantels instead. A mantel was a marble frame for a few coals in a grate. . . . So the *integral* fireplace became an important part of the building itself. . . . It comforted me to see the fire burning deep in the solid masonry of the house itself."

Wright's early design also showed his first tentative attempt to experiment with an open floor plan, i.e., to dispense with an interior partitioned into boxlike rooms, each with its specific function, that had characterized the Victorian house and was becoming an anachronism in American life. He is usually given credit for having pioneered this idea even though others were using the same concepts before him, among them Baillie Scott. However, according to the writer James D. Kornwolf, the shift toward a feeling of spaciousness and greater internal flexibility began even earlier, in the 1870s, with the work of H. H. Richardson and other architects of the period. Not only did they create designs that were a revelation in showing the possibilities of this new idea, but they began to experiment in the use of movable partitions in place of walls, another innovation usually given to Wright. Wright is often the target of criticism for his low ceilings, a criticism he artlessly brought on his own head by his comment that he designed them to accommodate his own modest height of five feet eight and a half inches, but the truth is that he was a master of the theatrical manipulation of space, the idea he had first used with his children's playroom. Since he realized that the human eye cannot distinguish readily between slight differences in ceiling heights, he made them either very low or very high—sometimes, with virtuoso aplomb, in the same room—so as to intensify the dramatic effect. That kind of experimentation, of varying room heights and levels rather than floors, also came from Richardson and his contemporaries.

Wright would also become famous for his characteristically low, massive, all-encompassing roofs with broad overhangs, another concept that may have evolved from the work of Voysey and Baillie Scott, as seen in the *Studio, Dekorative Kunst* and American journals such as *House Beautiful* and *Indoors and Out*. These roofs, symbolically protective and reassuring, also had immediate practical advantages in a region of harsh summers and bitterly cold winters. Other details, such as Wright's use of leaded casement windows, built-in furniture, art glass, broad and low doors, stained plaster walls edged with wood stripping and another very typical Wright touch, the hidden entrance, can also be seen in work of British architects of the movement. All this is not to imply, however, that Wright's designs were slavish imitations. Part of his strength lay in his ability to transform the ideas and concepts of others so that they looked distinctively new. And in absorbing the teachings of the movement, he particularly distinguished himself in the way he integrated his Prairie houses with the flat, unending American horizons of the Midwest—hence the name—stressing the horizontal with his spreading roofs and bands of windows, and stretching out porches and pergolas into the surrounding gardens so that the house and its setting would merge and blur into a single harmonious whole. Even his insistence on the use of natural materials inside and out, wood, brick and stone, following another Arts and Crafts dictum, with its overtones of the rural cottage or medieval castle, seemed peculiarly right, suggesting that the landscape's uncompromising vistas required a similarly direct, unadorned response.

It has been argued that Wright quickly parted from the Arts and Crafts Movement because of its rejection of the machine (following the dictates of William Morris) and because of his own belief that the machine was a boon to mankind—as Jenkin Lloyd Jones had argued—provided that it remained in control of artists who designed with its strengths and weaknesses in mind. This difference is so central, it is said, that Wright cannot be called an Arts and Crafts architect. However, David A. Hanks, the authority on Wright's decorative designs, furniture and objets d'art has questioned in *The Art and Craft of the Machine* how much weight should be placed on this difference of opinion, which seems more apparent than real. Many of Wright's designs for machine-made furniture required extensive finishing by hand; conversely, many other Arts and Crafts architects did not subscribe to the strict belief that the machine should never be used. The point is so often made that the fact that Wright had no quarrel with the movement's other beliefs, as was clear the year he made his famous speech, 1901, has been overlooked; Ashbee wrote then, "We are thoroughly at one on first principles. . . ." To judge from Wright's description of his ideal, "organic" house, in a lecture he gave at Princeton University three decades later, he never deviated from those first principles. He set out nine points; six of them are quoted below. These six are identical to the goals set forth by Baillie Scott in the *Studio* thirty years before.

1. To reduce . . . the separate rooms to a minimum, and make all come together as enclosed space.
2. To associate the building as a whole with its site.
3. To eliminate the room as a box and the house as another.
6. To eliminate combinations of different materials in favor of mono-material . . . to use no ornament that did not come out of the nature of materials.
8. To incorporate as organic architecture . . . furnishings, making them all one with the building and designing them in simple terms for machine work.
9. Eliminate the decorator. He was all curves and all efflorescence, if not all period.

Wright's felt lack of any drawing talent may have sent him in search of activities that did not require this particular ability. As an adolescent he had spent hours experimenting with an old printing press in the company of his devoted friend Robie. He would go on to become an accomplished graphics designer, inventing numerous variations for his own stationery, often ingeniously folded, his own posters, exhibition leaflets, brochures, programs and the like. His lifelong interest in graphics and typography was soon joined to an enthusiasm for amateur photography, and when an opportunity developed to use both, he seized it. That was provided by William Winslow, his first client after leaving Sullivan, and Chauncey Williams, for whom he had also built a house in River Forest, who joined forces in 1895 to found a small publishing firm. Winslow was an amateur and presumably chief financial backer. Williams was a publisher by profession, and Wright seems to have joined the firm immediately as chief designer.

In 1895 the Auvergne Press, as it was called, printed its first book, an edition of Keats's *The Eve of St. Agnes*, for which Wright designed the title page. They then set to work on a second, Wright contributing photographic studies of dried weeds and several pen-and-ink designs of highly stylized flower patterns. The book's title was *The House Beautiful*, a reprint of a sermon by William C. Gannett, editor of *Unity* and close friend of Jenkin Lloyd Jones. Gannett's account of the construction of the Lloyd Jones family church made the first public mention of the family's "boy architect." Gannett's sermon is not inspired, but his title was most up-to-date and symbolic, echoing as it did the central concern of the Arts and Crafts Movement. (The concern was so central, in fact, that a magazine would be founded in Chicago of that same name the same winter of 1896–97, but by another publisher, to promote the ideals of the movement.)

The chance to experiment in a new field was obviously a great lure for Wright, but what seems to have meant most to him was the importance of the message being put forward by this old friend of his family, one that he could "clothe with chastity," as he noted in the book itself. Later, he explained to Gannett, "its [*sic*] good to catch a glimpse sometimes of what the world will be like when cultivation has mellowed harshness and gentle unselfishness is the rule of life."

When Wright referred to this publishing experiment years later, he confined himself to a dismissive reference to his design and did not have a word to say about its central message. He must have liked it then; he must have felt that it expressed all that could be said about his own life at the time, and he must have shared the sentiment expressed by the sentimental poem Gannett quoted to close his book. The last stanza reads as follows:

> Together greet life's solemn real,
> Together own one glad ideal,
> Together laugh, together ache,
> And think one thought—"Each other's sake,"
> And hope one hope—in new-world weather,
> To still go on, and go together.

7

A House Divided

See: this wood has come to make you
Remember the hands that carved it, to take you
Back to the love and the pledges you shared. . . .
                      "The Husband's Message"
                    Poems from the Old English

The broad-brimmed hat, the cane and the swirling cape with which Frank Lloyd Wright strode through life and which was the costume most people conjured up when they thought of him, was adopted during his first great period as an architect, from the turn of the century to the outbreak of World War I. The instincts of the aesthete would have led him to choose the hat most flattering to his rather elongated and aquiline features (the brim, pulled down snappily over one eye, looked so good in profile), along with the flaring cape that when photographed from below, a trick he eventually adopted, made him tower over the scenery, as if being viewed from front-row stalls. The effect was completed by the perfectly superfluous cane, which Wright used as a decorative adjunct and for making broad gestures that would outline a new scheme or jab home a point. No one who ever saw him make an entrance in that regalia ever forgot him, so it is not surprising that he should have capitalized on such a useful tool in the game of self-promotion.

No one remembers nowadays, since it is so long ago, that the

Frank Lloyd Wright, circa 1905

Elbert Hubbard in 1904

costume was not Wright's invention but came from another prominent member of the American Arts and Crafts Movement, Elbert Hubbard. This pioneer in advertising, cofounder of the Larkin Company, a mail-order soap company in Buffalo for which Wright would design a famous building, then leader of an Arts and Crafts community in East Aurora, New York, had joined forces with his British counterparts to reject the drab and sober uniformity of Victorian attire, establishing themselves as reformers in this field, as in everything else. Instead of the closely fitting suits of the businessman, they adopted looser, more comfortable country tweeds, such as the American craftsman's sack suit. There is a photograph, taken in 1904, of Hubbard wearing just such a tweedy outfit and the kind of expression designed to silence comment. With it, Hubbard also wears the black satin bow, dashingly tied at the neck, that was de rigueur for the artist, as may be seen from photographs of Charles Rennie Mackintosh at the same period, another sartorial flourish that Wright would adopt. Hubbard's hair, like Wright's, was rather longer than the fashion, which would have seemed more of an affront to American than to British sensibilities of the same period. He also wears the broad-brimmed, soft-crowned hat that Wright would make his own. In all essential ways, this is a close cousin of the flat, clerical soft bowler worn by Protestant clergymen of the time, although somewhat more exaggerated—a pardonable ostentation. Those Arts and Crafts men whom Hubbard emulated were campaigning for sanity in an age when women still endured the tortures of the whalebone corset, lending their influence to a movement for dress reform that had begun in the 1850s and was considerably enhanced when Oscar Wilde, that nonconformist in dress along with everything else, took to the platform for dresses that would allow ease of movement and normal waistlines. So to advocate what was radical, because it was so eminently sane—" 'T'would ring the bells of Heaven / The wildest peal for years / If Parson lost his senses / And people came to theirs," as Hodgson wrote—would always have a great appeal for Wright. In years to come he would sport such novelties as trousers buttoned at the ankles for protective country wear, made to his own design. However, one has to believe that his main motive was to differentiate himself from the common herd by the shortest possible means. The hat, the cape, the flowing tie, the cane—all these labeled him as a presence, someone to contend with and, above all, an artist.

Hubbard, a pioneer in mass-marketing techniques, was a singular entrepreneur whose gift for business and self-promotion was coupled with an interest in the arts and a belief in the need for the reforms the Arts and Crafts Movement advocated. He had made the pilgrimage to visit William Morris in 1893 and on his return set about establishing a model Arts and Crafts colony called the Roycrofters in East Aurora, New York, with its own English Tudor workshops and surrounding cottages of stone, to demonstrate what could be done with book-binding, metalwork and furniture making if, as he liked to say, the aim were to provide the worker with real satisfactions rather than just a job. Like everything else he did, Hubbard was so successful in promoting his colony that the Roycrofters were obliged to build an inn to house all the people who wanted to buy their souvenirs: hammered copper trays, inkwells, leather bookends, stained-glass lamps and maple-sugar candy. There are some evident parallels between Hubbard's experiment at the turn of the century and Wright's own colony at Taliesin thirty years later. Both would emphasize the joys of work, both would advocate and teach a great number of arts and crafts, both would be successful at establishing a loyal community that was largely self-sufficient and even monkish, and both men benevolently and autocratically insisted on running the place themselves. Like Wright, Hubbard rather disliked being responsible for weekly wages, preferring to make things right with handsome presents at Christmas instead. Hubbard, with his dashing appearance, his conversational gifts, his eternal curiosity and his almost magical ability to capture the world's attention, was, John Lloyd Wright remembered, a frequent visitor at their Oak Park home. He and Wright talked art, poetry and philosophy by the hour, John wrote, adding that Hubbard one night declared, "Modesty being egotism turned wrong side out, let me say here that I am an orator, a great orator! I have health, gesture, imagination, voice, vocabulary, taste, ideas—I acknowledge it myself. What I lack in shape I make up in nerve. . . ." Going Hubbard one better, Wright rephrased the thought and quoted it for the rest of his days: "Early in life I had to choose between honest arrogance and hypocritical humility. I chose honest arrogance. . . ."

Another Arts and Crafts community with distinct resemblances to Wright's Taliesin Fellowship, the Guild of Handicrafts, was the invention of C. R. Ashbee in the late 1880s. The guild's reputation was soon established with some outstanding examples of metalwork, furniture and books that Ashbee had designed. (Some of these wonderful objects can now be seen at the Victoria and Albert Museum, London.) Ashbee was a gifted designer, architect and leader, a devoted follower of William Morris's and advocate of the simple life in a bucolic setting, where one acquired skill in one's métier while participating in such activities as calisthenics, drama and music, a prescription that would be repeated at Taliesin. Ashbee's own contribution as an architect had begun in the 1880s, and he had shown a design for a chair at the first exhibition of the London Arts and Crafts Society in 1888. His gifts as a proselytizer for the movement, along with his tireless willingness to travel and lecture, made him a natural leader when William Morris, worn out by his own herculean efforts, died in 1896. That was the year, according to Wright's son Lloyd, that Ashbee and Wright had met while the former was making his first trip to the United States. Ashbee's biographer, Alan Crawford, could not confirm that Ashbee had visited Chicago on that trip, but was able to discount Ashbee's own claim, made in later years, that he and Wright had met as early as 1892: "Ashbee was very vague, or rather, precise-and-mistaken, in giving dates. . . ." he wrote. The first real piece of evidence for the start of the Wright-Ashbee friendship is an entry in Ashbee's voluminous and famous *Journal*, in which he describes his meeting with Wright at a supper party given in Hull House in December 1900.

Since the friendship was to endure for four decades, its origins are worth exploring. Whether they met in 1896 or 1900, it is clear that Wright recognized in Ashbee a kindred spirit dedicated to the same goals. Perhaps Wright saw, in his friendship with Ashbee, an entrée into Europe and an introduction to other luminaries of the London scene. This would seem plausible, since Ashbee's letter to Wright in the spring of 1901 contains a cordial invitation to come and stay with them that summer. "I suggest you let me work out that itinerary for you, that you put a fortnight in London and another three weeks in other parts of England and be our guest for as long as you care to during the time," he wrote. Wright was certainly eager to be friendly, as his willingness to act as secretary of the Chicago committee for a new National Trust in America, a cause Ashbee was espousing, demonstrates. (It would seem most ironic in later years, given Wright's ruthless willingness to remove from his path whatever piece of flotsam history had left there.) Wright must have found it especially flattering that this prominent Englishman should consider him "far and away the ablest man in our line of work that I have come across in Chicago," as he wrote. "He not only has ideas but the power of expressing them. . . ." That same *Journal* entry records that Wright introduced him to Louis Sullivan (demonstrating that, by 1900, Wright and Sullivan were back on cordial terms), but that Ashbee believed Wright was destined to become far greater than his master. Wright would have been most gratified by that verdict too. And if they disagreed about the role to be played by the machine in the movement—"I want to have a good fight with you on the matter some time," Ashbee wrote—then the difference was not crucial because they were so much in agreement otherwise.

On that first visit of the Ashbees to Oak Park, in 1896, according to Lloyd, because there were only four children then, Ashbee and his wife taught them morris songs and dances and old English rounds such as "Great Tom Is Cast," and spoke of the extraordinary work being done by the young Scottish architect Charles Rennie Mackintosh. In fact they both took a genuine interest in the Wright children and would eventually invite daughter Catherine to spend the summer with them in London. It was a splendid family, Janet Ashbee wrote later in the same *Journal*, and Kitty, with her wide-open gray eyes, wispy yellow hair and the exquisite poise of her head and neck, put one in mind of the young Ellen Terry. There was something endearingly tender about her, and she was so light on her feet, so youthful in her smiles and gestures, it was hard to believe she was the mother of six. "Every tone of her voice rings with fearless honesty—almost a defiant cry against sham—compromise and all disloyalty. . . ." That radical original thinker, her husband, was as prepared as ever to stick to his principles. "He has the head of a musician—a sad, thought-worn face, that smiles whimsically between almost fanatic earnestnesses." As he approached his fortieth year, he seemed pursued by a sense of inadequacy: "How I have wasted half my day, / And left my work but just begun," as a poem of the period expressed it. That haunting inner reproach began at an age when most people would have been well satisfied. Writing to thank his mother for her birthday present, he wrote, "Birthdays have gotten to a point with me, however, that makes them unwarranted reminders of lost opportunities and untouched possibilities." He was just thirty years old.

If Wright looked fatigued, he had good reason. In retrospect it is hard to see how he could have advanced any more rapidly in his career than he did, or accomplished much more in terms of maturity of concept, completed buildings, staff, physical equipment and general acceptance. Between 1894 and 1911 he built 135 buildings. He lectured widely, published at least ten articles, was known nationally through his designs for the *Ladies' Home Journal* and major architectural magazines, was an acknowledged leader of the new Chicago, or Prairie school and, when his monumental work, the *Ausgeführte Bauten und Entwürfe von Frank Lloyd Wright* was published in Berlin in 1910, would make his mark in Europe as well. Just nine years after he built a small house for his family, he had already enlarged it substantially and then, in 1898, doubled its first-floor space by adding a studio for himself and his staff. He had taken this obvious step because of the increasing pressure of work; having worked out this arrangement, he would incorporate it into all of his later designs for his homes in Wisconsin and Arizona.

This first studio, comprising a reception hall, drafting room, library and private office, was placed along the Chicago Avenue side of his lot at right angles to his house and connected by a passage. It faced a street that was becoming commercialized and, since it had a streetcar, was much more heavily traveled than Forest Avenue, presenting him with the paradox of designing a building that would advertise itself as an architect's office while allowing privacy for the work being carried on inside. He solved this problem in an interesting way, one that he would often employ in designing houses facing busy streets. On the first floor his suite of rooms presents a largely impregnable facade; it is a locked series of angled walls, distinctive enough in appearance to look like an architect's office but quite private. All that changed at the second-floor level, with expanses of windows and skylights, and the architectural contrasts of solid masonry below and light and air above would be used to great effect in other designs.

Unlike many of his later designs, in which the entrance to a building is almost perversely difficult to find, the studio's main door was prominent and centrally located, but, as one might expect of the master, it opened into a closed and mysterious space that seemed, in comparison to the busy street, almost muffled. It was low-ceilinged, and its heavy dark basswood trims emphasized the horizontal, further heightening the feeling of being in a sanctum, that is, until one caught sight of the ceiling's panels of art glass, geometrically patterned in green and gold and glittering with reflected light. To the right one entered an octagonal library, used usually to entertain clients, its windows set high enough to screen out the distractions of the street, and benefiting from the same use of skylighting; to the left, one found the dramatic open space of the handsome two-story drafting room,

square on the first floor, changing to an octagonal drum on the upper
level, and encircled by a balcony. Each direction contained its own
surprise, in other words; but perhaps the most engaging room of the
four was the architect's own office. This demonstrated the same use
of horizontal bandings, matte-finish walls and exposed brick, the same
groupings of oriental potteries and beautifully arranged dried flowers,
the same severely simple effects, and the same jewel-like windows in
geometric patterns abstracted from natural forms. The effect was universally admired, but so was what in lesser hands would have been a
utilitarian corridor connecting the studio suite to the house. Finding
his way barred by a willow tree, Wright simply built around it,
allowing it adequate space to grow. The idea that one should incorporate a part of the natural world into one's dwelling, rather than
destroy it, caused great comment and was certainly consistent with
the values Wright was espousing. It was not, however, entirely original. A book about the Japanese house, published three years before,
contains a drawing of a living room in which the trunk of a tree has
been included in the design. Buildings spread out along the length
of their lots, mysterious without and full of treasures within, horizontal
emphases, unified concepts, discriminating use of wood, stone, brick
and other materials, contrasting textures, delicate oriental touches,
ceilings of dramatically different heights, earth tones, jewel-like
glass—all these aspects would be incorporated into his first great
houses. Almost from the start he seemed intent upon stating in sym-
bolical terms what Ruskin had implied in his collection of essays,
Sesame and Lilies, thirty years before. Proust would translate the essays
into French, and Proust's biographer, Painter, wrote, "The most significant note, however, is on the organic unity which underlies the
apparent deviousness of Ruskin's construction. In the last paragraph
of *King's Treasuries*, Ruskin gathers together the diverse meanings
latent in the Sesame of his title: it is a seed, a spiritual food, a magic
word which opens a long-hidden, underground treasure-house. . . ."
Nothing about Wright's buildings is conceivable at first glance, as if
he felt that the hidden treasure at their core was a prize that must be
won. To that end he worked with the cunning of a watchmaker and
the sleight of hand of a magician. The narrow entryways leading to
vast rooms, the square room on one level that becomes an octagon on
the second, the glimpses of deep perspectives and the obstacles presented by blank screens, the flash of light in a dark corner, the ability
to conceal and reveal, the sense the viewer has of being drawn into

an ever more mysterious exploration, mark aspects of his work that set it apart. When one considers that along with these great gifts was allied the eye of an aesthete, one begins to have some measure of the size of his achievement.

To chart the evolution of every great house is beyond the scope of this book, and, in any case, Wright's architecture has been extensively studied and described. Most writers agree that, with the houses Wright built for Isidor Heller (1897) and Joseph W. Husser (1899), he was on the verge of a breakthrough. He was certainly proud of the Husser house since he took Ashbee all over it, "showing me every detail with the keenest delight," Ashbee noted. Ashbee was suitably congratulatory: it was "one of the most beautiful and most individual of creations I have seen in America," he wrote. Wright's design for the *Ladies' Home Journal*, "A Home in a Prairie Town," published in 1901, seemed to have resolved something in his mind and released his energies for a decade of unparalleled creativity. That same year he designed his acknowledged masterpiece, the house, gardener's cottage and stables for Ward W. Willits, a wealthy client in Highland Park, another Chicago suburb. The house, although large, was split into four wings so as to minimize its bulk, and was sited behind trees so that, from the road, all that was visible was a series of rooflines and the chink of light in windows half-hidden under the eaves. As in all his Prairie houses, Wright set his massive fireplaces at the heart of the structure, with rooms flowing out from that central anchor to the four points of the compass, and he had arranged circulation inside the house so as to give a constantly changing kaleidoscope of views. The result, William J. R. Curtis wrote, was to produce a kind of " 'pinwheel' rotation, experienced in three dimensions as a spatial tension which varies as one moves through the interior spaces. . . . To Wright this dynamism was perhaps equivalent to the life force he sensed in nature: it gave his dwellings something of the quality of a spatial music in which rhythm, movement, repetition, and variation of similar elements achieved moods and emotions of different pitch and intensity."

As with the rooms in his studio, the walls were plastered and smooth and outlined with horizontal bands of wood that helped relate the scale of the house to its furnishings. These were all designed for that particular house. Even such details as "grilles, brick textures in the fireplace, window mullions [and] the leaded lines of the glass, bear the imprint of the same formal intelligence which conceived the whole, as if the smallest parts all had the generating idea implicit within

Detail of interior of Wright's studio, circa 1898, showing lamp he designed

Wright's home and studio buildings, taken in 1965

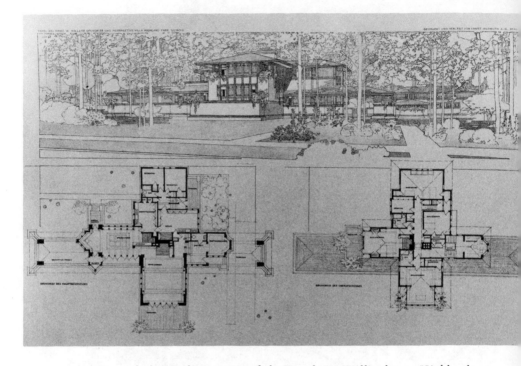

*Ground plan and perspective of the Ward W. Willits house, Highland
Park, Illinois, 1902*

Drawing of the Susan Lawrence Dana house dining room

Perspective drawing of the Susan Lawrence Dana house, 1903

them," Curtis wrote. The house did not impose itself on the street so much as suggest its formidable presence by means of its extensive rooflines. The rooms, while restrained, were elegant, their details fastidiously thought out. The scale of the house was handsome, and its mien sober and discreet, without being spartan. It suggested, in short, a family so well established in prosperity and social status as to have no need to emblazon that fact; they have arrived, and arrived in grand style. Wright had, in other words, found a symbolic language for a particular amalgam of qualities, and done so in a way that his particular group of clients would find exactly right.

The Willits house also has its appeal for theoreticians, who believe that its design demonstrates that a radical shift has occurred in man's relationship to his environment. In contrasting it with the Villa Rotunda of the sixteenth century, for instance, Vincent Scully points out that Palladio created a cylindrical void, a "stable, vertical volume of space which dramatizes the upright human being at its center and keeps him fixed where he is." Palladio was designing in a "preindustrial, humanistic world" where, as Kenneth Clark wrote, man was the measure of all things. By contrast, Wright's house, with its massive central chimney and elongated vistas leading the eye out to the horizon was, Scully wrote, "an image of modern man, caught up in constant change and flow, holding on . . . to whatever seems solid, but no longer regarding himself as the center of the world . . . a specifically American image. . . ."

The theoretical basis for Wright's infinite number of themes has already been described. Since he always organized his floor plans using the intricate patterns he had learned from Froebel blocks—he once said that he saw the method's possibilities anew when his own children began playing with them, and, of course, his wife was also teaching Froebel's method—this gave his designs, however modest or ambitious, uniform dimensions and properly orchestrated axes and directions to his houses. When he came to design his justly renowned Darwin D. Martin house in Buffalo (1904), his sense of design had advanced so far that he could conceive of its surrounding lawns, pergolas and connecting spaces as another kind of abstract pattern that required a similarly sophisticated solution, and was able to weave house and grounds into a single flowing and interpenetrating design. Since the same principles lay behind all of these outwardly disparate houses it is possible to see the resemblances between, for instance, the small, enchanting Arthur Heurtley residence in Oak Park and the mansion Wright designed that same year (1902) for Susan Lawrence Dana, a wealthy socialite in Springfield, Illinois, the façade of which is as imposing as the former's is understated and discreet. At this glorious moment in his life there seemed no end to the ideas, the inspired marriage of materials, the infinite ingenuity of the floor plans or the success of the results; he went from strength to strength. His comment that he could shake the designs out of his sleeve seems irrefutable, as if each new commission represented a new opportunity for fusing the real with the ideal.

As has been noted, Wright was hardly the first to reject the idea of a house and rooms as a series of boxes, but he took its possibilities in new directions. By positioning his rooms on the diagonal he avoided the error of creating, by the simple removal of walls, a larger box in place of two smaller boxes, and went much further than his predecessors in replacing those divisions, which had formerly dictated the use of individual spaces, with screens or freestanding slabs that merely suggested them. "Destroying the box" in this way still did not go far enough to suit him; he wanted to achieve the same effect with exterior walls as well. His solution was, first, to expand vastly the size and numbers of windows and, then, by inventing a method of turning the corner with windows, placing the panes of glass edge to edge with no intervening supports, he created the trompe l'oeil effect of appearing to make the corner disappear. But the less exterior walls were used as shelters from the weather meant, given the harsh Midwestern climate, a further shift of emphasis to the roof. Wright's roofs became ever longer and wider until, in the Robie house of 1906, he had built a cantilevered roof that extended twenty feet beyond the last masonry support.

Wright's practical solutions have been much admired and were advanced for his day. His roofs, for instance, were always angled so as to protect the house from the harsh summer sun while allowing winter sunlight to come in through the windows. Given these large expanses of glass, Wright's houses are remarkably livable, thanks to his central heating system using hot-water pipes that encircled the rooms and that were usually concealed in the wainscoting. If there were window seats, these would be warmed by a radiator positioned directly underneath them. In those days before air conditioning, Wright was scrupulous about providing cross-ventilation in summer and might compensate for the massive overhangs of his roofs and the danger of penumbral shade within by astute placement of clerestory windows, a trick hardly used since. One has to believe that, with Wright, aesthetic considerations always predominated, but these included the human fact of living in a house, not merely admiring its exquisite interiors. Wright's inner standard of excellence encompassed the healthful life, and that meant providing protection from sub-zero temperatures, creating between-season terraces sheltered from the wind and striking the right balance between the competing claims of spaciousness and privacy, adequate heat in winter and air circulation in summer. His final demand on himself was that these mechanics of living should be hidden if they were ugly or seamlessly incorporated into the room's design if they could not. A famous example of the latter is the way he has included a series of overhead electric light fixtures into the design of his Robie house sitting room.

Once Wright's houses became low and spreading, and his roofs vast and overhanging, the idea of opening up the interior spaces to include cathedral-ceiling living rooms followed inevitably. It was too good to miss, as Wright remarked of his early design for such a living room for the *Ladies' Home Journal*. That meant the quiet demise of the traditional attic, and Wright's basements disappeared along with it. Wright never really explains why he thought this space, which is still an integral part of many American houses, should have been eliminated. He makes a passing reference to its unwholesomeness, but his main objection appears to have been aesthetic. The universal cellar was an excrescence that stuck up above the ground for a foot or so, decorated with some halfhearted windows, making the house look as if it was sitting on a chair. That would not do at all. What Wright wanted was a harmonious unity and so, beginning with the Winslow house, he developed, as Charles White explained, a "grammar" of exterior design, which he then used consistently. This was to set his house on a base. The first-floor wall would extend to the second-story windowsills; from this point, Wright might use a frieze that would end at the roof, followed by a cornice and wide overhang.

Wright's celebrated prejudice against storage space is harder to understand. One knows only that it was deeply rooted, since it is a theme of his speeches from the beginning. It is conceivable that he resented devoting to a utilitarian function the money and space that might be used to greater decorative effect. However, his antagonism seems so pronounced that it suggests he may have felt on the defensive about having invaded, in pursuit of his goal of total design, a traditional female province. No housewife in a cold climate will willingly dispense with curtains, as Wright's clients were obliged to do, and no seasoned city dweller will endure, after dark, the absence of blinds and the miserable feeling that she can be spied upon without her knowledge.

The reminiscences of Frederick C. Robie, the prosperous young bicycle manufacturer who commissioned Wright to build his house, provide an excellent illustration of this point. When he chose Wright, Robie recalled that he wanted certain features, fireproofing for instance, and a living room that would allow him to look up and down the street without being seen by the neighbors, and separate quarters for his children, and a walled garden to keep them from wandering. What he did not want was "a lot of junk—a lot of fabrics, draperies, and what not, or old-fashioned roller shades with the brass fittings on the ends—in my line of vision, gathering dust and interfering with window washing. No sir. . . ." One notes that Robie's wife of five years is never mentioned. Like most wives of Wright's successful and opinionated businessmen clients, she presumably knew better than to interfere and, like Mrs. Darwin D. Martin, even appeared in clothes her architect had designed. The lady of the house might have been allowed a certain latitude for self-expression on the question of what was to be planted in the urns, boxes and planters, on steps, trailing from balconies and window ledges and enhancing the foundations of their houses, those accents of graceful greenery that did so much to soften the sometimes austere exteriors, that is, until Wright began to collaborate with landscape architects. Only a very headstrong female could have prevailed against a will like Wright's. One of the few, curiously enough, was his daughter Catherine Wright Baxter, mother of Anne, the late actress and film star. Catherine expressed her preference for frilly white curtains at an early age and clung to her antique-filled interiors all her life, rejecting her father's efforts to inform her taste.

Darwin D. Martin, that colossus in the life of Frank Lloyd Wright, who would have such a pivotal role in sustaining that talent, was a protégé of Elbert Hubbard's; Hubbard had spotted Martin slaving away (every day from 7 a.m. until 6 p.m.) in the bookkeeping department of the Larkin Company. Martin had left school at age eleven and an awareness of his lack of education led him to compensate industriously for that shortcoming. This, along with his natural aptitude for business, made him a most valuable employee. He invented a system of bookkeeping, then took over a crucially important aspect of the mail-order business and, by the time he met Wright in 1902, had become a Larkin Company of Buffalo chief executive with the amazing annual salary of $25,000 a year.

Martin adored Elbert Hubbard, that free spirit who never seemed to need the stimulus of alcohol or tobacco, who bounced into the office each morning ready for a new day's work and had been known to enliven the atmosphere with an Indian war whoop. It must have been a blow to him when Hubbard, a major contributor to the success of the company, left to enroll in Harvard University and launch himself, at least temporarily, on a writing career. When Martin met Wright a decade later, he may have seen that architect, in the first flush of his creative powers, as filling the gap in his life that Hubbard had left. One is tempted to think so, since from the first, Martin's attitude toward Wright, two years his junior, is a model of admiration and fraternal forbearance. Whatever Wright proposed was sure of a sympathetic hearing from Martin, and although the latter sometimes made a show of exacting stringent conditions, these seldom survived the full force of Wright's charm. His indulgent attitude toward Wright was exceeded only by that of his brother, W. E. Martin of Oak Park, with whom he owned a small business in Chicago, the E-Z Polish Factory; the latter was the first member of the family to commission Wright. W. E. Martin liked to ride around with Wright looking at buildings in progress. During one such outing, Wright stopped off at a new house for a few minutes, leaving W. E. Martin outside, and was invited to dinner. "Three hours later," John Lloyd Wright recalled, "Papa remembered Mr. Martin, waiting in the automobile. . . ."

Darwin D. Martin might have been prejudiced in favor of this young Chicago architect, but he was also prepared to make use of him. As he made his way up the corporate ladder, Martin was well aware that the company's founder, John D. Larkin, now manufacturing perfumes and powders as well as soap, and with offices in Pittsburgh, Boston and Philadelphia, was grooming his sons, Charles and John, Jr., to take over the manufacturing and mail-order divisions. There were plenty of heirs, because the upper echelons of the Larkin Company were linked by a series of intermarriages. John D. Larkin had married a sister of Elbert Hubbard's; W. R. Heath, the company's attorney, had married another; and even Darwin Martin's sister had married George Barton, who worked in the secretary's department. Sons, grandsons and nephews of the founder all worked together in reasonable

*Frederick C. Robie house, Chicago, 1906, showing famous
cantilevered porch roof*

Art-glass detail from the Robie house   *The formal dining room, brought to
a state of perfection in the
Robie house, circa 1911*

The Larkin Building

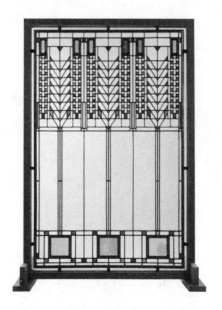

The famous Tree of Life *art glass from
the Darwin D. Martin house in Buffalo*

An example of the concealed entrance: the Darwin D. Martin house,
Buffalo

Darwin D. Martin house living room, showing the wisteria-mosaic fireplace wall

Entrance hall to the Martin house

harmony, but Darwin Martin, who had carelessly neglected to make the right marriage, knew that his continued prominence would depend on the extent to which he could consolidate his position. Once it became clear that Larkin intended to build a new headquarters beside his group of factory and warehouse buildings in a suburb of Buffalo, Martin was maneuvering to make that building a monument to himself and keep his rivals, chiefly Charles and John, Jr., out of it. What he needed was an architect of attainment but not too much status who could be counted on to protect his interests and who would know to whom he owed his allegiance. In fact, not just an office building was being discussed, but a mansion for the Darwin D. Martin family. W. E. Martin, who had talked of Wright in the most effusive terms, calling him "one of nature's noblemen," knew just whom "Dar" wanted. Wright, seeing the Larkin project as his chance to break into the world of large building commissions, was even surer. He shamelessly exaggerated the importance of his role at Adler and Sullivan (Martin later told Larkin that the "$500,000 Wainwright Building and the Union Trust Building of St. Louis; the Schiller Theatre and the Stock Exchange in Chicago; the Seattle and Pueblo Opera Houses, all Adler and Sullivan's work, were, I inferred from Mr. Wright, largely his creations. . . ."), showed himself eager to respond to every suggestion and meet every objection. For his part, Martin skillfully steered Wright through the politics of obtaining the commission and the many treacherous undercurrents. However much Wright may have accomplished for Martin by his design of the new Larkin Building, in years to come Martin would do immeasurably more for Wright and, as the latter knew, if one wants to be liked by a powerful man, one must be sure to place oneself forever in his debt.

The Larkin Company Building no longer exists, a casualty of the zeal of the immediate postwar period to replace outmoded buildings with parking lots, and photographs alone are left to give some indication of its impressive scale and monumental effect once construction was completed in 1906. On the outside, its severe, almost fortresslike appearance (Jack Quinan, expert on the building's design and construction, believes that it may have been inspired by the grain elevators to be seen within a mile of the site) was a response to the need to screen out the noise and air pollution in this industrial area. From the outside, the building might present an impregnable façade, but inside, its interior was a single vast rectangular space, an inner court rising to five stories and ringed by tiers of balconies, with stairwells at each corner. The space was lit from above by a skylight, and additional windows were positioned to provide natural light for the galleries. If the design spoke more or less clearly to the company's desire to have its employees feel a part of one united family, to European visitors the idea that the head of the office worked equably, side by side with everyone else, was most amazing of all. The building was technically advanced for its day, with central heating and also a form of air conditioning (using blocks of ice), and was furnished with metal desks and chairs now considered outstanding examples of Wright's ability to combine function and utility with sensitive use of materials. The Larkin Building's qualities were recognized by a few prescient critics at the time, and the building has acquired an almost legendary status; it has been called "one of the seminal works of the early modern movement." What Wright was demonstrating in terms of power and originality for his first office building he was also bringing to bear on the complex of buildings Darwin D. Martin wanted on his corner site along Summit Avenue in Buffalo. After some halfhearted objections, Martin provided almost unlimited funds to build a ten-thousand-square-foot house, greenhouse, two-story garage, stable and also a conservatory connected to the main house by a long pergola. As has been noted, the architect's ability to enlarge the scale of his Prairie Style house while keeping its proportions intact has been much admired. The Martin house is also an excellent example of a house that seems ostentatiously, almost aggressively, on display, while maintaining a paradoxical privacy for its owners. Those open porches and balconies are far less accessible than they appear at first glance, in part because of the wide, hovering roofs, but also because of walls calculated to screen from view whoever may be sitting there. Another curious aspect about the house is its apparent lack of a front door, putting one in mind of a castle the drawbridge of which is pulled up, and also making one think of Sullivan's comment to an imaginary listener in his book *Kindergarten Chats*: "Your suggestion that a building is a screen behind which a man is hiding is decidedly interesting and novel." Yet another idiosyncrasy of the Martin house is the complexity of its silhouette, to some extent true for all of Wright's houses, but so marked in this case that, as might be predicted, the house is impossible to fully comprehend except by treating it as a mammoth piece of sculpture. Although the Martin house did not quite suffer the fate of the Larkin Building, it was badly neglected for years, part of its lot sold for apartment buildings and some of its buildings torn down.

Symbols figure prominently in Wright's early work, as can be seen
by his consistent and inspired use of the same motifs throughout the
interior furnishings of his glorious early houses. The Celtic cross he
used as his personal emblem has been mentioned earlier. It was accompanied by further symbols at the entrance to his studio: a pair of
figures crouched over their knees (representing the struggles of creativity) and a bas-relief comprised of two storks, a book of knowledge,
a tree of life and an architect's plans, perhaps meant to propitiate the
passing gods. Wright took equal pains with his first business commission for John D. Larkin. Working with the sculptor Richard Bock
he developed the motif of a globe of the world (held up by angelic
figures), on which the name LARKIN was superimposed, to act as the
chief ornament for the building's exterior. There were also intaglio
reliefs on the outside walls with such messages as HONEST LABOR
NEEDS NO MASTER and similar exhortations to right conduct around
the balconies inside. Corporate pride was certainly a factor, but the
desire to put it in writing as well as state it symbolically must have
been uppermost in Wright's mind at the time, as if he was not entirely
sure that the building alone could convey the message he intended.
It is therefore fascinating to discover that by the time Wright designed
Unity Temple, a new church for the Unitarian congregation of Oak
Park a year later (1904), such statements of intent have all but disappeared. Cost could have been one factor, at least where the building's
exterior is concerned, because the congregation was operating on a
tight budget, but the fact that no words are inside either—and paint
is cheap—suggests that the architect's confidence was advancing by
leaps and bounds, and he was prepared to let his building speak for
itself.

Darwin Martin may have been the most prominent of Wright's
sponsors, but he was not the first. Before Martin came into his life,
Wright had been a protégé of a well-to-do inventor named Charles
E. Roberts. It is thought that the Wrights met the Roberts family
through the Aunts, Nell and Jane, and then became good friends of
Anna, whom they knew as Madame Wright. They referred to her son
as "Frank" or "Frank Wright." Roberts, who was of Welsh origin,
had invented a machine that could make the tops and bottoms of
screws in a single operation. He founded a machine company, and
soon sold it for the handsome price of $1 million so as to devote his
life to his other inventions. Despite the fact that one of them was an
early horseless carriage (now in a museum), Roberts never managed
to strike it rich again, and gradually lost his fortune. When he met

the Wrights, however, he and his wife and children, among the earliest residents of Oak Park, were prominent there as members of the
Unitarian congregation. (They were Universalists.) Being introduced
around by someone like Charles Roberts would have been crucially
important to Wright at the time when he was looking for clients and
needed solid recommendations; in fact, Roberts paid him the further
compliment of engaging him to do extensive remodeling of the interior
of his own house in 1896. Mrs. Joseph F. Johnston, Roberts's granddaughter, recalled that a master bedroom and bath were added to the
first floor, the bed designed to fold into the wall by day so as to make
a spacious sitting room; upstairs, there were a library, staircase, fireplaces and extensive interior remodeling. Mrs. Johnston said that the
outside of the house remained typically Victorian, but inside was
"lovely, with a lot of Wright details."

Roberts, his granddaughter said, was a gentle philanthropist who
took a kindly interest in Wright's affairs and often lent him money
—the total amount became a matter of dispute, but it was several
thousand dollars. Once the Unitarian church decided to build, Roberts
was named chairman of the building committee and appears to have
gone straight to Madame Wright's son. The story becomes extremely
interesting at this point because, if one posits that both Wright and
Roberts would be disposed to consult Welsh models, one would expect
to find resemblances between the interior design of their new Unity
Church (often called Unity Temple), and old-country prototypes. This
is exactly the case, according to Anthony Jones, former director of the
Glasgow School of Art, now director of the Art Institute of Chicago
art school and author of a book about the Welsh chapel. The main
concern of eighteenth and nineteenth century architects was to provide
a church in which the minister could be in close and intimate contact
with his audience. A cube-shaped building was considered especially
appropriate, because of its good acoustical qualities; it also obeyed the
scriptural injunction that ". . . the City of the Lord shall lie foresquare
and the breadth shall be no greater than the width." By arranging
the congregation around the room and in balconies on three sides, the
minister might see each listener and he or she might be close enough
to catch every inflection and nuance of feeling. This is, essentially,
the design Wright chose for his building, and although there is no
evidence to suggest that Wright ever did consult Welsh models, the
coincidence is striking. Jones commented, "This kind of interior is
uniquely Welsh nonconformist, with the synagogue as the only other
parallel. I find it a lively and very plausible connection."

It is, of course, a glorious interior, illuminated from above with ample skylights that flood it with light and also by clerestory windows embellished with his characteristic geometric designs. Architects admire the cunning of the raised auditorium space, the strong horizontal effects produced by the running bands of wood decorating every conceivable surface, and the way the architect has used his trompe l'oeil techniques to minimize the room's corners and further heighten the overall effect of his sanctuary as having been composed, like a jigsaw puzzle, of intricately locked blocks. It seems unique, yet as Jonathan Lipman, an architect and Wright scholar, has demonstrated, it shares common elements with Wright's design for his studio and other buildings in that it uses the same technique of dramatic surprise. One enters Unity Temple by means of a colonnade that links the structure to a second, smaller building (to provide meeting rooms, a kitchen, space for a Sunday school and the like), presenting no easy path for the visitor. To call this access labyrinthine would be to overstate the case, yet the tenacity with which Wright clung to this device suggests that it satisfied his need to heighten the moment when, having threaded his way around all the obstacles put in his path, the visitor would at last find himself in a marvelous, serene inner space bathed in light. This same concept, according to Lipman, can be seen to have influenced the design of the Larkin Building and such later triumphs as Wright's great Japanese building, the Imperial Hotel. However, to explain the effect created by Wright's sanctuary as due to his theatrical manipulation of space alone would be to trivialize his achievement. He himself called the building a "temple," indicating how seriously he took the call to create a "true reflection of man in the realm of his own spirit," as he wrote. "His building is therefore consecrated space wherein he seeks refuge . . . and repose for body, but especially mind."

One writer has seen a resemblance between Wright's design for Unity Temple and the work of his contemporary, a Viennese architect named Jose Maria Olbrich. Some believe they see the influence of pre-Columbian and Mayan architectural forms and motifs in Wright's work at an early stage, arguing that he would have seen such architecture on display at the World's Columbian Exposition in 1893 and that he consistently expressed his admiration for these cultures. Still others, notably David A. Hanks, the authority on Wright's decorative designs and objets d'art, have speculated that Wright, given American knowledge of each development in the British Arts and Crafts Movement, would have been aware of directions in taste from the start and used them as points of departure. The "presidential armchair" designed by Ashbee and shown at the first London Arts and Crafts Society exhibition in 1888, for instance, demonstrates the use of natural oak, rectilinear lines, slatted sides and high back that would be characteristic of Wright's early chairs. There are other interesting parallels between Wright's designs and those of Charles Rennie Mackintosh in Glasgow. Like Wright, Mackintosh parted from the Arts and Crafts Movement over the issue of handicrafts and traditional methods of construction, never hesitating to use unorthodox methods whenever necessary. He also shared Wright's fondness for linear, abstract design, in his case so heavily weighted with Gaelic symbolism and Celtic references that he and his circle became known as the "Spook School." At least one Mackintosh interior, the entrance hall for "Hill House" (1903–04), with its unified composition of carpets, woodwork, furniture and lighting fixtures, all of which repeat the motif of the square, could almost have come from the pencil of Wright himself. Then there are the further parallels between Wright's high-backed, slatted chairs for the Willits dining room of 1902 and Mackintosh's similar designs of the year before. Most writers have given the edge to Mackintosh: "If there was any interchange of ideas through journals," Roger Billcliffe wrote, "it can only have been in one direction, because Wright's work was not published in Europe until 1910, while Mackintosh's work would have been known . . . through . . . *The Studio*. . . ."

M. H. Baillie Scott and C. F. A. Voysey, the influential Arts and Crafts architects, also designed furniture that could be seen as having inspired specific designs by Wright. Hanks cited, for instance, a sofa by Voysey with broad armrests that is very like another sofa Wright designed a year later with the same kind of armrest, further exaggerated. Perhaps one of the most striking examples of Wright's omnivorous visual appetite and his responsiveness to the latest trends is given by the Louisiana Purchase Exposition at St. Louis in 1904, at which a number of German designers showed complete room interiors. Wright went, and was fascinated. He must go to the fair, Wright told his new draftsman, Charles White, in May 1904; "it is a liberal education." Among the objects on view were some unusual barrel-shaped chairs by Jose Maria Olbrich. That same year Wright designed his first barrel-shaped armchair with upholstered seat, for Darwin D. Martin's new house. Wright must have known that the lead in advanced design was moving from London to Germany and Austria, following the creation of the Viennese Wiener Werkstätte in 1903,

Unity Temple in 1908

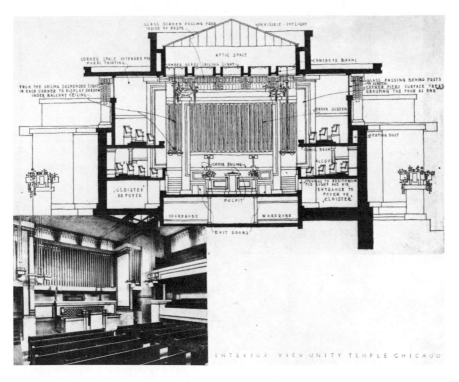

Unity Temple cross-section and interior view

Wright's curved armchair design for the Martin house

Wright's straight-backed oak side chair, 1904

a center for the decorative arts that had been founded by Josef Hoffmann. Along with Olbrich, Adolf Loos and the older Otto Wagner,
Hoffmann rejected both the Classical Academic tradition and also the
influence of Art Nouveau, a movement that was sweeping Europe.
These architects, however, shared the Arts and Crafts ideals of simplicity and integrity that Wright also espoused; in shifting his attention to these developments, in other words, Wright would not have
been abandoning first principles.

Evidence for a shift of interest by about 1904 comes from his personal
symbol, always the most reliable of weather vanes. Wright was gradually substituting a new motif for the Celtic cross that had appeared
on his earlier designs: that of a plain red square with an ocher outline.
Letters from Wright now in the Darwin D. Martin archives date this
shift fairly closely. From them, one finds that he was still using the
Celtic cross until early in 1904 and that the plain red square came
into use in the autumn of that same year. Most authorities on Wright
agree that this new symbol owes its origins fairly directly to Japanese
prints, in particular those of Hiroshige, and that Wright was hardly
the first to show an interest in this kind of signature, since many
artists, among them Henri de Toulouse-Lautrec, were using pseudo-
Japanese symbols that they had taken from the seals of Japanese censors.
What is interesting about this particular symbol is that Wright should
begin to use it just a matter of months before his first trip overseas
in February 1905: he, his wife and their friends and clients, Mr. and
Mrs. Ward W. Willits, sailed for Japan.

Most writers agree that Wright's interest in Japanese art probably
began with the Chicago World's Columbian Exposition of 1893, if
not before—one recalls that, as a member of Sullivan's office, he would
have had detailed knowledge of the advance planning—and, in particular, with one of the most popular exhibits, "The Ho-o-den," a
wooden temple of the Fujiwara Period, which the Japanese government
erected on a small plot of ground set in an artificial lake. It was the
first real introduction of Japanese art and architecture to the Middle
West. In terms of the enormous interest in all things Japanese that
had followed Commodore Matthew C. Perry's trip to Japan in 1845,
this discovery must be considered rather late. Bronzes, lacquers, fans,
ceramics and, above all, prints had been flooding to Europe for twenty
or thirty years, and artists as disparate as Redon and Steinlen had
drawn new inspiration from these exotic and unfamiliar objects, seizing
on the lessons they had to teach as a way to revitalize their imagery.

Architects were just as susceptible and, after the Philadelphia Centennial Exposition of 1876, where Japanese pavilions had been built,
and especially after publication of the first English-language book on
Japanese architecture in 1886, they focused their attention on this
aspect of Japanese culture. For Americans oriented toward the Arts
and Crafts Movement, Japan offered "the example of an indigenous
culture that embodied the organic quality they found in the middle
ages," as Richard Guy Wilson wrote. He added, "Japanese motifs,
from curved gable ends to nearly wholesale replication of pagodas and
torii gates, appeared in Arts and Crafts houses and bungalows from
coast to coast." One believes Wright's new interest to have been at
least partly connected with the exhaustion White had noticed and
remarked upon just before his employer left for Japan. It began the
year before, White wrote, when Wright seemed very "petered out."
However, in the last three months it had been impossible to get Wright
to give his office any attention at all. In fact, Wright had been confined
to bed for several weeks that winter with a case of tonsillitis that had
made its way around the family. He returned from Japan in May
sounding more like his old self. Writing to Darwin Martin he said,
"We, Mrs. Wright and I, have come back much improved in health
and spirits—can lick my weight in wild cats. How would you like
to be a wild-cat?" His interest was, nevertheless, entirely genuine,
and his visit would have a lasting influence.

Several writers claim to see a more or less direct connection between
the Japanese temple that Wright saw at the World's Columbian Exposition of 1893 and some of his own buildings. Vincent Scully
demonstrated that the treatment of exteriors in the Willits house
resembled those of the Ho-o-den, and Wright's use of light-colored
stucco panels edged with bands of darker wood seemed to suggest
Japanese models as well. Scully published copies of the two floor plans
to support his assertion that the house Wright designed for Willits
was modeled almost exactly on that of the Japanese shrine. Another
authority on Wright believed he had been most influenced by the
Japanese print, and he had certainly begun to collect ukiyo-e (pictures
of the floating world) sometime before his first visit to Japan, because
photographs of his interiors showed such prints prominently displayed.
He returned from Japan with over two hundred woodcuts by Hiroshige, considered the artist to have had the greatest influence on the
West, and lent them to the Art Institute of Chicago a year later for
the first ukiyo-e exhibition to be held in that museum. He bought

them as investments, making no bones about being a dealer, and was so successful that he had a sizable collection of Japanese prints on hand all his life, to be cashed in when necessary, and some famous collectors as clients. But he was also passionately interested in the subject, almost obsessed, and would talk endlessly about the exquisite qualities of these prints, their serenity, simplicity, sense of the natural world and reduction to essentials. While on that first trip he wore native robes and took extended trips into the interior to collect his prints and porcelains. All of this indicates that the feelings aroused by Japanese art were wholehearted, yet there is a suggestion that, at some level, Wright was made acutely uncomfortable by that most conformist, ordered and rigidly circumscribed culture that he apparently admired for its "spirituality." Writing to Ashbee in 1910, he exclaimed, "Do not say that I deny that my love for Japanese art has influenced me —I admit that it has but claim to have digested it—Do not accuse me of trying to 'adapt Japanese forms' however, *that is a false accusation and against my very religion.*"

Their sixth and last child, Robert Llewellyn, always called Llewellyn in the family, was born in the autumn of 1903 and would have been walking and perhaps saying his first words when his parents left for Japan in February 1905. Robert Llewellyn Wright's widow states that, when his mother returned, Llewellyn did not recognize her, causing her much anguish. She also suggested that Kitty knew then that her marriage was in trouble, and had been driven to take the extreme step, for her, of leaving her baby for three months in an effort to save it. Those years from 1904 to 1909 were to be pivotal in Wright's life and so it is worthwhile examining fairly closely the chain of events during that five- or six-year period just before he decided to walk away from his wife, children, home, his flourishing architectural practice and the considerable reputation he had built for himself in Chicago, never to return.

The fact that the Wrights had such a large family now seems like sheer carelessness, but one has to remember that methods of birth control were unreliable in those days, that both Frank and Kitty came from large and boisterous families, and that William Carey Wright also had six children (by two wives). Six may have seemed the right number, and the birth of the last child may—if there had been a suspicion in Wright's mind that he was destined to act out the role his father had played before him—have had an ominous finality to it. By the merest chance, William Wright died just seven months after the birth of this last child of Frank's, not one of which he had seen, on June 6, 1904. Elizabeth Wright Heller wrote in her memoir that one morning their father had just returned from the drugstore when they saw that he was pulling open his shirt in evident distress. He collapsed and died a few minutes later. He was seventy-nine years old. His body was transported to Lone Rock, Wisconsin, and he was buried in Bear Valley Cemetery beside his first wife. Anna's children, Jennie, Maginel and Frank, were not at the funeral, and Lizzie wrote that, two decades later, Jennie told her that they had not known about it. Lizzie noted her belief that they had been informed, but the reference was casual enough to suggest that she and her brothers would have considered such notification to be a very low priority. One assumes that Frank learned of his father's death from a relative or friend. One notes that he inherited nothing.

For a son who had been taught to think of his father as dead, it must still have been a jolt to have him actually die, a reminder that would be likely to release some long-repressed feelings of bitterness, along with self-reproach, a sense of lost opportunities and a host of buried memories. It is almost axiomatic that married couples in conflict will review the problems in their parents' marriages and begin to see some parallels. Wright gives some clues that one area of conflict in his marriage had to do with his wife's absorption in their children. They were never "our" children in his references, but always "hers," an echo, perhaps, of the old Celtic pattern and one that could have been reinforced by Kitty's enthusiasm for motherhood and child raising. One can hardly reproach a wife for being too good a mother, and Wright's carping on this score has been dismissed, but perhaps the criticism carried with it his feeling that he had been replaced. Given his emotional insecurity and undoubted narcissism, one can see what he expected from Catherine and understand how he might consider the normal distractibility of the mother of six as evidence of the withdrawal of love. That suspicion would have been intensified, given what he knew about his own parents. His mother had successfully pushed his father out and devoted herself to him and his sisters. He had won his mother's complete and unconditional love and must have expected that some day he would be ousted in his turn. He was also quite sincere in saying that he never felt like a father. What he meant, perhaps, was that in emotional terms he was still a child among children competing for love as his mother had competed in her marriage. In family photographs of that time (1904), Wright, who took the pictures, shows his mother, sister Maginel, wife, baby Llewellyn and other sons and daughters grouped along a wall of the house while he sits on the wall at a distinct distance. Frank Lloyd Wright, Jr., is much to the fore and dominates at least one of the poses. A family story has it that he and his father came to blows when he was an adolescent, just as his father and grandfather had done. It is said that Lloyd won. The possibility that Wright saw himself, at some level, as fated to leave his marriage, just as his father had done, is also somewhat buttressed by the following curious parallel: when William Carey Wright left home, his last child, Maginel, was just six years old. When Wright left home, Llewellyn was about to celebrate his sixth birthday.

Those years between Llewellyn's arrival and Wright's departure showed periods of calm and reconciliation, as well as renewed hopes. The return from Japan appears to have been such a time, to judge from a few clues in Wright's letters to Darwin Martin. In one, for instance, he exclaimed, "I am used to rebuffs and bumps—they don't count so very much except to make a fellow look kind of battered up, but as long as his wife loves him what's the difference?" One would expect his handling of money to be a continuing cause for conflict, somewhat mitigated perhaps by his fondness for giving extravagant presents. For Catherine however, what probably counted more than the lack of hard cash was the emotional accounting. At some point she seemed to be keeping a silent ledger and a tally of bills that would soon be presented.

There is the further question of the normal changes that her development from enchanting adolescent to mother of six would have brought about in her personality. As she struggled heroically to make the transition from princess to chatelaine, following the example of her resourceful mother, in those long hours of her life when Frank was working all day and all night as well, being thrown back on her own resources was bound to develop in her a certain self-reliance. But it would be enough, for Frank, who had to manage and control every aspect of the life of someone close to him, to feel that Kitty was no longer so willing to let him dominate, or to feel hurt and neglected. Perhaps her attempts to assert herself were clumsy; she was known for her sharp and critical tongue. That normal part of maturing would have seemed, to Wright, evidence that his wife no longer loved him.

He was in the curious position of finding himself intellectually attracted to clever women whom he wanted, once he had won them, to become extensions of himself, merging utterly with his ideas, his comforts, his goals, his achievements and his disappointments. What he was seeing was the normal development of a young woman from insecure adolescent into a confident matron who was becoming a leader in church and club activities, who gave speeches, organized playschools, did volunteer work at Hull House and had her own friends. The fact that his own neglect might have brought this about would not have occurred to him. Kitty had her life and her children, and he, he told himself, had become the odd man out. If he left, she would not even miss him.

Furthermore, one wonders how well suited they were after twenty years of marriage and the inevitable process of inner development. Whether he knew it or not, he was abandoning his stance of socially respectable man-about-town and, within the decade, would have become a genuine outcast. She, who had looked like a Pre-Raphaelite painter's vision when they met, had evolved into an entirely conventional matron with a fixed set of expectations. Having come to certain conclusions about how one lived one's life, and about obligations morally owed, she never altered her opinions, but nursed her grievances until they became self-wounding. Perhaps she felt cheated at every level, not just because she was being supplanted by another woman but because, in common with her generation, she expected that her reward for years of selfless devotion would be recognition and personal fulfillment. Instead, her own needs were ignored, her accomplishments went unrecognized, and she was about to lose her status as a person, a somebody, the wife of a famous man. The attitudes of her day would have heightened this sense of injury, since a married woman with six children whose husband had left her expected her life to be over— even if she were still only thirty-eight years old. It is a measure of her courage that she subsequently found a job and even a career, as a social worker. She was very much interested in the feminist movement in later years. During World War I she patrolled the city parks in order to warn adolescent girls against soldiers on the loose.

She was, of course, still very beautiful when Frank's attention began to wander. Being the person she was, she would not have remained silent about the evidence of her own eyes. And, by the winter of 1908, overlooking certain developments would have been difficult. The underlying tone of Janet Ashbee's diary entry about the Wright marriage,

Catherine Wright with her youngest child, Robert Llewellyn, 1907

Portraits of the family, 1909. From top left: David and Catherine;
second row, from left: John, Frank, Jr., and Mrs. Wright;
bottom row, from left: Robert Llewellyn and Frances

which she observed then, was that it was under severe stress and that Catherine's mood was one of indignation, if not outrage. "Every tone of her voice rings with fearless honesty . . . against sham—compromise and all disloyalty. . . ." After all, Frank had helped publish that book about *The House Beautiful*, a paean to the ideal marriage, the union of two souls, bound together forevermore. How could he, how dared he, repudiate that? If Frank Lloyd Wright were withdrawing from Catherine emotionally, this was his characteristic solution for those moments when the women in his life began to criticize, reproach, find fault and place too much emotional pressure on him. Catherine, however, never seems to have understood this. Like Anna, and then his second wife, Miriam, she became anxious and clinging as she felt him slip away. There were, Mrs. Ashbee noted, lines of tension around the mouth of that exquisite face.

Sometime in 1903 Frank Lloyd Wright began to design a single-story brick house with wood trim for Edwin H. Cheney and his wife, Mamah (pronounced Maymah), and, as it happened, the building permit to begin work on the house at 520 North East Avenue in Oak Park was issued in June 1904, a week after William Carey Wright died. Edwin Cheney was an electrical engineer and shared Wright's enthusiasm for those new mechanical marvels, automobiles. His wife, intellectually adventurous and bookish, had a B.A. from the University of Michigan, where they met, and an M.A. She was born in June 1869, making her exactly two years Wright's junior. She was one of three daughters of Marcus S. Borthwick, an employee of the Chicago and Northwestern Railroad, who held the position of superintendent of the repair department when he retired after forty years. After graduation, Mamah Borthwick seemed in no rush to marry, working as a librarian in Port Huron, Michigan. Her interests encompassed translations of Goethe and the writings of the Swedish feminist Ellen Key. She was thirty when she finally married Edwin in 1899 and moved to Oak Park; their first child, John, was born in 1902. Some time after her arrival in Chicago, she enrolled at the University of Chicago and was a student under Robert Herrick. It was said that she aspired to be a writer.

Although Mamah Borthwick Cheney was fairly reclusive, she did belong to the Nineteenth Century Women's Club, where she met Catherine Wright, then very much a leading light of that club along with Grace Hemingway, Ernest's mother. Subsequently the two women were "much in each other's company," according to a newspaper account. It is conceivable that the commission for the house was an outgrowth of Catherine's friendship with Mamah. If so, it would help explain Catherine's eventual feelings of deep betrayal. If, in addition, Catherine Wright's marriage was in trouble by early 1905, as she believed, then the relationship between Frank and Mamah must have developed fairly rapidly. From the tantalizing and fragmentary memories of people in Oak Park who still remember them, one is given the impression that Edwin Cheney was far more popular than his wife. He was, by one account, "a prince of a man." A neighbor, Verna Ross Orndorff, continued, "he was middle-aged, dark-eyed and bald. You could hardly call him a Don Juan, but he was so charming and gracious that he didn't have an enemy. Whereas Frank Lloyd Wright was very swashbuckling, a buccaneering type." As for Mamah, she was nice-looking without being glamorous. She has been described as capricious and temperamental, and perhaps she was, but she must have had some charms, judging from Wright's reactions. An element of that attraction may have been her guarded attitude toward her children. Mrs. Orndorff, who was once their playmate, had the impression that Mrs. Cheney was not a very devoted mother (in those days, any woman with intellectual ambitions would have been so judged), and she certainly gave Frank that impression, since he, according to one newspaper account, referred to her three children—as if he would rather not know how many she really had.

As for the house he designed, it is now so overgrown that it is almost impossible to see from the sidewalk, but even before the forest had moved in, the home's air of discreet withdrawal had been remarked upon: one could, it was noted, see those in the road without being seen oneself. Mrs. Orndorff had a memory of dark and gloomy rooms decorated in green and brown and without curtains on the windows, another indication of Mamah's lack of interest in her traditional role. In Oak Park, where the only women Wright met would have conformed to social expectations, it must have been intriguing to meet someone so obviously apart from the crowd, almost an outsider, just as he was giving up the struggle to conform himself. Since Wright would subsequently choose partners who were distinctly different and individualistic, if not plainly eccentric by the standards of their day, it is safe to assume that this aspect of Mamah Borthwick had the most allure for him. Nevertheless, the affair might have come to a quiet end, bearing in mind that Mamah and Edwin did have a second child, Martha, in 1906, had it not been for another event that threatened

Wright's emotional equilibrium and threw his Lloyd Jones family into an uproar: the death of Uncle James. That came "in a summer twilight after a day, like all his days, of unremitting labor," his niece Maginel wrote. "They had been threshing oats, he and the others, and he had gone home tired and hot. The threshing machine, the water tank, and the hayracks were proceeding to another of his farms to be set up for the next day's work.

"The procession, led by the threshing machine and its tender, approached a small bridge over a stream. As the heavy engine crossed, the bridge gave way. There were shouts and a sickening crash. The engine and tender fell to the dry stream bed, spraying steam and hot water." The two drivers, George W. Smith and Charles Culver, were pinned under the engine and scalded to death.

"James raced to the scene of the accident. He climbed onto the engine wheel leaning far over, trying vainly to reach and rescue the victims; shock and haste made him clumsy, his foot slipped and he fell, breaking his leg which had caught in the spokes of the wheel." He sank into a coma after ten hours and died six days later, on October 22, 1907, without ever regaining consciousness. He left a wife and seven children, four girls and three boys. Jenkin Lloyd Jones officiated at the funeral, and all those left alive—John, Margaret, Anna, Enos and the Aunts, Nell and Jane, along with their children and grand-children, their nephews, nieces and cousins—were surely at the funeral in Unity Chapel because, the *Home News* of Spring Green reported, "people from all over the state gathered in an assembly larger than has ever been seen on such an occasion in this portion of Wisconsin."

Once the funeral was over and the Lloyd Joneses had assessed James's affairs, the true horror of the situation dawned on them all. In the years when James had been buying up small farms in the valley, his actions would have been seen as a progressive desire to improve and mechanize, farm on a cost-cutting scale and thereby increase his profits. For years his brothers and sisters, more prudent, one would have said, but certainly less adventurous, having declined to follow his example, suffered no losses for having made him loans. At first the crops were good and so were the prices. Other members of the family, finding no risk, joined the backers of James. But, during the depression years of the 1890s, prices began to fall. In 1890 a farmer could get fifty cents a bushel for corn; by 1898 he was lucky to get half that. "Oats, cattle, butter—it was all as bad, and volume simply could not beat the intricacies of an economy that now included something Wash-

A contemporary view of the Cheney house

The only known photograph of Mamah Borthwick Cheney, published in the
Chicago Tribune *at the time of her murder, in 1914*

ington called 'the foreign market,' " Maginel observed. Mortgage payments were in arrears, and creditors were banging on James's door. What looked like prudence had become the rashest folly, and everyone in his family was at risk.

Among those who had "signed" for James many times was brother Enos. He was forced to sell everything at a heavy loss, and was left with little more than his homestead. The others suffered to greater or lesser degrees. (Anna seems to have been the only one spared, having benefited more from James's largesse than the other way around.) The Aunts, James's other principal backers, were always ready to acknowledge they were not skilled businesswomen, and, no doubt, by 1907, they spent more than income from tuition fees provided; nevertheless, they had increased the school's size and outward prosperity. They had found the money to commission their nephew to build onto the property in 1901–03 an assembly room (also serving as a chapel), space for a library, a manual-training room, a kitchen, an arts and science hall and a gymnasium. Aunt Jane wrote, "They told the architect they wanted a Welsh feel about that [assembly] room which the material, oak druid and stone, would make possible. Over the stone fireplace a tablet was inserted, inscribed with an appropriate stanza of Gray's *Elegy* for [their] mother's sake. The . . . fender was formed of the conventionalized Welsh hat." The Aunts instructed the architect to carve on the balcony a verse from Isaiah that had been their father's favorite: "They that wait upon the Lord shall renew their strength; they shall mount up with wings as eagles; they shall run and not weary; they shall walk and not faint."

By 1907 Hillside was said to contain nearly a hundred teachers and pupils, most of them from Chicago. As an enterprise the school was flourishing, but by agreeing to back brother James, the Aunts had risked everything. Frank Lloyd Wright's brother-in-law, Andrew Taylor Porter, a Canadian who had met and married Wright's sister Jennie and had an import business in Montreal, where they lived, was drawn unwittingly into the middle of the crisis. He was persuaded to become business manager for the school in the summer of 1907, and began his work there just before James died. It is conceivable, though nowhere stated, that Andrew Porter could have realized just how heavily involved the Aunts were, and how debt-ridden James was, that summer; Porter later revealed that James owed $65,000—an immense sum in those days. Whether Porter challenged James with this information will never be known; in any event, he worked without salary for two years in a desperate attempt to save the school. But by September 1909—interestingly, just a month before Wright left his wife and family—the Aunts declared bankruptcy, and Hillside was up for sale. As for the wretched James, as Maginel wrote, "Despair, I think, was the executioner."

In mid-December 1907, two months after James's death, Wright explained to Darwin Martin that he had been unable to work on plans for some of his buildings because of numerous petty details that had assaulted him like "an aftermath of ruthless fate." He continued, "Work seems at a standstill entirely and I guess for two years there is a hold-fast and hang-tight period ahead. I am ill prepared for it and what the outcome will be I can't say"—perhaps the clearest reference available to the crises that beset him on all fronts. A year later, in December 1908, he told Martin, "In my own life there is much that is complex at least. Life is not simple as it should be if within myself I could find the harmony you have found. It is difficult for me to square my life with myself, and I cannot rest until it is done or I am dead." That mood of fatalism was seen clearly enough by Ashbee, who wrote that same month, "Lloyd Wright who 8 years ago was with his school full of fire and belief, and meantime has become famous and practically made 'the school of the Middle West' has grown bitter, he has drawn in upon himself, it is the bitterness of an anarchic socialism."

Why Wright, at the peak of his influence and success, should throw up his practice and leave Chicago forever, not to mention abandoning his wife and six children, is a conundrum that has defied analysis. Some authors have concluded that it was the result of his inability to receive the national recognition that he believed was his due, but others have questioned that this was true. Some have put it down to his own conviction that he was never meant to be a husband and father, but an unsuccessful marriage alone cannot account for his throwing over a successful practice as well; one would expect him to settle the one without completely jeopardizing the other if he were shrewd, and Wright was shrewd. Wright's failure to capture a prized commission, that of designing a mansion for Harold and Edith Rockefeller McCormick, heirs to two of the country's greatest fortunes (it went instead to Charles A. Platt), is also given as a reason. This, too, seems inadequate, since Wright had designed many handsome houses that were never built. Wright himself is not very helpful. Writing about his flight, he omits all mention of one principal in the case, i.e., Mamah Borthwick Cheney, and acts as if explanations were in-adequate: "Because I did not know what I wanted I wanted to go away." The only clue he gives is the title to this particular segment of his autobiography: "The Closed Road."

It has been suggested that Wright's particular Welsh background, with its roots in the ancient animistic Celtic veneration for nature, along with his early indoctrination into radical Unitarian thought, had fitted him to be particularly receptive to Ruskin's ideas, i.e., that right emotion, true feeling and lofty thought were all included in the concept of what was beautiful, even that the perception of beauty was a test of one's morality and inner integrity. Added to this is the concept of the church as the true home, even one's only home (coming from the Welsh experience), and the Arts and Crafts manipulation of that thought into the idea of the home as a kind of church, a place in which to celebrate the sanctity of family life. Perhaps because of Wright's awareness of what a failed marriage meant, he was determined to make his own work, to make it into a perfect marriage. His whole architectural philosophy was based on the Arts and Crafts concept that a house should express an ideal of marriage and family life. No doubt he thought, sincerely, as had Ruskin, that "all architecture proposes an effect on the human mind, not merely the service of the human frame"; therefore the perfect house would bring forth the desired result, and if it did not there was something wrong with the house—or the architect. To reject the concept of marriage as a sacrament in favor of the radical notion that it was simply a convenient social arrangement was also to reject the Arts and Crafts Movement as well, since this belief was so central to its scale of values. He must also have felt that, as an artist, he had taken its concepts as far as he could go and that the movement was losing momentum. The road had come to a dead end—this particular road, at least.

There are some useful clues to his feelings at the time in his letters to Darwin Martin. He wrote, "I cannot make the standard of conduct I raised for myself—the moral standard for any human being—I believed it was right—but superhuman." Perhaps in his heart of hearts he longed to be able to admit that he was not the colossus he aspired to be but simply a flawed human being who had made the same mistakes in his personal life as everyone else. Faced with a superhuman task, he did what he had done as a boy, left alone in a field to tackle a man's work, and what Uncle James had just done: he let the whole edifice come crashing down, taking him with it.

His actions would be bound to have a major effect not just on his wife, children, clients and friends, but the whole Lloyd Jones clan as well. Jenkin Lloyd Jones might be particularly censorious—they had, after all, been estranged by the Lincoln Center fiasco—and ready to condemn this nephew about whom he had grave doubts. Wright was on the defensive, in view of the Lloyd Jones censoriousness, therefore taking pains to justify his acts and portray himself as a man obeying a higher law. The manner in which he condemns the hypocritical attitudes of his society is especially naïve, and there is an element of wounded pride in the way he proposes himself as the model of a superior man, and something more ominous in his conclusions: at one time, he wrote to Martin, "I go to the cross. . . ." An even bolder theme can be discerned in an essay he wrote for an exhibition of Japanese prints four years before, in 1906. This essay has less to do with prints than it does with the role of the artist. If Wright's original idea of the architect had been in the terms proposed by his mother —"Jenkin preached; Frank builds"—then his abandonment of the Celtic cross for the pure square heralded a philosophical shift. It meant that he was rejecting the dictates of his religion and its morality and was preparing to place himself beyond their reach, on a pinnacle far removed from the world-as-it-is, a hero of mythical stature, a poet, a Druid. His statement makes this very clear: "All the sheer wisdom of science, the cunning of politics, and the prayers of religion can but stand and wait for the revelation; awaiting the artist's conventional-ization of life principle that shall make our social living beautiful, organically true."

In taking this view, Wright may well have been attempting to relieve some inner pressures. Instead of seeing himself as ordained for an elevated, perhaps unattainable goal, he has shifted to the idea of Taliesin, the artist as Superman, divinely endowed, and therefore never to be challenged or questioned. Not only did this Romantic conception rid him of the weight of moral censure, but it lightened some impossible inner burdens. Whatever he did was a work of genius, because he did it. It was a very successful view from an emotional standpoint, and he held to it for the rest of his life, but it did contribute to the impression he gave of being impossibly stiff-necked and authoritarian, and his arrogance became legendary. Few people realized how compensatory those comments actually were.

Wright's lonely conviction of righteousness—Truth Against the World—was to provide a source of strength in the difficult years ahead. But it had a dark side: the ideal of himself as misunderstood and persecuted genius encouraged him to see motes only in the eyes of others. He looked at life from a distorted perspective, and the picture he saw, or thought he saw, embittered him.

Whatever else can be said about Wright's state of mind at this pivotal moment, it is safe to say that he was the most un-self-aware of men. The women who attracted him would, therefore, always seem to have a superior knowledge of human behavior—certainly, they were clever manipulators—and a way of making him feel at home with himself. This may have been Mamah Borthwick's great strength, and the evidence will show that Wright was incapable of living alone and would always look for an immediate replacement once "the woman" was out of his life. "I am a house divided against itself by circumstances I can not control," he wrote to his mother from Europe in the summer of 1910 when he had decided, at least temporarily, to return to his wife and children. "I can face them and down them or go down with them trying to get whole again within—but *again* is not the word— I have always as you know lived a divided life, but always with a hope—undefined—but a hope. Now it will be without the *hope*. . . ." Anna kept his letter and folded it into a book of mementos.

8

Flower in the Crannied Wall

Smoke leaps up,
Grey like a wolf, and all the world
Crackles with the sounds of pain and death.
"Storm on Land"
Poems from the Old English

By early 1909 Wright was looking for a pretext to make his first trip to Europe. He had been urged to visit London by Ashbee for several years. He was interested in the latest developments in Germany and Austria, and he also had the further encouragement of Mamah Borthwick Cheney, who had visited the Continent on her honeymoon and wanted to return to Berlin. Everything was conspiring in that direction and, as luck would have it, a German philosopher, Kuno Francke, in Boston for a year as visiting lecturer at Harvard, came to see Wright's work and subsequently put the architect in touch with a Berlin publisher, Ernst Wasmuth. This led to an invitation from Wasmuth. He intended to publish a complete folio of Wright's work to that date, a handsome edition known as the *Ausgeführte Bauten und Entwürfe* that would become a collector's item. It was the first such invitation from any direction and it seemed heaven-sent. Wright would, ostensibly, go to Berlin to prepare this volume of drawings, photographs and floor plans, and only those close to him would know the true circumstances. As might be expected he entrusted the work of closing down the studio to the first likely candidate, a young architect named Herman von Holst, and spent his remaining time assembling his materials and working out a complex business arrangement with Wasmuth by which he would buy the American rights. To do this, he borrowed ten thousand dollars from Francis Little, a former client and dedicated collector of Japanese prints, at 6 percent interest. Little held a portfolio of prints as collateral.

Wright and Mrs. Cheney made their plans with care. Sometime in the summer of 1909 she went to Boulder, Colorado, to visit a friend, taking her children John, aged seven, and Martha, aged three. Her husband had his suspicions, he said later, but did not believe them until he received a letter from her asking him to come and get the children. This version of events is contradicted by his testimony at the divorce proceedings, which was that she had left him in June of 1909 and had told him then that she did not intend to return. Cheney arrived in Boulder in early October to find that his wife was gone. She had met Wright in New York and had embarked for Europe.

The lovers arrived in Berlin, giving as their mailing address Wasmuth's office on the Markgrafenstrasse, and took rooms in a hotel, registering as Mr. and Mrs. Wright. All this was discovered and became front-page news shortly afterward, two or three weeks at most, since it was published by the *Chicago Tribune* on Sunday, November 7. The ostensible explanation for the article was that an alert foreign correspondent had discovered the false hotel registration. Since the possibility of a newspaper reporter's scanning the hotel registers in any city in pursuit of irregularities is remote, one is left to conclude that someone in Chicago wanted the elopement exposed and told the newspaper where to start looking. It is the kind of maneuver Anna was capable of because, at least at first, she saw Mamah Cheney as more of a threat than Catherine, and took the latter's side. It is also possible that Edwin Cheney may have been looking for evidence, since he soon filed for divorce. As for the papers, ever since the architect Stanford White was shot and killed by Harry K. Thaw over a scandal involving the latter's wife in 1906, journalists had been alerted to the exciting possibilities provided by the world of architecture; here was an almost parallel case. The deserted wife and the deserted husband were subjected to almost daily grillings, and when these failed to solicit sufficient indignation and outrage, the writers of the articles themselves were obliged to fall back on their own speculations about "two abandoned homes where children play at the hearthsides," a "fly-by-night journey through Germany," "strange infatuations" and a love "now trampled upon and spurned."

If the Cheney marriage was ending more or less by mutual consent the same cannot be said of the Wrights'. Catherine's early comments were that she and Frank were united in their determination to break the terrible hold of this "vampire." Her curious explanation was that he was the innocent victim, in other words, but with her help he would win out. She continued to believe with a faith that amounted to self-delusion that he would return, her son Llewellyn thought. During that year of 1909–10 she kept a "day book," marking each child's birthday with a lock of hair and a photograph and enclosing pictures cut from magazines, jokes, poems and the like, her theme being her love, her lonely vigil and her conviction that all would end happily.

If Catherine was grieving she was also understandably angry and resentful. When Frank did return a year later and she discovered that the affair was not over, she gave vent to her feelings in a letter to the Ashbees. Her words reveal not only her sense of being the helpless pawn in a game played by others, but almost of being an object, something to be bartered and sold like a stock market commodity. Or, their marriage was a bank account and Frank was the banker. Now some "upstart" had come along and closed out the account, the one that had been nurtured lovingly through the years—and with her husband's vigorous support. It was all too much. Not surprisingly, future arguments between Frank and Catherine would revolve around money. It was said that she refused to give Frank a divorce on her mother's advice, fearing that it would mean the end of any financial child support. Perhaps the best measure of Catherine's state of mind is provided by her son David. He recalled that when his father left, he, aged thirteen, was told he was now head of the household. They were left with a grocery bill of nine hundred dollars, he said. His indignation was still vivid some seventy years later.

There are no letters or diaries to chart the course of the love affair between Frank and Mamah, but, from the evidence, one can safely assume that he was blissfully happy. She seems to have decided on a divorce almost at once, and he, his zest for life renewed, threw himself into preparing the Wasmuth edition. They divided their time between Berlin and Fiesole, and when Lloyd was sent for, to join his father and a draftsman, Taylor Woolley, in preparing the new book, he found his father "already established in the little villino 'Fortuna' just below the Piazza Michelangelo and the David statue—in Florence." Italy had the predictable effect on Wright. He wrote lyrically to Ashbee about the beauty of the Florentine valley and catching sight of it "in the drifting mists or shining clear and marvelous in the Italian sunshine—opalescent, irridescent." He had been reading Howells, Ruskin and Vasari in Florence and was entranced by this "wondrous brood of Florentines . . . sculptor painters and painter sculptor architects. . . . I declare you cannot tell here—there was then no line drawn—between mediums—." Mamah had settled in Berlin and took a job teaching at a "young ladies seminary." Wright decided to return to his family, and his letter to his mother, that summer of 1910, was lengthy, justifying himself and accusing his family of failing to give him emotional support in his time of need. He enclosed with it a copy of his letter to Catherine that spelled out the terms of his return.

Wright reached Chicago's Union Station at five o'clock on the afternoon of Saturday, October 8, 1910, from New York, where he had disembarked a few days before. He drove to his Oak Park home, which was ablaze with lights. "The faces of the younger Wright children were wreathed in smiles," a reporter wrote, "and Mrs. Wright's countenance reflected the pleasure. . . . She was in buoyant spirits and conveyed the impression that a burden of care had dropped from her shoulders. Her younger son threw his arms about her and laughed. . . ."

"*It's true this time*," W. E. Martin wrote to his brother Darwin two days later. "He has returned as stated . . . and I have just seen him in the 'flesh.' " He looked much grayer, with long hair that just missed his shoulders, his manner had lost none of its mischievous charm, and he was wearing the kind of outfit Martin had not seen except on a Quaker Oats package: knee trousers, long stockings and broad-brimmed brown hat, worn with panache. Martin wrote that Wright had telephoned to ask if, as a test of his affection, he would drive Wright to the station to get his luggage? "His nerve was staggering," Martin wrote, "and I could not for the moment know what to say . . . and in my embarrassment told him would call for him as we went to church and so would go on down for his 'luggage,' but Winnie [Mrs. Martin] positively refused to be seen with him in the

auto and I didn't know what the duce [*sic*] to do. . . ." Martin
compromised by agreeing to meet Wright at the station. The latter
appeared promptly, apologizing for having put his client's friendship
to so acid a test. Wright's mien, however, was hardly what one would
expect of a repentant sinner. He called for his luggage in the loudest
possible voice and made a perfect spectacle of himself shouting, "All
aboard, all the way to Oak Park by auto!" Martin took the back streets
home.

As Bernard Shaw, writing in 1908, observed, ". . . open violation
of the marriage laws means either downright ruin or such inconven-
ience and disablement as a prudent man or woman would get married
ten times over rather than face." All those in Oak Park who had seen
him hurtling down their streets in the "Yellow Devil," wearing
"funny" clothes and his hair too long, or who had disliked his houses,
or had had painful financial dealings with him, rose up in righteous
wrath. Mrs. Johnston, Charles Roberts's granddaughter, recalled, "It
was the most awful scandal that ever happened. I was very young and
they tried to keep it from me—'That wasn't nice'—but it really
finished him in Oak Park. No one would have anything more to do
with him." Her mother's, Mrs. Charles White's, explanation was that
Wright had somehow got himself mixed up with Mrs. Cheney because
he never had "a bit of sense" about women. That was the charitable
view. That month Rev. George M. Luccock of First Presbyterian
Church in Oak Park preached a sermon on the theme of adultery.
Such a man had "lost all sense of morality and religion and is damnably
to be blamed," he said.

Wright had expected criticism but seemed genuinely taken aback
by its intensity. As he wrote to Darwin Martin two weeks after his
return, "I am accustomed to being alien but not to see women drawing
their skirts aside as they pass and my old friends (?) crossing the road
to avoid me. . . ." He had already lost some clients, and would lose
others. Arthur Heurtley, who had written so glowingly about Wright
to his German friend in 1908, had nothing but bad news to report
by 1912. Wright's friends had all deserted him, and his future was
in ruins. His former draftsman, Charles White, who left to set up his
own practice, wrote to his former employer to say he had heard about
the exodus and asking him to send such clients his way. (One assumes
that the request was ignored.)

The reason Wright gave for leaving Mamah, that he did not want
the beauty of their relationship soiled by too much daily contact,

sounds like a rationalization and a grossly unkind one at that. It seems more likely that Wright had worked out a careful strategy before he went home. This was that Mamah should stay in Germany until her divorce could be obtained, in the summer of 1911, on the grounds of a two-year separation. She could then discreetly return. Meantime he would remodel his home and studio, providing one-half for Catherine and the children and for income property in the other half. His mother, who had decided that the break was inevitable and had now thrown in her lot with her son, would cooperate by selling her Oak Park house and buying land in Spring Green on which to build anew.

He had told his mother he was returning without hope, but this was hardly true. He was back full of dynamism and high spirits and prepared for battle. One guesses that he had chosen Darwin Martin as his next financial backer because of the large sums his ambitious plans required, but if he were going to persuade the hidebound Martin to play this role, Wright would need to present a façade of repentance and reform, at least for a few months. Since, of all people who might have helped him with his luggage, Wright telephoned Darwin Martin's brother, one assumes that his strategy began at the Oak Park train station. He wanted to make sure the right person had proof positive that he was not only back but also back in his own house.

If this was the plan, it was brilliantly carried forward. Wright's first letter to Martin, written just four days after his return, was an artful amalgam of flattery, noble sentiments, feigned remorse and flowery vows to reform. "What I have seen and felt in this old world . . . has mellowed many harsh crudities and rubbed off many corners. I think I am a stronger man and a better architect." It was also clear from this letter that Wright was entirely in earnest about restoring his architectural practice. He could not let his work die, he wrote, and was prepared to fight for it. Meantime, Wright wrote to Larkin asking for the preposterous loan of twenty thousand dollars, which he must have known he stood no chance of getting. He spelled out his needs: money to pay a first installment on the Wasmuth publication, due in a month, money to repay Little and release his collection of prints, and money to remodel his house. Then he sat back and waited for Larkin to refuse, and Martin to unleash the predictable lecture.

That soon arrived. "You see I am bad, bad to the core, so what's the use," Wright wrote to his "dear lecturer," nevertheless managing to defend himself nimbly. He sent Martin a copy of his letter to Larkin, merely to inform him about his financial position. That was at the end of October. By mid-November Wright had not only extracted a loan from Martin to pay for the German publication installment but was talking him into settling the Little debt. "I suppose you have a lurking suspicion that Wright having been swept off his feet once may be again—if he gets large sums in his hands—but this is wide of the mark—I am due to make good all around, pay my debts and stand clear. . . . Go cautiously as you like you will find no trickery. . . ." Wright wrote earnestly, and no doubt sincerely. Once the debt with Little had been settled, releasing a Japanese print collection that Wright soon claimed to have sold (for twenty-one thousand dollars), he moved into phase three of his plan. His mother had bought "a small farm up country," meaning Spring Green, and was pressed for cash, because she had not yet sold her house in Oak Park, he told Martin. Perhaps Martin could help? Martin obligingly assumed the mortgage on Anna's house. The next step was to finance the remodeling project for the home and studio. Martin allowed himself to be talked into giving Wright something called a "trust-deed" loan. He would discover that Wright had been cheerfully selling off bits of his equity in that property for some time, a practice he enjoyed, since he used it forever after, sometimes with such calamitous success that the legal knots thus tied were impossible to unravel. In this particular case it seemed Little had an interest, and so did Mrs. Wright, and there were mechanics' liens on the property; Martin was undeterred. By the autumn of 1911 Catherine was writing, not to her husband, but to their banker, asking for his help in settling persistent creditors who were besieging her hourly "by the phone and door-bell." Wright eventually persuaded Martin to advance a total of twenty-five thousand dollars and was loud in his praise of the latter's sterling qualities. Martin wrote, "What you term 'a fine nature and a good heart' is commonly termed 'sucker.' . . ."

As for the borrower, he was in peak form, insisting that he never intended to see Mamah again while jumping on the first boat for Europe the moment he had some money in his pocket. (The ostensible reason for the trip, he told Martin early in 1911, was to resolve some problems with the Wasmuth edition in Berlin.) Some indication of the single-mindedness of his determination to establish his life on a new footing may be gathered from his comment, at this time, that "I am trying to live up to a more severe and extended scheme of human conduct than a man may perhaps but I shall die trying—and perhaps—*of* trying." Only one indication survives that Wright could, just the same, have been experiencing some anxiety as his plan moved successfully forward. Mamah Borthwick Cheney was divorced in August—she then reverted to her maiden name—and a month beforehand, Wright had a car accident that injured his arm and made his hand useless for months. That, oddly enough, had happened just three months after he had determined to "die trying." As for Catherine, she vacillated between an uncomfortable awareness of the financial and emotional abyss and her typically obstinate belief in a happy ending. She just had a feeling, she told Martin, that it would all be over in two years' time. It was December 1912.

In one of his letters to Martin, Wright mentioned that he would "see about building a small house" for his mother. That was in April 1911, and although he did not dare tell Martin, what he really had in mind was a house for himself. Anna was buying the hillside that she knew Frank loved, on land immediately adjoining the Hillside Home School, owned by one of the uncles. This would help to explain why Anna, that penny-pinching lady, had taken the highly imprudent step, for her, of buying a new home before she had sold the first— someone in the family must have urgently needed the money. The idea of Taliesin seems to have taken shape in her son's mind during his stay in Florence. In Fiesole, he had been much struck by the enchanting Villa Medici, which, according to Vasari, had been designed by Michelozzo for Giovanni, the son of Cosimo de' Medici. As Wright was admiring it, the house was being acquired by Lady Sybil Cutting, a socially prominent and wealthy widow and occasional writer, who would marry Geoffrey Scott, a brilliant young architectural historian, himself the future author of a classic, *The Architecture of Humanism* (1914). The Villa Medici, one of the great country houses of Italy, is situated on a hillside with commanding views of the Tuscan countryside and is terraced with gardens on the steep slopes around it. True to his nature whenever he was arrested by a vision of beauty, Wright spent part of his year designing *his* version of a Tuscan country house on the slopes around Florence. Surviving sketches show that while the overall feeling of the design, planned for Mamah and himself, is Prairie Style, it has been strongly influenced by classical dictates and surrounded by high walls enclosing secret gardens, in imitation of the Villa Medici.

The Villa Medici was on the side of a hill; Wright placed his own Wisconsin country house in the same position and emphasized the importance of this choice forever afterward. The experience of designing for Fiesole seems to have galvanized his imagination and brought it to bear on the challenge of designing a house for himself that would express everything he thought and believed, the summit of his mature development as an architect. The passage describing the birth of the idea of Taliesin in *An Autobiography* gives a fascinating insight into the way his mind worked when stimulated to its finest achievements. "I saw the hill-crown back of the house as one mass of apple trees in bloom . . . I saw plum trees, fragrant drifts of snow-white in the spring . . . I saw thickly pendent clusters of rubies like tassels in the dark leaves of the currant bushes . . . I saw the vineyard . . . I saw the spirited, well-schooled horses. . . . I looked forward to peacocks Javanese and white on the low roofs of the buildings. . . . Yes, Taliesin should be a garden and a farm behind a real workshop and a good home. I saw it all. . . ." As Norris Kelly Smith wrote, "Perhaps it is the distinguishing gift of the genuine artist that he thinks directly in terms of shapes and expresses himself verbally only afterward, if . . . at all." The maze of courtyards, terraces and flower borders interleaved within the Taliesin compound, with their unobtrusive retaining walls and shallow flights of steps, call to mind the hill gardens around Fiesole, as if the walls had always been there and the vines of ivy and low shrubs, the rock plants taking root in the crevices, had sprung from the stones themselves. At about this time Wright gave pride of place to a sculpture by Richard Bock, an artist with whom he often collaborated. The work, *Flower in the Crannied Wall*, named for the famous poem by Alfred, Lord Tennyson, had originally been designed for the house Wright built for Susan L. Dana in Springfield, Illinois, some years before. It depicts a nude (presumably the muse of architecture) constructing a tower from geometric blocks. Both shapes—the delicately rounded upper body and arms of the nude, and the phalliclike tower she is building—are arising from the same piece of stone, presumably meant to be read as a statement of Wright's belief that architecture receives its power from the life-force and that both man and his creation are in an identical state of becoming. He placed the statue in a pivotal position, with the house below it, growing like a ledge in the rock, and the undisturbed hillside above. Neil Levine wrote, "The sculptured figure . . . no longer points to a distinction between geometry and nature, or abstraction and representation, but rather signifies a continuity or identity of the two." To another observer, Wright's figure has a totemic significance. He sees

*Flower in the Crannied Wall: an original terra-cotta sculpture by
Richard Bock for the entrance to the Dana house*

her as a kind of corn dolly, guardian of the garden, seated beneath
the oaks reminiscent of Druid groves, meant to symbolize "the spiritual
forces which tie the architect, the house, and the land together,"
Thomas Beeby wrote. He also pointed out that the sculpture is placed
so as to face water spilling into a stone basin, originally designed to
have a masonry circle that would seem to indicate "its sacred nature.
. . . The sacred hill temples of the Druids often had a well of oracular
nature, the spring of Poetic Imagination." Exactly what *Flower in the
Crannied Wall* meant to him was never spelled out by Wright, but
then, none of the symbols that seemed to mean the most to him were
ever explained and there is enough of a clue in the poem itself to make

his reference clear. Speaking of the flower, Tennyson writes, ". . . but if I could understand / What you are . . . / I should know what God and man is."

Wright was probably well aware that the construction of Taliesin must be kept secret because, if it were known, the news would threaten the shaky façade of his marriage, with unknown repercussions on Martin. It was his bad luck that the *Chicago Examiner* learned of its construction in the autumn of 1911 and published an article remarkable for its insinuations, portraying a man still maintaining a pretext of family harmony while actually preparing what would soon be called a "love nest" or "love cottage" for the new woman in his life. A similar accusation, containing numerous inaccuracies, appeared three months later in the *Chicago Tribune* under the headline ARCHITECT WRIGHT IN NEW ROMANCE WITH 'MRS. CHENEY.' The article claimed that Wright and Mamah Borthwick had been living quietly at the new bungalow for some months and that he had been seen fording a stream, up to his shoulders in icy water, carrying the lady aloft, who was exhibiting, the article continued, "a good deal of lingerie of a quality not often on display in that part of Wisconsin." Back at Oak Park, questions were being adroitly fielded by his seventeen-year-old daughter, Catherine: "Just say for Mr. Wright and Mrs. Wright and all the little Wrights that we don't know anything about this awful story and it must be untrue." It was a brave try, but unsuccessful. Two days later Wright was forced to make his first public statement, in which he went over the arguments that had been well aired in letters to Martin. His version of the story, which tended to be given in the third person as if he were retelling a universal legend, had to do with the fact that they had married too young, had grown apart, and he believed he could do more for his family by separating. He concluded brightly, "The ordinary man cannot live without rules to guide his conduct. It is infinitely more difficult to live without rules, but that is what the really honest, sincere, thinking man is compelled to do. And I think when a man has displayed some spiritual power, has given concrete evidence of his ability to see and to feel the higher and better things of life, we ought to go slow in deciding he has acted badly."

If Wright thought this amiable description of the case would set everything to rights, he was to be disappointed. As transparently self-serving as his argument was, it did have a hidden motive: he had been goaded into it because of the effect his notoriety was having on the Lloyd Jones family and especially the Aunts. The Hillside Home School had been saved from ruin, but barely. At the bankruptcy proceedings two years before, an "unnamed friend" had come forward to buy the stock in the Aunts' interest; the friend turned out to be Jenkin Lloyd Jones. As Wright's affairs became front-page news, Nell and Jane were attempting to buy back their lost control and argue their brother out of the conviction that they did not have enough business sense to run the school. The last thing they needed at that moment was to lose money, and now one parent after another was withdrawing his or her children. As a Chicago businessman bluntly explained to Wright, he was a bad influence, and unless he could be persuaded to move from Hillside the school would be ruined. Wright's solution was to carry forward the fiction that he was nowhere near Hillside, geographically speaking, and had nothing to do with the school. It was unfair that anyone should think so, he wrote in a public statement, which was then notarized. Meantime the Lloyd Jones family leaked the news to the papers that it was about to sit in judgment on its erring member. In the middle of it all, the sheriff of Spring Green, W. L. Pengally, was under pressure to have Wright arrested. He refused, saying that he could not see that the architect was violating any state law. Mamah Borthwick said not a word for publication. Edwin Cheney quietly made plans to remarry.

If Wright's public statements were designed to place his acts in the best possible light for his family's benefit, his letters to Martin were more revealing. After two years of delicate maneuvering, he had achieved all that he had set out to do when he returned to Oak Park, and felt free to let his defiance show: "I can no longer endure the position in which as a husband and father I found myself placed. It grew up on me as a property institution always grows, with its mortgages and restrictions and absurd demands that one feel what others declare one ought. It is a barnyard institution. I am a wild bird—and must stay free [et cetera]." No doubt the immediate need to dissociate his address from that of the Hillside Home School played a role, but the declaration of independence must also be considered significant: he signed his address, that January of 1912, as Taliesin.

In 1905, at the peak of his success in Oak Park, Wright received thirteen commissions; when he left in 1909, he had ten. The following year it dropped to five, and then, in 1911, the number increased to eight. However, in the years 1912 and 1913 the total for each year dropped to three. One, however, was enormous: a project to design a "pleasure gardens" that would fill an entire city block in Chicago and serve all year-round as a center for concerts, dancing, drinking and dining. Work on the Midway Gardens, as it was called, came the same year that he was pursuing an even more tantalizing commission, that of designing a new hotel in Tokyo that would cost $7 million and garner architects' fees of from $40,000 to $50,000. Wright's name had been put forward by Frederick W. Gookin, a prominent Chicago banker and print collector, who had bought from Wright and who had high connections in Japanese government circles. An invitation to submit preliminary plans followed in due course. Then Wright went to Japan with Mamah Borthwick in January 1913, staying for six months. While there he drew up preliminary plans, studied the soils and suggested some choices for building materials, besides purchasing more prints. They returned in May, and, a month later, Wright was telling Martin he had won the prize, somewhat prematurely as it turned out, because he was not formally named as architect until 1916. That year of 1913 went by in a predictable fashion. Wright was building a sumptuous new mansion for his former client Francis W. Little, his first in Minnesota, with a fifty-five-foot living room overlooking Robinson Bay on Lake Minnetonka, and a beautiful library. When the house was demolished, both rooms were spared and are now in museums. John and Lloyd had joined their father in partnership in his offices in Orchestra Hall, Chicago, and Wright was fending off demands from Martin for interest payments due on his various loans. Wright was complaining that "the other architects are doing their best to put me out of business."

As the pace of work on the Midway Gardens quickened in an effort to get the vast project opened by the summer of 1914, Wright was spending every waking moment on the site and, he wrote, had barely time to sleep or eat. He had somehow managed to arrange for an exhibition of his recent work at the Art Institute of Chicago as well, because "It was imperative that I do something to let people know that I am up and doing." He had been trying to get the Oak Park property either rented or sold, and had asked Catherine for a divorce. A copy of his letter, dated November 22, 1914, is in the Taliesin Archive, but research has shown that the date was actually 1913 and has been altered. (No one knows why.) Wright did his best to persuade her that she was "conserving nothing, destroying much by your present unfair hold," and suggested that she accept a share of the profits "of the time during which our partnership lasted and as much more as I could reasonably make it." He argued that if she used the grounds of desertion, the matter could be settled with discretion. He ended with the thought that her position was as demoralizing as his own and that her objections were no longer valid. Given Wright's usual eloquence, it was a surprisingly lame letter, and it had the predictable result: Catherine was not to set him free for another nine years.

Catherine, at that period, was using every remaining card. Since "the woman" was still in Wright's life and was likely to remain so, Catherine's terms were that the children could see their father only if his mistress were not there. Frank considered that a rank injustice, she wrote in a letter to Janet Ashbee in the summer of 1913. She went on to describe complacently how distressed and agitated Frank was becoming and how (she had heard) the stress of his new situation was gradually undermining his self-confidence. It was awful to think of him in that predicament, but she knew how stubborn he could be once his mind was made up. It was the same confused mixture of sentimentality, unwarranted optimism and a kind of pious resentment. On the one hand, she felt as if her load was being lightened at last (while Frank sank deeper into his self-imposed morass); on the other hand, she never knew from one moment to the next what new disaster would bury them all.

Meantime Frank and Mamah were publishing her translations of writings by Ellen Key, the Swedish feminist, especially those having to do with free love and "The Woman Movement." Mamah was living quietly at Taliesin and was reported to be working on a book. She was no doubt delighted to leave household affairs to Frank, but was definitely interested in his projects. He was arranging a new exhibition of his work, to be held in San Francisco, and a number of his employees were living temporarily at Taliesin so as to make the work easier; Mamah was very much involved with their progress. For his part, Frank seems to have been genuinely proud of her attainments and was proposing to buy the local Spring Green paper, the *Weekly Home News*, and make her its editor. Andrew Porter and his wife, Jennie, Wright's sister, were spending the summer in Tan-y-Deri (Under the Oaks), the cottage beside Hillside school that Wright had built for them in 1907. With them were their two remaining children, Anna, aged eleven, and Frank Wright Porter (born in 1909 and loyally named for his uncle at the height of the crisis). James Andrew Porter, aged thirteen, had died two years before.

Mamah Borthwick had her children there for a month every summer since, unlike the other injured spouse in the case, Edwin Cheney had not imposed conditions on her contacts with John and Martha. Judging from the reminiscences of Edna Meudt, their local playmate, a nine-year-old from Dodgeville who became a Wisconsin poet, Mamah Borthwick's children were frequent visitors. The story of that summer in 1914 belongs, in a way, to the children who witnessed it, or were its victims. Edna's special friend was Martha, who would be nine in September. She had a beautiful sapphire ring, to match her eyes, and the two of them liked to play house with their dolls between the triple trunks of a gnarled tree in Willow Walk. Edna recalled that neither John nor Martha liked Taliesin very much, and usually wanted to go home after a few days. Perhaps it was the strangeness of the house: "Incense, on the floors creamy bears with no insides, birds that talk back, showy flowers she never knew, wall-hangings to be put out of her country mind," Edna wrote in her poem *A Summer Day That Changed the World*. Or perhaps it was the undercurrent of gossip and disapproval from grown-ups who kept children away from Taliesin because of the "goings-on." This censorious attitude had certainly been the reason why their other friend, Verna Ross Orndorff, had not been allowed to join them that weekend. She had been invited, and her mother was prepared to let her visit, but her father refused. So she went with her parents and the second Mrs. Cheney, the former Elsie Millor, and a niece of the Cheneys', Jessie, on a two-day trip to Lake Delavan in Wisconsin, some sixty-five miles north of Chicago. Edwin Cheney was on a business trip that weekend. Frank Lloyd Wright had dashed back to Chicago in midweek for some last-minute work on the Midway Gardens. Mamah Borthwick and her children were at Taliesin along with a work crew that included William (Billy) Weston, thirty-five, a tall, spare man with a sandy mustache who had, as master carpenter, built Taliesin; his son, Ernest, aged thirteen; Thomas Brunker of Ridgeway, aged fifty-six, the foreman; Emil Brodelle, architectural draftsman, aged thirty; Herbert Fritz, another draftsman, aged nineteen; and David Lindblom, a landscape gardener. That day, August 15, 1914, was, Edna wrote, "Saturday, our Lady's Assumption in August, / Church again tomorrow. Oxeye daisies suggest / picking for the altar, gophers run a rickrack / across dusty roads. Their pretty valley / dozes that near-noon hour." Dressed in her best clothes, and astride the mare Beauty, Edna was on her way to Taliesin three miles distant to invite Martha and John back home to see the threshing.

Julian Carlton and his wife, Gertrude, were originally from Barbados and had been recommended to Wright by John Vogelsang, the Chicago restaurateur who had the contract for the Midway Gardens. Carlton waited at table, did the work of the house and was general handyman; his wife did most of the cooking. He was young, of medium height, and slender, intelligent and quite well educated. He was not known to drink and appeared to have an equable disposition, but was nevertheless generally disliked and distrusted. Billy Weston had been overheard by a Spring Green tavern keeper to say, two weeks before, that Carlton was polite and smart, but "the most desperate, hotheaded fellow" he had ever met. A witness subsequently recalled Lindblom's saying that Carlton had given him an "awful calling-down" and said that "if anyone around there ever did him any dirt he would send him to hell in a minute." There was the further matter of a dispute that had taken place between Carlton and Brodelle a few days earlier. It was believed that Brodelle had called Carlton a "black son of a bitch" because he refused to saddle his horse. Carlton subsequently referred to this argument with Brodelle and said he had to defend himself because everyone there (not only Brodelle) was "picking on him" and complaining about him to Wright.

As one newspaper account had it, the Carltons had been at Taliesin for only a few weeks when they gave two weeks' notice, the reason being that only Gertrude was homesick for Chicago. This version is contradicted by that given in another local paper, the *Dodgeville Chronicle*, a day later, which seems more plausible. According to this account the Carltons seemed ideal servants at first, "but something seemed to cause Mamah Borthwick to dislike Carlton. What it was may never be known. . . . One of the survivors of the tragedy said whatever happened had led Mamah Borthwick to tell the negro and his wife that their time would be up on Saturday night." Perhaps Mamah Borthwick sensed that something was going very wrong, that August Saturday morning. She is said to have sent a telegram to Wright, which arrived that afternoon at two o'clock. It read, "Come as quickly as you possibly can. Something terrible has happened." Then there was the statement given by Carlton's wife. She said that for several days before their departure her husband had been acting strangely and slept with a hatchet in a bag beside his bed. She said, "De las' I seen he was runnin' round de house, actin' crazy and talkin' bout killin' folks."

The two draftsmen, Brodelle and Fritz, foreman Brunker, Billy Weston, his son, Ernest, and David Lindblom, the gardener, were all having lunch in the main dining room on the west side of the house, a small room about twelve feet square. Mamah Borthwick and her children were sitting elsewhere, in an enclosed screened porch overlooking the Wisconsin River. It was separated from the main dining room by a passageway some twenty-five feet long.

Carlton, dressed in a white coat, saw both parties to their seats and served the meals. Once they were eating, he came to Weston and was given permission to get some gasoline that he needed, he said, to clean a rug. He then went quietly outside, bolted the doors and windows and splashed several buckets of gasoline on rugs inside the house and all around the outside. He seized his hatchet, warned his wife to flee and apparently—the exact sequence is unclear—set a blaze going and dashed to the screened porch. His very first victim was Mamah Borthwick. He plunged his hatchet into the center of her head as she sat. The weapon went through her skull into her brain just above her forehead, with one tremendous blow. She must have died instantly. He then attacked her son, John, who also died in his chair; his charred bones were all that could be found. It was theorized that Carlton may have doused both corpses with gasoline and set them ablaze. Martha was trying to escape when he caught up with her and landed at least three blows behind her right ear, one above the other; one penetrated her skull. There was also the imprint of the head of the hatchet under her right eye. She was found lying in the inner courtyard, her clothes burned off, with burns on her arms and legs.

Herbert Fritz was able to give a detailed account of what happened in the main dining room. He recalled that there were two doors, one leading to the kitchen and the other opening onto the court. They had just been served and Carlton had just left the room when they noticed something flowing under the screen door that led to the courtyard. They thought it must be soapsuds. The liquid ran under his chair, and he suddenly smelled gasoline. Almost at the same moment, a streak of flame shot under his chair and the whole side of the room was ablaze. They all jumped up, and Fritz realized that his clothes were on fire. Since he was near a low window he plunged through it, landing on a rocky slope. His arm was broken by the fall, and flames were eating through his clothes and burning his body. He rolled over and over down the hill and managed to put the flames out. He scrambled to his feet and was about to start back up the hill when he saw Carlton running around the house with the hatchet in his hand. Emil Brodelle had also escaped through the window, but Carlton had buried his hatchet in his brain at the hairline. Brodelle staggered and fell to his knees.

Meantime, Billy Weston was on his way through the same window when he was attacked. Interestingly, Carlton chose to use the back of his hatchet this time, catching Weston with two stunning blows that knocked him to the ground but did not kill him. Carlton, perhaps thinking him dead, raced off in search of another victim. He had already attacked David Lindblom, dealing him a hatchet wound to the back of the head that had not penetrated his skull, but Lindblom was suffering from severe burns over his back, arms, legs, head and neck. Thomas Brunker, whom Carlton caught as he burst through the door into the courtyard, received a lethal blow that penetrated his brain. He, too, was badly burned. As for the thirteen-year-old Ernest Weston, his skull had been beaten in with the hatchet and he had severe burns.

By this time Taliesin was in flames. Despite two fierce blows to the head, Weston managed to get back onto his feet. He found Lindblom, bleeding and burned, and the two of them somehow ran half a mile to the nearest house with a telephone to call for help. Weston's actions that day were truly heroic. Wright wrote that, after giving the alarm, Weston went back to the house, "ran to where the fire hose was kept in a niche of the garden wall, . . . got the hose loose, staggered with it to the fire and with the playing hose stood against destruction until they led him away." The first to arrive on the scene were Frank Sliter, whose home was closest to the house, Jack Farries, Albert Beckley and Fred Hanke. Farries said he ran into the courtyard looking for Carlton. He did not find him but saw Brodelle on his hands and knees, on the point of collapse. He also found Ernest Weston, covered with blood but still on his feet. Ernest managed to walk a short distance and then fainted. Farries carried him into the shade of a tree. Then he found Martha Cheney, her clothing almost burned off her body.

The *Wisconsin State Journal* in Madison, which ran the first account of the disaster in its late editions Saturday night, reported that attendants from the Hillside Home School half a mile away had quickly reached the scene. The Spring Green fire department rushed across the three miles of prairie, and a bucket brigade of workers from Tower Hill was dispatched in an effort to save the house. Their work was in vain; by three o'clock that afternoon, it was reported, Taliesin was completely destroyed. Jenkin Lloyd Jones was directing the rescue and attempts to control the fire. The first person to reach Mamah Borthwick was Wright's brother-in-law Andrew Porter. He found her body ablaze and thought it had been saturated with gasoline. Her corpse was badly burned, and her hair almost completely burned off. It was then 12:45 p.m. He carried her, with the other dead and wounded, to a neighbor's cottage. When his wife first heard the news from the *Wisconsin State Journal*, she refused to believe it because, she said, Carlton was such a mild-mannered man.

Edna was on the road to Taliesin when she saw a thin curl of smoke coming from the hillside. There was a scream. She heard men's shouts, and cries of children. She slid from her horse and looked at her trembling hands. She began to cry and pray, "Hail Mary, full of grace! The Lord is with thee. . . ." over and over again. Then she found herself climbing the stone steps up to Taliesin, into the courtyard and past shapes "like statues in Lent fallen over." One of those shapes was half-hidden under towels. Her hair was burned and her eyelashes were gone, but she was still conscious. The lips in that face moved to mouth her name. Edna stared at her silently, thinking, "That is not Martha!" even as she recognized the ring on her playmate's swollen hand. Martha Cheney lived for only a few hours longer. Mamah Borthwick, John and Martha Cheney, Emil Brodelle and Thomas Brunker were dead or dying at the scene; Ernest Weston would die of his burns; so would David Lindblom. Of the nine who had sat down to lunch that Saturday, only two, Herbert Fritz and Billy Weston, survived.

Within an hour after the murders, hundreds of farmers, their wives and their children had arrived to beat out the flames; others combed the cornfields looking for Carlton. He was found at about 5:30 that afternoon. He had crept down to the basement of the house and was hiding inside the unlit furnace, protected from the flames. It was thought that he had planned to slip away after the search had been called off, and make his escape during the night. He had swallowed some muriatic acid and was only semiconscious. Three carloads of men were instantly ready to "string him up," but the guns of the sheriff and his posse held them off. He was incarcerated in the Dodgeville County jail, where his mouth and throat were found to be badly burned. He died in jail two months later, not from the effects of the acid, which were not judged life-threatening, but from a successful attempt to starve himself; he had lost almost sixty pounds. There was no trial, but there were preliminary hearings at which evidence was given. The day before one of them, Carlton, sick as he was, made trouble for Sheriff John T. Williams. It was stated that he had tried to throw a glass tumbler and tin pail at Williams, and "in the scuffle which followed the negro grabbed hold of the sheriff's leg." Help soon arrived, and Carlton was thrown back into his cell.

John Lloyd Wright, who was superintending the work at Midway Gardens, was having lunch on a scaffold that Saturday. A sandwich in one hand and a paintbrush in the other, he was painting a mural for the tavern wall. His father was eating lunch at the other end of the room. The door opened, and an office secretary appeared to say that Mr. Wright was wanted on the telephone. Wright disappeared for a few moments, and when he returned, John, absorbed with his work, did not pause. He soon became aware of an unnatural silence, his father's labored breathing and then a groan. John spun around; Wright's face was white and he was clinging to the table for support. There had been a fire; John must get a taxi. They took the first train for Spring Green. It was a slow local, and, as luck would have it, Edwin Cheney was on the platform. The two men looked at each other and clasped hands in silent sympathy. John pushed them both into a compartment to save them from being crushed by reporters. Journalists would tell them both the frightful news as the train inched forward, and they would see the headline: TALIESIN BURNING TO THE GROUND, SEVEN SLAIN. The Aunts, Nell and Jane, were at the Madison station awaiting their nephew's arrival. So was Richard Lloyd Jones, Jenkin's son, by now a journalist with the *Wisconsin State Journal*. Wright had sagged visibly as the journey progressed and, by the time he arrived, seemed about to faint. "Cousin Richard grabbed him by the coat collar, pounded him on the back, shook him vigorously and thundered, 'Stand up, Frank! It couldn't be worse, get hold of yourself!' " When the news came through to the parents of Verna Ross, vacationing in Lake Delavan, the second Mrs. Cheney collapsed and Mrs. Ross was up all night. All any of them could think of was that Verna might have been one more victim. Franklin Porter, then aged six, retains a confused memory of that day, of teams of horses rushing up the road from school and loud shouts as black clouds of smoke rose from Taliesin. "Those who had been burned fighting the fire were brought over to Tan-y-Deri and laid on improvised beds on the porch, right below the room in which I slept. Mingled with the memory of intense excitement of the fire is that of men moaning in the night with pain, and of a whippoorwill singing during moments of quiet," he wrote. "For ever after the song of a whippoorwill at night at Tan-y-Deri seems infinitely sad." Cheney left the next day on a train for Chicago, accompanied by a single casket containing the remains of his two children.

There was a hailstorm that weekend, resulting in much damage to corn and other crops in the towns of Spring Green, Wyoming, Arena and Dodgeville. That evening Wright's cousins, Orin and Ralph Lloyd Jones, and his son John, placed Mamah's body in a simple pine box. They loaded it onto a cart and drove it to Unity Church. It was then placed in an unmarked grave and heaped with zinnias, dahlias and nasturtiums from the Taliesin garden. A witness at the funeral said that, as the casket was lowered, the clouds opened and Wright asked everyone to leave. Looking back, he saw Wright standing alone in the rain. Wright later wrote, "All I had left to show for the struggle for freedom of the five years past that had swept most of my former life away, had now been swept away." However imperfectly, he had believed in the good, the true and the beautiful and had tried to incorporate those beliefs into his life, his work and his love. Nevertheless he was being punished, by that same hand he had always feared, the wrathful God of Isaiah. "Fate has smashed these wonderful walls, / This broken city, has crumbled the work / Of giants. . . ." Boils broke out over his back and neck. As one more victim after another died, he stoically went to their funerals. That there might have been a powerful desire, at some level, to share Mamah's fate is suggested by a small item that appeared in a local newspaper the following week. It seemed that on Tuesday, August 18, the heavy rains of the weekend forced the dam of the artificial lake below the ruins of Taliesin to break. Wright was standing close to the edge when it happened—too close. A sudden rush of water thundered down the creek and swept him into it. But then the shock of finding himself in actual physical danger brought about the moment of truth he had, perhaps unconsciously, courted. He fought his way to the bank with the help of Billy Weston, coming to his rescue yet again. He still, it seemed, wanted to live.

9

Lord of Her Waking Dreams

. . . while I
Go struggling deep in the ocean, thrashing
In its darkness. . . .
> "Storm at Sea"
> *Poems from the Old English*

The persistence with which Wright would cling to his hill in The Valley for the next half-century ought to settle the issue of how much of a Welshman he really was. In fact, he himself provided the evidence when he wrote, "I turned to this hill in the Valley as my grandfather before me turned to America—as a hope, and a haven." When the immigrants arrived in Wisconsin and claimed their newfound land, they set up an ideal to which at least one grandchild was forever faithful. It was the end of *hiraeth* and the beginning of fulfillment as human beings and representatives of an ancient and honorable culture. The terrible events of August 1914 might have sent some men to the other ends of the earth. Instead, the tragedy seemed to have sharpened his awareness of his Celtic heritage and to have drawn him closer to his companions in isolation, the Lloyd Jones family; it also reinforced his inner conviction of a special destiny. Two years before he had thrown in his lot with the name of Taliesin. Whatever could have caused him to choose the name, it provided an apt symbolism for the trial by fire through which he was passing. If something in him had

died with Mamah, the legend of Taliesin offered the hope that what
was imperishable in his nature might be born again. "The Prophet
Johannes called me Merddin / But now all kings know me as Taliesin."
He resolved almost immediately to rebuild.

That autumn of 1914, Frank Lloyd Wright might have been the
Lloyd Jones who had met misfortune most spectacularly, but he was
only the most obvious example. Not one member of his mother's
generation had remained untouched by hardship and private tragedy,
and as a result of the crisis of 1907, there had been a drastic dwindling
of their collective land holdings in The Valley as well. As long as
Wright remained on his hill he, as representative of the next generation, offered the best hope that the Lloyd Jones name might one day
be restored to its old prominence. And, as companions in adversity,
his relatives could not be improved upon. His son John, who had
accompanied him on that terrible five-hour trip from Chicago, had
quietly left after convincing himself that his father preferred to be
alone. His sister Maginel, by then married and pursuing a successful
career as an artist in New York, knew better. She returned to The
Valley to be with her brother, taking long rides over the hills to
Pleasant Ridge, Blue Mound and beyond. "He would stop the horses
on a hill and stare down at the Valley, with its cloud shadows. Then
he would talk; and he talked late into the night, too, when we
returned, pacing back and forth."

Maginel could be counted upon to find just the right note of encouragement, and she obviously believed there was something magical
about his newest home. In it, she saw a subtle interplay between
poetic, fanciful and very human qualities. To her, the house seemed
both romantic and profound, full of unexpected and transient delights,
yet somehow timeless. It always had a particular and distinctive smell.
"Set down in it by magic with my eyes closed I would know that I
was there by breathing the scent of wood smoke, dried pennyroyal,
pearly everlasting, and the faint elusive fragrance that emanates from
oriental *objets d'art.*" Taliesin's living quarters were destroyed, but the
studio remained, with a small bedroom behind it. This might have
seemed an omen, a clear signal that Wright was meant to restore and
redesign more wonderfully than before. If Maginel had spoken to him
in this vein, she would merely have strengthened her brother's resolve.
When she returned a few months later she found twenty-five workmen
engaged in reconstruction. Their sister Jane, "staunch as always in a
crisis," fed them all, providing gargantuan feasts that reminded Ma-

ginel of those she had seen at threshing time. The phoenix was rising, and whatever had been retrieved from its ashes—shards of porcelain, fragments of statuary—was being set into the cement of the stone piers. It was a triumph of imagination and will.

Wright wrote that he had not, at first, wanted Anna's company and that she had been very much hurt. This decision must have been short-lived, because she would seldom be far from her brilliant son's side from that time onward, until her death nine years later. She had become the formidable grande dame everyone had foreseen in Oak Park, model leader of the community—she was one of the founders of the Nineteenth Century Woman's Club and gave classes in Emerson and Browning and papers on one of her favorite authors, the naturalist John Burroughs. A scrapbook she kept late in life gives some indication of her interests in those years: clippings about Susan B. Anthony, Carrie Chapman Cart (president of the National American Woman's Suffrage Association) and Rev. Anna Howard Shaw. There are photographs of her former homes, of Unity Temple, of David Lloyd George, as Member of Parliament, and of a meeting to celebrate the centenary of Ann Griffiths, Welsh writer of hymns. Anna also kept old letters from Jenkin when he was fighting in the Civil War, homespun homilies written by her in a shaky hand and poems exhorting the reader to remain steadfast in difficulty. Yet to her intimates, Anna remained the same volatile mixture of piety and capriciousness, aloofness and malleability, childlike delight and poetic responsiveness, as shifting in her moods as the weather. Wright had built living quarters for her at Taliesin and, during his absences, often left her in charge.

At a moment when no expense was being spared to restore Taliesin, the fate of the Oak Park home and studio, now split into separate units, hung in the balance. Wright had somehow neglected to pay back taxes, and the town was about to foreclose. Wright still owed money to Little, the Forest Avenue unit remained unrented (Catherine and family having moved into the remodeled, studio side), and, as Darwin Martin was aware, his own financial share in the property, the result of his "trust-deed" loan of four years before, was jeopardized by Wright's irresponsible behavior. Martin scolded his architect for his frequent absences in Wisconsin, away from the path of duty, in pursuit of "dalliance and self-indulgence," but Wright, at this point, was immune. He had taken the measure of his man and had perfected his defenses; besides, he had long since accepted such reproaches as the price he paid for never having to face a final accounting. Behind the clearly self-defeatist behavior were the instincts of a survivor, and these always surfaced when he most needed them; with his back to the wall, Wright was magnificent, unconquerable. As Taliesin was being rebuilt, Wright bent every nerve to compose masterpieces of placating prose, combining plausible explanations for past behavior with appeals to friendship and apparently genuine offers at quasi-solutions that served his immediate purpose, the only one he cared about, of buying more time.

Had Martin known just how ambitious the reconstruction was, and just how extensive a household Wright was now supporting, he would have been even angrier. The house was "not by any means a modest affair," wrote Antonin Raymond, a young artist and future architect who came to join the master's atelier as work was being completed. Raymond, a Czech who had been educated in Prague, studied painting in Italy and trained as an architectural draftsman in New York, provided a vivid account of the Taliesin household that he found when he arrived with his young French wife, Noémi, in the spring of 1916. They took the train to Spring Green, where they were met by the master himself in a handsome carriage, and taken to Taliesin, up and around the hill, through the porte cochère and into the inner courtyard. The building complex was extensive: not just an enlarged studio, with new living quarters for several draftsmen, newly erected farm buildings, stables, guest quarters, servants' quarters and so on, but also a handsome residence for the master. Several workmen were in permanent attendance, including a Czech stonemason, aged eighty, who spent his days building walls, refreshing his efforts with a flask containing pure alcohol. Raymond made a mental note of handsome horse carriages and a collection of horses—Wright was "an experienced and fearless rider"—including Kaiser, a large black horse with vicious yellow teeth that the architect alone could master, and Shots and Silver, two gentler animals. Riding was everyone's chief form of relaxation because, "Roaming through the Wisconsin countryside . . . was magnificent in those days. The roads were all dust or mud or nonexistent. Motor cars were few, and horses shied at their sight. All our leisure time we spent in discovering the rolling hills, fertile valleys and the bluff overlooking the Wisconsin River. . . ."

The main residence was a masterpiece. Wright had built it in his usual style, with immense roofs and massive fireplaces, of stucco and plaster, staining his lines of moldings with Cabot's stain or creosote,

The earliest-known view of Taliesin, Spring Green, Wisconsin, circa 1911

A contemporary view of the Taliesin living room

*The entrance to Frank Lloyd Wright's "bungalow" as it looked
at a later period*

*Architectural details, now lost, from a view of Taliesin as it looked
in the mid-1920s*

An early view of Taliesin in winter

Taliesin's inner courtyard

as a fitting backdrop for his extensive collection of furniture and ornaments. He had gilded the joints between bricks, made wide use of ornamentation, even around windows and doors, and incorporated numerous Japanese screens, sculptures, prints, lacquerware, statuary and other objects into his famous overall schemes. Rugs and upholstery were of the finest materials, and animal skins further embellished couches and floors; there were great bouquets of flowers everywhere. The host himself, then aged forty-eight and at the height of his mental and physical powers, put Raymond in mind of a latter-day Diamond Jim Brady: underwear of chamois leather, hats made to order, swirling capes, complete outfits handmade by the finest tailors. They were shown to a suite of guest rooms and entertained with panache by their cordial and generous host. A few days after Raymond arrived, he remarked that the studio in which the draftsmen worked was not well enough lit or large enough to permit seeing things from a distance. Their host promptly encouraged them to take down the roof and start again. Wright was planting fields, orchards and a new vineyard, but, the Raymonds noticed, as soon as these ambitious projects needed work, he would lose interest. His inventiveness and energy were prodigious and he worked ceaselessly, although the actual building for clients was almost nonexistent. His draftsmen were at work on his new idea for the mass manufacture of low-cost prefabricated houses, ingenious and practical and far ahead of its time: more evidence of his ability to combine artistry and shrewd business sense. Despite all of his imagination and energy, Raymond thought Wright's interest flagged whenever practical matters were concerned, at least in his own establishment. He had constructed a dam to generate electricity at the foot of Taliesin, one fed by a brook, and the equipment was always getting stuck. Raymond wrote, "The other draftsmen and myself were then called upon to dive into the pond among the frogs and mud turtles and try to get it going again. This was very typical of anything around Wright in the matter of mechanics. Mechanical equipment was always in the state of needing repairs and adjustments. In its design, as in the design of the buildings as a whole, fantastic imagination was the chief guide. . . ."

He was a man of prodigious courage, energy and imagination; he gave generously of himself, and he was a reliable friend. The Raymonds had met "Dan," a former schoolmate of the master's, now a jack-of-all-trades around the place who kept the complicated establishment functioning and took care of the horses, wagons and so-called farm.

Dan was also a heavy drinker who would periodically disappear. Whenever that happened, Wright would go searching for him and bring him back in the buggy. That showed how charming he could be, and how loyal—too loyal. When Noémi made a sketch of one of his daughters, Wright "unveiled an, up to now, totally new and unexpected part of his character. He became rude and insulting, claiming that Noémi intentionally made his daughter look like an imbecile. . . ." On another occasion, Wright forcefully criticized one of Antonin Raymond's paintings because it was clearly in the style of an experimental new school he happened to dislike—not, one would have thought, the tactful thing to do.

The tact and diplomacy with which Wright had managed to gloss over differences between himself and his early clients and ease his upward struggle when he was making a name for himself seemed to have largely vanished, and in their place was a readiness to take sharp and sarcastic exception to people and actions whenever his feelings were hurt. One of the first-known examples of this can be traced to 1907, that year of tumult in his life, and an exchange of letters between himself and a Chicago poet and critic, Harriet Monroe, who was also sister-in-law of the architect John Welborn Root. She reviewed an exhibition of Wright's designs at the Chicago Art Institute in what one would have called a friendly way, but without the lavish approval and unqualified praise the architect plainly expected. Characteristically, he tore off a lengthy epistle, the gist of which was that she did not know anything about the noble cause he espoused, and although her writings had "no power to harm the inherent virtue of good work," her thankless remarks had power to "hamper the man." The two patched up their differences, but this experience no doubt influenced Monroe's final opinion of Wright's work. Summing it up in her book *A Poet's Life*, Monroe judged him to be far below Sullivan in stature, and a publicity hound to boot.

Wright's pattern, a belligerent willingness to strike back harder whenever he sensed hostility, followed at length by a temperate response, was unvarying. Some were able to shrug off his pique and remained to become good friends. Others were permanently offended. One of them appears to have been his gifted assistant, Marion Mahony Griffin, only the second woman to receive a degree in architecture from the Massachusetts Institute of Technology. She joined Wright's Oak Park studio in 1895 and became indispensable as his delineator. Many have judged her to be more of an artist than an architect; at any event, it is known that many of the designs for Wright's 1910 Wasmuth portfolio were actually drawn by her, and Plates 14 and 15 bear her monogram, MLM. She was also a fine designer, and at least some of the designs for interior furnishings, mosaics, stained glass and murals for which Wright took complete credit are now thought to have been created by Mahony. When Wright left his family in 1909, Mahony stayed on in the office and was the creative force behind the completion of his projects. But the relationship ended badly. A letter from Wright, accusing Mahony of stealing his ideas, taking clients away, betraying him to the world at large and other words to that effect, has not survived, but her reply to it has. She was leaving Oak Park to join the office of Walter Burley Griffin, another Wright ex-apprentice, who was to have a distinguished Australian career as an architect, and a man she soon married. With a formal politeness that could not entirely conceal her sense of outrage, Mahony spiritedly defended her work while in Wright's employ, work that he was now attacking as inferior. She concluded, "Forgive my heat—You should be slower to condemn."

He should have been slower to condemn: it was a fair comment. From about 1911 onward he was completely wrapped up in the resentful conviction that lesser men and women, many of them his former students, had broken away, taking his ideas with them, and were throwing up sordid little imitations of his work all over the Midwest, cheapening the ideas he had first formulated and, all alone, had championed. This was of course a distorted view, but it did contain a germ of truth. It was a fact that a number of architects, now part of the New School of the Midwest, among them Walter Burley Griffin, George Grant Elmslie, Barry Byrne, George W. Maher, Robert C. Spencer, Jr., Eben E. Roberts, John S. Van Bergen, Charles E. White, and the architectural firm of Tallmadge and Watson, were designing in ways that, to the casual eye, looked Wright-inspired and influenced. What would have rankled most was his belief, as he wrote to Martin in the autumn of 1913, that "the other architects are doing their best to put me out of business."

He may also have felt, with more justification, that he was far too often praised, in American professional circles, with faint damns. That Harriet Monroe tendency, as he saw it, to commend with one sentence while removing the grounds for such approval with the next, had become a positive plague of dismissive articles. When his first really important publication, *Ausgeführte Bauten und Entwürfe von Frank Lloyd*

Wright, was published in 1910, only one magazine published a review, and the noted critic Montgomery Schuyler, who wrote it, could not bring himself to praise the book unreservedly. As H. Allen Brooks observed, "One senses that Schuyler's concern was over ornament—without such ornament as Sullivan would supply, Wright's architecture was too severe."

All of this might not have mattered had Wright felt in his usual fettle, with all kinds of new tricks up his sleeve. As has been noted, he was seeking a source of inspiration in the Japanese as early as 1905, but there were, as might be predicted, myriads of strands, any one of which could be pursued with profit in the game of speculating about the particular influences on his work at any particular moment. It is known that, while in Europe that winter of 1909–10, he studied the new movements in art and interior design, and, as might have been expected, some of these elements crept into his work after his return. His designs for the Coonley Playhouse of 1912 are frequently compared, in their use of circular motifs, which had appeared in Wright's work for the first time, with the paintings of such European artists as František Kupka, Roger de la Fresnaye and Robert Delaunay, which predate them. Other designs by Wright, including murals for the Midway Gardens, an intricate pattern of interlocked circles in floating configurations, and even the dinner service he used for the Imperial Hotel of 1916–22, show the same affinities with these European precursors. The influences, however, were far from being in one direction alone. As is evident, Wright inspired a host of sympathetic imitators, and his magnificent early designs in stained glass, with their geometrical formalism, would be enthusiastically rediscovered once the great Paris exhibition of 1925 brought about a rage for the Art Deco style. One would have to compare Wright with Picasso in his restless willingness to follow a radical path wherever it led, so long as it took him into a fertile field for experimentation. Other artists, such as Wassily Kandinsky, whose famous *Improvisation No. 6* of 1913 directly predicted the coming upheaval, sensed that the world was moving inexorably toward famine, fire and death. Wright would not have been Wright if he had not, somehow, been thrown off stride by that sense of foreboding.

As might be predicted, the great movement that had built on the teachings of Ruskin and Morris, the Arts and Crafts Movement, was coming to an end. H. Allen Brooks's history of the rise and fall of the Prairie school dates its waning influence very precisely. He wrote that, in 1914, the Prairie school was still a driving force in Chicago, and its work was well represented in an exhibition of the Chicago Architectural Club. A year later, its architects were having difficulty obtaining commissions; by 1917, some of the most famous had moved into other fields and there was not one example of Prairie school work in the annual architectural exhibition at the Art Institute. Wright's position, as World War I began, was analogous to that of a theoretician whose main themes will soon be considered irrelevant and whose main body of work will soon be as outmoded as the Gibson Girl and the horse and carriage—left alone to preach a message no one, any longer, believed.

What was equally distressing for Wright, perhaps, was a contemplation of the direction that modern art was clearly taking. If he had been following movements in Germany closely, as no doubt he had, he would have seen the similarities between the landscape Raymond had painted, to which he had taken such a dislike, and similar landscapes painted by Kandinsky in 1909. Raymond's exaggerated distortions of line and color and his radical simplification of the actual scene being illustrated, all of which were meant to produce a far greater emotional impact than, say, the serene and naturalistic landscapes of the Impressionists, were in the accepted manner of the new group of Expressionist painters. Kandinsky, a major theoretician of the movement, and one of the founders of the *Blaue Reiter* (Blue Rider) group in 1911, had just published a book, *The Art of Spiritual Harmony* (1914), which would be the manifesto of the then-emerging style of Abstractionism. Kandinsky would go on to teach at the Bauhaus— the famous school of architecture, design and craftsmanship that was yet to be established. (It did not come into existence until 1919.) Yet with his uncanny prescience, Wright somehow knew that Expressionism and its closely related school, Abstractionism, were taking art, and architecture along with it, down a path to which he would become absolutely opposed. It gave Raymond great pause for thought. Was this man truly a part of the modern movement, or could it be that he did not understand what was coming, and was destined to be left behind?

Just as in England the Arts and Crafts Movement paved the way for Neo-Georgian, which became the conventional and preferred style for the middle-class suburban house, so in the United States the vogue for individuality and original design was being superseded by a revival of the colonial house, the new symbol of genteel culture. The last Prairie house designs were published in *House Beautiful* in 1914. That magazine was moving its offices from Chicago to New York, reflecting the growing influence of younger magazines already being published there: *House and Garden* (founded 1901) and *American Homes and Gardens* (1905). These publications lent editorial weight to the new view that the words *Americanism* and *democracy* could best be applied to the colonial style, which, some wrote, was the only distinctly American one. But in fact the trend was toward an eclectic romp of styles: Beaux Arts, Tudor, French Château, Italianate and the like, which would clutter up the domestic scene until World War II, bringing with it just that claustrophobic visual chaos Wright had so much abhorred and against which he had set his energies decades before.

Wright's hostility to any interference from the lady of the house has already been described, and it would not have made his task any easier. The Darwin Martin correspondence provides some apt examples of Wright's readiness to flatten the first sign of feminine mutiny. In the early stages of designing their house, Darwin Martin wrote to Wright that "a question has occurred to us . . . regarding your French windows—Mrs. Martin says what will Mr. Wright do with a window which it is desired to fasten open and draw the shade which is often the case in bedrooms at night. . . . The shade will rattle all night." Wright replied airily, "The fear of shades rattling is an hallucination which might bother you in advance but will seem extremely insignificant when it has come to pass." He went on to do battle, that same March of 1903, with Mrs. Martin's expressed dislike of the kind of exterior he had in mind. The samples he submitted were merely "evidence of a capacity on the part of your architect to understand and appreciate your feelings and wants," he wrote soothingly. Many other clients had been just as doubtful as Mrs. Martin was, until they had seen the results. She—and her husband—must learn to have faith. Two years later, when Mrs. Martin popped her head up again, it was with a meek little squeak. She wanted a round table, her husband said. Perhaps the architect might be inclined to grant this request. Once Mrs. Martin had been put in her place Wright could afford to be generous, although his praise might sound offensive to some ears: she was to be commended, he wrote in 1908, for her "gentleness of spirit." A woman who knew her own mind was the kind of client Wright emphatically did not want, unless it was a special kind of woman (the kind he would have considered enlightened) who wanted exactly the kind of house he wanted. He found her in Mrs. Avery Coonley, the former Queene Ferry of Detroit. She came from a family that had made a fortune as early developers of seed companies, which ought to have made her a member of the idle rich. That she certainly was not. Shortly after graduating from Vassar she spent her first year doing volunteer work at one of the first Chicago settlement houses, then trained to be a kindergarten teacher. She took an advanced interest in progressive theories of child raising. She became interested in women's rights, a cause she shared with her husband, also the child of a wealthy, progressive and distinguished family.

Naturally, both Coonleys took politically liberal positions, which would have endeared them to a Lloyd Jones, and they were also devout Christian Scientists. Queene Coonley's progressive views made her most receptive to Wright's innovative architecture—"My grand-father," Celia Clevenger recalled, "would have been happy in a house with green shutters"—and Wright responded with one of his most superb creations, called "the palazzo among prairie houses." Since one of Mrs. Coonley's great interests was early-childhood education (she had founded five schools in the Chicago area before she was forty-five), the idea of having Wright also build them a "playhouse," actually a school, on the grounds of their Riverside, Illinois, home was a natural extension of those interests. Her enthusiasm for Wright's ideas, and his character, never lessened, despite the fact that she was "straight-laced," her granddaughter said. When someone made a derogatory remark about "all his wives," she responded, "Well, he only had one at a time."

Catherine's prediction to Darwin Martin, in December 1912, that the Mamah Borthwick episode would end in two years, was uncannily prescient. But the reconciliation that was also foreseen by some of the Chicago papers during their coverage of the Taliesin murders had not taken place. Catherine seemed to have forgotten about her own pre-diction when she wrote to Janet Ashbee a month after the murders. Her letter was mostly taken up with the news that the children, whom she had prevented from seeing their father as long as Mamah was alive, were now staying with him, and daughter Catherine was even proposing to keep house for him. The tragedy had been traumatic, and they would have to wait for time to do its work. Catherine did not expect their marriage to be reestablished any time soon, but if that day ever came, she knew she would hear from him. That was enough for her. It was a new note of resignation, and there might have been a chance for a reconciliation, but a letter from Wright to his wife, sent in December 1914, ruled it out. He enclosed his monthly check, and the manner in which he described the financial sparring with Darwin D. Martin in which he was then engaged suggests that the house had, in some sense, become a substitute for the battleground of their marriage and all of its lingering resentments. Their daughter would not do as a housekeeper. "Catherine and I are a failure I am sorry to say," he wrote. "She has too much of the old poisonous idea of me in her system to give me any comfort. . . ." Quite soon thereafter, he hired a housekeeper for Spring Green. Her name was Nellie Breen.

Two days after Wright wrote that letter to Catherine, and as Christmas Day, 1914, approached, a stranger wrote a letter of sympathy and commiseration. Knowing how acutely one felt such a loss during the holidays, she was writing to express her horror at the dimensions of his tragedy and tell him that she, too, had known such a loss. Several paragraphs followed having to do with learning to forget, consoling oneself with thoughts of the beloved's blissful present state and similar thoughts couched in phrases that made one think, as D. B. Wyndham Lewis wrote in his preface to his anthology of bad verse, of "the spinster lady coyly attuned to Life and Spring." All too soon such language and the sentiments it expressed would be ridiculed out of existence, but for the moment it was the height of fashion. The letter, which made a pleasing impression upon the recipient, was signed "Madame Noel."

Maude Miriam Noel, who was forty-five when she met Frank Lloyd Wright, and two years his junior, was born in a suburb of Memphis, Tennessee, on May 9, 1869. She was descended from a distinguished family of Southerners whose origins went back to the 1700s in colonial Virginia. Her father, Andrew J. Hicks, M.D., was son of one of the wealthiest plantation owners in western Tennessee, holder of several thousand acres and master of numerous slaves before the Civil War. Dr. Hicks was one of nine sons, all well educated. He studied medicine in Philadelphia and spent the greater part of his life in Texas and New Mexico. His daughter, called "Aunt Maude" by the family, preferred to be known as Miriam; she had married very young (she claimed she was fifteen) to Emil Noel, son of a wealthy Southern family. They moved to Chicago, where Noel became a department store executive with Marshall Field, and had three children, Norma, Thomas and Corinne.

Miriam Noel probably never went to college; "Southern women in those days were not well educated," her relative, Norma Noel Cawthon, recalled. She was, however, accustomed to a comfortable, if not elegant, life, had excellent taste in furniture and objets d'art and was famous for her wardrobe. Whenever she traveled she took trunks full of clothes, probably custom-made, since she dressed for theatrical effect rather than style, wearing capes and turbans and all manner of chokers, necklaces, brooches, rings and a monocle suspended from her neck on a cord of white silk. When war broke out, she had been living in Paris for the past decade (to judge from her memoir), her husband having died three years before. It is a family belief that she was a sculptor of some accomplishment, although no samples of her work are known; it is said that one of her works, a pair of hands, was accepted for the collection at the Louvre. Whether or not this is true, the fact that she tied for first place in a Paris sculpture competition with Mrs. Harry Payne Whitney seems plausible. She was socially well placed and moved in a circle of American and British expatriates and dilettanti.

To judge from Miriam Noel's account—she left Paris after war was declared to join her married daughter, Norma, in Chicago—she had been leading a life of refinement and luxury, surrounded by a circle of prominent friends including Leon Trotsky. Her house in Paris was full of treasures: "a painting by Scott Dabo, a drawing of my beautiful daughter by George Ade, etchings by Ade, a painting by René Castaigne, figures by Rembrandt Bugatti, a head of my little daughter done by Prince Paul Troubetsky [sic], exquisite figures by Elie Nadelman and Zadkine, drawings by Richard Wallace, all treasured gifts I had received from friends."

She was still beautiful, with a trim, erect figure, a mass of reddish brown hair, eyes with a greenish tinge and pale, unlined skin. Wright would call her "truly brilliant," and also clairvoyant. She was a follower of Mary Baker Eddy's, and it would later transpire that she was attracted to spiritualism and consulted mediums. He saw her remarkable qualities but would not have seen an aspect of her character that was not immediately apparent: she was dangerously self-delusory. She had a hidden script, a fantasy that she had woven around herself, in which she was destined to become the leading lady in a heroic, legendary romance. Being a woman of her generation, her own abilities and accomplishments would not have counted for much in her own estimation. She would have seen herself as, say, another Eleonora Duse, a woman of marked gifts who might only attain immortality if her name had been linked with that of a man of even more unique and remarkable gifts. In Duse's case it was the Italian dramatist and poet Gabriele D'Annunzio, then at the height of his fame in Paris. To judge from her memoir, Miriam Noel had marked out Wright to play such a role in her life before she returned to Chicago. This fantasist quality, which would become so evident, is immediately apparent in her writings. In a scene so false as to be a parody of the genre, she describes the sorrow of the disappointed lover she leaves behind in Paris. She: " 'I cannot love you as you . . . deserve to be loved. You must forget me.' " He: " 'Never, never! . . . I cannot forget. I shall love you always, hopeless as I know my love is.' " He moved toward the door, "his footsteps suddenly grown uncertain, like those of an old man who has come unexpectedly face to face with despair. . . . 'Tomorrow,' he said, 'I shall join the French foreign legion. . . .' " Whether there really was such a suitor, and what actually happened is not known, but given Miriam Noel's predilections one may safely assume that it was probably the reverse of her account. The truth, the world as it is, facing facts: none of these necessities had any charm for Miriam Noel. Her mission in life was to mold the world closer to her own illusion. Given opposition, she would simply try harder, displaying a tenacity and conviction that were admirable, if one could overlook the fact that this herculean force of will was being exerted upon an unrealizable objective.

The feelings of defeat, despair and worthlessness that may have fueled this manic fantasy world can only be guessed at, but that there was an air of tragedy about Miriam Noel was instantly communicated to Wright when they met. He noted that her head shook slightly but continuously. She talked about an unhappy love affair that, she said, paralleled his own; it had broken her health. Perhaps inadvertently, she had hit upon the approach most calculated to bring forth Wright's indignant and warmest sympathies. He could not resist a victim of fate and, from Robie Lamp onward, could be counted upon to be loyal and fiercely defensive of anyone he thought had been unfairly treated. And Miriam's secret was that she had a severe handicap. For all her poise and authority, her refinement, social status and artistic accomplishment, she must have seemed as much an outsider and as emotionally adrift as he was. He would discover only later that she was a morphine addict.

Throughout the nineteenth century, the United States was the only major Western nation to have no laws restricting narcotics. Opium and morphine were widely used, and in the mid-1880s it was perfectly legal to sniff, smoke, inject, rub, eat or drink cocaine. Morphine's value as a pain reliever and sedative was known long before its addictive qualities, as well as its undesirable side effects—circulatory, respiratory and gastrointestinal—were understood. It is also known to be a depressant.

He was fated to like her and he wanted to like her; that much is clear. The next woman in his life had appeared before him, just as Kitty had done when she collided with him on the dance floor, without any effort on his part. He might, from the beginning, have had some reservations, but she never had a moment's doubt. She had angled for, and received, an invitation in just a few days, as the correspondence shows, and never looked back. She had gone to meet him in his studio, a mere pinpoint of light in the canyons of stone, brick and glass of downtown Chicago, and saw at a distance a short, stocky figure in the doorway, with a halo of almost white hair and a face as deeply lined as Holbein's portrait of Erasmus. This unprepossessing figure was a distinct disappointment, and she did not like his hands. But then, he looked at her "with eyes that became strangely, subtly, brilliantly alive and magic happened to me. . . . In that one glance, I '. . . had fed in honeydew / And drunk the milk of paradise.' "

A man with a marvelous gaze, instant, headlong capitulation: the plot had long been written in advance, but no first act could have played itself out more satisfactorily. But more was to come. They talked for "hour after glorious hour," about "kings and slaves and troubadours; . . . we ranged the whole world of art and literature, our minds in perfect unison." At the end of the evening he had declared that he was in love with her, just like that! And she had, with eyes averted, blushingly and et cetera. Duse could have created no more palpitating portrait of a heroine responding to the ardor of a gallant new suitor, or shown more appreciation for the interior decorating talents of her D'Annunzio than Noel did for the modest little house Wright inhabited in Chicago and that, by virtue of his gifts, had become "as rare and lovely as a miniature Palace of Baghdad!" Her memoir describes the whirlwind of breakfasts, luncheons, dinners, drives into the country and visits to art exhibitions staged by Wright for her benefit. On that first Christmas at his house she wore a Paris gown of almond green velvet; he was in a black velvet dinner jacket and Chinese trousers. She wrote, "Everywhere there were bowls of deep red velvet roses. . . ." No heroine from D'Annunzio's romances could have been more fastidiously courted; nor found a more perfect setting for the drama of true love that was unfolding.

"Lord of my Waking Dreams!" she wrote by way of salutation on Christmas Day, 1914, barely two weeks after her first letter. They had met, she had been conquered, they had shared the midnight hours, and she, in perhaps unconscious imitation of "Perdita" (by Mary Robinson, a minor nineteenth-century poet), meant to do it full justice. "Piercing the air, a golden crescent towers / Veiled by transparent clouds; while smiling hours / Shake from their varying wings celestial joys!" Perdita wrote. It was precisely right, if one can judge from Miriam's winged phrases, scattered in girlish abundance over page after page as her pen raced to keep up with her tempestuous feelings. Exclamation marks were liberally employed. Multiple references were made to classical allusions that may have puzzled her classically illiterate swain. But all, no doubt, was forgiven in the avalanche of compliments that was descending upon him. Every fiber of her being ached with desire. He was her first true love. They had reached heights of bliss hitherto unknown to humankind, and she, an ardent slave to passion, writhed at his feet. But, no! There she need not stay. He would enfold her in his purple pinions and together they would soar starward where, entwined in chrysolite, they would find emblazoned the eternally conjoined names of Frank, and . . . Oh, by the way, would he mind calling her Miriam? she added. As posterity would demonstrate, Maude Miriam Noel did not have much of a sense of humor.

Her letter reveals that they became lovers with a speed one would have thought breakneck for their times. It also suggests that Wright uncritically accepted her self-portrait along with her version of events, and complacently took as his due the cataract of compliments one might have expected him to write to her, rather than the reverse. By some uncanny sixth sense she had hit upon just the right note. As his adoring helpmeet she was prepared to provide as much approval and praise as he needed, or could stand. One must, of course, make allowance for the poetic conceits of the epoch as well as Noel's natural desire to apply balm to a wounded soul, but these reservations aside, one has to conclude that her panegyrics reached new heights, or depths, of hyperbole. Someone less gullible and self-absorbed than Wright would have been put on his guard very quickly, but Wright, sometimes so astute at discerning the motives of others, appeared not to suspect that her calls to noble conduct, some biblical citations, a high-minded use of the words "spiritual" and "pure" and similar references were calculated to soothe his Puritan sensibilities. She was even prepared to accept an unconventional liaison, after learning that he was not free to marry, although with a kind of dignified recoil. In short, she gave an impression of being exquisitely cultured and refined, a woman of the world who was wise in the ways of the human soul yet still capable of living with passionate abandon, truly courageous and noble of heart. He must have thought her perfection itself. Had he looked beneath this shining surface he might have discovered a certain thread of pessimism that, even then, clouded her emotional horizon. Their love was, perhaps, doomed to be fleeting, she continued. He would be bound to tire of her. He would cast her away, with only her shattered hopes for companionship. It had happened before and would happen again. What was it about men that made them turn on their women and blame them for their own shortcomings? What agonies she had suffered before, and what an effort it had taken to drag herself from the abyss. There was a veiled reference to another lover whom she had forced to confront his "cowardice." Years later, Wright would learn that Miriam Noel was referring to a fracas in Paris in which she had been engaged. It seemed she had set out to wreak "vengeance" on someone who had wronged her, with such deadly intent that she had been arrested by the French police.

However, if Wright had any reservations in 1914, these had less to do with Miriam's defects of character than his needs at the time. Before they met, he wrote, "I know how to be a lover but have never learned how to be a friend. (I feel that now I must learn.) And I have been so utterly flung back upon myself, damned at flood-tide—, finding more pitiably human now the 'self' I have lifted so proudly over circumstance for 'love' than was ever the case perhaps in many whom I have scorned—as I hunger for the living touch of some-one —something, intimately peculiar to myself—inviolably *mine.*' Yes —at times almost *anyone* or *anything.*" Five years later, he would confess to her that "I had not loved you much" (read, at all) "until I began to understand my hungry need at first and your gifts came to me in the dark like a ray of hope. I was, like you, in love with love . . . I took you as I take everything. . . ."

Long before Wright made this attempt at amends, in fact barely weeks after her ecstatic declaration of love, Miriam Noel had genuine cause for complaint, she later wrote. In those first days and weeks of their courtship she had taken extreme care with her appearance: "I put on the simplest, most expensive dress I owned, a soft brown velvet that outlined my neck and arms . . . with delicate shadings. My hat was a very small affair of cloth of gold. . . . My only jewelry was a ring representing a scarab . . . a gift from my daughter's father. It had come down as an heirloom in his family and was fabled to have been worn by Cleopatra as a charm against faithlessness in her lovers. A plain loose cloak completed my costume. . . ." Wright admired the results extravagantly, as he did everything else she wore, that is, until she had moved in with him at 25 East Cedar Street in Chicago. This meant, according to him, that they had "settled down," and he now began to complain that her clothes were far too conspicuous, worldly and sophisticated. Miriam Noel was taken aback, but since she had determined to "stay and do my best," she set about converting her wardrobe to satisfy his Puritan tastes. She also removed her family coat of arms from linen and stationery, which Wright thought un-American, and replaced it with his plain red square.

Then there was the matter of their menus. He disliked her Continental dishes and disapproved of the use of wine at meals, preferring bananas, codfish, salt pork and "such foods," she wrote. He knew that she smoked, but now he began to condemn it "bitterly." He went to Taliesin without her. He said that this house must be kept pure and unsullied, in memory of Mamah Borthwick; "[a] dead woman whom you tortured as you have tortured me and to whose memory you have given no real loyalty," she flared back. That Wright might have balked at installing a new mistress in his "love bungalow," and cringed at the thought of yet another scandal, was an idea that came to her only belatedly. Wright may also have known about a recent act of Congress, the White Slave Traffic, or Mann Act, named for its sponsor, the Chicagoan James Robert Mann. It was passed in 1910 as part of an international effort to suppress the worldwide trade in prostitutes and provided stiff penalties for the interstate transportation of women for "immoral purposes." Anyone, in short, who took an unmarried woman across a state line—as Wright did every time he went from Chicago to Spring Green—could be placed in an embarrassing position if charges were brought. And, in fact, Wright really did not want to continue what he would term his "entanglement" with Miriam Noel. He took his personal effects and moved out of 25

East Cedar Street. She conceded defeat: "I am going—the 'menace' to your safety no longer exists."

Early April of 1915 found her in Albuquerque, New Mexico, writing to "Dear Frank" instead of "Lord of my Waking Dreams!" He had returned to Taliesin and had been enjoying a visit from Llewellyn, Catherine, David and Frances, riding, singing, playing and having a good time. But he was troubled at the thought of her, left alone. He wrote, "It cannot continue Miriam. The disparaging discrepancy is too great it counts too heavily against me always—and I can not be or do the things you need to give you happiness—Your demands are beyond me—Your expectations sinister in my sight—I can not even *promise* to be '*true*' to you whatever you mean by it, I can only be true to myself and that is difficult enough. . . ." He was sending her some money, "which I felt necessary in this case," and encouraged her to pass him by because "perspective is gone! Reason is gone! Charity is gone—Now comes Fear—Hate—Revenge—Punishment—Then Regret—Shame, Humiliation—Ashes, It is the accepted Road—all ambitious Souls hear me! Sex is the curse of Life!"

It was the perfect moment for Wright to have ended a relationship he already knew could have only one outcome: "It is to be a narrow hard suspicious affair then? Another suffering ego to contemplate in the name of love?" he wrote sarcastically. Yet by the summer of 1915, Miriam Noel was living at Taliesin and some months after that, early in 1916, he was telling Darwin Martin that "I am beginning to see the light—at last—I know that it is love in the truest deepest sense and that it will by its sheer *goodness* dispel the darkness that has made me and mine so miserable." The lightning shift of mood seems inexplicable without additional information, which has not been uncovered. Anna had an operation sometime in 1915–16, and it is conceivable that faced with the prospect of losing her, he moved toward the remaining woman in his life who offered some comfort, who was willing to lay her entire life on the altar of his needs, as she wrote.

Frank Lloyd Wright and Miriam Noel left Chicago on August 30, 1915, and went to Taliesin. They stayed for two weeks, returning to Chicago on September 12. After a week they were back again, on September 19. These dates are known from the testimony of Nellie Breen, the housekeeper Wright had unwisely put in charge of Taliesin that year. She was small and elderly, carried an ear trumpet and had a highly developed sense of propriety that Miriam Noel's arrival had offended. She later explained that duty forced her to protest, since

Mr. Wright's children were also in the house. Her concern seems to have been somewhat forced given that, by then, Lloyd and John were married, Frances was in college, Catherine was taking a kindergarten course in Chicago and "cadeting" at Hull House and the baby of them all, Llewellyn, was in seventh grade. Nevertheless Mrs. Breen's displeasure was so marked that Miriam fled to her room and shut the door. Next morning Wright was singing hymns with his children and the crisis seemed to have passed. Miriam was delighted with the establishment and full of praise for its rare and valuable statuary, pictures and books. Nevertheless she found it somewhat stiff and formal. There were no curtains, cushions or comfortable chairs because Frank considered such embellishments "worldly." This did not suit her at all. She set about remedying the omissions, while Frank grumbled about the "effete" atmosphere she was creating.

Nellie Breen was dismissed in early October. Shortly thereafter she marched into the Department of Justice, claiming that Wright had violated the Mann Act by transporting a "sculptress of note" to and from Chicago and Spring Green during August and September. She handed the authorities a group of letters from the sculptress to Wright to bolster her case and demanded that deportation proceedings be begun against the lady since she was not an American citizen. Wright realized he was in trouble and engaged the services of Clarence Darrow, a lawyer already famous for his courtroom skills in defense of the underdog, and who would become nationally known in 1925 when he would defend a schoolteacher who had taught Darwin's theories of evolution in defiance of a Tennessee statute. Darrow presented as evidence five letters written by Mrs. Breen to support his countercharge that Miriam Noel was being threatened by her with bodily harm. The deportation charges were soon dropped, and no formal charges were ever brought against Wright under the Mann Act. That suspicion, however, had been raised and would return to haunt him.

Miriam Noel's memoir, understandably, does not mention this embarrassing episode or the fact that her letters had been stolen and subsequently published in a Chicago newspaper. At the time, however, she seemed charmed by the attention and even wrote a statement, published in the *Chicago Sunday Tribune*, in which she denied that she had been a victim of unrequited love, as those letters suggested. "Well might any woman proudly stand in my place and count the cost as nothing." In fact they both seemed to be enjoying the unusual opportunity to present themselves as the injured parties. A reporter who interviewed them in Taliesin noted, "Mrs. Noel appeared in a clinging gown of shimmering white. 'I have prepared a statement,' Mrs. Noel said, 'which embodies all I care to say about this affair. Mr. Wright and I have smoothed out all our little misunderstandings. I am here at Taliesin to stay. . . .'"

She was there to stay, but to say that all their misunderstandings had been set at rest would be an overstatement. A great deal of them would arise from her emotional insecurities, making her hypersensitive to slights, real or imagined. She attacked the Darrows for not including her when they invited Frank Lloyd Wright to dinner, and even dared to suggest that Mrs. Darrow was being far too warm and friendly to him. These charges have been deduced from an undated reply by Ruby Darrow. Mrs. Darrow parried the charges adroitly by poking gentle fun at Miriam Noel's contention that the relationship between her and Wright was "more delicate and sacred" than marriage, but in a way it was true. Without the security of a socially sanctioned union, Noel was at the mercy of any sudden shift in her lover's affections and, in fact, had shown how fearful she was from the start by wearing the amulet Cleopatra had supposedly owned to guard against such a possibility. Wright had only to look at another woman, and he was always loudly appreciative of feminine beauty, for her to go into a panic.

"O, it was really very terrible in its importance," she wrote, "and nearly destroyed my faith in you. Apart from your relations with me, I did not think you were that sort of man—a D'Annunzio type of talented dilettante—and my disillusionment and disappointment were appalling and my actual respect for you suffered seriously."

She knew from bitter experience just how unpredictable he could be. Once, when they were staying in a Chicago hotel, she had innocently gone off to a matinee of a play. He returned to the room in her absence and, angry and impatient to find her gone—Wright was incapable of waiting for anyone—threw their clothes into their suitcases and checked out. She, perfectly bewildered, not knowing of the change in plan, finally found him outside the hotel, one foot on the sidewalk and the other on the running board of a taxi. She was to get in the car; they must make a dash for it and catch a train; he had to be in Taliesin by nightfall. They roared to the station, arriving with seconds to spare. "It took a swarm of red caps to get the bags on board and he paid our train fare after we started. When the scramble was over and we were settled in the Pullman drawing room, he continued his silence."

He was obviously furious, and she, rather than take offense, artfully launched into a charming account of the play she had just seen. What a pity he had missed it! He must be sure to see it next time. His anger immediately evaporated, and he was all eager desire to see the wonderful play now, that very day. They got off the train at the very next station, commandeered the only telephone, reserved tickets for that evening and hired a car to take them back to Chicago. He had a wonderful time at the theater and "bubbled over with good nature and compliments."

Wright adored the challenge of catching a train and took it as a personal test of his mettle. "The nearest railway station, Spring Green, was two miles distant. Frank frequently arrived at the outskirts of the village just as his train whistled for the station. Standing up in the carriage with hair and coat tails flying, he grabbed the reins in one hand, the whip in the other, and the race was on. He got there just in time to board his train, breathless, ticketless, but there."

He also loved to entertain. When guests were expected, he was all over the house, demanding "upheavals" of cleaning, polishing and minute attention to the decor. Then he would dress himself in the very height of fashion, often in Japanese costume, and greet the arrivals with perfect courtesy. As Antonin Raymond confirmed, Taliesin was a heavenly place to visit—and yet. Wright was not an easy person at close quarters because "his nervous energy did not allow things to flow smoothly," Raymond wrote. If the day seemed to be proceeding calmly, Wright could be counted upon to stir things up.

Noémi was a particular friend of Miriam's and, because of this, was privy to her confidences and knew more about her life with Wright than she was comfortable with. Bit by bit, Antonin and Noémi found themselves becoming sucked into the whirlpool of emotions, insinuations, charges and countercharges that swirled around the central characters. As an example, Antonin described an evening that took place not long afterward, when they all found themselves in Japan. He was working in Wright's office on construction of the Imperial Hotel, and he and Noémi occupied an apartment near that of Wright and Madame Noel, as he called her.

In the middle of the night Miriam, in her nightclothes, "burst in" on them, crying hysterically. Frank had behaved badly, accusing her of heaven knows what in the crudest terms. She could not stand it a moment longer. They were calming her when Wright himself appeared, wearing an old-fashioned, short-sleeved nightshirt. He struck a dramatic pose, pointed his finger at Antonin and accused him of giving aid to "this creature," of being "a traitor" and more to this effect. Then he climbed into bed with the three of them, threw the bedcover over his shoulders and continued his caustic accusations. As Noémi began to crumple under the strain of such concentrated venom, Miriam, oddly enough, seemed to be feeling better. Whatever could be wrong, Miriam asked. Noémi was trembling! She began to console her. Wright calmed down. Miriam looked at him, and he looked at her; perhaps they smiled. Quite soon afterward, they left arm in arm. The Raymonds realized that in some way they did not understand, they had been made the cause of the quarrel. It was a very uncomfortable feeling.

10

The Cauldron

. . . I travelled
Seeking the sun of protection and safety
Accepting exile as payment for hope.
"A Woman's Message"
Poems from the Old English

The studio in which Antonin Raymond worked when he arrived at Taliesin in 1916 had spacious windows with a view of magnificent birches and the broad sweep of the Wisconsin River valley. In the center of the room was a stone vault in which Wright kept his superb Japanese prints, so as to be available for inspection at a moment's notice and, in a mezzanine above the vault stood his precious Steinway grand. This had been dragged out of a window two years before to save it from the fire and had lost its legs; for years it stood on drafting stools. In those days a portrait of Anna, which Wright had commissioned, hung in the room. It was the one painting he would tolerate in it, and the motto he had placed on the wall for periodic contemplation was "What a Man Does, That He Has." Its blithe assumption spoke to the optimist in him, the one who believed he was capable of anything, and it is interesting to contrast this public statement with that made by another flamboyant extrovert, his contemporary, Gabriele D'Annunzio, at the entrance to his own estate: "I have that which I have given away."

Work was far more than dutiful toil to Wright; it was the very stuff of living. In common with Arts and Crafts spokesmen from William Morris to William Price, Wright believed that work should be "the creative and joyful essence of daily life," and he was his own best example of just how exhilarating and revivifying the right work—that which called forth the individual's gifts and spoke to his profoundest needs—could be. He even wrote a song to celebrate his theme, dating from the earliest days of his independent practice, that speaks volumes for his lifelong beliefs:

> I'll live as I work as I am
> No work for fashion in sham
> Nor to favor forsworn
> Wear mask crest or thorn
> My *work* as befitteth a man
> *My* work
> Work that befitteth the man.

That defiant, here-I-am, take-it-or-leave-it quality that was his greatest strength and weakness finds clear expression here, and so does a Whitmanesque celebration of an individual's choices, his rights as a free man, along with the Romantic belief that fixity of purpose was the paramount virtue. It demonstrated an exuberant, unconquerably optimistic conviction that right attitudes would bring about the humanistic and organic architecture that was his lifelong obsession.

He was an early riser and often at work long before breakfast. He often said his best ideas came on the farm, in the fields and woods or beside the stream banks. "Thus he mentally designed great buildings when he was riding the road grader or directing the bull-dozer," his chief draftsman, John H. Howe, wrote. "Many times he came to the studio, direct from the farm, refreshed and bursting to put new ideas on paper. . . ." Or he might be there even earlier, carrying the back of an envelope on which he had sketched the germ of a new idea that had come to him in the middle of the night.

"He would enter the studio, sit down at the drafting board and immediately start 'playing' with T-square, triangles and compass on the plot plan or topographical map for the particular project to be designed. The resulting plan and sometimes a cross-section would contain the entire essence of his design. . . .

"It was this central 'idea' which constituted the soul of his buildings, all parts being integrated with the whole." He worked with enormous patience and concentration, giving extreme attention to detail, and the design inevitably went through innumerable revisions while he eliminated what might be "extraneous, discordant or capricious," Howe wrote. Such periods of concentrated effort would be interspersed with intervals at the keyboard playing Bach, Beethoven or his own improvisations. Or he might pull out a new group of Japanese prints to be admired at extravagant length. No matter how chaotic or tempestuous his personal life might be, Wright always stepped into the studio a happy man. "He was agile on his feet and often hummed snatches of favorite tunes, quoted the punch-line of a familiar joke or did a make-believe juggling act indicating that he was 'keeping all the balls in the air.' . . ." One of Wright's many apprentices to study in that studio recalled that one day when he was buried underneath the Steinway making another of the innumerable attempts to restore its legs, he saw the master saunter into the room. Believing himself alone, Wright arranged three or four objects on the window ledge, then stood back admiringly. He walked over to the piano, still oblivious of the hidden observer, struck a few chords and pirouetted out of the room, singing to himself, "I am the greatest."

One of Wright's charming qualities, Howe wrote, was his staunch championing of his clients. "He had the highest regard for each of his clients simply because they were *his* clients; he found virtues in them which were indiscernible to others and almost refused to acknowledge their shortcomings. . . ." In the case of the Imperial Hotel, it took no great effort on his part to be excited and challenged by such a great Japanese commission, but it had taken considerable patience. From the first hint, in 1911, that there might be such an opportunity to the day when he actually set sail for Japan took five years. Wright pursued the tempting possibility with unflagging zeal, aware that it was the opportunity of a lifetime.

The Imperial Hotel also presented an immediate objective along a path that was increasingly unclear. His Wasmuth portfolio, published in 1910 and 1911, had received far more attention and acclaim in Europe than in his own country. By that mental telepathy linking the best and brightest in any profession, young architects in Germany, France, Holland and elsewhere had immediately sensed the importance of Wright's ideas. The brilliant young German architect Georg Walter Adolf Gropius, founder of the Bauhaus, had, by 1914, already built the "Fabrik," a model factory and office building at the Werkbund Exhibition in Cologne, which was clearly influenced by Wright's designs for a bank and a boat club published by Wasmuth three years before. Dutch architects like Theo van Doesburg were turning to Wright for inspiration and, to at least one architectural historian, the Dutch *De Stijl* movement owed more to Wright's "interwoven stripping details and plastic masses" than to French Cubism, with which it is usually compared. Another Dutch architect, Robert van t'Hoff, built two houses in 1914–15 that were a direct outgrowth of Wright's ideas, and H. P. Berlage, another well-known Dutch figure, introduced Wright's work in lectures and exhibitions.

Then there was the young French architect Charles-Edouard Jeanneret, better known as Le Corbusier, who would become reluctant to acknowledge a debt to Wright. A letter of his, written in 1925, has been discovered in which he waxed eloquent about his first discovery of the latter's work: ". . . the sight of these several houses in 1914 strongly impressed me. I was totally unaware that there could be in America an architectural manifestation so purified and so innovative. . . . Wright *introduced order*, and he imposed himself as an architect. . . . Although I knew almost nothing about Wright, I still remember clearly the shock I felt at seeing these houses, spiritual and smiling. . . ." As for Richard Neutra, the young Viennese architect who would become one of Wright's assistants, the discovery of the Wasmuth portfolio was a revelation. "Whoever he was, Frank Lloyd Wright, the man far away, had done something momentous and rich in meaning. This miracle man instilled in me the conviction that, no matter what, I would have to go to the places where he walked and worked." Germany was clearly the next adventure, but Europe was at war, and Wright wanted to go somewhere. "I still imagined one might get away from himself that way," he wrote wistfully. The events of August 1914 had left him with a terrible sense of foreboding. As he wrote to his mother, "I feel the swerving of the financial helm occasionally, as I steer out of the dark that has always threatened to engulf my frail bark but I no longer feel the damp sweat on my forehead at night as I used to do at Taliesin waking in dread—of 'What now! I am at the bottom of my pile! The reserve that stood between me and utter defeat.' But that defeat was only material defeat out of which had it come at any time I might have won real success. So I do not really worry any more—although the habitual qualms of a lifetime echo and re-echo through me in this waking dream wherein we all seem somnambulists, walking innocently on the ridges of churches and the edges of precipitous banks— . . ."

The plural case was, no doubt, a reference to the Lloyd Jones family and the recent closing of the Hillside Home School. That distinguished institution never fully recovered from the combined shocks of Uncle James's bankruptcy, Wright's "love cottage" scandals and the terrible murder-fire of 1914. So many parents removed their children that autumn that the school did not complete its next term, and, in the spring of 1915, the Aunts were close to bankruptcy once more. This may have been the reason why a plan was worked out by which Hillside Home School, its gardens, acreage, outbuildings and all its furnishings, would be sold to Frank for one dollar. In exchange, he agreed to care for Aunts Nell and Jane by providing them with three rooms, bath and board, along with a small annual allowance. This arrangement seems to have satisfied everyone at first. As Raymond had discovered, Wright was at his most expansive just then, in the middle of a dozen ambitious projects, and as early as 1916 seems to have entertained the idea of reviving the school. He was equally ready to sell it if the price was right, and thought he had a buyer a year later, although nothing came of that. The Aunts had moved out to Los Angeles, where Lloyd and his new wife were living, but they soon had a new complaint: Frank would not send them any money. Jane's letters of the next two years become increasingly frantic. All too late she realized that Frank could not, or would not, provide a monthly check, and they had not insisted upon a penalty clause. The school's facilities had been deteriorating for some time and, when Antonin and Noémi found it, just a year after it had closed, Hillside was already in a bad state of disrepair. "Vandals got into the building and precious books and other objects littered the floors; many windows were broken."

After some months, Wright agreed to let the Aunts return to Taliesin, where they were under his roof and at his table. They were grateful for that, but agonized by the daily sight of their ruined school. Maginel wrote, "One day Aunt Jennie went back to the school. . . . She crept back into the great, echoing, empty building that had been her home, and up to her old room. She died there, alone." Aunt Nell, left at Taliesin, died there in 1919, but not before her nephew had been driven almost frantic by her daily fights with Anna. He wrote to his sister Jane Porter to say that he had been obliged to send Anna to visit her for a couple of weeks, because "the situation between her and Aunt Nell has got to such an acute stage that her misery pervades the whole house and her state is unbearable. . . . Mother herself is impossible to live with quietly but when Aunt Nell enters into the proposition then there is a perfect hell. . . ." It must have been clear to him that the "jealousies that burn fiercely and induce the fickleness and treachery that have poisoned the air . . ." threatened to light a new conflagration. Anna and Miriam must be separated, and soon. Japan was the solution.

The vast hotel Wright would spend the next six years of his life building (1916–22) belongs in concept to his Midway Gardens, rather than to any of his previous structures. It was to replace an older building that had outlived its usefulness, and it was basically designed in the form of an **H**, with a central block containing lobby, dining room, ballroom and other facilities. These public rooms were surrounded by large garden courts decorated with parapets and terraced with exquisitely selected plantings in the Japanese manner. Bedrooms were contained in the two long parallel wings. This was the plan in major outline, but so refined and elaborated that, at ground level, it seemed more like a Byzantine maze than a single building, and it was so ornamented and refined in finish that it strikes contemporary taste as far too "ornate and mannered." So cunningly was it put together that almost every guest room in the two enormous wings was different from every other bedroom. There were endless tiny terraces and miniature courts, tight passages opening into vast public areas, floors and ceilings of a bewildering number of heights, pools everywhere (not just for ornamental purposes, but in case of fire), windows in unexpected places, glazed doors leading to secluded balconies: it was all a stunning demonstration of spatial showmanship in the best Wright manner, brought to a high polish. For the hotel, which would eventually cost four and a half million dollars, was entirely under his control. He would design its every detail from exterior decoration to interior furnishings, right down to the plates and notepaper. One suspects that one explanation for this degree of fine detailing had to do with the architect's chronic shortage of funds. The exact amount of his fee is unknown, but if it was 10 percent, as is the case for another commission he received at this period, and not considered exorbitant, given the titanic amount of work undertaken, he stood to gain handsomely, even if his earnings were to be spread over a five-year period. It was, in short, in Wright's prudent business interest to design with a lavish hand, and in years to come he would gain a well-deserved notoriety for the way his costs magically rose far beyond the original estimates.

The Imperial Hotel was one of his favorite buildings, and he boasted about it all his life, whether because he believed it a milestone in his artistic development, or because it withstood a famous earthquake, is not clear. Norris Kelly Smith believed that, as a building, the Imperial Hotel was peripheral to Wright's main achievements, providing him with a challenge that "turned more upon an objective problem in engineering than upon metaphorical expression." The comment refers to the fact that the hotel had to be built on a site that would slither like a jelly in an earthquake: eight feet of surface soil riding on sixty to seventy feet of soft mud. Traditional Japanese houses had been built of wood and anchored with individual posts that were designed to withstand such stresses, but a structure of brick, stone, steel and reinforced concrete was another matter. It was a tricky problem, but it is fair to say that Wright was not entirely unfamiliar with it, since the first architects who rebuilt Chicago following the great fire faced a similar situation. They knew that the mixture of sand, clay and boulders underlying the surface of the city was unstable, making it highly undesirable as a foundation for the new skyscrapers that they were then in the middle of constructing downtown. One of the architects of this new building style was William Le Baron Jenney, in whose office Louis Sullivan worked when he first arrived in Chicago. Jenney, whom Sullivan always described as more of an engineer than an architect, was a pioneer in the design of foundations for such soils. The methods developed as a result subsequently became famous as the Chicago "floating foundation." Buildings were either supported by enormous pilings or caissons of concrete and steel or by "pads" of the same materials, resting, or "floating," on the clay, which would sustain and distribute the weight.

Sullivan had worked for Jenney; Paul Mueller, Wright's contractor for a number of major projects as well as for the Imperial Hotel, had worked for Sullivan. So the line from Jenney to Wright is direct, and it is likely that Wright had learned something about the proper distribution of weight on an unstable surface from this Chicago experience. His solution for his hotel was to build concrete "posts," or "fingers," under the center of each section; the floors were cantilevered from these pivots so that each unit was supported as it "floated" on its unstable base. Similarly, the hotel's walls were supported with a complicated system of pins, or fingers, allowing each part of the building to jiggle independently and return to its original position once the earthquake was spent. But Wright went even further in his

Interior view of Midway Gardens, Chicago

The Imperial Hotel, Tokyo, Japan, 1921

The Aisaku Hayashi residence in Tokyo, designed by Wright in 1917

determination to build a hotel that would not one day be a death trap, perhaps in memory of the new wing to the State Capitol in Madison that he had watched collapse so many years before. Instead of the customary Japanese roof tiles, which turned into murderous projectiles during an earthquake, he ordered a hand-worked, green copper roof. To prevent the walls from collapsing, he kept the center of gravity low, designing his walls thicker at the base than at the top. Instead of piping and wiring laid within the structure, which an earthquake would rip apart to devastating effect, his would be protected by covered concrete trenches and laid separately, in the ground. In short, whatever could be done would be. These decisions, some made over the heated objections of the financiers, would prove their worth even before the hotel's doors opened for business.

In the long years during which the new hotel was being built, Wright, always accompanied by Miriam, spent the bulk of his time in Japan, particularly from 1919 to 1922. He liked to arrive early in the year, returning shortly after the annual Imperial Garden Party, held at the height of the cherry blossom season and before the rainy season (May and June). Wright also spent months at Taliesin, particularly in the early stages, preparing the working drawings. In Japan, the work was supervised by Arato Endo, a Japanese architect who was almost a collaborator on the project and was, in any case, absolutely indispensable as liaison since Wright spoke no Japanese. The hotel was to replace the first Imperial Hotel, then still in use, which had been the height of fashion in the 1880s: high ceilings, vast halls, immense staircases and numerous dark, gloomy passages. The humid Japanese climate had ensured that the hotel smelled constantly of mold, but it was the only place in Tokyo large enough for balls, banquets and weddings, and its accommodations had been improved by the addition of an annex. One of the reasons why Wright remained in Japan for so many years was not just because of the laborious nature of the construction but also because, in 1920, when work was in full swing, the annex burned to the ground, and the pressure for an immediate substitute became intense: Wright designed a new wing in eight days. (The first Imperial Hotel was also destroyed by fire two years later.) Wright's energy was, as always, prodigious, but even he required an enormous staff, and he engaged several promising young architects who could act as supervisors during his absences. One of them was his son John, who, Ashbee noted in a letter to his wife, Janet, had become "a rather curious and dreamy person" with "beautiful reflective eyes." He was married to an artist, "dramatic and musical." Antonin Raymond, promised a handsome salary and all expenses paid, was another, and a third was Rudolph Schindler, an attractive and highly cultured Austrian who had studied in Vienna with Otto Wagner and Adolph Loos and then emigrated to Chicago, where he had worked for several years with an architectural firm before being hired to work on drawings for the Imperial Hotel. He would settle in Los Angeles and, with Richard Neutra, who worked for Wright a few years later, would become a leading exponent of the International Style on the West Coast.

As has been observed, it was characteristic of Wright to make himself entirely comfortable, no matter where he was, before any work could begin. At the old Imperial Hotel he was provided with a five-room apartment and a grand piano, and he had a car and chauffeur in constant attendance. After the new annex was built, he stayed in accommodations that he had thoughtfully designed for his own personal comfort. He called the suite "a modest little nook." No work began in the studio until a temporary office had been built at the job site; his staff was then put to work preparing detailed drawings and perspectives of the interiors and exteriors. The Raymonds, John and his wife, Wright and Miriam Noel, and Paul Mueller and his jolly, German-American wife were the only Westerners at the hotel. Most businessmen lived in the port cities of Yokohama, Kobe or Nagasaki, and the few Western diplomats and missionaries in Tokyo had their own compounds. Wright never altered his first impression of that city as ugly, redeemed by a few beauties hidden behind unpromising façades, and he moved up to the mountains at Karnizawa, where he would stay at local inns during the rainy season, making other trips to Kyoto, where the climate was better and temples and gardens purer in style. For, busy as he was, he always had time to hunt for treasures: Japanese prints, or "Chinese paintings and embroideries . . . old lacquer boxes, carved ivories, brocades, jade and all sorts of beautiful things," Miriam Noel wrote. As notables, they were invited everywhere, and Madame Noel was always included—a factor that probably contributed to her favorable memories of these events, because an invitation, now in the Taliesin Archive, shows that she was styled as "Mrs. Wright."

There were long intervals in Japan that seemed to go happily, perhaps because Miriam became so involved in Wright's work at an early stage. She wrote, "I felt warm and friendly toward people but they were not necessary so long as we had each other and the work that was our heart and soul. I didn't know there could be so much joy." There is a tradition that she even helped design some of the textiles used in the hotel, but this has not been verified. What is clear is that she had abandoned any thought of resuming her own career as a sculptor (because he objected), and that she focused her energies on "the work that was our heart and soul," that is to say, on his movements, his goals, his aspirations and his well-being. An incident took place in the spring of 1922, shortly before they left Tokyo, that would have reinforced Wright's belief that Miriam had psychic powers. After saying, at first, that she wanted to attend the annual garden party at the American embassy, and becoming angry because Frank forgot to get tickets, on the day of the party Miriam could not bring herself to leave the hotel. One might think this was the result of pique but, no, a sense of foreboding made her stay, she told him when he came to collect her in the car to go for a drive in the country. So the chauffeur was dismissed and Frank left her alone. He returned in a panic some time later: the hotel was on fire. They must save everything they could. He rushed to rescue his collection of Japanese prints, worth at least $40,000, and other valuable items in his possession, and she took charge of their personal effects: clothes, rugs, furs, jewelry, throwing them out of the window to the chauffeur waiting below. Had she not refused to leave the hotel they would have lost a substantial part of the collection he had worked so many years to amass. He must have been limp with gratitude to think that, for once in his life, he had been spared from the fire.

She was, perhaps, a woman of mysterious gifts but not an easy person to live with. He wrote that for many years she had "been the victim of strange disturbances," when she would become ill and the prey to various kinds of symptoms. "Then peace again for some time and a charming life."

Miriam does not mention these "strange disturbances," and there are no other eyewitnesses. Ashbee did, however, provide a vivid portrait of the exotic Madame Noel, of whom he evidently disapproved, though he gave her a kind of grudging admiration. Writing to Janet, he noted that she used face powder, which he disliked, and wore clothes ten years too young for her, to put it mildly. But there was, just the same, something rather engaging about the amused look in her soft gray eyes, and she definitely had panache, in her curious and somewhat skimpy homespun dresses, wearing an embroidered Turkish towel, looking like a toque, around her hair. Ashbee also thought that Madame Noel had Wright "absolutely in the palm of her hand," and was giving him a valuable introduction to the fine points of French manners and mores. As evidence of Miriam Noel's superior will, he recounted an incident that took place while he was at Taliesin. Wright had joked that she must not appear for lunch unless she changed her dress. She took him at his word, locked herself in her room and refused to emerge even though he made a personal appeal. "In the evening she appeared, radiant, in white silk, with a black velvet zuave and a diamond crescent—a sort of Diane de Poitiers. Then she made her conditions—publicly bringing him to heel before me.

" 'There's one thing I cannot allow—that you come to meals with me in your riding breeches!' " Ashbee's comment was, "Chicago being whipped into grace."

Frank and Miriam spent the remainder of the evening absorbed in designing a new dinner costume for him to be made of white linen. It was one more of the artistic costumes Wright would affect, while at home in Taliesin in those years, and was on a par with his all-velvet suit, complete with lace collar and cuffs, in which he was photographed beside his immense living room fireplace, managing to

Frank Lloyd Wright at his desk in the early 1920s: a probable self-portrait

The west façade of Hollyhock House

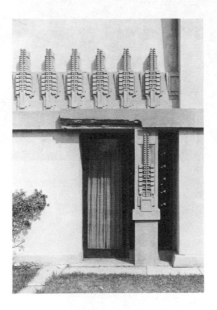

The Hollyhock motif: detail from the southwest terrace

The fireplace in the living room of Hollyhock House

look manly despite it, and decidedly aesthetical. The same cannot be said for the freakish clothes he affected in Tokyo: curiously shaped and draped hats, immense bows dangling from the neck, tasseled cummerbunds, trouser legs folded over and buttoned at the ankle to create a disconcerting, bloused effect, and high heels. It is likely that such sartorial excesses were encouraged not only by Miriam but also by his new friendship with Rudolf and Pauline Schindler, advocates of unfettered Bohemianism: nude sunbaths, fresh fruit and vegetables and loose garments of natural fibers, cut on the bias and anchored only with ties.

Everyone knew that Wright was a pacifist. Ashbee listened toler-antly, merely suggesting that Wright be sure of his facts as the latter belligerently proclaimed his pro-German sympathies and attacked the British position; Miriam, agonizingly concerned about Paris, was less diplomatic. Wright remained a convinced pacifist through both world wars, a belief that stemmed from his conviction that these wars were entirely due to British imperialism. This would have been perfectly consistent with a good Welshman's belief that any war the British aristocracy was fighting was bound to be wrong and therefore no concern of his. When his patriotism was later questioned, the Federal Bureau of Investigation concluded, according to a report in its files, that Mr. Wright was not un-American, just violently anti-English. Apart from his bias, it would be a point of pride for Wright to rally around that other noted pacifist in the family, Jenkin Lloyd Jones, as he sailed into the war zone trying valiantly to stop the conflict. Once it appeared that the United States was about to enter the war on the British side, Jenkin Lloyd Jones became the target of intense criticism and was even harassed by the United States government, which refused to accept his magazine, *Unity*, for the mails. It was Uncle Jenk's last, heroic cause, and it proved too much for him. As he fought to have the ban lifted, Jenkin Lloyd Jones was oper-ated on for a hernia, then had a heart attack. He was recuperating when the news came that *Unity* could once more be mailed. His last act would be to read the proofs for the new issue. He died on September 12, 1918, not quite seventy-five years old, and two months short of the armistice. Ashbee wrote, "The puritan chapel in the valley is now empty and the voice of 'the Lord' no longer heard there."

* * *

With his design for the Imperial Hotel, Frank Lloyd Wright did everything possible to accommodate his building to the conditions of its site, and it is curious, given his adoration for all things Japanese, that the result is so un-Japanese in character. Numerous explanations have been advanced for this unsatisfactory state of affairs, but the most plausible is the most obvious, i.e., that for some time Wright's roving eye had been focused in a new direction, this time on other venerable cultures, the American Indian and pre-Columbian. His interest in the former had been vivid since childhood, and the two murals he commissioned for the walls of his and Catherine's bedroom in Oak Park took the Indians of the Midwestern Plains as their subject. As has been noted, the World's Columbian Exposition provided a cornucopia of architectural ideas for a young man with Wright's impressionable tastes: not just the Japanese buildings, but everything from Persian bazaars to Lapland villages. Faint echoes of these diverse influences, what Vincent Scully has called Wright's "continual 'condensation' of multiple sources into 'new unities' with a special richness of their own," have been discerned in many of Wright's early designs, but the first clear evidence that he was now exploring pre-Columbian themes did not appear until 1915, with a warehouse design for his birthplace of Richland Center. This is evidently derived from the Temple of Three Lintels at Chichén Itzá in the Yucatán. "What Wright wanted is . . . clear: maximum mass, sculptural weight, a monumentality even more dense and earth-pressing than he had achieved before—and one more primitive, separate from his earlier culture, exotic to his eyes, and deep in time." Certain aspects of the Imperial Hotel—its scale, its monumental entrances and its particular kind of ornamentation—attest to the fact that Wright was continuing in this same direction, but another project that he undertook at the same time takes these ideas to a triumphant fulfillment. It was one of his most ambitious residential endeavors: Hollyhock House, built for a Los Angeles oil heiress, Aline Barnsdall. Once dismissed as hopelessly imitative and dated, Hollyhock House has been reconsidered in the light of postmodernism and is now seen as one of Wright's "most significant works and modern architecture's most splendid achievements," Neil Levine wrote.

Its owner, born Louise Aline Barnsdall in Bradford, Pennsylvania, was the granddaughter of a pre–Civil War oil pioneer and daughter of Theodore Barnsdall, an astute businessman who vastly increased the family's prosperity. From the start, her interests were cultural and intellectual: she spent her adolescence in Europe pursuing a career in theater and music. She then moved to Chicago during what has been called the "Chicago Renaissance," a period just before World War I when the newly established Little Theatre was a leader in the production of avant-garde plays, Harriet Monroe's *Poetry* magazine was publishing T. S. Eliot and Ezra Pound, and a new literary magazine, *The Little Review*, with editorial direction from Pound, was serializing that shocking new book, James Joyce's *Ulysses*. Kathryn Smith, a Wright scholar who has written extensively on the early histories of the Imperial Hotel and Hollyhock House, found evidence that Barnsdall approached Wright at an early stage with the idea of designing a new and larger building for the Little Theatre. This idea fell through, perhaps because Barnsdall soon became eager to establish her own theater in Los Angeles and again approached Wright to design one. The fact that he had never built a theater in his life would, of course, be a minor detail, one Wright would have dismissed as easily as he had turned aside objections from Uncle Jenk that he did not know how to design a church, all those years ago.

Besides, he liked the site. In 1919, Aline Barnsdall bought a thirty-six acre tract of land in Los Angeles called Olive Hill, a prominent local landmark at the edge of the Los Angeles Basin, with unimpeded views of the city to the southeast, the San Gabriel Mountains to the north and the Pacific Ocean in the distance. It must have seemed like a golden opportunity to create a second Taliesin and, in fact, Wright's first sketches for Olive Hill are marked TANYDERI TALIESIN, Tany-deri being the house Wright had designed for his sister Jane on the family property. Since Barnsdall, who had just inherited her father's fortune, was prepared to turn the whole hill into an artists' encampment, complete with a movie theater, stores and satellite residences as well as a handsome house for herself, the opportunity was too good to miss. The commission seemed to take Wright a step closer toward a move he had been considering intermittently. Years before, his daughter Catherine, newly arrived on the West Coast, had written to tell him that a development boom was on and he ought to come west to take advantage of it. This would become even truer during the postwar building boom of 1919–22. Wright's eldest son, Lloyd, who had begun as a landscape draftsman in the Boston offices of Olmsted and Olmsted (1910–11), had moved out to the West Coast to join the offices of Irving J. Gill, a prominent architect, where he worked as a draftsman and delineator and established himself in independent practice in 1915. A year later he became head of the design department at Paramount Studios and would work closely with his father on the construction and landscaping for Hollyhock House and Olive Hill. Wright finally decided to move his own offices out to the West Coast in the spring of 1923, but the venture was short-lived, and he returned to Chicago barely two years later. In the years 1914 to 1924, Smith writes, Barnsdall gave Wright commissions for forty-five buildings.

In our own age Aline Barnsdall would be remarkable enough; given her epoch, her attitudes, ambitions and independent life-style are little short of amazing. Long before it was intellectually fashionable she supported the Russian Revolution and had a close friendship with a Russian-born anarchist, Emma Goldman, who was deported from the United States in 1919. The theater company she formed in Los Angeles—unfortunately, it ran for only one season, 1916–17—attracted some first-rate talents. Among them were Kira Markham, formerly with Chicago's Little Theatre, who would marry Lloyd Wright; Norman Bel Geddes, a talented scene designer who would have a brilliant future; and an artistic director named Richard Ordynski. Barnsdall discreetly began living with Ordynski and shortly thereafter gave birth to her only child, Aline Elizabeth. Her daughter took her mother's surname and was known for years as "Sugar Top."

The history of Olive Hill faithfully reflects the quixotic elements of Barnsdall's personality. She was, like her architect, living outside of conventional morality, as scornful of it as he was, freed by her wealth to build a community of her imagination on a tract of land that would conspicuously proclaim her freedom from petty constraints and flaunt her unconventionalism before the world. She was, however, a woman of as many facets and fleeting moods as the man whose talents she engaged; never quite able to build a theater, though she flirted with the idea for years; never there when she was needed during construction, always appearing at the worst moments; picking up new ideas and abandoning others with a speed and arbitrariness that matched Wright's. In the end, only Hollyhock House, two studio residences and a kindergarten were ever built, partly because of her inability to make decisions, the gradual decline in her income and a kind of final reluctance to have her dream of perfection become tainted by grubby reality. After building a magnificent house she hardly ever lived there and finally gave the whole property to the city of Los Angeles. One of her letters of impossible instructions is worth quoting: "We are going ahead with it," she wrote of the house, "but worry because you are not here to decide on the color. I don't want it to *look* green but to *feel* green. . . ." Wright would have some pertinent comments to make later about these "arbitrary conditions." If she thought he was spending too much money she was capable of stopping him in his tracks with a kindly reproof. Artists were perfectionists by nature. In pursuit of beauty they would cheerfully bankrupt anyone, but she did not intend to allow that to happen to her. Since they were both Celts they were too much alike not to be at loggerheads, she concluded. This did not prevent her from admiring him enormously. She had never met anyone more delightful, fascinating, charming, gifted, and genuinely nice, she told him. If only he were not so old-fashioned. It was high time he read George Bernard Shaw and realized that there was a new kind of woman in the world. "You judge me by a deep-rooted conventionality within your self," she concluded. "You are free in your art but not in your relation to life."

As for Wright, after defending the completed Hollyhock House as a miracle that had somehow been built despite the obstreperous interference of his client and her staff—"You will marvel then, perhaps, as I do, that a thing so harmonious, strong and unlike anything of its kind in the world—should be there at all," he wrote after it was finished—he was all too ready, a mere nine years later, to dismiss it. It seemed that Hollyhock House had an intractable roof problem. It insisted upon leaking (not that Wright blamed himself for that, of course). But, he wrote, "let's forget it. The damned thing will float away some day and be forgotten. It was a transition building. . . ."

Almost anyone who visits Hollyhock House (named for the flowers found growing wild on Olive Hill) is irresistibly reminded of a Mayan temple deep in the Yucatán, imposing, awe-inspiring, monumental and forbidding. Its fortresslike appearance, however, conceals an inner courtyard in the local Spanish Colonial tradition, to which its numerous rooms, symmetrically organized, have easy access. A stream, wandering through lush foliage, connects circular and square reflecting pools, adding to the impression of an oasis in a desertlike climate— a secluded, precious refuge from the heat and the blare of a large modern city. The house is, as one would expect, extremely spacious and luxurious in feeling, with guest quarters, library, music room and a roof terrace, but its most dramatic space, the living room, is a symmetrical double square crowned by a tentlike ceiling; the room contains a massive fireplace actually surrounded by a miniature moat, or pool, and crowned with a skylight placed so as to reflect the starry sky and the flickering flames of the fire. Nothing, in short, could be more outré, more Hollywood-in-the-nineteen-twenties in its romantic symbolism, or, as it turns out, more poetic and mythmaking: "Fire and water emerge from the cracks and crevices of the earthy stone floor under the blistering sun of the California sky to condense in one complex form Wright's perception of the violent forces of nature," Levine wrote.

For years Hollyhock House was viewed as an aberration, a romantic and iconoclastic detour from the master's great purpose. It was thought that his career as an architect had reached its peak in 1910, with his great Prairie Style houses, and that everything that followed (at least before the 1930s) represented a falling-off of concentration and inspiration, attributable to the chaotic events in his personal life. Levine, however, is one of the authors to see Hollyhock House as further evidence of Wright's superb responsiveness to the natural world and the connotations of the site, in short, the spirit of place. In Wisconsin, nature was benevolent, lush and bucolic, but in Japan, where he would design much of Hollyhock House, he would have his first experience of another kind of nature, destructive, terrifying and awe-inspiring. That exquisite sensitivity made it inevitable that Wright would then begin designing in an entirely new way and one that, to him, summed up his instinctive response to life on the Pacific rim of the world, to its grandeur, its unpredictability and its implacable power. Wright, who had always emphasized that his goal was an "organic" architecture, however inadequately he might have defined the term, became, if possible, more emphatic about this as he aged. It was an important clue, if one believes, as does Levine, that he was remaining faithful to a classical view of architecture as an art of representation, or the imitation of nature. Seen in this light, there was nothing deviative about his design for Hollyhock House. Levine wrote, "It represents an abstraction and an idealization of the forces of nature through a form of expression that helped release Wright's architecture" from whatever limits the fashions of the moment might have imposed.

If one accepts the view that Wright had the rare gift of being able to experience moments of heightened perception, then one also has to suspect that he had another such "moment of vision," as such experiences were termed by Kenneth Clark, at some time during his stay in Japan. There are several reasons to think that this happened, and at least one of them is persuasive. To begin with, he is known to have designed yet another house for himself shortly after his return, this one for a site in the Mojave Desert, probably at a time when he was planning to move from Chicago to the West Coast. (The house was never built and exists only in a sketch.) It is a small building folded into the rear of an octagonal court, its walls as fortresslike as those of Hollyhock House and its interior rooms designed in the same manner, to face an inner courtyard and a circular pool. Its shape, however, was hardly Mayan. To find an analogy, Levine believes, one would have to look at the oriental cisterns, pots and jars he was collecting at this period. This itself is significant since Wright's designs for his own houses may safely be taken as primers for his most experimental thinking at any given point. But there is even stronger evidence for Levine's thesis, made in a fascinating essay, "Frank Lloyd Wright's Own Houses and His Changing Concept of Representation," that the shape of the vessel suddenly suggested, to Wright, a whole new way of looking at architecture. Indeed, one of the maxims he invariably quoted in later years, from Okakura's *Book of Tea*, was by Lao-tse and defined a building in terms of the space it enclosed. This definition clearly influenced Wright's subsequent description of his own buildings as "vessels of space" and his architecture as "architecture of the within." Once Wright returned to Taliesin he removed *Flower in the Crannied Wall* from its place of honor, replacing it with an enormous Ming tub, perhaps the clearest evidence that a momentous shift had taken place in his thinking. Referring to the ability of artists like Thomas Bewick and Rembrandt to turn "human experiences directly into graphic symbols," Clark wrote, "We are reminded of the burning glass, casting its ray brighter and deadlier as its focus grows sharper, till suddenly a feather of smoke warns us that it has achieved, through intensity, a transformation of matter."

The years during which Wright was working on the Barnsdall projects and the Imperial Hotel seem to have been one of the few periods during which his helter-skelter finances were almost under control. The Barnsdall correspondence shows that, by the end of 1921, he was expecting a total of $90,000 in commissions from that account alone, and had worked out an agreement with his client and the Bank of Wisconsin, the main mortgage holder for Taliesin, that future payments (with the exception of some $36,000 already received) would be sent directly to the bank in settlement of his debts. By the summer of the following year, he could tell Darwin Martin that Taliesin, with its two hundred acres, was now owned free and clear. All he owed at that point was his debt to Martin plus a $15,000 mortgage on Oak Park (or so he said). By his estimate he had amassed an extremely valuable collection of Orientalia, not just prints but gold screens, Chinese paintings, sculpture, antique rugs, bronzes, pottery and embroideries, to a total value of $60,000 to $70,000 and worth twice that on the New York market. (One of his steady customers was the Metropolitan Museum of Art, which had acquired about $20,000 worth of Wright's prints between 1918 and 1922, but that source of sales dried up after a group of prints he had, in good faith, sold as genuine, were judged almost worthless because they had been reworked.) After a long round of negotiations of baffling complexity, Wright had wrested back control of the Oak Park property from his debtors. Both units had been renovated and rented out, and he would soon sell the entire property to a prominent real estate dealer in Chicago for $33,000. While he was still, with characteristic charm, beguiling his way out of repaying his remaining debt to Martin, he might have been perfectly able to do so, at that moment at least. What held him back could have been a divorce settlement, which seemed possible at last. Word had come through his daughter Catherine that Kitty was willing to agree to a quiet divorce (legally available on the grounds of five years' separation). Her terms were a cash settlement of $10,000 plus possession of the household furnishings, and $150 a month alimony. All this was signed and settled on November 13, 1922, the decree to become final one year later. Not surprisingly, he immediately felt poor again. He wrote to his *"Lieber Meister"* two weeks later, "I am going to tell you a secret which I hope you will keep—: I am extremely hard up—and not a job in sight in the world. My 'selling' campaigns have failed. . . ." It must have been a relief, nevertheless, to have the reality of their estrangement acknowledged, after thirteen years. A year later, when the divorce became absolute, he expressed his satisfaction in a letter to his son John. That phase of his life, at least, was over.

Wright had created so much elaborate detailing for the Imperial Hotel's façade that the work could be guaranteed to creep along at a snail's pace. Raymond wrote that this was "the result of doodles over initial drawings by myself and other draftsmen, executed with amazing dexterity by Wright with the aid of triangles and a T-square." On the other hand he was also capable of complaining, as he did to Martin, that the Japanese project was not profitable because it had "dragged out too long—about five years—." For despite, or because of, the skill of Japanese carpenters and masons, who were willing to spend months transferring Wright's designs into the intricate tracery that covered every square inch of the hotel, the patience of the backers was at an end. Raymond states that Wright was discharged before the building was finished; Wright states that he left because he was no longer needed. The truth is probably somewhere in between, the skyrocketing costs and a perpetually delayed opening having had the predictable results. By April 1922, the month that the first Imperial Hotel burned down, the backers were mutinous. This must have been the moment at which he was called to a meeting and questioned relentlessly. He wrote, "The foundations. Always the foundations— and the money. The money!"

Just as matters looked blackest, fate intervened to give the architect his first vote of confidence. Four days after the Imperial Hotel fire, on April 26, 1922, while Wright was working in his office on the top floor of the hotel's new left wing, Tokyo received the worst earthquake it had had for thirty years. He wrote, "The structure was literally in convulsions. I was knocked down by the rush of workmen and my own boys to save their own lives. . . ." He heard a fearful crash and was convinced that the new section, containing the banquet hall, had fallen. He discovered that what did fall were the five chimneys of the old hotel, all that remained from the fire. His building had stood and he could write, "The work had been proved."

This put everyone back on speaking terms with the architect. He could now make a graceful exit and did so three months later, in the wake of much ceremony and expressions of genuine regret by his Japanese associates. It was a splendid victory, and it was only the first. The Great Kanto earthquake, the biggest to hit Japan in the twentieth century, took place a year and a half later, on September 1, 1923. By a perverse coincidence, this was the day that the hotel, now completely finished, was to be formally opened. An official luncheon had been planned for that noon and, a few minutes before, the earthquake struck. During the next twenty-four hours there were continuous aftershocks, winds of hurricane force and then the dreaded fires that destroyed nearly half the city. About 150,000 people lost their lives. All communication was cut off with the outside world, and when the first rumors reached the American newspapers it was reported that the Imperial Hotel was in ruins. Miriam Noel wrote, "We had word that the building was destroyed and Frank was so wounded I thought he would die that week. Finally word was received that the hotel had survived the shock with only slight damage." In fact the building had been used as a home for refugees, where free meals had been dispensed to thousands, and it had become the temporary headquarters for embassies, public utilities and the press. "Within a matter of days," Kathryn Smith wrote, "the hotel became an object of praise for Japanese and foreigners alike and Wright was hailed as its architect." Now well into his fifties, Wright's oeuvre, hundreds of structures built or projected, his inventiveness, his methods and his skill, seemed to be crowned by the triumphant success of the Imperial Hotel. He had arrived, at last.

Young men, like the architects Schindler and Neutra, and the equally gifted German architect Erich Mendelsohn, were beginning to knock at his door and beg for the privilege of studying at the master's feet. After one such meeting in 1924 Mendelsohn, then at the start of his career, wrote that his conversation with Wright had ranged over every conceivable subject, from aesthetics, society and mankind to the future of religion. "He says," Mendelsohn wrote, "that the dualism of God and man is disappearing: man is himself a god; there is only one creator, just as there can only be one architecture, only one space. Am I a dreamer because I am younger, because I still *believe*, where he already knows?" Next day, Mendelsohn left Taliesin in a daze of admiration. Wright's development as an architect, great as it was, had only just begun. "His genius is beyond doubt." The term began to enter descriptions of Wright. Aline Barnsdall was willing to concede only his "genius for getting into trouble."

Without being ill, Wright was never really well during those years when he was traveling between Los Angeles, Tokyo and Spring Green. The sea voyage invariably upset him, which did not prevent him from hoping optimistically that the sea air would act as a restorative, on occasions when he was recovering from a bad cold or a bout of influenza. He had at least one accident on the job. He wrote to Pauline Schindler in the spring of 1922:

A small four-cornered wood block has just laid me up here— unable to put my foot down—since I stepped down upon it weeks ago—

Cyrano you remember, whose whole life was one heroic adventurous gesture got knocked out finally by a flower pot dislodged by a careless servant from the window sill above his head as he was passing below.

I am sure the flower in the pot was a Geranium. Pessimism can go no further. . . .

Despite the lighthearted tone, letters of this period indicate that Wright was experiencing, for the first time, an awareness of his own mortality. He wrote to his daughter Catherine and her new husband, Kenneth, "Once upon a time I never could strike the bottom of my physical resources—but now I find out that my grey hair and fifty three years—indicate something that I will have to pay attention to—." Then there was the continual anxiety about Taliesin, left to the mercy of workmen, caretakers and friends, and his fears were sure to be reinforced by his mother's bulletins, which invariably contained some new complaint that an employee supposedly there to safeguard the property was loafing or neglecting a repair. He missed having a "good old-fashioned home," as he put it to Catherine. He was loneliest of all at Christmas, despite Miriam's company. He wrote to his daughter, "Christmas and New Year's used to be so lively and full of everything from candy to grief—that of late years I rather dread it for its lack of little children—." Most of all, he was tired of being a perpetual exile. "I have had a terrible quest for the repose of heart and mind that meant *home* to me," he told his mother. "Have waded through rivers of tears and blood to find it with a ruthlessness seldom if ever heard of—but always with a fool's sincerity and hope at least and a man's courage." What he wanted and needed at this stage of his life was a loving relationship and a calm and tranquil home, the one boon, it seemed, that life withheld.

For several years past he had been aware that his mother presented him with an almost insoluble dilemma. To turn her out of Taliesin was unthinkable. The best that could be hoped for was an occasional respite from her presence when she visited Jane or Maginel; yet to live with her was a guarantee of continual turmoil. She created so much dissension, suspicion and doubt around her and had such a way of interfering in his affairs that she was making his life unbearable. Yet, whenever he complained of this to his sisters he invariably provided Anna with a defense. She could not help being the way she was; she was made that way. Behind this reasoning can be seen a conviction that Anna was so much on his side and so fiercely loyal that, naturally, she would be bound to resent any other woman in his life and see her as a rival. That was forgivable, even lovable in a way, and her letters were so full of tender concern and affection that it was easy to forget how destructive she could be at close quarters. Besides, she was now very frail and subject to frequent fainting spells when she would fall, whatever she was doing, and be disoriented for days afterward so that she could no longer be left alone with any confidence.

However, there was no doubt that a return to Taliesin meant trouble ahead, if Anna remained there. He and Miriam had managed to live together now for several years in occasional peace and harmony. He wrote in the early summer of 1919, "We ride about a good deal, buy a little here and there, have a little time for two or three friends—Read together, study some each in his or her own way, work at prints—walk over Tokio—and eat three meals every day and sleep ten hours or so every night." Nevertheless, their relationship had been scarred by her pathological jealousy of any woman in whom he appeared to show an interest. Barely weeks after he wrote to his mother giving her this description of their tranquil life, Miriam Noel fled to a country inn outside Tokyo because, she claimed, Wright was attracted to Madame Krynska, a Russian friend of hers. No doubt he expressed his usual naïve enthusiasm for an attractive personality, and, no doubt, Miriam Noel took it as proof that her precarious position in his life was about to be usurped. The rest was predictable; storms of reproaches and rage from her, after which she would throw her clothes into her suitcase and flee, composing a barrage of future letters as she went. The latest scene had taken place one terrible night when they were all together. Piecing together the evidence it appears that Miriam Noel had pulled out a gun, threatening to kill Madame Krynska or herself or both, and that Wright had wrestled it from her. (She, by her own admission, once threatened him with a knife.) He had, subsequently, intercepted a wounding letter she had written to the lady, defending that as his right as her "husband." Interestingly, Wright nowhere reproaches Miriam Noel for her insane suspiciousness. Rather, it is his fault for his shameful behavior, for the suffering he has inflicted upon her, for his chicanery and innate crookedness. It was as if he took a kind of melancholic pride in their violent encounters for, as he later wrote of her, "I loved her enough to kill her and myself." He needed such proof of the indispensable role he played in Miriam Noel's life, as he did in his mother's, to keep at bay some terrible inner insecurities. For, however irrational Miriam's behavior, it is clear that there was more than a core of justification for it. So long as they remained unmarried, she was socially as well as emotionally vulnerable, however much he might consider her his wife and style her as such in his letters. Ideals of free love were one thing; the reality of life in the straitlaced Middle West was something else. If they were to live together in Wisconsin and Illinois, nothing less than an old-fashioned marriage contract would do.

She left him at least once more while they were in Japan, spending several weeks in a secluded village. This may have been the occasion when Wright wrote to tell Maginel that the affair was over and received her congratulations. The date was the spring of 1920, by coincidence the moment that Anna was visiting Frank in Tokyo. She had made the trip because one of Frank's attacks of a Japanese fever had proved intractable. For some weeks he seemed critically ill, and Anna insisted upon going to his side. (She found him much improved and immediately took to bed with an attack of sciatica.) Perhaps Anna's arrival was the reason for Miriam's departure, or perhaps she had left some weeks before, precipitating an emotional upheaval in Wright that expressed itself in physical terms. To judge from a fragmentary diary Anna wrote while in Japan, Frank had been alone for some time, and apart from a single reference to the "enraged woman," Anna makes no mention of her rival, though she goes into long descriptions of the life she observed, the drives through avenues of cherry blossoms, and magical garden parties.

Maginel feared that the separation might not last, and this was well founded. Once at a distance, and under less emotional pressure, Wright felt his usual remorse and regret. He could then write to Miriam in the heartfelt and unguarded way in which he invariably wrote to Anna, judging from the handful of letters that has survived. One in particular is remarkable for its revelations about the extent of his sense of guilt and self-disparagement along with his resolutions to improve. He was prepared to do anything to win back the one who had become his ideal, and if she was suspicious and resentful, jealous and subject to sudden moods, the time might come, he wrote to Anna, when "her fears and suspicions born of an experience with me at my worst" might gradually subside. "And I guess her better self . . . lies mostly with me. She is very proud and sensitive and she is mostly in the right."

The most likable aspect of Wright's nature, the one that was capable of admitting his faults and making a heroic effort to understand the feelings of his nearest and dearest, could have been counted upon to make major accommodations once Miriam was to be moved to Taliesin as its new chatelaine. The one factor over which he had no control was his mother's opposition, and that was relentless. It was obvious, she wrote to Jane soon after his affair began, that Madame Noel had changed Frank's whole nature. Anna was convinced that this lady was Russian, which would explain her "cruel, tyrannical" ways. And now Frank was becoming a tyrant. She was very sad about that. To Miriam Noel, Anna was far more tactful but evidently not diplomatic enough, because Miriam soon attacked her on the most sacred grounds of all. Anna might have been Frank's confidante during his childhood and adolescence, but she did not seem to understand that things had changed. The person closest to Frank's heart nowadays was not Anna, but Miriam. This letter, written barely two years after she had met Wright, was a clear provocation, and even sharper reproofs were to follow. The battle lines had been drawn at an early stage despite Anna's protestations to her son that she had gone out of her way to make Miriam feel accepted and at ease.

Frank and Miriam returned to Spring Green in mid-August of 1922, and a month later, Wright was writing to his sister Jane and begging her to do something about their mother. His suggestion was that she be installed at Tan-y-deri, with a woman to take care of her. He wrote, "I say Tanyderi because . . . she won't go out of the Valley. Oak Park doesn't get a rise of any kind no matter how hard I try. I have no home here while mother is here." In other words, Miriam was refusing to live at Taliesin, and he was forced to put her up in a hotel. "The situation between Mother and M. is utterly—irreparable. And, maybe, now that I have allowed her to be kept out of her home with me . . . by 'Mother' she will not return to Taliesin again.

"This is painful and expensive and wasteful but I can't help it," he continued. "And it is miserable for both. You can say I could change it to a reasonable basis if I would. You know nothing about it. I can't, there you are." Jane had suggested that Anna be moved to a sanitarium, but, "[a] sanitorium [*sic*] is out of the question for Mother unless you want to take her there chloroformed. She won't go," he declared. As for her falling sickness, that was not going to end her life. "She comes through wherever she is. She has just come through another—sunk so low I thought she was dying and sent for Uncle Enos. Next day (yesterday) she sat up bright and dressed and snappy as ever."

Jane's reply to this is not known, but from the scanty evidence available it is clear that Anna's fate had been sealed, because Wright was, at the same time, writing to tell Darwin Martin that he would soon be all alone and inviting them to "run up" to Spring Green for a week to view his oriental treasures. He wrote, "A reunion on my own ground . . . of myself and my old clients whom I have truly so unconscionably abused would do my drooping spirits much good." The rare display of contrition, the warmth of the invitation and the picture of abandonment hinted at in this letter are all indications of the emotions that had been aroused by this latest crisis. And if Wright had managed to avoid choosing between Mother and Catherine, or Mother and Mamah, he could no longer evade the issue, because Miriam was determined to make him choose. He had, with no doubt an extremely uneasy conscience, taken sides with the woman he had treated in Japan as his wife. "I have no right to indulge her [Anna's] wish at the expense of my nearest obligation," he told his sister.

Anna Wright left Taliesin forever in September 1922. She knew that she had been exiled, and her last letters sound a new note of pathetic resignation, along with some half-hearted attempts to justify her past actions. Perhaps she stayed for a time with Andrew and Jane in Oak Park, and then, some weeks later, perhaps she had another crisis and needed around-the-clock nursing care. All that is known is that she was transferred to the Waldheim Sanitarium in Oconomowoc, Wisconsin, a small hamlet about thirty-five miles due east of Madison, not far from Milwaukee, sometime that year. There she died on February 10, 1923, after a stay of three or four months. She was buried two days later in Unity Chapel, freshly decorated with pine boughs and spring flowers, and then laid to rest under the tall, dark pines she loved. Not one of the many obituaries makes any mention of her son's presence at the funeral, and it is known that the casket bearers were her nephews and one of her grandsons, not her own son. These clues would indicate that he was not there, and the available records suggest that he had left Chicago and returned to Los Angeles a few days before her death. Miriam Noel, of course, did not attend either. Distance had separated them, and more than distance. The year before she died, Anna seemed to sum up the frustrations of a lifetime in her final words to her beloved son. Now she was old, and it made her sad to think that Frank, and Maginel as well, had not found happiness. She hoped her children would support each other and share each others' burdens. As for herself, she felt so alone.

Miriam Noel Wright

In November 1923, the month that Frank Lloyd Wright's divorce became final, he married Miriam Noel. The ceremony took place secretly, at midnight, on a bridge over the Wisconsin River. He gave her a wedding ring inscribed, "Frank to Miriam." It was, she wrote, her most precious possession.

11

The Cause Conservative

It's easy to smash what never existed,
You and I together.
                    "Wulf and Eadwacer"
                    Poems from the Old English

In one of his letters, written soon after his relationship with Miriam Noel began, Wright called it an "entanglement," and this description, made in a moment of exasperation, was truer than he knew. A woman he had taken up because she was sexually available at the moment when he was at his most vulnerable had insinuated her way into his life by calculated degrees and had become indispensable to him. When they first met his needs were uppermost; she had, as Ashbee noted, brought him to heel. She had accomplished what two other women in his life had not: she had defeated Anna. She had finally married her longtime lover and was now the legal mistress of all he surveyed. She should have been savoring the victorious moment and perhaps she was, but the triumph was brief.

They had only lived together as husband and wife for about six months when, in May 1924, she left him. Something about the fact of being married was enough to overtax a stormy but enduring relationship, and it is tempting to speculate that, once securely installed, Miriam dropped a façade that she had intermittently maintained in the past, that of pretending to be all things to her lover. She would have been well aware that there was no end to his need for uncritical acceptance, praise and reassurance, and that any woman close to him had made a bargain: to give up her own sense of herself in order to live a life through him, have no thoughts but his, no needs but his, no life outside his own. Fortunately for her, the Imperial Hotel project was so lengthy and genuinely absorbing, their life in Japan so full of the delights of travel and connoisseurship, and her status, through him, so exalted, that the relationship had lived up to her demands upon it for a considerable time. Once back in the United States, Wright was no longer the master architect but a middle-aged figure thought to be out of step with his times, trying to drum up some work. Instead of a man in command of armies, he was to be found riding machinery on the farm around Taliesin. Instead of being socially courted, she was looked upon as simply the latest inhabitant of the infamous "love cottage," and was no doubt cut on the street by her social inferiors in Spring Green and marooned in the countryside miles from a decent art gallery. When she had left him in Tokyo, the letter he wrote then gave a vivid description of the ruthless Old Testament conscience lurking behind his apparent veneer of breezy self-confidence. This inner censor weighed his acts and found them wanting; it believed he had "no personal culture"; that he was selfish and made everyone else suffer; that he was self-deceptive; that he would always "slip and slide and cheat" to escape censure; that he would not hesitate to "slay or betray or desert"; that he was "crooked"; that he was weak; that he had pet vanities; and that he was a hypocrite. This lengthy accounting is further evidence of the insecurity behind that shield that Wright had successfully erected between himself and the world, one that also kept at bay his private conviction that "this inner chamber I call my heart has been very long neglected—the prospects are not beautiful, the air is not sweet." Given Wright's typical reactions, one can make a safe guess that it would be one thing for him to accuse himself of failings, but quite another to have a once-adoring woman turn into an avenging angel. Nothing could be better guaranteed to arouse his defenses and make him reflect upon the folly of having made an honest woman out of her.

As has been noted, even if Miriam had possessed the necessary insights, she was in the thrall of demons of her own. Morphine, so widely and casually available when she was a young woman, was becoming increasingly difficult to obtain. A federal law to limit the use of morphine, cocaine, opium and heroin had been enacted in 1915 as a result of an increased awareness that drug addiction was a problem with no easy answers. Most physicians, believing that an addict was a moral reprobate, would not offer treatment; others tried to popularize questionable cures. International concern was growing throughout the 1920s, and the supply was tightening, but detoxification was uncertain and clinics were few. A morphine addict faced alone the terrors of withdrawal: ". . . frequent yawning, nasal discharge, tears, widening of the pupils, sweating, erection of the hair, and restlessness are usually observed 12 to 16 hours after the last dose. Later, muscular aches and twitches, abdominal cramps, vomiting, diarrhea, hypertension, insomnia, loss of appetite, agitation, profuse sweating and weight loss develop. . . ." These symptoms of morphine withdrawal reached their peak after three days. If the addict took a single dose they subsided dramatically, but would be back with renewed ferocity as soon as four to six hours later. (It took at least six months for all symptoms to fully disappear.)

This description provides explanation enough for those "strange disturbances" Wright described in his autobiography. That Wright wished to leave the reader with the belief that Miriam was insane is evident, and in fact it was a fashionable theory in the early 1920s that drug addiction did not have a physiological basis but was a symptom of a disordered libido, needing psychoanalytic help to channel it along "higher thought and emotional levels." So Wright was simply taking the course advanced by progressive thinking when he took Miriam to be examined by a Chicago psychiatrist, the best in the country, as he told his son Lloyd. He wrote, "It seems that I have been combating not willful perversity all these years, hoping for a turn for the better—but a disease which is hopeless.

"She is not a commitable case—but will never improve. Dr. Hixon, his wife also who aids him, says I have been batting my brains out against a brick wall so far as any impression I might make is concerned—and that my life has been actually in danger—for some years past. Reason has no part in the matter—she is going, owing to hereditary taint, insane—. Will ultimately have to be confined, when, no one can say. . . . Defective affectivity (Praecox.) Tradgedy [sic] strikes at me through my personal life—in extraordinarily drastic fashion. . . ."

The meaningless diagnosis cited: "defective affectivity," and the generally ambiguous tone of the remarks supports the theory that having convinced himself that Miriam's drug addiction was proof of severe emotional disturbance (at the very least), Wright could give up all hope of curing her himself, for, as he had written, "I think in your extremity as I saw it then I came to really love you." In short, he had accepted that he could not "save you for myself." She was beyond cure, beyond anyone's help. The explanation was useful indeed, because it shifted his dilemma—Miriam's addiction—from a subject that could not be discussed to one that would explain everything. It removed any possibility that he might be tarred with that execrable label, "moral reprobate," for living in proximity to her. And it made her restless wandering from town to town look like the dementia of a mentally disturbed woman instead of the likely search of an addict seeking a ready supply of morphine.

It is easy to see Miriam Noel Wright as a physically addicted, deeply disturbed and vengeful woman, but to dismiss her as insane is harder. Her testimony in support of a divorce is far from that which one would expect of a madwoman; on the contrary, it portrays a calculating intelligence, one making adroit use of the very few legal avenues available. When she finally made her petition in 1927, she claimed that shortly after their marriage in November 1923, Wright began to be abusive. Court transcripts read, "That said treatment consisted in part of neglecting, ignoring plaintiff; calling her vile, vulgar, indecent, abusive and opprobrious names and epithets, and referring to her in such terms; unjustly, harshly and severely criticizing her; and by violence inflicted upon her person. . . . That on or about December 15, 1923, . . . the defendant, without cause or provocation, struck, beat, bruised and otherwise mistreated the plaintiff, bruising her flesh and causing black and blue abrasions thereon."

A wife suing for divorce naturally wants to paint the blackest possible picture. However, the fact that Wright did not challenge this testimony points to the possibility that it may be true. By her own admission, Miriam Noel had drawn a knife on Wright and had threatened to use a gun. Wright also admitted, all his life, to "hot flashes" of malicious and vindictive behavior, and his actions, past and future, demonstrate that he was prepared to use his fists if pushed far enough. So one is inclined to believe Miriam Noel Wright's claim that he beat her, and surprised only that she does not mention this in her memoirs. She writes only that the quarrel had been precipitated by an "unfortunate encounter with a guest at Taliesin," and she decided to leave. Frank drove her as far as Chicago, and then sent emissaries asking her to return. She replied by saying she was going to Mexico

City. He should give her six months, and then they might try again.
She moved on to Los Angeles and heard nothing further until receiving
a letter from his lawyer asking her for a divorce. Miriam's actions
during the years 1924–28, when their divorce became final, have to
be seen, just the same, as those of a wife who did not really want to
leave her husband even if he was capable of covering her with bruises.
That mention of an encounter with a guest was, no doubt, a discreet
reference to yet one more explosion of jealous rage. But now that she
was securely his wife, Miriam Noel may have taken less pains to arouse
his contrition and become more openly sarcastic and derisive. There
is some evidence that this may have been true, judging from his
comment to her, "Enough of 'crawling back' as you say." Perhaps he
had hoped to inspire in her that deep love for Taliesin, which was his
most cherished possession. All the blood, tears and pain extended had
been in vain if, at the end of it all, Miriam refused to be happy there.
Something finally changed in him, for, as he also wrote to her at that
time, "whatever was in me for you is absolutely dead." She had, in
short, tested his love too far, and if she thought he would crawl back
once more, she was wrong. She had predicted when they first met
that he would eventually fall out of love with her, and it had become
literally true.

As has been suggested, the tremendous upheaval in the worlds of art
and architecture that was ushered in with World War I had been
sensed by Wright almost as it was being formed. In art, a new wave
of Italian Futurists, in love with progress and technology, was celebrating the arrival of the train, the airplane and the motorcar in
drawings whose attempts to portray movement were also being echoed
by a famous Cubist painting of Marcel Duchamp, *Nude Descending a
Staircase* (1912), which caused an uproar at the famous New York
Armory show a year later. Futurism, Fauvism, Constructivism, Abstract Expressionism, Dadaism—such developments were giving rise
to an equal revolution in architecture as men like Le Corbusier, Walter
Gropius, Adolph Meyer and Ludwig Mies van der Rohe ushered in a
new era. The machine age had arrived and turned upside down all the
old values. Now what counted was the extent to which the architect
could successfully adapt his métier to the requirements of the new
materials and mass production, how well he could build for the new
spirit of progress, revolution, industrialism and social betterment. The

Bauhaus complex, as designed by Gropius and described by Sigfried Giedion, one of the principal exponents of the new architecture, in his famous book, *Space, Time and Architecture*, was built as an arrangement of cubes of differing sizes, materials and locations. "The aim is not to anchor them to the ground but to have them float or hover upon the site. This is the reason for the winglike connecting bridges and the liberal use of glass . . . called in for its dematerializing quality. . . ." Giedion added that this was the first large building of its date (1926) to exemplify so completely "a crystallization of the new space concept."

The new buildings, whether houses, apartments or commercial structures, shared the qualities of the ground-breaking Bauhaus complex; that is to say, they were uncompromisingly boxy, streamlined, uniform, regimented, looking like the factories in which they had probably been assembled and certainly like "machines for living," that phrase of Le Corbusier's that was to haunt him ever afterward. Ornamentation, whimsical shifts of direction, unexpected nooks and crannies—all these, being evidence of the bad old days, were abolished. The new architects espoused the doctrine of simplification, purification, the nobility of glass-curtain walls and transparent volumes, and dedicated themselves to a Utopian, technological and functional future swept clean of individual and idiosyncratic fantasies. In so doing they abandoned the aesthetic of beauty, as Ruskin had defined it— Duchamp, in fact, had discredited the very idea of a work of art. What these architects liked was Sullivan's phrase "form follows function," or their reductionist interpretation of that phrase, and they sought what has been called a "symbolic objectivity." As described by William Jordy, "The goal of symbolic objectivity was to align architecture with the pervasive factuality of modern existence, with that 'ineloquence' (to call up Bernard Berenson's tag) which characterizes the modern imagination. The aims of simplification and purification at the core of the movement, providing it with a morality of Calvinist austerity, actually stemmed from a diffuse convention on the part of many progressive designers and theorists during the nineteenth century to the effect that architecture should be 'honest,' 'truthful,' and 'real'. . . . During the twenties this moralistic heritage acquired an antiseptic cleanliness, and irreducible bareness. . . ." Future arbiters of taste, such as the critic Lewis Mumford, who would become one of Wright's staunchest supporters, would eventually criticize this very purism and impersonality: "Mies van der Rohe," Mumford wrote in 1964, "used the facilities offered by steel and glass to create some elegant monuments of nothingness. . . . His own chaste taste gave these hollow glass shells a crystalline purity of form; but they existed alone in the Platonic world of his imagination and had no relation to site, climate, insulation, function, or internal activity. . . ."

These comments raise issues that touch directly on Wright's dilemma as he attempted to re-establish his reputation in the United States after having spent so many years in Japan and the Pacific Rim. Instead of being in the avant-garde, in courageous opposition to all that was specious, wasteful, inartistic and untruthful about architecture, carrying the flag for simplicity, truth to materials, relationship to site and a uniquely American vision, he returned to find himself relegated to the camp of those whose nineteenth century precursors practically guaranteed their eclipse. He might still see himself as a trailblazer, but to conventional opinion he was a distinguished American whose best work had been summed up, and ended with, the Wasmuth portfolio of 1910. Or he was considered a valiant forerunner for concepts that better men would bring to fruition, which was almost as insulting.

On the other hand there was little point of contact between his own work and that of the European avant-garde. True, he shared their interest in the machine and experimented with new materials, as his work of the 1920s and 1930s would show. However, the point is not always made that Wright's advocacy of the machine was as one more tool to be placed at the command of the artist. Given this emphasis, he must have felt that the European modernists were taking a step beyond which he would not go: they were letting the machine dictate their art. This would have been absolute anathema to Wright, and their claim of "truth to materials" would have seemed like an empty boast to him. But the central conflict had to do with what Jordy and Mumford saw as the soulless materialism and "ineloquence" of the new imagination. Whatever one wanted to say about Wright's imagination, it was certainly eloquent. Soon there were two opposed camps: Wright in one, versus The Rest. That archaic notion that beauty existed to convey a society's absolute values had been thrown out, but Wright, to his cost, was irretrievably wedded to it. He was still a man with a mission and with a message left to preach, but he had lost his audience. He must have looked at these constructions of glass and steel and thought of Ruskin's succinct phrase: an "absence of grace."

Norris Kelly Smith has perhaps best described Wright's position at that time. "He prided himself upon being a revolutionary trail blazer, responsible for the principal innovations that have determined the character of all modern architecture, but at the same time he regarded himself as the defender of a universal organic ideal whose nature has been misunderstood by virtually all modern architects." Wright wanted it all ways and would probably be most likely to accept the contemporary view that he was a "radical conservative," working in the classic architectural tradition of evolutionary change, as argued by the British architect and author Richard MacCormac. For, as Wright had declared in 1908, "radical though it may be, the work here illustrated is dedicated to a cause conservative in the best sense of the word. At no point does it involve denial of the elemental law and order inherent in all great architecture." In 1922 he would tell Dr. Hendrick P. Berlage, the state architect of Holland, "my heart is still where it was in 1908," but Wright was not then using the term "radical conservative" for himself and might even have shied away from it. It might have seemed uncomfortably reminiscent of those eloquent Arts and Crafts spokesmen whose principal message had been a return to sensible values, sensible attitudes and conservative reform: and that had made it radical for their day and age. Even to breathe the term Arts and Crafts would, one guesses, reveal the kind of horrid secret concealed in the French phrase *"femme d'un certain âge."* This may explain why Wright's writings from the 1920s onward make no reference to this formative influence and allude only to Louis Sullivan, who at least was kindly regarded by the modernists, since he had been so clever about skyscrapers. One concludes that as the decade of the 1920s progressed, Wright decided it was far better to present himself as so far ahead of the pack that no one had yet caught up with him, than to risk being seen as a relic whom the march of time had left behind. To be a radical, if not an outlaw, had the comfort of the familiar and held its own kind of allure. Had not Jenkin Lloyd Jones, "Lincoln's soldier of civic righteousness," as he was called, preached freedom of religion, harmony between nations, justice for the oppressed, equal rights for women and animals and all those other noble causes, however lonely and persecuted he might have been? Had not the Lloyd Joneses before him suffered ostracism in Wales for their high-minded beliefs? What was the world's antagonism and ridicule if, in your heart, you knew you were right? But, on the other hand, suppose you did not prevail? One of the stories Wright greatly liked and told to several people (he also used it in an article) concerned the fate of a certain monkey that had been caught by a planter and roped to his porch. The monkey escaped during the night and returned to the jungle. But, Wright continued, with obvious reference to his own "outsider" status, "there he was torn limb from limb because he was different: he had a rope around his belly no other monkey had." Wright wrote in his article, "Our own tribe destroys on similar suspicion the man who might impart something of immense importance and value to his tribe such as this poor 'suspect' might have imparted: how to avoid being caught and tied up, say—or if tied up,—how to escape."

He was, he told his son Lloyd in the midsummer of 1924, learning to be alone, "by degrees. It is a long time since anything warm and human has transpired in my life with M—She left about May 5th but for years before that, really." To master the art of living required a technique, just as art did. "Let us learn it." In the meantime he was, as usual, acutely short of cash and in the hole to the tune of $47,000, but was determined to keep Taliesin a showplace so as to make it a "job-getter"; and he was on the job.

His prospects would continue to look the same for the next six or seven years. That is to say, there were always a few large exciting commissions of potentially great promise that never quite came to fruition, while the actual buildings that he saw constructed were excruciatingly few. In the former category, he would soon be asked to design a thirty-two-story skyscraper on Chicago's Water Tower Place for the National Life Insurance Company. Although this project did not materialize, it resulted in a brilliant design that he would adapt later for an even more ambitious project in New York, his future St. Mark's-in-the-Bouwerie tower. At the same time he was working on another commission that was even more challenging. This was for a tourist attraction to be built on Sugarloaf Mountain in Frederick County, Maryland. Gordon Strong, a Chicagoan who had amassed a fortune in real estate, had bought the mountain and the three thousand acres surrounding it and proposed to maintain it as a nature park. His idea was that weekend drivers from Washington, Baltimore and the surrounding area would drive up the mountain to park and enjoy the picturesque views from observation platforms while also patronizing the restaurants, gift shops, movie theater, planetarium and so on that Wright would design. It was an up-to-date idea for a brand-new age; Wright rose to the challenge with an equally daring concept based on the beehive, or ziggurat, shape (surrounded by tiers of driving ramps) and prepared hundreds of drawings in the months that followed. This work eventually resulted in some exquisite presentation drawings, strongly Japanese in feeling, and colored in purples, yellows, greens and blues—but no building. Strong never made up his mind whether he preferred Wright's concept or one of the other four ideas he had commissioned from other architects, which ranged from the most formal and eighteenth century to the most naturalistic. Another disappointment for Wright, but he put all that work to excellent use three decades later, as will be demonstrated.

That neither of these potentially lucrative projects should come to completion must have been a severe disappointment, but at that period Wright was still looking hopefully toward Los Angeles, where Lloyd had successfully established himself and where "real opportunity" awaited, he wrote. The opportunity to which he referred had to do with the four houses he built in 1923–24 in Los Angeles, Hollywood and Pasadena. In terms of their design, these exquisite small buildings—built for Alice Millard, a rare-book dealer, in Pasadena; Harriet and Sam Freeman (he was a jeweler, and she was a modern dancer); John Storer, a dentist; and Mr. and Mrs. Charles Ennis, a wealthy couple—are obviously closely related to Hollyhock House, that is to say, they are monumental, aloof and irresistibly Mayan in feeling. They are all, in fact, much smaller—the Freeman house is only 1,500 square feet—but so artfully proportioned that like the Millard house, known as La Miniatura, they present a teasing conundrum in photographs. Are they cottages or palaces? Only a human figure can establish the actual scale. All four are built on slopes, which gave Wright an opportunity to design an entrance, as in the Freeman house, that had an unobtrusive door in a garden wall facing the main rooms onto the glorious vistas hidden in the background.

What also distinguishes these houses is their method of construction. Working with his son Lloyd, Wright had hammered out a variation on the design of the humble and inexpensive concrete block, which was easy to manufacture, easy to assemble and apparently easy to maintain: he called it the textile block system. It could be made in a variety of patterns, sizes and surfaces, and linked together with a method of horizontal and vertical steel rods that he and his son invented. The result was wonderfully solid and imposing inside and out, with an overtone of theatricality that seemed natural, if not required, for the Los Angeles of the 1920s, but the method was not as trouble-free as it looked. Recent study has established that the small Freeman house alone required over eleven thousand blocks and that

*The corner window and an interior view of the Freeman house,
Hollywood, California*

The Millard house, La Miniatura, in Pasadena, California

the intricate patterns of the blocks, cast in a dry, porous concrete, did not usually come out cleanly on the first pass through the mold. As many as four stampings might be necessary before the results could be called satisfactory. In addition, far more patterns had been used than had first been thought (there were more than forty), and each block had to cure for twenty-eight days before it could be used. That was not the end of the matter. The material used meant that the resulting block, seemingly so solid, was actually very fragile and extremely vulnerable to chipping and crumbling. The concrete was also porous: the present curator of the Freeman house has declared that he can turn a water hose on full blast against a wall, stand there all day and not have a drop of water hit the ground. Being so porous means that these blocks have absorbed, along with the rainwater, the dissolved acids from Los Angeles's notorious smog: the blocks are now being literally eaten away.

These disadvantages, along with the obvious problems of flat roofs—and Wright began to make extensive use of them in his designs—are evident nowadays, but even in his day Wright was on the defensive about them and eager to prove he had cured their drawbacks. Some historians have deduced a new note of austere turning away from the world in these California designs of Wright's, but, given the lack of a comment from the architect that would support this notion, one is inclined to believe that the seemingly fortresslike aspects of the textile block houses had more to do with the architect's superb sense of place. "Surely one reason for the thick walls and inward-turning courts was the climate of the south-west," Curtis wrote. "Wright's regional sensitivities required a new response, and he followed some of the cues supplied by traditional adobe structures with their thick sloping walls and flat roofs. . . ." All four houses, as Hitchcock remarked, are further evidence of Wright's ability to "renew again and again his architectural imagination" with the stimulus of a new problem and new materials—in this case, the very last word in modern construction.

Wright's contingent of young assistants on the West Coast, besides his son Lloyd, included Rudolf Michael Schindler, who had joined his office early in 1918, had worked on plans for the Imperial Hotel and was then dispatched to Los Angeles two years later to supervise Hollyhock House and its adjacent buildings. As one of the advance guard for the European modernists, Schindler was a remarkable figure, highly original and creator of a studio on Kings Road in Los Angeles for himself, his wife, Pauline, and another couple. The structure is now considered a landmark, not only for its radical design but also for the manner of living it imposed on its inhabitants: both bohemian and austerely demanding.

As might be predicted, it was all very well for a former assistant to ask the master's permission in advance to say that he had made designs for him or, as Wright preferred it, "Sometimes if they are in luck, or rather if I am in luck, they make them with me." It was something else entirely, Wright decided two years later, when, without any advance warning, Schindler allowed an art school at which he was teaching to publish in its catalogue that he had been in charge of Wright's Chicago architectural office for two years during his absence. Wright was livid. He wrote, "Get this:

"Where I am my office is. My office is *me*. Frank Lloyd Wright has no other office, never had one and never will. . . ."

The real issue behind his rage seemed to be the added fact that Schindler was now claiming a substantial contribution to the design of the Imperial Hotel and, as he had told the state of California, "I had worked extensively both on the structural and architectural plans of the Imperial Hotel. . . ." Wright was inclined, at first, to be indulgent: "The fact that these plans were all thrown away when I got to Japan and I built the building myself out of the office there is no reflection upon the work that you and the other men . . . did. . . ." But now, Schindler was actually having the gall to assert that without his work the hotel would not have withstood the earthquake. Writing to Lloyd the same day he had mailed his withering letter to Schindler, Wright observed, "I do not know to what he refers when he says: 'structural features that held the Imperial together incorporated only after overcoming my resistance.' . . ." But a few weeks later he decided, "I suspect on thinking the matter over that Rudy must refer to the omission in the wings of the solid implastered continuous slab I designed and wanted in favor of the beam-slab. . . . That is the only thing I accepted reluctantly and wished afterward, and now, that I had not consented to do. . . ." To Wright it must have seemed that Schindler was not only taking cheap advantage of his reputation but pushing him down a notch or two by attempting to steal credit that was his alone. That was unforgivable, and Wright would never forgive.

In short, his former apprentices had to be extremely diplomatic if their genial *"Lieber Meister,"* so capable of large generous gestures and paternal encouragement, were not to metamorphose into a monster. Even the tolerant and tactful Antonin Raymond had been dismissed from the Imperial Hotel project because, it would seem, he had set up an office of his own and now looked like a competitor. The ostensible cause for the break was a rendering he completed for Wright that the master called "hopeless" and "intended to resemble nothing so much as a dung hill in a mud puddle." Wright ended his letter with the comment "And to this I want to add that from now on I prefer your honest enmity to any friendship you . . . may profess. . . ." There almost seemed to be a pattern to this sequence of friendships with all those talented young men and women that began with so much hope and goodwill and ended in such bitter partings. Wright's explanation, as he wrote to Mrs. Schindler in happier days, was that the fault lay in his own guileless nature. "I am recklessly open in my communications, trusting always to be liberally understood—why—God Knows!" he wrote. "My 'world' has been a great fool! No malignity nor any form of petty mischief has been disappointed of its gratification, at my expense, because of this reckless habit. . . . Why I am continually hurt and surprised at proofs of what I have come to expect is strange. . . . But it is true. I never get used to it. . . ."

Part of the problem appeared to be that even when he and his assistants remained on excellent terms and there was no ostensible reason for a break, Wright could not bear to have anyone leave him. He would pretend it was not happening, load the favored one down with more work and eventually complain, "Anybody can leave, but only a few are allowed to stay. So why leave and not enjoy this place and this situation?" His was a fond, indulgent and seldom arbitrary love, for, as has been said of his clients, he was ready to see special qualities in anyone with the heartwarming ability to admire his work for the right reasons. Richard Neutra, the other young Viennese architect who would work for him, and a friend of Schindler's, had made a methodical pilgrimage to all of Wright's buildings in Chicago, finding them even more admirable than he had expected. In 1923 he was using Schindler as an intermediary to fulfill his ambition to work for Wright, despite his friend's warning that "he is devoid of consideration and has a blind spot regarding the qualities of other people." Schindler added, "I believe, however, that a year in his studio would be worth any sacrifice. . . ." Neutra's first reaction on meeting Wright, that he was "truly a child but not a well-behaved one. God only knows," is evidence that his admiration for Wright's work did not blind him to Wright's possible shortcomings. These reservations faded once Neutra and his young wife, Dione, were invited to visit Taliesin in the summer of 1924, and he was immediately invited to work for the master.

They were met at the Spring Green station by Werner Moser, a Taliesin apprentice and son of the architect Karl Moser, under whom Neutra had briefly studied in Zurich, and had driven across the vast Wisconsin River and up the curving driveway. Arriving at the house Richard Neutra felt "as though I were in a Japanese temple district, whatever I thought that might look like." His wife was meeting Wright for the first time and was apprehensive about being introduced to a genius, but felt immediately at ease. Wright was at his most agreeable and winning, being "well built, elegant, of middle height, with a significant head, which could best be compared to that of Liszt."

That evening they were conducted to the wonderful living room, "[v]ery low with a beautiful fireplace-corner and, above all, an indescribably magnificent view" to meet Albert Johnson and his superficial wife. He was an elderly, dull little man, whom everyone was most eager to please because he was about to award Wright the commission to design the skyscraper for the National Life Insurance Company in Chicago. It seemed painful to Dione Neutra that Wright, this "outstanding man," should have to abase himself before a boring little businessman because he needed the work.

The Neutras woke up next morning to the chirping of brilliantly colored birds—"[I]t was a glorious day which seemed fabulously unreal. . . ."—and were taken on a tour of the house by Moser. It had been built at different periods and contained innumerable nooks and crannies. In one of them the Neutras discovered stacks of copies—several hundred at least—of the famous Wasmuth edition of 1910. Wright had bought up all the copies and had hoped to sell them but there they were, covered with mildew and literally rotting away. There was something equally sad about the discovery that Wright had become a tourist stop on the sight-seeing tour of the area. "We were told that on Sundays hordes of strangers come, go through all the rooms, sniff around everywhere, leave this famous house astonished. Long caravans of cars are standing on the street, even in the courtyard. According to his mood, Wright serves as guide, or is angered by them."

Moser took them for a drive around the idyllic estate, and then they returned to Wright's room for a display of his drawings. "Moser had told us beforehand that he loses his drawings due to his disorderliness and carelessness, but supposes, nevertheless, that everybody robs him, so he is full of distrust. In fact, he began to search, became excited, rummaged in all drawers, and said helplessly: 'Everything is gone.' " He was wrong, of course; drawings were eventually produced, and the Neutras were eloquently silent. In the evening they all lay on the grass watching the fireflies while Wright talked on in his warm, caressing voice, and Dione was mesmerized even though she barely understood what he was saying. "In spite of the many . . . stories that are spread, his heart certainly seems pure. He can't be measured with the yardstick of the ordinary citizen. Those who condemn him are incapable of understanding his art. . . ."

Neutra spent nine happy and constructive months in Wright's studio working on drawings and design studies for Mr. Johnson's skyscraper and several other projects, including Wright's beehive for Sugarloaf Mountain and another extraordinary complex of buildings, never built, for the Edward H. Doheny ranch in the Sierra Madre of California. They were ideal additions to life at Taliesin. Dione could play the cello and sing at the same time, an accomplishment Wright found quite astounding, and their evenings, spent artistically grouped around the living room fireplace, as seen in early photographs, are a model of the intellectual, bohemian way of living that Wright would perpetuate in his Taliesin Fellowship of a decade later. Despite Wright's protestations to Lloyd, so long as these charming young couples were in residence he could hardly be considered solitary, and indeed he recalled later that they kept up his spirits and became, in effect, his "immediate family. A happy one because they were all good to what was left of me at that bad time."

Lloyd Wright was a frequent visitor. When it came to dealing with the children of his first marriage, Frank Lloyd Wright managed a better accommodation with his eldest son, and also with John, David, Llewellyn, Catherine and Frances, than his father had done in his own case. True, he would always talk about them as Catherine's children, as if their existence had been no affair of his, and it seems clear, from family reminiscences, that Catherine tried to get her children to take her side, just as Anna had done, in the tug-of-war that continued for years after Wright left home. Lloyd and John, perhaps equally jolted, fared a little better than David had. For although Wright had told

Catherine Wright in Michigan, summer of 1917, with her son David

Lloyd, then in his first year at the University of Wisconsin, that he was on his own and it was up to him to support his mother—something he also seems to have told David and John—in fact, he soon coaxed Lloyd and John to Europe, paid their way, found them work, wrote cautious letters to them and kept in touch for the rest of his life; Llewellyn would eventually become Wright's lawyer. Given the destructive family patterns Wright had experienced, it has to be counted as a considerable achievement that he could maintain contact with his brood at all, and if his attentions were sporadic and his largesse undependable, he did his best for them after his fashion.

This is not to say that relations were ever ideal, particularly with David—he and his father always seemed to be circling around each other—Llewellyn, John or, especially, Lloyd. As the firstborn, Lloyd carried the heaviest load of parental expectations, for it is axiomatic that a father's demands on his son will exactly mirror those he has of himself, and the harsher these are, the more exacting his attitude will be. And, for undoubtedly complex reasons, Lloyd chose to involve himself in his father's business affairs. He had built the first concrete block house—before his father's more famous houses were ever conceived—and took the role of intermediary between the clients and his peripatetic father. Under these circumstances something was bound to go wrong, and Wright aroused could be the wrath of Jove himself. There is, after all, nothing more exasperating for a father than to find in his son shortcomings he particularly detests. "You are 'spongy' and you don't know . . . why. But I will tell you why. It is because you are not really *reliable*. You will say a thing *is* so when you only *think* it is so. You will promise and not keep it. You will buy when you can't pay. You will attempt anything and blame failure on others. You will believe what you want to believe or think you ought to and never live up to either—. . . . It is *hard work* to overcome faults at your age. But it is the only man's work. Believe me.

"Go *to* it—Stop preaching and *practice*—No one will be quicker to get the evidence or effects of improvement than your father. I see your hard work . . . and it makes me ache to see you get so little out of what you get *for* your work—The value of a dollar is a blank to your mind. Your sense of time is loose. Your step is loose—Your grasp of your work is loose—Your sense of Justice is loose—Your idea of right and wrong is loose— . . . Hell is paved with such as my son—'good intentions' loosely strung as selfishness and self indulgence and aborting at the end!" Most interesting of all, perhaps, Wright even accused his eldest son of doing exactly what he himself was in the very act of doing—"You are quick to impute to others the quality that is rankling in your soul"—perhaps the best evidence of his utter and complete inability to understand what was happening to him. But, as he also commented at about that same time, "I do not know myself—or very much care."

Having thus demolished any hope Lloyd might have of joining the human race, Wright was then capable of adding that the lecture rose from a father's full and loving heart, and that it would do him good. It would not have helped that Lloyd, according to his son Eric, had no equivalent of Anna in his life to give him the necessary inner confidence and make him believe he was destined for great things; but if he had compared notes with his brother John, as no doubt he did, he would have found that he was hardly alone in being singled out for criticism. For his father was far too judgmental; it would be fairer to say that he was too critical and too indulgent by turns, sometimes simultaneously, acting exactly as his own parents had acted toward him. And once the mood had passed, purged no doubt by these endless denunciations scrawled over pages of paper, Wright was impulsively warm and confiding, would address Lloyd or John as his "dear boy," inquire after their well being and press them to come to Taliesin for a long visit. And there was always that redeeming quality, his sense of fun. Writing to Lloyd from Chicago, after he had recently returned from the West Coast, Wright complained, "I waited until the last fifteen minutes before train-time for you—and then dashed into a cab—tore the insides out of it to make the station in fifteen minutes on the dot as the train pulled out.

"The red-cap jumped on the running board, told the taxi where to head off the train and we were soon running up alongside it—I got out on the running-board next the train—watched my chance and jumped into the open hatch—the red-cap passing up bags and coats as the taxi kept alongside threw the fare into the cab—

"That's how I got away.

"Where were you?"

Another of Wright's complaints about Lloyd—his "lack of consideration or whatever it is that emanates from you"—was the one most often made about him by his children. He seemed oblivious to the feelings of others and could exult, of a drawing, "That's the greatest thing your father ever did," conveniently forgetting, as he praised himself before Lloyd, that Lloyd had made that particular rendering.

And by general agreement, Lloyd was the better artist. He was also the son who inherited a good deal of his father's talent. After moving to Los Angeles to design the gardens for Hollyhock House and Olive Hill, Lloyd took up architecture and, it is now said, if he had carried the name of Wright Lloyd instead of Lloyd Wright, his reputation might have been much greater. As it was, he was destined to be compared unfavorably with his father and to have his own work confused with that of the master's. One had to expect that, of course, if one were the son of a famous man, particularly one as insecure and reflexively competitive as Frank Lloyd Wright. Even John—everyone's favorite because he was so full of fun and good humor, whose way of dealing with conflict was to turn it aside with a quip, who had written the openly admiring memoir, *My Father Who Is on Earth*—having taken up architecture, found himself living in his father's shadow. It took years before he could let his father's derogatory remarks roll off his back. For, as John said, one simply could not predict Wright's reactions. "When he hears about my enemies attacking me his feathers rise and he becomes a fiercely protective bird. 'John,' he calls, 'I'm coming down there and clean them up.' Yet at other times his opposition to my development as an architect seems almost compulsive. . . ." They parted once over a serious quarrel involving John's wages. They eventually reconciled, but it had been a lifelong struggle to "avoid being destroyed."

Both Lloyd and John shared their father's delicate responsiveness to poetry and beautiful objects; they all loved The Valley and were as capable of being moved to tears by the first patch of violets in the grass as was Wright himself. But Lloyd, in particular, was not easy to deal with either, having acquired that ominous Lloyd Jones penchant for flying into a rage when crossed, and Eric recalled that his father would actually froth at the mouth. If Lloyd and his father were continually at loggerheads, some of the responsibility had to be laid at Lloyd's door. Eric gave an example of the kind of battle that might occur between his father and grandfather by relating an incident that took place while he was working as a young apprentice at Taliesin. He said, "They were working on a cottage and Wright wanted a very light wood for the roof frame to keep the structure light in feeling. Jack Howe, his chief draftsman, said it wouldn't hold up. They were putting up this frame at the time, but they had just talked Wright out of the idea when my father appeared. He said, 'What are you doing?' Wright told him. He answered, 'How stupid can you get?'

Wright immediately became defensive. 'What do you mean? Of course it will hold.' Jack Howe turned to me and said, 'Your father has just undone half an hour of persuasion.' So of course the flimsy roof went up, and quite soon after that a workman was tarring it and fell through it carrying a pot of tar. Fortunately no one was hurt." He concluded, "My father always chose the wrong way—always would."

One by one they were all dying off, those mentors of former years. Elbert Hubbard and his wife had gone down with the *Lusitania* a year after World War I started (in 1915), and Louis Sullivan was in frail health. Although Wright stated that he and Sullivan did not meet for twenty years after their break in 1893, there are indications that they were reconciled, if not back on former terms, some seven years later. Ashbee's diary for December 1900 notes that Wright had introduced him to "his master, Sullivan," and that same year Wright had (presumably) approved an article by his fellow architect, Robert C. Spencer, acknowledging the early influence of Sullivan on his work; Wright again made clear his debt to Sullivan in his essay of 1908, "In the Cause of Architecture." Given these significant straws in the wind, it would be a fair guess that Wright was never completely out of touch after 1900, and that he was aware of the shift in Sullivan's fortunes. For, as Sullivan had predicted after the World's Columbian Exposition of 1893, the tide of architecture had moved away from him. The building boom in Chicago was over, and the decline in his practice was subsequently exacerbated by the dissolution of his partnership with Dankmar Adler. Curiously, the year of 1909 was as momentous for Sullivan as it was for Wright. Sullivan separated from his own wife and was forced to dismiss George Elmslie, his invaluable assistant for twenty years, for lack of work.

By about 1920 Sullivan's reputation was international—Schindler and Neutra, recently arrived from Vienna, were going to enormous lengths to see his work and meet the great man in person—while his actual practice had dwindled to some remodeling and a few small banks. He was sometimes desperate for the fifty dollars a month he needed to keep his office going. Early in 1918 Sullivan made a telephone call to Wright in Taliesin, and that call re-established the friendship on a new and warmer footing, lasting for the remainder of Sullivan's life. Even at his most formidable, Sullivan had always shown an indulgent attitude toward his brilliant young assistant, and now that the tables were turned, the boy who had been called "Wright" was ready with numerous gifts of cash and visited him whenever he was in Chicago. What may have made Wright most indignant was receiving a letter from Sullivan that stated, "with the future blank I am surely living in hell. To think I should come to this at 61." The plight of his *"Lieber Meister,"* rejected, ignored, his magnificent gifts scorned, had galvanized Wright to rush to his side. Now that Sullivan was penniless and friendless he could count on Wright to the end, for, as Wright wrote in late 1922, ". . . you must know I would share my last crust with you. . . ." He was determined that he would one day restore Sullivan to his rightful place. He wrote in 1919, "When I am strong [enough] to lay my own enemies in the dust yours won't go unscathed!" The biography Wright belatedly wrote (in 1949), made good on that promise and placed the blame where Wright felt it squarely belonged, on the "mobocracy," which was unable to appreciate a genius. Wright's description of Sullivan's last days is similarly indignant and heartfelt. Referring to those days, he told Aline Saarinen, "I saw 'him' die deserted and in awful misery—alone except for little but myself. . . ." Perhaps the truth was that Wright identified with Sullivan—he must have seen that the fate of his *"Lieber Meister"* could easily be his own—and the ordeal of watching Sullivan die must have been made more agonizing by the knowledge that his own marriage with Miriam Noel was disintegrating. Curiously enough, Miriam left Taliesin (on May 9, 1924) just three weeks after Sullivan died. This could have been the moment that, writing to Lloyd, he observed, "I don't know where to turn at present but I know I've got to work like hell. That's all I ever really know."

The Oak Park home and studio sale had been settled in the summer of 1924; Catherine was well established in her career as a social worker and was, at that time, living elsewhere in Chicago and working as a juvenile protection officer. However, the papers were not drawn up until early in the new year. At the end of January Darwin D. Martin received a letter from a Chicago attorney involved in the proceedings who needed Miriam Noel Wright's signature on the deed of sale. The lawyer had written to her husband and found, to his surprise, that this gentleman did not know the whereabouts of the second Mrs. Wright.

Darwin Martin replied, "It is entirely of a piece with Wright's usual carelessness to have mislaid a second wife." He soon heard from Wright that the documents had finally reached Mrs. Wright in Los

Angeles and were expected back soon. If he, Martin, knew anything at all about wives (and he did not, since he had only one), he would know that wives were not so easily mislaid, although their husbands might be misled. Wright continued his bantering tone with some light-hearted references to "being laid" and "mislaid," and concluded, "You gave me a good laugh."

He had reason to be relieved. He had not seen Miriam for almost a year, and as far as he knew she had decided to settle at a safe distance. He felt free to start all over again and was engaging in a number of flirtations, including one with a Wisconsin author that may have been somewhat serious. Her name was Zona Gale. She was a member of a large family for whom Wright had designed some entirely conventional, Queen Anne style houses on Lake Street in Oak Park before he left Sullivan, and she had worked her way up from jobs on Milwaukee and New York newspapers to become a famous novelist. Her satiric novel, *Miss Lulu Bett*, was a great success and won a Pulitzer Prize in 1921 after the author turned it into a play. When Wright returned from Japan, she was at the height of her reputation; she was then in her mid-forties and had not married. (She married in 1928, ten years before she died.)

When they first met, Zona was an adolescent living in Oak Park; finding her a woman of accomplishments, Wright decided to advance. He appeared at her home one day accompanied by two Japanese houseboys bearing gifts, and several armfuls of flowers including goldenrod. Her biographer, August Derleth, wrote, "They found the house on Edgewater Place, invaded it, and placed the flowers in her parlor. . . ." But her father arrived first, "saw the flowers, clapped one hand to his nose and shouted, 'Get those things out of here!' He was suffering from hay fever. . . ." That, according to her biographer, was the beginning and end of her friendship with Wright, although the latter intimates it had more substance. He was in search of amorous conquest but, perhaps, not quite as indiscriminately as he had been after Mamah's death. He was, after all, surrounded every evening by charming young women, even if they were the wives of other men, and no one thought it too significant when, one evening during the visit of the Neutras to Taliesin, a young European made her appearance. Her name was Olgivanna Hinzenberg, she had recently arrived from France, and she danced before the fire while Dione Neutra played Schubert's setting of a poem by Goethe on the cello. It was "The Elf King."

12

A Stern Chase

How gaily, how often, we'd fashioned oaths
Defying everything but death to endanger
Our love. . . .

"A Woman's Message"
Poems from the Old English

Olga Ivanovna Lazovich, who would play a central role in Frank Lloyd
Wright's life until his death, and whose language, cultural background
and upbringing were almost exotically alien to his own, might seem
to have been a bizarre choice as the third official Mrs. Wright. She
was more than thirty years his junior, having been born in Cetinje,
Montenegro, on December 27, 1898, the ninth and last child of highly
unusual parents. Her father, Ivan Lazovich, was chief justice of the
tiny principality; her mother, Militza, was daughter of a famous general, Marco Miliyanov, or Milanoff, a man of almost legendary courage,
who had been commander in chief of the Montenegrin army.

Montenegro, on the Adriatic coast of Yugoslavia, takes its name
from the Venetian *Monte Nero*, or "Black Mountain," so called because
of the dark-leaved shrubs that grow on the stony peaks of this geo-
graphical landmark, the historical center of the country. Nature has
made it a natural fortress, and its statehood dates back to the fourteenth
century and the dissolution of the Serbian Empire. From that time
onward Montenegro was engaged in a continual battle to defend its

autonomy. When the Turks fought their way into Albania and Her-
cegovina, Montenegro's ruler, Ivo the Black, was pushed back to the
remote mountain village of Cetinje but not defeated. There, in the
late fifteenth century he founded a monastery and bishopric and set
up the first printing press in the Balkans. For centuries the moun-
taineers were subsequently ruled by bishops (*vladikas*) elected in popular assemblies, their statehood continually threatened by invasions
of the Turks, whom they kept at bay for two centuries. Their success
led to political recognition far out of proportion to their numbers.
Early in the eighteenth century, Vladika Danilo I, the first hereditary
vladika, was able to forge an enduring alliance with Russia; then,
under Peter I, the Montenegrins cooperated with the British and
Russians against Napoleon and won substantial additional territory.
Peter I was succeeded in due course by Peter II, who became renowned
in Montenegrin history as a soldier, statesman and the greatest of
Serbian poets, and then by Nicholas I. In short, centuries of knowing
themselves surrounded by hostile and well-armed armies had bred
extraordinary resilience, cunning and self-reliance. Montenegrins were
known in Europe for their innate dignity, love of poetry, willingness
to use their fists and aversion to work (still a standard joke in Yugoslavia). Their successful resistance became, by the nineteenth century, almost a byword for guerrilla warfare. Tennyson wrote, "O
smallest among peoples! rough rock-throne / Of Freedom! warriors
beating back the swarm / Of Turkish Islam for five hundred years."
Montenegro has been part of Yugoslavia since World War I, and its
population is now three million.

Louis Adamic, a Montenegrin author, left an eloquent description
of Nicholas I, during whose reign Olgivanna was born, in his memoir,
The Native's Return. He wrote that Nicholas "made the hamlet of
Cetinye into a tidy little town and built himself a 'palace,' which still
stands today and looks like a neglected town hall in a small American
community. Every Sunday afternoon he dispensed patriarchal justice
under an elm tree near the palace. . . . His subjects called him *gospodar*
(boss) and he greeted them by their first names. . . . A tireless worker,
he personally kept track of everything. If you, a foreigner, came to
Cetinye and registered at the Grand Hotel, which he owned, he knew
your name and business ten minutes later. If you wanted to send a
registered letter, the clerk at the post-office . . . sent you over to the
'palace,' for the king kept all stamps of higher denomination in his
private safe. . . . His wife, the queen, kept house. . . . Mornings,

with her basket and petroleum-can, she went shopping in the market place. She bore him ten daughters and three sons. . . ." Given such a comic-opera setting, one would expect the Montenegrin dynasty to have quietly slid into obscurity. In fact, this stamp-dispensing king managed to marry off his daughters most advantageously and could, through them, claim dynastic links with the king of Serbia (Prince Peter Karagjorgjevic), the Russian aristocracy (two grand dukes) and the throne of Italy (his daughter, Princess Elena, married Victor Emmanuel).

A small-town atmosphere, connections in high places, a physically arduous existence, a proud heritage, an embattled past—it is not difficult to see the points of contact that Wright found between his family's origins in rural Wales and this Serbian beauty from the shores of the Adriatic. Olgivanna Lloyd Wright subsequently wrote about her famous grandfather, but nowhere mentioned the even more astonishing fact that her mother was also a general in the Montenegrin army. She, too, gained such a reputation for ferocity that, it was said, the Turks declared if they ever caught her they would tie her between two horses. When Olgivanna left home to go to private school, her mother gave her a photograph of herself in uniform to take with her. She was too embarrassed to display it, so she kept the picture in a drawer. One day, a classmate found it and wanted to know who the military lady was. Olgivanna replied, "I've never seen that woman before in my life." Olgivanna also recalled that on another occasion she was riding on a streetcar with her mother when the latter caught sight of a man she believed to be a crooked politician, a few seats away. She stood up and launched into a denunciation then and there. That was Olgivanna's enduring memory of her mother: fierce, domineering, distant and almost recklessly brave.

Olgivanna's way of doing things was very different. One sees her as a young girl, very beautiful in a grave and stately kind of way, with a slim figure, hair dressed very simply, head bent forward in studious attentiveness and, as the above makes clear, painfully shy. As the youngest in a large family she appears to have been brought up as much by her older sisters as by her mother; in any event, her memories of childhood seem to center on her father, Ivan Lazovich, who had become blind and had given her the task of reading aloud to him: everything from legal briefs to newspapers, poetry and philosophy.

When Olgivanna was eleven, she was sent to live with her married

*Gurdjieff dancers executing a dervish prayer, Olgivanna Lloyd Wright in
left foreground*

sister in the port city of Batumi, in the Caucasus on the Black Sea.
Olgivanna was enrolled in a private coeducational school that, according to another former pupil who knew her there, was considered
most progressive for its day. It was particularly renowned for its
teaching of foreign languages, perhaps because, at the end of the
nineteenth century, the Black Sea "was an international highway which
permitted free movement between Russia, Turkey and the Balkans,"
and its student body was a polyglot of Turks, Germans, Poles, Greeks
and Armenians as well as Russians; in such a setting, the arrival of a
Serb would have caused little comment. Olgivanna was taught fluent
French and learned her Russian from a distinguished man of letters
who had written for a progressive magazine in the 1860s. Her friend
Vera Leikina-Svirskaya, four years her junior, was one of the editors
of a school magazine; Olgivanna was another. Together they laboriously wrote out the short stories and poems that filled its pages.
Reckless confrontation was not Olgivanna's style; she preferred the
tactics of psychological survival, that is to say, sharp attention, silent
conclusions and the value of the surprise attack, followed by retreat
into the darkness. She also learned the value of self-discipline.

She later recalled, "I lived some very rich years with my sister, with
so many servants I couldn't count . . . and I had everything one could

desire. But my sister was a strong disciplinarian; . . . she made me do things, notwithstanding the luxuries that surrounded me—including the governesses and music teachers. . . . It was a very high society at the villa, with counts, countesses, princes, and princesses coming in from the villas around us. But my sister, who studied medicine, was a rather advanced person, and she said to me that work was the most important thing. . . ."

Olgivanna's move to Russia appears to have coincided with a parental separation, since her father is known to have accompanied her, leaving her mother in Montenegro. All that is known about the latter is that she traveled widely in later years, lived to a great age and kept in touch with her last child. (Olgivanna periodically sent money, but the two never met again.) Olgivanna grew up with the concept of a mother for whom the career or the cause—both were probably interchangeable concepts—counted for more than the emotional needs of any individual, and of a father who perfectly fitted the traditional pattern of benevolent patriarch but made unusual demands upon her. A youthful marriage would have been expected for her, but she seems to have been bent upon making any kind of marriage as soon as possible. When her first love affair was thwarted by the boy's father —who sent him to Rome—she looked elsewhere and was soon being courted by a Russian architect ten years her senior, Vlademar Hinzenberg. This shadowy figure said later that he was working in Tiflis in the central Caucasus when they met in 1916. He was slightly built, polite and well educated with a soft, calm voice, and was a chain-smoker. He seems to have pursued her impetuously; that winter, while he was courting her, he wired a bare tree outside her window full of hothouse flowers. She told a confidante that she had never loved him and married him when she was eighteen to fulfill a promise she had made to his dying mother. The explanation sounds a little too pat, and one wonders whether she might have been pregnant; their daughter, Svetlana, was born in 1917, the year Hinzenberg said they were married. In any event, the marriage was not a success.

By the time Svetlana was born, Olgivanna Lazovich Hinzenberg had met a man destined to have a lasting influence on her life. He was Georgei Ivanovitch Gurdjieff, an intriguing and sphinxlike figure best known for having founded the Institute for the Harmonious Development of Man in Fontainebleau, outside Paris, in the early 1920s, to which Katherine Mansfield came at the end of her life and where she died. Gurdjieff's early life, his biographer has written, is almost as shadowy as that of the historical Moses. It is known, however, that he was the son of a Greek father and an Armenian mother, born in the town of Alexandropol (now Leninakan) on the Russo-Turkish border, in a part of the Caucasus perpetually fought over by Turkey, Russia and Persia. When shifts of allegiance were the rule, minority peoples, such as Armenians, were in particular danger of persecution, and the Gurdjieff family moved frequently. The Gurdjieffs were also poor and there was no hope of an advanced education for Georgei, but he was intellectually curious and ambitious to become, if not a philosopher, certainly someone skilled in esoteric knowledge. He studied Sufi and shamanistic teachings and, by early adulthood, was making his living as a professional hypnotist and teacher of the occult. But his main interest was in founding a philosophy of spiritual development, and by the time he was in his early forties, he had developed a highly idiosyncratic set of beliefs he called "The Work," which taught by means of cryptic and apparently contradictory directives in the tradition of Zen Buddhism. Gurdjieff's methods would eventually encompass exercise, dance, arduous physical labor and psychological disciplines designed to awaken his followers from what he called the profound slumber of humankind. Work, suffering, self-discipline, sacrifice, conscious effort and self-awareness—this was the path toward inner enlightenment, Gurdjieff believed. Years later Olgivanna Wright would publish a book, *The Struggle Within* (1955), and her reiteration of these goals would attest to the strength of Gurdjieff's influence.

Numerous reminiscences from former devotees have described the allure of Gurdjieff's personality: his mesmerizing gaze, his ability to seemingly read others' thoughts and his superhuman strength, as well as his capricious shifts of mood, his dictatorial ways, deliberate obfuscations and the difficulty of ever really knowing who he was. Like Wright, he was at his most confiding and least elliptical with women, and there are some fascinating parallels between their two temperaments. Both were emotionally unpredictable, extremely loyal, family-centered and generous; both were from militant minorities; both were pitiless with themselves and others; both were seignorial about money; both loved fast cars and pretty women and were extremely susceptible to flattery. Both presented themselves as authorities—Gurdjieff was almost the archetypal Magician; "the Man Who Knows," he was called—and there was no doubt that Olgivanna would be attracted to commanding figures, before she became one herself. As James

Webb, the biographer, also said of Gurdjieff, he tended to attract men and women in search of "a pair of shoulders broad enough to carry their burdens," and when Olgivanna first met Gurdjieff her marriage was failing, her father was ill or dying, her mother was far distant, and she was still an adolescent who had been catapulted into motherhood. Their immediate link was Gurdjieff's passionate interest in the music and dances he had learned in Turkestan, Belugistan and Tibet since, she wrote, "Turkish and Albanian music was the first I heard." Soon after they met, he asked her if there was something she really wanted from life. She replied, "I wish for immortality."

In 1917, as the Bolshevik forces went into action, the political situation in Tiflis became confused and dangerous. Webb wrote, "In addition to the Soviet-inspired 'Trans-Caucasian Commissariat,' the White forces had to contend with Caucasian separatists—Georgians, Armenians, and Azerbaijanis—who were not content with establishing claims to their resurrected nations, but vied incessantly with one another. In the south, the Turks, who were still at war with Russia, occupied Batum. The issue was further complicated by troops of the Allied Powers which were attempting to help the anti-Bolshevik elements and at the same time, prevent the Turks from advancing further into Russia." To his entourage, a sizable group composed of impoverished aristocrats and intellectuals, as well as refugee members of his own family, Gurdjieff must have looked like the one man with the necessary cunning and contacts in high places to conduct them all to relative safety, and they were right. In the summer of 1918 the group, cagily renamed the "International Idealistic Society," were temporarily living in Essentuki in the Caucasus. The town had a Bolshevik government, but White forces were on the offensive, and it seemed only a matter of time before they would invade Essentuki. Using his contacts, Gurdjieff adroitly secured permission for them all to leave on the pretext that they intended to make an archaeological expedition to the mountains. They immediately made for the port of Sochi on the Black Sea outside the battle zone and, after innumerable adventures, sailed for Constantinople, where they arrived in the early summer of 1920. A year later they had reached Berlin, and after examining the possibility of settling in Germany or England, Gurdjieff decided upon France and Fontainebleau.

For Olgivanna, a château outside Paris—reportedly built for Madame de Maintenon—in the idyllic French countryside must have seemed heaven-sent. Exactly when she and Hinzenberg separated is not clear, but it is apparent he felt that her intense involvement in the Gurdjieff movement and her unwillingness to set up a separate household with him had doomed their marriage from the start. In fact she was completely committed and, by dint of intense application, had become one of the master's best dancers. She spoke fluent French, there was even a kindergarten at the institute (where mothers took turns caring for the children), and by the time she arrived at *Le Prieuré*, as it was called, she had become one of Gurdjieff's six assistant instructors. As C. S. Nott, another dedicated student, wrote, "Like all the women who really worked with Gurdjieff, she was remarkable and unusual; she possessed an inner something, she had individuality, and she could turn her hand to anything."

The members of the institute had already given a series of demonstrations in Paris, and Gurdjieff had resolved to take them to New York for another introductory group of performances, early in 1924. This would have been welcome news for Olgivanna, since Hinzenberg, who had immigrated into the United States in 1922, was practicing architecture in Chicago (they would soon agree to an American divorce), and her brother Vladimir, or "Vlado," an agent for the United States Lines, was living with his family in Hollis, a suburb of New York.

They opened early in January with performances in Leslie Hall (260 West Eighty-third Street), the Lenox Theatre, the Neighborhood Playhouse and Carnegie Hall. Their reputation had preceded them, and the first audiences were packed with famous names: John O'Hara, Theodore Dreiser, Gloria Swanson, Rebecca West, Elinor Wylie and, strangely enough, Zona Gale, who became an enthusiastic supporter. They were all curious to see what superhuman feats this maguslike figure would devise, and they were not disappointed. One writer described in detail one of Gurdjieff's most celebrated exercises in which, on hearing a command that might come at any moment, the pupil had to instantly stop whatever he or she might be doing: one of his ways of waking people from the "sleep" of their automatic daily routine. This became the highlight of the evening. The troupe lined up at the back of the stage and began running full tilt toward the footlights. "We expected to see a wonderful exhibition of arrested motion," one observer wrote. "But instead Gurdjieff calmly turned his back, and was lighting a cigarette. In the next split second an aerial human avalanche was flying through the air, across the orchestra, down among empty chairs, on the floor, bodies pell-mell, piled on

top of each other, arms and legs sticking out in weird postures—
frozen there, fallen, in complete immobility and silence.

"Only after it happened did Gurdjieff turn and look at them as
they lay there, still immobile. When they presently arose . . . and it
was evident that no arms, legs, or necks had been broken . . . there
were storms of applause, mingled with a little protest. It had been
almost too much." Newspaper headlines stressed the sensational aspects of the demonstrations, and a British writer likened Gurdjieff to
a riding master with curious and unsettling powers. Despite the note
of repellent fascination in the reports, or perhaps because of it, Gurdjieff pronounced the debut a success and planned a sequel. Along with
Gurdjieff and others in the troupe, Olgivanna Hinzenberg made her
way back to Paris after she had, it is said, declined an invitation from
Cecil B. DeMille to become a dancer in Hollywood. Plans were going
ahead for the return visit. Then, on July 5, 1924, Gurdjieff, who was
a notoriously bad driver and had been known to fall asleep at the
wheel, was driving back from Paris after lunching in an Armenian
restaurant when, one report had it, his steering failed and the car
collided with a tree. According to some accounts, he was badly hurt.
Another writer believed that he had staged the accident as a way of
disbanding his institute, which had become tiresome. In any event,
as soon as he could lift his head off the pillow, most of them were
given two days to leave. Those in the inner circle, like Olgivanna
Hinzenberg, were allowed a longer period of grace, but the day of
reckoning could not be postponed for too long. Nott recalled that in
the autumn of 1924, he and Olgivanna worked with a crosscut saw
every day for two weeks, cutting up logs for the winter, and each day
Gurdjieff came around to talk to her. "From what I could follow of
the conversation it seemed to be about her plans for the future. . . ."

Gurdjieff was suggesting that she and Svetlana return to the United
States. He said that he had taught Olgivanna all he knew, and it was
time for her to "go out and live." She: "But I don't want to leave,"
and "Where will I go?" She should go to her brother, Gurdjieff said,
and that settled it. Exactly when she took that step is not clear, but
she probably arrived in New York in late October or early November.
Then she traveled on to Chicago, where her divorce from Hinzenberg
was now in the courts. Besides, some Americans who had spent time
at *Le Prieuré* were living in Chicago, and it is conceivable that Olgivanna Hinzenberg had thoughts of helping them form a new center
for the work there. She had been in the United States for three weeks

when, one afternoon, she went to a ballet performance starring Tamara Karsavina. She had noticed Wright in the lobby crowd and been attracted to him; then, to her surprise, she found herself conducted to the same box as he.

He wrote, "An usher quietly showed a dark, slender gentlewoman to the one empty seat in the house. Unobtrusive but lovely. I secretly observed her aristocratic bearing, no hat, her dark hair parted in the middle and smoothed down over her ears, a light small shawl over her shoulders, little or no makeup, very simply dressed. . . . I instantly liked her looks. . . ." They began to talk, and Wright remarked casually that Karsavina, whom they had just seen perform, would not do. She was "dead." He gestured toward the audience below. "They are all dead: the dead is dancing to the dead." He could not have known that this remark, of all those he might have made, was the one best calculated to have a dramatic effect on Olgivanna, recalling as it did one of Gurdjieff's major dicta. She gave him a "quick comprehending glance," he wrote; he felt a "strange elation." He invited her to a tea dance after the performance, and the conversation was as animated as that first celebrated meeting with Madame Noel had been, but this encounter was, by contrast, being described from his viewpoint. He liked the fact that, in a few words, she had dismissed Karsavina with the right kind of criticism; that she was perfectly straightforward and natural, yet diplomatic. He liked a certain severity about her manner. He liked the fact that she was well bred and sophisticated and had titled friends. Most of all he liked her "low musical voice" and her "sensitive feminine brow and dark eyes." As for Olgivanna, halfway through the encounter, the orchestra struck up a Strauss waltz and he invited her to dance. She later explained, "I fell in love . . . very simple . . . just like that."

Given Wright's impulsiveness, one would have expected him to sweep the lady off her feet; this seems to have happened. He wrote that he was committed to make a trip east for a week, but contacted her after he returned and invited her to the theater. The next move was an invitation to Taliesin, which she accepted. That was the evening she danced before the fire, and the Neutras, the Mosers and the Tsuchiuras, from Zurich, Vienna and Tokyo, respectively, were enthusiastic. They were "sure" that Olgivanna would be a wonderful addition to Taliesin. Wright wrote, "none so sure as I."

As for the actual date of their meeting, correspondence that autumn of 1924 in the form of telegrams between Wright and his son Lloyd in Los Angeles pinpoints Wright's movements fairly closely. Lloyd Wright was overseeing construction of the textile block houses for Storer, Freeman and Ennis, and Wright would make lightning trips to the West Coast in response to crises of one kind or another. He liked to take the Santa Fe California Limited. He could leave Chicago one evening and be in Los Angeles three days later. An analysis of his movements shows that he was in Chicago around November 22, when he could have met Olgivanna. He was off to New York on November 25 and back in Chicago, where he liked to stay in the Congress Hotel, by December 1, just long enough to take the fast train to Los Angeles. He had returned to Chicago by December 20, just in time for Christmas at Taliesin. It seems likely that Olgivanna had moved into the house that would be her home for the next sixty years early in the new year of 1925.

This may be the moment to recall Wright's first meeting with Miriam Noel and that slight but perceptible trembling of her head that first aroused his compassion and concern. Here, now, was a woman just as cultured and elegant, while far younger and prettier, and perhaps more reminiscent of Anna in her simply dressed hair, her sharp-eyed attentiveness, her unsmiling gaze and her regal bearing. He would have discovered before long that this seemingly self-possessed foreigner was as much at a loss as he was himself. The mainstay of her life had been pulled out from under her, and his indignation and sympathetic determination to take her side can be predicted. For, as he told Aline Barnsdall after she dreamed about him as a Roman singer in a Technicolor movie, that was not the right image at all. Could she not imagine a situation in which her house was about to collapse and he was standing over her, so as to take the falling beams on his own back? Or could she not see herself on a bark gliding down a stream, in an echo of John Everett Millais's painting of Ophelia perhaps, and then imagine him swimming to her rescue, so as to steer her boat into shallow waters where the lotuses grew and "golden carp raised questioning eyes?" He continued, "You see how easy it is."

That message was a remarkably consistent one. Olgivanna Lloyd Wright described an incident that took place years later, one evening when they were staying in a luxurious suite in a hotel in Paris. He wanted to make love; she was too tired. So, by way of persuasion, he began to invent a hypothetical situation: she was out for a walk in Paris; before long, she discovered that she was being followed by a man. Then a second joined in the chase. She began to run faster and faster, but the men were gaining on her. All seemed lost; in her extremity, she called her husband's name. And suddenly, he was there. She flew into his arms, and, he concluded, there she found all the safety she needed. He knew her well enough, in other words, to believe that the most seductive image he could paint of himself was as her defender, her savior.

In a photograph taken in the early 1930s, a few years after their marriage, Wright is dressed in a dark suit, carrying a cane, with a pale, broad-brimmed hat pulled down over his forehead. He is seen in profile, looking at something over his right shoulder, his gray hair swept back behind his ears. Olgivanna Lloyd Wright stands beside him, her slender body folded around his left side, one arm tucked into his and the other hand placed possessively on his chest in a gesture that is both self-conscious and eloquent. She wears an identically shaped hat at the same angle, and she, too, is in profile, her hair swept back behind her ears. Wifely devotion and identification with the beloved can go no further. She had found her new reason for being.

In his autobiography, Wright gave the impression that by the time Olgivanna and her daughter, Svetlana, had moved into Taliesin, he had filed for divorce from Miriam. He explained that he and Olgivanna felt morally free to live together; that he had filed for divorce was not quite true. Olgivanna had done so, but he did not until July 1925. His hesitation seems out of character, but there was at least one practical reason for the delay. The sale of Oak Park, so long postponed, was inching toward its conclusion in early 1925, and Wright needed the settlement and the cash. He dared not run the risk of antagonizing Miriam until he had, at least, obtained her signature on that deed, and, as has been noted, for a while she could not be found. She finally signed it in March 1925, the same month that Olgivanna obtained her divorce. There may have been, too, a certain suspicion in the back of his mind that getting Miriam to agree to a divorce might not be as painless as, no doubt, he made it appear. It was true that she had left him, but, on the other hand, he knew just how "tricky" she could be, how adept at emotional blackmail, how calculating and how vindictive. If he had ever thought about the matter, he must have been puzzled by the conundrum his relationships with women seemed to present: none of them ever wanted to let him go. His mother had clung to him through every vicissitude of his fortunes, and contemplating the final months of her life, when he finally shook her off,

must have given him some very remorseful feelings. Catherine, blind
to every rebuff, had been mesmerized by her obstinate conviction that
he would one day return, and perhaps loved him still. Now there was
Miriam; how would she jump? And if she did agree to a quiet divorce,
there would be the problems of a financial settlement and alimony
and another set of monthly payments to hound him. But if he wavered,
it could not be for long. That same March of 1925, perhaps in a mood
of euphoria, he and Olgivanna made an impulsive decision to start a
family of their own. By the time the last papers on Oak Park had
been signed and he was free to file suit for divorce (he charged Miriam
with desertion), she was four months pregnant. Olgivanna had assumed
her mother's maiden name of Milanoff and perhaps it was then that
Wright launched the transparent fiction that she was at Taliesin as
his housekeeper. He had used this ruse with Miriam in 1918, even
persuading her to sign a formal agreement to that effect (for sixty
dollars-a-month salary). The new explanation seemed no more likely
to work than had the first.

The Oak Park sale was the chief reason for the delay, but there was
another, this time a catastrophic piece of misfortune. It happened early
one evening in April just as lightning began to flash in the sky; the
wind was rising, and a heavy thunderstorm appeared imminent. Coming down from his evening meal, one he took in a small detached
dining room on the hillside above the main house, Wright learned
that something was wrong with the new system he had recently installed between his bedroom telephone and a buzzer in the kitchen.
This, by itself, was nothing new since, as Raymond had observed ten
years before, mechanical equipment frequently malfunctioned at Taliesin, but the buzzer would not stop ringing, and that was a nuisance.
Wright went to his bedroom to investigate and discovered that the
wall near the telephone was on fire, and a bed and curtains were
blazing. Undoubtedly there was a short circuit in the wall, but there
was no time to investigate because smoke was pouring out of the
windows. Wright immediately organized a bucket brigade, and had
just quelled the flames when he heard an ominous crackling noise
above the bedroom ceiling, in the dead space beneath the roof: the
fire had spread. He sent out a call for help to Spring Green, but by
the time the fire brigade arrived, the fire was already out of control,
spread by the high winds. Wright wrote, "Water! More water was
the cry as more men came over the hills to fight the now roaring sea
of devastation. Whipped by the big wind, great clouds of smoke and

sparks drove straight down the length of Taliesin courts. The place seemed doomed. . . . That merciless wind! How cruel the wind may be, cruel as fire itself.

"But I was on the smoking roofs, feet burned, lungs seared, hair and eyebrows gone, thunder rolling as the lightning flashed over the lurid scene. . . . I stood there—and fought." Their living quarters were doomed, and the next battle was to save his studio and work-rooms. These, too, seemed lost. Then, almost on cue, a dramatic roll of thunder brought a deluge of rain and a shift in the direction of the wind. Suddenly, the conflagration was under control. It had all taken just twenty minutes, and in that time the heat was so intense that the plate glass in the windows had melted; it lay in pools among the ashes on the stone pavements. The loss of their house was a terrible blow, but the building, which he had insured for $39,000, could at least be rebuilt. What were not insured, but what were valued at half a million dollars by his estimate, were a number of priceless tapestries, screens, bronzes and other treasures. He still had his print collection, as he explained a few months later to the daughter of his old Oak Park patron, Charles Roberts. Those at least were safe, but the market for the moment was poor, since impoverished Europeans had been putting their collections up for sale at auction in New York for what-ever prices they could get. Values would eventually return to their rightful levels, but for the moment he himself would have to borrow against his own collection and use it as a security. He added, "The fire knocked me flat just as I was . . . ready to realize on my investments . . . My Tokio earnings all went up in smoke—." He might have been secretly pleased that newspaper accounts made no mention of his marriage to Miriam Noel; that did not become public knowledge until he filed to divorce her. Better yet, there was no mention of Olgivanna, although she was there. At the end of the terrible fire, she crept toward him from the shadows, with a splendid message: "Taliesin lived wher-ever I stood!" He believed her.

His indomitable spirit rose to the new challenge. He picked through the ruins of Taliesin, putting aside many of the stones along with the "partly calcined marble heads of the Tang Dynasty, fragments of the black basalt of a splendid Wei-stone, soft-clay Sung sculpture and gorgeous Ming pottery that had turned to the color of bronze by the intensity of the fire." These would be lovingly incorporated into the new building. Taliesin had grown piecemeal, as the need to expand arose. This was his opportunity to design better than ever, to a unified, orderly plan. He made forty sheets of pencil studies in pursuit of his latest vision for Taliesin reborn: "Taliesin, gentler prophet of the Celts, and of a more merciful God. . . ." He was soon out walking again, swimming in the river and driving over the hills. His appetite for life was as good as ever; better in fact, because now he had Olgivanna and would soon be a father once more. He sent his usual group of masterly letters to Darwin Martin in search of the latest loan. By way of explaining his perpetual predicament, he liked to say about this time, and said it often, that "A stern chase is a long chase. If I had known how long I would have laid down long ago perhaps, I don't know. But I didn't know and I have gone on working and paying, yes and *praying* too. . . ." Tiring, no doubt, of Wright's perennial ability to cast himself in the role of the injured party battered by a hostile fate, Martin replied to the new appeals that Wright's words "would draw money from a stone image—but I am harder than that." Martin relented, as he usually did, and revived a plan to have his architect design a summer cottage. It was not, of course, enough to pull Wright out of his latest financial hole. If he really hoped, as he wrote to Harriet Monroe a few months before the fire, that he would soon be free of debt, "in spite of the gift I have for increasing the load as I travel on—the gift amounts to genius—really," that blissful state seemed farther away than ever. But, as he said in his autobiography, cheerfully, "Life is like that!" There was, nevertheless, a limit even to his sunny ability to find a silver lining in every financial cloud. When informed that he owed storage charges for a cabinet he had bought, he replied, "You are hereby invited to go strictly to hell, wherever that is, with the cabinet you mention. . . ."

On the first of January 1925, Wright had moved his studio back to Chicago and announced the opening of an office at 19 Cedar Street. Commissions were scarce that year, but he did capture one exciting new project—it would take various shapes and appear in new guises for the next four years—commissioned by William Norman Guthrie, Episcopal minister of a small church in New York and a man he had known for years. Guthrie asked Wright to design a cathedral that would hold a million people in numerous churches and chapels, all under one roof. Wright set to work that year on his idea for a triangular glass-and-steel pyramid a thousand feet high, with cathedrals and chapels grouped around its base to form a hexagon. He called it the

steel cathedral. He planned a new system of cantilevered floor construction resting on immense pylons, and an exterior of copper and
glass, as he explained to the Dutch architect H. Th. Wijdeveld. They
wrote to each other often that year, because the latter, who was founder
and editor of an architectural magazine called *Wendingen*, was planning
to publish a book about Wright's work.

Wijdeveld had conceived the idea of devoting seven consecutive
special issues of the magazine to Wright, and then binding them
together to make a book. The issues contained essays by noted writers,
including H. P. Berlage and J. J. P. Oud, an essay praising the
Imperial Hotel written by Louis H. Sullivan shortly before his death,
an essay on the social background of Wright by the interesting young
critic named Lewis Mumford, and similar studies. The resulting book
was prefaced with an introduction by Wijdeveld titled "Some Flowers
for Architect Frank Lloyd Wright." In admiring if sometimes un-
grammatical prose, Wijdeveld advanced the thesis that Wright's greatness lay "in the lofty attitude of his proportions, in the severe and
stately rhythm of his walls, in the simplicity of his masses and through
these in the proof that in all this renewing of material and form may
lie a spiritual depth which promises the certain return of Beauty." He
also wrote, "Who supports is fortunate, who leads is the chosen
one! Such a chosen one is the architect Frank Lloyd Wright."
Wright naturally termed the book "a charming and graceful compliment. . . ." After his death, his widow noted that, as he had done
with any object that was particularly precious—a vase, a piece of
sculpture or a Japanese lacquer box—Wright kept the *Wendingen*
edition close by his side for the rest of his life.

After receiving word of the divorce suit, Miriam Noel Wright
returned like a whirlwind with a cascade of letters and tearful, daily
telephone calls. Her missives have not been recovered, but at least
one letter from Wright, addressed to Judge Frederick S. Fake of
Chicago in the summer of 1925, has survived, indicating the kinds
of claims she was making. She was insisting that she wanted a reconciliation. He replied, "I look upon her return against my will
. . . as a betrayal. . . ." She was making wild and unfounded charges,
but the behavior, he believed, was simply evidence of "the usual rule-
or-ruin tactics" that she always used; she was a desperate and dangerous
woman. She sounded hysterical on the telephone. In short, he did not
know how to calm her, but if money was what she wanted, he would
make the best settlement he could, and even agree to let her bring

the suit on a charge of desertion, if she preferred. After a few months they had agreed on $10,000 in cash, $250 a month and a half-interest in the Spring Green property. Wright was willing to throw in another $1,000 if Miriam went through with her implied intention to return to Paris. To get that money, he added cleverly, she had to leave within six weeks of the agreement, which was dated November 18, 1925. It seemed as if the whole issue might be settled at the eleventh hour; the birth of Olgivanna and Wright's child was expected early in December.

It seems fair to believe that Miriam was at first negotiating, one would have said, in good faith, i.e., ignorant of the real reason for Wright's uncharacteristic willingness to accept a hard financial bargain. Being cast off in this way hardly fitted her inner fantasy world. If anyone was going to do the leave-taking, that person was supposed to be she. It was not in the cards at all for him to be heartily glad to see her leave, and in such strange haste to repudiate those solemn vows said over water at midnight just two years before. It was hurtful. It offended her very delicate and sensitive amour propre. Such a man should not think he could get off scot-free, even if his financial terms are generous. He has to expect some public embarrassment; he has to understand that his wife is going to tell her version of events. She had a press conference two days before the agreement was to take effect. The reporters were most attentive.

All this was bad enough from Wright's point of view, but worse was to come. It is perfectly likely that Miriam hired a private detective immediately. It was fashionable in the 1920s, a realistic way of ensuring that the financial settlement was exactly as you wished.

You would not, of course, ever make this public. No, you would simply let your information leak out innocently, as if you had found out by chance. Miriam told the press that she had visited the Art Institute in Chicago and was passing by the Congress Hotel, at Michigan Avenue and Congress Street, when she happened to see Wright's car standing outside; his chauffeur, Billy, was at the wheel. Billy told her that his employer was staying at the hotel. Then Billy told her something else.

Miriam Wright said that she then went to the manager's office and demanded to see the hotel register. The manager refused, so she called the police. Before they arrived, the man changed his mind and there, under her horrified eyes, was the incriminating evidence.

Did she really find out in this way, or was Wright being followed?

At this point it hardly mattered. It was a gross miscalculation on his part to check in to his favorite hotel with Olgivanna, given his sorry experiences with Mamah Borthwick in an identical situation, given the vital importance, at that particular moment, of doing nothing to compromise some delicate negotiations and given what he knew about Miriam. This repetitious flaunting of convention was more than characteristic; at this point it had to be compulsive, so much so that the need to defy had blinded him to all other considerations. If there were any one point in this latest imbroglio at which Wright took a fatal wrong turn, this was it, and because Miriam Wright was so vengeful he could argue that she was responsible for wounds that were actually self-inflicted.

Miriam began her press conference quietly and reasonably, by observing that it was quite wrong to say that she had left him. She had merely gone on a holiday to recover her health. He was the one who no longer wished to live with her. The fact that they had only been married for a few months before she left was similarly embellished, but in acting out her role of the wronged wife, Miriam was a past master of the art of putting herself in the best possible light, no matter how much glossing over of uncomfortable facts and invention of others might be required.

Olgivanna's second child and Frank's seventh, a baby girl named Iovanna, was born less than a month later, on December 2. Any hope that a discreet veil could be drawn over this unhappy turn of events had long vanished. The local Spring Green newspaper noted that, for several days past, the road between the town and Taliesin had been "warmed" by reporters and photographers from Chicago, Milwaukee and Madison, which had "had the world famous architect warmed up also." By December 5 Miriam had tracked down mother and child in their Chicago hospital and raised such an uproar that they fled. Olgivanna said that she and her baby were taken to the train, bound for New York, on a stretcher.

Announcement of the marriage of Olgivanna and Frank Lloyd Wright,
showing a picture of Iovanna, age three

Olgivanna and Iovanna at the height of the divorce crisis

13

Truth Against the World

Alas, you glorious princes! All gone
Lost in the night, as you had never lived.

Fate blows hardest on a bleeding heart.
"The Wanderer"
Poems from the Old English

The angry prophet had destroyed Taliesin twice and might smite again. "No doubt Isaiah still stood there in the storms that muttered, rolled and broke again over this low spreading shelter. . . ." Never mind. Let the worst happen, the thunder roll and lightning strike. He could face it, so long as he was behind his newly restored battlements and had the loving support of this unsmiling, self-possessed beauty who was as utterly devoted to him as he was to her. But how secure were they? If he had thought that Miriam's rage was assuaged by her moment in the limelight that autumn, he was soon disabused of that notion. Not only had she harassed Olgivanna in her hospital bed but also a few days before that, she had actually lodged a complaint with the immigration authorities. According to her testimony, "Olga" Milanoff "came to their home as a servant and has stayed on as Wright's sweetheart." Miriam added that he was the kind of man who would fall in love with any woman who flattered his art. If Miriam really intended to go on making trouble, he knew how easy it would be.

Taliesin, that serene symbol of all that was safe and secure, his sacred place, his enchanted domain, now appeared to be the one place in which neither of them dared be found if Miriam were determined to pursue them. Building it for the third time was a constant drain, and being rebuffed by Darwin Martin was another unwelcome development. "I came to you as a brother in need and really my need was deep and wide for I am unable to go on to meet the load this last misfortune heaves upon my shoulders—and carry on my work at all," he wrote, in a last-ditch effort to persuade Martin to take his print collection as collateral, something he always declined to do. "My chief assets as print purchasers—three of them—dead! Where to turn?" he asked forlornly. He was pressing everyone he could think of, and had written so forcefully to Gordon Strong, his client for the Sugarloaf project, that Strong sent a check in an envelope without a covering letter. Wright replied that he hoped he had not offended him. "I tried to show you what you must already know that I am carrying on my house-building under great difficulties. No doubt a foolish thing to do. But I must do it." Meantime he would have to make good on his first alimony payments to his wife. She claimed that there were no funds to cover his checks at his bank.

A note of panic was clearly evident, and as invariably happened when his back was to the wall, Wright turned on his tormentor. He had plenty of charges of his own to make early in February 1926, when a hearing was held in Dane County to have him explain why he should not pay his wife's attorney fees and personal expenses (of $1,500) until the divorce trial, planned for a month later. Wright's attorney, Levi H. Bancroft, said that his client had been tailed by "gunmen," an apparent reference to private detectives, and "dope addicts," a clear reference to Miriam herself. He said that he had copies of a hundred letters Mrs. Wright had written to bankers and creditors in an attempt to blacken her husband's name and destroy his reputation as an architect. He said, "And if I turned them over to federal officials she'd go to the penitentiary for writing obscene matter."

For her part, Mrs. Wright claimed that since her husband had not paid any alimony, she had repudiated that contract and would not give him a divorce after all. What she wanted now was separate maintenance of $250 a month. Her husband could easily afford it; he was capable of earning between $10,000 and $25,000 a year, with an estate worth $50,000. Wright's attorney, per contra, argued that his client was insolvent. The architect's earning power, he said, had been destroyed by her attacks.

Wright did not attend the hearing. His attorney stated that he was in hiding, claiming that he feared for his life. As for Olgivanna, she had also disappeared; it was rumored that immigration authorities were moving to deport her as an undesirable alien. From her expensive room in Chicago's Southmoor Hotel, Miriam Wright said complacently that the Russian "danseuse" had fled to Canada. Miriam had already succeeded in disrupting their lives and was the likely informant for yet another piece of mischief, this time a complaint lodged with the Department of Justice's Bureau of Investigation (later, the FBI). The files on this complaint reveal that someone, name deleted, who refused to give an address, had charged early in February 1926 that Frank Lloyd Wright (subject), and Olga "Millinoff" (victim), posing as a housekeeper, had actually been living together in Spring Green for at least a year. The subject had taken the victim on frequent trips between Spring Green and Chicago, making it a "possible violation of the White Slave Traffic Act": charges that Olgivanna should be deported and he thrown in jail under the Mann Act—it was all terribly familiar. It must have given Miriam Wright, now the oh-so-legal wife, all kinds of satisfaction to be adroitly turning the tables on her successor and making her suffer, just as she had been made to do a decade before.

It is likely that Wright knew nothing, as yet, about the Justice Department's renewed interest in his movements, but he was rightly concerned about the possibility that Olgivanna might be deported. Since Miriam had forced mother and baby to leave, they might as well be conducted to Hollis and the relative safety of her brother and sister-in-law's home. "Love and protection around her," Wright wrote. "A great change from the humiliation and misery of the last fortnight." They spent Christmas at "Vlado's" and he accompanied his almost-brother-in-law into New York every day. While Vlado worked, he walked the streets, jotting down impressions of the big city that he would eventually use in a series of articles. He had always lectured; now he began to teach himself to write, using stream-of-consciousness passages in which he tried to describe the visual bombardment that a walk along its streets represented. His solution when beset by a problem was to take instant refuge in a new challenge, one in which he could cheerfully become absorbed, one he could write about and pontificate about. Despite their present predicament (attorney Bancroft had urged that they disappear for three months while he worked out a solution), Wright was tolerably optimistic. Olgivanna, his temperamental opposite, was evidently reacting very differently. She was painfully thin and could not eat. She needed a warm climate, and he hit upon the idea of a trip to Puerto Rico. Since it was now a U.S. possession, there would be no awkward questions about passports; still, to be safe, they traveled in a first-class cabin under the pseudonym of Mr. and Mrs. Frank Richardson. This detail was of interest to the Bureau of Investigation, which compiled a list of "aliases"; its files read, "Frank Lloyd Wright, alias Frank Richardson, alias F. W. Wilson," and "Olga Hinzenberg, alias Milanoff, alias Anna Richardson, alias Emily Richardson. . . ." According to these same files, the Richardsons were in Puerto Rico for about a month while an assistant U.S. attorney debated whether to press charges. After reviewing the files he advised that the evidence was insufficient to warrant an arrest. The case was closed. The couple then went to Washington, perhaps in pursuit of some resolution for the immigration problem, though Wright does not mention this. Olgivanna did not improve and he became worried. "These peregrinations had to cease. . . . And so, braving the persecution, we returned to Taliesin. . . ."

By May, Wright's spirits were on the rise again, and he was inviting the Darwin Martins to come for a visit. The new house was in good shape and the countryside had never looked lovelier. The immigration proceedings, apparently, were in abeyance. "All traces of misfortune have disappeared here." He spoke too soon. Miriam had made the Chicago papers again, claiming that she faced eviction from her expensive hotel room because she could not pay her bill, and would be obliged to sell her valuable collection of pieces of jade, prints, shawls, fans, inlaid furniture and oriental trinkets, given by her husband in happier days. Meantime her suit for separate maintenance was still pending. Her lawyer advised her that Taliesin was community property, therefore her home. She had as much right to live there as her husband did.

"I had no money, but a Chicago newspaper man and his wife were driving over to Madison and offered to take me. We arrived at Spring Green late in the afternoon. Next morning the newspaper man and his wife came to the hotel for me and we continued our journey to Taliesin." For once, Wright was ready for her. When she arrived (armed with a warrant for Olgivanna and a peace warrant for him, which she had obtained on a trip to Dodgeville), she found the front gate locked. William Weston, Wright's chief employee, explained that he had instructions to keep everyone off the premises. Miriam knew that there was also a back entrance, and she attempted to enter through this route but found that a truck had been wedged across the passageway, and there was another guard of men there. Her demands to talk to her husband were also fruitless. He was not at home, his daughter, Frances Wright Cuppley, declared. Newspaper accounts state that she proved "an efficient defender of the fort." Miriam Wright ripped a sign off the front gate stating No Visitors Allowed and flung it away, to the delight of watching reporters and cameramen. She discovered a second in a glass frame, took a rock to it and battered it to smithereens. It all made very good copy.

She was back next day waving warrants and succeeded, for a few hours, in actually having her husband arrested. (He was soon released.) Olgivanna was nowhere to be found. On Miriam's third attempt, a county prosecutor intervened with the news that her husband would provide $125 a month if she would give up. It was hardly a victory, given the sum she was demanding, but it was better than nothing. Miriam Wright conceded defeat and left Madison on the 5:30 train. Wright felt a certain cautious hope. Now, if people would only let him alone, he wrote, in an article for the local *Weekly Home News*, he could get on with his life, come "right side up" and make his neighbors proud of him yet. "I feel that I belong to this region just as the . . . horses and cows and barns do. My grandfather began my life here. My mother and her people continued it and . . . loved the valley to which I have come back as the third generation in a struggle to develop, an old family soil, some of the finer elements of what we call civilization. . . ."

Another hurricane was brewing, this one at the bank. Alerted, perhaps, by Bancroft's reluctant admission in February that his client was "insolvent," the Bank of Wisconsin took the matter in hand and found Wright's mortgage in arrears and his debts mounting. Although he had an estimated $150,000 invested in his house, outbuildings, farm and 193 acres of land, he owed $25,000 on the mortgage, a further chattel mortgage of $1,500, and there were liens for unpaid bills of $17,000—for a grand total of $43,500. On the advice of his lawyer, and an old friend, Judge James Hill, Wright went to the bank to solicit a new mortgage that would cover everything he owned: plans, collections, drawing instruments, studio tools and farm implements. Although the bank's idea of the balance due to him was far less than he had hoped for, a measly $1,500, it did put his debts into a certain tidy order. The problem being shelved, as he thought, he characteristically forgot about it. He had started a correspondence with the young critic Mumford, who had written about him in *Wendingen* (Wright seems to have reproached him for not being more enthusiastic), and received a graceful reply in which Mumford explained that he had been hesitant because he had not yet seen Wright's work, but hoped to do so soon. He thought that foreign critics had misinterpreted these buildings by seeing in them more mechanistic rigor than was actually there. "They have merely caught up with the machine; whereas you have carried the machine, as it were, into a new phase. Is this misreading you, too?" That summer of 1926 Darwin Martin sent him a handbook about Wales, annotated in Martin's characteristically firm hand. Wright wrote, "I am glad to have it from your hand and I only now learn just what the word 'Taliesin' means. It is worth knowing." Meanwhile he was struggling to concentrate on Martin's new cottage and finding it difficult; it refused to "grow from the ground" but sat bolt upright on the landscape. He was, perhaps, too distracted by the relentless parade of bad news in his personal life to give the matter his full attention. Hill and Bancroft were urging him to leave Taliesin for another three months. He rather finesses the point in his autobiography, but no doubt they reasoned that if he were to cut a believable figure as persecuted spouse he could not go on living in flagrant adultery. Wright was all for staying and fighting it out; his legal advisors urged a discreet withdrawal, and, naturally, so did Olgivanna. The decision was made for them on August 30 when Miriam Wright made another lightning strike: an alienation-of-affection suit against Olgivanna for $100,000. After writing an "open letter" for the *Capital Times* saying he was going abroad, they packed up and left, so hastily that blueprints were scattered all over the floor of his studio and the table was still set for a meal. The second Mrs. Wright announced next day that she would move in.

They were advised to go as far away as possible, Canada preferably, but Wright was afraid that if he and Olgivanna crossed the border, he might never get her back. Minneapolis seemed a good compromise. Autumn was beautiful there and they had friends staying in Wildhurst, an exclusive summer resort colony on Lake Minnetonka, twenty miles southwest of Minneapolis. On August 30 they set off in his Cadillac with a maid, Svetlana and Iovanna, following the Mississippi River and arriving in Minneapolis on September 2, where they stayed for a few days. Wright could not have known that his movements were being investigated by an agent for the Justice Department's Bureau of Investigation, and that by driving Olgivanna across the Wisconsin-Minnesota state line, instead of having her get out and walk (presumably to demonstrate that she was not a "victim") he had given the bureau new evidence under the White Slave Traffic Act. Meantime, warrants were made out in Baraboo, Wisconsin, for their arrest on charges of adultery. They had escaped just in time.

A week after they left Taliesin, Miriam Wright appeared again at Taliesin's door. This time she was carrying a "writ of entrance" signed by a court commissioner in Dodgeville that essentially acknowledged her legal right to live there. The loyal William Weston tried to stop her but was forced to concede defeat. "I'll go in alone but I will fire those in charge and then I will invite my friends to come in," Mrs. Wright declared. "This is my home." Then she entered the "love bungalow" for the first time in two years.

Her Chicago attorney, Harold Jackson, said that his objective had been to demonstrate his client's legal right to return to Taliesin. He conceded that she could not expect to stay for long. As she walked through the front door, two bankers, H. H. Thomas of Madison and R. L. Hopkins, manager of the Bank of Wisconsin, drove up the hill. No doubt they had appeared in the hope that the joint owner of Taliesin would write them out a check. Wright had forgotten to pay his bills again—perhaps he was in arrears on the mortgage payments by a month or two. It seems likely that the bankers were tired of dealing with him and looking for a pretext to close the account and dispense with him as a client. In any event, Wright's indebtedness had the effect of checkmating any plan Miriam might have been concocting to take over Taliesin herself, unless, of course, she could immediately pay up. Since she evidently could not, Messrs. Thomas and Hopkins had the painful duty of informing her that a date for foreclosure proceedings would soon be fixed. Until this was announced there was very little Mrs. Wright could do. She certainly could not fire the servants.

Jackson, the ace lawyer from Chicago, was, by an odd coincidence, also acting as counsel for Olgivanna's divorced husband. Miriam Wright's demonic determination to "hound" her husband to "the ends of the earth" and the news that Wright and his dancer planned to go abroad had had their effect on the courtly Hinzenberg. He said, "I heard rumors, and read notices that [Svetlana] was to be taken out of the country. . . . I was frantic for fear that I wouldn't see her again."

He was the one who had obtained adultery warrants for the arrest of Wright and his former wife, a writ of habeas corpus to secure Svetlana's custody, and was offering a $500 reward for information leading to Wright's capture. Soon after that, he also sued Wright for $250,000 for alienating the affections of his ex-wife and daughter. Meanwhile, Mrs. Wright had initiated an involuntary bankruptcy suit against Wright. She also asked for his arrest on Mann Act charges. The sheriff of Sauk County, Wisconsin, circulated photographs of the fugitives. It seemed the right moment for a Madison, Wisconsin, construction firm to bring suit for $4,000 said to be owed for the latest rebuilding of Talicsin. Rumors spread that Wright and his companion, fugitives from the law, were in Europe, or in Mexico, or on their way to Seattle in their commodious Cadillac, about to embark for Japan.

Wright, of course, was perfectly happy and in no rush to go anywhere. They took a friend's sailboat on the lake and went for walks in the countryside. Having all that free time and nothing to do with it, he thought he might as well write an autobiography, and hired a stenographer. It was going well and he was sure, he told Martin expansively, that it would sell for $50,000 and provide a steady income thereafter. "It is very simple and truthful—and a surprise no doubt to most everybody as the truth always is."

The Bureau of Investigation agents had been patiently picking up clues. They learned that "Anna Richardson" and her two children had checked into a room of the Nicollet Hotel in Minneapolis, and a certain "F. W. Wilson" had taken another. Mr. Wilson had such a distinctive appearance—perhaps the first time in his life that he had cause to rue it—that an informant remembered him very clearly. The same kind of luck pursued them at Lake Minnetonka. No one suspected that "Mr. and Mrs. Frank Richardson" were not man and wife until someone happened to read an article in the Minneapolis paper, to the effect that Vlademar Hinzenberg was looking for his little girl, and had overheard the Richardsons calling their daughter "Svetlana." There was a Wisconsin license plate on the Cadillac, and, well, one thing led to another. An agent for the Bureau of Investigation wired the secretary of state for identification of the license plate number and was advised by return wire that it belonged to Frank Lloyd Wright of Spring Green. Although she was not there to experience that moment of triumph, it was Miriam Noel Wright's finest hour.

* * *

The law caught up with Wright, Madame Milanoff, Svetlana and baby Iovanna one October evening about a month after their arrival. There was a knock at the door, and a dozen burly characters, led by Miriam Wright's Chicago lawyer, Harold Jackson, burst into the room. They were placed under arrest, and they and the children were taken to the Hennepin County jail to spend the night. Next morning they were brought before county court, where they were charged with conspiracy to violate the Mann Act and required to post bonds of $12,500. They then went to municipal court, where Wright had to deposit another $3,000 to avoid spending further time in jail on the adultery warrant. According to a newspaper account, "Wright was as debonair as usual and outwardly as urbane and unconcerned as ever when he appeared before the commissioner. He was wearing his customary flowing bow tie and carrying a cane which he swung in a jaunty manner. . . . The Montenegrin woman was calm and composed as she faced the commissioner but her eyes were red as if with weeping, and her face looked drawn and haggard."

The first person to see reason was Hinzenberg. Once he had been convinced that his daughter was in no danger of being kidnapped, he readily agreed to drop his charges of adultery and make arrangements with her mother for joint custody. The sheriff of Sauk County then released them from charges of being fugitives from justice. That left the Mann Act charges, which seemed serious, and all the suits Mrs. Wright was bringing, including her attorney's new insistence that there was something sinister about the murder-fire trial of 1914 and that the whole issue should be reopened. The "involuntary bankruptcy" charge had been dropped, apparently on the urging of Wright's principal creditor, that is, the Bank of Wisconsin, which managed to convince the implacable Mrs. Wright that her husband would never be able to support her, or pay off his debts, if she did not relent on this score at least. Most troubling for Wright, perhaps, was the discovery that the immigration authorities were taking a fresh interest in Olgivanna's case, and she had innocently given them information against herself by a reference to their trip to Puerto Rico. It could now be argued, he wrote, that he had brought her back to the mainland for "immoral purposes." As soon as they were released, Olgivanna and the children prudently moved in with friends, and another friend offered Wright the hospitality of the Minneapolis Athletic Club.

" 'Morally we are right, legally we are wrong.'

"This statement has become more or less famous in Minneapolis since Frank Lloyd Wright, internationally famous architect, and his companion, Mme. Olga Milanoff, were arrested," said an editorial in a Minneapolis newspaper, the *Twin City Reporter,* a week later. The surprising fact was that most people agreed with the public position Wright was now taking. "Genius that he is in his chosen profession, his life so far as the married side is concerned has been one blunder after another. Perhaps it is the obvious mercenary attitude . . . Miriam Noel, of Chicago, is taking in her attitude toward Wright that has aroused so much sympathy." The editorial added that her attorney's ruthless tactics had not endeared her either. "Ordinarily, a man in Wright's shoes would be condemned, but [this] is a strange case in which the sympathy of the people is with the man who has violated the social code. If he loves Mme. Milanoff, is willing to marry her and provide a home for her and the children . . . then why not make the road to happiness . . . easy? . . ." It was the first indication that opinion might be shifting from the victimized wife to the unfairly hounded husband, but there were others. It was considered a "moral" victory for Wright when the first Mrs. Wright telegrammed that she was prepared to come to Minneapolis if she could help him in any way. It was another victory of sorts when the lawyer for Miriam Wright resigned, in disgust, after having made three attempts to negotiate a monthly settlement for her, all of which she rejected. "I wanted to be a lawyer," he declared, "and Mrs. Wright wanted me to be an avenging angel." That there might be something irrational about Mrs. Wright's behavior began to be suspected. She actually brought suit against the Bank of Wisconsin on the ground that it had conspired with Wright to deny her access to Taliesin. The case was brought to court but considered so preposterous that it was expunged from the record. She was awarded fifty dollars in court costs.

The cumulative effect of these attacks had their usual invigorating results on Wright's spirits, but the same could not be said for Olgivanna. Nothing Miriam Wright had said or done could destroy her love, but it had deeply shaken her faith in herself. She had not gained any weight since Iovanna's birth. Photographs of her, published at the time, show her thinner than ever, hollow-cheeked and grave of face. A week after she and Wright were arrested, and the day before she was to appear in court for preliminary hearings of the Mann Act charge, she collapsed and was taken to a Minneapolis sanatorium.

The problem seemed to be that, in contrast to her lover, who blamed everyone else when embattled, Olgivanna Milanoff blamed herself. A letter to Wright's sister, Mrs. Andrew Porter, addressed as "Sister Jane," written from Minneapolis in mid-November, makes it clear that what had unnerved her most was to find herself on the wrong side of the law, she who was the daughter of a dispenser of justice. Speaking of the law, she wrote, "I lived in it. It was just as natural as the air I breathe . . ."; now, she was told, the law was out to destroy her. What was equally mortifying was her inability to find the inner peace she needed, she who had helped so many in the past. Wright made a copy of this letter and sent it to friends. Among them was Alfred MacArthur, an old friend from his Oak Park days, now a publisher in Chicago. MacArthur had been one of the tenants in the rental part of the home and studio and, as general agent for the National Life Insurance Company, gave Wright some sage business advice, seldom followed. He had also been the lender of small sums. His daughter, Mrs. William V. Hansen, said emphatically, "My father was not well off. I should say not!" MacArthur was a brother of the famous playwright Charles MacArthur, who married Helen Hayes, and they were all friendly. Yet another brother, John, would establish the famous MacArthur Foundation in later years. No doubt Wright had a certain ulterior motive in passing along Olgivanna's letter, which he thought very fine.

In fact, Wright's friends were beginning to rally to his defense. A group of architects, professors and writers that included MacArthur, the poet Carl Sandburg and Ferdinand Schevill, professor of history at the University of Chicago, had made an appeal to Lafayette French, Jr., the federal district attorney in Minneapolis, urging him not to press charges against Wright that were transparently instruments of "persecution and revenge." Even Aline Barnsdall, whom he had exasperated by threatening to sue over their latest fracas involving past business dealings, could separate her annoyance about that from her indignation at the unjust treatment Wright was receiving. How anyone could accuse a man like himself of such ridiculous, trumped-up charges was beyond her. Anyone could see that what he was trying to do was set matters to rights, and there would have been less friction between herself and him if he had had a proper helpmeet in those days and not "a wild cat." He had been too prominent a figure and unlucky—that was his verdict, and she agreed with it entirely and told people so. She well remembered his telling her about the evenings when, as a young man, he went for long walks over the hills, dreaming of his Ideal Girl. Far from being a man of loose morals, he was a "hopeless romanticist."

The tide was turning in Wright's favor, and the next major battle would be the threatened foreclosure proceedings by the Bank of Wisconsin. Wright had attempted to bluster his way out of this and received a very tart reply from R. L. Hopkins, bank manager, early in November. It was not going to be easy. He had to concede that the bank had given him ample warning, but, from habits long ingrained, he had continued to think that the bill could be indefinitely postponed or that, when all else failed, someone else would pay it. In the old days that had been his mother. For many years now, it had been Darwin Martin. Some recent refusals ought to have given him pause. In declining to pay one bill, Martin had explained that it was too reminiscent of the old days when Wright had been "the world's best advance collector." Wright had missed the emphasis on the past tense. In fact, Martin had retired the year before, was now living on a fixed income, and was ambitious to endow a chair at the University of Buffalo. (He accomplished this with a check for $100,000 in 1928.) His determination to leave this legacy gave him, for the first time, considerable immunity. As before, Wright's reflex upon news of foreclosure proceedings was to write to him. Wright observed, "I am like the boy who cried wolf when there was no wolf—when the wolf came, no one would believe him. . . . The wolf has arrived and you will not believe me. . . ."

At last, Wright faced reality. He might actually lose Taliesin! He must have thought it could never happen. It was about to happen unless he thought fast.

Wright immediately began to negotiate with the bank using his last card, his precious collection of prints. These ought to be worth $250,000, as he assured Martin, but what they would actually fetch in the present depressed market was another matter. Still, an offer to arrange a New York exhibition and sale might stave off disaster for a few more months. Then what? It was at this point that Wright had his cleverest idea. He would sell shares in himself! In other words, he would mortgage his future by persuading a group of, say, ten wealthy people, to buy shares at $7,500 each. This would give him enough cash to pay his debts, satisfy the bank, get back on his feet, pay off Miriam and establish his career anew. It would all be above board, of course. There would be dividends perhaps; but this was an issue over which he tended to glide. Looking like a good prospect was what counted most. One of the first to be sounded out on the idea was, inevitably, Darwin Martin. He cautiously allowed that, under the proper circumstances, and if nine other backers could be found, he was willing to become the tenth. He had to hand it to Wright; the idea was "very ingenious."

The question of why Wright, later in life, subtracted two years from his age, is often raised. The evidence suggests that the new birth year of 1869 did not come into use until November 1925. Conceivably, the imminent arrival of his seventh child and the fact that Olgivanna was so much younger were the precipitating factors. However, a year later, when the idea of incorporating himself came to him, it would have occurred to the prudent side of his nature that it was far easier to sell shares on the future of a man still in his fifties than on one who is almost sixty. In any event, the 1869 date was adhered to for the rest of his life. A few years later, he even joked about the subject with Darwin Martin (who knew the truth). "We celebrate a year younger each year," he wrote in June 1934, "and began soon enough to make this my sixtieth. Next year I shall be in my fifties. . . ." He was sixty-seven.

The next person to be approached was the lawyer William R. Heath, another old friend from Oak Park days, former client and Larkin Company official, whose advice he had solicited as he negotiated his way through the complexities of divorcing Miriam. Finding himself in Buffalo at about that time, Wright had made an unannounced call on Heath but no one was at home. He left a note pinned to the door: "By the look of this house you need me as much as I need you!" In fact, he needed every good prospect, and Heath seemed especially promising. Wright sent him one of his most masterly appeals from the Hotel Brevoort in New York, where he was staying in 1927 to attend the auction sale of his more than three hundred prints at the Anderson Galleries on January 6 and 7. Was Heath willing to put his shoulder to the wheel and protect Wright and his future? "You have the temper and the mind to be of great value to me . . . I should see more of you—And out of that might come something valuable to us both as we grow on—I am very anxious and none to [sic] certain without you."

He conceded that his present misfortune was deserved though the punishment seemed harsh. But he was willing and eager now, with the help of friends like his dear "WR." He begged him to "try me out," and enclosed a photograph of Olgivanna and Iovanna for Mrs. Heath. It was masterly, but it failed. Heath replied, "My dear Frank . . . I just can't do it!" He longed, nevertheless, to see Wright's troubles ended and would help all he could. Similar expressions of reluctant but firm regret came from other quarters, but enough people—among them Professor Schevill, Darwin Martin, Wright's sister Jane, his former client Mrs. Avery Coonley, the designer Joseph Urban and others—were willing to risk their $7,500. "The world's best advance collector" had done it again.

He needed this encouragement because, as he had probably feared, the print sale was a disaster. Like a horrid dream it summed up and characterized so much of what was happening to him at this period: so many crises, most of his own making, to which he would rise heroically, inventing eleventh-hour solutions to snatch, as he liked to say, victory from the jaws of defeat, only to have his most ingenious efforts wiped out and destroyed by what must have seemed an especially virulent fate. The collection, valued at $100,000, was to be sold at the order of the Bank of Wisconsin to satisfy Wright's debts: a total of $52,576. What Wright probably neglected to mention until absolutely necessary was that the collection itself was mortgaged. The Anderson Galleries had first call on the proceeds, since he had borrowed $25,000 from them in 1925 and had used the collection as collateral. So, to pay off these immediate, pressing debts Wright needed to net $77,000 from the proceeds. No doubt this was a reasonable expectation. One print alone, a two-color by Toyonobu dating back nearly two hundred years, was considered extremely valuable since it was very rare and in superb condition. There were many other beautiful specimens. There was an unusual number of Hiroshige prints, including the celebrated *Monkey Bridge*, of which only seven of this quality were known to exist, and a series of seven uncut sheets of a Korean wedding procession by Utamaro. A writer for the *New York Times* noted that Japanese prints of this quality would soon be unavailable since Japan was belatedly realizing that its national treasures had almost disappeared into European and American collections.

The *New York Times* advance review was admiring, and the prospects looked good. Then, just before eight o'clock, when the auction was to begin, a New York lawyer representing Mrs. Miriam Noel Wright appeared on the scene with a warrant of attachment for the prints. Mrs. Wright argued that the proceeds should be diverted to herself, because, while living with Wright, she had advanced him $35,000 of her personal funds, which he never repaid. She further claimed that, under a recent separation agreement, he owed her a further $15,000. The gallery's lawyer made a counterclaim, and it looked as if the gallery's doors would not open. At the last possible moment,

Mrs. Wright's lawyer agreed to let the disposition of the proceeds be decided by a New York court.

This danger averted, the auction began. It was well attended but disappointing. The jewel of the collection, the two-color Toyonobu, valued at $10,000, went for $2,500, and other prices were far lower: the Hiroshige *Monkey Bridge* sold for a mere $1,500 and the Korean wedding procession for a paltry $900. At the end of two days the final total from this sale of Wright's treasures was $36,975. He never saw a penny of it, but neither did the bank or Miriam Wright. The state of New York decreed that the Anderson Galleries, which presented a final bill (loan plus costs) for slightly more than $37,000, should take the lot.

The Mann Act charges were dropped in March. The federal district attorney, Lafayette French, Jr., perhaps influenced by the appeals of Wright's distinguished group of friends, finally removed that threat just as a grand jury was about to sit. He concluded that the evidence pointed to a "technical rather than a criminal violation." Miriam Wright's alienation-of-affection suit similarly petered out, and that lady went to the West Coast to recover from the exhaustion of her pursuit. She had not yet, however, run out of ideas. Shortly after her arrival, she filed a new suit asking for Wright's arrest on a charge of desertion. She was scraping the bottom of the barrel, legalistically speaking, and was quickly rebuffed on the ground that no crime had been committed in California. In a rare mood of dejection, Miriam Wright declared, "Alone, deserted, desolate, I must now find my way out without him." There was another reason for celebrating that spring: The Académie Royale des Beaux Arts of Holland had elected him a member. Wright dashed off an exultant letter to his friend Alexander Woollcott with the playful comment, "And there's a diploma and an 'order' which I'll let you wear around your neck. . . . Sometimes—if you will be good."

Plenty of bad news continued to roll in. There had been another fire at Taliesin in February, fortunately minor—since the bank owned the chattels as well, everything of value had been removed—apparently again caused by faulty electric wiring. There was about three thousand dollars in damages, and the fire had the unexpected but salutary effect of delaying foreclosure while the bank totaled up its losses and made a new appraisal. Miriam Wright still declared she would never agree to a divorce, and immigration authorities continued to display a sinister interest in Olgivanna. While Wright and Olgivanna were visiting

Maginel in New York, officers actually appeared at the door of her apartment to arrest Olgivanna. Wright cashed in his last Liberty bond to pay for her bail. It was all too much. "My sense of humor began to fade."

The new company, Frank Lloyd Wright, Inc., had been formed in January but no money had, as yet, changed hands. Nothing could be done until the divorce was final and a complete list had been compiled of all the creditors. While trying to stave off the approaching deportation proceedings, Wright was also (perhaps it was a reflex) trying to avoid knowing how much money he owed. One of his lawyers finally wrote, "You say that the corporation is waiting to know the exact amount which it will take to settle your indebtedness. Permit me to ask you in all fairness, how the devil do you expect me to know who all your creditors are? . . ."

For months Wright had been giving a spectacular imitation of a man riding a spinning log while it plunges headlong toward the rapids. For months his gaze had been steady, his steering agile, his demeanor loftily nonchalant and his balance impeccable. Nevertheless, he was only human. "Getting somewhat warm and weary," he confessed to his favorite correspondent, his "Dear DDM." His letter was received by that friend, always meticulous about recording such things, on the afternoon of April 21, 1927. The letter was, however, dated "May 21st 1893." Such an amazing slip had never happened before, or ever did again, and cannot be explained by the usual reason, i.e. by an absentminded transposition of numbers. No, the 21st of May 1893 had some powerful significance, but apart from its possible connection with his decision to leave Sullivan and strike out on his own, it has not been identified. One is tempted to think that as he faced the imminent prospect of losing Olgivanna—who was, after all, his reason for this long and gallant fight—he felt as jittery and frightened as he had all those years before. It is also possible, at some level, that he wished he were back in 1893, when life seemed so full of promise and so much simpler.

The fact that a corporation of sponsors had been formed seemed to work its magic on the Bank of Wisconsin. Wright had taken the prudent step of engaging Philip F. La Follette, member of a prominent Wisconsin family, as his lawyer, and his astute advice came just in time. La Follette, who would serve two terms as governor of Wisconsin, persuaded the bank to give Wright time to work out a financial settlement and won an agreement in May 1927 for a year's grace. This was fortunate for more than one reason. Wright could now return to Taliesin. He would be given access to his studio, so that he could work off his debts. Miriam was enjoined from entering. It had been a frightful struggle, but Miriam was close to conceding defeat for, as La Follette told Wright early in June, her children were urging her to settle and threatening to withdraw their financial support if she did not.

Bargaining went on from day to day that July as they waited it out in Jane's cottage on the grounds of Taliesin. Miriam Wright made one final effort to punish Wright by proposing that she would agree to a divorce only if he did not marry again for five years and forever renounced Olga Milanoff, but her hopes were dashed. She accepted $6,000 in cash, a trust fund of $30,000 and $250 a month for life. Judge A. Hoppman granted the decree in Madison on August 26, 1927. Wright wrote to Woollcott, "In other words, all is bright again and while still smarting from recent humiliating gestures and attitudes—yes, and *acts*—here's hoping!"

Two months before the divorce, the feared deportation proceedings had been averted. Wright wrote to tell Martin that his lawyer's father, the distinguished former governor of Wisconsin, now a U.S. senator, had intervened with the State Department using the argument that Olga Milanoff's "illegal" husband was doing his best to become a legal one. Wright's decision to choose La Follette as his lawyer had been most astute; the immigration authorities agreed not to interfere. It was all a tremendous relief—Wright had even contemplated moving to Canada—but there was a catch. Until the decree became final in a year's time, Wright had pledged himself to lead a "moral" life and stood to lose everything if he gave Miriam reason to claim that he was defying the law. The voice of Philip La Follette is always the voice of reason in Wright's life, although the truth of what he had to say was sometimes more than his client could stomach. Wright was particularly incensed by La Follette's insistence that he and Olgivanna must not live together for a year. He absolutely refused to leave Taliesin again; no one was going to turn him out this time. He transferred his fury at the law to his lawyer, who was a more immediate target; as might be expected, however, La Follette was right and Wright was stubbornly and rashly wrong. All sentiment aside, he ought to have known how dangerous Miriam Wright was. According to his autobiography, at one point during divorce proceedings she "snatched a revolver from the district attorney's desk and telling the reporters to 'come on,' started for Taliesin." Whether or not this is true, there is no doubt that she was not about to let a divorce decree deter her.

Miriam Wright's next move was to send Wright a letter his lawyer gleefully claimed was so obscene it should not have been put through the mails. She had, in short, gone too far. She was arrested, charged with an offense and released on five hundred dollars bail. At last, Wright had a bargaining position, and he used it. When the trial was held a few days later he refused to testify against her. He had agreed not to press charges if Miriam would leave them alone. When she had failed to receive a sympathetic hearing, Miriam Wright had demanded an audience with the governor of Wisconsin, Fred R. Zimmerman, appealing to him to force the local authorities to act. Finding the governor in a Chicago hotel, where he was attending an advertising convention, Miriam Wright went in full pursuit. "I want to see you, Governor," she shouted across the lobby. He told his aides, "I don't want to see her—I won't see her," and beat an undignified exit through the hotel kitchen.

Another setback! But she was not finished yet. In the months that followed, Frank and Olgivanna had moved to Phoenix, Arizona, where he was acting as consulting architect for the construction of a new hotel. As he told Martin, "She—'the bad smell'—went to Phoenix first and by representing that she was still my wife, only separated—estranged as she put it, and having had no alimony paid since last December, being penniless, asked a warrant for my arrest, alleging I had installed another woman in luxury in her home. She got it."

Meanwhile they had moved on to La Jolla, California, where Wright immediately hired a Los Angeles attorney to protect him against his bloodhound, now in pursuit of a warrant for his arrest there on the charge that he and his lady were "lewd and dissolute persons." By chance the lawyer, James Farraher, arrived at the district attorney's office just before Mrs. Wright did, and the two met there. Farraher subsequently told his client that the lady jumped to the conclusion that he and the D.A. were conspiring against her and gave them some choice pieces of her mind. She then went on to describe all prosecuting officers and lawyers "crooks," which was a wonderful piece of luck for Mr. Wright. She then left in a huff, Farraher said. He added that, since Wright would marry the moment he legally could, he was confident that the authorities would not bring charges until they became moot.

As Miriam Wright told the story, she found out where they were living and made a phone call to the house. Having learned that the coast was clear, she took a taxi there and discovered that the back door was unlocked.

"I went in . . . and found my own belongings all over the place.

"I decided to get on the front page of the newspapers and see what effect publicity would have upon the situation. I thought the happy home belonged to Frank, so I wrecked the place inside, and as a wreck it was a perfect success."

She was tried and given a thirty-day suspended sentence.

In September 1928, a month after the marriage, Miriam Wright, who had moved to Hollywood, announced plans to begin screen tests for a movie career. She also intended to return to her sculpture and would study philosophy in Paris. There was a new plan in October: now, she said, she was going to have her face lifted. But there was more. She had just given birth to a baby girl; the child's father was an heir to a throne of Europe and would soon marry her. Since she was fifty-nine years old, that latest report seemed to have stretched credulity as far as it would go, and no more was heard of Miriam Wright in the news columns. She was, whatever she told the papers, living very quietly and writing her memoirs. She was in bad health; her death certificate would list several degenerative diseases. Her account was published in 1932, two years after her death.

It is difficult to reconcile the tone of her narrative, which is dignified and restrained, with the reality of her behavior during the three years she fought with Wright. The account is heavily edited, of course. That one would expect, but the story told sounds perfectly rational. The only safe conclusion is that Miriam remained consistent. She never really relinquished her inner image of her ideal mate. He was supposed to be the man she thought he was, and when she found out that this charismatic figure was, in reality, a flawed human being with all kinds of quirks and crotchets of his own, she could not deal with it. They were both, essentially, in the grip of a fantasy. Hers was that sheer willpower alone could bend life to her illusions; his, that whatever the reality of a situation, he could go on indefinitely defying the odds and getting away with it.

Philip La Follette played a heroic and largely thankless role in Wright's life at this time. It was his painful duty to remind his client of all the things he could not do, restraining his spending while also bringing him face to face with a most unpleasant list of debts, one that kept growing. Among the young lawyer's most inspired contributions was his brilliant strategy at that delicate moment in Wright's life, when one false move could have destroyed the whole edifice he was painstakingly restoring. After much thought La Follette decided that Wright's debts must be liquidated first. If his creditors believed Wright was living in Arizona and unlikely to return to Wisconsin, they would be more likely to see reason and settle for a small cash settlement than if they believed Wright had a number of wealthy backers and would soon return to Taliesin, all expenses paid. That meant months of patient negotiating on the lawyer's part, followed by agreements drawn up and duly signed that the creditors either take a third (in the case of actual goods purchased, most of them construction materials) in payment or, in the case of labor costs, to accept further ten-year notes at 5 percent interest. La Follette pursued a similar course with the Bank of Wisconsin, making promises designed to give that august institution some hope, but not too much. It was a clever strategy, the only one that could work. It was, of course, exactly the kind of cautious, deliberate approach Wright most hated. He sent periodic explosions of rage by way of epistles mailed from Arizona and California, asking how long he could be expected to live on a measly five hundred dollars a month while Taliesin stayed empty, in need of urgent repairs, etc., etc. La Follette was long-suffering but Darwin Martin and Professor Schevill, who were in close consultation with Wright, had less patience. Professor Schevill began by making a joke of Wright's indignation and the heroic effort he was making to be guided by La Follette. As to the future, they needed money urgently and were looking everywhere for backers, but finding them would not be easy. Something about the mere mention of Wright's name put people instinctively on their guard. Never mind. They were all hard at work so as to put their architect back in his house and restore his career.

The debts were staggering but, by October 1928, La Follette had reduced $30,000 in general claims to a cash settlement of $10,000 and continued credit on the remaining labor bills of $11,000. La Follette had also watched and waited while the Bank of Wisconsin put Taliesin up for sale. On July 30, 1928, the *Chicago Tribune* reported, "For sale: One romantic, rambling, famous picturesque home on a hill with 190 acres of farm and park, known as a 'love nest,' murder scene, fire scene, raid scene and showplace." The sale took place and, since there were no other bidders, the bank bought the property itself for $25,000. For the next two months La Follette was negotiating to buy Taliesin back. The bank had added on all kinds of extra charges, and the bill was now close to $60,000, but La Follette whittled that down to $40,000 and arranged for a new mortgage of $25,000 plus a cash settlement of $15,000, provided by Martin and a newcomer to the group, a businessman named Ben Page. The corporation was reorganized under the new name of Wright, Inc., and Taliesin was reclaimed at last. Not quite two months after Olga Ivanovna Lazovich of Montenegro married Frank Lloyd Wright of Taliesin at Rancho Santa Fe, in San Diego (Martin did not know how Wright had managed to obtain permission for the California ceremony and hoped he had not "strong-armed" it), they were home at last. WRIGHT, OLGA, CHILDREN BACK TO 'LOVE NEST,' the *Capital Times* of Madison reported in mid-October. Kenneth F. Schmitt, staff reporter, wrote, "The patter of little children, the antics of a big Newfoundland dog, and the marital bliss of a happy pair of lovers has replaced the troublesome atmosphere at Taliesin—for Frank Lloyd Wright is back home."

The great man himself appeared to greet the journalist. He looked very much better than he had the year before. His eyes were brighter, and although his hair was now silvery gray, he had all the enthusiasm of a man half his age. "Sauntering about the estate in his usual informal dress, Wright seemed very happy to be back, after a stay of nearly a year in the west. He wore a leather jacket over his colored shirt and the usual flowing scarf was knotted around a high stiff collar. His glasses hung from a ribbon around his neck."

Wright was vague about just how this return to Taliesin had been accomplished. He certainly did not mention that, one way or another, it had taken almost $100,000 to clear his debts, or that everything he had was now owned by Wright, Inc., or that his financial transactions were being reported to La Follette and a certain Ben Page of Chicago. Page was disapproving; there were much better uses for that money, right then, than buying a new car, he wrote. He would have been equally disapproving had he seen the letter Wright had received from the N. Porter Saddle & Harness Co. (Silver Inlaid Bits and Spurs; Hand-made Harness a Specialty) of Phoenix, Arizona. The company was writing to thank him for the saddles, bridles and blankets ordered while Mr. Wright was in Phoenix. "We have made you four mighty fine saddles and we feel certain that they will please you," the representative wrote. The writer was sorry there had been a slight misunderstanding about the price of Mr. Wright's new coat. As for his jacket and vest, the lady who was now making these was designing some hats and caps which they respectfully hoped would be to his liking. In the interim the writer wanted to thank Mr. Wright for this very nice piece of business.

14

Work Song

The funeral
Pyre sprouts a rounded apple
Out of a bed of ashes. . . .
"The Phoenix"
Poems from the Old English

When E. L. Meyer, a columnist for the *Madison Capital Times*, and a colleague took a canoe trip down the Wisconsin and Mississippi rivers in the summer of 1928, they stopped to see what the passage of time had done to The Valley. They went first to Shot Tower Hill, where, in Civil War days, a whole town had grown up to manufacture cannonballs and whence barges weighed down with their cargo made their way south. The shifting sands on the river bottom had effaced the channel, but the shot tower itself, a tunnel impressively constructed through two hundred feet of solid rock, was still intact, if beginning to decay. "Already the frosts and thaws are eating at its base. And here, in this vault, once vibrant with industry and the shouts of toiling men, there is no sound save the thin piping of a frog in a puddle. . . . So perished the war makers, with a croak for an epitaph."

Above the river, on the crest of Tower Hill, they found the forlorn relics of more recent undertakings, the encampment of cottages built by Jenkin Lloyd Jones, now deserted. That indomitable old preacher had built one for himself, which he named Westhope, and it, like the others, stood with its windows broken, its floors littered with old books and its walls fast disappearing behind vines and weeds. Moving on to Hillside, they found that the years had not dealt any more kindly with that building to which, long ago, young ladies came to be trained in deportment and recited poetry under the pines. "There, too, the wreckers have visited. The grand piano has been crashed in. When you pluck one of the twisted wires the room throbs to a mocking note until silence again settles over the debris like water over a deserted pond." As for Taliesin, that, too, had suffered. Its beautiful treasures were gone, its owner, the "romantic architect," was in exile and the "dust, the mice and the moss are claiming empire over their invaded dominions."

Meyer returned to Taliesin four years later to record an extraordinary transformation. "The fragrance of fresh-hewn wood is in the wind, the smell of plaster, and the pungency of stone-dust under the chisel. Here is the uncompleted and vast drafting room. . . . Here the dormitories. Here the public playhouse, newly built, and there the sculptors' studio, the painters' studio, the study hall. . . . Tradition, fealty to Welsh ancestors have, too, their place in the cloister. 'Gosod by Galon Ar Addysg,' reads the motto on the great stone fireplace in the playhouse, meaning, 'The Soul Without Knowledge Is Not Good.' "

A lesser man would have been defeated by the vandalism and neglect or, perhaps, fled superstitiously from "the dust of old tragedy that has settled" on the crests of the hills, as Meyer wrote four years before. But Wright's spirit was indomitable. Now that kind friends had restored Taliesin to him it might be, as he described himself to Mumford, "battered up," but it was still in the ring. The situation he found, however, was worse than Meyer had described. The main problem, he explained to Martin, was that a great deal of new construction had been left half-finished as a result of his forced departure the year before. For example, he had almost finished an upper terrace with rooms below it before he left. It lacked only a coat of concrete that would have cost twenty-five dollars, but the bank refused to spend the money. As a result the rooms below were continually water-soaked during his absence. The furnishings they contained—rugs and furniture—had been left outside, at the mercy of the weather, and were ruined. In fact, all of the carpets and upholstery were soiled because the bank had had so many parties there, or so he claimed. The telephone system had been destroyed, and the electric wiring throughout the house was in urgent need of an overhaul.

All kinds of household linens were gone: sheets, pillowcases, bed-

covers, towels and ten pairs of blankets. Almost every tool and all of
his office equipment were gone from the property, including a valuable
collection of colored pencils that he had begun in Germany in 1910
and had taken to Tokyo. A set of dishes from the Imperial Hotel that
he had designed had been stolen, with the exception of three pieces,
"and I don't understand why they were left. They look very nice to
me," he added dryly. As for his pictures, these had been pulled off
the walls, leaving the thumbtacks still in place. It was all very
disheartening.

His first priority was to stop the leaks, patch the broken plaster,
restore the water system, fix the broken doors and get the long driveway, impassable in wet weather, back in operation. They were up
every morning at 6:00 and fell into bed every night at 9:30. But they
were home at last. More than that he would not ask of life, because
"pioneers—that is what we are—take pioneers' fare and no dessert,"
he had once told his son Lloyd. It was worth everything to be able
to stand, barefoot, in the hill garden of Taliesin and see, below him,
the clump of fir trees surrounding the chapel where his grandparents,
his mother, his aunts, his uncles and his cousins were now buried;
survey the same hills where he once went looking for cows and beyond
them, the far fields where he had lain in a kind of trance while Uncle
James called, "Come back, Frank, come back!"

He wrote, "Moments of anguish? Oh yes—but not of regret. I am
enjoying more, day by day, the eternity that is now, realizing, at last,
that it *is* now. . . ." And, as always when he had emerged victorious
after tremendous effort, Wright was at his most affectionate, elegiac
and contrite.

"You see hope and courage are still 'as was,' " he wrote to Woollcott
in January 1929, "notwithstanding the failure of our illegitimate
intrigues. As a financial promoter, it is to laugh at me. I like myself
less in that role than in any other I have tried to 'play.' When I think
of trying to get you . . . to let me carry some thousands of . . . hard-
earned dollars in my basket, something very like chagrin makes me
moist and uncomfortable under my back hair.

"You know, Alex, I didn't realize then that $7,500.00 was a 'lot
of money.' I know now.

"It seemed so natural and reasonable to me that . . . there would
be no trouble getting all I needed and more. . . . Can you believe it?"

Wright thought that the biggest lesson he had learned during the past four years was the value of friendship. "I got naturally into a hell of a fix—where I needed my friends and I hadn't really myself earned the right to make any demands. . . . I had never really invested anything deep-heartedly or seriously in 'friendship' either." The fact that Woollcott still had an affectionate regard for him was "beyond anything I deserve."

As for their first Christmas at home, they had hardly been back in Taliesin for two months when Svetlana came down with the flu. Then Iovanna got sick. Olgivanna was next, and finally himself. It laid him low for a month. Now he and Olgivanna were recuperating, sitting up in bed reading Woollcott's book, *Two Gentlemen and a Lady.* "And if the laughter provoked in our little family, [*sic*] follows your book through the country, the ripple will be felt in the back-wash at New York City." He was aging, of course; about to be sixty, he said, perpetuating the myth. And, if he really had reached the age of wisdom, he kept forgetting to act that way. Isabelle Doyle, a native of Spring Green, started working evenings at Taliesin as a secretary at about that time. She had a full-time job at the State Bank of Spring Green, and recalled seeing Mr. Wright come sailing into the bank wearing his smartest outfit, topped by one of the big Stetson hats he favored, and swinging his cane. That particular day the bank manager looked him up and down, and said, "You certainly look comfortable." Wright replied, "You could do this if you weren't so straitlaced." It was then she realized that he was not wearing any shoes.

In those months when it became clear that Hillside Home School had failed and Aunt Nell, almost mad with worry, would moan aloud as she paced up and down, he had made a vow. He had promised the Aunts and he had promised his mother, somehow ". . . to see their educational work go on at beloved Hillside on the site of the pioneer homestead," he wrote. "That filial promise would go along with me wherever I went. If I settled down, it settled down with me." Almost as soon as he had walked through the doors of Taliesin, he was reviving the idea of Hillside. It was completely illogical to think of launching such an ambitious undertaking, but barely a month after his return he was describing to Professor Schevill his idea for a new school, one that he had been refining for some time past. (It would eventually be published as a booklet, *The Hillside Home School of the Allied Arts*, in 1931.) Wright's concept took as its starting point the idea of a coeducational boarding school dedicated to progressive ideas where students would also work on a farm. When he came into architecture as a young man, the debate over the relationship between the artist, artisan and the machine had been in full swing. He had declared then that the machine should be put to the service of art; thirty years later he still believed it. He proposed that a consortium of seven manufacturers—in glassmaking, pottery, textiles, the forge, casting in all materials, woodworking and sheet-metal working—come together to buy the land and buildings, hire him as architect to build anew and then run the school. This consortium would finance the venture until its artist-teachers and students had produced a sufficient body of work to be sold for mass production. He wrote, ". . . the nature of our livelihood, commercial industry . . . must be put into experimental stations where its many operations may come into the hands of sensitive, unspoiled students inspired by such creative artists as we can obtain to help them." The machines would be the tools of their study, and the new school would serve machinery "in order that machinery itself, in the future might honestly serve what is growing to be a beauty-loving and appreciative country now borrowing or faking its effects because it . . . has none other."

It sounded hopelessly ambitious, but his idea was firmly grounded in the Arts and Crafts concept of workshops, which had flourished in the 1890s: Elbert Hubbard's colony of Roycrofters and also Ashbee's Guild of Handicrafts in the Cotswolds, both of them based on earlier experiments of William Morris. Hubbard's colony in East Aurora, New York, would have been on Wright's mind because he and Olgivanna had stayed there with the Heaths not long before. He would have been reminded that it was run as a school, a farm and a series of workshops. Hubbard had begun with a print shop, which led to a bindery, then to leather and copper crafts and cabinetmaking. His machine-made souvenirs, for sale in his hotel, were also obtainable through a mail-order catalogue. But there were more recent examples with which Wright would have been conversant. Walter Gropius's academy and school, the Bauhaus, which moved to Dessau in the late 1920s, was training its students in the use of machinery and new materials for household objects. Closer to home, the Cranbrook Academy, founded by George Booth, millionaire publisher, in Bloomfield Hills, Michigan, was conceived as a school, atelier and art colony with the same Arts and Crafts goal of producing tasteful designs to replace the shoddy objects in American homes. His Finnish architect, Eliel

Saarinen, with whom he joined forces in 1924, shared his goal of establishing an institution in which "all the related arts, sculpture and handicraft included, should be gathered together." In fact, Cranbrook would become famous in the 1950s for elegant, mass-produced objects based upon its original designs, the work of its artist-teachers, Saarinen and Charles Eames among them, and its metalwork, bookbinding, letterpress printing, carpentry shops, ceramic studios, textile workshops and so on. How soon Saarinen and Wright met is not known, but it is more than likely that Wright knew of the Cranbrook experiment when he planned his own, and Saarinen certainly knew about Hillside. His Kingswood School for Girls, built on the Cranbrook campus from 1929 to 1931, is generally acknowledged to have been inspired by the Prairie Style buildings Wright had built in Oak Park a quarter of a century before, and is also reminiscent of the design Wright made for Hillside in 1903.

Saarinen had found a millionaire philanthropist for his "experimental station." Whether Wright was likely to find manufacturers prepared to build and support a project along the same lines with uncertain financial returns seemed unlikely. He, however, had no doubts and thought he had already found his first sponsor, a Dutch glass manufacturer. He also wanted a connection with the University of Wisconsin and naïvely believed that this institution would be prepared to match the investment dollar for dollar. Professor Schevill quickly disabused him of this notion; on the contrary, the university would expect a handsome endowment if it took part, he explained to Wright. Nevertheless, he did not want to take the edge off Wright's enthusiasm. He thought it a splendid idea and urged him to take it further. While exhorting Schevill to "put his shoulder to the wheel," Wright was also soliciting the advice and help of Jens Jensen, a distinguished landscape architect, and was even trying to interest Darwin Martin. The latter replied that, much as he admired Wright's plan, he would have to be left out of it as it was "beyond our scope." He also wondered whether Wright ought to be devoting time and attention to this. Ever the pragmatist, Martin recommended that his efforts might be better employed with the work already at hand.

As 1929 began, those prospects looked handsome, perhaps the best for several years. Wright was being commissioned by the Rosenwald Foundation to design one of the schoolhouses that this philanthropic organization was building for black children in La Jolla, and had signed a life contract with the Leerdam Glass-fabriek of Holland to design on a royalty basis. There was a commission for a 23-story copper-and-glass apartment tower in New York, called the St. Mark's-in-the-Bouwerie project, and Wright was using his design for the National Life building as the prototype for this new design. Wright's cousin Richard, Jenkin's son, was now a prosperous newspaper publisher in Tulsa, Oklahoma, and wanted him to build a $75,000 house. He also told Lewis Mumford in January 1929 that he had been working on a luxury hotel in the "Simon-pure Arizona desert" that would be built using his textile block construction method. There was yet another prospect in Arizona, this one for an even more lavish hotel, that would absorb months of his time.

The textile block hotel, the Arizona Biltmore in Phoenix, was a project that appeared in February 1928, just as his prospects looked bleakest. He had been approached by Albert Chase McArthur (no relation to the Alfred MacArthur family), a former apprentice from Oak Park days, now established as an architect. McArthur's two brothers, Charles and Warren, owners of a successful car dealership, had bought several hundred acres of land eight miles northeast of Phoenix some years before, and had persuaded a hotel chain to build a winter resort and bungalow group on the site. The ambitious undertaking would be designed by McArthur, and the original cost was to be one million dollars. The architect decided that he wanted to use the textile block system Wright and his son Lloyd had successfully developed in California. Wright had designed four houses with this method, and since Lloyd had supervised their construction and built eleven block houses of his own, he had had even more practical experience. As a method it was handsome and cheap; Lloyd estimated that Mexican labor, on a piecework basis, could make each block for an average of fifty-six cents. Perhaps McArthur assumed that the Wrights had taken out a patent on the system. Perhaps he received such assurances from Wright. The latter is likely, since McArthur had assured the hotel corporation that the construction method he had contracted to use had been patented. McArthur contacted Wright, who was very happy to be hired for a thousand dollars a month for seven months, with a further seven thousand dollars due when the hotel opened.

The building project in what was then the Arizona desert was unbelievably difficult and expensive, even in those days of cheap labor. The development needed its own water system, and the first underground electrical system in Arizona went to the Biltmore. A master plan to develop the site with a nursery, fruit orchards, a mile-long

The Arizona Biltmore Hotel as it looked in the early 1930s

Detail of the block design during construction of the Arizona Biltmore

An early view of the main lobby

An early view of the men's smoking room

canal and an adjoining housing estate was also prepared. Then a large temporary tent community took over the site. An actual textile block factory worked around the clock to produce the 250,000 blocks required. It was soon clear that the original cost estimates were inadequate; new backers were brought in to provide an additional million dollars. When the doors opened for the first time in February 1929, much comment was made about the hotel's luxurious and costly fittings—gold leaf ceilings, a roof made entirely of copper, uniquely designed furniture, murals, wrought-iron fixtures—and its air of refined opulence. But it was already in financial difficulties. Its principal backers had had the bad luck to invest in the year of the great stock market crash. The McArthur brothers could not meet their financial obligations and were forced to sell out for a pittance to the one backer not affected by the crash, the chewing-gum magnate William Wrigley, Jr. He was able to buy out other stockholders advantageously and continued to develop the property when the hotel reopened in November 1929. It survived the Great Depression and went on to become one of the nation's most famous hotels.

To this day, it is stated in brochures published by the Arizona Biltmore that its architect was Albert Chase McArthur, and a statement made by Wright in 1930 is reprinted; in it, Wright disclaims authorship. Wright, McArthur maintained, licensed him to make use of the textile block method, acted as advisor during construction, criticized the plans and details, made sketches of the decorative designs and was paid for those services. That was all. However, the low horizontal lines of the building, its complex silhouette, its Art Deco formalism and, in particular, its handling of interior space and idiosyncratic details bear the stamp of Wright's personality. For years it has been generally thought that Wright was the designer and that McArthur's role was confined to the working drawings. This theory is supported by references in Wright's letters to the fact that he was working on drawings, to the fact that McArthur commissioned him to make a set of presentation drawings, and to the fact that he spent so much time in Phoenix before construction began. If McArthur did design the building, he leaned very heavily on Wright's ideas and got them for a bargain price: a fraction of the fee Wright would have been paid had he been the official architect with his usual 10 percent commission. There is even clearer evidence that Wright considered himself its author. When McArthur died in 1951, his widow wrote to ask Wright to write an article praising McArthur's achievement in this building, which, it seemed evident, had been his major accomplishment. Wright replied by saying that he regretted he had needed the money so much that he had allowed McArthur to call the hotel his own. He wrote, "The whole office knew how the building came to be as it is and probably talked although the building talked enough. Nevertheless I have always given Albert's name as architect . . . and always will. But I know better and so should you."

The intriguing question is why Wright should voluntarily renounce this major accomplishment, his first hotel in the United States, at a time when he needed all the acclaim he could get. The correspondence of the period suggests that the answer is to be found in the textile block construction agreement. Early in 1930, McArthur received a letter from a Los Angeles law firm on behalf of another inventor of concrete blocks, William E. Nelson, holder of two U.S. patents, claiming that Wright's system violated his own. Shortly afterward Wright received a letter from a Phoenix law firm questioning him closely on his patent. Wright conceded fairly readily that, for technical reasons, he had never quite managed to patent the method he had licensed McArthur to use. At the same time McArthur was writing to Wright to say that rumors were flying around Phoenix that Wright had actually designed the Biltmore. McArthur was ambitious to get other hotel commissions, and these pernicious rumors were destroying his chances. Exactly what agreement was hammered out between Wright and McArthur is not described in their correspondence. However, it seems clear that it was not to Wright's advantage to be seen as the "real" architect at a time when all kinds of lawsuits and countersuits seemed imminent and he had no real defense. By then, no doubt, he had had enough of lawsuits. At any rate, letters from lawyers to Wright soon ceased, and a "To Whom It May Concern" statement by Wright soon appeared, giving credit for the Arizona Biltmore to Albert Chase McArthur.

Wright was also working on San Marcos-in-the-Desert, another luxury resort hotel project near Chandler, Arizona, that would also have used his textile block system. The timing was such that, had it been built, he would almost certainly have faced the same patent-infringement charges there and with more serious consequences. Nevertheless it was unfortunate that this magnificent project was never built, because it provides an immediate refutation of the argument that, during the late 1920s, Wright's creativity was at a low ebb. Not only did the sizable project for a hotel complex give, according to Hitchcock, a convincing demonstration of the large-scale possibilities of the textile block system, but Wright's concept provided, "perhaps for the first time in history, an adequate expression specifically suited to a desert environment."

As he could see, Wright told Lloyd, the whole idea was based on the triangle. "The slope of the talus is a triangle, the spurs of rock come down into it as triangles, the mountains themselves rising behind, —triangles. The cross sections of the Sajuaro (cactus) and all other desert plants, —triangles." He had already designed the simple geometric relief he wanted for his blocks, a modified zigzag that gave a fluted effect. From a distance it looked like a dotted line, the line Wright thought typical of the desert. Wright continued, "These dotted-horizontals drip into the walls with a mixture of straight and dotted lines . . . as a glaze is poured over a vase from above, — running where and how it will." The comment is an indication of the pains he took to get a particular effect. His surviving drawings show a building so spread out, its wings of private suites improbably attenuated, that it looks like a hill town. That he had a vivid internal picture of it in his mind is, however, clear: "Deep loggia spaces with planted terraces and wall enclosed gardens should be features," he continued. The floor-to-ceiling windows should be treated with long, heavy curtains in a uniform color. "The color of the building will be that of . . . the desert. . . . The drawing should show the character of the site with desert growth and the rock masses as they are, —the building horizontally drifted between the rock ledges that terminate it, —belonging to all—naturally." All these fascinating experiments of working on a vastly reduced scale would prove their worth ten years later when he came to design his first Usonian houses. In short, Wright was challenged and excited by the possibilities, and thought he had found in the scheme's promoter, A. J. Chandler, a former veterinarian turned hotelier and entrepreneur, the right man to bring the project to completion. The opportunity came at a pivotal moment, just as he most needed to prove to his corporation that his future prospects were bright. He wired to Martin, IDEAL COMMISSION SETTLED WILL BUILD AND FURNISH SAN MARCOS IN THE DESERT A PERFECTLY APPOINTED HALF MILLION DOLLAR HOTEL, in the spring of 1928, just a month before the Bank of Wisconsin put Taliesin up for sale. His choice of verbs, *build* and *furnish*, was pardonably optimistic but premature. At that moment, all he had was a commission to make the designs, prepare the working drawings and give an informed estimate of costs.

Since he needed to see a full-fledged opportunity in what was, essentially, only an overture, he was in the unusual position, for him, of being at the mercy of his client. When Chandler, who lived in the town named for him, sent Wright an urgent wire in January 1929 to return to Arizona—ostensibly to advise some newcomers who had bought part of the land and wanted to build on it—Wright took the summons as a command to begin work. He assembled an office staff with dispatch and by mid-January was ready to drive to Arizona with his band of fifteen. Once they arrived in Chandler there was nowhere to stay. Olgivanna Wright told Mrs. Darwin Martin that they spent a few days in a hotel, but could not continue to spend so much money so they decided to build a temporary camp on Chandler's land. The draftsmen were pressed into service as builders and carpenters, and, in less than two weeks, the little band had constructed a sizable camp complete with living room, guesthouse, dining room, draftsmen's offices, kitchen, court, garage and even an electrical plant, using battened lower walls and wood-frame roofs covered with canvas—a glorified tent city. Photographs of Ocatillo, as the camp came to be called, show low divans and floors covered with Navajo rugs, artistically draped greenery, a (rented) grand piano and a telephone.

By February 1, the studio roof had been canvased over, and work on the hotel drawings could start. Back in Madison, Philip La Follette was infuriated. Just three months after Wright's return to Taliesin (and after endless loud complaints about being denied the right to live in his own house), after all that money and energy expended, Wright had gone off on some harebrained scheme to make drawings in the middle of the Arizona desert. But La Follette's principal concern was what the cost of transporting, housing and feeding fifteen people for this kind of expedition implied. It was clear to him that Wright must have received a sizable check from Chandler if he were now building a camp for himself. This really rankled because, a week before Wright left, La Follette had warned him that the Wright, Inc. account was down to its last two thousand dollars, and current bills, plus Wright's monthly salary of five hundred dollars, would wipe it out. He made a point of stating that Wright had himself turned in bills for payment just that month. La Follette had put his finger on the issue and the reason why the Wright, Inc. arrangement would never work. Wright took the view that whatever money he earned was his, while the responsibility for meeting his monthly expenses belonged to his backers, indefinitely, or so it seemed. La Follette knew that he had to make an issue of this. As soon as he learned that Wright had decamped, he wrote again, insisting that Wright's earnings be placed in the corporation's account. He took steps to ensure that by contacting Chandler directly.

Wright's reply, when it came, went on for five pages. After going over old ground and attacking La Follette's actions in his turn, he demanded that he be given the right to make whatever expenditures he saw fit. He intended, he said in a lordly way, to send La Follette money to cover the obligations due in April; meantime, he would have to go on expending thousands each month in pursuit of the fee he expected to get, $60,000. (This would come when and if construction began, a detail he omitted.) In short, instead of having La Follette, as chief officer of the corporation, control income and expenditures, Wright wanted this function returned to him. It was an impasse, and La Follette turned for support to Schevill and Martin. The latter obliged with a letter that began by lecturing Wright and reminding him of his contractual obligations, but that ended with an unsuccessful attempt at conciliation. If they would revise the terms of his contract Wright was prepared, he told La Follette in May, to give up Taliesin, the cause of all his problems ("loving it too much and trying to hang on to it at this price. . . ."). La Follette jumped on the idea. If he was really serious they could start selling the property immediately, he wrote. Wright hastily withdrew the offer, and, after more months of negotiation, he had won the right to amend his contract. La Follette conceded defeat. Some time after that, exactly as he had foreseen, Wright, Inc. was bankrupt and its shareholders had lost every penny. But reading between the lines, it is evident that Darwin Martin well knew (however convincingly he maintained the fiction that his frequent checks were simply loans) that he would never see his money again. Had he switched tactics and turned his loans into outright gifts, he might have aroused Wright's conscience and ensured that the money would be repaid. He was, however, by long habit and emotional predisposition fated to play out his role, and Wright was bound to cling to such an advantageous relationship. But perhaps Martin, with his indulgent view of the license due a great artist, had the larger vision. Something about the desert setting was acting on the master like an elixir. He was responding to its challenge with unusual zest and a heightened creativity. That camp of Ocatillo, such a seeming waste of time and money (and destined to be vandalized the moment his back was turned), had given him the germ of a new idea. It would be brought to a triumphant fulfillment a few years later when he built his masterpiece, Taliesin West.

They were working at Ocatillo for five months. Back at Taliesin,

Wright told Chandler, "Of course I am still staggering financially under the costs of plan-making in the Desert, my 'corporation' none too sympathetic with that expenditure of time and money," but his faith in the project was strong and he hoped building could begin that autumn. Chandler kept up a barrage of phone calls and telegrams, asking for more sketches and new estimates. Wright's hopes soared. Even in late October he believed Chandler was on the verge of putting together the $500,000 Wright estimated (although he told Martin privately he expected the cost to be closer to $750,000). This hopeful news was conveyed to Lloyd on the day of the stock market crash, October 29, 1929. Weeks later, he and Chandler continued to tell each other that the crash had been a good thing because it would release investment capital that had been diverted to speculations on the stock market. Wright went on assuring everyone that Chandler was just about to come up with the money, and Chandler, indefatigably optimistic, pursued his goal for the next eight years writing, as late as 1937, that the clouds were lifting. By then he sounded marginally less hopeful.

Wright, too, kept up a good front, but by the spring of 1930 he could no longer appease his creditors with incantations to Western deities. He wrote to Chandler in April, "The set-back of San Marcos financing has put a serious crimp in the financial situation here—a somewhat staggering blow. . . ." Not surprisingly, all work had also stopped on the St. Mark's-in-the-Bouwerie project, and the bank was about to foreclose, again. Martin told La Follette that this could be explained because, as a friend said of him, "All Wright's plans go 'flooey or phlooey.' . . ." Meanwhile Wright was sending out appeals for more subscriptions to anyone he could think of, including the millionaire Harold McCormick, heir to a great farm-machinery fortune, and went on spending money like the trooper he was. Vladimir Karfik, a young Czech architect who worked for him at that time, recalled, "Wright didn't seem to have any troubles with money. We were having breakfast, lunch and dinner together with Mr. and Mrs. Wright every day and listened to his wonderful stories. . . . Wright didn't pay us regularly but he dressed [our group] nicely, we got our meals and had one of his cars for our use. . . ." He chiefly remembered accompanying the Wrights to the Czechoslovak Art Shop in Chicago to look at some Yugoslavian clothes. "He picked the dresses in his usual . . . arrogant manner with his stick," asked his wife if she liked them, and bought a dozen.

Miriam Noel, whom he fervently hoped had dropped out of his life after his marriage to Olgivanna, continued to make her baleful presence felt. As late as November 1929 she brought a new suit against him claiming unpaid alimony of seven thousand dollars. Wright refused to pay much attention to her Milwaukee lawyer's letter. He had learned that she was in the hospital and had only a few weeks to live. In fact, she had been operated on that month and seemed to be recovering when she had a relapse. She went into a coma and died at noon five days later, on Friday, January 3, 1930. Cause of death, according to the death certificate, was "exhaustion following delirium due to pelvic cellulitis, and chronic salpingitis with septic spleen and hypostatic pneumonia." She was not yet sixty-one. She was buried the next day in the Forest Home cemetery, Milwaukee, and her former husband did not attend the funeral. By the time her will was probated and the major claims against her estate had been made, the net value of it was about four dollars. It was pathetic and sad, but Miriam Noel's death did have the effect of releasing what was left of the trust fund Wright had set up at the time of their divorce to pay her monthly alimony. The balance was now due to revert to him. Seeing his opportunity, Philip La Follette, whose bill Wright had indignantly refused to pay, presented it for settlement against the fund and was successful. Another creditor, the Wisconsin Foundry and Machine Company, saw its chance and jumped in with a bill for nine hundred dollars. Nevertheless, the balance due was over five thousand dollars and very welcome that February of 1930.

Once Philip La Follette withdrew, the complex and thankless task of riding herd on Wright's finances was taken over by the corporation's treasurer, Benjamin Eldridge Page. Page was a Chicago businessman who still kept an office there although, having made his fortune, he had retired from active life five years before. He was comfortably off but not wealthy, a friend of Schevill's with, the professor thought, a talent for accounting. He was a widower with one son studying for his master's degree in philosophy at the University of Chicago, played a fast game of tennis and was proud owner of Speedwell Farm in the corn belt of Illinois, a historic property that had been owned by one family for a century and that he had recently bought. Wright found him agreeable enough. Page seemed more amenable to Wright's ingenious arguments (usually revolving around the wisdom of spending

money now so as to save it later), and the two had a lively exchange
of letters; Page was a welcome visitor at Taliesin whenever Wright
was there. Another person on the fringes of Wright's life at that period
was his first wife, Catherine. What had happened between them was
ancient history, as far as Wright was concerned, and now that he had
his freedom from her (and perhaps in light of his experiences with
Miriam Noel), he was much more kindly disposed. He had commented
in 1926–27, at the height of his troubles with Miriam, that he and
Catherine would be friends if the world would let them, and even
argued shamelessly that she was his prior responsibility when Miriam
was in the middle of making her biggest financial demands. Catherine
Wright's attitude is harder to gauge since she was much more cautious
about revealing her feelings on paper, but she seemed genuinely concerned about him, or so she said. After Wright left her, and once the
children began to need her less, she became increasingly involved in
social work at Hull House. She moved to Greenville, South Carolina,
in the early 1920s, where she worked for the Red Cross and the Juvenile
Protective Association, then returned to Chicago (in 1924) to continue
her social work there, with frequent trips to North Carolina and
Knoxville, Tennessee. By 1929 the only child still living at home was
her youngest, Robert Llewellyn. He had graduated from college a few
years before and was working for a large law firm while studying for
the bar. In the summer of 1930 he was due to take his state bar
examinations and planned to move into an apartment of his own. Her
lease would be up in the autumn of 1930.

Catherine Wright was now fifty-nine. She had gained weight and
seemed "bosomly and motherly" to her nieces, but she was still handsome and as much a talker as ever. She met Ben Page at some point
during the year 1929–30, and a romance developed. It is just possible
that Wright learned of this by chance. While in Chicago he dropped
in unexpectedly on Page, who was staying with friends overnight,
and found him "playing around with a friend of his," he told Schevill.
That friend is not named, but if it was Catherine Wright one imagines
that both she and Page might have enjoyed the effect of the revelation
on Wright. Robert Llewellyn believed his mother's problem was her
refusal to accept the reality of her situation and her delusory hope that
his father would one day return. That hope must have vanished once
they were divorced, but they kept abreast of each other's lives through
their children, and if Catherine Wright harbored some lingering
resentments—and money, or the lack of it, carries a heavy symbolic
freight—the appearance of Ben Page in her life, with his hand on

Wright's purse strings, would have presented an intriguing turn of events, a chance to savor a kind of advantage over Wright. There might even have seemed something retributive about it. If this were true, the triumph was destined to be short-lived. Like so many others, Page became a victim of the stock market crash and some poor investments. He soon lost his attraction for Wright, who did not want an insolvent businessman for a treasurer. (It looked bad.) After a year or so, Wright successfully maneuvered to have Page dropped from the inner circle, and Catherine found their tastes incompatible. Saying she did not enjoy her isolated life on a farm, she moved back to Chicago. (The Pages were divorced in 1937.)

All this was to come. In the summer of 1930, Catherine Wright was facing the prospect of a lonely old age and knew she would soon have to renew the lease on her apartment or move. It is clear from a letter she wrote to the Ashbees that the strain of holding down a full-time job and running an apartment as well made the idea of marriage that much more attractive. They married in mid-June. "Why didn't you say who Page married? I received the announcement," Martin asked Wright a month later. The event took Wright by surprise, and he was most annoyed to find that Page had deducted a full month's alimony for June from his account—for a man who seemed to have no head for figures, Wright kept a surprisingly careful track of certain items, at least. He sent them a congratulatory telegram. "Thanks for your wire," Page wrote in a postscript. "We are both very happy."

The day of the stock market crash Wright was also writing to his lawyer in Washington in pursuit of a goal that had persistently eluded him, that of removing the threat to the immigrant status of Olgivanna and Svetlana. After believing that the deportation proceedings had been quashed, he was unpleasantly surprised to find that the whole issue had been renewed, the result of Miriam Noel's ceaseless complaints. The government now felt impelled to hold a pro forma hearing. It took place on Ellis Island in the summer of 1928, and although no decision was made—to give him time to become legally married—the specter would not be lifted until Olgivanna Wright had been properly admitted to the United States. This meant that she would have to go to Mexico and apply for re-entry as a non-quota immigrant. It was all just a formality but an expensive and time-consuming one. They made the trip early in January 1930, and their efforts were rewarded at last when, two months later, they finally received word that all proceedings had been dropped.

Among the very few building projects of Wright's that would not

Richard Lloyd Jones in 1916, as editor and publisher of the Wisconsin
State Journal

Westhope, the Tulsa, Oklahoma, home of
Richard Lloyd Jones
Detail, showing the design of the window openings for Westhope

fall victim to the stock market crash was Darwin Martin's summer house, Graycliff, on Lake Erie, and the house in Tulsa, Oklahoma, for his cousin Richard Lloyd Jones, founder and publisher of the *Tulsa Tribune*. Wright and Richard, who was six years his junior, had known each other since childhood. Like Frank, Richard was the only son of an adoring mother. He studied first for the law at the University of Wisconsin and at Chicago Law School, taking a master's degree, and then went into journalism. There he rose rapidly, first as editor of the *Stamford* (Connecticut) *Telegram*, editorial writer for the *Washington Times*, editor of *Cosmopolitan* magazine, editor of *Collier's*, editor and part owner of the *Wisconsin State Journal* in Madison and, after 1919, editor and publisher of the *Tulsa Tribune*. He married Georgia Hayden (always called George) when he was thirty-four, and they had three children, Richard, Jenkin and Florence. Richard was articulate, feisty, and a natural writer. Like his cousin Frank, he had an unusual ability to express himself on paper and was willing to spin out his thoughts endlessly to ensure that his reader knew exactly what he meant. This made him an eager correspondent and sometimes a formidable one. His letters as his house was being built provide an unvarnished account of the hopes, fears, disappointments, frustrations and satisfactions of a Wright client.

Richard Lloyd Jones shared his father's veneration for Lincoln and went to Hodgenville, Kentucky, in 1905 to buy Lincoln's boyhood home when it was sold at public auction. He then launched a successful subscription drive (the contribution was twenty-five cents) to raise money for a granite memorial on the site and collected the amazing sum of $400,000. President Theodore Roosevelt laid the cornerstone. Richard was also a great collector of authentic Lincolniana and, at one time, owned Lincoln's death mask and the mold of his hand. He later became one of the organizers of the Grass Roots Republican convention (1935) in Springfield, Illinois, and ran the pre-convention campaign of Alfred M. Landon of Kansas for the Republican presidential nomination against Roosevelt. He held many committee appointments, including one on the Federal Prison Labor Committee (1905–11), and became something of a legend in his own time for his fearless editorials, staunch Republican views and moral probity.

Richard Lloyd Jones had, in short, inherited all the Lloyd Jones intellectual energy and physical stamina (he lived to be ninety), along with the family's love of a pulpit and its combativeness. Since his political views were diametrically opposed to those of his cousin and since neither ever scrupled to spare the other's feelings, the battles were ferocious. There is some indication that Richard was jealous of Frank's greater eminence; having grown up in the shadow of one famous man, he had no intention of playing second fiddle to another. But it was more complicated than that. Richard genuinely admired Frank's art and liked his charm, his warmth, and his expansiveness and secretly knew that, for all his improvidence, he was the most generous of men. And to discover that a Lloyd Jones was in trouble was, for any other Lloyd Jones, a battle cry to the ramparts; the enemy's forces had to be bravely faced, even if the cause was hopeless. He also wrote that he would not disagree with Frank so much if he did not love him so much. This was probably perfectly true, but their relationship was put to its ultimate test with the building of the enormous (8,500 square feet) and very expensive house (named Westhope in honor of his father) that Richard had, in an indulgent moment, asked Frank to build—because he knew Frank needed the money. Finding himself in this sentimental trap seemed to arouse Richard's feelings of exasperation with his impossible cousin and reminded him of the disagreeable past. For instance, he was editor of the Madison paper when, in 1911, Wright had scandalized public opinion by moving Mamah Borthwick into the newly built Taliesin. Richard had been one of the principal backers of the family caucus and had written to tell his cousin the effect the scandal was having on the Aunts and the Hillside Home School. Frank was incorrigible; everybody knew that. Richard liked to tell the story about the time in 1905 when Wright appeared in his office at *Collier's* in New York asking for his rail fare back to Chicago. Richard dug the sum up and, an hour later, Frank was back again. He was carrying a beautiful Japanese print that he had just bought, and he still needed his rail fare back to Chicago.

The Lloyd Joneses had bought four acres of land on an open knoll on the outskirts of Tulsa and began leisurely negotiations about the kind of house they wanted sometime in 1928. Their son Jenkin believed that Wright's original sketch was for a rambling wood-and-stucco house around a courtyard with off-angled rooms and one of Wright's characteristically low-pitched roofs. This would have been appropriate for the Oklahoma landscape and better attuned to the kind of comfortable, old-fashioned furniture Richard and George liked (wing chairs, for example) than the house Wright gave them. If there were any discussions these were on a very informal basis because sometime in November 1928 Wright fired off the first salvo. Noting that

Richard and Lloyd were "the only ones to vent their outrage on outrageous me," Wright went on to say that his cousin was not a bad fellow and he was truly fond of him. However, he was "a Puritan and a publican of the worst stripe. The hypocrisy necessary to be these things is bred in the bone, dyed in the wool. . . ."

That did it. Richard tore off a nine-page letter, typed and single-spaced. He was outraged to be called a hypocrite, which he thought was name calling and unfair, unleashing a thunderbolt of criticism that would have done justice to Jove (or Wright) himself. If Wright found hypocrisy around him it was because of his grandiloquent, "I-own-the-world" ways, his outlandish appearance, his selfish determination to have his own way at all costs, his contempt for society, his lack of sympathy for others.

This ferocious attack would have daunted anyone less thick-skinned (or less financially at his mercy) than his architect at that moment. Perhaps Richard Lloyd Jones knew that. At any rate it was accompanied by a second letter, which made it clear that he was serious about a new house. For his part Wright had decided that their house should be built of the textile blocks with which he had been working. He wanted this time to try a different effect, dispensing with Mayan themes altogether and emphasizing the vertical in a free-form composition that would also incorporate an up-to-date version of the conservatory, or sun room. He would build his blocks into pillars and intersperse them with columns of windows of the same width. It was the end result of his theoretical interest in dispensing with walls entirely since, as Hitchcock wrote, the result could hardly be called a wall at all. Instead, it was "a screen of closely spaced piers between which space flows . . . freely. . . ." Wright had already tried this effect for the living room of the Millard house a few years before, spacing his piers between double panes of glass. He increased the effect with his next attempt for the Storer house, moving the piers closer together, with a single rectangle of glass placed horizontally between them. Now he proposed to move them even closer, by positioning the rectangle of glass vertically. He had never tried for this particular effect before, but the more he thought about it, the more he wanted to design it whether Richard and George were enthusiastic, or not.

Richard Lloyd Jones had immediate reservations about the blocks. A friend had told him that he had a house like this in New Mexico and liked it so much that he tried the same thing in Ohio but found that the blocks seemed to absorb moisture from the air because the house was always damp. It rained in Oklahoma, Richard reminded his cousin. He wanted to be sure that the blocks were moisture-proof before he approved them. Meantime Wright should give them a very rough floor plan, not even to scale, for them all to discuss. If they approved, he could then go ahead with a detailed plan and they could begin to build. On the ground floor they wanted, in addition to a vestibule and living room, a dining room to accommodate twenty, a sixteen-by-twenty-four-foot study for himself, a billiard room not less than twenty-two by sixteen, a kitchen, pantries and four-car garage. They wanted five bedrooms in all and a roof garden. There should be a courtyard for the cars.

Wright's letter was reassuring. There would be two layers of blocks, an outer and inner, reinforced vertically and horizontally with steel joints. All the grooves would be poured with water-resisting cement, and the inner seams of the outside blocks would be coated with asphalt. He preferred this to using exterior waterproofing, which spoiled the color and texture of the blocks. A house like this might be somewhat harder to heat, but it would hold its heat, and the inside of the house would never be damp. It would also be fireproof. He described the usual schedule of payments for a total of 10 percent and smoothly interjected the idea that it was usual for the contract to include furnishings and plantings so that the client might have "the full benefit of a harmonious scheme fully completed."

Wright and party went off to Chandler, Arizona, early in 1929, and nothing much happened on the Lloyd Jones house for several months, except a call for money. Richard sent off a thousand dollars as an advance against fee and said he would be very glad to send more as needed.

A month later Richard Lloyd Jones wrote again with a few alternative sketches, Plans A to D. His cousin might get a good laugh. In the first plan he had simply tried to take Wright's idea, square it and add a room he called the "Bissorium." This was a reference to his daughter, Florence, called "Bisser" by the family, who was ambitious to make botany her career, so he had added a flower room, or greenhouse, for her. On the second floor he was giving George a room with a south, west, east and northeast exposure, which should be delightful.

In Plan B, he had put the study beside the living room and arranged the rest of the house accordingly. He thought that was the least successful. Plan C provided living room exposures to the west, south, east and north. But then he thought that the Bissorium had better have an eastern exposure so he switched to Plan D. They all liked this the best, apart from the placement of the swimming pool and lily pond. In short, he would see what his architect had to say. His only concern was that he had indicated a half-million-dollar house and his limit was $50,000. In fact, he would like the final price better if it were $48,865.45.

By April it was possible to discern a strategy behind Wright's moves. He was working in his Chandler, Arizona, camp on the San Marcos project, but keeping a staff of fifteen housed and fed was a bigger financial drain than he had bargained for. Wright's court of last resort, Darwin Martin, was feeling the effect of the stock market crash and, in light of the dispute with La Follette, unlikely to slip Wright any money under the table. So Wright was transferring his hopes to his cousin, who was obliging by sending him checks directly. Richard was also dispensing free financial advice (get rid of La Follette) and even offering to act as a guarantor for 6 percent interest on money others might invest in Wright's corporation. Finding his cousin this amenable gave Wright the necessary tolerance for the inevitable sermons that accompanied the checks. Another advance of a thousand dollars (on April 19) was sent with an observation that Wright should be a millionaire by now and would be, were it not for his ability to shoot himself in the foot, the result of his self-centeredness, his arrogance, his intolerance of others and his vaingloriousness. Bit by bit Richard Lloyd Jones revealed the real reason for what he called his "vitriol." The Lloyd Joneses, he said, had been split between those who put on airs, wove fictional romances around themselves and thought themselves too good for the rest of the world and those, like Uncle Thomas and his father, who despised such posturing. If Frank would just drop the fake act and allow his achievements to speak for themselves he would be universally admired and respected instead of being an outlaw and outcast. And so on. Wright took the scolding with good humor, and Richard, all unsuspecting, went on sending money, unaware that his shrewd cousin was closing in for the kill. Wright finally wrote to say that Chandler had advanced $7,500, but that the desert adventure had actually cost about $12,600. He would soon have that money and more, he wrote, with a reference to November when construction on San Marcos was due to begin. In the meantime, if "Rich" could possibly advance a further $1,500 he would be happy to give him a few valuable Japanese prints, saved from the New York debacle, as collateral.

The appeal was a success. More money came by return mail, although his cousin was aware that he had now sent the bulk of the $5,000 architectural fee for a $50,000 house ($3,500) and had nothing to show for it and certainly not the choice of floor plans he had requested weeks before. He was beginning to doubt his cousin's motives, and that made him angry again. He did not want Japanese prints as collateral. He did not intend to continue advancing money, which his cousin would then treat as a gift. Frank was headed for total disaster unless, at the advanced age of sixty-five, said Rich, adding a few years (Wright was then sixty-two), he could make some basic changes in his character, renounce his false philosophy and stop expecting the world to serve him, or he might end up in jail. Four days later another thousand dollars was accompanied by a different kind of scolding. Cousin Rich was horrified to hear that on the return journey to Spring Green, Frank had let his police dog ride on the running board, at sixty miles an hour. No wonder the poor dog fell off. He could have been killed. Richard could not stand a man who treated dumb animals this way. It was one more example of Frank's general thoughtlessness. Richard had written a little tract, "My Dog's Bequest," which he was sending along. It had been translated into seven languages, including Chinese.

The house project continued to be a battleground for old grievances and resentments. Richard continued to send money while working himself into a rage over any hint that Wright might be patronizing him or showing evidence of the same bad old habits. Wright, aware that he was walking a tightrope, kept his letters short and his response muted. Apart from his prudent business reasons for doing so, he appeared to know enough about his cousin to discount some of his more outrageous statements, waiting for the generous impulses that invariably followed the storm. At these moments Richard was at his most malleable, and Wright took full advantage. In fact he showed great restraint, although he did allow himself the comment that behind his own apparent "bravado" was a hidden sadness, ". . . and though you may not know it, I too have fought a good fight." With his sister he was less guarded. He was very sorry for his cousin, he told Jane, who was meeting the fate of all negatively good people. Then he added carelessly that he had always regarded his immediate relations as enemies, a comment hardly designed to endear himself to his sister.

Richard and George spent the summer of 1929 in Europe. He returned as crotchety as ever, muttering imprecations about the average Welshman's level of intelligence, but he was still talking about building and wanted Frank's plans. However, Frank had tested their generosity too far. When he appealed again, in October, for a $7,500 subscription to his corporation (so as to finance another trip to Arizona), he came up against serious resistance. Richard and George were ready to throw in the towel because they were not convinced that the house Wright was offering them was the one they wanted. What gave rise to their gravest doubts was Richard's belated realization that his willingness to help Frank get back on his feet financially was being misread as a readiness to back one speculative project after another, in this case San Marcos: the leopard had not changed his spots in the slightest. Another reason for his unease was the suspicious way the price of his house kept jumping. First it was $65,000, and now it was $75,000 and maybe $80,000 or more. It was unnerving. He could not afford it. But if he did build he did not intend to cut corners, as Wright now suggested, doing without steel bindings for the blocks or steel frames for the glass. If Wright originally thought they were necessary, they were still necessary. Richard had a horrid feeling that Wright was making pictures for his own satisfaction and that he, as client, was expected to take a chance on an experimental house to accommodate his architect; it was an $80,000 bet. He absolutely insisted that his architect accommodate him instead. He also begged his artistic cousin to worry first about practicalities and let the aesthetics look after themselves.

Wright responded with an eight-page letter. The San Marcos project was all but certain. He knew it would go through, but, to make his cousin feel better, he would not go back until it was definite. Meantime, like the superb salesman he was, he did his best to allay his cousin's reservations about investing in his corporation and to get him to continue with the house. Richard remained adamant on the former but was ready to concede the latter. Plans were sent and he was deeply disappointed. He had asked for several choices. Instead, he had received a completed plan that took no account of the requests they had made. He did not want a breakfast room, and he wanted that extra space thrown into the billiard room. He was specific about the way he wanted the ground floor rearranged. He wanted a servants' toilet in the main part of the house. He wanted five feet taken off the hall upstairs. He wanted a fourth bedroom and told Wright how to get it. He wanted the servants' quarters on the second floor over the garage, and he wanted a bigger garage. There were other details, but what worried him most was that Wright had ignored the evidence of his own eyes.

The plan as presented would not go on their lot because it did not take account of the topography and the slope in the land toward the north corner. He reminded Wright that he had offered to provide a topographical survey, and Wright said it would not be necessary. As drawn, the garage and servants' quarters were going down a ten-foot incline. That was not good enough for "the greatest architect in America."

Realizing he had made a mistake, Wright did his best to minimize it and make hasty adjustments—"What you now say about the slope of the ground would modify the arrangement of the house some-what. . . ."—but he thought varying the floor levels would improve rather than hurt the design. However, he could not visualize it clearly and asked for a new set of photographs. Wright was amenable to most of the suggestions, though he advised against having servants' quarters adjoining the family bedrooms. Still, if that was what they wanted, he would give it to them. As for orientation, Rich ought to consider that the use of pillar and glass would turn the whole living room wall into "a window with vertical mullions." This would make for an outlook in every direction. He added, "I admit this is a novel proposition and it is quite natural for you to question it." Question it his cousin did. He could not see how Wright's new vertical plan could possibly be an improvement on the strips of horizontal windows he used to build. He sent a drawing to illustrate his argument. He really wanted those nice old windows but that would, as his architect said, have required another kind of house, and Wright was not going to give it to him.

Westhope, which is now on the National Register of historic build-ings, has to be considered a mixed achievement. From the evidence it would appear that Wright was at his best when given a free hand artistically; thus the ideal client for him was sensitive to his special gifts, intelligently receptive to his ideas and raised a minimum of objections during its design. The relationship between the two cousins could never fit that model, despite Richard Lloyd Jones's genuine pride in Wright's achievements and his respect for his art. He was too suspicious, too distrustful and too prepared to pounce on what he perceived as Wright's personal shortcomings, and this biased him in the direction of seeing devious behavior where none was intended. His blanket denunciations had the predictable result of producing exactly the wrong kind of attitude in his architect. Wright, when convinced he was right, as has been noted, would persist blindly on a wrong course even when he knew better. If this thesis is valid, it would help to explain the disappointments of the experimental method of building textile blocks in vertical rows that he tried with Westhope and never repeated, a design that resulted in a house that was stripped-down, forbidding and almost belligerently lacking in charm. From certain aspects it still looks like an armed camp (the window slits acting as gun emplacements) or, as Hitchcock wrote, a penitentiary. Richard Lloyd Jones had opened the dialogue by stating that the house was being built for his wife, but he soon dropped this fiction, and if Westhope can be said to have been influenced by Richard Lloyd Jones's character, it mirrors his prickly exterior to perfection. Even the interior runs true to form, being vastly more comfortable, spacious and pleasing than its exterior would lead one to think, and that would have reflected its central character too. But, as Richard's daughter, Florence L. J. Barnett, commented, the house remains an anomaly since its vertical emphasis is perversely inappropriate to its setting and its method of construction made it the most uncomfortable house possible: too hot in summer and too cold in winter. The blocks went on absorbing water like a sponge as Richard Lloyd Jones knew they would, despite repeated attempts at waterproofing. His wife never liked it (she wanted a wood house and got a concrete one), and she gratefully surrendered it to a dedicated young architect and his family after her husband died.

Richard Lloyd Jones was very happy there, which did not stop him from being fully aware of the unsatisfactory nature of the design. He saw that in the autumn of 1930, almost as soon as the house went up. He wrote to Wright that, now that he could see the wall taking shape, he realized how right he had been about the lack of a panoramic view from the interior and how wrong Wright had been. Once inside, he was not going to be able to see out unless he went right up to the window, and then he would have only a forty-five-degree-angle view. He felt like a horse wearing blinders. It was too late now; the die was cast, but if he had it to do over again he would never accept this "slat device," he wrote. Construction continued through the winter of 1930–31. Wright had recommended that Richard employ his favorite builder, Paul Mueller, the German-born engineer who had moved to Chicago and had begun working for Dankmar Adler (on the Chicago Auditorium project). He became foreman for Adler and Sullivan shortly thereafter; he then joined a construction company as partner and rose to prominence in Chicago in the 1890s when he built thirty-three of the Chicago World's Fair buildings. Besides the Imperial Hotel, he and Wright went on to collaborate on many of Wright's most notable projects, including Unity Temple, Midway Gardens, and the Larkin Building. He was, in short, vastly experienced and knowledgeable, and Richard Lloyd Jones, after objecting that he was being given no choice, was grateful for Mueller's patience and expertise. But at some point during construction, a problem developed. Various versions are given, but the most authoritative is that of Jenkin Lloyd Jones. He wrote that, halfway through construction, work almost ceased. His exasperated father demanded an explanation. Mueller, accompanied by a lawyer, appeared at his office in tears. He confessed that there had been cost overruns, that he had diverted a large part of his advance to pay off old debts and, in short, that he was out of funds. Richard Lloyd Jones very gamely refused to prosecute, but the result was to add $20,000 onto the final cost of the house, so that he could not afford the furniture and plantings that Wright had also designed. That might have been an advantage as, Mrs. Barnett said, they used family antiques instead, which helped to "warm up" the place. Perhaps this unfortunate episode is responsible for the name Richard Lloyd Jones used to describe it. His son wrote that his neighbors were increasingly baffled as the house took shape and wanted to know what it was. Richard Lloyd Jones replied, "A pickle factory." He was then asked, "Do they have to build them like this?"

Westhope is probably the original setting for the anecdote that is linked with many other houses of Wright's flat-roof design. The roof, of course, leaked almost immediately. Roofers were summoned to give it yet another surface; it was all in vain. Finally Richard Lloyd Jones, in a fury, went to his desk and made a long-distance call. "Dammit, Frank," he raged, "it's leaking on my desk!" Wright calmly replied, "Richard, why don't you move your desk?" Westhope is also the setting for another wonderful comment, this time by Mrs. Lloyd Jones when, during a cloudburst, she and her family dashed around the living room with buckets and pans trying to spare the rugs as the rain poured in. "Well," she said, "this is what we get for leaving a work of art out in the rain."

He was glad, Richard Lloyd Jones wrote at the height of the depression, that no one had any money. Now that they were all "busted," they were all on common ground. It gave him a virtuous democratic sort of feeling. He had heard good things about Wright's ambitious plans for a school. He did not know how in the devil Wright proposed to pull it off, but his cousin had proved that "a man doesn't need any money." That comment was made early in the 1930s, no doubt after one of those famous winters everyone remembered about Taliesin when, as another frequent visitor wrote, icicles as "big as your thigh" hung from the eaves and the hillside stood wrapped in snows as deep and profound as any Hans Christian Andersen had invented for his heroine in *The Snow Queen*. Frederick Gutheim, the distinguished architectural historian who was first taken to Taliesin by Philip La Follette in the winter of 1928, had a vivid memory of what he called Taliesin's rural poverty: "Peasant meals of potatoes and cabbage, occasionally if memorably enlivened by a roast pig or a case of lettuce. . . ." Jenkin Lloyd Jones, another frequent visitor, remarked that the simple fare was served with panache, and the living room would be full of pussy willows or bouquets of wildflowers. That was Mrs. Wright's doing: "She never permitted them to look poor. There was always that patina of success." When all the commissions dried up (and every architect one knew was out of work), she was the one who had encouraged her husband to turn to lecturing and writing and had given him such emotional support while he wrote *An Autobiography*.

Dozens of Wright's early essays, some so annotated and vandalized that they never could be published, exist in fragmented manuscripts. He was obviously willing to abandon these trial efforts but was determined to have *An Autobiography* published and sent it to Woollcott for a reading at an early stage, in late 1927. Woollcott prudently replied that he had two cardinal rules, one being to refuse to join a committee, and the second, never to read other people's manuscripts. Wright replied by return mail with three sentences that are classic illustrations of the predictable train of his mercurial reactions. His first comment was to damn the manuscript. Woollcott could forget all about it and he liked him better for having pushed it away. His next response was to damn himself. He never would, or ever could, become a writer. Finally, a wave of self-pity struck him. "More and more a stranger in my own land—Alexander," he observed mournfully. He did not mean it for a moment, of course, and if there was a certain pique to be discerned, that was effaced by a generous closing paragraph in which he told Woollcott how much he loved and admired him. Unlike another friend of those years, the architectural critic Lewis Mumford, who could not be cajoled into visiting Taliesin, Woollcott could and did. Like many who came after him, Woollcott would perceive, from that serene and smiling vision, some rare qualities in its creator: "So good a mind, so leaping an imagination, . . . so fresh a sense of beauty," and had, it was clear, decided to like him before they met. Under such circumstances Wright was at his very best, and the two became instant friends. They often traveled from New York to Chicago together in a Pullman car, and on one such occasion, Wright, who was on his way home from a speaking engagement, brought with him a small secondhand organ or melodeon that folded up into a small suitcase. It was the kind that traveling evangelists were wont to take to camp meetings and had become Wright's inseparable companion since he had found it in a secondhand shop in New York.

On that particular occasion, other Pullman passengers were surprised and amused to see these two middle-aged gentlemen, obviously artistic and distinctly eccentric, with the melodeon set up in the aisle between them, regaling themselves with ditties and having a perfectly hilarious time about it. One, it was noted, was heavyset, with pendulous jaws and a shock of long, untidy brown hair. The other seemed older but "better preserved," had a handsome head of curly white locks, wore homespun clothes, a flowing black silk tie, and had a delightful twinkle in his gray-blue eyes. The consensus was that the two must be a pair of itinerant musicians, or religious fanatics having a weekend off. Not one person recognized the famous humorist, much less his companion, the world's most famous architect. And in fact, if that appellation was being used with increasing frequency, Woollcott was at least partly responsible. He had recently written an article about Frank Lloyd Wright for *The New Yorker* that closed with, "Indeed, if the editor of this journal were so to ration me that I were suffered to apply the word 'genius' to only one living American, I would have to save it up for Frank Lloyd Wright." That charming encomium may well account for the new note of aggressive self-confidence that can be discerned in Wright's letters shortly after the summer of 1930, when the article was written. To Claude Bragdon, another New Yorker, architect and stage designer, he wrote, ". . . my fellows are trying to dispose of me in any damned old way just so they get the cuss out of the way." That would not be easy. Wright intended, as he advised Lloyd, to keep his courage up to "fighting pitch." He also wrote, "There is probably something coming before they shove your old man under."

15

The World's Greatest Architect

If I had to say which was telling the truth about society, a speech by a Minister of Housing or the actual buildings put up in his time, I should believe the buildings.

—KENNETH CLARK
Civilisation

For all his professed lack of interest in himself—he once told his mother that he did not know himself, and did not care—Wright was intrigued by his own psyche; in fact, the criticism most often made about him is that Frank Lloyd Wright was the only person he was interested in. Numerous comments at differing stages of his life confirm the impression that his view of himself remained that of a misunderstood genius, lonely and embattled, faithful to the truth though all the world should stand against him. Continuing evidence that he identified himself strongly, if not exclusively, with his Welsh heritage is as clear in his letters as elsewhere. To Catherine, he spoke about their common heritage of "Welsh ire"; to Lloyd, he made the playful observation that, like most Welshmen, he was not a convincing liar. At least one visitor to Taliesin described him as a "modern Druid"; another, not Welsh herself, observed without rancor that anyone named Jones was accorded preferential treatment there. A broad hint that his sister Maginel considered him not only quintessentially Welsh but also a worthy descendant of his bellicose Unitarian ancestors is provided in her description of their forebear Dr. Charles Lloyd, "a man of wonderful ability, bad temper, jealous to a degree, and always in hot water of his own boiling."

Like many master salesmen and entrepreneurs of the business world, a crisis of any kind was a test of Wright's resilience and ability to triumph; it almost seemed a necessity. Speaking of such special personalities, Anthony Sampson wrote in *The Changing Anatomy of Britain* that "they have to feel they've got their backs to the wall to perform properly. If they make a lot of money they have to get rid of it, like gamblers, so that they're at risk again." Wright was, at least in public, a model of brazen self-confidence. One of his characteristic quips, usually quoted with mingled disapproval and awe, is, "Early in life I had to choose between honest arrogance and hypocritical humility; I chose arrogance." On another occasion he referred to himself in court as the world's greatest architect. Asked if he did not think this self-assessment somewhat inflated, he replied, "Well, I was under oath, wasn't I?" That would have been said with just the right blend of effrontery and guile, with a suggestion of self-mockery thrown in; with Wright, one was never quite sure. He was equally able to joke about his braggadocio, as when he told Woollcott that "the only man three times as entertaining, twice as instructive, and five times as attractive as I am, is you. . . ." Evidence that there was also a punitive and disparaging, if not pitiless, self-assessment behind the façade is equally consistent, down through the years. On the subject of reading the autobiography he had just published, Wright also told Woollcott, "And I can understand what a bore it would be just as I am afraid I am one." A similar theme can be discerned from his comment to another friend, "You see, I am naturally rather dumb, having come in from the country on a load of poles." He also wrote, after meeting his Dutch admirer Wijdeveld, that the man was a bigger egotist than he was, which surprised him. "I thought I was the limit."

One could easily have missed this muted minor theme, hidden as it was behind a barrage of charm. A man who can dissuade a thief in the act of burgling a house can do anything, and Wright invariably used his guile to extract himself from the hot water that he himself had brought to a rolling boil. For instance, when one of his early patrons, C. E. Roberts of Oak Park, wrote in 1906 to say that Wright still owed him $5,000, he replied with exquisite formality that he could not reconcile his own accounts with such a large figure. "It seems gross injustice on my part to question it, I have fought against it for a long time but I believe it better to confess that the mystery has grown more puzzling instead of less so," he wrote. He ended his letter with the charming confession that he could not clear the debt as yet and asked for another loan, this time to help the Aunts and Hillside. For, as he also vowed, "I think you wanted sincerely to help and I loved you more than I ever loved a father. . . ." The response to this piece of shamelessness is not known, but it was typical of him. It was almost beyond his control; he simply had to try his luck and did so with such success that, as on one occasion when he was invited to lecture at the University of Oregon, he not only wheedled a larger fee out of the administration but so touched the sympathy of the professor involved that he kept sending Wright money. Wright finally had to tell him to stop. The Roberts family, which was not repaid, took a slightly more jaundiced view of Wright's charm, but they kept the letter he wrote after his former benefactor died in 1934. Wright, who had not seen him for years, told his widow, "I shan't miss him because he will always be right where he has been these many years —close by." Jean Cocteau, that master of the gilded phrase, could not have done any better. It goes without saying that Wright could turn any incident to his advantage. A minor example of this was the occasion when, as he was lecturing in a college department of architecture, he was interrupted with cries to speak up. Some men might have been unnerved. Wright merely paused, then inquired, "Are the acoustics in this hall as bad as I think they are?"

He was interested in himself, but his comments to most of his friends are unrevealing. He usually explained that he was the way he was, and that was that. He told Mrs. Darwin Martin after his old patron died, "Character is fate and mine got me into heavy going. . . ." He also told a friend, Oskar Stonorov, late in life, "I think I am too many people ever to be put into one presentment." It is likely that he knew far more about "this inner chamber I call my heart" than he was willing to concede, and a certain formality in his manner kept at arm's length some who loved him and were baffled by him, men in particular. As the architect Edgar Tafel, who wrote a revealing book about his apprenticeship with Wright, commented, "I never had the courage to invade the privacy of his mind. I wish I had." Only with women did Wright ever let down his guard and then only after their reproaches had pushed him into an agony of confession.

At such moments he might say something quite revealing, as he once had to Miriam: "I guess my talent has screened me from myself all along. . . ." Perhaps Taliesin, that cunning labyrinth, is the best metaphor for the personality of its creator, with its sunlit, expansive vistas and chiaroscuro, its wide-open windows and blank walls, its veiled allusions and sudden revelations, its perfectly composed and inviting rooms and its stiffly formal chairs. His impulsiveness, his mercurial shifts of mood and the complexity of his responses made him an easy man to misjudge. The immediate impression gained from his thousands of letters is that he reveled in handing out insults whenever he was infuriated (and that was as unpredictable as everything else about him). There are only a relatively few witnesses left alive to attest to his inability to state his grievances at close quarters. One of those friends, Professor Marya Lilien, who came to know him in the 1930s when she was an apprentice at Taliesin, said, "He never wanted to hurt anyone. I remember one time that Wright had a laborer in Spring Green who used to do odd jobs, but he was a real bum and he had never liked him. One day Wright was out digging in a field —he liked to work off his energy that way—when his secretary, Eugene Masselink, appeared with the man in tow, whose name was Joe. Could he get some work shearing sheep? Without looking up, Wright vehemently retorted that he never wanted to see the man again. Then he suddenly saw who was standing there. 'Oh, hello, Joe,' he said without missing a beat. 'What would you like to do for us?' That was one of Mr. Wright's most charming inconsistencies, very characteristic. He used to tell me, 'If you want something from me, come in person because it's terribly easy to say no in a letter.' "

This taboo against being directly rude, if that is what it was, did not extend to lecturing, where his actor's instinct for the provocative statement, allied with his compulsive rebelliousness, ensured that he would take the offensive for, as he also said, "I've always wanted to take the dust off people." Or, as he explained to Lawrence C. Lemmon, another apprentice of the 1930s, "When I go out on a lecture tour I don't hand them a lot of bromides. I kick them in the shins and step on their feet and get them to listen to me." His granddaughter, Nora Natof, Frances's daughter, thought he had no awareness of his effect on others. Once, when she was dining at Taliesin, her grandfather began to make rude remarks about the rapidity with which she was eating. She got up and left the table. He apologized for that later. "What some people called vindictiveness I simply think of as a lack of sensitivity to others' feelings," she said.

However, one makes this kind of generalization about Wright at one's peril, along with all the others. Just as many anecdotes are told about his delicacy of feeling. Elizabeth Kassler, another early apprentice, recalled that on one occasion when she was in the middle of a divorce she wrote to ask whether she might come to Taliesin for a while with her young son, Fritz. She was in a state of emotional turmoil, but her letter was so discreet that, Olgivanna Wright said later, they had not realized how desperate she was. Kassler and her son took the train to Phoenix, where the Wrights were, by then, spending their winters, arriving at three in the morning. They were met, taken to the new Taliesin and slept late. When they came out onto the loggia it was a cool, crisp sunny morning. Wright looked at her penetratingly, then said, "Betty and Fritzli! You know I think what you should do for the next few days is paint the insides of your quarters white." He had, in other words, immediately sensed her need and was offering her his indefinite hospitality. That he had showed such generosity and understanding was still deeply moving to Mrs. Kassler forty years later.

Throughout his life many women found Wright irresistible, often in a way they could not really explain. Miriam Noel wrote about the allure of his fleetingly unguarded gaze, and so did Olgivanna Wright: "He gave me that wonderful swift look and there was an extremely brilliant sheen in his eyes," she wrote. His ability to be gallant was almost a reflex, though, one has to add, it trembled on the verge of being pornographic. Writing to Aline Saarinen, the writer, wife of Eero Saarinen, the famous architect, Wright, who was then in his eighties, thanked her for the bouquet of flowers "containing the baby-adder—I kiss you for the flowers and allowed the baby-adder to bite me on the lips. There is some swelling. . . ." As a rule he saved his best insults for men and, as might be gathered from his letter to Richard Lloyd Jones, easily descended to name calling. Writing to Oskar Stonorov, Wright made several references to the former's ample outlines: "You buxom idealist," he called him, and "dear old buxom," and, in a flash of irritation, referred to his "ample fanny." Examples of his ability to switch from malice to remorse are equally numerous. Speaking of the young architectural historian Henry-Russell Hitchcock, Wright told Mumford in 1930, "You know, Lewis, I am sorry I called poor Hitchcock a fool and am writing to take back a swipe at his latest book. . . . Why should I try to hurt him? He is at least sincere. What if he doesn't know? He may learn. Anyhow, I can't strike the blow. . . ." Then there was the saving grace of his humor.

Eric Wright said, "After a horrible outburst he'd make some sort of witty comment and you'd have to laugh." His way of apologizing was characteristic and showed a certain insight. To Woollcott, he remarked, "I was so disappointed I had to damn everything. . . ." To Aline Saarinen, referring to a similar occasion, he wrote, "Here is apology for breaking down when I could rightfully be expected to contribute a telling note to the occasion. . . . But it was either that or sobbing, and I chose to swear—the male substitute for tears. . . ."

In many respects Wright was shrewd and calculating, and yet, the English writer C. S. Nott thought, he was essentially gullible. "Like all geniuses [he] . . . was . . . naive and would believe anyone who was nice to him and flattered him; he could not see through people." One day while Nott was staying at Taliesin, Wright came to him with a letter from a man in Mexico who claimed to know where a fortune was hidden (but who, for some reason, could not go there himself). Nevertheless he guaranteed that if Wright would advance him a thousand dollars, he would be repaid fivefold. Wright wanted to know whether Nott was willing to join him in the scheme. Nott continued, "After I had read the letter I said, 'You don't really believe this, do you?' 'Why not?' he said. 'It seems genuine to me.' 'It's one of the oldest swindles I know,' I said." Wright refused to believe him, and was with difficulty dissuaded from parting with his cash by another friend who happened to be staying there. The anecdote is revealing because it goes some distance toward explaining Wright's injured feelings when others were not as ready to accept his facile explanations as he wanted them to be, or to gamble their money on whatever get-rich-quick scheme he had thought of that week. When rebuffed, his amour propre would become involved, and on that point he was, as Nott said, "prickly." Those who became close to him learned he had to be handled with care; "managed" is the word they used. By all accounts one of the masters of this tightrope walking was his indispensable assistant Gene Masselink, another was his wife Olgivanna, and a third was Jack Howe. He said, "It took Mr. Wright two whole winters to get out working drawings for the Johnson's Wax building [of the 1930s] because he was under pressure to get it done in one. My explanation is that if Mr. Wright saw any evidence of efficiency he struck it down. He thought it was antipathetic to the creative process." Furthering that thought, Howe added, "If Mr. Wright wanted something, we had to have it ready yesterday because he couldn't wait. But if his clients were applying pressure, they could wait because, he said, 'I am an artist.' "

That he made severe demands on himself went without saying. The Lloyd Jones insistence that he, as a young farmhand in the summers, "add tired to tired," something he had so fiercely resented, became, as he aged, a maxim he quoted with relish and applied with most vigor to those who were his nearest and dearest; "the closer you were to him, the higher were his expectations of you," Eric Wright said. Frank Lloyd Wright insisted that they be as stoical as he was. One of the most vivid examples of this is given by Olgivanna Wright, who described an evening boat party that he had organized for the pond below their hill the first summer she went to live at Taliesin. He had draped their boat with mosquito netting, but it was not fine enough, and, as they got out into the middle of the lake, thousands of insects found their way under the net and began to persecute her and a visiting friend. The women frantically begged him to make for the shoreline; he became more and more stubbornly determined to continue. It was up to them not to mind. By the time they reached dry land both women were covered with bites, and one of Olgivanna's eyes was completely closed from the swelling. They made up their differences later. He praised her; she was "made of strong metal," he said. His daughter Iovanna thought his ability to endure pain quite extraordinary. "He had sciatica as he got older and I can remember him lying on his back on the couch and moaning, but he would not take anything stronger than Empirin." Perhaps most amusing, in retrospect, was his indomitable self-assurance. Catherine Wright's niece, Jeanne T. Bletzer, said, "Of course he was vain. He'd be talking to me and if there was a mirror in the room he'd be looking into that the whole time and not at me." She did not mind. "He had to believe in himself. Nobody else did for a long time."

The truth was that one wanted to be around him because, as the architect Wesley Peters, who would become his son-in-law, explained, "He had so much life and energy; it shaped everyone around him." Nott's reaction was, "With all his genius as regards architecture, with all his strong personality, in essence he was a boy. Perhaps this was one of the reasons why we all loved him." He could surmount one disaster after another and jauntily declare, as he did to Woollcott in 1929, "You see hope and courage are still 'as was,' notwithstanding the failure of our illegitimate intrigues. . . ." At the end of his life he was able to sum it up and call it happy: "I have had the very worst and the very best of anybody in the world." He had his own way of surviving: he never looked back. Howe said that he never reminisced about his past. He dismissed what he had once built, for the most part; what counted was whatever he was working on now. So one can take as genuine his comment to daughter Catherine, in 1921, that, "Every day life is the important thing, not tomorrow or yesterday but today. You won't reach anything better than the 'right-now,' if you take it as you ought—." And one never knew what he would do next. His close friends Herbert and Eloise Fritz of Spring Green, who went to many of his famous Sunday picnics, like to tell about the time he appeared wearing a beautiful white suit and a new set of false teeth. He presided benevolently over the meal and after it was over, took out his teeth and sat there, calmly cleaning them with an onion. Another former apprentice related an anecdote that had been told to him by Gene Masselink. It seemed that on one occasion in Madison, Wright went to a wholesale house to buy tumblers. As he walked through the store he was pursued by a persistent salesman who had a particular tumbler he wanted to sell because, he said, it could be dropped and would not break. He kept on demonstrating this. Wright ignored him for as long as he could, then turned to him and said, "Here, give me one and let me try." With that, he dropped the tumbler in the identical manner and it broke into a thousand pieces. Wright turned to the salesman and said, "Good. I'll take twelve dozen." Dorothy Meyer, wife of the *Madison Capital Times* columnist, refused to categorize him except to say, "One felt in the presence of a great man." Herb Fritz said, "He'd either shock you or amuse you. He was two hundred percent alive."

Wright's autobiography first appeared in 1932, with the modest first printing of 2,500 copies, the publisher having no confidence in his ability to sell, at the height of the depression, what are now collectors' items. He had started writing it in the autumn of 1926 when he and Olgivanna were in hiding in their Lake Minnetonka cabin. He kept up his pace with his usual energy and persistence so that, well before a divorce from Miriam Noel seemed possible, he was fretting about how to copyright the book so that she could not claim part of the proceeds. (His sister Jane suggested that he put it in Olgivanna's name.) It has been written in a self-consciously "poetic" style that must have gone through many revisions before its author, self-taught as ever, had hammered out the kind of prose he wanted. He might have been influenced by Sullivan's *The Autobiography of an Idea*, in which Sullivan describes his childhood in the third person, since Wright also uses this device as if aiming for a certain mythological tone. He could also have been influenced by the highly mannered storyteller's tone Carl Sandburg adopted for his multivolume biography of Abraham Lincoln, the first volume of which was published that year, and which Wright would have known about since Sandburg was a friend of his. Typical of that tone is Sandburg's statement that "she believed in God, in the Bible, in mankind, in the past and future, in babies, people, animals, flowers, fishes, in foundations and roofs, in time and the eternities outside of time. . . ." He wrote, that is to say, in a seemingly simple statement of the eternal truths that now seems self-conscious and clichéd, although it was once much admired. Woollcott seemed to believe Wright had been influenced in this direction since he grumbled about the latter's "Lincolnesque" writing style. The fact that Wright would adopt this particular tone is consistent with his desire to present himself as a homegrown product of the American Midwest, just like Sandburg, but his imitation stops short of parody and, to a surprising extent, conveys the dreaming image of a farm boy, moving through a magical world of exquisite sights and sounds intermittently interrupted by demands that he face the grim realities of a pioneer's life. These twin themes—the almost hypersensitive responsiveness to nature and the influence of his Welsh family's puritanical beliefs—along with his sense of rootedness in both, are conveyed with remarkable swiftness, clarity and economy, when one considers that this was the author's first attempt. One wag commented that the book reads as if it had been translated from the Welsh, and, indeed, the author's fondness for eliminating verbs (which became a mania as his book went through numerous revisions and reprintings) contributes to this effect. It is a safe guess that whenever the language becomes impenetrable it is either because Wright does not want to make a certain confession or because his thoughts are far more disorganized and unfocused than he would have it appear. In fact one can see a great many aspects of his character in his narrative's shifting tone, which tends to develop from melodically sustained passages of description to exhaustive recapitulations—of, for instance, the highminded reasons why he left his wife in 1909—to ingenious arguments in which he shifts the blame for his sensationally spendthrift ways onto all those who had made it so easy for him to borrow money. The poet, the aesthete, the dazzling creator, the scamp tirelessly bent on ways to excuse himself and accuse others, the Welsh moralist thundering from his pulpit—they are all here. Wright is at his best when he is content to describe the vivid past: his first memories of his parents, of his Welsh clan, of his early struggles, the chapel and, always, his beloved Valley. He divided his narrative into five sections or "books." Every one of them begins with a scene set in The Valley, as if that were the eternal point of return.

Like all autobiographies, his glosses over some facts and misrepresents others. In common with Lloyd George, his truth seemed to be curved, and this casual attitude toward facts and figures made some uncomfortable, unsure whether to take it as evidence of a superior imagination or proof of severe personal shortcomings, on a par with having changed his middle name. (At that time, too, he was experimenting with new initials, having hit upon the Welsh abbreviation for Lloyd as a double L, hence his signature of "F.LL.W" and, finally, "F.Ll.W.") There was something too unsettling about his airy refusal to be bound by other people's realities, something too mocking in his picaresque mood, so that it would be easy to miss the underlying seriousness of tone. If, early in the 1930s, Wright felt embattled and alone, if he knew how drastically the tide of architecture had turned against him, leaving him in the position of lonely survivor of an outmoded aesthetic, then the only way to counteract that impression would be the energetic argument that he was the standard-bearer for a new, quintessentially American vision that owed nothing to European influences, particularly not those becoming admired in the early 1930s. He needed to appear as an individualist, even an anarchist in architectural terms, and so, apart from the predictable references to his *"Lieber Meister,"* and some safe comments about peripheral influences, Wright continued to avoid the dangerous subject of the Arts and Crafts Movement. He was perhaps aware that, by 1930, no one remembered that the concept of an organic architecture had originated with Ruskin, or even that the phrase "in the nature of materials," which became identified with him, had also been coined by someone else: in this case, the English architect Joseph Twyman, follower of William Morris, and one of the early proselytizers for that master's ideas in Chicago. As Albert Bush-Brown wrote in the *Atlantic* after Wright's death, "His themes are nineteenth-century themes. First there is the hero, of Wagnerian dimensions, capable of great public service, as Plutarch would have him, but a Carlylean hero forced to breast the wave of ignorance around him. This hero, a Messiah in the lineage of Christ, a philosopher like Lao-tse, owes his strength to nature; his parables come from the field; his metaphor is the root and flower, never the machine. . . ."

In Wright's narrative one could find all the themes that had been historically celebrated in American literature, i.e., that the true life was lived close to the soil, that small settlements were superior to large ones, that the city was the source of all evil, and that the purpose of American democracy was to create "an original form of natural life in which the individual stands supreme. . . ." Whatever the shortcomings of Wright's buildings, and there were many, one had to concede (this author continued) that their creator had the courage of his high convictions and they reflected his belief that architecture's noblest function was to build memorable works of art. As Wright himself wrote, "Let us all willingly confess that modern architecture is, first of all, in the nature of a spiritual conviction—detail, curtail, appropriate or falsify it how you may. If the primal spiritual insight as conviction is lacking, no more than reiteration of certain bald, machine-age commonplaces will be the barren result of any devotion, however esthetic." That this notorious figure should turn out to be a man of courageous convictions, as well as someone with beguiling wit and charm and the gusto of a man half his age, was a distinct revelation. *An Autobiography* sold out its first printing almost at once, went to a second, was reprinted in 1938, revised and enlarged in 1943 and eventually published in a new, handsome edition some years after his death. Wright was at last telling his version of his "stormy life," and this was considered news enough to warrant half a column in *The New York Times* of March 30, 1932. "The Autobiography has astonished everyone including me," Wright told Cyrus Adler a month after publication. "The publishers say no such spontaneous flood of favorable publicity in their experience. . . ." Perhaps he was exaggerating, but not by much. If he had once thought, as he wrote to Louis Sullivan shortly before the latter's death, that "Most autobiographies are a form of auto-intoxication—something like getting a man crying drunk in order to get him to tell you all he knows," the gratifying reception his own was receiving had changed that view, particularly when reviewers referred to him as "one of the few really great men of our time."

In his famous book, *Space, Time and Architecture*, Giedion suggested that Wright's oeuvre was a quintessential example of the "irrational

and organic" versus the rational and geometrical. The comment followed the general trend of seeing Wright, exemplified by Albert
Bush-Brown, as exemplifying the great nineteenth century romantic
tradition of those artists who had, as Kenneth Clark wrote, "appealed
to our emotions by analogies, buried memories or the sensuous use of
color. . . ." Johann Joachim Winckelmann, one of the great early
theorists of classicism, had said, "Beauty resembles the most limpid
water drawn from a pure source, which is all the healthier for being
tasteless." The centuries-old dichotomy between those whose work
called forth a passionate emotional response and those whose work had
its primary appeal for the intellect and the logic of order seemed to
be played out once again in the lonely fight Wright was waging against
the European modernists, those architects whose work repeated the
commonplaces of the machine age because it lacked "spiritual conviction," and that had absolutely no flavor whatsoever. Some sharp-
eyed observers of Wright's writings also thought they perceived a
sanctimonious or "preachy" trace of Ruskin's baleful influence, and
they were right. This was evident everywhere in the autobiography,
as might be gathered from other references to the "soul" of a design
and to his belief in art, like religion, as a form of inner experience.
Nature, truth, goodness, the "countenance of principle," the perception of beauty as a moral test, as Thoreau wrote—it was quite out of
vogue to be talking in these terms, if not verging on the ridiculous.

As James D. Kornwolf pointed out in his biography of M. H.
Baillie Scott, there were other basic differences. The Arts and Crafts
Movement had been, essentially, a British rebellion against the new
industrial-economic system and a society that made the "ultimate goal
of human endeavor—of civilization—not the welfare of man but the
production of wealth." What made the Arts and Crafts Movement
unique was its insistence upon a healthful and beautiful environment.
It was also a revolutionary idea "because each man would share in it,"
and if the movement's attempts to ruralize the towns and their social
structure failed, along with the equal attempt to "wrest the production
of goods . . . and even building itself, from the control of industry,"
it was a noble failure. "For a short time it replaced the false aesthetic
of greedy industry with a true one, creating new, living forms that
are unsurpassed . . . for their formal and functional integrity." Like
Morris, Baillie Scott and others, Wright placed his emphasis upon
man as a being with emotional and spiritual needs that transcended
his physical ones. Speaking of the dangers of materialism, of tech-

nological advance divorced from any other considerations, Aldous Huxley wrote, "The mortal peril to humanity of thoughtlessly accepting
these conveniences (with their inherent disadvantages) as constituting
a philosophy of life is now becoming apparent. For the implications
of this disruptive materialism . . . are that human beings are nothing
but bodies, animals, mere machines. . . ." Huxley was not alone in
believing that there was something remorseless and dehumanizing
about the new movement, and what one of its leading figures had to
say on the subject was not reassuring. Le Corbusier more or less
consciously revealed his scale of values by the comment that "considerable sacrifices were demanded of the inhabitant of the machine in
order that purely abstract formal development . . . might be carried
as far as possible." For his part, Wright came to the crux of the
argument quickly by asking, "Why should architecture or objects of
art in the machine age, just because they are made by machines, have
to resemble machinery?" That humanist position, which would receive
belated recognition, was hardly fashionable in 1930 as those in the
new wave in France and Germany joined the ranks of the new aes-
theticians. What must have been an added irritant to Wright was the
assertion by the new generation that "complete renunciation of past
architectural developments, both literary and stylistic, was a prereq-
uisite for the creation of any valid new architecture and the parallel
claim . . . that they had created that architecture," as Kornwolf
observed. "Wright's generation was as shocked by the anarchism of
the program as by the egotism of the claim of success. It countered
with equal vehemence, asserting the importance of precedent for principles and forms in art." As for that, Wright could be just as dogmatic
and egotistical as they were. At the end of his life he said loftily, "I
would consider myself in my dotage if I were to in the least go out
of my way to institute comparisons with those who are comparative
children in the realm I spiritually inhabit."

Perhaps by then he meant it, but, in 1930, comparisons with
younger colleagues were exactly what he meant to make, and the
obverse of his assertion of spiritual superiority was the suspicion that
leaders of the new movement were forming a conspiracy against him.
His letter to that effect has not survived, but his fears can be assumed
based on a reply by Lewis Mumford that, if there were such a cabal,
it was wholly unconscious. Wright's main cause for concern at that
moment was the architectural historian Hitchcock, then an art in-
structor at Vassar, who had just published an essay on Wright's work

for *Cahiers d'Art* that, while complimentary, had placed Wright as an old master of the period before World War I, too tied to old influences (such as Sullivan's regrettable penchant for ornamentation) and wedded to the picturesque. This last was perhaps the most "anti-architectural" of qualities, so that despite Wright's stature as an artist, architect and engineer, he lacked those "literary" influences that were so much more acceptable to contemporary taste. Hitchcock concluded, "He remains, it is time to say without reservation, the greatest architect and perhaps the greatest American of the early twentieth century."

The tone was meant to be friendly, but for Wright there seemed a complete inability to understand the underlying principles of his work, no doubt judged on the basis of a few bad photographs. What perhaps rankled most was the compliment that relegated him to a defunct epoch (and there was worse to come, since he would soon be called the "greatest architect of the *nineteenth* century"). He would flash his own challenge to Hitchcock, two years later: "And I warn Henry right here and now, that having a good start, not only do I fully intend to be the greatest architect who has yet lived—but the greatest Architect who will ever live—." Wright's bravado may be taken as an indication of the threat he felt Hitchcock's views represented to his own position. Indeed, as Kornwolf observed, Hitchcock (and other critics) could hardly wait, in 1930, for the "immediate and total" acceptance of the new architecture, even though he might suspect that it lacked some "spiritual" qualities. Hitchcock tended to dismiss the problem: "If Humanism be not, so much the worse for it." Mumford tried to mediate by explaining that this young writer's sympathies would naturally tend toward the postwar generation. "Like the Frenchmen he admires, & like some of the Germans of the same guild, his esthetic ideas are biassed by an inadequate sociology: he fancies that the age of art is over, and (like Spengler) he thinks the architecture of the future will be engineering or nothing." Mumford continued, "Root's and Sullivan's early skyscrapers are the equivalent of Corbusier's designs today: they are both primitives of the machine: while your work is a step beyond this, with fuller mastery of the materials & freer expression. Expressed in time, you are still 30 years ahead of Corbusier."

Lewis Mumford, the great American social philosopher, city planner and architectural critic, was, fortunately for Wright, an early champion in the face of what seemed an avalanche of approval for the new architecture. Long before he wrote his most influential books, such as

Technics and Civilization (1934) and *The Culture of Cities* (1938), Mumford had seen the threat that uncritical adoption of the machine posed for modern man, and deplored the same dehumanizing trends that he also saw in the new architectural aesthetic, or anti-aesthetic. The very qualities now seemingly outmoded in Wright's work, the respect for materials, the reverence for place, the organic quality of the building's design and the architect's attempt to satisfy the emotional and spiritual needs of the occupants—all those qualities now dismissed by the new critics—were precisely those Mumford thought most worth having. Wright was suitably grateful: Mumford, he declared, had a mind of "Emersonian quality." He needed Mumford's ability to mediate with the opposition; most of all, he needed his generous encouragement. "Your recent work has made my heart leap with joy," Mumford wrote at a particularly bleak moment. "[I]f it is the work of a 'dead one,' the sooner the rest of us stop living the better." Mumford was Wright's great support during that period, but he was by no means the only writer to see his unique qualities.

Fiske Kimball, then curator at the Philadelphia Museum of Art, whose sympathies were with the classicism Wright now deplored, had referred in his history of architecture (*American Architecture*, 1928) to the shameful neglect of this giant in the field. That led to a reply from Wright in Arizona: "Yours was no donkey's kick at a 'dying lion.' Nor am I a lion, nor dying—nor am I in exile." Fiske Kimball responded with a card containing a quotation from the German poet and dramatist Johann C. F. von Schiller—"Art is living, breathing form"—that Wright took everywhere. Then there was Douglas Haskell, at that time a writer for the *Architectural Record*, who published a spirited defense of Wright in the *Nation* in 1930 when it seemed that plans for the building of the Chicago World's Fair in 1933 would not include him. This was unconscionable, because it was perfectly obvious that Wright had, for thirty years, been sending "a powerful original impulse" around the world. His conceitedness might be hard to take and his views unpopular with some, but, in the ruthless game of architecture, it took someone as brash and rebellious as he was to "push a whole civilization in front of him." But there was even better to come. In the late spring of 1930 Wright was invited to give the famous Kahn Lectures on Art, Archaeology and Architecture at Princeton (published in book form the following year), and with that great honor went the privilege of mounting an exhibition of his work that would then travel around the country. It arrived in New York in June

1930 at the Architectural League headquarters, 115 West Fortieth Street, the first time an exhibition of Wright's had been seen there. *Time* magazine noted that the East had now made common cause with the Midwest in acknowledging Frank Lloyd Wright as a "pioneer in modernism." It was "Wright's Time," the magazine stated. That exhibition led to a flurry of articles by authors rediscovering the home-grown talents of this neglected artist and writing admiring paragraphs, in particular, about the model on display for his office tower close beside St. Mark's-in-the-Bouwerie, which had been designed as a central trunk with reinforced concrete piers running up it and, like a tree, growing wider as it spread upward. It was now conceded that, as H. I. Brock wrote in the *New York Times Magazine*, "at the very beginning of the century he was doing those very flat-topped houses with horizontal bands of windows which are now being exploited by our most advanced young architects as the newest thing. . . ."

Yet another factor that may have educated critics' eyes to find new value in Wright's work was the arrival of the Art Deco style. Such geometrical and angular designs and decorative motifs, ostensibly inspired by Cubism, had their origins, according to some writers, at the turn of the century, in the work of the Vienna Secessionists, Charles Rennie Mackintosh and Frank Lloyd Wright. The Art Deco style had been introduced in a famous Paris exhibition, the *"Exposition Internationale des Arts Décoratifs et Industriels Modernes"* of 1925, hence its name. It would be followed four years later by another famous exhibition at the Metropolitan Museum of Art, "The Architect and the Industrial Arts," which introduced the new vogue to New York. Wright's early work had, it was noted, the "refined geometrical formalism" found in much later Art Deco, and his Los Angeles design, Hollyhock House in particular, was almost the prototype for the California Deco style—more than a decade before the East had discovered it. Wright sent Mumford the tongue-in-cheek comment that "the New York boys" were suddenly being nice to him, which must mean they were no longer afraid of him, a very worrying development. And he subsequently commented to Haskell that the day might be saved for organic architecture after all.

This new flurry of interest was not confined to the East Coast. A few months later architects might be seen "snooping around" the houses he had built in Oak Park and taking copious notes, a lawyer in Racine, Wisconsin, reported. This was of a piece with another incident in which Wright took even greater pride. When the Illinois chapter of the American Institute of Architects decided to hold a banquet in his honor in late 1929, 105 people bought tickets (55 being the most they had ever had before). There had never been such a gathering, and so it looked as if the profession no longer had any ill feeling toward him, Wright told Lloyd.

He kept his own pen sharpened to a fine point. When he learned that the *Architectural Record* planned to publish a review of Hitchcock's latest book, *Modern Architecture*, in late 1929, he shot off a telegram to its editor asking for the right to review it. "Believe I can do it justice, at any rate only justice I am asking," he said. The barb was unmistakable; the editor diplomatically replied that the review had already been assigned. Meantime there was the matter of an article about Wright's office tower for the Bouwerie, which the editor planned to give prominent mention. Wright's doublesided approach: a flattering courtship of writers, editors and critics who favored his work and dogged pursuit of those who did not (in the hope of changing their minds) was the method he had developed for three decades. The value of manipulating the press was something he had learned from his father; those years of being pilloried in the papers had left an indelible scar. And when *Vanity Fair* published an article in December 1931 dismissing him as an "aging individualist," and calling Raymond Hood (then organizing the Chicago World's Fair, which had excluded Wright) the better architect, Wright thrashed around for a way to retaliate. He hit upon the idea of having the famous photographer Edward Steichen take his cause up with the magazine. "Don't you think this commits Crowninshield [the publisher] to a portrait by you and a come-back by me—?" he wrote. Then he thought better of it.

At a time when Wright was making such a valiant effort at a "come-back" and keeping his creditors placated ("Very well then," he told Martin, "I am a horse, —with a race to win in record time")— he had not yet settled on a phrase that successfully defined his own work and distinguished it from the rest. At times he called it "organic architecture"; at other times he appeared to speak of himself as a modernist, a term he would later drop and heatedly denounce. As for those exponents of the sleek, austere new steel-and-glass edifices, Le Corbusier, Mies van der Rohe, J. J. Oud, Walter Gropius and the like, Hitchcock had tried calling them the New Pioneers in his book *Modern Architecture*, and some other writers were using the term New Architecture, but both had their flaws. Alice Goldfarb Marquis, biographer of Alfred H. Barr, Jr., founder of the newly formed Museum of Modern Art in New York, states that Barr was the one who came up with the label that would take hold, the International Style. "His name was an echo of the fifteenth century's international style of painting, so called because artists in many European countries began to use oil paints, linear perspective, and secular subject matter as part of the High Renaissance." Philip Johnson later commented that he had taken on the work of publicizing the new style: "I was the drummer and screamer-arounder."

Philip Johnson, an early collector of modern art, an intellectual and a wealthy connoisseur, had studied classics at Harvard and had become fascinated by the new European modernists, as exemplified by work at the Bauhaus, after reading an essay on the subject by Hitchcock. He met Barr at Wellesley, where the latter was then teaching, and happened to remark that he was thinking of founding a museum of modern art. Barr invited him to join it and take charge of the department of architecture. The two men made overtures to Hitchcock, and all three were soon planning their first exhibition of modern architecture, to feature the International Style they fervently admired. (It opened at MOMA on February 10, 1932.)

As soon as he knew, through Mumford, that plans were in the works, Wright was ready to denounce the whole process. The fact that Hitchcock was involved was enough, but he also doubted whether Johnson, that youthful unknown, would be sufficiently respectful; and his fears were well founded since Johnson is the one credited with the quip that Wright was "America's greatest nineteenth century architect." Although he was soon invited to exhibit, Wright was still on his guard against this small group of propagandists relentlessly promoting a narrow cause, as he called them, but he allowed Johnson to persuade him against his better judgment. Having agreed to cooperate, he very characteristically decided to pull out at the eleventh hour, that is to say, a month before the show was set to open. He explained to Johnson that he did not object to being seen beside Le Corbusier and Mies van der Rohe, or even George Howe and William Lescaze, whom he respected and thought were "good men." What he did object to was the inclusion of Raymond Hood, that builder of mediocre skyscrapers, in the exhibition, and also Richard Neutra.

By 1931 Wright had become as disenchanted with Neutra as he had with Schindler (the one Wright thought had traded so unscrupulously on his reputation). Fortunately for Wright, Schindler's work had not met with favor from Hitchcock and Johnson, and despite his pleas to be included Schindler at least was not going to be shown on an equal footing with his mentor, just a few years after he had been a lowly assistant (in Wright's view). But Neutra had been more fortunate. In common with Schindler, he was now considered one of the leading practitioners of the International Style on the West Coast. That would be enough to make Wright mutinous, but, as fate would have it, he had been further antagonized by an unfortunate incident involving another exhibition that Schindler's wife, Pauline, had organized in Los Angeles the year before. Wright agreed to be included and sent material, only to find that the exhibition was being titled "Three Architects of International Renown"—or, as he later described it, "Frank Lloyd Wright middle, Neutra right, Schindler left." That happened in the spring of 1930; he immediately demanded that his work be withdrawn. As he explained it, "All novices, in the nature of the Cuckoo, have not hesitated to lay their eggs in my nest. . . ." It had been too big an affront to his pride, and the memory was green the following year when, it appeared, the same insult was about to be perpetrated all over again. He wrote to Johnson, "It seems to me I see too much at stake . . . to countenance a hand-picked group of men in various stages of eclecticism by riding around the country with them [a reference to the three-year tour that was planned] as though I approved of them and their work as modern when I distinctly do not only disapprove but positively condemn them. . . ."

Johnson was naturally horrified. He had gone to enormous pains to placate the prickly architect, and so had Hitchcock. Both men knew that they were skating on thin ice but were determined to have their old master; indeed, given Wright's prominence and his controversial status, they could hardly avoid including him. Two days later Johnson responded with an anguished telegram stating that they needed him and could not do without him. He had saved the day for the moment, at least. And it was a good thing that Wright would be included, Mumford told that architect a few days later. Hood's supporters "would probably have gone to the length of hinting, as that rascal did in the *Vanity Fair* article, that you had nothing to show." Despite Mumford's fervent hope that Wright would be glad he had been included, the architect could not have been very happy with the final outcome since the catalogue, as written by Alfred Barr, echoed Hitchcock's dictum that he was forerunner of a movement that younger men had now brought to a triumphant fulfillment. Wright's importance, in other words, was not on his own terms, for what he had thought and accomplished for forty years, but only in the context of a movement that he detested and believed wholly opposed to his central philosophy. The sop thrown to his pride, that he was "the embodiment of the romantic principle of individualism," whose work remained "a challenge to the classical austerity of the style of his best younger contemporaries," would not have given him much comfort.

The damage had been done. The Museum of Modern Art's assessment of Wright became the one generally accepted by the proselytizers of the International Style, which did not mean that Wright ever accepted his subordinate status or ever stopped denouncing it and them. His relationship with the museum remained basically antagonistic, despite that institution's attempts to make amends with subsequent exhibitions. As late as 1953, Wright was charging that MOMA had made "a sinister attempt to betray American Organic Architecture." As for the young Philip Johnson, who would go on to become a famous architect himself, Wright's attitude veered between a willingness to let bygones be bygones and a mischievous impulse to get even with him for the exhibition of 1932. Years later, referring to the all-glass house Johnson built for himself in New Canaan, Connecticut, just after World War II, and upon meeting Johnson again, Wright joked, "Ah yes! Philip Johnson! You're the man who builds those little houses and then leaves them out in the rain." It became a famous anecdote, as well as a demonstration of Wright's adroit ability to make good use of a quip that, all those years before, had been used against *him*. As for the International Style itself, no words could express his contempt for this "evil crusade," this manifestation of "totalitarianism. . . ." As the 1930s began, there was something admirable and even courageous about Wright's loyalty to those ideals that stood for sanity and humaneness in an increasingly uncertain world, and something wonderful about the fact that his imaginative gifts were still intact—ageless, almost. He was, as Harold Nicolson observed with great prescience of Churchill in 1931, a man who led forlorn hopes. There was every likelihood that when architecture became disenchanted with the new movement, as he knew it must, he would once again be accepted on his own terms and "summoned to leadership."

16

Taliesin

No colors fade, no leaves decay,
No fires char that beauty nor ever
Can until the world is changed
And ended.
    "The Phoenix"
    Poems from the Old English

The belief of the International Style's exponents that Wright, at the age of sixty-five, should be relegated to the background, while profoundly mistaken, was understandable given the circumstances. It was Wright's bad luck that two of his most brilliant designs, for St. Mark's-in-the-Bouwerie and San Marcos-in-the-Desert, would never be built. True, Wright had exhibited, along with his model for St. Mark's, another promising idea, for a modernistic-looking house on a western mesa, although this, too, would not be built. He had finished the design for another ambitious and unrealized project, a series of Chicago apartment towers. He did show at the Museum of Modern Art one house design that would become a reality, the Malcolm Willey house in Minneapolis, which, for all its scaled-down size and traditional materials (brick and wood), represented several important breakthroughs in terms of design that Wright would incorporate into his later houses: the first use of a kitchen work space that was part of the living room, the first use of a carport, the first use of radiant heating in the floors and the first use of a balcony parapet of lapped siding. But the most exciting works were his designs for St. Mark's and San Marcos. Had these been under construction when the MOMA exhibition opened, the tone might have been distinctly more respectful and Wright's "come-back" an accomplished fact.

As it was, even admirers like Harold Sterner, a New York City architect, spoke in elegiac terms about him some years afterward. "In Europe the names of Sullivan and Wright are famous and respected, but both of these men were given relatively few opportunities to practice their genius, and now Sullivan is long since dead and Frank Lloyd Wright approaching the end of his career," he observed. It did not help that Wright had steadfastly refused to join the professional organization of his peers, the American Institute of Architects. For whatever reasons, he dismissed it as a political body and, as a writer explained, "attacked their integrity, antagonized their officers, and defied their right to set fees, write codes of ethics and influence the centers of finance, government and education." He liked to quip that the name should have been the "American Institute of Appearances," and called its members "old gentlemen afraid to go out without their rubbers." These quips sound like vintage Wright and not particularly cutting ones at that, but his slights had the effect of maintaining the gulf between himself and other professionals and of adding further weight to the idea of himself as a gifted maverick, an iconoclast. At least one wag in Chicago called him "Frank Lloyd Wrong," and the nickname stuck. These kinds of professional gibes would have further isolated him in his rural kingdom at a time when he was frantic for any help he could get. As it was, he faced the depression years with no money, no prospects (apart from the Willey house), a staff of seven or eight draftsmen, a farm to run, a wife, a stepdaughter and a little girl.

Like his sister Maginel's, Wright's hair went gray at an early stage, so for a long time he looked every one of his years, and he eventually needed glasses, although he is seldom photographed wearing them. But his physical and creative energies had scarcely diminished. Two years before he died, when he was examined by a specialist in geriatrics, he was pronounced in such good health that he would live for another twenty years. (He was then eighty-nine.) He said he would settle for three more, and then added irritably, "I wish people wouldn't remind me of my age." That was characteristic. Mary Matthews, wife of a British architect who studied with Wright, recalled conducting a group of visitors around Taliesin. During the tour one guest exclaimed that he thought Wright was dead. She retold the anecdote to the architect, thinking it would give him a laugh, and was sent in disgrace to Mrs. Wright's room to be instructed about the taboo subject of death, because "he was so afraid of it."

His Welsh family's straitlaced horror of tobacco—one of his grandmother's regrets being, apparently, that she never persuaded "Ein Tad" to give up his pipe—ensured that Wright would similarly regard smoking as a moral flaw and become more vehement on the subject as he aged. Like the Lloyd Joneses, he regarded alcohol with disgust, although, in that respect, he mellowed slightly. He had established a vineyard, and Olgivanna succeeded in arguing that if they were going to grow grapes, they should make wine. After that he would partake occasionally, and he developed a taste for whiskey after Alexander Woollcott brought him a bottle of Bushmill's Old Irish. Herbert Fritz recalled seeing him hold up a bottle with the words "Boys, you have your youth and I have this." But his conversion hardly amounted to capitulation; he might have a small glass once or twice a week. Plenty of exercise, afternoon naps and a lifetime spent eating homegrown food had sustained his health so that his bearing, mien, attitudes and robust appetite for life were those of a much younger man.

He was without prospects, and the depression had hammered the final nail in the coffin of his corporation. Although "Uncle" Ben Page clung to his overseer's right to supervise Wright's spending, before long there was no more money to worry about, and that paragon of virtue, the long-suffering Darwin Martin, was as poor as everyone else. Martin wrote to say that he had seen Wright's autobiography for sale in the bookshops but, alas, could not afford to buy a copy. He continued, "I have not dared to ask you how affairs are coming on with you, but I dare now, because I am immune to any tale of woe. . . ." Wright replied it was hard to believe that the financially astute DDM could be down to carfare and lunch money. For Wright's part, his pockets were full of holes from carrying around the small change for "vegetables, meat, laundry, petty office supplies, chicken feed, wood, butter, milk, eggs, gasoline, carbide, kerosene, oil, petty repairs to cars and engine, license plates, pump repairs, etc. etc." He apologized for not having written, that spring of 1932: "What use writing when struggling to survive? Like a drowning man taking time for a 'hulloa' to a friend on the bank." He also used the curious

metaphor of hanging. His book and other work had netted him about
$14,000 over the past two years, but even so he had been hit again.
He wrote, "The trap fell—and no hood to pull over my eyes. So I've
been kicking at the end of the rope—gurgling and choking some—
but my hands were free and I could hang on. . . ."

The calamity to which he referred was, no doubt, the very real
threat that Taliesin would be sold again for unpaid insurance, mortgage
and back taxes. For two years he had managed to stave off disaster at
the eleventh hour, most recently by a last-minute appeal to his brother-
in-law, Andrew Porter, for $500. But, as a general rule, the mortgage
of time, as he wrote, was always threatening to foreclose on human
fallibility. His wonderful idea of founding a school for the applied
arts had fallen flat, despite his clever use of the forum of his Princeton
lectures to promote his concept. At that point he should have given
up, but the Wrights were desperate. Sometime in 1931 it occurred
to the Wrights that if they could attract twenty or thirty students at
a tuition of $650 a year, a steady source of income would be provided
for Taliesin, and his extra income as a writer and lecturer would make
up the difference. Even after they had written and sent out a circular
letter in the summer of 1932 they still hoped to get a prominent
figure to run their school. Wijdeveld had inspected the premises but
had not yet definitely declined, and when he did, Wright turned
hopefully to Mumford. (He declined.) Jens Jensen, the distinguished
landscape artist, leader of the movement to use native materials in
landscaping, who had numbered the two Henry Fords, Sr. and Jr.,
among his clients, as well as Rockefeller, had been courted and had
given liberal advice ("You cannot get away from yourself") but no
commitment to actually teach. The brilliant woman artist, Georgia
O'Keeffe, was then approached, and even Alexander Woollcott; both
demurred.

No one wanted to be ensnared in what must have seemed like one
more of Wright's foolhardy schemes, particularly since, at some point
in the discussion, he would have made it charmingly clear that he had
no money. More to the point, perhaps, Wright's concept of what was
basically an arts-and-crafts workshop was being launched at a moment
when the concept of the architect was changing, in common with a
general shift toward professionalism, from the idea of master builder
and toward the theoretical and scholarly. His insistence upon the
importance of direct experience and an apprenticeship to the master
must have seemed almost an anachronism. Furthermore, he was con-

tinuing to place what must have seemed an old-fashioned emphasis upon beauty and creativity just as many were jettisoning such theories in favor of the idea of architecture as an activity that should be directed toward the pressing social and economic problems of the age. Wright's loud praises for the virtues of unpaid work, for early breakfasts, hand labor and long evenings in the drafting room must have sounded far too bracing to contemporary tastes, and later bulletins from the front were not reassuring: "Taliesin is probably preaching . . . the old gospel of hard-work: adding tired to tired. . . ." When he first heard about the forming of the Fellowship, Jenkin Lloyd Jones, Richard's son, quipped, "Frank has invented slave labor."

It should be noted that Taliesin's later emphasis upon spiritual development, or what might be called group therapy on the Gurdjieff model, was absent from the first manifesto, which still echoed the goals he had outlined for the revived Hillside Home School. He would take on the responsibility of instructing his students in the use of machinery, for furniture, textiles, metalwork and so on, and the actual products, including architectural models, would then be sent around on traveling exhibitions. He envisioned a flourishing cottage industry and still clung to the idea that industry would eventually be brought in to sponsor the work. And, even at that early stage, he was thinking on an even grander scale, about the formation of an Arcadian community, his future "Broadacre City," an idea that would come to fruition three years later. As usual, Wright was full of expansive and optimistic goals for the future. There was just one hitch. If he could not get Wijdeveld, Mumford, Jensen or Woollcott, who would run the school?

Olgivanna Wright was in poor health as 1932 began. She felt more and more tired, so exhausted that she could no longer climb up their hill. She went to Chicago for X-rays, and the doctor discovered several tubercular spots on her left lung and ordered her to gain weight. So she went on a regime of two quarts of milk a day, along with five raw eggs, raw cabbage and orange juice, and gained eight pounds in a month. Her energy returned, and that was good news because the Fellowship was due to begin in October and she was in charge. She was touring the countryside asking for donations of plates, cooking equipment and spare beds, anything she could find. Her husband had charmed twenty local workmen into making repairs at Hillside, with the promise of a share in tuition fees once the students arrived. Getting the necessary supplies was a little harder. In years to come Wright would boast that he had managed to circumvent the suspicious local merchants by ordering directly from wholesalers. The school's kitchen had been restored, as had the dining room, and the workmen had been given sleeping quarters when Olgivanna Wright described their progress in a letter to Mrs. Martin in the summer of 1932. As for the enrollment, they had a number of students already, including five Vassar graduates. "There was no stopping to mourn," Wright wrote. "What had been beautiful at Taliesin should live as a grateful memory . . . and, come who might to share Taliesin, they would help in that spirit. I believed it. . . ."

Herbert Fritz, the architect son of the man who survived the 1914 Taliesin fire, remembers going to Taliesin when he was about seven and Olgivanna Wright and daughter Svetlana had just come to live there: "I remember the sunny day, the stone walls, the beautiful spreading roofs, the hollyhocks and delphiniums. . . ." At the time of the murder-fire, his father had been working there as a draftsman and had had gymnastic training. This was what saved him because the window he crashed through was a story and a half above the ground. Even so, Fritz recalled, he had broken an arm. He said, "My father never talked about what he saw happening. I think he had emotional problems, because he would just stand and stare off into space." His grandfather Alfred Larson had been a farmer-mason from Norway and had built most of Taliesin. Since his father's time, aunts, uncles, sisters, nieces, nephews and brothers-in-law had worked there; Aunts Emma and Mabel, Alfred's daughters, would become the cooks for the Fellowship. Fritz has another memory of Wright's riding horseback through the meadows and over the winding country roads. "Those were, in those days, scarcely wide enough for two buggies to pass, and one could reach up or down . . . and pick wild asters, ragged gypsy, brown-eyed susans, or wild plums from the branches of the thickets." Fritz had grown up with horses, and after his sister Frances had struck up a friendship with Svetlana, they visited Taliesin often, and he made himself useful by catching, saddling and harnessing the horses. Svetlana rode a spirited white horse, Beauty, which they talk about still. Beauty would occasionally allow herself to be used as a packhorse, so they took her on a picnic. Mr. and Mrs. Wright and the rest of them hiked past Phoebe Point and up into the hills above the river. The weather was perfect, the scene Arcadian. Wright sat down with his back against a tree and said, "Let us loaf and invite the soul."

Fritz had found some elegant old carriages in the Hillside barn: a brougham, a victoria, and a wagonette that had been used to bring the Hillside students from the train in Spring Green. So he polished up the victoria and mended the cushions, hitched up Curly and Dick, the farming team, and he and the Wrights drove over to Cousin Dick's. That meant passing through the Rieder farmyard to get to the main road. Farmer Rieder had a barnyard on one side of what is now the present driveway and a pigpen on the other. Wright said he did not enjoy driving past the pigpen and would buy that farm one day.

Taliesin was their playground, and Fritz, who loved the farm life, climbed trees, rowed boats and went swimming, as well as mowing, raking or pitching hay and cultivating corn. Not only did he love horses, but he was just as bedazzled by fine automobiles as Mr. Wright was. There was one Cord Phaeton in particular, a masterpiece of design, that was Wright's pride and joy. When the driveway had dissolved into liquid mud, the beautiful Cord would sink in up to its axles and Fritz and the other boys would get out the Caterpillar tractor from down near the dam and pull the Cord out of the mud. It seemed natural, once he became a high school sophomore, that he should work at Taliesin during the summer vacation. He and Frances also spent winter vacations at Taliesin, and he has an enduring memory of the living room, which seemed to radiate a light of its own, ". . . with the warm waxed cypress floor, the fire in the golden limestone fireplace, the view of the Wisconsin River and the hills beyond. . . ." There was always the faint smell of pearly everlasting or Indian tobacco and another aroma, indefinable but peculiar to Taliesin. They would play records on the Victrola—Wagner, Dvořák and Spanish songs sung by Tito Schipa, a great favorite of Mr. Wright's—and examine his collection of musical instruments: a lute, a harpsichord, a balalaika and some Dushkin recorders. His eye was uncanny. He had bought an exquisite Storioni violin for Svetlana and would confound the experts with his knowledge of the size and proportion of a violin. On another occasion, Fritz remembered seeing him study the proportions of their two Lincoln Continentals and correctly conclude that one was two inches higher than the other. Wright also said he could identify the work of every mason who had ever built a wall at Taliesin, although, since the same stone had been used, it was impossible for an untutored eye to see the difference.

That Christmas week ended with a New Year's party for Svetlana and her friends, and Fritz asked her mother to dance. Mrs. Wright answered, "No thank you. I only dance with Mr. Wright." As for her husband, he spent hours in the drafting room while the day slipped away. One evening Mrs. Wright took him to task, and he replied, "Well, who am I doing it for?" They played checkers and charades and games like "Coffee Pot" and "Ghosts." A few years after that, one of their favorite games became "Murder." Fritz and his sister had invited a group of apprentices, along with Iovanna, to their house and the game was in full swing that evening when Mrs. Wright arrived to get Iovanna. Just as she drove into their yard, all the lights went out and someone yelled "Murder!" It was a long time before Mrs. Wright could laugh about that.

Herbert Fritz was, in other words, growing up at Taliesin just as the Fellowship was being organized, and sharing quarters with the pioneers, students like Rudolph Mock from Switzerland, and Wright's Danish secretary, Karl Jensen, who could not pronounce his r's and would say things like "wed stwing" and "womb." Wright's chief draftsman at that time was Henry Klumb, a native of Cologne who had joined him early in 1929 and worked on San Marcos, then supervised a traveling exhibition that went to Amsterdam, Berlin, Stuttgart, Antwerp and Brussels, the first such review of Wright's work in Europe since 1909. Fritz watched the old laundry building at Hillside, made of green wood shingle, and the least vandalized, being transformed into a kitchen and dining room for the workmen. Pretty soon plowing corn lost its appeal, and he was given permission to dig foundation ditches. Mr. Wright always said yes.

On a bright sunny morning in that summer of 1932, a gangling (six-foot-four) twenty-year-old college student who had been studying engineering in Evansville, Indiana, and at the Massachusetts Institute of Technology in Cambridge wandered into The Valley, having heard that Frank Lloyd Wright planned to open a school. His parents had driven him as far as Madison in the belief that he was about to enter the University of Wisconsin, but William Wesley Peters had other plans. He took the bus to Spring Green and walked the three and a half miles to Taliesin. Approaching the estate he saw a great many No Trespassing signs, so he went over to a farmhouse (one he would eventually own) to ask directions. He found the farmer sitting on the front porch in his underwear. "Oh, you mean the bungalow?" He should give the signs no mind, and just walk in. Peters was following this advice when he met up with Karl Jensen, who told him to return that afternoon. So, to fill the time, with the energy of a superb constitution, he ambled off for a ten-mile walk. (His physical prowess would become legendary; he said, modestly, "In those days when I pushed a piece of machinery I expected it to *move*.") Returning later in the day, he was finally ushered in to meet the architect. "I had thought he was tall and he wasn't, but he dominated the room. I can't explain what happened but something did. I felt my whole life would be changed." They discussed terms. Peters, son of a wealthy Indiana newspaper publisher, did not balk at the cost of tuition. The architect added engagingly that he needed seven hundred dollars right away to pay a road gang. Peters handed over a year's tuition in cash and moved right in.

Despite Wright's well-deserved reputation for never paying anyone "except under the greatest duress," as Jack Howe put it, he had attracted some fine craftsmen because he was offering room and board and the promise of cash at a time of severe unemployment. There was Ole Anderson, a Norwegian carpenter; Bill Schwanke, a master carpenter from Spring Green; Charlie Curtis, a master mason from Mineral Point; Manuel Sandoval, a superb cabinetmaker from Nicaragua; and many others. They were quarrying rock to rebuild Hillside, and lime for the mortar was being burned at Will Rogers's farm some miles to the south. Men would take turns staying there all night to keep the kiln fires burning. Sand was hauled from the river, and a sawmill had been set up to cut the oak beams for a new, enlarged drafting room at Hillside. This would replace the architectural studio adjoining the main house, connected to it by an entrance loggia, which was now too small. (The new room would not finally open until 1942.) Peters—always called "Wes" because Wright already had too many "Bills" about the place—became a familiar figure, digging ditches, hauling buckets, fitting pipes and driving trucks, in his wrinkled overalls and with the hair over his eyes. He was given immediate responsibility for one of the major chores, i.e., providing wood for the three steam boilers, in a climate where it could get as cold as minus thirty or minus forty degrees Fahrenheit, in a desperate attempt to keep a house warm that was, despite its beauty, as flimsy as a stage set, with drafty floors, no storm windows and no insulation. In years to come Herb Fritz would be given the job of stoking the boiler underneath the Taliesin living room. His second day on the job he went to see a film and let the fire go out. He wrote, "I have never received such a lecture [from Mrs. Wright] before or since. I can't remember what she said, but I do know . . . no drill sergeant in the marines could have been more effective."

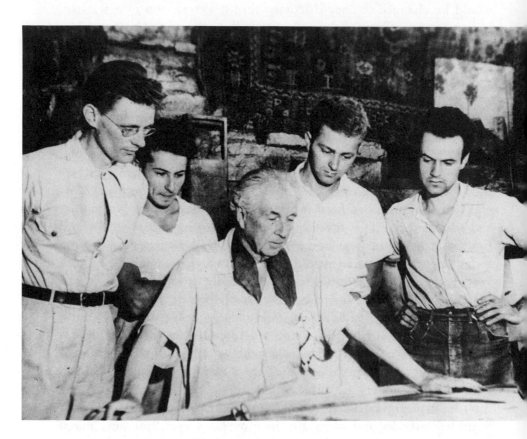

A 1932 photograph of members of the Taliesin Fellowship. From left: Eu-
gene Masselink, Benny Dombar, Frank Lloyd Wright, Edgar Tafel and
John H. Howe

Wright went out every day on a search for building lumber and wood for the fires, "often driving in an open car and wearing a magnificent black polar bear car-coat," Jack Howe recalled. Peters was in the forest felling oaks and putting them through a steam-driven saw. He said, "One of the heaviest jobs I ever had was carrying away those slabs of wood. I went from 190 pounds to 178, but it was all muscle." Very soon after Peters's arrival, Mendel Glickman joined the Fellowship as a teacher in structural engineering, having just returned from Stalingrad, where he had been chief American engineer at a tractor plant. He and Peters became fast friends, and they would devise ingenious strategies for hauling the wood across a local farmer's fields, in spite of his objections that the trucks made tracks in his soil. That winter of 1932, Svetlana, who was just fifteen, started riding along with Wes in the truck. She was a willing worker and could heave stones with the best of them. That was the winter they fell in love.

Peters was famous for his practical jokes. Anyone who dared lie too long in bed ran the risk of being catapulted out of it by Wes with a bucket of water. He had the kind of humor, Howe recalled, that absolutely mystified Olgivanna. Wright thought he was hugely funny and egged him on. There was the time that Wes and Edgar Tafel, another early apprentice, led Iovanna's pony up the steep stairway to Jack Howe's bedroom and then hid in the room next door waiting for him to return. Then there was the time Karl had a big party for several girls in his room. Once it was in full swing, with the drinks handed around and the fire blazing, Wes and Edgar crawled up on the roof and put a board across the chimney.

Another of the major outdoor projects that first year of the Fellowship was working on the dam below Taliesin. It had been neglected for years, and Wright had brought in a power shovel to dig out the accumulated silt washed down from neighboring fields, and Blaine Drake and Cary Caraway, two new recruits, hauled the dirt back to the fields in dump trucks. A new concrete wall was poured, a new spillway built, and revisions were made to the masonry. Wright loved that kind of work and would supervise for hours. Then he installed a new turbine at the dam, which provided electricity for Taliesin, and each night one of the students would go down the steep path through the woods to turn it off. "Repairing this one time, Wes dropped a pipe wrench into the water; he told that while recovering it a snapping turtle struck at the wrench and actually dented it," Fritz wrote. "I know Wes believed that, but I never could." Another urgent project was replacing the woven-wire fences with electric ones, because Mr. Wright was always trying to do away with such visual barriers. There was, naturally, far more work to be done on the property than in the drafting room in those first years, and so the order of importance for the articles an apprentice was required to bring with him or her was a saw, a hammer, a pocket rule, T square and triangle. Similarly, enthusiastic youngsters who knew nothing about architecture were to be preferred—university training being considered a distinct drawback—and the younger the better. Young women were also accepted, reluctantly, but the main objective was to gather together an ambitious group of young men he called "sparks" willing, as Wright wrote, to get their hands dirty with the mud from which the bricks are made. He wanted a year's commitment from everyone but made some exceptions to that rule. If the applicant had written to say that he had been inspired by Mr. Wright's autobiography (no one ever called him Frank, not even Wes Peters, and when a few old farmers did, the Fellowship members bristled), that was an even better way to introduce oneself. A number of young idealists, fired with enthusiasm, would trudge up to his door with backpacks and their love of his books as their sole introduction. Edgar Kaufmann, Jr., another early apprentice, wrote, "I had no inkling of the character of his art, and his story flowed into my mind like the first trickle of irrigation in a desert land."

The enormous work of organizing the estate fell, from the first, on Olgivanna Wright. She considered herself co-founder of the Fellowship and was, by general agreement, the secret of its success: "He would have lost his patience and sent us home after the third week," Howe said. She had charge of all the meals, and she was most particular about the food, which had to be well cooked and substantial. She made up the lists of activities to which all were assigned by rote: firing the boilers, cleaning the chicken house, scouring the pots, hoeing the fields, weeding, digging, carting, hauling, polishing, sweeping. It was hard physical labor. Her rugged experiences with Gurdjieff at Fontainebleau would stand her in good stead; she had mastered all kinds of practical tasks and did them well. She was the one who sent an apprentice away in disgrace; the Wrights were at their most unyielding about transgressions of sexual mores, something they might have been expected to be understanding about. But although she hired and fired with a free hand (and was expected to lecture when lecturing was called for), hers was not the court of last resort. On one occasion, a young offender was told to pack up and leave and, after making his farewells to Wright, was given a last-minute reprieve. Wright's explanation for that was, "Something in his smile reminded me of Louis Sullivan and I could not let him go." The day was planned with great care so that everyone was busy, from the time he or she awoke (Wright himself was an early riser, up at four-thirty or five at the latest) until the generator was turned off at ten in the evening. During the winter months, chorus rehearsal took place immediately after breakfast, even when it was still dark. In spring, everyone planted the garden, then went on to the drafting room, or put in some of the thousands of trees Wright was planting on the estate, or milked the cows, or arranged their rooms, rebuilding the interiors to their own design (which then had to be approved). Apprentices soon mastered one of the unwritten codes of Taliesin, which was to seem to be doing whatever Mr. Wright wanted to do next, preferably just before he did it. If he went to hoe, one should be hoeing; if he was going to work on the dam, one rushed there, and he had only to make steps for the drafting room for a crowd to appear in short order. Howe, who became chief draftsman, said, "Mr. Wright loved to show off. When he'd sit at the drafting table it was a production and the more people around him the better he liked it." This became fairly annoying to Howe in later years because "I knew how much work there was to get out. He was making a show of something that required solitude and concentration."

But, in the early days, one forgave a great deal because they were all doing it together, and the way to relax was not to "rest" but to switch activities, the way he did. Because he loved variety, there were plenty of parties, including picnic excursions every Saturday, usually to one of the many limestone outcroppings that crowned the hills, a foreign film every weekend, and services on Sunday mornings in the old Lloyd Jones's Unity Chapel. (Wright had rewritten the words of Bach's "Jesu Joy of Man's Desiring" to read "Joy in Work is Man's Desiring," and it became the Fellowship hymn.) There were Halloween parties and birthday parties and boat trips and sleigh rides and charades; Wright was always ready for fun. He invented a game in which someone left the room and returned as another personality, and the other players had a limited time in which to guess who was being imitated. When it was his turn, he came back and started moving the furniture around. That was too easy, so they sent him out again; he returned with undulating hips, a leer and "Come up and see me sometime." In fact, he was so insistent on their not falling into a rut that he kept changing the time of the main midday meal, which caused havoc. Sunday evenings were great occasions, when everyone dressed formally, a stylish dinner was served on carefully decorated tables, and the Wrights sat on a dais like royalty, accompanied by Svetlana and Iovanna, for the entertainment afterward. In later years Iovanna performed on the harp; in the early days the musicians were Herbert Fritz on the cello, Svetlana on the violin, Jim Thompson on the recorder and Blaine Drake on the viola. Wright liked to call them the "Farmer-Labor Quartet." Believing that no one could ever have too much good music, Wright positioned speakers at strategic locations in the house, studio, garden and all over the countryside so that the joys of Bach, Beethoven, Brahms and Schubert might not be denied his students, wherever they were. Howe said, "There were amplifiers on the hill garden right next to my room. You couldn't get away from Beethoven and it's a wonder I can still listen to it."

The "sparks" were kept continually occupied for a reason: many were still minors, and Wright wanted them closely supervised. Young single women were chaperoned, at least in the early days. He did not want them wandering because they might make the wrong impression on Spring Green and vice versa. Isabelle Doyle, who grew up there, explained that the town was half Catholic and half Lutheran and divided between those who disapproved of Mr. Wright's personal peccadilloes and those to whom he still owed money. "They knew too much and did not appreciate his great gifts," she said. Olgivanna Wright believed, in the 1930s, that people crossed the road to avoid her. So, for whatever reasons, the Wrights were unyielding if any of their charges broke this rule, and their wrath was not limited to minors. Elizabeth Wright Ingraham, John's daughter, recalled visiting Taliesin with her parents when Aunt Maginel was there. They all heard a wonderful concert at Taliesin, and then trooped off to a local bar. Next morning they were summoned to Wright's studio to explain themselves. How could they possibly go off to a bar? Maginel told her brother they would go anywhere they "damn pleased." Mrs. Ingraham's comment was, "He had to have total control."

In those early days, to be at Mr. Wright's elbow was to be in the most privileged position, but those who served in the kitchen regularly also had a certain insider status. Larry Lemmon, a practicing landscape architect with several years' experience, found himself out of work in 1937, with a wife and baby girl to support, and hit upon the idea of their applying for jobs as cooks at Taliesin. His brother thought he was making a great mistake. "I was going out there to waste my life with a crazy man," but Lemmon was optimistic and his application was accepted. The Lemmons arrived in East Coast clothes—he was wearing a suit and hat—and found girls in shorts and dirndl skirts and boys in overalls and wearing long hair, all very friendly and very much at home. The job was remarkably pleasant, even though kitchen facilities were primitive (an old wood-fired stove that also heated water), because there was plenty of help for the tedious work of preparing vegetables and considerable leeway for imaginative preparation of food. His whole-wheat bread made a great hit. Mrs. Wright would say, "Your bread is always so good because you have the strength to knead it." He always kept a pot of yogurt simmering, used plenty of paprika, and took the trouble to learn the special Russian dishes that Mrs. Wright liked: borscht and shish kebab. As for the menus, one day there would be steak and the next only cabbage, and Wright would start talking about new ways to cook radishes.

Although in theory all work was rotated, to do one job well was a kind of guarantee that this was the one you would end up with. "I never looked at the lists because I knew what I was supposed to do and it was always the same," Fritz said with resignation. He became housekeeper for the Wrights, which meant making beds, building fires, waxing, dusting, tidying, vacuuming and arranging the floral decorations. They were both exacting to work for. He recalled that one time when they were camping out in Arizona, and had planned a special dinner, he set out white napkins instead of colored ones and incurred Wright's wrath: "Can't you see the tables need color?" One of Wright's biographers, Grant Manson, who was a guest in those days, learned that family and guest quarters were privileged accommodations, rather like first class on a ship, and off limits to everyone else, although he added dryly that the "roofs leaked equally upon all, and the facilities throughout were iffy. It was mere guesswork as to what, if anything, would come forth out of faucets labeled 'hot' and 'cold.' . . . ." A separate, well-trained group of students served these quarters, and one of them appeared at Manson's door each morning with a breakfast tray of ambrosial buckwheat pancakes cooked in the family's own kitchen. This is not to say that meals for the rest of the Fellowship were inferior. Herb Fritz's Aunts Emma and Mabel were in charge of the two kitchens at Hillside and Taliesin, and were engaged in a friendly rivalry to see who could cook the best meals.

Both had their advocates, but only Wes Peters could polish off both meals at a single sitting, that is, until Wright found out about it. In those days Wes's appetite was as celebrated as his strength. Taliesin's telephone system was always rudimentary, and at that time Wright had a party line (which meant that all his farmer neighbors knew everything that was going on), served by Esther, the town's switchboard operator. Her office was located on a strategic corner, just above the drugstore, and so when Peters could not be found, someone would ask Esther if she had seen him and she would invariably reply, "Oh yes, he just went in to Pope's Cafe for some of their banana cream pie."

That an intense loyalty and camaraderie should spring up in this motley band of people is a tribute to the Wrights' joint ability to make each member feel a part of the group. A new arrival, as Elizabeth Kassler found out, would be shown to his or her modest quarters, handed a paint brush and smilingly urged to go to work. Professor Lilien, exiled from Poland, called it her second home. Jack Howe said it was his substitute family. Kay Rattenbury began to think of herself as almost a daughter. Wesley Peters actually did become a son-in-law, after marrying Svetlana, whom Wright adopted. Edgar Tafel, another of the founding group of apprentices, signed himself, "Your adopted son." There was, of course, the comradeship in adversity that they shared as they wrestled with the challenge of turning trees into lumber or learning how to make cabinets, shelves, trim, doors and windows from scratch for, as Tafel wrote, workmen came and went, and they had to learn fast. They also had to become instant farmers. Once, when Wright told an apprentice to "slaughter a pig," he, not being a farm boy, went to his room to get his gun. Stopped toilets remained unusable until they fixed them. Tractors remained broken until their mechanisms had been mastered. It was one long, intense, backbreaking struggle to become self-sufficient, and it united them, although there were the inevitable accidents. Tafel wrote, "Apprentices were forever falling off horses, out of trees, down steps, off tractors . . . cutting themselves on saws, hammering their fingers. . . ." But miraculously, there were no severe injuries. And for the inevitable hangover, Wright would march them off to his bathroom and force a tablespoon of castor oil down their reluctant throats.

It was communal living at its most idealistic, at a moment when the socialist system looked like the solution to the evils of capitalism, and the exploitation of labor, a new opportunity to rebuild the world along more equitable lines, which was not to say that this particular experiment, taking place in a setting of great natural beauty, was entirely equitable. Taliesin was more like a tiny principality presided over by a patriarch, or benevolent monarch, who had given each newcomer a share in his life and called them his boys and girls, just as the Aunts did at Hillside. Indeed, many of his own children would come to resent the special place held in their father's affections by these children of his imagination. There are many stories about his kindly manner, his patience in teaching, his willingness to praise and ability to criticize constructively, and it must be added that, at least in the early days, he worked beside them. Jack Howe said that one of the lessons he learned was the value of loving the work. "Mr. Wright played at working. He didn't do anything he didn't enjoy, but he enjoyed most everything. I remember that he and I waxed the wood floors on Saturday mornings. I put polish on the floor and he pushed the lead weights; it is one of my fondest memories of him." And when the inevitable mistakes were made Wright had a way of turning them into assets. Larry Lemmon recalled that his daughter, Ruthie, then just a toddler, had once found a bucket of red paint and had done her own fingerpainting all over a new redwood balustrade. Lemmon was vainly trying to clean it off with steel wool when Wright came along. "Don't touch it!" he was told. Ever afterward, Wright would point out the impromptu mural on the balustrade with a smile, calling it "the work of my youngest apprentice." As Wright explained it, "our hopeless ship" was finally coming to port, and he could not have been happier. Herbert Fritz said, "After being at Taliesin, you never accept reality again. It's so perfect. You don't ever think the world is what it should be."

They were unhesitatingly and ardently his—part of his truth, against the whole world if need be—and at a surprisingly early stage. That first autumn the loyalty of the Fellowship was put to the test almost at once. A running battle was in progress between Wright, who had promised his workmen the balance of their wages once the buildings were complete and occupied, and those who wanted to leave and be paid. The law was on their side, since it stated that deferred wage payments were illegal; in addition, many of them wanted to quit since, as unemployed workers, they could now get far more on "relief" than from their impecunious employer. He argued that they had not yet fulfilled their contracts, since the buildings were unfinished. But in any event he had no money, and they probably knew it. His delaying tactics, aided and abetted by the nimble-minded Jensen, were ingenious, but a few men would not be put off much longer. One, named Jones, attacked him late one afternoon in his studio. Jones's hands were at his throat; Henry Klumb, who was also in the room, jumped up and yelled so loudly that Jones was scared off.

Everywhere one looked there were half-completed projects, but that was consistent with the Taliesin that Antonin Raymond had found almost twenty years before, in a continual state of flux, half of it being built and the other half falling down. Herb Fritz wrote, "One Saturday evening Eloise [his wife] and I returned from Madison to find that a large part of Hillside had burned down—the theatre and the wing between it and the living room. Mr. Wright had lit a brush pile near the building. I thought he might be devastated by the loss, so I went to see him soon after. . . . He said, 'I thought you knew me better than that. I always wanted to remodel the theatre and that wing of the building. But thanks for your concern." As the British architect Peter Matthews, a later apprentice, said, "The important point to grasp about Wright is that nothing was ever finished. It was the ideas that interested him; the actual building was secondary." Jack and Lu Howe soon learned, as so many others had before them, that the price of being part of Wright's inner circle was that one could not avoid being swept up in a maelstrom of activity, of last-minute deadlines, eleventh-hour crises and the constant need to escape from another looming catastrophe. Wright was the eye of calm in the center of this storm, the only one who never felt rushed, although, as they well knew, the crises were of his making.

Once commissions started coming in, Wright would sometimes offer his students practice in designing for a particular site. They would be given a topographical map and property survey and told to go to work. Herb Fritz remembered working on a design for the John C. Pew residence, subsequently built in Shorewood Hills, Wisconsin, on a sharply descending hillside with a view over Lake Mendota. The apprentices finished their designs and then gathered for a critique. Each apprentice allowed for setback requirements and had made fairly conventional designs. They were all found to be inadequate by the master, who produced his own version a few days later. He had, Fritz wrote, noticed a small ravine on the property and had designed the house as a bridge over it and cantilevered into the woods, close to the water's edge. This, he told them, was a lesson in taking advantage of a site's natural features, something they had ignored. Twice a year, at Christmas and on his birthday, each apprentice was expected to produce a design to be included in boxes that were built for the occasion, each one crafted with originality, with a unique hinge, or some kind of clever opening and closing device. These were important occasions, Howe noted, because students could seldom work on their own projects; as a rule, they were put to work on Wright's projects. Wright would review each work and make a constructive comment, as was his habit, giving each student a kindly pat on the back. He was always helpful, and yet there seemed to be an invisible hurdle that the beginner could not cross because, as one apprentice later observed, "If your designs were too much like those of Wright's, they were considered imitative, but if too different, people said, 'He didn't get it.' " As in so many other areas of his life, Wright had mixed feelings about how good he wanted his students to be. He genuinely cared for them, and wanted them to learn. But if they were too good, that other side of his nature that feared and resented competition (with reason, since there was not enough work to go around) would rise to the surface and he would become resentful and dictatorial.

One of the first to encounter this kind of opposition was Henry Klumb, his gifted assistant, who would go on to have a major career as an architect in Puerto Rico, as an urban planner and also designer of schools, shops, low-cost housing, health centers, libraries, government buildings, airports, residential developments and the University of Puerto Rico. Everyone already knew that he was an architect of promise and, after having worked at Wright's elbow for four years (1929–33) he was ready for something more challenging. Wright vacillated between encouraging Klumb to strike out on his own and trying to tempt him back to Taliesin. For his part, Klumb would have liked an informal liaison allowing him to do outside work while remaining connected with Wright's studio. Wright, however, had made up his mind that he would allow no "moonlighting." He decreed that any architect at Taliesin must agree to work as an anonymous member of the group and plow all profits back into the Fellowship (his own included, he said). It sounded logical, but in effect they were arguing at cross-purposes. Wright charged that Klumb only pretended to be a part of Taliesin but, like so many others, was merely awaiting his chance to make influential contacts through Wright and get his own work as fast as possible. Klumb believed Wright was refusing to face the real issue, which was that he did not want his students to develop their own gifts. At a certain point, the student had to develop his own ideas if he was to make any contribution at all. Since Wright himself had experienced the identical dilemma when he was young, Klumb hoped he would eventually understand how his "sincere and loyal" students felt. There was no getting around the truth of Klumb's words, but Wright never would concede the point, and Klumb left Taliesin forever. But, as everyone knew, just to say you were going to leave, once you had been taken into the group, was "a betrayal; you had stepped off the end of the world," Howe said, an observation that was made by many others. The clever way to leave Taliesin was to do or say something outrageous so that the Wrights would make the decision for you. More than one apprentice made his or her escape in this fashion, by accident or design. Larry Lemmon was overheard in the kitchen one day complaining because, during a lean period, the only butter in the house went to the Wrights' table. He did not think that was very democratic and was openly critical. His remarks were reported to Mrs. Wright, who told him he and his family must leave. He said, "I hated to go away with her angry at me, but I had family reasons for wanting to go at the time, so I allowed it to happen." They packed up their belongings and drove away with a clear conscience.

Jack Howe entered the Taliesin circle in 1932 and soon became a vital member of Wright's drafting-room staff, taking over the position of chief draftsman from Henry Klumb in 1934. Howe was extremely able and intelligent, and he had the gift of learning by close observation, which was the quality one needed most if one worked for Wright, because his methods of teaching were unorthodox. Another gifted apprentice who became disenchanted was Manuel Sandoval, the cabinetmaker from Nicaragua. He had come to study architecture with the great man, but instead of being instructed, he felt he was kept doing fine cabinetry for Wright, work for which he was being highly paid in the outside world—in other words, exploited. Howe commented that Sandoval had expected an old-world, master-pupil relationship and did not understand that Wright taught nothing in the accepted sense.

Howe had a natural artistic gift and the rare ability to perceive what

Wright wanted from the sketchiest of outlines. Another apprentice from the early days said, "He could take a theme and play it like a piece of music." He became so good at this kind of interpretation that he was, in effect, the pencil in Wright's hand. Something like 90 percent of the drawings from the 1930s that are credited to Wright were actually made by Howe, a point he has never insisted upon. As was his custom, after approving the work, Wright affixed his own red square.

Howe was extremely well organized and made sure that the work was finished on time. That was another indispensable attribute. He was so valuable in the drafting room that, other people said, Wright never wanted him to leave—not that Howe wanted to go. Those were the wonderful days when Wright, waking early, would have a new idea. He would go to Howe's bedroom and call softly up the stairs, "Oh, Jack!" and Howe would get his clothes on and go straight to the drafting room and, "I'd miss my breakfast again," Howe said with a rueful smile. "It was very demanding but it was a real challenge and I learned to work fast. It was always exciting. Right up to the end."

Those who knew the inner workings of the drafting room placed great stress on Howe's ability to "manage" Wright in the nicest possible way and find solutions to the problems Wright himself would pose. After the drafting room had produced a complete set of working drawings, which could be as many as twenty or twenty-five sheets for a large building, the work would be presented to Wright for approval. True to form he would want extensive changes and would make marks all over the neat work. Then he would want a revised set in a hurry.

So the drafting room's leaders hit upon the idea of making a duplicate set of drawings at the same time, keeping that fact a secret from Wright. He would make his changes, these would be transferred to the second set, and the neatly revised work would be presented for the architect's approval in record time. Wright never learned of the harmless deception.

As for the clientele, it went without saying that Wright would promise them anything, always happily convinced that the building could be constructed for a fraction of its eventual cost. Then his staff would have to cope with the problem of trying to live up to his rash promises, which they had not been apprised of, since they were excluded from the client conferences. Fortunately, Gene Masselink, who replaced Jensen as Wright's secretary in 1933, and who had an office adjoining Wright's, was within earshot. Masselink would take notes on the conversation and brief the drafting room in detail later—another way of saving Wright, once again, from himself.

Howe and Wright had their differences, as everyone did who worked on close terms with the master. Wright called Howe "the How" when he was not in a good mood, and if they had quarreled and he wanted to make amends, it would be "Jackie" or "Jackson." Howe was receiving such priceless training and loved his work so much that he was content for far longer than Klumb had been. The moment did come, however, when he wanted his chance to supervise the actual construction of a building, but Wright would not let him go. He finally won the master's grudging permission to oversee the building of a house for Herman T. Mossberg in South Bend, Indiana. It was such an exhilarating experience that, once it was finished, Howe kept postponing his return and took a leisurely tour of other houses Wright was then building in Michigan, his first textile block designs in that state. Finally a telegram arrived from Wright: WHERE ARE YOU, AND WHY? It was as much of an overture as he was capable of making, and Jack Howe went back to the drafting room.

Edgar Kaufmann, Jr., had an interesting simile to describe the effect of Wright's work on his life—"The first trickle of irrigation in a desert land"—that seems curiously appropriate, given what followed. Kaufmann was the son of a wealthy Pittsburgh department store owner and must have been an early and persuasive advocate for his new mentor, because his father soon wrote to ask whether Wright would be interested in collaborating on a number of civic projects for Pittsburgh that were being planned at the end of 1934. Letters and contacts followed—Wright seems to have seen in Kaufmann, whom he called "EJ," a candidate to replace the impoverished and aging Darwin D. Martin—and before long, the Kaufmanns suggested that Wright build them a weekend cottage in the countryside, near a beautiful waterfall and ravine called Bear Run, in Connellsville, Pennsylvania. Years later, Wright recalled, "There in a beautiful forest was a solid, high rock ledge rising beside a waterfall, and the natural thing seemed to be to cantilever the house from that rock bank over the falling water. . . ." The Kaufmanns wanted their house to be placed on the other side of Bear Run, looking at the falls from below; Wright, as his description makes clear, had a very different idea from the start. However, he was in no hurry to talk about it or even commit it to paper, in common with his often-stated dictum that nothing ought

Fallingwater

Using Fallingwater to promote a new kind of insulating material

Edgar Kaufmann, Sr., and Wright conferring in Wright's desert camp, Taliesin West. A Welsh harp can be seen in the background.

to be attempted until an idea had taken clear shape in an architect's imagination. He had visited Bear Run for the second time by the summer of 1935, and his apprentices knew that the house had not yet been designed. Still, the weeks went by. Cary Caraway said, "At tea he'd talk about things and not setting them down until the idea was clear in his mind. As I remember it, Mr. Kaufmann came to Milwaukee for some other function and said, 'I'd like to know how you are doing, Mr. Wright,' and Wright replied calmly, 'Your house is finished,' and we knew nothing had happened. Then we heard that Kaufmann was about to drive the 140 miles from Milwaukee to Spring Green. It could have been the morning of that day when word went out, 'He's in the studio.' Then the next report was, 'He's sitting down!' " It was one of the most famous moments in architecture and one of the best documented—it was witnessed by Blaine Drake, Edgar Tafel, Bob Mosher, John Lautner, Jack Howe and others as well as Caraway—tantamount to being at Mozart's elbow the day he dipped his quill pen into the ink and began to compose *The Magic Flute*. They were waiting to see how this champion juggler, who had kept so many balls up in the air, would retrieve this one. Wright calmly began work, and, Caraway continued, "took three sheets of tracing paper in different colors, one for the basement, another for the first floor and a third for the second floor and sketched it to a scale of one-eighth inch equals one foot. We were all standing around him. I'd say it took two hours." Section, elevation and details: they were all pouring onto the paper, and pencils were being worn down and broken off as fast as they could be sharpened. As he worked, he kept up a running commentary: "The rock on which E.J. sits will be the hearth, coming right out of the floor, the fire burning just behind it. The warming kettle will fit into the wall here. . . . Steam will permeate the atmosphere. You'll hear the hiss. . . ." He had even decided upon the name of the house; it was a tour de force.

Then Wright threw down his pencils, and two apprentices, Tafel and Mosher, stayed on to draw views, one of which Wright selected for presentation. Wright also worked on the perspective drawings later. Howe said, "I particularly remember Mr. Wright as he worked with relish early one morning on the perspective drawings . . . he was dressed in his bathrobe, seated at a table by the fire in his study-bedroom. I had brought the layouts in from the studio, and was standing by with a supply of colored pencils, while he worked on the drawings. The most satisfactory and beautifully executed of these

drawings was later published on the cover of . . . *Time* magazine.
. . . This drawing is one which was executed entirely by Mr. Wright
himself." When the moment finally came to present the finished design
to the client, Wright, as was his custom, would not allow any of his
apprentices in the room. But, Caraway said, "he came out of the
meeting all smiles. Kaufmann had said, 'Don't change a thing.' " It
was the genesis of one of the most beautiful houses in the world:
Fallingwater.

17

Broad Acres

First the heavens were formed as a roof
For men,. and then the holy Creator
Eternal Lord and protector of souls,
Shaped our earth, prepared our home,
The almighty Master, our Prince, our God.
"Caedmon's Hymn"
Poems from the Old English

Edgar J. Kaufmann, president of Kaufmann Department Stores, Inc., in Pittsburgh, self-made son of an immigrant Jewish peddler was, when he met Wright, no stranger to the realms of architectural design. He had already commissioned and brought to completion at least ten building projects and would, by the time of his death in 1955, have commissioned half a dozen different architects. These projects not only included reconstruction of his own store and numerous civic projects like hospitals, museums, a planetarium and a public parking garage, but also six houses he built himself and nine others he bought or commissioned. One would have to compare him with Aline Barnsdall for the scope of his vision, his instinctive eye for quality and his restless imagination, which would ensure that he always had more projects in mind for himself, his store or his city than he could conceivably support or promote. As a human being he was forceful, commanding, the model of a farsighted entrepreneur, with a secret insecurity. He was, as the historian Franklin Toker has argued persuasively, aware of his socially inferior status and attempting to compensate for it by a civic-minded largesse; and he was defensive and apologetic about his own métier. "After all, we are only trades people and cannot see things quite as clearly as others," he wrote to Wright, perhaps only half ironically, early in their relationship.

He was, one might say, a connoisseur of architects. He would commission and build a $400,000 Neutra-designed house in Palm Springs for himself, in spite of Wright's determined ridicule, and although he had confined himself to supporting conservative architectural design to this point, it is reasonable to suppose that his eye was now ready for something more daring, more contemporary and more American. Professor Toker has suggested that Kaufmann's reflexive competitiveness may have had something to do with it, since Stanley Marcus, owner of Neiman-Marcus, the famous Dallas department store, had just commissioned Wright to design a house for him, and, in fact, Marcus had "made the pilgrimage" to Wright's studio at Taliesin that same autumn of 1935.

For whatever reasons, Kaufmann decided to make Wright "his" architect almost immediately, commissioning him not only to design the weekend house at Bear Run but also to remodel his own office and, later, to add further embellishments to Fallingwater in the way of a guesthouse and gate lodge. It is perfectly possible, given the rapidity of the commissions themselves, that Edgar Kaufmann, Jr., had been sent to Taliesin as a scout; he certainly did not stay there long, leaving, to Wright's clear disappointment, some months later to join his father's department store. There would be many more commissions from Kaufmann, something like twenty projects over the next two decades, most of them destined never to be built. Although Wright protested that he did not have much more time to spend on paper dreams, he never told his patron to go away, because Kaufmann had appeared in his life at an extraordinarily fortuitous moment. He arrived in September 1935; that dear old former patron, Darwin D. Martin, had a stroke early in December of that year and died soon after, but not before calculating that Wright still owed him exactly $37,976.29, most of it, presumably, in the form of the Taliesin mortgage. Shortly after that, Edgar Tafel recalled visiting the Martin house with Wright. The family was no longer living there, but it was still in mint condition. This state of affairs was destined to be brief, since Martin's son, Darwin R., could not afford upkeep and taxes.

He offered the house to the city or to the University of Buffalo as a branch library. Neither offer was accepted, and ten years later the house would be sold to recoup $75,000 in back taxes. Martin's death caused Wright the remorseful reflection that "I only wish I had been less taking and more giving where he was concerned. . . ." But his words lacked the note of despair one would have expected from someone who sees his last hope for a backer disappearing. In fact, he was very well suited with Kaufmann. It suited Wright to be designing for this daring Pittsburgh businessman; it suited him to be able to get another check on demand; it suited him to collect advances against a print collection, the usual ruse, and Kaufmann was as openhanded and less scrupulous about an exact accounting than Darwin D. Martin had been. For when it came to well-heeled clients, Wright's point of view had not varied much since the days when he and Aline Barnsdall were haggling (his version) over her costs compared with his optimistic estimates. Money was power, as he explained to her in 1927. A wealthy client would naturally want to live on a grand scale, as a way of demonstrating this power before all the world. So when money was there, he as an architect considered it almost a crime to use an inferior material when something perfect would make all the difference. By way of reply, Aline Barnsdall made a pointed reference to those in-dolent, spoiled figures of the nineteenth century such as Gordon Craig or Isadora Duncan, who let their patrons pay their bills and justified it in the name of "Art." One never heard this same lament from Kaufmann, even though the house that he had told Wright must not exceed $35,000 eventually cost $75,000, not to mention further ad-ditions and embellishments for an additional $50,000. He did, it is true, balk at gold leaf for the walls, but only because that extra flourish seemed, to him, to take Fallingwater too far from the original concept of a cottage in the woods.

Kaufmann's first idea had been of a place to entertain within sight of the falls. He did not get this once Wright had fixed on his idea of placing the house over the falls—one had to go out onto the terraces for that kind of view—but he did get the wonderful living room, thirty-five by forty-five feet, with views in all directions, that he had asked for. Wright's conception was to build Fallingwater as an in-terlapping series of reinforced concrete trays supported by piers and anchored to a central masonry core. The chimney was made from local stone laid rough, the floors were of quarried stone, and a rocky out-cropping was incorporated into the hearth. There were no walls as such, just uninterrupted vistas of glass that repeated the horizontal and vertical rhythms. On that famous day when Wright committed his vision of Fallingwater to paper and talked about what one would hear as one sat by the fireplace (the hissing of steam), he, no doubt, was also thinking of the background splash of water, the rustle of wind moving through the boughs, the shifting patterns of dappled light and shade, the feeling of being deep in a cave, sheltered by low ceilings and overhanging eaves, and the sense of rocks behind, as one sat beside a vast and friendly fire. At the same time, the lack of any walls as such would give one the paradoxical feeling of living in a boundary-less world. "There was the sense of a vital, ever-changing order as elements and context shifted into new relationships. The spaces around the waterfall and the screens of the trees were all drawn into the composition: nature and art were made to complement one another." And, as Edgar Kaufmann, Jr., would later write, "the materials of the structure blend with the colorings of the rocks and trees, while occasional accents are provided by bright furnishings, like the wildflowers or birds outside. The paths within the house, stairs and passages, meander without formality or urgency. . . . Sociability and privacy are both available. . . ."

In feeling, Fallingwater most resembles Taliesin. All of Wright's interiors play with the contrasts between bold, dramatic textures and decorative elements of extreme subtlety and refinement, such as his beloved oriental prints, pottery, porcelain, statuary and the trailing tendrils of hanging plants, but here the contrast is marked, as if deliberately reminiscent of medieval great halls with their crude, massive walls and rude stone floors half-hidden behind tapestries and strewn with fur throws. Wright's hidden entrances with their curious, one might say perverse, angles, grow smaller and more mysterious at Fallingwater, as at Taliesin; they seem hewn out of the walls or the rocks themselves. Stairways are narrower and steeper, recalling flights of stone steps descending into the gloom of an ancient fortress. Garden paths, half overgrown, hug the steep hillsides or disappear into thickets of trees. Great pillars of stone are spaced at intervals throughout the house; desks, cupboards, tables and benches are welded into the design, and boulders jut out of unexpected corners. Cavernous depths and dazzling perspectives, the sense of an impregnable fortress, a house of limitless spaciousness—the comparisons are inevitable. It has been pointed out that Wright's favorite way of signing his initials is contained, by accident or design, in the name of FaLLingWater.

Fallingwater may, like Le Corbusier's masterpiece, the Villa Savoye, have made use of man-made materials and the machine, and, as John H. Howe recalled, Wright may have wanted to show advocates of the International School "a thing or two" when he designed it, but the building has only the most superficial resemblance to that school, as several writers have pointed out. Scully compares Fallingwater with an earlier design by Neutra, the Lovell house (1929–30) in Los Angeles, to demonstrate Wright's superior mastery of concept. For although Neutra's house makes a similar use of concrete trays cantilevered over a ravine, its silhouette is essentially that of a rectangular box imposed on a hillside, whereas Fallingwater is intricately united with its site, its shape is complex and asymmetrical, and its overall form is essentially that of a pyramid. Like Palladio's Villa Rotunda and the Villa Savoye, Fallingwater was the fruit of a mature creativity and a deeply felt aesthetic. If the Villa Rotunda expressed the Renaissance artist's confident belief that man was the measure of all things, if Le Corbusier's pure geometric forms summed up all that a classicist's severe poetic vision might bring to the challenge of expressing, with man-made materials and machine forms, the triumph of man over nature, then Wright's Fallingwater has to be viewed as the antithesis of that belief. Wright's houses, with their massive masonry centers and flowing balconies and terraces that blend with their surroundings, may well speak, as Vincent Scully believed, to modern man's belief that he is no longer the center of the world and must hold on to whatever seems solid. There is, nevertheless, an air of indomitable American optimism and expansiveness about these spacious dwellings, with their axes "like country cross roads in the boundless prairie. . . ." And one cannot visit Wright's buildings (looking at photographs of them is a poor substitute) without feeling that still more is implied in his best work. For, as Peter Blake observed, Wright's buildings were indicative of "the mysticism that has always governed northern man's relationship to nature. They hark back to the mounds that conceal the ancient graves of the Vikings, to Harlech castle growing out of a Welsh hilltop, to Mont St. Michel. . . ." The fact that he dared to place a house actually over a waterfall, the fact that he wrestled with the elemental forces of nature (forging fire and earth with water, as he had with Hollyhock House): the fact that he spoke in terms of "consecrated" spaces: these state more forcefully than words Wright's almost demonic determination to weld man (the newcomer in an alien land) to his environment, make him inextricably part of it. They also show what one can only call Wright's essentially religious impulses of respect, wonder and celebration of the natural world. Man in tune with the primal forces of nature, man partaking in the great creative impulse—these are two of the lessons one can perhaps draw from a work that was, almost from the first, recognized as a masterpiece. Fallingwater was a stunning synthesis of all Wright thought and believed and spectacular proof that, at the age of sixty-eight, when most men are ready to retire, Wright was launching himself on the final great phase of his astonishing career.

As with all his patrons, whom he alternately charmed (in person) and castigated (on paper), Wright was invariably hospitable and ready with the usual unsolicited advice at moments of crises in their lives. After EJ's wife, Liliane, committed suicide, Wright solemnly warned Kaufmann against marrying again, since he was bound to be vulnerable to the first flattering female who came along, and once the sexual appetite had been satisfied, "again ashes and vain regrets." As usual he was making a fairly accurate assessment of the reason why so many of his own relationships had foundered. That he, with his spectacular lack of awareness and his own disastrous marital relationships, should be attempting to advise someone else, no doubt struck EJ as comical. For the fact was that Wright's attitudes toward women continued to reflect the clichéd thought of his generation, since the days that he had written (of the Romeo and Juliet windmill), "Romeo, as you will see, will do all the work and Juliet cuddle alongside to support and exalt him." A woman's success in life, in other words, depended upon how faithfully she reflected the light shining from the really important person in the marriage, as an article he wrote for *Cosmopolitan* in 1938 makes clear. When he listened to his wife as she worked and played "with such intense artistry," she was himself, he wrote. His daughter, Iovanna, was himself; his students were himself; Taliesin was himself. Others, in short, only existed to the extent that they reflected his personality, his ideas, his values, to the extent that they flattered and mirrored his image of himself. For someone as acutely aware, visually, as Wright, the myopia is terrifying, and since it was coupled with such a lack of awareness about his own motives, and a complete inability to admit a mistake, it did not bode well for any relationship. Once, when he was discussing the case of a man who had been divorced after a twenty-year marriage, Wright commented that he wished he could give that person some advice. "What would it be?" his friend asked. "I'd tell him that I was married three times, and each time they became Mrs. Wright."

Olgivanna Lloyd Wright (she took his middle name) is often described as emotionally and spiritually advanced, but she was not a particularly easy person to deal with. One of Wright's biographers, Grant Manson, recalled that after his first visit to Taliesin in 1938, he had spent much time and thought deciding on just the right gift, and arranged to have a dozen exquisite and expensive Spode cups and saucers sent to Taliesin. Some months later he made a brief stop there and found the atmosphere distinctly chilly. Mrs. Wright finally told him, "I was never so insulted! Two weeks you lived with us last time and never so much as a word from you after you drove away!" Manson protested that he had written a letter of thanks; she insisted they had never received it. What about the gift he had sent? "Cups? From you? I know nossing of cups. I received no gift from you!" After careful investigation, it was clear that the china had been sent and delivered, but Mrs. Wright continued to disclaim all knowledge of it and hold it against the hapless visitor.

She could be stubborn, if not implacable. In one of her columns for the *Madison Capital Times*, she described a running battle she had had with Elizabeth Enright Gillham, daughter of Maginel (always called "Bitsy"), a short story writer and author of children's books. The fight centered on an apron pocket. It seemed that Olgivanna had bought a green apron and did not like its pocket. She took it off and threw it away. Bitsy, for a joke, retrieved the object and pinned it to a flower and placed it where it would be found by Olgivanna: on her mirror. Olgivanna smiled and threw the pocket away again. She did not think about the subject until the next time she used the apron: the pocket had been neatly stitched back into place. So she took it off again, wrapped it in tissue, placed it in a large box, tied it with a yellow ribbon and sent it back to Bitsy with her compliments. The object of the game became to see who could be tricked into accepting the pocket under various disguises and which woman could outsmart the other. Each ingenious ruse simply spurred the receiver to invent more fiendish ways of returning the hated object: Olgivanna said, "Oh, to have fallen into such a masterful and well-timed trap set by my incomparable adversary!" The battle of the green pocket went on for years.

Olgivanna Wright was equally capable of warmhearted sympathy, generosity and active help. Tales of her generous gestures are legion, along with those of her unpredictability. One simply never knew what to expect of her, which must have seemed familiar to her husband, part of the reason why each of his women seemed to become the same "Mrs. Wright." (One notes that he addressed Catherine and Olgivanna, at least, as "Mother," but that might simply have been the remnant of the old country form of address for the mother of one's children.) There are many accounts of Olgivanna's tender solicitude for him. She watched over his health, she supervised his day, she mediated in disputes, she soothed and supported him. Loren Pope thought Olgivanna regarded her husband as "something like a national treasure that she was protecting and she was extremely particular about having the proper deference shown. I remember he had lectured in Washington on a hot summer evening and I went to see him afterwards. I think my shirt was open and my tie undone, and I got the distinct impression that she did not approve, because she was not as gracious as he was." She also influenced him. Dr. Joseph Rorke, who became a Taliesin Fellow, observed that one of the first things Olgivanna did was to persuade Frank to abandon his flowing artist's tie and shorten his hair, presumably because he was beginning to look faintly quaint and old-fashioned. After that, he switched to a regular tie, although he usually disdained the Windsor knot in favor of an intricate wrap-and-tie of his own invention, the ends tucked under his collar. Wesley Peters also noted that Olgivanna became adept at intervening in disputes and intercepting letters that Wright had written in a fury and would, she was convinced, regret once he had calmed down.

Professor Lilien commented, "You know, she had this very delicate appearance. She looked like a Byzantine Madonna with narrow eyes, and she was very slender, with graceful movements, but with all this, she was as strong as steel. His first wife never had time for him, and this is what Olgivanna excelled in. She was always with him, and if he wanted to go anywhere, she went, even if it meant getting out of bed." Olgivanna Wright says much the same thing in her memoir of her years with Wright, *The Shining Brow*. For years she suffered from intermittent tachycardia (rapid heart beat), which might incapacitate her for hours. Wright was always solicitous, but as soon as the immediate danger was over he thought she should be ready to go back to whatever they were planning, a picnic, for instance. She, with knees buckling and fingers trembling, would get dressed and go out because he wanted her beside him and that was enough.

He continued to flirt with women. She recalled an incident that was entirely typical of him. Once, going to the theater with a group of apprentices to see one of his favorite actresses, Lillian Harvey, Wright announced loudly, as they all took their seats, "Boys, she's mine!" It seemed grossly insensitive to her (he refused to apologize), but then, she was even jealous of his admiration for Marlene Dietrich. He was just as ready to suspect her of infidelity. Once he dreamed that he had found her in bed with a black, and was very huffy about it. She replied, "Frank, are you out of your mind? I'm not responsible for your dreams." But logic had nothing to do with the matter. It must be her fault, because "there must have been something in you that led me to the conclusion of such a dream." They went on arguing, and the subject was dropped, she thought, but he remained distant. Finally he said, "Well, how do I know that you are faithful to me?" He thought she had been looking at one of their visitors, Douglas Haskell, in far too friendly a way. He concluded, "You may be a woman of very easy conduct."

Wright had once called her "a darling sensitive soul, the only woman I have ever known to be honest all the way through," apparently never discovering that she had become most adept at manipulating him. In one particular case, realizing that he could not be reasoned with, she leaned toward him and said tenderly, "Frank, where did you get that beautiful necktie?" He looked surprised. Then he melted and became as anxious as he could be to make amends without actually apologizing. He took her to Madison and they spent a delightful afternoon. Like Miriam Noel, Olgivanna Wright had discovered how easily distractable Wright was and no doubt realized their marriage would last as long as she was prepared to manipulate him as one would a child, someone at the mercy of ambivalent and irrational swings of mood. This would mean subjecting her own feelings to an iron control. That might be difficult to do when, as often happened, Wright would submit her to his highly developed version of the double bind. He would argue a point vehemently until she, to end the fight, would drop her opposition. Sometime later, having changed his mind, he would chastise her for having allowed him to make such a fool of himself. One also believes that he also encouraged, by accident or design, a hierarchy of blaming others. If someone in his own life infuriated him but, for whatever reasons, he could not vent his anger on that person, he would pick a fight with Olgivanna. Even while she knew this was happening, she seemed helpless to prevent the chain reaction and would turn on someone else, often a junior apprentice, as a way of relieving her own feelings. Any woman who wanted to live with Wright, in other words, not only had to live up to his expectations of her and be prepared for unpredictable attacks and irrational scenes but also would be swept up in the roller-coaster atmosphere of crisis that surrounded him. It is not surprising that one of Iovanna Wright's early memories, of around November 1933, is of the night when her father almost left them. She wrote that it was a frosty evening, with a thin layer of snow on the ground. She had gone to bed but was not asleep when she overheard a loud argument between her parents.

She rushed into her mother's room and found her opening her closet doors. Olgivanna's pulse was rapid and she was trembling. "I am leaving him," she said. "I cannot bear this abuse any longer." Then she saw her father going by the open door, wearing his hat and coat, carrying a cane and a small suitcase. Soon, they heard the front door bang. "Stop him, Iovanna!" her mother suddenly cried. It was an echo of the days when Catherine used to have her children write heart-tugging letters to Fiesole, begging Daddy to come home. Iovanna ran out into the snow in her nightgown and bare feet. She continued, " 'Please come back, Daddy,' I said. 'We love you—we need you. Mother is suffering—please don't go away.' He stopped, silent. . . . I said, 'You're my whole life—and you're Mother's life.' He was still silent. 'Daddy it's cold—the snow pains my feet—come back.' He turned around, and walking together we went into the house. I left them alone and went to my room, my whole body shivering. What makes them fight? I wondered then. I know they love each other. Why did this happen?"

Georgei Ivanovitch Gurdjieff first came to Taliesin in the summer of 1934. Up to that point, Howe remembers overhearing frequent "shouting matches" between these two strong-willed personalities, and after Gurdjieff had paid his lightning visit, the furious battles came to an end. "I am sure Gurdjieff told her to be devious, because it all changed," a friend said. It would have been like Olgivanna Wright to turn, in her moment of panic, to her old mentor and put her faith in whatever she might interpret as his methods. After his visit, her husband actually wrote a short essay about Gurdjieff, comparing him to Gandhi and Whitman and praising his solid, fatherly manner. It is entirely unrevealing. A more telling description of the encounter that took place between the two men came from Nott, who observed, when they met in London in May 1939, that Wright was behaving "rather like a brilliant undergraduate, and it was clear that of the ideas he understood nothing. He seemed to regard Gurdjieff as having achieved almost the same level as himself. . . ." On another occasion, just before World War II, when Gurdjieff was at Taliesin and they were all seated in the living room, drinking coffee, Wright grandly remarked that perhaps he should send some of his pupils to Gurdjieff in Paris. " 'Then they can come back to me and I'll finish them off.'

" '*You* finish! You are idiot,' said Gurdjieff angrily. '*You* finish! No. *You* begin. I finish.' " It was clear that Wright had met his match.

The apprentices at Taliesin were, Nott thought, fascinated by Gurdjieff's prowess as a cook. He could take a number of spices, peppers and herbs and produce a delicious meal from the toughest of chickens. That is Nott's version; Tafel had another story. He recalled that Gurdjieff told them all how to make vast quantities of sauerkraut using whole apples, including the cores, herbs, raisins and cabbage. It was horrible, and after making a pretense of eating, they were happy to throw the remains in the garbage. Unfortunately, mountains of sauerkraut were still left, and Mr. Wright insisted they take two fifty-gallon barrels of it to their desert camp in Arizona. Tafel and other members of the Fellowship loaded the barrels onto a truck and got as far as Iowa. Arriving in bitter cold, they perceived that the sauerkraut had frozen solid. "We loosened the tailgate ropes and dumped the barrels into a ditch."

Making sure that Iovanna should be guided by, and properly respectful of, Gurdjieff's dicta was, naturally, much on her mother's mind. Luckily, the little girl whose arrival had thrown her parents' lives into so much turmoil, took an instinctive interest in music, was a natural dancer and loved poetry. She had, some people thought, a genuine poetic gift. Once she asked her mother when her favorite flower, jack-in-the-pulpit, preached. Her mother replied that he preached all day long to the other flowers. "Do all of them listen?" the little girl wanted to know. This child's poetic fancy—she appeared to have clear memories of having lived before as Jane Porter's son, and described it in enough detail for her mother to write a letter to her sister-in-law about it—was usually hidden behind the outward stance of the tomboy. Everyone remembers Iovanna's riding over the countryside, her head of golden curls bouncing, or clumping into the

Olgivanna with the young Iovanna, date unknown

The Wrights at Taliesin, circa 1936–37

Sunday-evening music and discussion in the main living room in 1935. Io-vanna is on the floor at the feet of her parents, seated on a dais; Svetlana is seated behind her mother and looking directly at her future husband, William Wesley Peters (center in profile).

Wright as paterfamilias, with Svetlana, Iovanna and Olgivanna

dining room smelling of manure. She was passionately interested in cowboy movies and "always impatient for the shooting to begin," her mother observed with distaste. Her favorite outfit was leather chaps over blue jeans, with a western hat, red kerchief, cowboy boots and a double-gun holster that she refused to remove, even while taking her obligatory lessons on the harp.

She stayed at home for the first eight years. Her father built a miniature schoolhouse for her, and one of the apprentices, Philip L. Holliday, later a graphics designer, was elected to serve as a teacher. One would hear screams of laughter coming from the schoolroom as Iovanna pulled her teacher's hair, and he, feebly protesting, tried to prevent it. There are other stories of Iovanna's pounding over the hillside, beating her pony's flanks until the blood came. Around the Fellowship the consensus was that her parents did not discipline her.

It is true that her father was soon referring to his baby in royal terms. Iovanna had recovered from a recent attack of scarlet fever "as a princess should," he told Darwin Martin in 1929. That was part of the problem, another observer thought. "Mrs. Wright put an image of greatness in front of her and expected her to conform to it." Others believed the trouble was that the attitude of both Iovanna's parents was unpredictable and inconsistent, so that their daughter never knew what to expect from one moment to another.

Iovanna's first memories of childhood are of sitting in her father's lap with her mother standing by, and she was brushing his hair over his face and calling him "Spider Man." She thinks she may have been about three and a half. Her next memory is of being given a doll when she was six. She had never had a doll and wanted one badly, but her father refused to allow it as it would spoil his architecture, he said. She chuckled about that. One day, her beloved Uncle Vlado brought her a beautiful baby doll dressed in pink gauze. That night, she left the doll outside on the porch. It rained in the night, and in the morning the doll's wax cheeks were covered with raindrops. She tried to grasp the doll's face and her fingers sank into the wax; she screamed with fright. Her father said, "Cheeky [the name he always called her], this is your first experience with death." She said, "I knew nothing about death then, but I always connected it with something horrible after that." Her next memory was of the time that she had been given Blackie, the Shetland pony of four and a half hands, was dressed up in riding clothes and placed in the saddle. Her father gave her a few instructions and slapped the animal's side. Startled, Blackie jumped over a puddle. Iovanna flew into the air and fell on her back in the water. She was screaming for help and her mother was concerned, but her father insisted that she get back in the saddle. He told her, "Life is like this. Learn how to fall, but keep at it." In retrospect she thought it had been a valuable lesson, if a hard one. "When it came to music I was forced to play an instrument. I had my choice, but I had to play something. You know, I am an ex-harpist. If you stop for a week, you have to begin all over again and I stopped several times, taking up the piano and recorder instead. Mother wanted me to play the cello. I used to sit there with tears streaming down my face. I did not want to displease anybody, but I couldn't stand it." Although these seemed to be painful memories, Iovanna refused to feel any anger or resentment, describing the experiences as good discipline, and praising what she saw as her parents' exalted standards. "I loved my father so dearly and deeply, as I do now. I used to kiss his hands. I equally loved my mother. She was extremely beautiful, highly talented and gifted. No one could have had a more wonderful mother, and Father was very indulgent, although he could lose his temper." What was he like then? "Like a torrent, a hurricane. I felt awful." People might not think so, but there were times when "I was bad." She smiled and looked roguish. She also remembered times when her father would point accusingly and say, "You sent me to jail." She added, "As I got older, I learned to say, 'You sent yourself.' "

If Iovanna's childhood was troubled, Svetlana's seems to have been amazingly serene, given the chaotic events of her early life, the flight from Russia, the uproar over her supposed abduction and all the other crises she would have been old enough to understand. True, she had spent most of her time in private school or with Uncle Vlado and Aunt Sophie, generally considered to have been ideal parent figures. She was a gifted and accomplished musician, leader in doing the chores, inventing games, even floral arrangements, and mature far beyond her years. Wesley Peters said, "She could talk to Mr. Wright and her mother when they quarreled and iron it out when she was only fifteen or sixteen." She was also gifted artistically, sensible and very well liked. "She shone in every way," he said. He called her "My Svet." The image of Svetlana, the girl who did everything right, became fixed in the lore of the Taliesin Fellowship. An apprentice recalled that when they were all in their twenties, Iovanna organized a surprise party for him. After all the guests left he had insisted on doing the dishes instead of what Iovanna wanted, which was to relax and have a good time. She said accusingly, "You're just like my sister!" and it suddenly dawned on him. "That's the answer! Cain and Abel."

That first winter of his stay in Taliesin, when Svet and Wes fell in love, she was not yet sixteen. Olgivanna and Frank were, naturally, the last to find out. Wright wrote, "When we did wake up—there were some accusations and unkind words. Too soon! Both too young!" It looked like a kind of treachery, he added. Peters said, "Mr. Wright thought I had deceived him. He was fonder of Svet than any of his children." (Wright had formally adopted her by then.) "Possibly, he was jealous. So I told him we were going to leave. Mrs. Wright was upset, but she had encouraged us. About June of 1933 I put all my stuff in my car and left. I went to my parents' home in southern Indiana and Svet had got a job in Winnetka, a suburb of Chicago. She moved in with the family of the first violinist of the Chicago Symphony, keeping house in exchange for violin lessons. She worked for over a year that way and she and I went on seeing each other.

"Meantime Mr. Wright had written my father a very strong letter saying, 'By subterfuge he has betrayed me.' He intimated that I had attacked Svetlana, which certainly wasn't the case. It was a nasty letter and my father wrote back saying that he could not believe what Wright was saying about me. Mr. Wright thought about it for a while, then responded handsomely. He wrote, 'I wrote you a bad letter and you sent me a good one.' "

They were married in Evansville, Indiana, on April 1, 1935. By then Peters had obtained his architect's license and was building two houses in Evanston, Illinois. About six months after that, overtures were made from Taliesin, and they returned for good. Then Wes's famous father, the publisher who had driven the Ku Klux Klan out of Indiana practically single-handedly, died, Wright wrote in his autobiography and Wes came into his inheritance.

The original reasons for founding the Fellowship made a certain kind of sense for Wright at the height of the depression. Having twenty or thirty young men about gave him a steady pool of willing and enthusiastic, if unskilled, labor. So far so good, but given Wright's perennial expansiveness and improvidence, he was bound to overextend himself with the Fellowship as he did with everything else, and although there are no balance sheets for that period, the indications are that he was, as usual and if possible, more in debt than ever. He wrote, "But altogether thirty-five thousand dollars a year would not keep us going for materials—and Fellowship upkeep. I had found that I had got into something that only a multimillionaire should have attempted. . . . 'I don't know whether you are a saint or a fool,' said my lawyer. I said, 'Is there a difference?' "

When Schevill, Martin, Page, La Follette et al. had saved Taliesin for Wright, consolidated his debts and paid off his creditors, they had also settled with the Bank of Wisconsin for a cash payment of $15,000 ($10,000 from Martin and $5,000 from Page) plus a note from Wright, Inc. of $23,500, essentially a first mortgage on the property for a period of five years. That took place in September 1928, and two months later, on November 9, 1928, ownership of the property was transferred to Martin (two-thirds) and Page (one-third). Since Wright had arranged to have these men take responsibility for mortgage payments, interest and taxes on Taliesin, he might have been forgiven for taking the lordly attitude that such financial matters were no longer his responsibility when he and La Follette had their famous fight. Very soon thereafter Page was penniless, and so was Darwin Martin. Given Wright's cheerful assumption that he did not have to worry about Taliesin anymore, it is not surprising that there were periodic threats of foreclosure and last-minute attempts by Wright to stave off disaster. Records showed that interest payments on the mortgage were not met from 1932 onward, and nothing was paid on the principal note when it came due in the autumn of 1933, nor thereafter.

In 1932 the Bank of Wisconsin sold the Taliesin mortgage to the First Wisconsin National Bank of Milwaukee, and when Martin died in December 1935, Wright finally realized he had to act. Within days of Martin's death he had contacted Page and somehow charmed him into signing over his one-third interest in Taliesin for the sum of one dollar. This was remarkable, and perhaps Wright thought it would be equally easy to wrestle the remaining two-thirds interest from Martin's widow and son. His position was that Martin had wrongly taken title, instead of leaving it with the corporation, and had allowed thousands of dollars of interest to accrue on the loan and back taxes at a time when he himself was "helpless to turn a penny from my work." That was his story, but it seems clear that it did not go down well with the Martins, who were in no hurry to make Wright a present of Taliesin when their own circumstances were almost as desperate. Still, they too could not protect their interest by paying its debts, and the bank was pressing to foreclose again. The situation was at a stalemate when Svetlana and Wes came back. About a year after Wes and Svet returned, on September 14, 1936, the First Wisconsin National Bank issued a mortgage in Olgivanna Wright's name. Somebody, in other words, had put up the money to buy out the Martin share. That someone could only have been William Wesley Peters since, twelve days later, the mortgage was transferred to him. It was an adroit move, born of Wright's long experience at evading the rightful claims of creditors. By making Peters the owner, he effectively blocked any attempt the Martins might have made to use their part ownership of Taliesin as a weapon to attempt to recover some of the $38,000 he owed. There was no great risk involved for Wright now that Peters was a relative, linked to him and his wife. Peters represented Wright's stake in the future, and Wright was prepared to do anything to save Taliesin because, as he told Darwin R. Martin three years later, "I saw no good reason why I should lose my home and my earnings of a lifetime because of any benefactor, even your father. . . ."

Martin's son had been outflanked, which did not prevent him from trying to get redress for years. There was another foreclosure threat in 1939, and perhaps this is the reason why Wright took the further step of transferring all of his personal property to the Frank Lloyd Wright Foundation, a nonprofit, educational Wisconsin corporation. Martin continued to raise the issue periodically but had to concede defeat in 1949 when an exhaustive investigation by La Follette's old law firm regretfully concluded that, as his father's heir, he had no enforceable rights.

Wright's immediate objective was to add to the Taliesin holdings, which had dwindled to seventy acres by the time it was put up for sale in 1928. Wright may have been motivated by a determination to recover the family land that had been sold off, farm by farm, all those years ago. In any event, one of the first acts was to buy farmer Rieder's property at the bottom of the driveway for the giveaway price of twelve thousand dollars. They then tore down the house and removed all traces of the barnyard and the abominable pigpens. This purchase also gave Taliesin 350 acres on the waterfront, its first direct access to the river. Then Peters bought the farm at which he had made inquiries on that fateful morning in 1932. He bought Uncle Enos's old property, and the two-story house was demolished; so many of those old houses were in bad shape, he said. Perhaps the choicest purchase of all was Uncle James's farm across The Valley, comprising another 350 acres. During the next thirty years of his ownership, Peters enlarged and remodeled the old homestead, naming it "Aldebaran," one of the stars in the Taurus constellation meaning "follower." Once this property had been bought, Taliesin had assumed control of about a thousand acres including three miles of waterfront. The acquisitions did not end there. Wright wanted a gentleman's estate, to be owner of all he surveyed and beyond. They kept buying until Taliesin had acquired three thousand acres and its boundaries reached to the edges of State Highway 14 and Tower Hill, by now a state park, site of old Helena and so many Jenkin Lloyd Jones camp meetings. A few broken-down buildings, remnants of the old town, were on the land, including two clapboard farmhouses, c. 1850, about which local folk were becoming nostalgic. A few more black marks were added to Wright's name when he burned them down. It has to be confessed that Wright could not resist a good fire. Another famous event of the postwar period took place at Stuffy's Bar, a disreputable building near the river that had become a hangout for Taliesin apprentices, who sneaked out after ten o'clock curfew for a few drinks. Once he found out, Wright naturally disapproved. So he bought the property (Stuffy was glad enough to sell) and announced a celebration. Everyone assembled with picnic baskets at a hillside spot that afforded an excellent view of the scene of so much illicit carousing. Then, without turning a hair, Wright gave the order to "pour the gasoline, boys!" and while the whole Fellowship watched, Stuffy's Bar went up with a roar. To put the final touch on the evening, Wright arranged to have John Amarantides, his star student musician, fiddling while Stuffy's burned.

Jack and Lu Howe thought Wright's eventual ambition was to buy up enough land to make Taliesin a state park. He also encouraged some of his apprentices to buy land and settle in The Valley. Henning Waterston bought Uncle John's old farmhouse, which for many years served as the official post office for the town of Hillside. (John was the postmaster, and after his death, his wife carried on.) Frances and Cary Caraway took over the small, red gambrel-roofed cottage once owned by Margaret Lloyd (Evans) Jones and her widowed stepdaughter. Davy and Kay Davison bought half of the beautiful old property, all orchards, pines, vegetable and flower gardens and sweeping lawns, that had belonged to Aunt Mary and Uncle James Philip, and Herb and Eloise Fritz bought the other half. Eloise Fritz recalled that the Wrights came up to dinner one evening, and he was very complimentary. "My, Herbert, you have got this looking nice," he said. As he left, he proposed that his former student give his property to the Fellowship. Of course, they could go on living there during their lifetimes. Eloise said, "Herb's mother was so worried because she thought Herb would actually do it." He said, "Not quite."

In the early 1930s lecturing was the chief source of Wright's income, before architectural commissions began to roll in. University engagements were particularly lucrative, according to Howe. He would usually be invited by the students, and Masselink, Fritz, Tafel or Howe would act as chauffeur for the Cord or the Lincoln Continental and make the trip while Wright napped in the back seat. As has been observed, he became very skilled at extemporaneous lectures, although his archives attest to the fact that he also spent hours writing speeches and laboriously amending them. Elizabeth Wright Ingraham, John's daughter, recalled that Wright once made a brilliant speech at a local school without using notes, and afterward she looked to see whether he had hidden notes on his cuff or written on his hand. He told her, "What notes I speak are from the heart and the head." She said, "I was very impressed." Sometimes he made the trip by train. Henry Sayles Francis, then a young curator, although acting director of the Cleveland Museum of Art, recalled having Wright to dinner in the spring of 1932, when he was on the lecture circuit to talk about his autobiography.

"I went to meet him in the cavernous Cleveland depot and saw him approaching across the vast space in sombrero and sky-blue, silk-lined cape." Wright was not amused, they thought, to be received by such a junior member of the museum, and appeared to become more and more disapproving once they took him back to their modest home; "no pomp and no trustees," Francis explained. After dinner, Wright went to the bathroom to prepare for his lecture and was gone for some time. Finally he summoned his hostess. He had dropped a bridge of false teeth down the toilet. She arrived, and they peered down together but there was nothing they could do as he had already flushed it.

The subject of Wright at train stations cannot be left without recounting another incident that took place some years later when a former mayor of Louisville, Charles Farnsley, invited Wright to lecture. Farnsley was unable to meet the distinguished visitor personally, so he sent two chauffeurs to the station. One of them happened to be a policeman, and when Wright, coming along the platform, saw the policeman approaching he got back on the train.

Some of Wright's senior apprentices were occasionally engaged to make speeches of their own. Bob Mosher, whom Wright had placed in charge of Fallingwater and defended when his client protested that he deserved a more experienced overseer, told the story that he, Peters and Caraway were all in New York one time when an invitation came from the architectural department at Yale University. One of them was asked to make a speech; Mosher was elected. He went to New Haven, delivered his speech and was delighted to find that they were paying him twenty-five dollars. While he was away, Wright breezed into town, arriving unannounced as he liked to do. He immediately wanted to know where Mosher was. As luck would have it, Mosher returned at that moment and was obliged to confess that he had given a lecture. Mosher was no match for Wright's determined questioning and soon conceded that he had been paid.

Wright said, "Bobbie, come with me for a moment." They walked up Fifth Avenue to a handsome store, the one from which Wright bought his ties and hats. "Let's step in here for a moment," Wright said. "I'm looking for a beret." He tried on several and then found a cap he liked. "How much is this?" The price was twenty-five dollars.

"I think I can use it," Wright said. In a trice he had expertly ripped off the visor. He turned to Mosher. "Bobbie, can you lend me twenty-five dollars?" Mosher laughed and paid up.

Everyone knew what a terror Wright was in a store: how he haggled over discounts, how he tried to beat down the merchant, using his characteristically shameless mixture of brashness and guile. Henry-Russell Hitchcock recalled accompanying Wright to Abercrombie and Fitch in New York, where Wright was drawn like a magnet to a rack of the most expensive men's coats. After settling on the one he wanted, Wright went into a brilliant monologue about the reasons why the store should give him a coat, since it would be so advantageous for them to have him, a famous man, as a walking advertisement. After twenty or thirty minutes of this kind of pressure, the manager finally agreed to waive the price. "Fine," said Wright briskly, "and I want one for my friend, too."

Part of his motivation, it was thought, had to do with his urge to reform his friends. If he particularly liked someone, he would attempt to take him or her in hand. Sophia Mumford recalled, "He was always trying to get Lewis to spell his name with a double L, in the Welsh fashion, and taking him to task over small things, such as the temperature of his whiskey or the way he walked." Arthur Holden, the architect who worked closely with him when the Guggenheim Museum was being built, quipped that Wright's main motivation was his desire to improve the scenery: "One day he said to me, 'Arthur, why don't you wear your brown suit more often? You look your best in brown.' Then he took me into a store to buy me a tie, and when I chose one that had a connecting-rod design, he was very disapproving. I was color blind, he said." Carl Sandburg, Lincoln's biographer and famous poet, with whom he was on distant but cordial terms for decades, grumbled that Wright once made him dress up in a velvet suit with a frilly shirt, and he was in an agony that someone might recognize him in that outfit. Wright later observed that he had tried to mold Carl but had had to give up, because he was "too far gone on along the lines of Lincoln. . . . I couldn't do much with him." As he liked to tell his appreciative audiences during his lecture tours and seminars on campuses all over the country, "First of all, my father was a preacher and his father was a preacher . . . and way back they're all preachers. . . ."

As for his next great client of the 1930s, Herbert F. ("Hib") Johnson, Wright's approach was the same carefully calculated combination of flattery, impudence and guile. He knew that Hib Johnson, grandson of the founder of Johnson's Wax, had already chosen an architect to design a new administration building for his Racine, Wisconsin, company, S. C. Johnson and Sons. Wright was determined to shake whatever confidence remained in the architect of choice and persuade Hib of his superior merits. As soon as word went out that the Johnson delegation was to appear, everyone was pressed into service for the newest emergency, washing windows, raking grounds, cleaning and waxing the floors and filling every room with great armfuls of flowers. The group was given the grand tour, followed by an elegant lunch, and then Wright went on the offensive. "He insulted me about everything," Johnson later recalled, "and I insulted him, but he did a better job. I showed him pictures of the old office, and he said it was awful. . . . He had a Lincoln-Zephyr, and I had one—that was the only thing we agreed on. On all other matters we were at each other's throats." Johnson nevertheless left thinking, "If that guy can talk like that he must have something." Having thoroughly unsettled Johnson, Wright exerted the full force of his charismatic personality in describing the kind of building he would design, unconventional, imaginative, trend-setting, a visual symbol of a great company. Alistair Cooke later described the special quality of Wright's speech, "delicate and warmly modulated," that voice that had "for 50 years seduced wax manufacturers, oil tycoons, bishops, university boards of trustees and at least one emperor of Japan. . . ." They became enormously fond of each other despite, or perhaps because of, Johnson's conclusion that he was no match for Wright. On one occasion, when both were to appear before an important meeting of company officials, Johnson said, "Please, Frank, don't scold me in front of my board of directors!"

Those who know Wright best have said that, in his art as in his life, the one constant was his mutability, his restless inventiveness. Perpetual renewal was the rallying cry for, as he told Tafel, "what we did yesterday we won't do today. And what we don't do tomorrow will not be what we'll be doing the day after." In that respect he was temperamentally at the opposite pole of an architect like Mies van der Rohe, someone he came to like personally, whose goal it was to polish his particular style to a high gloss. It has also been suggested that Wright was capable of capitalizing upon whatever new movement was in the air. And, in 1936, when he came to design the S. C. Johnson and Sons Administration Building, the newest vogue was Streamlining. The style was an outgrowth of the development of the new field of industrial design and pioneered by men like Raymond Loewy and Norman Bel Geddes, whom Wright already knew since he had worked on theatrical productions with Aline Barnsdall. It expressed all that could be summed up in the glorification of speed and the machine, a kind of exultation of power itself, one that Marinetti, leader of the Italian Futurist movement, had celebrated twenty years before: "A roaring motorcar, which runs like a machine-gun." The ideal form, the ultimate symbol of efficiency and untrammeled movement, became that of the teardrop, or parabolic curve. Inevitably, the first industrial designs in the new style centered on such automobiles as the Lincoln Zephyr and the new locomotives, but the style caught on so rapidly that everything from radios to jukeboxes, cameras, lighters and cocktail cabinets was redesigned to reflect the sleek lines and rounded edges of this symbol of the new age, representing as it did "the machine and the hope it held for the future." Given Wright's avid eye, not to mention his long-standing interest in the subject of art and the machine, it was only a matter of time before the streamlined curve would appear in his work, and the Johnson Administration Building was the obvious place to start. So one would expect to see, in its sleek horizontal lines and rounded corners, a new symbol of advanced and progressive ideas.

In fact, the Johnson Corporation, with its liberal policy toward its employees (it was one of the first in the nation to institute profit sharing), must have put Wright in mind of the other company he had come to know so well and for which he had designed another precedent-shattering building thirty years before. Benevolent paternalism: for the Larkin Company, that concept had been expressed by a single vast work space surrounded by balconies, and since the Johnson Corporation also wanted to portray "a sort of extended family under a beneficent patriarchy," Curtis wrote, it seemed logical that Wright would use the same design principle. The flat lot in an ugly urban setting had no views worth exploiting, so Wright, as he had in Buffalo, designed a large, windowless rectangle decorated, at the roofline, with a frieze of glass tubing that admitted light but no view. The same glass tubing was used in the roof. Inside, the central work space was interspersed with rows of slender concrete columns sometimes described as mushroom or lilypad in shape; the whole was surrounded by curving tiers of balconies designed to accommodate the offices of middle management. Jonathan Lipman, the architect who organized the exhibition "Frank Lloyd Wright and the Johnson Wax Buildings," has observed that however up-to-the-minute Wright's design might appear, it actually had all major points in common, not only with the Larkin Building, but also a number of other public spaces Wright designed during his long career, including Unity Temple, the Imperial Hotel and others. For instance, Wright made sure that one entered through a low reception hall, which gave no hint of the interior drama and the superb, glowing, cathedral-like space that was to be discovered. It was a trick that had not failed to work since he first tried it out in Oak Park. As he had before, Wright built a smaller building beside it, connected by the common entrance, for utilitarian purposes: garage, exercise deck, squash court and so on. A dazzling variation on an unchanging theme: it was vintage Wright, and Wright at the top of his form. From the day the building opened, Samuel C. Johnson, Hib's son, wrote, "We achieved international attention because that building represented and symbolized the quality of everything we did. . . ."

Since, as Professor Jack Quinan has noted, Wright saved his most daring experiments with new materials for his largest and most important commissions, a number of the Johnson building's innovations presented the inevitable problems. Building permits were delayed because the authorities did not believe that the columns, as designed, would support the necessary loads until Wright, in a famous demonstration, proved that they could. The building made use of the new technique of air conditioning, then in its early design stages, which was never really satisfactory. As for the glass tubing in the walls and roof, Wright invented a new system of glazing that always leaked, Tafel wrote. As Samuel Johnson observed, the idea of having fifty typists at work in a vast, echoing space is one of those concepts that may look attractive on paper but which tends to grate on the nerves once it becomes a reality. Naturally, the building's cost had more than doubled over its projection, but none of that really mattered since it had become such a successful symbol for the company. Johnson went on to commission an addition, a research tower, ten years later. He also asked Wright to build him a house.

As its name would imply, Wingspread was a two-storey house that isolated various activities into wings: one for sleeping, another for the kitchen quarters, a third for the children and so on, in a cruciform pattern, with an enormous, two-story, skylit living room in the center. It was the biggest house Wright ever built (fourteen thousand square feet), and most architectural historians consider it to be the last of his Prairie houses, although, like the Johnson building, it did usher in Wright's interest in curved and circular forms, shapes he had not entertained seriously to this point. (The centerpiece of Wingspread, for instance, is a horseshoe-shaped fireplace.) Although only in his twenties when he met Wright, Hib Johnson had already had a complicated marital life. He and his first wife were divorced when his firstborn, Samuel C. Johnson, was six years old, in 1934. Two years later he married Jane Roach, who had two boys of her own, leading him to commission the house. However, there were soon signs that all was not well, as the Wright-Johnson correspondence shows, despite Wright's cheerful comment that his design, which gave everyone privacy, as well as immediate access to the outdoors, would provide a basis for domestic tranquillity for, as he wrote, "I think half the divorces in America could be prevented by a sensible plan for living. . . ." A handwritten letter to Wright from Johnson on University of Michigan Union stationery stated that Jane had had a terrible time following an unspecified hospital visit in the summer of 1937. Two months later she was at home recovering, but had expressed reservations about the design of the house as building began. Wright responded with the characteristic observation that Mrs. Johnson's reaction, of seeing the parts rather than the whole, was typical of a refined woman. "Architects have most trouble because of this characteristic trait of women. It makes them useful in other ways though and indispensible in still others. I guess we wouldn't have them changed, would we, Hib?" Mrs. Johnson's ideas do not appear again in the correspondence, and there is only a terse note from Johnson thanking Wright for his condolences a year later. Wright wrote that before the house was completed, an old workman observed that a white dove, which had been frequenting a belvedere, had flown away. "The workman shook his head. . . . 'The young mistress will never live in this house,' he said." He was right; she died of alcoholism before it was completed. It is strange that both wives of clients with the money and will to build lavishly, who had commissioned Wright almost at the same moment, would take self-destructive paths.

Johnson later married Irene Purcell, a film actress, and brought her to live at Wingspread. Samuel Johnson noted that Irene "did not relate" to the house and went to some lengths to redecorate the interiors and add paintings and objets d'art more to her taste. That gave rise to an incident that would be repeated often, whenever Wright returned to visit a house he had designed. Hib and Irene invited him to stay overnight a few years later. Wright was up with the lark at four in the morning and redecorated Irene's decorations. Johnson wrote, "He took some of the furniture that he didn't think was particularly appropriate and put it in a storeroom. He changed many of the paintings, and then waited for Irene to come down for breakfast. . . . I don't think she and Mr. Wright ever spoke seriously together after that. . . ." Of course the roof leaked. For the first year or so, Johnson had workmen at the ready with putty guns whenever it threatened to rain. Inevitably, the same story that was reported at Westhope became part of the lore at Wingspread: the same thunderstorm, the same outraged owner, the same telephone call, the same message—"Frank, . . . it is leaking right on top of my head!"—and the same reply, given with his usual insouciance.

Wright almost lost the Johnson commission because he was close to insisting that Johnson abandon his ugly industrial site and relocate his entire business four or five miles out of town, to be serviced by a railway, and surrounded by a "Johnson Village" for his employees. It was, of course, far too ambitious and visionary, but entirely of a piece with Wright's new ideas, which centered on a concept he called

Broadacre City, which he made into a model, exhibited widely and talked about for the rest of his life. Given his temperament and his penchant for telling people not only how to dress but how to arrange their furniture and what pictures to hang (if any), it was only a matter of time before he would become fascinated by the issue of social planning, which was, in any case, one of the central concerns of his day. Le Corbusier had introduced his concept, the *Ville Radieuse*, basically a series of apartment buildings and office towers grouped together in a park, and directed his entire architectural effort toward this vision of an idealized society. Wright's concept derived from entirely different models—inspired, perhaps, by the early garden cities of Morris and Sidney Webb, as interpreted by the famous English firm of Parker and Unwin—attempts to resettle city dwellers from the urban slums into healthier environments. Like these pioneering British concepts, Wright's was humanist, nature-oriented and arts-centered. He envisioned whole communities where each family would live on an acre of land, hence the name. These new towns, more like expanded villages, would be self-contained and self-sufficient, with carefully planned centers for art and recreation, worship, education, instruction, relaxation; an idyllic life in an environmentally sound setting, one that the car and the railway had now made possible.

Wright's social-planning ideas, after decades of being dismissed as freakish, have been reconsidered in recent years and, it is argued, were entirely in accord with the enlightened thought of his day. Lionel March, writing on Broadacre City in *Writings on Wright*, believed that Wright had been influenced by the ideas of the German author Silvio Gesell, who wrote that a new system of finance was needed if society were to avoid the pitfalls of monopoly capitalism and the credit system that had brought about economic collapse. Gesell's concept of a new system of "free-land" and "free-money," a currency that would lose its value over time, encouraging its use as soon as possible, was more than just a Utopian idea. During the early 1930s the free-money concept, one that Wright espoused for Broadacre City, was actually in use in many parts of the United States, and in 1933 a bill was presented in Congress "directing the Federal Treasury to issue a billion dollars worth of free-money," March wrote. "So this idea . . . was in its time and place a practical political economic proposition."

In Wisconsin, a new political party, called the Progressive, had been formed by Robert La Follette's eldest son Bob, just elected senator from Wisconsin at the age of thirty, and Philip, that erstwhile secretary of Wright's corporation, was now governor of Wisconsin. The Progressives believed in the right of men and women to own their homes, farms and places of employment, opposing corporate and absentee ownership. They lobbied for the public ownership of utilities and banking, for social security, cooperative movements of all kinds, in short, for a broad-based democracy. This socialist manifesto was essentially that adopted by Wright. He had realized, March writes, that "a city is not an arrangement of roads, buildings, and spaces, it is a society in action. . . . The city is a process, rather than a form." March concluded, "To my mind, Broadacre is one of the most brilliant examples of what is today described as 'futuristics'—the study of possible futures—applied to man's environment."

Just as the concept of the city itself needed to be redefined in the context of a reformed society so, too, the idea of the house needed revision to reflect the needs of the new age. During the same period, Wright was working intensively on his idea for a new kind of low-cost dwelling that he called the Usonian house, his attempt to bring designs of beauty and humanity within the range of ordinary people. He said he had taken that name, as John Sergeant writes in his excellent study of these houses, from a Utopian novel by Samuel Butler, *Erewhon*, of 1872, but no one has been able to find the reference. "It has been suggested that Wright picked up the name on his first European trip in 1910 when there was talk of calling the U.S.A. 'U-S-O-N-A,' to avoid confusion with the new Union of South Africa." Whatever its origin, the term came to symbolize for Wright an idealized way of living in a landscape, a vision in miniature of what a perfectly designed house could be, despite the severe constraints on size and the shortage, at first, of materials and, later, in the face of continually rising costs. The modern house might be modest by Oak Park standards but would remain true to his concept of the Prairie house with its elongated, one-floor plan and its respectful relationship to its site. It would dispense with servants' quarters, and basements and attics had long since gone from Wright's houses. Carports would replace garages, and the separate dining room, that sanctum sanctorum for the Arts and Crafts architect, would be folded into a corner of the living room. The kitchen and laundry, once banished to a corner of the house, were now placed in a pivotal position so as to give the homemaker instant access to the living quarters. The fireplace was never abandoned, and Wright continued to play with an infinite number of variations on that theme as if aware that, whatever items the modern family might be willing to dispense with, the central hearth would never be one of them, as posterity has demonstrated. Wright's designs for the Willey, Hoult and Lusk houses were early experiments with the Usonian idea, which he brought to a triumphant fulfillment with his house for Herbert Jacobs, a Wisconsin journalist, and his family. Working with a budget of $5,500 and on a small suburban lot, Wright audaciously placed his building flush with the street but without windows, saving these for the garden area, and provided 1,500 square feet of living space in all.

He redesigned everything, from a new system of central heating (in which hot-water pipes were inserted into a drained bed of cinders and sand, so as to warm the concrete-slab floors) to a wide overhanging roof made from a simple, insulated slab and containing a ventilation system, to a new method of prefabricating walls using three layers of board and two of tarpaper. During the next two decades he would continually experiment with better and cheaper methods of building, although radiant floor heat remained his method of choice. The Usonian house would, in short, be built with every possible labor and money-saving shortcut that ingenuity could devise. But since the house was the work of a master, it retained all the essential attributes: the same adroit use of space, the same quality of spatial surprise, the same aesthetic awareness and the same meticulous attention to the natural setting. The Jacobs house, built in the shape of an L, with its central kitchen work area, its abundant natural light provided by harmonious banks of floor-to-ceiling windows and doors opening onto terraces, and its sleek, distinctly Japanese lines, became one of Wright's favorite floor plans, and, Howe said, he was always looking for a way to use it again. The Jacobs house was economical if not spartan, but full of so many trend-setting ideas that it was an instant success. Herbert and Katherine Jacobs, who wrote a book about it, stated that almost from the first, they were besieged by visitors. They finally charged fifty cents to give a tour and calculated that, by the time they sold the house, this modest charge had paid back their architect's fee. Curtis wrote, "It was no accident that Wright's formula should have been adopted so rapidly by building contractors and cheap home catalogues. For its free-plan interiors and exterior patios captured precisely the ethos of an emergent middle-class suburban existence." Wright can hardly be blamed for the fact that the imitations "were all too often clumsy 'ranch-style' shoe-boxes, laid out in jerry-built monotony on the boom tracts of the 1950s."

In the winter of 1936, however, plans for the Jacobs house had come to a temporary halt. Wright had a rare collapse. He had been in the middle of a resurgence as he fought with Kaufmann, the contractor and everyone else on the scene at Fallingwater; made weekly trips to Racine, Wisconsin, to supervise construction of the Johnson Administration Building and Wingspread; and negotiated with the Hannas, a prosperous new set of clients as well as the Jacobs family. He was, after all, about to be seventy, although, apart from the occasional accident (in June of that year he fell off the road grader as he was making a new road to Hillside, broke a couple of ribs and wrenched his neck and leg), his physical stamina had seemed as good as ever. However, that winter his secretary Eugene Masselink wrote to tell one of his correspondents that, after returning late in the evening from Racine, he had contracted pneumonia in early December. Masselink made light of the illness but, in fact, it was serious. Wright ran a high temperature every day, was delirious, and it was a week before his temperature returned to normal and the doctor pronounced the crisis over. Iovanna said, "My mother pulled him through. He was in bed for a couple of weeks and finally asked for some speckled trout and a glass of champagne." There were further setbacks early in January when he had phlebitis in his left leg. Finally he was on the mend.

By mid-January Masselink was able to report that Wright had emerged from his sickbed at last, was seated in front of his own fire and even playing the harpsichord occasionally. He had been given a radio as a Christmas present and, "Mr. Wright controls the world from his chair." Although he made a fine recovery, the effects took months to dissipate completely because, in May, after Johnson took photographs, Wright complained that he still looked "pretty ragged" from his bout with pneumonia. The illness was a reminder that, healthy as he was, he was not immortal. It was also a demonstration, if one were needed, that without him, nothing could be decided or accomplished. It seemed prudent, perhaps, to begin thinking seriously about spending winters in a warmer climate.

Wright had, of course, been making forays to Arizona since he first began work on the Arizona Biltmore and San Marcos-in-the-Desert. Interestingly, as early as that, he was talking about the Ocatillo site as if it were a second Taliesin, as a letter to one of his "boys" in Switzerland, Werner Moser, shows: it was dated the summer of 1929. By the summer of 1930 he was prepared to abandon what remained of the temporary Taliesin. That was not much, to judge from a report that the kitchen, dining room, cooks' dormitory and a cottage had gone up in flames. He offered the camp to Dr. Chandler, who declined politely, observing that the cost of keeping a caretaker on the premises would be more than the camp was worth. There matters stood, but Wright had not given up his idea of transferring operations for the winter months. It was becoming clear that the effort involved in keeping all those people warm within Taliesin's drafty walls was becoming more and more of an ordeal every year. If they could go south, he probably reasoned, they would save so much money that the trip would pay for itself.

There was a further reason, as he told Cousin Richard. Olgivanna did not like the bleak Wisconsin winters and was drawn to the sand, stones and desert growth of the Arizona landscape. She recalls telling him, "I wish we had a home in Arizona. This is such a different world from Wisconsin—like another planet." He promised her that some day they would. He was, perhaps, looking for a reason to return, and the irrepressible Dr. Chandler was back in his life again, asking for a scaled-down version of the original plan, or a "Little San Marcos," as he called it. He thought he could now finance it with the aid of a government loan. Chandler offered them living quarters at a ranch complex, La Hacienda, on the edge of town, and they set out early in 1935. Howe wrote, "The sunny courtyard, upon which the various rooms opened, became our 'studio' and here we constructed the Broadacre City models. . . . The characteristic Taliesin life was transplanted to Arizona and we entertained guests from the nearby San Marcos hotel with Sunday evening dinner and . . . music. . . ." The Fellowship spent a second winter at La Hacienda early in 1936. Again, Chandler had to concede defeat: the government had turned down his application to build San Marcos. That should have ended the matter, but, after his illness, Wright was more determined than ever to find a permanent home in Arizona. Tafel recalled that, in 1937, Wright bought about eight hundred acres of land at $3.50 an acre on a southern slope of the McDowell Range overlooking Paradise Valley outside Scottsdale. In those days, hardly anyone lived there. It was perfect and unspoiled, but there was a hitch. The land had no history of water, the reason for its bargain price. Wright refused to be discouraged. He hired a well digger and kept spending money—the sizable sum of $10,000 in all. Finally the good news came that water had been found. Their desert camp could be built at last.

Memories of what became an annual exodus to Arizona, beginning in January 1938, frequently focus on the vicissitudes of the trip, which took several days. Jack Howe recalled the earlier caravans to visit Dr. Chandler: "We always seemed to leave in the middle of a blizzard. Usually the big truck we needed would be in the garage with a broken axle waiting for repairs." They would drive as far south as Dodgeville, where lunch would be waiting for them provided by Etta Parsons, the wonderful, large-hearted owner of a grocery store who willingly extended infinite credit to Mr. Wright and, perhaps for that reason, was one of the few creditors whom he willingly repaid. On that particular trip, by dark they reached Iowa City, where a professor of architecture had agreed to give them beds for the night. Wright appeared, saying "Here we are!" with twenty-seven people behind him. The professor took a long look, then gamely put up all the men in a large attic room over his school (most of them having brought sleeping bags); the women slept in his classroom. Another night was spent camping out in Richard Lloyd Jones's new house in Tulsa. Howe said, "I slept on the pool table in the billiard room with one guy, and two others were underneath." The one unvarying rule of the trip was that all the trucks and cars, eight vehicles in all, would meet at the same service station in order to get their gasoline wholesale. For subsequent trips, Howe recalled, Wright bought them an English Bantam car designed as a mobile kitchen that became known as the Dinky Diner. It had been built to carry food in pots in the center, along with plates, cutlery and accoutrements. Mabel, the cook, was in attendance, and Howe recalled grumbling one time because there was no ketchup, which became a standing joke. "We had our favorite picnic spots," he said. "Usually a schoolyard was a good place because we could get water there. We'd pull our cars around into a circle and build a fire in the middle to cut down on the wind.

"I remember one time that Mr. Wright decided to go by way of Death Valley. He had seen paintings in Germany of the Grand Canyon, giving the view from the north side where you can see for about a mile, and was ambitious to see it for himself. First we got into a sandstorm in Death Valley and could not move until all the carburetors had been cleaned out. Then we went onward until we were approaching the north rim in Utah at night. We had no headlights and did not know where we were, but Mr. Wright kept telling us to drive on. Finally he said, 'Better stop here,' and we all pulled up. When we got out we discovered we were fifteen feet away from the edge."

Taliesin West took several years to build, and while waiting for more permanent quarters, apprentices took their sleeping bags and erected temporary structures for themselves and their families. Larry Lemmon, who was on the first expedition, recalled that each was issued enough canvas and lumber to build a temporary house. He built his against a paloverde tree but had to cut off one of its branches and received a stern lecture from Wright. As one of the cooks, he had constructed an earth closet in which to keep provisions and recalled cleaning maggots off a piece of meat. They had to eat it, so he disguised the meat with plenty of garlic and recalled, "It was one of the tastiest meals we ever had." At night there was the cry of coyotes. There were plagues of grasshoppers, scorpions and lizards. But the desert in spring was enchanting. Olgivanna Wright remembered the "staghorn cactus, prickly pear, saguaros, and the red feather-like cluster of ocotillo blossoms ending each angular branch. We often stopped to crush the leaves of the grease-bush and inhaled the sharp medicinal odor. . . . The desert floor was covered with tiny orange colored blossoms and silver grass disappeared into the golden sands. . . ."

Work began at once. Fritz remembered seeing Wright draw the plans for the camp on brown wrapping paper, aided by Jack Howe. "No blueprints were ever made, and I think that sometimes what was drawn one day was built the next." Wright began by devising what he called "desert concrete," a combination of cement and large chunks of rock, poured into slanting walls and topped off with superstructures of redwood and canvas. Wright wanted massive walls, in those days before air conditioning, to keep rooms cool in the daytime and warmer at night. Blake wrote, "Through the canvas, light would filter and fill the interior with a lovely glow; just under the deeply cantilevered roof rafters, there would be viewing slots that opened up the great desert horizon; and all around the base of the concrete-and-rock parapets, there would be stepped-down terraces, pools, and gardens that made the entire group of buildings a dreamlike oasis in the desert."

It was an oasis and it was dreamlike, but not achieved without an immense amount of work. The "desert concrete" walls were built throughout the camp, which became nine hundred feet long, and they did all the work themselves. It became a point of pride, Fritz wrote, to be able to take a wheelbarrow filled with rock or concrete up a plank runway to the top of a chimney, one pulling it up with a rope while the other pushed. He added, "Wes [Peters] greatly accelerated the construction time of some of these walls by promising the crew a

dinner out if we reached a certain distance by a certain time. . . ."
They transported interesting-looking boulders, perhaps four feet high,
and covered with Indian petroglyphs, down to the camp as decorations,
using Caterpillar tractors and a "stoneboat" made from a sheet of steel.
They moved cacti to new locations and transplanted a saguaro that
probably weighed a ton, using an improvised sling and plenty of
ropes. They laid roads and wired up lights and sometimes found
themselves in comical predicaments, as when Charles Samson, newly
returned from New York, tried to jump over a cholla cactus in his
beautiful new jodhpurs and riding boots and missed, covering his
posterior with hundreds of painful burrs.

Everyone developed an enormous respect for the desert depressions
called arroyos, or "washes," that could turn into raging rivers, and
there were many such between Taliesin West and Phoenix. Wright
wrote that they might be marooned for days on end and, "At times
on the way to and from Phoenix for supplies I would sit in the car,
Olgivanna by my side, when my feet were on the brakes under water
up to my knees." There was the famous occasion when Gene Masselink's parents, on their way out from Phoenix, were several hours late
arriving at camp. One of the apprentices took a station wagon out to
look for them. Fritz wrote, "He came to a flooded wash and decided
to back up and cross it by sheer speed. He was soon adrift in five or
six feet of water and had to swim for it." There were disappointments
and discouraging setbacks but, for most of them, the desert camp, as
it was usually called during Wright's lifetime, was an escape and a
release.

From Wright's description it is clear that the great allure of his
campsite was the dazzling, unobstructed view it offered in those early
days, stretching for miles. He wrote, "Just imagine what it would be
like on top of the world looking over the universe at sunrise or at
sunset with clear sky in between. . . . An esthetic, even ascetic,
idealization of space. . . ." As the grandson of pioneers, he was too
close to the experience not to want a newfound land of his own. Living
in the desert was a "spiritual cathartic." It swept one's character clean
of old ways of thinking, and one was ready for "fresh adventure."

By 1937 Wright had become known for his fearless attacks on such
subjects as American politics, economics and the general level of
architecture, not just his opposition to architects of the school favored

Taliesin West

*Olgivanna Wright in the great room of Taliesin West
after her husband's death*

A classic example of "streamlining": the Johnson Wax building

Interior of the Johnson Wax building showing the "lilypad" columns and the diffused overhead lighting

*William Wesley Peters, Wright and Hib Johnson on site
during construction*

Forecourt of the Hanna house

by the Museum of Modern Art. When he arrived in Washington in
the summer of 1935, where his model for Broadacre City went on
view at the Corcoran Gallery of Art, he was pounced upon by journalists
in the hope that he would say something controversial. Was it true,
one asked, that he was against capitalism? Wright was in a mellow
mood that day. "I'm not against capitalism," he answered, smiling.
"The time to hit capitalism is not when it's down. Let the dear old
thing die." A statement of that kind might have led many an observer
to conclude that he was anti-capitalist and perhaps anti-American as
well. Writing about Broadacre City that same year, Stephan Alexander
observed in *New Masses* that "the significance of Mr. Wright's project
is that it points inexorably to the necessity for the removal of capitalism
and the creation of a socialist society as the primary condition for the
progressive development of architecture."

On the other hand, Wright was perfectly capable of exclaiming
that "I believe in a capitalist system. I only wish I could see it tried
some time." The fact was that, where politics were involved, and as
a loyal nephew of Jenkin Lloyd Jones's, he would always side instinctively with the most liberal position, and in the early 1930s, as has
been noted, he was emphatically in favor of public ownership and the
decline of big business without ever being a communist; he would,
perhaps, have declined to be called a socialist as well. It would be a
mistake to look for a consistent position about politics, in particular
from someone as mercurial as Wright, given that it was far from being
one of his major concerns. It would be fairer to say that he began the
decade as an enthusiast and soon discovered some shortcomings that
he, characteristically, committed to paper. But when he was invited
to attend the First All-Union Congress of Soviet Architects in Moscow
in June 1937, these reservations were not uppermost. He was ready
to like the Russians themselves, out of loyalty, perhaps, to his wife
and daughters. He had always been ready to go anywhere when the
invitation was cordial enough, as might be gathered from his years
in Japan and Germany, and was none too scrupulous about the shortcomings of a country's particular political system or the reasons why
he might have been asked. He was actively engaged in furthering his
"renaissance," and by 1937 was enjoying something of a revival elsewhere in Europe, where his architecture had been exhibited or his
writings published in France, Belgium, Holland, Germany, Italy,
Poland, Hungary and England, as well as Japan, although not east of
Poland. The Moscow invitation presented new opportunities for self-

promotion, and Wright was not loath. Besides, Olgivanna had not been to Russia since she had escaped twenty years earlier, and had relatives and friends still living there, including her mother. And, if there was an aspect of his nature that still courted the role of outsider, beyond the pale, this Russian trip would give it a new outlet. The idea that he and his Fellowship had elected themselves as part of some universal brotherhood, and were therefore outside the petty constraints of conventional mores or international boundaries, had a great attraction for Wright at this period. Holden recalls his boasting at about this time that he was the first American anarchist. He became quite deflated to learn that this was not the case, Josiah Warren having come first. Wright immediately took up the cause of Warren's life and began to lecture about him, Mrs. Wright told Holden later. They had attracted the attention of the FBI, she said, only half jokingly.

There were six days of speeches. Wright's came at the end, giving it more the character of an "after-dinner" commentary than a keynote address, as Donald Leslie Johnson pointed out in his essay, "Frank Lloyd Wright in Moscow: June, 1937." All things considered, it was a carefully phrased statement of his own philosophy and one that Olgivanna had no doubt translated into Russian with even greater care. He cautioned that the new Soviet society should shun what he called "grandomania," i.e., the unthinking replication of outmoded European forms, just as much as the sterile reductionist approach of the "new" architects, both of which, he noted elsewhere, he found in Moscow but not much else. He urged them to build "organically" without describing what that meant, and spoke about their opportunity to plan for new societies without defining what kind of "correct" planning he had in mind. In short, he made a diplomatic speech into which official opinion could read anything it chose. It was received with somewhat less than the overwhelming ovation he describes in his autobiography. However, he returned full of admiration and affection for the people he had met, and perhaps this new enthusiasm for what he called the "Russian spirit" accounts for the combative statements he made upon his return, centering on his claim that American journalists had not been telling the truth about Russia. He also said, "Were I in Stalin's place I would kick them out, all correspondents, and for the good of everyone concerned." In that first flush of his ardor he also made the remark that "if Stalin has betrayed the Revolution, he has betrayed it into the hands of the Russian people," which led to some heated exchanges when he returned home.

It was an early indication that Wright was slipping into a new role as senior statesman of the arts and that he was perfectly prepared to exploit every opportunity to make pronouncements on any and every subject, rashly made and soon regretted. By then he would have predicted, and rather enjoyed, the storm he stirred up, but he could not have dreamed that his family would one day be linked, through Wesley Peters, whose second wife was Svetlana Alliluyeva, to the great Stalin himself. Nor would he have liked very much the fact that the second Mrs. Peters would leave her marriage in part because of the stresses of the "psychological yoke" of the Fellowship he had founded.

However, it seems clear that the trip to Moscow had the fairly immediate result of producing some serious reservations about Soviet Russia, as may be seen in the book Wright wrote with Baker Brownell, *Architecture and Modern Life*, published the following year. Both authors took the view that Nazi Germany, Fascist Italy and Communist Russia were already demonstrating the evils of centralized government. Their emphasis was upon the opposite, i.e., decentralization, the disappearance of the city, and the return to a truly participatory democracy that would, by allowing individual liberties to flourish, also correct the evils of capitalism short of a revolution. That this remained Wright's view is suggested by an "Our House" column that Olgivanna Wright wrote some years after World War II. In it she told the detailed story of their arrival in Russia and the incident, one gathers, that helped bring about this change of attitude.

They had crossed the Atlantic on the *Queen Mary*, disembarking at Cherbourg, and traveled onward toward Paris and Berlin for short stays before taking the train for Moscow. Arriving at the Russian border, they got off the train at Njegorieloje for the obligatory customs inspection of luggage. Olgivanna Wright, acting as translator, began to open their trunk and suitcases while her husband walked around. He was carrying a roll of drawings under his arm, and one of the customs officials, a woman, showed a sudden interest in what might be concealed inside the roll. She demanded to see it. Wright looked at her and stated in plain terms that she was not to put her unclean hands on these architectural drawings, which he was taking to a convention in Moscow. The woman became red in the face, and another official, a man, became hostile. Wright, so ready in theory to find every virtue in Russian society, was just as prompt (in reality) to tell them all what they could do with their rules and regulations. He would never, ever release the drawings. They would have to remove them by force. Didn't they know who he was, and so on.

Olgivanna Wright was becoming more and more apprehensive as she tried, on the one hand, to persuade the Russians to rescind their order while, on the other, attempting to reason with her outraged and pugnacious husband. She was convinced that it would end in an "international incident," and became even more frightened when Wright, who had stormed away from them across the platform, was escorted back by a soldier at riflepoint. The male official went to telephone. Olgivanna was trembling, and even the woman customs official seemed flustered. Only Wright, his usual magnificent self, was daring anyone to come an inch closer. After what seemed an age, word came to allow them to proceed. Once they arrived in Moscow they received a huge welcome and were shown every courtesy, but Olgivanna never forgot that frightening experience. Even her husband, as he wrote, could not repress an apprehensive "glance now and then at the walls" the day they lunched with the American ambassador and his wife after his firsthand experience of what lay beneath the surface of Soviet society. They never went back.

One of the comments that received the most applause during Wright's speech in Moscow that summer of 1937 was his attack on the modern skyscraper, construction of which had, until the depression, boomed and which had transformed the profile of American cities. As Curtis wrote, this modern solution to the problem of cramming as many people as possible onto smaller and smaller parcels of land had led to "the rapid growth of highways, and the creation of suburban sprawl. The resultant pressures on urban services were overwhelming, but perceptions of this crisis of mechanization were far from most architects' minds," with the exception of Wright. He, it has been noted, had not benefited from that boom and disapproved of the architects most involved with such design, such as Raymond Hood, George Howe, William Lescaze and Walter Gropius. It is true that he himself had experimented with designing skyscrapers in Chicago and New York City, using his metaphor of a tree with a central trunk and cantilevered concrete slabs for branches, but by the 1930s he seemed convinced that the building style was doomed because the car would bring about the death of American cities. "Americans, he believes, want spaciousness. Their buildings should express that desire, instead of huddling together. Buildings, he insists, should be spread out horizontally, instead of being thrown toward the sky." As for the "vainglorious skyscraper," that was one of the most abominable inventions of mankind. Wright also liked to ask, "Who but the landlord and the bank are benefited by skyscrapers? They are Molochs raised for commercial greatness," and should be taxed out of existence.

Denunciations were, of course, his specialty, the more sweeping the better. The state of New York was the most "provincial of all provinces." As for Pittsburgh, "It would be cheaper to abandon it." Speaking of Los Angeles, he said it was "the great American commonplace. It is as if you tipped the U.S. up so that all the commonplace people slid down here to Southern California." (He liked this so well that he kept polishing it and finally evolved the comment that, "You know, the U.S. tips as you go West and everything loose ends up in Los Angeles.") All American architecture was terrible, save for its industrial buildings; archaeologists of the future would excavate the ruins and find "only bathrooms." One notes the relish behind the condemnations, as well as a new note of respect that had crept into descriptions of his views in the newspapers. He was no longer so easy to dismiss as a crackpot. He was becoming someone to reckon with. He had designed the front cover for *Town and Country*, July 1937, and made the cover of *Time* magazine in 1938. His project of a house for a family with an income of five to six thousand dollars appeared on the cover of *Life* that same year, and, perhaps most significant of all, a complete issue of *Architectural Forum* (January 1938) was devoted to his work, and he was invited to design it himself. Universities like Wesleyan in Middletown, Connecticut, began to confer honorary degrees upon him, and academies of art in unlikely places, Berlin, for instance, elected him an honorary member. The winds of change were blowing, even at the Museum of Modern Art.

Frank Lloyd Wright went to Middletown, Connecticut, to receive his honorary degree in June 1938. By a coincidence, Henry-Russell Hitchcock was teaching there. Wright's relationship with that architectural historian had not noticeably improved in the five or six years since they had met. The year before, in the summer of 1937, Hitchcock had written an article in the *London Review* that had prompted an angry letter from John E. Lautner, Jr., a Wright apprentice, because Hitchcock had referred to Wright in the past tense. Hitchcock wrote, "For, I suppose, there might conceivably grow up in a vacuum, without benefit of intention, a sense of form wholly of the twentieth century and wholly American, as was Wright's in the days when he was an active architect before the war." Lautner pointed out that Wright was in the midst of building five major works and hardly qualified as a man who had faded into the background. It looked like another gratuitous snub from Hitchcock, and Wright could not help capitalizing upon it. He did not know how or why Hitchcock had managed to appoint himself the arbiter of taste in architectural matters, he wrote. However, he did recognize the depth of ignorance behind Hitchcock's dicta, and suggested that the latter join his Fellowship for a year or two. "We will take you . . . and see if we can't put some fundamental understanding of the great art you only serve to abuse and confuse into the empty hole. . . ."

Hitchcock never answered that letter but, the following year, extended a polite invitation to the Wrights to stay with him during commencement. Wright promptly accepted, adding, "I feel that a good talk will straighten out our 'differences.' " By then he knew that he had acted hastily. As usual, when faced with the prospect of meeting a living, breathing human being rather than an abstraction, Wright's anger evaporated. After their visit he wrote to thank his host, with the comment "Yours is a master hand at heaping coals of fire." But Hitchcock, too, had decided to make his peace with Wright, as the fact of his invitation showed. Berthold Lubetkin, a Russian architect who founded the Techton group in London and went on to build High Point I in Highgate (1933–35), which Curtis called "an intelligent adaptation of Le Corbusier's white forms of the twenties," recalled that he and Hitchcock were traveling through France in the summer of 1937 when the latter received a letter from John D. Rockefeller, Jr. The message was that the Museum of Modern Art's enthusiasm for the International Style was waning, and its new interest was the work of those homegrown American architects whom Hitchcock thought might, entirely by chance, have evolved something worth calling a native style. The shift to Wright, in other words, had taken place. Hitchcock's studied lack of interest in Wright, as his article showed, had been a tactical error, and he was about to be brought up to date by the museum itself. Its curator of architecture, John McAndrew, was one of the first visitors to spend a weekend at the curious new house the Kaufmanns had built at Bear Run. He went there in the autumn of 1937 and returned full of praises for Fallingwater. A photographic exhibition was promptly organized. Of all the events that were conspiring to bring Wright back to the public eye, this shift of emphasis at the Museum of Modern Art has to be considered one of the most important. It gave Lewis Mumford, Wright's dedicated ally, the opportunity to praise him once more in print, as he did early in 1938. The structural elements of Fallingwater were part of its great appeal, Mumford wrote, but so were some of the telling details, such as the rectangular pool Wright had designed above the river level, "proof that Wright never thinks of architectural design except in relation to the third dimension, plus movement through space. Hence the perpetual breathless sense of surprise one receives. . . . One looks at two-dimensional compositions and exhausts them in a view or two, but one must go through Wright's work, finding new compositions, new revelations, new relationships at every step." The exhibition, he wrote, showed Wright at the top of his form, "undoubtedly the world's greatest living architect, a man who can dance circles around any of his contemporaries."

Two years later Wright was paid another compliment by MOMA, a retrospective exhibition devoted to his career: plans, drawings, photographs, models and plenty of captions. Through what seems to have been a misunderstanding there was, however, no catalogue, and the installation was confusing, critics pointed out. Wright, always supersensitive to any hint that he was less than perfect, responded with his usual defensiveness but recognized the validity of the criticism. Someone was needed to write about his work and put it in the proper chronological order. What he needed was not so much a critical review as an interpretation of his ideas. He even had a title: *In the Nature of Materials*. The month the MOMA exhibition opened, November 1940, Wright wrote to Hitchcock inviting him to be the author. He offered to pay all expenses plus a further five hundred dollars and to split the publisher's royalties between them, two-thirds to Hitchcock and one-third to Wright. Hitchcock jumped at the chance.

Hitchcock saw his work on Wright's oeuvre as "purely archaeological," unearthing the old photographs, documents and drawings, which he would then present to Wright, "so that a history of almost sixty years of architecture will glow with . . . that life which is in all your work . . . and which the work of scholars like myself is usually so devoid of," he added handsomely. He also thought he would need more money soon, and Wright, in the spring of 1941, was at his most welcoming. However, that did not make him an easier man to deal with, since he was always ready to fancy himself ill served whenever money was involved. He did not like the oblong format that the publisher had settled on, and thought that the fault must somehow be Hitchcock's, writing revealingly to one of the publishers, Charles

Duell, that he was suspicious of this "young academic whiskers." He was then outrageous enough to tell Hitchcock he distinctly remembered that he had suggested a royalty split of fifty-fifty, but had reconsidered and, in light of all the work he had done himself, and money spent, now thought he should get three-fourths to Hitchcock's one-fourth. It was Wright at his least attractive, settling old scores perhaps, and Hitchcock ought to have held him to their earlier agreement, since he had it in writing. Instead, he wrote that he would be happy to accept whatever arrangement Wright wanted. He just hoped he was not being asked to pay for the book out of his own pocket since he could not afford it. That defused another potential storm, and Wright had the grace to thank the author, once the book appeared, for having done "a good job."

The publisher for *In the Nature of Materials*, Duell, Sloan and Pearce, had taken up Wright's cause with enthusiasm and was planning to publish three books about him. The second was an anthology of his writings, *Frank Lloyd Wright on Architecture*, edited by Frederick Gutheim, and the third, a new edition of *An Autobiography*. Gutheim said, "I was a friend of Cap Pearce [another partner] and I remember him calling me to say that Longmans, Green and Company, which had published his autobiography in 1932, had gone bankrupt. The plates of that edition were for sale." Gutheim suggested he buy them, which he promptly did: for four hundred dollars. "Then we had to persuade Wright to bring his autobiography up to date by another ten years and cut 35,000 words from his early life. We finally managed to do that." Gutheim was the one who suggested that the three books appear as a group, as they eventually did: his own in 1941, Hitchcock's in 1942 and Wright's in 1943. All of them were valuable additions to the slim collection of books about Wright then available. Hitchcock's was particularly important because it was one of the first evaluations of Wright's career by a fully trained architectural historian, as Gutheim said. Evaluation may, however, be too strong a word. Hitchcock's commentary is, by and large, blandly diplomatic, as one would expect of a book the copyright of which is jointly owned by the writer and the subject of the text. It would be decades before Wright's work was subjected to independent critical scrutiny; not that this was anything Wright wanted or needed at that point. In terms of his growing public, what he needed was precisely what Hitchcock provided: a levelheaded, impeccably researched survey, placing his work in precise chronological order and showing its coherent development. *In the*

Nature of Materials became one of the standard reference works about Wright and has never been out of print.

Wright's choice of title, emphasizing materials and their use, seems partly defensive, as if to rebut the charge that he was no longer modern and "up-to-date," concerned with the latest technology. This may have been a reason why he was so ready to experiment with relatively untested materials in his most ambitious and visible projects such as the Johnson Wax buildings. Articles he wrote for the *Architectural Record* in the late 1920s are almost entirely concerned with technical questions, in the use of sheet metal, concrete, glass, stone and so on. He had to be continually pushing the limits of his craft if he wanted his claim to be far in advance of the crowd taken seriously, but it would be doing him a disservice to believe this was the only motivation. His temperament would have ensured that he explored new methods even if no question of status were involved. And he belonged to that small band of architects who had seen, as Curtis wrote, that mechanization had reached a crisis. This particular subject was very much on his mind after he returned from London in the summer of 1939, where, to general surprise, he had been invited to give a series of lectures by the Royal Institute of British Architects. Two years later that august institution would present him with the same award it had also offered to John Ruskin, the Royal Gold Medal for Architecture.

Wright was also invited to dine at the Art Workers Guild. In his letter of invitation, his old friend Ashbee expressed the belief that the dinner would be far less stuffy and pompous than the one he had attended, held by the R.I.B.A. The guild's present master was a cabinetmaker and designer; Ashbee himself had been master in 1929, and Lutyens had followed him. William Morris was master in 1892 —wasn't that the year they had met, Ashbee asked, incorrectly. As it happened, Wright could not be there. He was on his way to Paris after having given "four hard lectures," but was delighted to say he had met some of Ashbee's old comrades, including Lutyens and Voysey. The trip had brought back a host of memories and old associations, and perhaps this was the reason why he decided to address the Arts and Crafts Society at Hull House in November of that year. When he had first given his famous lecture "The Art and Craft of the Machine" there almost forty years before, he had truly believed it could become a tool for creative expression, if placed in the right hands. That dream had died as, by degrees, he saw advertising and commercialization take over to such a degree that the machine now owned man and the depression had demonstrated the havoc that this state of affairs could cause. He had returned out of "parental solicitude" to exhort the young to learn to see life as structure and to grasp the essential nature of materials so that they could, in their turn, develop a truly indigenous, organic architecture. The speech was, in its rambling way, quintessentially Wrightian: quixotic, contentious and idealistic. It was clear—as he panned the British for the revival of the Neo-Georgian style that had driven out the Arts and Crafts Movement in the same breath that he denounced the vogue for the colonial that had accomplished the same thing in the United States—that what he was mourning was the death of the Arts and Crafts Movement and all that it had symbolized. In a sense he had not resigned himself to it, and never would. In all essential ways he remained true to his statement of 1908 that "radical though it may be, the work here illustrated is dedicated to a cause conservative"; but the words *radical* and *conservative* were coming closer than ever before: "Were our eyes opened we would see that the radical is the actual conservative." He had, in other words, remained true to his belief in himself as a radical dissenter who, by virtue of his personality and conviction, would cleanse his art of its stylistic sins and create a Utopian present. He was still responding to beauty in the only way that Ruskin would have approved of, that is, with his whole moral being. He had, like Ruskin, kept intact that most vital aspect of himself, his imaginative and spiritual responsiveness. In common with many British artists of the twentieth century, he had instinctively rejected modernity, clinging to his "unashamed preference for an older, romantic and spiritual tradition," as Peter Fuller wrote. He had remained faithful to the good, the true and the beautiful, and always would.

18

The Revolutionist as Architect

Because I never forget the fate
Of men, robbed of their riches, suddenly
Looted by death—
                "The Wanderer"
                Poems from the Old English

The image of Wright as embattled advocate, the one with which he became identified during his struggle for recognition in the 1930s, had the effect of attracting some loyal adherents. As the decade drew to a close Wright was emerging as something between a prophet and a public scold, but certainly an artist whose work was keeping alive "a rich and poetic conception of architectural metaphor at a time when the theory of architecture was being reduced . . . to a matter of petty problem-solving and of desiccated technics," as Norris Kelly Smith wrote. If he was still a highly visible target for his critics, he was, at the same time, the logical choice for those clients who were instinctively opposed to modernism as defined by the Bauhaus. Almost the quintessential examples of these were Dr. and Mrs. Paul R. Hanna, both college professors who earnestly desired to build to the highest principles—they were children of ministers—but who had rejected the International Style's purism and austerity. Then they discovered

Wright's volume of Princeton lectures and sat up half the night reading it to each other. They immediately wrote to congratulate him and were promptly invited to visit Taliesin. They subsequently spent a day there, most of which seems to have been spent listening to Mr. Wright espouse his now-familiar themes. In short, they were the ideal clients, intelligent, malleable and adventurous, although it would be almost five years before Hanna joined the Stanford faculty and they were ready to build on a handsome scale. They wanted a house big enough for themselves and their three children, and to accommodate up to thirty people for dinner and a hundred guests for receptions, cocktails and teas, as well as overnight guests and student seminars. They expected to be surprised but were taken aback to discover that the architect intended to experiment on them by building a house on the hexagon. Every corner, in other words, would be 120 degrees, and the inevitable bedroom "tail" that, in the Jacobs house, formed the end of its L shape, could now be more completely integrated with the main part of the house. The Hannas gamely agreed, insisting only that Wright's original plan for a single large bedroom for their three children (with screens between beds) be amended in favor of separate rooms. Once the final site had been approved, a hilly slope of about an acre and a half on the Stanford University campus in Palo Alto, California, Wright responded by designing a magnificent, U-shaped, wood-and-brick one-story plan, with immense walls of glass taking advantage of the view, while other rooms turned toward intimate terraces, the same concept that he had followed for Taliesin. Wright continued to experiment with the hexagon for some time before returning to his tried-and-tested module of the square. At least one reason seems obvious; most furniture is designed for rooms with 90-degree corners, and the built-in furniture and hexagonal tables, chairs and the like meant steadily rising costs, as the Hanna correspondence shows. Nevertheless one can see why Wright was attracted to the honeycomb motif, since it gave him enchanting opportunities for the constant shifts of direction and emphasis in which he delighted, the patterning of the maze. It was as if, like a player absorbed in a solo game of chess, he were setting himself ever more baffling challenges as he arranged these kaleidoscopic shapes to form complex and seamless unities. If the Hannas believed that theirs was the most amazing house Wright ever built, their pride is pardonable.

Squares and hexagons having lost some of their mystery, Wright then began to tackle triangles, parallelograms and, more and more in later years, the ultimate challenge of spirals, crescents and circles, themes he had begun with the Johnson Wax building. It was his good fortune that the kinds of clients who sought him out were invariably from the educated and articulate, but not necessarily well-heeled, professional classes. Like the Hannas, they were often on the fringe of the arts. There was, for instance, Isadore J. Zimmerman, a prominent physician who was, along with his wife, Lucille, a passionate amateur musician. The Zimmermans also pounced upon the Princeton lectures and subsequently commissioned a Usonian house for their site in Manchester, New Hampshire, in 1952. Or there were Herbert and Katherine Jacobs, struggling along on a journalist's tiny salary, who had given Wright a present in disguise by challenging him to build them a cheap house. That had turned out brilliantly, and when the Jacobs family, having outgrown its Usonian prototype, asked Wright for a larger one, the architect seized upon the opportunity. His demonstration that small houses could be aesthetically satisfying had been a triumph. His plan for Broadacres was proof that he had found it extremely interesting and instructive to consider social needs as well as personal ones. His experience of designing a tolerable environment in the inhospitable desert had been another resounding success, and during World War II the idea of saving on heating costs would have been newly fashionable. So when Jacobs invited him to design a five-bedroom house for his family in Middleton, Wisconsin, and presented him with an exposed hilltop site swept by icy winds in winter, Wright wrote enthusiastically that they were to be made "the goats" for his latest experiment, a solar house.

The Jacobses were duly presented with a crescent-shaped structure cunningly built into the hillside, where it was protected from severe winter weather by a berm of earth and, on the opposite side, faced a beautiful view. There, banks of windows would be surrounded by a half-circle of garden sunk four feet below floor level so as to provide, he explained, a pocket of air immediately in front of the windows and dead calm whatever the weather. This was a solution he had used once before when, at an early stage in his career, he had designed a boathouse and shed in Madison that had required a windless mooring shelter. Wright's term for his design was "streamlining," the fashionable word; nowadays it is looked upon as an audacious early experiment in solar design. He had envisioned a roof that would protect the windows from the sun's summer heat but allow it to penetrate the rooms in winter. In short, it was further proof of the way his imagination soared

The castlelike exterior of Wright's second design for
Mr. and Mrs. Herbert Jacobs

Another view of the Jacobs house, north side
Detail: South façade of the Jacobs house

when stimulated by the requirements of a demanding but beautiful site. It is rightly celebrated for its innovations, and yet, from the perspective of Wright's personality, what seems most notable is the fact that this most contemporary of dwellings looks, from one direction, exactly like a medieval fortress—turrets, gun emplacements, stone walls of gray limestone and all. This façade is reminiscent of those interpretations of the castle that were being made by a gifted English contemporary, one of the few architects Wright admired. Sir Edwin Lutyens successfully re-created the same sense of enclosure and security in his designs for castles that were, for all their fidelity, clearly the reinterpretations of a twentieth century sensibility. Only Lutyens rivaled Wright in his ingenious ability to breathe new life into ancient traditions, and perhaps this is why one is reminded of Lutyens's design for Lambay Castle (1905–08), Dublin, built on the site of an old house, surrounded by a circular rampart also constructed of gray limestone and including a range of buildings that was also partially sunken. At Lambay, the inhabitant is also protected from the elements, and Wright's design for the second Jacobs house is a reminder of the way visual metaphors took charge of his imagination whenever certain needs were uppermost. Absolutely impregnable from one vantage point, ravishingly open to every influence from the other, the second Jacobs house reconciles its opposites in one perfect statement of stone and glass.

The story of his houses that Herbert Jacobs, like the Hannas, felt almost compelled to write, makes it clear that a great deal of the construction of this second venture was done without Wright's involvement. Something terrible happened. Jacobs had made a written mention of the fact that Wright, then working on revisions to *An Autobiography* for a new edition (published in 1943), had "sought his help" in going over the manuscript. It seemed innocent enough, particularly since Jacobs had found nothing to add, but it struck Wright as meaning that "he sought my help in writing it," Jacobs continued. An awful schism opened between the two men that was later repaired, but it did demonstrate the perils that even ideal clients might expect to face in the delicate business of employing an architect of temperament. Another friendship was put to a similar test at about the same time, revolving around the building of a house for Lloyd and Kathryn Lewis.

Wright and Lloyd Lewis had known each other almost back to the days when he was known as Frank without the fancy middle name

and certainly without the abbreviation of a double *l*. They met in
1918 at the Tavern Club for writers, journalists, playwrights and
artists at the top of a Chicago skyscraper when Lewis was a sportswriter
for the *Chicago Daily News* (he later became its editor) and struck up
a friendship. During Wright's years of crisis, he took the ingenious
step of hiring Lewis to keep his name *out* of the newspapers. (Wright
fired him when he failed.) There was some Welsh in Lewis's background, or Wright thought there was, and he periodically addressed
his friend as Llewis, demanding to know why he refused to employ
the double *l* abbreviation. They were both friends of Wright's old
friend from Oak Park days, Alfred MacArthur, who later became a
Chicago banker and would finance Lewis's house. In the old days the
three of them would steal off on Friday afternoons for a picnic, roasting
corn over an open fire, and MacArthur's daughter recalls their yodeling
songs about the Buffalo Skinners at weekend parties. All this would
have been enough to endear Lloyd Lewis in Wright's eyes but then,
one afternoon in the mid-1930s, when they were staying at Taliesin
in Wisconsin, Lewis turned to his host and said, "Frank, I want you
to design a home for Kathryn and me, a home that will have the same
feeling and repose that this room has. I don't care what it is, just let
me feel, in whatever house you design, that I am sitting here in this
incredible room." That was the start of it all.

Wright knew Libertyville, the area on the Des Plaines River where
Lewis had bought a lot, and was aware that the flattish, dampish,
shady site presented problems. He therefore designed the house high
above the ground, with a handsome second-floor living room that
would provide the same kind of panoramic view of the river and
marshes that Taliesin commanded over the Wisconsin countryside.
The house, a long, low structure supported by brick pillars, represented a return to his earlier rectangular plans, with the added fillip
of an entrance at ground level that gave no hint of the glories to be
encountered at the top of the stairs, the splendid hearth, the screened
terraces and the expansive vistas. Naturally enough, the Lewises were
thrilled with the plans even though the estimated cost jumped rather
quickly from the $15,000 they had called their top figure in June
1939, to a total of $17,600 a few months later. It jumped again after
Lewis received an estimate of $19,500 from the contractor Wright
had recommended.

As Lewis was recovering from that blow, Wright and MacArthur
were engaged in a bantering correspondence having to do with the

architect's disinclination, the banker said, for using standard materials and practice. MacArthur reminded him that bankers must be practical, that the money must be repaid, and that the house must look like a good resale proposition, concepts that were loftily spurned by Wright: "Since I've been pretty damn near jail or assassination every moment of my professional career expect no tear from me in this business of helping to get houses built which will be safe investments. . . ."

Meantime the architect was exerting the full force of his persuasive powers. The points Alfred raised showed that he completely misunderstood what the architect intended, not that the misunderstanding would last for ten minutes if they were to sit down together. And Wright apologized for having asked for architect's fees in advance from Lewis. He was in Arizona, he had been extravagant as usual, and he thought someone would lend Lewis the money if Alfred did not. "I always think people have more money than they have—especially me." Then Lloyd and Kathryn drove adventurously to Arizona to visit him in the company of their friend Marc Connelly, the playwright, and once they were back home in April all the difficulties had been resolved. By early summer, construction was underway.

Almost from the start, problems surfaced. Inspecting the work in the summer of 1940, Lewis was horrified to discover that the cypress boards that had been erected on the back wall were of inferior quality, uneven in color, full of knotholes, and some were cracked. Lewis was insistent that Wright do something at once. He urged Wright to inspect the work himself. Wright did not, but instructed Edgar Tafel, who had been sent to supervise construction, to reject the labor and have the unacceptable boards removed and replaced. Other reproofs soon followed. The balconies, as designed, were so high that no one sitting in the living room, bedrooms or study could see the ground or the river—the tops of trees alone were visible. If Wright simply removed the top board, the problem would be solved. Lewis had also realized that the kitchen, as designed, would be far too dark—he called it "a friar's cell"—and would require artificial light in the daytime, an expense he would like to avoid. In a telegram that followed, Lewis called the balcony heights "ridiculous." Perhaps it was that word that did it. At any rate, Wright fired back a wire of his own saying he had been insulted and was withdrawing from the project.

Lewis was stunned. "You say in your wire that I regard myself as a greater architect than you. You misread the letter . . . and there is nothing to that whatsoever. You are, in my opinion, just where you were in 1918, only now more people over the world recognize it. To go along for years arguing and speaking freely and then get mad at one item and toss over the job and an old friendship isn't fair to me," he wrote. What could be insulting about his discovery that the balcony was high? It seemed a natural enough mistake and easily corrected. However, if it meant that much to Wright, he, Lewis, was not going to insist upon a change and have it destroy their friendship because Wright was worth more to them than any house. His letter was indignant, heartfelt and sorrowful, and it had the desired effect. Wright had not, he wrote by return mail, made the balconies an arbitrary height. Such decisions were calculated to the last inch, and for aesthetic as well as safety reasons they had to remain that height. But if Lewis really insisted upon it, Wright was prepared to perforate the top board (so as to give glimpses of the view). As for the kitchen, he had given it four toplights that would solve the problem. Wright thought Lewis and Kathryn had been "swell" to that point. Lewis called Wright's letter "swell," and the crisis passed.

It was to be the first of many, revolving around the fact that Wright simply had not made the proper allowances for the extremes of heat and cold in that climate. This elementary error perhaps stemmed from his understandable desire to give his friend what he had asked for, i.e., another Taliesin living room. By elevating the main living floor up a level, he had resolved one problem but created another. MacArthur put his finger on the flaw when he pointed out that the air constantly circulating under the main living floor would make it impossible to heat. It would be far better to redraw the house as a one-floor plan and place the heating pipes in the usual concrete slab. He also rightly pointed out how much heat would be lost through the large glass windows Wright had designed, and although storm windows were not mentioned, they were implied. He was quite correct, as Tafel later acknowledged; the hot-water pipes Wright designed to run under the main living floor never worked efficiently, even after insulation had been added. Furthermore, the lack of adequate insulation in the roof, walls and floor (it is unclear whether this was the fault of the builder or the architect) guaranteed a series of anguished letters from the new owners. They must have moved into the house just before Christmas 1940, because on December 19, Tafel wired Wright that the home's bedroom, entry and dining rooms were "uninhabitably cold." A letter from Lewis soon followed. The house was exquisitely beautiful and caused visitors to gasp with admiration, but the living room temperature sank to sixty-three degrees whenever the wind blew against the glass, the bedroom was colder than that, and the main entry had to have a radiator. To top it all off, the fireplaces refused to draw. He raised the taboo subject of storm windows, for which he was getting estimates. Wright, with many dark hints about "interference," vetoed the idea. They were expensive and ugly. What the house needed was the proper weather stripping, a better pump on the hot-water system and adequate floor and roof insulation; walls were not that important. The spring was on its way, he wrote from Arizona in March. The house he had built was intended to be beautiful and sensible. It was important pioneering, "not intended to coddle parasites. . . ." Lewis replied promptly that Wright's notion of comfort seemed to be that of a man living in the tropics, "viewing the cold north through a haze of heat waves." If Wright were living in his house, he would "bellow louder than I."

Problems with heating were followed almost immediately by the discovery that the house was impossibly hot in summer, and there were no screen windows. Again, Wright was unable to understand how anyone could be so bothered by "a passing petty epidemic of special little green bugs," but since Lewis was threatening to move out, Wright dispatched Caraway to oversee the installation of the proper screens, as well as rock wool insulation for the roof. Then, in the autumn of 1941, the house started to spring leaks. Lewis wrote to remind Wright that he had already told him the roof leaked and asked whether the builder would honor his year's guarantee to make the proper repairs. Now there was a new problem: water was coming in through the wall, as well, and that was decidedly novel. There were pots and pans everywhere. At last, Wright appeared personally to inspect the problems. One by one the issues were resolved, although the fireplace that refused to work properly defied even his ingenuity, he confessed in 1943. One day it would learn, he insisted.

Despite its flaws, it was clear that the Lewis house was a great success. Among those at the gala housewarming were mutual friends of the Lewises and the Wrights: the playwright Charles MacArthur and his wife, Helen Hayes; Harpo Marx; Marc Connelly; and Alexander Woollcott. The last-named was about to crown his career by becoming an actor; he would play himself in a comedy that had been written about him by Moss Hart and George Kaufman, *The Man Who Came to Dinner*. He was a frequent houseguest of the Lewises, perhaps a closer friend of theirs than of Frank's, and he penned many graceful tributes, writing in 1942 that "Just to be in that house uplifts the heart and refreshes the spirit." By then he was the toast of Broadway, but he had had another in a series of heart attacks and his days as an actor were over. He died a few months later. Lewis himself would die of a heart attack one evening in 1949. Writing to Wright, his widow said that her husband's last eight years had been his happiest, since he felt in such close contact with the creativity and proofs of Wright's affection in evidence all around him. Wright felt his loss acutely. What a dear man Lewis had been, he told Carl Sandburg in 1957. He missed him more than ever. "His admonition, 'Frank, just keep remembering that it takes all kinds! Never forget.' And of course I've found out that it does. . . ."

Although Wright continued to be primarily concerned with domestic architecture, it was almost faute de mieux, since he was always looking for the ideal scheme that would go on supporting his expensive habits for years to come. He had designed several apartment buildings, the first of these the Robert Roloson apartments (actually a series of row houses) at an early stage in his career (1894), and was delighted to be given an opportunity to design such units on a more sophisticated plan for a site in Ardmore, Pennsylvania. Suntop Homes, as they came to be known, were originally planned as a group of four apartment buildings, each having four units, based on his Broadacre City models, and amplified when Wright thought he had obtained a government contract to build them in Pittsfield, Massachusetts. He lost his chance when local architects objected, and only one, the building in suburban Philadelphia, was ever built. Instead of stacking units on top of one another or in a row, Wright conceived the idea of dividing a single building into quarters, each two stories high and containing a basement, carport and sunroof. The building was constructed of brick and horizontal lapped wood siding and must have looked promisingly low cost, even in those days of inexpensive home construction, since each unit cost only four thousand dollars in 1939. All the utility areas were buried in the center of the building, leaving outside walls free for expansive areas of glass. But the real triumph was the way Wright had fitted together his asymmetrical design so that no front door was beside any other, each dwelling had cross-ventilation, and rooms gave onto completely private gardens. It was a masterly demonstration of

An early photograph of Suntop Homes in Ardmore, Pennsylvania

how to achieve privacy and space on a tight budget, and so logical one would have thought it would now be common practice instead of remaining an apparent anomaly. Trees have grown up around Suntop Homes in Ardmore and modified the original concept of those roof terraces open to the sun, but the superior merit of the design is still evident on an otherwise conventional suburban street.

It has been said that the stages of Wright's development, from his first great industrial building, the Larkin, to the last of his great accomplishments, the Guggenheim, took him from an architecture that, although still rectangular, had its own elegant monumentality to "an architecture that was fluid, plastic, continuous, and has utterly changed our ideas of the nature of space and structure." One of the stages along the way was the commission to design buildings for Florida Southern College in Lakeland. It was the only college campus Wright would build, and he contributed a chapel, a library, a theater, an administration building and numerous classrooms. Work began in 1938 and continued to provide reliable employment for Taliesin's drawing boards for the next fifteen years. The campus was built on sixty-two acres of a former orange grove, sloping down toward Lake Hollingsworth, a pleasant but undistinguished site. Perhaps as a result, Wright's 1938 master plan is bold and complex. Of all the buildings he designed (the campus was not complete at the time of his death), perhaps the most successful is the chapel named in honor of Annie Pfeiffer, a generous contributor to the campus building fund. Based on the diamond, or double triangle, the Pfeiffer Chapel, built of steel-reinforced cement in Wright's textile block design and with a diamond-patterned tower of glass, steel and cement, has no windows as such. Light is admitted through the tower and through fifty thousand cubes of colored glass embedded in the walls and roof that create constantly shifting patterns of colored light, the kind of effect Wright delighted in. As the campus took shape it began to display other theatrical, if not cinematic, influences that may have been an unavoidable aspect of most "advanced" design of the period. One recalls that Wright was an enthusiastic admirer of Hollywood films, sometimes watching a particular favorite repeatedly, and that his son on the West Coast had worked as head of the design and drafting department of Paramount Studios. Lloyd Wright's designs for such unbuilt projects as his auditorium for the Institute of Mental Physics (late 1950s) have that otherworldly, science-fiction air one would expect, but his gifts as a delineator were such, his color so delicately nuanced and his line so ethereal, that one suspends disbelief, aware that one is in the presence of a powerful poetic imagination. Wright's designs for Florida Southern College are lacking in this kind of conviction, and for that reason it is doubtful whether they have changed anyone's concept of space and structure. The Pfeiffer Chapel, for instance, has some details—it is resting upon squat triangular pillars —that give it an almost comically spaceship look. It is perhaps possible that Wright's main motivation was a desire to beat the Futurists at their own game. One recalls that the chief emphasis of the New York World's Fair of 1939 was socially visionary, the brave new world of tomorrow that was just around the corner. Wright, who had been excluded from participation in the Chicago World's Fair of 1933, was not invited to participate in the New York event either.

Writing in the late autumn of 1940, in a review of Wright's exhibition at the Museum of Modern Art, a critic noted that the architect was placing more emphasis upon his recent work than the accomplishments of his Oak Park years, and that was a pity. The observation was certainly valid, and of a piece with Wright's willingness to focus his energies on the ideas that still lay, half-formed, at the back of his mind. But if he had looked backward he would not have found much to celebrate. The Midway Gardens, for which he had taken such pains, designed to stand for a century, barely functioned as the sophisticated pleasure palace that had been planned, was demoted to a beer garden and demolished (at considerable expense) in the late 1920s, an early victim of changing tastes in architecture. Various other structures, such as the Municipal Boat House in Madison (1893), in which he took such pride, came down in 1928, and anonymous garages, summer cottages, smaller houses and miscellaneous structures gradually vanished, their passing unremarked and unchronicled. The Larkin Building, which has now gained immortal fame, had already been substantially altered, and defaced, by the 1930s. In 1939, the Larkin Company faced bankruptcy, and the building's days were numbered. It would be torn down in 1950 (again, at some cost) to make way for a parking lot.

That jewel in Wright's crown, the Imperial Hotel, which took another phenomenal effort from him and demonstrated its worth through earthquakes, had become so rundown and neglected by the start of World War II that it was considered structurally dangerous. Nor were many of Wright's masterpieces of domestic housing in much better condition. As has been noted, Darwin Martin's heirs tried desperately to divest themselves of the punitive responsibility for keeping that mansion in good repair. Hollyhock House, which Aline Barnsdall gave to the city of Los Angeles in 1927, would suffer the same not-so-benign neglect. Some patchy attempts at refurbishing it did, however, have the result of protecting the original paint colors and providing specialists in restoring Wright's building with some valuable clues in years to come. His own home and studio in Oak Park, though still standing, had been subjected to some radical attempts to make them of some use to somebody. Other houses would be drastically remuddled, like the Tomak house in Riverside, Illinois, which subsequent owners attempted to transform into a Mediterranean villa, complete with classical balconies and round-headed windows. This attitude toward Wright's designs and buildings seems cavalier to the point of sacrilege nowadays, but one doubts whether it would have been particularly unusual for its day. Sir Hugh Casson recalled that in the 1930s he had radically remodeled a stylish country house owned by the dilettante Edward James in the style of his good friend, the Surrealist artist Salvador Dalí. Casson observed, "Nowadays you couldn't get away with redesigning Lutyens, but at that time it seemed acceptable." The survival of Wright's work depended, at that juncture, upon the whims of his original clients and their families. Twenty or thirty years after construction, the clients were aged or dying or had sold their houses.

One of the most ambitious houses of Wright's Prairie Style, and the first to be built with a two-story living room, was commissioned in 1902 by Susan Lawrence Dana, daughter of a prosperous railway magnate who had made a fortune with silver mines in Oregon and who had left her, by one estimate, a $3 million inheritance. The heiress, a socialite of renown but also a feminist with a passionate interest in spiritualism, took the adventurous step of hiring the young architect Wright instead of a well-established firm in her hometown of Springfield, Illinois, and once the house opened in 1906, she invited a thousand guests in two receptions that were the talk of the season. But, by the late 1930s, Dana was in failing health and hospitalized, her house abandoned and her finances a shambles. When it was announced that her house and its contents would be sold, enormous crowds came to view the layette set she had bought on her honeymoon in Paris but had never used, the seventy-diamond necklace Tiffany had designed for her, costing $24,000, the paintings, sculpture, furniture, china, cut glass, Japanese curio boxes and Orientalia that had filled her mansion. Few, however, would buy, and the bids were abysmally low. That summer of 1943, the auction opened with an admission charge of one dollar, which was higher than some of the prices that would be paid for Wright's furniture.

Since Wright's attitude toward much of his work was that it deserved to be torn down, it is not surprising, perhaps, that one finds little in his voluminous correspondence amounting to a call to action to save a threatened building. The exception was the proposed demolition, in 1941, of the Robie house, one of the great designs of his Prairie period. Built in 1906, the house, as has been noted, demonstrates all the hallmarks of his style at that time: the sleek, sculptural horizontal lines, the wide overhanging roof that in this case (and thanks to the early use of welded steel beams in the roof) was cantilevered twenty feet beyond the last masonry support, the tiers of balconies allowing the owner to sit and see without being seen, the flowing interiors, the massive central fireplaces, the glorious use of art glass, the mischievously hidden entrances, the sense of drama, surprise and of jewel-like corners of repose in the midst of a big city. Another aspect of the Robie house that is much admired was the way Wright integrated its mechanical and electrical equipment into the concept of the whole. For instance, the overhead lighting fixtures in the living room, a series of globes, were designed to form the visual punctuation points of the beamed roof, reinforcing a row of horizontals that is opposed by banks of French doors along one wall, with exquisite art glass inserts. Looked at in one way, the Robie house living room has such a powerful presence that it is difficult to find furnishings that can hold their own against such a dominating design. But from another vantage point, most of Wright's living rooms, in contrast to the antiseptic bareness of much modern design, and rooms containing nothing more emphatic than white walls and a window, are never empty, even when devoid of tables and chairs. At least one owner of such a room said it had always been his ambition to live in it with no furniture at all.

Frederick C. Robie, the enterprising manufacturer of bicycles who had commissioned the house, lived there with his family for only two and a half years. It passed briefly into the Taylor family, and was then sold to Marshall D. Wilbur, who lived there with his family until 1926. It was subsequently bought by the Chicago Theological Seminary, which used the building as a dormitory and conference center for the next fifteen years. Then the blow fell. It was too massive, too expensive to keep going and not well suited to the seminary's particular needs. Fortunately, the advent of World War II put a stop to plans to tear the building down. In 1957, when the seminary again proposed to demolish the Robie house, even more voices were raised in protest. As a result, the building was eventually acquired by the University of Chicago. It is on the city of Chicago's list of architectural landmarks and is one of seventeen Wright buildings designated by the American Institute of Architects as worthy of being retained as an example of his work. Because of a combination of luck and public opposition, the Robie house has been saved. Other Wright landmarks would languish for years before their plight was discovered, and repairing the damage decades afterward would cause other problems. But the idea, that Wright had made such an important contribution to American architecture that his buildings deserved to be preserved, and that destroying them would be an act of vandalism, was being taken seriously for the first time in those early days of 1941.

As Lewis Mumford observed, "It is easy to conquer posterity: the hard job for an original mind is to make any dent on its contemporaries." Where Wright was concerned, Mumford was always as generous as his strict sense of fairness would allow, no doubt from an awareness that the architect needed continual reassurance from one whose ideas he trusted and whose support he needed. In actual fact, Wright's original mind had more than made its influence felt by the time Mumford wrote that comment, well after the end of World War II. Geoffrey Baker's review of his Museum of Modern Art exhibition would not have pleased Wright since Baker had accepted the view that the architect's principal contribution was having "come closer than anybody else" to what was called "modern" architecture at such an early date. This critic did think it extraordinary, however, that he should have been neglected in the United States, without adherents or imitators, until the 1930s. Christopher Stull, reviewing Gutheim's collection of Wright's selected writings for the *San Francisco Chronicle*, was more respectful. If Wright was "ahead of his time" in 1894, he had remained so, and his latest articles were proof that the rest of the world lagged behind him even though his "authority" had been recognized at last. "For whether or not you belong among the ranks of his severest critics . . . you will find it impossible not to acknowledge him one of the greatest theoreticians of our century." A critic for another California paper noted that he was "one of the most challenging philosophers of our time." The *New York Times* thought that the ideas

Wright first formulated in 1894 were as relevant as they had been then: "Simplicity, repose, individuality; adaptation of the building to the owner, its purposes and its environment; bringing out 'the nature of the materials'; use of the machine to do the work it can do well; sincerity, integrity—these are virtues of architecture now as they were, or should have been, then." The *News* of Chicago thought no one since Leonardo had described so explicitly what he intended and, "It is difficult to find a flaw in his major theory." Wright's old friend Ben Page, who had once been in charge of controlling Wright's purse strings, was among those to notice the change in his fortunes. Page was full of admiration for his tenacity and courage and the "wonderful comeback." Page then went on to say that the years had not been kind to him. He was living on his old-age pension of thirty dollars a month and whatever he could recover from loans he had made in happier days. Page reminded Wright that he had contributed five thousand dollars to save Taliesin. Frank did not owe him a cent, of course, but if he felt able to send a few dollars once in a while, it would be a tremendous help—for old time's sake. Wright's reply to this letter, if any, has not been recorded.

Wright resurgent, Wright triumphant, one of the "greatest theoreticians of our century": it must have been a heady moment. If there was any criticism, it had to do with his insistence that the Europeans had simply picked up and assimilated ideas of his own that others had carried abroad; his strange reluctance to give full weight to Sullivan's influence on his work; in short, what looked like a streak of jealousy in his character. Since Wright's rivals in the International Style had already, generously, acknowledged his contributions, it was time America's "undeniably great architect" admitted that "new machines, new materials and new architectural ideas appeared almost simultaneously here and abroad, and that many men, great and obscure, had a part in making them productive." Wright would, of course, never have admitted anything of the kind. In the process of becoming himself, that is to say, in standing up stubbornly, almost recklessly, for his own opinions, however unpopular they might be, he had stumbled on the best of all ways to advance his own interests, having perfected the technique of "insulting you and making you like it," as the saying went. When dealing with important and influential critics he was always careful to antagonize no one, cultivating friendships with editors and publishers. It is probably true, as Peter Blake asserts in *The Master Builders*, that this tireless courtship made it possible for him to control what was said and written about him in the professional press so that, at least in later years, "no really critical evaluation of his work" appeared during his lifetime.

As has been noted, Wright's condemnations were becoming more inclusive and the targets of his attacks broader as World War II began. As might be expected, his opposition to war was, if possible, more pronounced than ever. Lloyd Lewis joked that since Alexander Woollcott was known to be in favor of helping the British, he expected the two to battle it out while their friends provided the necessary cooling breezes and buckets of cold water. He was referring to Wright's now-celebrated pacifism and his earnest conviction, as Uncle Jenk had preached, that war solved nothing. War was simply a political tool used by financiers, the ruling élite and corrupt politicians to advance their own ends, which usually boiled down to profit and power. Wright's suspicion of the motives of powerful nations, including his own, seldom extended to those countries that past experience had disposed him to like, such as Germany, Japan and Russia, focusing instead on the nation prejudice had taught him to hate. Like all good Welshmen he believed that Britain (and France as well) was fighting, not to preserve democracy or freedom, but its empire. His comment to August Derleth, "Democracy's real enemy is not the Axis but Bureaucracy here at home in the War for Gold," is an echo of the view held by an influential group of isolationists, who also believed that the principal threat to America was not Germany but war itself, since it would be bound to bring in its wake a curtailment of democratic freedoms and a dangerous expansion of bureaucratic control. So far so good, but then Wright began expounding upon the large issues. Modern warfare had made borders obsolete. It had made the concept of war itself obsolete. The only solution was a world without borders, the establishment of world citizenship and "Nature's organic law," whatever that meant. That his high-minded convictions might not be shared by Hitler or Mussolini was the hole in the argument, one he blankly refused to entertain. Wright embattled, as he himself conceded, was Wright ever more suicidally bent on retaliation. As luck would have it, this unfortunate chain reaction was set in motion by his principal supporter and proselytizer, Lewis Mumford, who happened to be the illegitimate son of a Jewish lawyer, Jacob Mack, from Frankfurt am Main. Wright must have seen the danger signals in April 1941, after Mumford wrote asking whether Wright's political views had caught up with his architectural ones, arguing for war, and

hoping Wright had outgrown his "Chamberlain" period—already an
effective insult. Wright's reply was measured: "I am sure we have no
quarrel. . . ." But then he rashly sent Mumford his latest broadside.
Mumford was horrified. He wrote,

> In this strange tirade you use the word gangster, not to char-
> acterize Hitler and his followers, but to castigate those who would
> fight to the death rather than see Hitler's 'new order' prevail in
> any part of the earth. You hurl reproaches against the system of
> empire, meaning by this only the British Empire, an empire that
> widened the area of justice and freedom and peace: but you have
> not a word to say against the Slave Empire that Germany would
> set on its ruins. . . .
>
> What a spectacle! You shrink into your selfish ego and urge
> America to follow you; you are willing to abandon to their terrible
> fate the conquered, the helpless, the humiliated, the suffering;
> . . . In short: you have become a living corpse: a spreader of
> active corruption. You dishonor all the generous impulses you
> once ennobled. Be silent! lest you bring upon yourself some
> greater shame.

It was a terrible rebuke, perhaps the most dreadful one Wright
ever received, and made worse by Mumford's further decision to submit
it for publication to a pro-war magazine (the *Leader*), as Wright noted
bitterly in his reply of a few days later. Worst of all, Mumford had
questioned Wright about just what position he thought his country
would be in once Hitler's "new order" prevailed. This was precisely
the issue Wright had evaded and would continue to avoid answering,
along with his indefensible double standard where Germany was concerned. He was obliged to fall back on the argument that there was
no such thing as a just war, that Mumford had misunderstood him
and twisted his words, and that Mumford must be "yellow with this
strange but ancient sickness of the soul: the malady that has thrown
down civilization after civilization by meeting force with force." He
was a deserter, a traitor, vengeful and conceited, "another writer out
of ideas." He was a hypocrite and should examine his heart, wherein
he would find "impotence and rage." What must have made it all
worse was the fact that the terrible quarrel took place just as Mumford
was putting the finishing touches to an article for *The New Yorker*
praising Gutheim's new book and "[t]he color of Wright's personality,
the wide range of his mind, his healthy aplomb, his deeply moral

feeling about life and art. . . ." Mumford's further comment, "When he is talking about nature, when he is finding a new beauty in the rocks or the vegetation of some little-known region, interpreting its values for architectural form, Wright is at his supreme best," published on June 7, 1941, four days after Wright wrote his reply, must have been the final twist of the knife.

To add to the ironies of the situation, Wright was being taken up by the London press, a direct result of his having received his gold medal from the Royal Institute of British Architects, almost a decade before that august body's American counterpart would see fit to do the same. In short, he was in a somewhat awkward position of snubbing his admirers, one that would have become most embarrassing had anyone known about his anti-British stance, which does not seem to have been the case. Even as he wrote, London was being bombed to ruins, and the *News Chronicle* invited him to write an article on how it should be rebuilt. The result was, perhaps, one of the strangest documents ever to issue from his pen, since his lack of empathy for the city that had asked for his advice could hardly be masked. The suffering and devastation were somehow the fault of the British for trying to hold on to their empire. His exact phrase was "one of the most evil games ever played *by* Empire." (Italics added.) London would have muddled along in the same old way had not these forces done it the favor of destroying the feudal monster so that "the Art and Science of human habitation" might enter. Given Wright's characteristic impatience with old buildings, one can see a certain Wrightian logic in his brisk admonition to the British to pull up their socks. But then the newer Wright, the one advocating radical reform, not just of housing and interiors but society itself, came to the fore in the form of vague and flowery exhortations to seek a cleaner, purer, more organic, etc. future. "1. No very rich nor very poor to build for. No gold. 2. No idle land except for common landscape. No realtors. 3. No holding against society of the ideas by way of which society lives. No patents." Since further bombings were inevitable, and since the machine age had ushered in a new scale for the city, twenty-five feet now being the equivalent of one foot formerly, the new London must be twenty-five times larger. He went on to describe a decentralized city that, not surprisingly, sounded greatly like his plan for Broadacre.

The reaction came quickly. That interesting Welsh architect, Clough Williams-Ellis, builder of Portmeirion, led the spate of letters criticizing Wright's Arcadian visions. He wrote, "I was startled to find him much more impractically Welsh than I was myself, full of fine and generous emotions that soared far away and beyond the sordid consideration of How and When that kept me doubtingly earthbound." He continued, "No one will disagree with his three clearly enunciated sociological and economic postulates demanding an end to exploitation, but what little else is clear seems to me highly dubious.

"We are apparently invited to replace London for the convenience of millions of motor-cars rather than for men: yet further to inflate it 25 times its already menacing size, and to build it on the hopeless assumption that 'bombing is here to stay.' "

In Wright's defense it must be said that he had, perhaps, too much time on his hands at that moment. His love of fast foreign cars (Mercedes-Benz, Jaguar, Riley) never faltered, nor did his lifelong habit of driving at a terrifying speed. Despite his wife's insistence that he was a very safe driver (because he had such good reflexes), he was bound to get into trouble and had his share of accidents from which, with his usual good luck, he escaped unscathed. On one occasion, for instance, he encountered a florist's delivery truck (entering the highway at a snail's pace, no doubt), and bounced it on its side. Fost Choles, the driver and owner of the business, went to the hospital; Wright merely made his way into Madison and continued his journey by train. His good luck was bound to run out, and, eight years later, driving the California roads near Fresno, he had a head-on collision with a truck. He thought so little of the matter that his miraculous escape hardly concerned him. Instead, he grumbled to Hib Johnson that "[t]he highways are now commercialized to such an extent that they are no place for a gentleman with a fine car," and joked that he was about to switch to horses. However, he had been thoroughly shaken up and put to bed where, having nothing else to do, he took up his pugnacious pen.

During those months before Pearl Harbor and America's entry into the war (on December 8), a storm was brewing that centered on an old and seemingly insoluble problem, the apprentice who had served long enough. For years, Edgar Tafel had been one of Wright's principal assistants, acting as supervisor for the construction of some major projects, including Fallingwater and the Johnson Wax building. He was ambitious to become a fully fledged architect, and since he had just married there were the practical problems of dentist's bills and clothes, impossible luxuries so long as his sole employer was Taliesin. In addition, he had attracted the attention of some new clients and thought, perhaps naïvely, that Wright would be delighted to get the work, particularly because he agreed to have his designs bear the Taliesin imprimatur and to split the fees.

However, the atmosphere soon became strained. "Mr. Wright saw the problem. Naturally, the apprentice would want to tend to his own work first. Mr. Wright wanted apprentices to attend to Wright's projects first." That was one issue, but the basic question appeared to center on the emergence of young rival architects at Taliesin, the issue Klumb had tried to resolve some years before. Wright was absolutely determined that this was not going to happen. If his helpers wished to bring in work that he would design, that was fine, but the split would be smaller: two-thirds to Taliesin, one-third to them. Tafel was even prepared to accept those terms and brought in a new client. But when no money was forthcoming, he went to talk the matter over with Mr. Wright and was handed a crumpled hundred-dollar bill. It was clear that the arrangement would never work. Once Tafel had talked the matter over with other "oldsters," he found a great deal of support for his position. One by one, seven of them left; some, like Tafel, were in tears.

The loss of some of his best and brightest may have been one reason why Wright fought so hard to keep those who remained. He certainly was aware that the entrance of the United States into the war would destroy the edifice he had built up so painstakingly over the past decade, denying him at one blow not only all that help in the new drafting room (which, by some irony, finally opened in 1942) and on his enormous farm, but also the raison d'être for all those new buildings in Wisconsin and Arizona. Even if he had not been so opposed to war, he would have fought to keep them and thought he had come up with the solution, in the spring of 1941, after a new law was passed requiring able-bodied young men to register for the draft. He would ask that his men be exempted on the ground that they were needed to keep his farm and architectural workshops going. That might have been a persuasive argument, but then a paragraph was included about the futility of war and asking that the twenty-six members of the Taliesin Fellowship who signed the document be put on record as objectors to the compulsory military draft. (Wright disclaimed authorship of this document.)

Once the United States entered the war the focus shifted from the Taliesin Fellowship to Wright or, rather, what the latter might have done to persuade all those young men to oppose the will of their government. The issue came to a head after Federal Judge Patrick T. Stone of the Western District of Wisconsin, while hearing the case of Marcus Earl Weston, twenty-seven, son of "Billy" Weston (who refused to appear for induction into the army), announced from the bench that he would ask the Federal Bureau of Investigation to enter the case. It was the judge's considered opinion that Wright was "obstructing" the war. Weston denied that he had been unduly influenced by the great man's opinions, but the judge was not convinced. He said, "I think you boys are living under a bad influence with that man Wright. I'm afraid he is poisoning your minds." Officials of the local draft board in Dodgeville, predictably, turned down the petition of the twenty-six Taliesin Fellows for exemption from the draft. Frank Lloyd Wright, of course, heatedly denied that he had unduly influenced his apprentices (as did they) or had encouraged them to shirk their patriotic duty. He published a letter to that effect and told anyone who would listen. Unfortunately, the FBI was now very interested in the opinions and possibly unlawful acts of Wright, an interest that reached to the highest levels. In March 1943, its director, J. Edgar Hoover, sent a memorandum to the assistant attorney general, a copy of which has been made available under the Freedom of Information Act. The memorandum asked whether there had been a violation of the sedition statutes and requested a ruling on whether the investigation should be continued. A month later the assistant attorney general replied that the facts did not warrant prosecution or further investigation. The now-familiar pattern had been repeated: the FBI detailing its suspicions and the government declining to prosecute. And, as before, the FBI was unwilling to let the matter drop.

It was, perhaps, just bad luck that the review of Wright's revised *Autobiography*, published that spring of 1943 in the *New York Herald Tribune*, should have as its headline, THE REVOLUTIONIST AS ARCHITECT, or that the reviewer should comment, "One might read it for the story of a man who does not fit into the common pattern in his living any more than in his art, and of how the world treats him for that subversiveness. . . ." That seemed curiously apropos, given Director Hoover's memorandum. It also fitted in with Wright's more recent acts: the fact, for instance, that he was a contributing editor to a magazine called *World Unity* (described by one source as a radical organization), or that he had agreed to attend a Russian War Relief

Benefit held in Madison Square Garden in the autumn of 1941 (as advertised in the *Daily Worker*), or that he had personally criticized President Roosevelt for having implied, during a speech about Lend-Lease, that he was prepared to send the U.S. Army and Navy into battle, or that he had made speeches, just two months before Pearl Harbor, to the effect that the Japanese were really nice people and Americans ought to let Japan have whatever it wanted in Asia.

It was perhaps inevitable that at least one family with a son at Taliesin did not approve of Wright. In this case the parents were those of Allen L. ("Davy") Davison, who had taken a degree in architecture from Cornell, then joined the Fellowship and met and married Kay Rattenbury. This union, in 1941, placed Davison, a young idealist who was a talented artist and photographer, inside Taliesin's inner circle by virtue of his wife's close friendship with the Wrights. It seemed more than an accident that Davison, who also declared himself a conscientious objector, was not to be dissuaded and served a prison term. (Weston and Howe were also sent to prison for failure to report for military service. Curtis Besinger, later professor of architecture at the University of Kansas, and Howard Tenbrink went to C.O. camps.) This made Davison's views suspect, but it is clear from his letters to his parents that he was sympathetic to Wright's ideas even before he joined the Taliesin Fellowship in 1938. (This would have buttressed Wright's argument, one aspect of which was that his apprentices came because they shared his views, not because they were easily persuadable.) Davison's letters are almost wholly concerned with reassurances that, far from being the negative influence they feared, Wright's work and philosophy, and the high standards he espoused, could only improve his character. But Davison made comments, artless or not, that were hardly designed to set his parents' minds at ease, making it clear that he thought the war was being waged to benefit Wall Street profiteers, and hurling defiance at "Mr. Roosevelt." His admiration for the Wrights, whom he called "his parents in Ideal," was another remark hardly calculated to reassure his own, and all the more remarkable since he admitted that he and Wright were not always on the best terms. Davison's respect continued despite a birthday party the architect used as an opportunity to reproach his followers for refusing to develop minds of their own and using the Fellowship as a refuge from the outside world. Those who had just left might have found that a curious accusation, coming from him. Davison took the rebuke meekly and expressed a new surge of loyalty for Wright.

In short, the correspondence seemed innocent enough and, in any event, simply reiterates views Wright had never tried to conceal from anyone. Once their son proved determined to go to jail, however, the Davison parents must have been looking for a scapegoat. Extracts of letters purporting to show the extent of Wright's influence were made available to the U.S. attorney in Madison and then passed to the Federal Bureau of Investigation. (This file was also released under provisions of the Freedom of Information Act.) In July 1943, Hoover wrote anew to the assistant attorney general enclosing copies and asking once more whether the sedition statutes had been violated. Again, the assistant attorney general advised that no action was warranted. Hoover subsequently told authorities in Milwaukee of the decision, asking them, just the same, to keep an eye on Wright and send along any more evidence that might come to light. As the *New York Herald Tribune* review of Wright's *Autobiography* concluded, the harassment Wright received for his "subversive" views did little credit to "American customs or citizens." As for Wright, he continued to speak out against the folly of war, although his admiration for Germany appeared to dwindle somewhat after it invaded Russia. Writing on the same day to Tafel and Burton Goodrich (who joined the marines), Wright suggested that each of them go to Russia and enlist to fight the Germans "on the only front that seems to matter."

Howe went off to the Federal Correctional Institution in Sandstone, Minnesota, to serve for almost four years. He said, "I was on the staff, teaching architecture and drafting and had a very interesting time of it. There were all sorts of people there: Black Muslims who refused to salute the flag, Trotskyites and Jehovah's Witnesses. I remember a farmer and his three sons from North Dakota who were very religious but who were just damned if they were going to join up. One of the high points was the day Mr. Wright came to lecture about architecture. Of course he didn't talk about architecture at all, but about the war, and the warden kept trying to shush him up. I'll never forget the sight of them all appearing in the courtyard below while we watched from our dormitory windows: Mr. and Mrs. Wright, Svetlana and Wes and Kay. They all crossed the courtyard and we just collapsed emotionally." Four more pivotal figures were gone, others had joined up and only a few were left, among them William Wesley Peters, Gene Masselink and Cary Caraway. Work at the drafting boards had ground to a halt, which did not stop Wright from inventing all kinds of new schemes. He had thought up a new method for building defense housing and was trying to interest a manufacturer in a prefabricated method of constructing planks three inches thick and a foot wide that could be used for interiors and exteriors. It looked promising, and a fiberboard manufacturer was intrigued, but then Wright asked $100,000 for the patent and the deal collapsed.

Wright was as full of breeze and bounce as ever, Herb Jacobs noted, whenever he visited them during those dreary winters of 1943 and 1944, although Olgivanna Wright seems to have been in poor health. Wright told his son Lloyd in the winter of 1943 that she "was and still is in a highly nervous state—unable to stand any strain . . ."—a state that continued for some months thereafter, judging from grandson Eric's report to his father. Her husband was keeping her close to home and working on the final section of *An Autobiography*, hoping the income would help keep the Fellowship on its feet. Meantime, he wrote, "we are hard to take—like Stalingrad." Uncle Enos had died at the grand old age of eighty-eight, and Wes was planning to take over his farm where, it had been decided, Gene Masselink, also a talented artist, would have his print shop. Wes Peters recalled that his father had been opposed to World War I. His earliest memory is of playing at his father's feet the day word arrived of the sinking in 1915 of the *Lusitania*. (Over 100 Americans died out of a total of 1,153, and the attack by a German submarine on an unarmed British liner did a great deal to shift American sympathies toward the British cause.) Peters immediately championed Wright's position during the early days of World War II and added that, before Pearl Harbor, most Americans felt the same way. He recalled the attacks of Judge Stone, as well as a spirited defense of Wright by William Evjue, founder, editor and publisher of Madison's liberal newspaper, the *Capital Times*, who asked in an editorial, "Upon what meat are some of these judges feeding?" Those at Taliesin knew that the FBI was conducting an investigation, but no one thought much about it. Peters recalled that, during the war, tires were in short supply and he had gone to some lengths to stockpile those they had in the basement.

"One day I came down into the boiler room where the tires were stored and saw two strange men looking them over." Thinking they were about to be robbed, "I performed a citizen's arrest. I was scared. I had a double-barreled ten-gauge shotgun so I came down behind them and told them to put up their hands. Then I marched them out onto the front terrace.

"They said, 'We're members of the FBI.'

"I said, 'That's a likely story.' I looked under their coats and saw they were wearing shoulder holsters. I made them drop them and picked up the guns. Then I asked to see their certification and demanded to know what they were doing without a search warrant. I threw their magazines out of their guns and told them to leave. They said, 'We'll be back with the sheriff,' and I said, 'When you do, bring a search warrant.' They were trying to prove that we had some bootlegged tires down there."

Peters modestly neglected to mention that most of the credit for the success of the farm was due to his herculean efforts. Eric told his father that Wes was the hardest worker there and put up fifty bales of hay single-handedly. Peters said, "Every winter we filled the cellar with root crops. It was the closest we ever came to Mr. Wright's dream of living from the land.

"All of our profits went directly back into Taliesin. People forget that Taliesin needs constant repair. It's an architectural sketch. Originally Mr. Wright had made use of the Welsh basement, that is to say, he built shallow trenches filled with gravel into which the foundations were placed, the idea being that water would drain through the gravel. He used this method with some success but, unfortunately, when the house burned in 1926, and they were rebuilding, they just leveled off the land, pushed the ashes off the hill and built right on the ground. That gave us a lot of problems later.

"Once when I was digging a new trench, five or six feet deep, I came across a Han [dynasty] horse's head in fragments and bits of Ming roof tiles. Mr. Wright said, 'Wes, finders keepers.' Did I keep them? Sure I did."

At the conclusion of the revised *Autobiography* published in 1943, Wright wrote, "Life always rides in strength to victory, not through internationalism . . . but only through the direct responsibility of the individual." As he was sitting out the war in Spring Green and living his dream of self-sufficiency in The Valley, a small, dark-haired Russian novelist with an arresting gaze was putting the finishing touches on a novel inspired by these and similar statements by Wright. She was Ayn Rand, born in St. Petersburg in 1905, whose ambition it had been to escape from her homeland to the haven of the United States. As a brilliant young university student her experiences during the Russian Revolution had stimulated her to formulate a pro-capitalist, anti-Communist philosophy later codified as "Objectivism."

It seems to have points in common with what Kenneth Clark called "Heroic Materialism," a new religion that took as its temples the iron foundries and in which was offered up "to Gain, the master idol of the realm, perpetual sacrifice," as Wordsworth wrote. Where others saw the exploitation and dehumanization of man, Rand saw in the growth of the free enterprise system a limitless expansion of the powers of mankind. It led to a lifelong belief in "the concept of man as a heroic being, with his own happiness as the moral purpose of his life, with productive achievement as his noblest activity, and reason as his only absolute," she would explain.

Kenneth Clark also wrote, "Certain philosophers, going back to Hegel, tell us that humanitarianism is a weak, sloppy, self-indulgent condition, spiritually much inferior to cruelty and violence. . . ." Rand would not have expressed it exactly in that way. She believed man had a moral imperative to be upright and heroic and to cultivate an inner integrity, but she feared and mistrusted altruism, since it could be construed to give the state, or society at large, power over human destiny. As a lifelong atheist, her antagonism extended to the church. She also valued reason and logic above all other attributes. The reasonable man, her ideal hero, acted from impeccable and logical postulates, and the notion that human emotion might have validity was, as her biographer Barbara Branden showed, as irrelevant to her view of herself as it was to her philosophical stance.

Once she had succeeded in emigrating, had settled in New York and met Wright through his writings, her next ambition (and Rand was nothing if not single-minded) became to meet him. She was not famous as yet, she wrote with a kind of artless hauteur, but she had already published two novels. She planned to write a third about an architect who would rise to triumphant heights despite every obstacle and whose life, although it would not be patterned after his, would reflect the superb qualities she had found in it. She quoted from his writings. She said that her new book would be a monument to his life and work, and asked only for the chance to meet him so as to be inspired. It was the kind of letter that, from anyone else, would have produced an immediate invitation to visit Taliesin; but perhaps something in it struck the wrong note. Or perhaps it came at the wrong moment. It was her bad luck to be writing in December 1937, just as Wright was absorbed by his plans to build a new Taliesin in the Arizona desert and the problems of moving his Fellowship there. The reply to her letter, written with evident haste by Masselink, made the perfectly truthful excuse that Mr. Wright had already left for Arizona and did not know when he could see her. (The letter was addressed to "Mr." Rand.)

She was disheartened but not deterred. Some months later, in the autumn of 1938, when Wright was to lecture in New York before the National Association of Real Estate Boards, Rand made plans to go, using introductions to Wright through Mrs. Alfred Knopf, wife of her publisher, and also Ely Jacques Kahn, in whose office she was then working to learn about architecture at first hand. "I spent three hundred and fifty dollars out of my savings to buy a black velvet dress and shoes and a cape, everything to match, at Bonwit Teller's, which I had never entered before," she said later. "I felt this would be an unrepeatable occasion, because I was to meet a man who was really great." They met after the lecture, but there was no immediate rapport, or not the one she had hoped for. So she wrote a letter, sending him the first three chapters of what would become her phenomenally best-selling novel *The Fountainhead*. Eleven days later Wright responded. He wrote, "No man named Roark with flaming red hair could be a genius that could lick the contracting fraternity." In short, he was not impressed.

Had Rand known more about Wright, and had she not been disposed to see in his work a man who was not there, she would have realized at once that her association with Louis Kahn, the American architect most influenced by Le Corbusier, had already made her suspect, and that what Wright had gathered from those first three chapters would have confirmed the diagnosis. Those chapters were enough to show him that she had perceived nothing about the essential Wright, and that her instinctive sympathies, he must have realized, were in accord with the rational and geometric purism of the International Style. Her hero ought to have been an ascetic like Le Corbusier, or any of those other Internationalists who, like Hitchcock, could have said, "If Humanism be not, so much the worse for it." She later stated that her hero was not Frank Lloyd Wright, but she acted as if he were, and Wright was rightly confused. Either he was or he was not, and if Roark was meant to be him, he was not at all sure he had been complimented. In taking as her model an architect who is rejected by the Establishment and reviled for his genius, Rand might have been confident of her ability to give Wright the mirror in which he wanted to look. But she did not understand that the Establishment now seeking to discredit Wright was the one whose ideas, ideals and political views she represented. The fact that she was an atheist ought to have made her aware of his profoundly religious impulses, instead of blind to them. As a proselytizer for capitalism, she, of all people, ought to have seen the ample evidence that Wright was at the other end of the political spectrum, supporting the cause of exploited masses and the international socialist movement everywhere, an error the FBI certainly had not made. She, a lover of the city, gave Roark a skyscraper as the crowning achievement of his career, as if she had not understood Wright's roots in the natural world, his conviction that the city was dying and his scorn for skyscrapers, those corrupt symbols of a discredited capitalism. The climactic moment of her novel comes when her architect is given the chance to build a housing project and then sees it defaced and degraded by other hands. Denied every other form of protest, he sends the building sky-high with a stick of dynamite. In the same circumstances Wright would have prevailed long before his design was ruined by anyone, but even if this had happened, he would have roared his defiance, then found something good to say about the result and cashed the check (because, in all likelihood, the money would have already been spent on Japanese prints). These essential differences were apparent to Wright, no doubt, which has not prevented the continued misconception that Rand's hero is somehow Wright personified.

After the novel became a best-seller Wright mellowed to the extent of believing himself marginally pleased. The author had, after all, found him a man of nobility and personal integrity, or so she said. She was still pursuing him. Her book had been sold to Hollywood, and Wright was approached to do the sets, an idea he flirted with before rejecting it. She then asked him to build her a house. All of this meant that Wright must try to find some virtues in this curious person, and try he did. She was invited to Taliesin and was as repulsed as delighted. He would have been equally put off by her dogmatic certainties and, in fact, all the ways in which certain aspects of her character resembled his: her imperious demands on friendship, her need for a circle of admirers, her alacrity in passing moral and psychological judgments, her readiness to blame others. Her personal habits certainly did not endear her. She smoked two packs of cigarettes a day and, it is said, kept chain-smoking and blowing the smoke in Wright's face. Finally he took the cigarette out of her mouth, threw it into the fireplace and walked out. That was the start of the absolute prohibition against smoking in Wright's presence and ought to have been the end of his friendship with Ayn Rand. But he persevered and designed her a house she absolutely adored, or so she said in 1946. There was one problem. It would cost $35,000. When she voiced her objections, Wright told her airily to go out and make some more money. Not too long after that, she and her husband found a stream-lined example of the International Style by Richard Neutra for sale in the San Fernando Valley. Neutra had built it for Josef von Sternberg in 1935 and it would become one of his most famous buildings. The price was $24,000, so they bought it. No doubt this act, which represented a symbolic rejection of Wright's philosophy and ideas, and her choice of an architect whose style was an absolute anathema to him, told this "uncommon man" everything he needed to know.

19

That Strange Disease, Humility

The Phoenix's breast is a flickering rainbow
Of color, bright and beautiful.
"The Phoenix"
Poems from the Old English

In those years just after the war a certain event, almost a ritual, was repeated over and over again at the gates of the Taliesins in Wisconsin and Arizona.

At any hour of the day or night, young men and women could be seen straggling toward them armed with letters of introduction or, almost as often, drawn there, uninvited, by some mysterious inner compulsion, proposing themselves for the night or the weekend or the rest of their lives.

They came by bus and train or hitchhiked, often with backpacks or no luggage at all, and two dollars in their pockets. Or, like Babette Eddleston, a young architect who became a water colorist, print maker and sculptor, they drove a thousand miles and arrived one summer morning. She had no invitation, but knew a former apprentice at Taliesin in Wisconsin. After driving west from Madison along Route 14, she caught sight of a building up on the hill, off to her right. There was a rural mailbox standing nearby, but the name was unreadable. She stopped to ask a farmworker driving a tractor whether that building above them, ocherous, sand-colored, the color of masking tape, could be Wright's house. It was, and that was the driveway. Arriving in the courtyard, she was introduced to Gene Masselink and explained that she would like to stay for the weekend. That was impossible, he said, but he would show her around. Then he went off to send a telegram, and she was left to wander through the rooms and garden terraces of this "magical kingdom," gaining a confused impression of drafting tables, stone columns, sheepskins and cushions, a fireplace bench padded with gold, branches of trees, patterns of leaves, petunias and the incongruity of this amazing building on the side of a hill after so many miles of farmland. She was meeting a host of young apprentices. "All the girls are terribly thin and plain-looking, with plain-looking clothes." Mr. Wright's daughter Iovanna, by contrast, was gaily, almost flashily dressed. They all talked about him. "Mr. Wright said, Mr. Wright thinks. . . ." At that moment they knew he was having tea. "Everyone knows where Mr. Wright is at every second, and what he is doing and, what's more, they know what he is thinking, and what he thought ten years ago on such and such an occasion and the exact words he used. . . ."

Then she entered the famous Taliesin living room and saw the great man himself in the middle of a discussion with an apprentice about cleaning the fireplace. She waited until the conversation was finished and walked over to him, "wanting to extend my hand, but his is so tight upon his cane, which is not touching the floor, [that] I hesitate." She introduced herself. "He looks at me squarely with his tiny blue eyes. His oatmeal-colored clothes, skin and hair. I say I am visiting and he turns his back on me and walks to the side with the beautiful light coming in, the ferns with the sun playing on them, the red blinds, the gold cushions and says, 'We are not interested in visitors.' The birds fly through the room."

She explained that she was a friend of Eleanore Pettersen, who had studied architecture at Cooper Union in New York, as she had, and spent two years at Taliesin during the war. The great man turned. She was a friend of Eleanore's; well, that was different. He supposed she wanted to stay for a month. No, just a weekend. He asked for news of their mutual friend. Then he told her to speak to Mrs. Wright. "If it is agreeable to her it is all right with me."

An unpromising reception and then a dazzling about-face because the arguments were persuasive: this kind of response was encountered more than once. Carter H. Manny, Jr., now director of the Graham Foundation for Advanced Studies in the Fine Arts in Chicago, said he had grown up in Michigan City, Indiana, and that his parents had been friends of Wright's son John and daughter Catherine. This was enough to get him an invitation to spend the weekend in Spring Green. He had a pleasant stay and was finally interviewed by Mr. Wright.

By then he was wondering how he had ever managed to get himself invited because the great man was so discouraging. His own hair was too short, Wright said. (It ought to be around his ears.) He should throw away his glasses and strengthen his eyes with exercises. The fact that he had graduated from Harvard in 1941, magna cum laude, was another mark against him. Finally, he had asked to be admitted for a part of the year, and Mr. Wright refused.

The would-be apprentice left, but his note of thanks for the weekend included an appeal to Mr. Wright to change his mind. He received a cryptic note. "All right Carter Manny, since you are in earnest, come along. $100 a month. We'll call you a professor. Sincerely, F.Ll.W." Manny reappeared joyfully, joining the Fellowship in Arizona, and his dexterity with a hammer and saw soon convinced his employer that he was capable of living down his Harvard background. The whole camp was the scene of intense activity as the Fellowship attended to the problems caused by the years of neglect during the war. The great redwood girders spanning the drafting room and garden room of the Wrights' quarters had to be straightened and reinforced and new, snow-white canvas stretched over them. A new cabinet was needed in the apprentices' dining room, a new door for Wright's quarters and a host of other repairs and improvements were to be made. Fortunately there was no shortage of help. By the autumn of 1946, the Fellowship numbered sixty-five, the largest group ever, plus assorted wives and children. Manny noted that almost half were from abroad—England, Ireland, France, Switzerland, Japan, Italy, India and even more exotic places—and several of the Americans had taken advantage of their G.I. Bill of Rights to pay their tuition. One of the postwar apprentices, for instance, was the twenty-one-year-old Prince Giovanni del Drago (from one of the oldest and most aristocratic families in Italy), who was doing kitchen duty along with everyone else, although he drew the line at serving a countryman, the Marquis Franco D'Dyala Valva, because that gentleman was beneath him socially. There were Indian apprentices representing the Brahman, warrior and merchant castes (each refusing to speak to the other), and wealthy American boys and apprentices like Andrew Devane from

Dublin, who arrived penniless, having spent his last dollar on a one-way bus ticket.

The day at Taliesin West began at about six. Breakfast was at seven, followed by a half-hour's choral practice led by Svetlana Peters— "Svet," as she was called—who rehearsed them in works of Bach, Palestrina and César Franck. Work began at 8:30, stopped for an hour and a half at noon for lunch and a rest, then resumed until about five. Dinner was at six and evenings were free. In these postwar years Wright had somewhat relaxed his dictum against leaving the camp, and a group would sometimes drive to Phoenix for a beer and a movie, though trips of this kind were usually saved for Wednesdays when everyone had the afternoon off.

In the evenings long discussions on architecture were the rule, but Manny soon tired of them. "It was quickly evident that admiration expressed for architecture other than Mr. Wright's was treated as heresy or breach of loyalty. . . ." Jack Dunbar, who became a Taliesin apprentice in 1946 on the G.I. Bill, found evidence of the same attitude one day when he discovered Homer, one of the hired help, in the back burning books, including Giedion's *Space, Time and Architecture*. The solution, for Manny in Arizona, was to escape into music. "Sitting in the still unfinished drafting room looking out across the vast expanse of desert as twilight faded and twinkling lights came on from settlements that were thirty or forty miles away, while the Scott [record player] gave forth with the Busch ensemble's rendition of the opening of Brandenburg No. 4, is a recollection that still brings a tingle to my spine." In fact, the drafting room was the scene of one of the most extraordinary events he would witness.

One morning Wright appeared at breakfast carrying a sheaf of drawings and asked three or four of his best aides to join him in the drafting room. Immediately all work stopped as Manny and the others gathered around Wright's table.

"My eyes boggled as he went over three drawings, each for a separate house project, all produced, he said, since he awoke at 4 a.m. . . .

"The drawings were in colored pencil drawn with a T-square and triangle for the most part, but also in . . . free hand. On each sheet, plan, section and elevation were superimposed on top of one another forming wondrous abstractions, but actually concisely depicting multiple aspects of each conception.

"After a brief explanation each drawing was turned over to a senior apprentice whose task would be to adapt a module to the conceptual design and prepare separate, conventional drawings for plans, sections and elevations for Mr. Wright's further scrutiny. I was astounded. . . . Imagine, three designs in roughly three and one half hours! This was a virtuoso performance. . . ."

Having completed a herculean amount of work, Wright was just as likely to hold up the final drawings indefinitely while he tinkered with them. Peter Matthews, the English architect who was also there after the war, said, "When he saw Mr. Wright coming, Jack [Howe] would say, 'For God's sake get that drawing out of the way,' because there were deadlines to meet. It was amusing to see the way people protected him from himself. And he had his own way of doing things. I remember giving him an adjustable set square and he said, 'Take that thing away and bring me a triangle.' "

After the hiatus of the war years, when many of the projects on which he was engaged—an ambitious complex of a hotel, shops and theaters called Crystal Heights (1939) in Washington, D.C., for instance—remained unbuilt, work was pouring in. In 1943 he had been given the great chance at his first building for New York City, a museum to house modern art commissioned by Solomon R. Guggenheim, which would absorb a large part of his energies for the rest of his life. A year after that, he was commissioned by Hib Johnson to design a new building, a fifteen-story research laboratory, as a companion to the Johnson Wax company's administration building. In 1947, some thirty-two commissions were in hand, and the pace would continue to quicken. The pressure of work, for a man close to his eightieth birthday, was formidable. He confessed to his eldest son, "I sometimes feel my flanks tremble as [I have] seen it in a race-horse just out on the track for a race." In those years after the war he had estimated that, to keep the foundation solvent, he needed to provide some $75,000 a year. He told a returning apprentice, "I keep nothing for myself and family but a living." However, he also boasted to Carter Manny at the same period that he had received $1 million in architect's fees. Assuming that this was an exaggeration, it still meant that he was retaining considerably more than "a living," although the truth of the matter is hard to unravel. What does seem clear is that he would always think of himself as poor, as if nothing had changed since those days when, during one of the innumerable reconstructions of Taliesin, he appeared at a Spring Green hardware store to pick up the supplies he had ordered and, when presented with the bill, opened his billfold and extracted a single ten-dollar note. For money came in

Wright at work in September 1956 with, from left, Alan Davison, Kenneth Lockhart, Eugene Masselink and John H. Howe

spurts, whenever the checks arrived. Wright was as disorganized as ever, capable of filing away checks in his back pocket until they were hopelessly crumpled and out of date, and in between, there were sixty-five mouths to feed. Peter Matthews confirmed that Wright was still looking for credit and being considered a bad risk, because he was sent farther and farther afield to buy timber in those days. Fortunately there was always another fee due from Edgar Kaufmann for one or another of his many visionary schemes. Wright's letters were unvarying: "Dear Edgar: We need Money. Yes—badly. . . ." Meantime, there were the interminable repairs. A window somewhere at Taliesin was always breaking, and tiny birds would fly about the room, beating their breasts against the tall glass doors.

Evidence that, after years of disastrous miscalculations, Wright had improved as a judge of character, can be discerned from the fact that by the late 1940s he had gathered around him a devoted, capable and sterling group of senior assistants. Jack Howe, who ran the drafting room with such a sure hand, had become absolutely indispensable, as had Wes Peters, the authority on engineering, and his beloved wife, Svet, who worked just as hard as he did. There was the equally loved Vladimir Lazovich, Mrs. Wright's brother, "Uncle Vlad," and his wife, "Aunt Sophie." Wright's daughter-in-law Betty Wright called Aunt Sophie "a darling old-fashioned woman with a wonderful voice." Uncle Vlad had been a great rake, a dashing officer in the czar's army and, even in old age, was a formidable figure, fully capable of intimidating anyone who wandered onto the premises by silently appearing and inquiring, with great courtesy, "Can I help you?" They did not stay in Fellowship quarters—"Aunt Sophie wanted her own nest," Howe said—but lived over the dining room where they, as caretakers, had a commanding view of everyone who arrived. There was Ling Po (Chow Yi-Hsein), who arrived in 1946 and would become a gifted designer and artistic delineator. There was Cornelia Brierly, whose special gifts as an interior designer had become so valuable to Wright. There was Tom Casey, a talented architect from Los Angeles, and the devoted husband-and-wife team of Charles and Minerva Montooth. There was the young art student Bruce Brooks Pfeiffer, who arrived not knowing "which end of the hammer you picked up," he said, and would become Wright's archivist. There was Marcus Weston, who had proved to be so loyal during the war years, Curtis Besinger and Davy Davison. There was Kenneth Burton Lockhart, whose expertise as a certified construction specifier was essential to the smooth functioning of what had become a large and successful business.

Wright would have been completely overwhelmed by success had he not, by then, put in place a first-class firm of architects. But to call them only that would be to ignore the underlying factor, the ability of the Taliesin group to work as a team. The old Lloyd Jones gift for gathering kindred spirits among The Valley families, with whom they had worked, fought and intermarried, had been continued and amplified with the creation of this extended family, men and women with whom Wright shared similar aspirations and ideals. They were the companions of his waking hours. They rejoiced at his triumphs and mourned his sorrows, looming inevitably larger than his own children, now scattered across a continent, or even his fond and devoted sisters. And Catherine was gone forever, or was she? Jack Howe said, "Did I meet the first Mrs. Wright? I don't know. Everyone was on a picnic one Sunday and I was left alone to work in the studio, when a group of ladies appeared. One of them came up to me and said, 'I just wanted my friends to see this place.' She evidently knew her way around and after a while she left. I always wondered if that was Catherine."

One of the pivotal figures in the smooth functioning of Taliesin was Wright's internuncio, Gene Masselink. Born in South Africa of Dutch parents, Masselink grew up in Grand Rapids, Michigan, and took a degree in fine art from Ohio State University. He had won a first prize in art at the precocious age of four, and his great love, all his life, was painting in oils. His younger brother, Ben, recalled that Gene met Wright in 1932. "It was like the Pied Piper. Frank Lloyd Wright spoke, and that was it. He practically followed him out of the door." He continued, "Wright didn't like people doing work in their own style and did not like Gene's work. So Gene taught himself to work in Wright's style and became very good at it." He began as Wright's secretary and became the indispensable intermediary between the architect and his clients. Howe said, "He'd write the letters and Mr. Wright would sign them. He could write Frank Lloyd Wright letters." Gene's brother continued, "Peters was the outside man and Gene was the inside man. He solved all the problems. When he died, no one knew what to do."

Richard Carney, who began as Masselink's assistant, recalled that "Gene would pay the bills on beautifully designed Taliesin checks if he could find the money. He somehow balanced the books. He took a casual attitude toward these kinds of problems. He would say, 'Things are never as serious as you think.' " Masselink recalled that when the first Lincoln Continentals appeared in 1937, he was invited on a trip to Chicago with Wright and his brother. They were driving down Michigan Avenue when, all at once, Wright commanded them to stop in front of a Lincoln Continental dealership. He grandly alighted from the car: "You know, he often wore two shirts because he liked having two collars. He walked in there with his pork pie hat and red lined cape and staff and his two shirts. Gene is behind him and I am behind them. The only thing bringing me in is the cars.

"Mr. Wright went up to the new Lincoln, tapped the fender with his stick and said, 'I want one of these and one of these. Gene, show him the color we want, the Cherokee Red.' The salesman explained that the color would have to be a special order. 'And,' Mr. Wright continued, 'I want a convertible top. Take that thing off. I will send you my own design'—something like a rolltop desk, made of accordion metal and wood. Then he declared, 'and I don't intend to pay for them.' He turned toward the door and added, 'I expect them to be ready in two weeks.' Then he left, leaving Gene to go to work. That was Mr. Wright. Gene would pick up the pieces. I can recall merchants running out of their stores as they passed by saying, 'Pay me!' 'Pay me!' and Gene would go in and tell them he would send them five dollars on account. He didn't seem to mind."

Ben Masselink thought his brother was absolutely selfless, and this was not without its problems. "I always called him a 'gofer' because he literally trotted between Hillside and the house and one time he stepped into a gopher hole, breaking his hip. It never set properly and one leg was a half inch shorter than the other and always hurt him; he eventually had to have a hip operation. Because of this, he was exempt during the war. He used to try not to limp. But he never complained. His attitude was, 'I am sorry I stepped in that gopher hole.' "

Over the years Masselink created Wrightian murals and paintings for clients. He helped establish the Taliesin Press, designed programs, stationery and invitations. Bill Calvert, another apprentice, remembered the exquisitely designed work lists that Masselink would draw up, minor works of art in themselves. Masselink was always hoping for some free time to work on his art, and would be promised time off "between two and four in the afternoon and then something would come up and he'd have to stop," Howe said. His brother said, "He worked all the time."

But then, they all worked hard. Another of the pivotal figures at

Taliesin was Masselink's assistant, Richard Carney, now managing trustee and chief executive officer of the Frank Lloyd Wright Memorial Foundation. He had been in the war and had enrolled at Washington University in St. Louis, but soon became disenchanted by the commercial emphasis of the architecture department. One of the requirements of the course was that he study in an architect's office, but he could not find an opening. Then he happened to meet one of the first Taliesin students, Bill Bernoudy, later an architect in St. Louis. "He started telling me what they did, and I felt, 'I must get to that place.' I had been searching and was almost ready to give up when, just at that moment, I found what I was looking for. It seemed like the hand of fate." His first letter went unanswered, but Carney persisted and was soon given his chance. His father had been a Baptist minister, and at the point when Carney met the Wrights, he had become practically an atheist. He said, "But I sensed that both Wrights had a deep sense of reverence for God and knew the difference between morality and ethics. If I had known about Taliesin, I would have been looking for it. After the disillusion of war I had a sense of life restored, of ethics, beauty and the development of each individual to his fullest capacity. I would listen to Mr. Wright on Sunday mornings and find myself so set on fire by the power of his ideas that I would want to run for three miles.

"Another time, something he said made me think. Before I came here I thought the expression 'a rolling stone gathers no moss' was a derogatory term. But Mr. Wright made me realize that the truth was exactly the reverse of what I had believed.

"I also learned that he was capable of gigantic anger because he once directed it at me. I had always smoked and thought I knew the rule, which was, no smoking in the house. I was walking in the upper court and just at the door, threw the cigarette away. Mr. Wright smelled my breath. 'Have you been smoking? I never want to see you again. Get out of my sight. Leave!' He was in deadly earnest. Mrs. Wright spent the next twenty-four hours trying to persuade him to change his mind. He finally agreed to let me stay."

As Taliesin's numbers grew, the demands on Wright as an architect became ever more pressing, and inevitable changes took place within the Fellowship. The yearly round, of traveling between Wisconsin and Arizona, continued, as did his weekly monologues on the nature of society and democracy and the organic, during which he "loved to quote himself and Mrs. Wright would look for a door to escape,"

The Taliesin Fellowship boat party

Howe said. Parties that had been small and unpretentious became more formal and the guest lists more distinguished; among their visitors were Sherwood Anderson, Mike Todd, Charles Lindbergh, Helen Hayes, Charles Laughton, Leopold Stokowski and Clare Boothe Luce, although Wright was never able to snare some of the others he wanted, including Thornton Wilder, Archibald MacLeish or Gertrude Stein. And then there were people who occasionally felt they were not wanted. Rupert Pole, Eric Wright's half brother, whose mother, Helen, was Lloyd Wright's second wife, took the writer Anaïs Nin to visit them in Arizona. They arrived unannounced, and Mrs. Wright noticed "this foreign-looking woman" talking to her husband, Pole said. "She came over to us and said without ceremony, 'Frahnk, who *is* this woman?' " He continued, "Anaïs wanted to laugh about it but couldn't. So we left."

Parties also became more elaborate. Ben Masselink recalled one birthday party at which an astonishing surprise had been prepared. The Wrights were escorted to chairs on the bank of the river, the word was given and, suddenly, a Spanish galleon came around the bend in full sail. It had been designed, built and outfitted by Wes

Peters and was manned by a crew in full regalia. The ship came alongside, and the crew landed, carrying a treasure chest, the birthday box for that year.

In the old days, Wright's personal imprint had been on every aspect of the work and daily round. He liked to call himself "the general cook and bottle washer." Now he was just as willing, but his resources of energy were no longer limitless, leading to the delegation of tasks he once led himself. The result was to somewhat sharpen the distinction Manson and others had noted before the war, i.e., between the private life of family and guests and that of the rest of the Fellowship. No longer did the Wright family, artistically grouped, with a dog at their feet, sit on a dais only on weekends when they listened to the evening's entertainment, but they ate on a dais as well. Ayn Rand noted disapprovingly that theirs was a special menu, while the rest of the Fellowship was served fried eggs. Some quipped, paraphrasing Churchill, "Never have so many people spent so much time making a very few people comfortable." But a larger split was developing between those whose lives revolved around the work of the architectural firm, known as the "studio crowd," and the rest, many of them wives. Mary Matthews, Peter's wife, said, "Mrs. Wright wanted to set up her own coterie with all those who were not exactly architects. They were supposed to come and sit at her feet. You gave her your spirit and she molded you." Mrs. Matthews, in common with other observers, believed that Mrs. Wright had become a masterly manipulator. "She would see an opportunity when someone was uncertain or slightly at fault, and she would tear them to shreds to see how they would react, find their weak points. I was given the task of typing up the cookbook and missed a detail on the method of making baba, and she started on me. But I was not about to let her get the upper hand, and she finally said, 'The trouble with you is you stand before me like a rod when you should bend like the grass before the wind.'" Speaking of these surprise attacks, which often came to the unwary apprentice before large groups of people, Mrs. Wright "sometimes had to crack heads open to put something new in them," her friends explained. Or, as she herself would write, "It is better to hear the rebuke of the wise, than for a man to hear the song of fools." Most people thought they saw evidence of the training Mrs. Wright had received in Fontainebleau in such tactics and, in fact, Gurdjieff's name was constantly being invoked. Mrs. Kassler said, "In the first six months when I was there, I rather doubt that any of the draftsmen or apprentices even knew the name. But when I returned in 1948 his influence was very evident. We all had to sit and listen to Mr. Wright reading aloud from this tedious book by Gurdjieff. Perhaps it was *All and Everything* and I remember my eyes closing." It was around that time that Iovanna, who was studying with the famous French harpist Marcel Grandjany, went to France to spend time with Gurdjieff and returned with the ambition to become a dancer. She said, "He was like the rising sun. He had no weaknesses," a view apparently shared by her mother and members of her mother's circle. That came to be called "the little kitchen crowd," so called because, it was said, people would sit there and wait, sometimes for hours, in order to talk over their problems with Mrs. Wright. It was as if Mrs. Wright were preparing to assume her aging mentor's mantle (Gurdjieff died in 1949), as well as his dogmatic certainties. Asked if she ever admitted that she was wrong, the Howes just laughed.

Now in middle age, Olgivanna Wright was still an attractive, even striking woman, with the same slim dancer's figure, although she was also "austere and distant, unless you were close to her," Jean Kennedy Wolford, wife of another apprentice, said. Rupert Pole, who was not one of her admirers, said, "As an actor, I saw through her. I thought she was a very designing woman, powerful and egotistical." She supervised every aspect of running the household, setting the tone and stamping out whatever she saw as pernicious influences, from smoking cigarettes and wearing beards to such details as the wrong color socks or even the way an apprentice combed his hair. Jack Dunbar, who would become a well-known New York designer, said, "I was very poor and had arrived there with a homemade pair of sandals, two T-shirts and two pairs of blue jeans. I had also made myself a leather belt of Indian design and a silk vest that I thought was quite smashing. So that was what I wore to Saturday-night dinners, and one evening Mrs. Wright stopped me at the door and said, 'We dress for dinner here.' I explained that I had no money to buy anything else. She said, 'Get something.' "

Mrs. Wright also supervised the state of each apprentice's room. Dunbar said he had been given a room at Hillside that was in total disrepair and had gone to some lengths to clean it up. Then he placed his sleeping roll at one end and whatever he had found, branches and other foliage and bric-a-brac, at the other end. "It turned out that mine was the nicest room in the place, and at the next meeting I was being singled out for praise by Frank Lloyd Wright because Mrs.

Wright had taken him to my room. I must say that these things profoundly offended me."

Not only did Mrs. Wright make herself available for counseling, she practically required that everyone at Taliesin, including her daughter, Iovanna, reveal the intimate details of their lives. And while Iovanna was an adolescent, just beginning to date, her mother, and father as well, were determined to keep a close watch on her movements. Iovanna said that, unknown to her, her father had wired her room to an alarm clock placed beside his bed so that whenever she returned to her room, sometimes late at night, his alarm would go off. "Then he'd rush into my mother's room, through the double Dutch doors, and shout at her, 'Your daughter came in at two o'clock. Do something.' You know something?" she continued. "He always wanted to be popular, so he would give her the dirty work. She'd be upset because he woke her up. In the morning, he would simply say, 'Did you enjoy yourself last night?' "

This attitude changed in a curious way in the years to come. Bill Calvert, who admired Mrs. Wright but was not blind to her idiosyncrasies, said, "I pretty much accepted a lot of Mrs. Wright's criticisms because I knew they were valid. However, I drew the line one time after I came back to Taliesin for a visit. I had been on good terms with Olgivanna, and she and Iovanna cooked up a surprise birthday party for me. Iovanna was the hostess and it was a wonderful party, but she kept insisting I stay afterward. At the same time I knew that a lot of fairly freewheeling liaisons were being arranged by the 'little kitchen.' By eleven or eleven thirty I could see the writing on the wall. I was thinking, 'Oh my God, I am getting sucked into something,' but I still didn't want to go through with it.

"I also knew that a lot of Monday-morning quarterbacking went on in the 'little kitchen.' A lot of us steered clear for this reason. You were expected to kiss and tell. And if you didn't perform . . . let's say, you'd be called in and corrected. I couldn't cope with it. Next morning I was up and left before anyone knew it. I knew what Olgivanna was capable of. We'd get someone new, a boy called Michael, and a couple of months later she would interview him and say, 'Oh, you are doing a wonderful job. Joe and Ken keep telling me how well you do. Now, why is it all the boys like you? What's the matter with you? Are you a homosexual?' and poor Michael would break down in tears."

Given this amount of eavesdropping on their lives, apprentices often left without much ceremony. Jack Dunbar says that Wright's influence on his ideas—the principles he absorbed while he was there—had a profound effect, but he rebelled at what he saw as an unscrupulous attempt to manipulate his private life. "I snapped," he said. "I walked back to my room and started packing." Several couples, including Peter and Mary Matthews, believed that a more or less determined effort was being made to destroy their marriages. After Mrs. Matthews moved out of the Fellowship, she said that she never received a letter from her husband, or he from her, although they were writing to each other frequently. Perhaps the most famous marital breakup was that between Wes Peters and his second wife, Svetlana Alliluyeva, whose book *The Faraway Music* places a great deal of blame for the failure of her marriage on the divide-and-rule tactics of Olgivanna Wright. But even when Mrs. Wright's Balkan suspicions were not aroused, married couples had difficulty with the problems intrinsic to Taliesin's communal life. Cary Caraway said, "I met my wife Frances through Taliesin and we had two children there. We left when the children were preschool age. Mr. Wright talked a good philosophy about family life but it never existed. He could never let go of the need to have your energies focused on his work. And the mother didn't have enough free time with the children. There are no successful apprentice families that survived staying at Taliesin."

Bill Calvert said of Mrs. Wright, "On balance, I am on her side. In many ways she was a second mother to a lot of people. I was only eighteen when I went there, and she filled a real gap in my life. There was a lot of warmth and acceptance coming from her too. There were a lot of wonderful things she did for us." People remember her thoughtfulness. Soon after both her husband and sister had died, Mrs. Kassler went to Taliesin for a visit. Perhaps it was a warm evening, but she found herself shivering. "Olgivanna said, 'Let me get you a stole,' and she found something right away. The message I received was, 'Get warm and get happier.' "

Calvert continued, "Keep in mind that Mrs. Wright was running a branch of the czarist court, and absolutely anything was possible. I am not exaggerating a bit. She was a master of intrigue but Mr. Wright hated it." Tony Puttnam, another member of the Fellowship, agreed: "I thought he was remarkably patient and good-humored. He'd suffer students. He'd make an attempt not to catch people out, so he would clear his throat before he came into a room." A great deal of effort was sometimes expended, Calvert said, to keep Wright from finding out. "Here is a typical example. Some guy would get a girl in the town pregnant. There would be the threat of scandal. Olgivanna's approach would be to try and solve it quietly. Talk to the girl and pay her off. But we all dreaded what would happen if Mr. Wright found out. He would call everyone in. The message would be, 'Don't stop to change.' The phone would be ringing extra loud. Your whole life starts flashing before your eyes and you are thinking, 'I'm going to be exposed. I'm going to have to parade around with no clothes on.' We'd all be sitting there, and Wright would say, 'Let's get this out into the open. Find out how many guys are sleeping with girls.' Then he'd say, 'Okay, Joe, why did you do it with this girl? Haven't you heard of prophylactics?' Putting on heavy boots and tramping through peoples' lives. He'd go around the room. 'Okay, Bill, you were living next door. Why didn't you stop this?' The worst sin at Taliesin was lying to protect yourself. All the wrath would turn on you and your crime was greater. But it was more subtle than that. You said what was necessary to get you through. You had to learn to perceive what was required. The little lie. The point at which they stopped. You had to be quick on your feet and know what role to play. Sometimes tell the truth and sometimes lie, and if you did it right, you'd be called in later and complimented. It made a skillful liar out of you, that's for sure. We none of us liked it. But you have to understand. She wasn't an ogre. It's hard to convey. She was operating on a different principle. Her goals were to keep Wright going and Taliesin intact, and she did it brilliantly."

Mrs. Wright became very adept at dealing with her husband too. Calvert recalled one occasion when Wright had brought back boxes of "little twinkling lights" from San Francisco, the kind that are "now used on Christmas trees. Well, we had a surprise party of some kind in the desert, and Gene, with Mrs. Wright's permission, opened up the boxes and decorated the theater with these lights. But it turned out that Mr. Wright had wanted to use the lights for something else. There was a big cocktail party with a lot of important guests, and everyone went into the theater and Mr. Wright saw the lights. He flew into a rage. Who could have done this? Olgivanna was asked whether it was her. She, for expediency, said, 'No, Gene did it.' Gene knew he would have to take the fall for public consumption. It was a charade; later on, he would be forgiven. To simplify the problem. The evening went on and they were having dinner. I'm serving at the family table but he had not stopped complaining. 'Gene, where do you get off? You've assumed too much responsibility. You don't know your place.' All this in front of guests. Finally Gene got up and walked out, which he had never done before. So Mrs. Wright ignored the guests and turned on Mr. Wright. She totally humiliated him, something she had learned from Gurdjieff. 'You've ruined the meal for everyone. No one has touched their plates,' which I knew was true, because I carried them out. 'You're acting like a child.' He threw down his napkin and left. She was trying to salvage the evening after that, and we all assumed we wouldn't see him again. I was aware of his pacing around outside. I was just serving dessert when I saw him coming back. 'Oh, my God, he is going to throw everyone out.' Not a bit of it. He had returned to apologize personally to Gene and all the guests. Then he embraced Mrs. Wright. 'Come on, Mother, let's have a party.' "

No one who saw them together doubted that the Wrights had a deep and enduring love for each other. He depended upon her completely for the day-to-day running of two vast estates, for dealing with the inevitable conflicts and antagonisms, for lightening his load in all major ways, for companionship, for a special kind of nurturing, for the constant challenge of her able mind. They continued, of course, to be jealous of each other's flirtations, if that is not too strong a word, and sexual jealousy, it is said, was the cause of any continuing friction between them in later years. Olgivanna Wright has provided evidence that jealousy was not exactly the issue. What seemed to have been happening was that her emerging role as the iron hand on Taliesin's smooth functioning had, inevitably, placed her in a much more powerful position than either of them had anticipated when the Fellowship began. It was one thing for a young wife to oversee the cooking, the cleaning, the laundry, the canning of fruit and vegetables and the making of wine and the organization of such mundane tasks, playing a subordinate role. It was something else entirely to be married to a woman at the height of her power and authority, who was on equal terms with him at home, however much she might be just a famous man's wife in the outside world. That the balance was shifting must have been apparent to him, and he was too narcissistic and insecure not to resent it. This much is made clear by Olgivanna Wright herself, describing her husband's reaction to the publication of her first book, *The Struggle Within*, by Horizon Press in 1955. She described his rage

A family portrait

At a Taliesin party in 1954, Wright, in his favorite white suit, being observed by, from left, Iovanna Wright, Mrs. Katherine Lewis, Mrs. Kenneth Lockhart, Edgar Kaufmann, Jr., and Olgivanna Lloyd Wright

and insulting behavior on several occasions, always an indication that he felt severely threatened. It was not enough that his wife should now rival him in importance at Taliesin, but now she wanted a position in the outside world. She had become an author, he sneered. He threw her book down, had temper tantrums and, in short, made himself thoroughly unpleasant. Wasn't it enough for her to be his wife, he wanted to know. Things reached such an impasse that, after an evening of more abuse, in 1955 Olgivanna Wright decided that she had had enough. She was going to leave him. She wanted to have a life of her own, not simply live in his reflected glory, but he, she told him, "wanted me to be the same as you said Sophie was to Uncle Vlado, a pair of trousers that you can put on and take off at your own will." That he should, at some level, see her emergence as an individual as a threat summarizes the dilemma he faced in all his relationships with women, one he never resolved, although in this particular case he patched things up by persuading her to stay. He gave her his word of honor that, from then on, he would only praise her work as a writer. When *Our House* was published in 1958, he was as good as his word.

Besides, Wright had his own way of getting even with Olgivanna. The story is told that she came into the drafting room one day to meet him, as they had planned to make a trip into Madison. The day was hot. He did not appear, and she left. Finally, Wright came into the room and wanted to know where she was. He was told she had left, so he went down to the parking lot at Hillside, thinking she might be waiting in the car. She was not there either, so he turned to an assistant and said, "Go back to the drafting room and get me some scissors." Although the day was sweltering he was wearing one of his beautiful English suits, tailor-made for him in London, of heavy tweed, with a hat and tie. The scissors were delivered. Wright commanded his apprentice to cut off his pants above the knee. That was the spectacle he presented when his wife finally found him. She was, the apprentice said, "in a rage."

Wright also knew that, in ways that really counted, Olgivanna would always play the right part. When the Philadelphia chapter of the American Institute of Architects awarded him a gold medal in 1950, Mrs. Wright went along, and gave the president, Alfred Bendiner, precise instructions about the food to be served to the great man. "One piece whitefish, and this is to be cooked not in the fire or on the fire or under the fire, but directly *over* the fire, dry without any butter or sauces or mishmash. Then maybe one baked potato but absolutely dry with no butter, and a little fresh peas, and then maybe a little raspberry Jello, and maybe a little coffee, and then you will go and buy one quart skimmed milk, Grade A, and bring it back and show this to me, so I am sure," she told him. She concluded by reminding Bendiner that her husband's life was in his hands.

There was one further factor affecting Olgivanna Wright's life in those postwar years. Svetlana, her beautiful, enchanting daughter, the one who greeted family members on their visits and saw that they were comfortable and well cared for—Svetlana was dead.

Ben Masselink said, "Gene and Wes and Svet went everywhere together, like the trio in the famous film *Jules et Jim*. I think Gene must have been in love with her. She was dark-haired, almost Tahitian, with full lips and dark eyes, of medium build, five-foot-four, and very slim. Gene was very self-effacing, like me, and Svetlana was very vivacious, the life of the whole place." For several years, she and Wes had no children. Then Brandoch was born; then came Daniel, and in the autumn of 1946 they were expecting their third child.

One September morning, Svetlana Peters was on her way to Spring Green from Taliesin driving a jeep with Brandoch, four, and Daniel, one and a half, inside. She had stopped at a garage near the river to make a few purchases before traveling the remaining mile and a half to Spring Green. She had crossed the river and was approaching a smaller bridge over a slough, protected from the running brook beneath only by a railing about a foot high. Then something happened. One theory was that she could have had a fainting spell—it was said she had been prone to them at the time. Another was that she was carrying a small kitten in the car and it had made a sudden movement. Wes Peters said his son's explanation was that Daniel started to fall out of the car. Peters said, "A wartime jeep responded very quickly, and I think that as Svet tried to make a grab for Daniel the car made a fast swerve." It leapt over the railing, plunged into four feet of water and landed upside down. Brandoch was thrown clear. His mother and brother were trapped under the partially submerged jeep. The little boy made his way to the road just as Glen Richardson, operator of the garage, and his employee, Donald Fogo, were on their way into Spring Green driving a wrecker. Seeing the little boy, they stopped, and he shouted, "The jeep ran into the water!" They raced to the scene and tried to pry the car loose, but it was stuck fast. Richardson reached into the wreckage and pulled out Daniel, but was unable to free Svetlana until they had hitched up a cable and lifted the car clear. That took five or ten minutes.

Peters said, "I remember I was working in the Hillside drafting room when I got the news. As I arrived, Glen Richardson was just getting the car out and we got Svetlana out of there." By then the local doctor was on the scene. He had no artificial-respiration equipment, and the nearest hospital was in Madison, so he ordered the two to be taken there. Peters drove them—an hour-long trip—with the Irish architect Andrew Devane. They took turns applying artificial respiration to Svetlana. "Daniel had been fatally hurt, so we concentrated on her. To add to the problems, as we got into Madison a tire blew out." The two were pronounced dead at the hospital. Peters said, "The doctors said that they both had internal injuries and couldn't have survived." He and Gene Masselink dug the graves for Daniel and Svetlana themselves in the Wright family cemetery in Unity Chapel yard. Perhaps it was after the loss of his wife, son and unborn child that Wes Peters, who had always stood so tall, began to stoop.

As it happened, both of the Wrights were in Chicago, and Jack Howe was delegated to relay the bad news. Howe said, "He absolutely couldn't believe it. He kept saying, 'It can't be that bad,' and I said, 'It can't be worse.'" As for Olgivanna, "She was inconsolable." Kay Rattenbury remembered going to the scene of the accident and seeing Svetlana lying on the grass, "white and inert." She was there when Olgivanna Wright came back to her room, cleaning it. "I knew she would be upset, but I had no idea. . . . She came into the room weeping and sobbing. 'Oh, Kay, leave me alone,' she said. Oh, God, it was awful. I hate to think about it." Olgivanna was prostrate, but Frank Lloyd Wright was magnificent. Peters said, "He never failed. He'd always rise to the occasion. When the cards were down, he always came through." He personally made arrangements for the funeral and would not allow Svetlana's casket to be placed in the living room, because, he told Olgivanna, "If we do that you will never go into that room again. We will put her in the garden room." Olgivanna Wright continued to mourn her daughter's death. Dr. Joseph Rorke, her close friend in later years, believed she refused to eat and that she was living in a tent; "Mr. Wright finally made her stop," he said. And, for whatever reason, she blamed Svetlana's death on cats. Bill Calvert said, "She would fly into a rage if a cat appeared and it would have to be removed." There is another story that, sometime after the death of Svetlana,

Wright at work in his study at Taliesin. The man with him is not identified.

Wright making an acceptance speech before the American Institute of Architects after receiving a gold medal in 1948

Wright went to visit a client. The client asked where Mrs. Wright was, and he replied, "She's in the car crying."

In 1949 still more commissions were coming in. That year Wright was asked to design twenty houses; eleven would be built. He was designing a self-service garage for Edgar Kaufmann in Pittsburgh; a vast concrete bridge, called the Butterfly Wing Bridge, to be built south of San Francisco; a theater in Hartford; a building for the YWCA in Racine, Wisconsin; and many others. He found time to publish a biography of Sullivan, *Genius and the Mobocracy*. Two years earlier the National Institute of Arts and Letters had made him a member, and other honors crowded in on him during those years: honorary degrees from Princeton, Cooper Union, Florida Southern College, Yale, Wisconsin and Temple universities, among others. Foreign organizations, such as the Académie Royale des Beaux-Arts of Stockholm, the National Academy of Finland and the Uruguayan National Academy of Architects, made him an honorary member. The University of Wales claimed him for its own with an honorary degree of doctor of philosophy. One of the other honors of those years was the gold medal for architecture, given by the American Academy of Arts and Letters and the National Institute of Arts and Letters. He was the stellar attraction the day he received the honor, but by no means the only one. Marianne Moore was receiving the gold medal for poetry, and Ivan Mestrovic, the award of merit for painting. Elizabeth Bowen was giving the address, Archibald MacLeish was in the chair, and Louis Kronenberger was conducting the induction of new members of the institute, among them Rachel Carson, Reinhold Niebuhr and Delmore Schwartz. In addition, the elegant nineteenth century New York town house in which the ceremony was held was the scene of an exhibition of the work of those being honored, and included the sculpture of Mestrovic and William Zorach and the paintings of Louis Bouché, Leo Friedlander, Hyman Bloom, Francis Speight, Jacob Lawrence and others —about a hundred items in all, exhibited in the main gallery and subsidiary rooms around it. Felicia Van Veen, the academy's former executive director, said they had invited Wright to contribute a small exhibit. He arrived with perspective studies and models for his major works at the time, including a perspective and general plan of the Guggenheim; a model of a proposed skyscraper for the H. C. Price Construction Company of Bartlesville, Oklahoma; a glass chapel for the family of E. J. Kaufmann; a circular house for his son David; perspective studies for a small library, to be called the Masieri Memorial and built on Venice's Grand Canal; and other items. Almost before she knew it, Mrs. Van Veen said, Wright had commandeered the choice exhibition space and was pushing Mestrovic's sculpture, which had a prominent position, out of the way, and replacing it with his own models. "He was terribly fresh and I had to speak up," she said. He took over her office and began making calls all over town to tell the press he had arrived. He made everyone work after hours because he was so demanding. She recalled that she had persuaded someone to donate a cheap rug for the occasion. It had a small red stripe around the edge. That would not do, Wright said. It had to be erased, not with a paintbrush, which would have been relatively simple, but with colored inks. His crew "sat up all night inking out this tiny red stripe," she said. "I thought he was obnoxious, but his men were his slaves. They'd stand on their heads for him. Anything he wanted, they did." Another staff member, Lydia Kaim, had a slightly more positive impression. "He came every day," she said. "He was in his eighties but he looked wonderful. I'd say, 'How are you?' and he would reply, 'Couldn't be better!' with a glint in his eye." Naturally, he did not approve of the introduction Ralph Walker, a New York architect of large industrial plants, office skyscrapers and housing projects, and the president of the American Institute of Architects, had seen fit to give. "I had no idea how outrageously inadequate this introduction . . . would be," was his opening remark. "Couldn't you do better than that?"

He continued, "As these honors have descended upon me one by one, somehow I expected each honor would add a certain luster, a certain brightness to the psyche which is mine. On the contrary, a shadow seems to fall with each one. I think it casts a shadow on my native arrogance, and for a moment I feel coming on that disease which is recommended so highly, of humility. . . ." It was an irresistible remark, much quoted, and it laid bare, artlessly or not, the roots of Wright's marvelously sustained outrageousness, and what lay behind it, try though he might to pretend it was not there. Architects were artists and poets, or they were nothing, and to be a poet in America "puts you rather in the backyard and out of things and the procession goes on without you," he explained. But the procession, at last, had paused, and invited him to join.

These heady tributes were accompanied by one even more illustrious, that of the gold medal of the American Institute of Architects, at its eighty-first annual meeting in Houston in the spring of 1949. The recognition came very late—as he was the first to remind them—and almost despite him, since he had made such a point of never becoming an A.I.A. member and had criticized almost every aspect of the profession. Given what the members knew must happen, it has to be considered an act of forbearance on their part to award to this contentious and maverick artist their highest honor. If they expected to be lectured and harangued once more, they were not disappointed. Wright, saying he came prepared to "look you in the face and insult you," launched into an attack on the inferior cities they had built, Houston being an excellent example (speaking of a new hotel, the Shamrock, he quipped, "I can see the sham—but where's the rock?"), and all the ways in which they had fallen short of their great and noble opportunity to build for democracy. Nothing of any value had been built, he said, sweeping away the achievements of the century as so much detritus. But it was not too late to reform, seek an organic architecture of spiritual qualities, internal strength, nobility of purpose and so on. And, in case they should want to pin on him the label with which he had been identified, i.e., as an early proselytizer of the machine, he wanted them to be disabused. Where he had once been enthusiastic he was now scornful, if not despairing, of the changes the machine had wrought on society; science had "ruined us. . . ." It was all vintage Wright, and no doubt the capacity audience, which jammed the Rice Hotel for the presentation dinner, would have been disappointed if he had acted otherwise. They gave him a thunderous reception, and perhaps there were only a few left that night who thought he did not deserve to be so received. Arthur Holden, who was attending the meeting as new regional director from New York, and had joined the A.I.A. board, knew something of the behind-the-scenes maneuvering that had taken place, with older men who thoroughly disliked and disapproved of Wright finally being outvoted by younger factions arguing in his favor. Among those opposed, Holden recalled, was Bronson Gamba, a member of the board of directors from Detroit, who told him that Wright would be awarded the gold medal "over his dead body!" Another enemy of Wright's was a former president of the Milwaukee chapter, Leigh Hunt. That night, he happened to be seated beside Holden. Holden recalled that Hunt had known Wright and his first wife, and remembered having supper with Wright one evening in 1909 when he appeared tense and on edge. Wright finally burst out with the news that he intended to leave Catherine. Hunt was horrified. That was the end of the friendship between Hunt and Wright, Holden said. "I remember Leigh Hunt telling me that he couldn't stay in the room while this presentation was taking place and he did step out a window to a balcony outside."

Mrs. Kassler also remembered the A.I.A. convention because she was arranging flowers in the dining room in Taliesin in Arizona when Wright appeared. "He strode in looking awfully pleased with himself. He had just returned from the convention and was so proud. Usually I was so intimidated I never talked to him, but this time I could not help asking, 'Why are you so pleased about this?' He replied, 'One is never too old to want the approval and admiration of one's peers.' I was really moved, as well as surprised." Then there was the time when Peter Matthews was asked to take Wright his breakfast in bed one morning. "I went into the room and he said, 'See that box over on the table? Open it.' I did so and inside was the gold medal. He said, 'Put it on!' I did as I was told, and he laughed, and said, 'Now you can't say you have never worn the gold medal.'" That was Wright, full of radiant good humor, his face glowing, striding across the platform to savor the victory, in Houston or New York, or, as he would do in Mexico City in 1953, the one man, among a host of his peers in formal evening dress, wearing a white linen suit.

20

The Shining Land

So the blesséd one survives his death
And goes back to the shining land that was his
In a former life.
                    "The Phoenix"
                    Poems from the Old English

Don Anderson, publisher of the *Wisconsin State Journal*, wanted Wright to sell him one of the portraits he had acquired at reduced cost from Karsh of Ottawa and, by the way, Anderson said, "Karsh also told me that you and George Bernard Shaw were the two most interesting people he had photographed." The United States Information Agency came to Spring Green to make a record of Wright at work and play: in the drafting room, walking over the hills and posing with his photographs, drawings and models, with Beethoven for the sound track. Wright observed that the federal government had never thought him good enough to award him a commission, and was now sending a film about him around the world—a supreme irony. Senator Alexander Wiley of Wisconsin read into the *Congressional Record* a statement about "the universally acknowledged architectural genius, Mr. Frank Lloyd Wright." He was so famous that taxi drivers, porters at stations and even waiters in modest side-street restaurants in New York recognized him. One morning, when he had unaccountably forgotten to bring any cash with him to breakfast, the manager of the diner cheerfully accepted an autograph in lieu of payment. Gone were the days when his perpetual last-minute dash placed him in peril of missing a train. Now, trains were held for him, and so were theater curtains. A friend was sitting in a Madison audience one evening, wondering why the play had not yet begun, when she saw the familiar figure appear. "As he was walking down the aisle, all eyes followed," she said.

As a national living treasure, he was an inviting subject for portraitists. One of the most successful, apart from Karsh (whose photograph captured the quixotic stubbornness of his subject), was the writer and television personality Alistair Cooke. He went to interview Wright in his Plaza Hotel suite and found him "stretched out on a sofa, his fine hands folded on his lap, a shawl precisely draped around his shoulders. In writing about him thus, I hope that I am not so much arranging a suitable atmosphere as conveying a psychological shock. One expected a tyrant, a man constantly caricatured by the press as a bellowing iconoclast. And here was a genial skeptic whose habitual tone was one of pianissimo raillery. . . ." And if he was still automatically *contra*—Cooke discovered that, when asked to turn his head for the right camera angle, the great man loudly refused—the damage could be repaired if one appealed to his sense of humor, and that made him "as malleable as an aging cat."

Those wishing to capture a physical likeness generally faced the greatest challenge. Back in 1931, when Wright was a comparative whippersnapper of sixty-four, he complained that the photograph Steichen had taken of him made him look "about ninety-five years old." For the fact was that his features had elongated in a way that made it difficult to flatter him. There were crevices in his cheeks, his upper lip had lengthened, his mouth had contracted into a thin line, and, as another artist, Arizona art teacher and critic, Dr. Harry Wood, noticed, it settled into a dour fold when he relaxed. Some daunting folds around his mouth, beginning at the nostrils and descending into the chin, would have to be addressed, and some way found to widen those eyes that, although "like gimlets," retained "a blueness and intensity and total focus I shall never forget," Dr. Wood said. Something else in his face, perhaps having to do with the heavy lids or perhaps the right eyebrow, as eloquently arched as Garbo's, gave another kind of impression, one Wright noticed himself. In the summer of 1944 he complained to Lloyd that he "looked like an old hag," and by the middle 1950s he was avoiding photographers altogether

Frank Lloyd Wright in 1957

because "they all make me look like an old woman." (As a curious
corollary, in some pictures Olgivanna Wright began to assume a
distinctly soldierly look.) Even cartoonists had a hard time making a
recognizable likeness. That veiled yet penetrating look, the mulish
set of the chin, the challenge of the mouth—if these presented problems enough, there was the further handicap of the sitter himself.
Wood, who painted Wright a few months before he died, wrote
revealingly that his sitter would give a minute criticism of his progress
at the end of each session, demanding that he remove details that, at
the end of the next, he would just as arbitrarily want restored. This
was not designed to inspire a relaxed mood in the artist himself, and
the better Wright knew him, the more likely the whole exercise was
to end in chaos.

A case in point was a bust begun by his friend Oskar Stonorov, a
German-born architect of distinction who had become director of the
Philadelphia Housing Association and was a noted town planner. He
had studied sculpture with Maillol, was a clever portraitist and had
conceived the ambition to sculpt Wright's head. That was a compliment, but then Stonorov decided he must work in Wright's bedroom.
Perhaps he hoped to insulate his subject from the demands of the
studio, but it made the work-in-progress far too tempting a target.
One evening, thinking her husband quieter than usual, Olgivanna
Wright went into his bedroom and found him at work on the bust.
She wondered what Stonorov would have to say about that. "I worked
on it before," her husband replied gaily, "and he did not notice
anything." This time might be different, she responded, since the
change was evident. Her husband conceded the point, but wanted to
know whether he had improved the result. She studied it, and concluded that the nose was somewhat too long and the spacing of the
right eye was at fault. Before she knew it, they were both attacking
the bust. They pursued their improvements for some time and, at
length, declared themselves completely satisfied. But, next morning,
she discovered that Wright had added some additional touches that
had quite ruined the effect. Stonorov seemed blind to the embellishments but eventually wondered aloud what could have happened to
his bust. The moment to confess was upon them. Wright looked him
straight in the eye and said that Olgivanna had done it. She concluded,
"Needless to say, the bust was never finished." The one sculpture of
Wright that they did like is now on exhibit at Taliesin. The artist
was a young apprentice, Heloise Crista, who hit upon the idea of

having her subject's eyes raised, making his habitually raised eyebrow seem logically placed, and having the effect of widening his eyes. The architect, at the moment of inspiration: it was a brilliant solution. Since it was only the second piece of modeling she had ever done, Wright must have reasoned that she could not do much harm, and left her to her own devices.

Stonorov's abortive attempt to portray Wright was the result of having been asked to organize a retrospective exhibition of the latter's work, "Sixty Years of Living Architecture," the largest that had ever been attempted. The idea was suggested by Frederick Gutheim, expanded upon by Wright and worked out in detail by Stonorov. It would capitalize upon an offer from the Italian Academy of Art to exhibit in the Palazzo Strozzi in Florence, one that could not be accepted because the Italian government was not able to pay for transportation, and neither could the architect. It was Stonorov's idea to seek the sponsorship of the Gimbel's department store in Philadelphia. If Wright were to allow that store to mount a preview, Gimbel's would pay travel costs (it eventually contributed $50,000 toward the project), and Stonorov's bust would have a place of honor in the Palazzo Strozzi. The materials used for the project—hundreds of renderings, nearly a thousand original drawings, photomurals, twenty-five models and an actual exhibition house—would form the prototype for another successful exhibition, "Frank Lloyd Wright in the Realm of Ideas," held decades later. The exhibition was an immediate success when it opened in Florence in May 1951.

One of the projects that most excited him during that period was the chance to build in Venice. A young Italian architectural student who had seen the exhibition in Florence, and who had been fired with enthusiasm for his work, was on his way to Arizona to commission Wright to build him a house in Venice when, outside Philadelphia, he was killed in a car accident. His family decided to commission Wright to build a memorial to their son in the form of a small architectural library, with space to accommodate twelve students. They had the site, at the rear of Santa Maria Novella on the Grand Canal, and Wright thought he had the design, in white Pavonazzo marble and Murano glass, punctuated with tiny balconies, that would reflect, in contemporary terms, the balance, proportion and classical grace of the adjoining Renaissance palaces. The Masieri Memorial, as it was called, was admired in Italian architectural circles but considered a sacrilege in others, and the Venetian Committee on Tourism finally

Wright before a model of his Price Tower in Bartlesville, Oklahoma, on exhibition at "Sixty Years of Living Architecture," New York, 1953

exerted such pressure on the project that it was abandoned. Among those opposed was another octogenarian and aesthete, a longtime resident of Florence, the Italian Renaissance art historian Bernard Berenson, and so was Ernest Hemingway. The latter's parents had lived in Oak Park, and Wright had met them in his younger days. Subsequently, Wright could be heard complaining about the narrowness of all literary men and artists in general, with the exception, of course, of architects.

Another favorite project of those years was the nineteen-story skyscraper Wright built for the Harold C. Price Construction Company in Bartlesville, Oklahoma. Wright's views about the skyscraper as a desirable form had undergone a number of shifts since the early days when he, influenced by Sullivan, saw it simply as an architectural problem to be solved. There the matter rested until he was invited to design St. Mark's-in-the-Bouwerie for New York, and it is clear from the resultant structure, with its concrete roots, hollow trunk and projecting, swastikalike wings, that he had fully grasped the potential possibilities. Vincent Scully commented, "St. Mark's Tower, rising like a jewel out of some of Wright's most tormented years, best expresses of all his projects the structural, spatial, and formal abstraction through which he hoped to evoke nature's organic forms." The depression had destroyed all hope that this masterpiece might be built. Somewhere, however, in the recesses of his mind there lingered an unquenchable fondness for what he had wrought with St. Mark's and a natural desire to see the idea resurrected. So when he was eventually given the opportunity to build a version of it, as an office and apartment tower in an Oklahoma town, it was perhaps not surprising that he decided to seize the chance first and worry about the rationalizations later. For the fact was that this modified version of the great St. Mark's project was, and is, a perfect delight. Its patrons, Mr. and Mrs. Harold C. Price, were a farsighted couple, lovers of the Orient, who had made a fortune in oil and natural gas pipeline construction and were generously willing to let the grand old man have his way. They cheerfully acquiesced to his proposal to build a building with no square corners (so much dead space, he told them), accepting his argument that he would have to design special furniture and fittings for the triangular- and parallelogram-shaped rooms. They agreed upon the reinforced concrete-glass-and-copper building, with its stamped copper plates of special design and the gold-tinted glass, paid an estimated $6.5 million for it, and allowed Wright to emblazon a quotation from Whitman in the lobby, a conceit that must have seemed most old-fashioned by the 1950s. ("Where the city that has produced the greatest man stands, / There the greatest city stands.") The Price Tower has been dismissed as a much-watered-down version of the original, but to at least one visitor, that was part of its charm. If Wright's Millard house looks insistently monumental, despite its miniature size, the reverse can be said for the Price Tower, despite its height of 221 feet. And, since every aspect of the building has a different facet, one has the overwhelming impression of a piece of sculpture, of sublime delicacy and refinement, unaccountably deposited at a modest corner of Sixth and Dewey streets in Bartlesville. It has been designated as one of the buildings worthy of being retained as an example of Wright's work by the A.I.A., and is on the Department of the Interior's register of historic buildings.

The success of the Price Tower seemed to convince Wright that a case could be made for skyscrapers after all. And, being Wright, to be persuaded was to become an ardent advocate. Four years later, in 1956, he was proposing that the city of Chicago erect an office building on its waterfront a mile high, that is to say, approximately four times as tall as the Empire State Building, to house one hundred thousand people. This monstrous project—the drawing alone was twenty-two feet long—seemed such an anomaly, coming from Wright, that most people did not take him seriously. Lewis Mumford, the old friend with whom he was by now reconciled, was perfectly disgusted and refused to have anything to do with it. Wright's "Sky City" died a quiet death.

These and other vast projects—a synagogue in suburban Philadelphia, a Unitarian church in Madison, a music building for the Florida Southern campus, a Greek Orthodox church for Milwaukee, an opera house for Baghdad and a gift shop in San Francisco with an imposing façade and a spiral ramp interior—show that, far from moderating his pace, Wright was even more productive than ever. During the last nine years of his life he executed three hundred commissions. One hundred and thirty-five of them were built, nearly a third of his total output. He kept up this astounding pace, in addition to the usual migration between Wisconsin and Arizona, more and more frequent trips to New York in connection with building the Guggenheim, and six trips overseas: to London (1950), Italy (1951), Paris (1952), Zurich (1955), Wales (1956) and Iraq (1957). None of it deflected him from the kind of work he loved best. Even before World War I, he had been an enthusiast for simplified construction and, he repeatedly said, would rather "solve the small house problem than build anything else that I can think of." In the face of constantly rising costs, some way had to be found to economize still further on his most successful idea, the Usonian house. Early in the 1950s he thought he had found a method of construction so simple that anyone could use it—his answer to the do-it-yourself movement. He decided to try using plain hollow blocks, lighter and less costly than the original versions, knitted together with reinforcing steel rods and grouting. In principle any child could play with the block system, usually designed on a two-by-four-foot module, since the system could span openings, accommodate glass and appeared to be easy to use. After one of his students, Arthur Pieper, managed to build himself a house using the method, with some help from Charles Montooth, Wright decided to launch these self-build houses, which he called Usonian automatic, and the most successful subsequent example was the Benjamin Adelman house in Phoenix, Arizona, of 1953. However, cost was again the problem. As John Sergeant, author of a valuable study of Wright's Usonian houses, explained, "Great care had to be taken in construction to ensure that block joints occurred on module, otherwise an incremental error soon built up, and the necessary fine tolerance was difficult to achieve in homemade blocks." The method, in other words, was impractical for the novice, and that meant skilled help, and the costs shot up once again. Wright had optimistically assessed the cost of the house at $5,000; the Adelman residence cost $25,000.

Undaunted, Wright came up with a new answer to the concept of prefabrication, a modern version of the ready-cut houses he had invented in 1911 and actually built. This time he would make use of panel construction systems that were, in later versions, wall panels made from synthetic fiber and externally boarded studwork. Wright designed four different versions, teamed up with the Marshall Erdman Company in Madison and announced that these standardized techniques would cut the cost of a new house to $16,000. Magazines gave the idea wide publicity and, according to the manufacturer, at least twenty such houses were built. But again, there were flaws in the scheme. Despite his best intentions Wright was constitutionally incapable of compromising and would insist, for instance, on such details as genuine mahogany paneling and piano hinges, far handsomer than the usual door hinge, but more costly as well. Once the extra costs of crating and shipping had been added, the price had jumped again,

The Unitarian Church, Madison, Wisconsin, from the southwest

Annuniciation Greek Orthodox Church, Milwaukee, which Wright designed but did not live to see built

The Robert Llewellyn Wright house in Bethesda, Maryland

to between $30,000 and $50,000: hardly the cheap house he had hoped for.

Those who knew him best, the members of his family, never expected Wright to give them anything inexpensive. Robert Llewellyn, his youngest son, who became a successful Washington lawyer, had wanted his father to build a house for his family for years. But Wright had always insisted that they buy a two-acre lot, and in the early days they could not afford that. Finally, in 1956, they bought a site a builder did not want because it was a steep wooded slope. That was quite perfect from Wright's point of view, and since by then all his experimental work was encompassing circular forms, he designed a two-story hemicycle made from concrete block and specially curved boards of Philippine mahogany, with plenty of extra mahogany used for interior detailing, no doubt to counteract the roughhewn appearance of the concrete block walls. Robert and his wife, Betty, loved the whole concept, but were dumbfounded to discover that his father's international reputation did not help at all when the moment came to finance the house. "We borrowed from a friend to get the house constructed," Robert Wright said in 1974. "Then we had a time finding an appraiser who would say it was worth half what it cost. It cost $40,000 and we wanted a $20,000 mortgage. . . . The appraisers didn't like the site or the slag block, but they weren't used to anything different." Their only regrets, in retrospect, were that they had scaled down some aspects of the original design because, as they also observed, the house was, for all practical purposes, impossible to enlarge.

The house Wright designed for his son David and daughter-in-law Gladys in Phoenix was even more of a tour de force, as he must have known when he put it on exhibit at the National Institute of Arts and Letters in 1953. This time he was making use of concrete blocks built by the Besser Company, with which David Wright was an executive. The house is reached by a spiraling ramp, decorated with trailing vines and with a trickling stream running alongside, and living space is raised above the ground in curved-line fashion. The concrete floors have been cantilevered from piers, also made of concrete block, and these carry the air conditioning and other utilities. Building curved forms from square materials was a virtuoso performance indeed, and placing the living quarters a level above the ground (so as to avoid the dust of that arid climate) had the further advantage of providing spectacular views of the surroundings. From the living room one looks past an almond-shaped pool and across citrus groves to the distant mountains. The house, with its bold, curving forms, its panoramic vistas, its wonderful, comfortable living room with its collection of Japanese prints, plates, bowls, jars and tiny potteries that once belonged to Catherine, and a glorious, custom-made carpet designed in circular motifs, has earned a prominent place in the pantheon of Wright's achievements.

David, the fourth child, cannot remember ever seeing much of his father, except on holidays and birthdays. He said that, for all practical purposes, he never had a father. As a young man, he served in World War I and took jobs in steel mills and then as a traveling salesman: "I was a man of all trades." He continued, "I've been in some tough situations. The thirties were the worst period of my life. Taking hold of myself and making do. But my mother gave me good training. She taught us to be responsible and self-sufficient. Llewellyn was his father's boy and I suppose I was my mother's.

"What I really care about nowadays is, I'd like to have my mother understood. I am appalled that, in Oak Park, they are telling stories about my father's last wife in my mother's quarters. Very few people have given the first Mrs. Wright her due in developing her family. She raised six successful children; my father didn't."

After Catherine Wright's marriage to Page ended, she went to live with her daughter Frances in West Virginia. Then, in 1933, she returned to Chicago and took an apartment with Llewellyn on the North Side. After that, she spent her time traveling between children, ending her days in a sanatorium in Los Angeles. She had a bad knee, and, David Wright thought, her daughter Catherine, with whom she often stayed, did not understand the problem and kept trying to make her walk. Eventually she fell and had to go to the hospital. For a while she managed to use a walker, but then she broke her leg and never tried to walk again. David said, "Catherine was very impatient and intolerant of her mother's condition. So she was a nomad in later life, not a very satisfactory arrangement." Mrs. Robert Wright added, "Catherine—she wanted to be called Nancy in later years, and that's what her grandchildren called her—never really adapted herself to life alone and not having a big place of her own where she could have her family. She was a very interested and loving grandmother, and I liked her a lot, although it was not easy having her in the house. She was very critical. Finally my husband found her a room near us and she lived there for a while. She became rather bitter and my husband would make excuses for her."

Her granddaughter Elizabeth Wright Ingraham added, "At the end of her life she was living in a twilight world and my father, John, would not go to visit her in California. I think he thought she was more of a child than he was. My own view was that nirvana, for Nancy, was being completely taken care of."

At least two large public building projects that should have come Wright's way during the final decade of a brilliant career did not, and a third was threatened, at least partly because of a widespread perception that he was a communist sympathizer, if not actually Red himself. These suspicions might have been put at rest after the FBI tried, and failed, to have Wright prosecuted on charges of sedition during the war. Unfortunately, Wright gave everyone plenty of reason to go on impugning his patriotism. He continued to insist hotly that the imperialist ambitions of Roosevelt and Churchill had brought about World War II, his comment to his daughter Iovanna, "Roosevelt has sold his country down the river," being typical. He caused a furor at a League of American Writers meeting in 1944 by telling them that if they wanted to do something useful they could start by getting the president out of the White House. He never hid his dislike of Truman for what he thought were similar predilections. He caused another commotion some years later by suggesting that his interviewer, Jinx McCrary, add a postscript to a letter she proposed to send to Mrs. Eisenhower: "You married a military man. Kindly restrain him." The interview was seen on television, and the subsequent headline was NOTED ARCHITECT APES MOSCOW'S LINE ON TV BROADCAST. The FBI files grew longer. Repetitious summaries of the reasons for suspecting Frank Lloyd Wright went back to 1915, reviewed all the old Mann Act accusations, drew a veil over the repeated refusals to prosecute and painted him as a notorious lecher, a champion of draft dodgers and now, in his dotage, a communist spokesman.

For, in those immediate postwar years, Wright's stance was as antiwar and pacifist as ever, and that made him ready to suspect American foreign policy and champion those who seemed, to him, to be the underdogs in the debate, i.e., the Russian people. Years ago it had been concluded that Wright was not so much pro-German as anti-British. Now it could be said that he was not so much pro-communist as against his country's militarism and opposed to what he saw as a disturbing development of the cold war: a climate of paranoia and suspicion. Wright on the defensive for his views was Wright alerted to the dangers facing free men everywhere. It was almost axiomatic that the more he was attacked, the more rash his pronouncements would become, the more defiant his attitude and the more prepared he was to damn the whole world.

Wright had, of course, never needed much encouragement to be controversial. In a speech at Princeton just after the war he proposed that all American cities be decentralized and higher education suspended for ten years. (He advised architecture students at Carnegie Tech in Pittsburgh to "Go home and make something of yourselves.") Two years later, in Washington, he avowed with a straight face that he had been trying to persuade Mr. Truman to join him in his campaign to "move the capital out West, west of the Mississippi." The president quite agreed with his project but "did not promise his support." The State Department ought to be abolished, but so should the presidency, as it presently existed. The atom bomb that the war had unleashed was a cataclysm; it had thrown everyone "off base," "making all we have called progress obsolete overnight." It became more imperative than ever to work for world peace. Wright added his name to a prominent list of supporters for the Cultural and Scientific Conference for World Peace, held in New York City in the spring of 1949. The group sponsoring the event was cited as a "Communist front" by the House Un-American Activities Committee the following year. A year after that, in 1951, Wright's name was on that committee's list of Americans who, it claimed, had been "affiliated with from five to ten Communist-front organizations," along with actors José Ferrer and Judy Holliday, singer Paul Robeson, artist Rockwell Kent, authors Dashiell Hammett and Thomas Mann, playwrights Lillian Hellman and Clifford Odets, composer Aaron Copland and scientist Albert Einstein. Wright's response was to continue his inflammatory statements about the need for world peace and the necessity for the United States to take the lead in disarmament, saying, "We have nothing to fear in abandoning the atom arms race. Russia wants peace just as much as we do."

In the summer of 1950, he signed a World Peace Appeal, another subversive act according to FBI memoranda, since the organization involved, the Permanent Committee of the World Peace Congress, had received the enthusiastic endorsement of the Supreme Soviet. He supported the establishment of the Emergency Civil Liberties Committee in 1951, formed in response to the perceived threat to constitutional guarantees of free speech and numbering a large proportion of professors and ministers in its ranks. This, too, was a suspect body, the main basis for suspicion appearing to be the amount of space its activities was being given in the *Daily Worker*. Further sinister connotations were seen in the fact that Wright had written an article on Russian life and architecture for the magazine *New Masses* in 1937, that he had shown Russian films at Taliesin during World War II, and that he was one of seventeen prominent Americans who had signed a Christmas appeal for the parole of eight out of an original ten Hollywood figures sentenced to prison as a result of their appearances before the House Un-American Activities Committee in October 1947. It was only a matter of time before the Taliesin Fellowship would also be suspect.

In the spring of 1954 someone visited the Los Angeles office of the FBI to report that the school of architecture being conducted by Wright in Spring Green and Scottsdale, which had Veterans Administration accreditation (meaning that the federal government was paying for the tuition of former G.I.s), had no actual classrooms. The

Fellowship seemed to be a religious cult following the teachings of an oriental metaphysician. Students, the informant declared, held dances to the moon and were told what to think. Their movements were closely monitored, their freedom restricted, and attendance was required at "certain meetings" that had nothing to do with schoolwork. The student body harbored draft dodgers, conscientious objectors and homosexuals. In short, it was a subversive organization whose teachings were contrary to the American way of life. This anonymous message was duly forwarded to the Veterans Administration by the FBI.

As it happened, Taliesin, which had qualified as a training ground for veterans in 1946, had again received approval, the year before this letter was written, from an elect governor's committee of distinguished educators. This new examination had been made to comply with amendments to federal law. The committee's report, given in Madison in the autumn of 1953, concluded that the Taliesin Fellowship was "unique in concept and operation," being, essentially, a well-structured and supervised apprenticeship in architectural training and, as such, should be approved for the training of veterans. That report should have been persuasive, but, unfortunately, Wright was then approaching the climax of a long battle with the town of Spring Green, which claimed that Taliesin should not be tax exempt. The amount owed the town was small (it was finally assessed at $886) but more was at issue, because if the town were successful then the state would have to be paid as well, and that would be expensive. Wright had explained to anyone who would listen that Taliesin had been run as a nonprofit foundation since 1940, and that all income from architectural fees went to maintain it as a school and farm. He had asked for a further ruling, and, as luck would have it, the case was to be heard by the state supreme court of Wisconsin in 1954 just as, Mumford wrote, "the fear and suspicion and poisonous hatred and irrationality now rampant among our countrymen" was at its height. Commenting on the subsequent verdict, the *Capital Times* observed, "In view of the conservative outlook of many lawyers, and of most judges, it is likely that Wright suffered from hostility before he even got into court. The judicial mind, which dwells so largely in the past, is probably not interested in a modern approach to architecture, or likely to recognize a school that does not conform to all the red tape and forms so dear to the legal mind." The verdict of the state supreme court of Wisconsin, handed down in November 1954, was that Taliesin did not qualify for tax-exempt status. The court found that, after expenses, the Fellowship had enjoyed a usual annual profit of between $12,000 and $40,000 (for the years 1946–50), that Wright had continued to exert the main financial control, and that the main function of Taliesin was architectural practice, not education and farming. Taliesin owed back taxes to a total of $18,646.

Editorial comment was uniformly sympathetic. The *Weekly Home News* of Spring Green published a front-page editorial, and other writers observed that Wright had twice offered to give a "butterfly type" bridge design to the state, one for the Wisconsin River near Taliesin and the other near Wisconsin Dells, and that the state had twice refused. Wright was outraged. He would leave Wisconsin. He would sell his sixty-head herd of cattle and Taliesin. He would burn Taliesin down. That was such a terrifying thought that his friends and supporters rallied at once. A former apprentice, Cary Caraway, now associated with the University of Illinois, was the leading spirit in organizing a testimonial dinner, attended by the governor and several hundred other dignitaries, which raised $10,000 toward paying the taxes. Wright declared himself deeply touched by the ovation and said he would not leave the state after all. He said, "After that demonstration of feeling and affection . . . I don't think it would be possible for me to leave my native state. I was born in Wisconsin and I belong in Wisconsin."

One of the public building projects affected by the accusations swirling around Wright in the early 1950s was his grand design to give his boyhood home of Madison a new civic center. He had first launched the idea in 1938, having been commissioned by several prominent citizens who were opposed to a routine scheme for a new city-county building. Wright's ambitious project would have required the filling-in of some part of Lake Monona to make a large graceful curve that would accommodate a garden park, fountains and walkways, and beneath this, levels containing auditoriums, convention space, exhibition halls and government offices, including courtrooms. There would even be a railroad station, a bus depot and a marina. The cost was staggering (an estimated $17 million), but there was no doubt it was a brilliant plan, conceived by Wright at the very peak of his renaissance. In arguing for it, Wright was at his most persuasive. The original plan was defeated by a single vote. However, that unfortunately meant the loss of several hundred thousand dollars in federal funds. Factions split for and against Wright, but then the war intervened, and the whole question of building Monona Terrace, as it came to be called, was shelved until 1953. By then the plan was simply the latest and largest of a series of Madison houses, churches, hotels, apartments and the like, thirty-two designs in all (not all of them built), that amounted to a decade-by-decade collection of Wright's oeuvre, beginning in the 1890s. A revised Monona Terrace plan would be the jewel in the crown, simply the latest and most brilliant of all his schemes. As before, the citizens were almost evenly divided between those who fervently supported Wright and those who condemned him. John Hunter, associate editor of the newspaper, the *Capital Times*, which consistently supported the Monona Terrace project, said the problem was that the good folk of Madison never ceased to disapprove of Wright's unconventional life and refused to believe he was anyone of real importance. Hunter cited, as an example, a decision made decades later by the congregation of the Unitarian church Wright had designed in 1947 to sell his furniture and uncomfortable chairs. "When the time came to put up the chairs for auction, to their astonishment they sold for five thousand dollars each," he said. Even so the city managed to approve a scaled-down version of Monona Terrace in 1954, the year its old city hall was torn down, and authorized a $5.5 million bond issue. Wright was narrowly approved as architect by a margin of 1,300 votes.

Almost as soon as the referendum was passed, and victory assured, his opponents sprang into action. Carroll Metzner, a prominent lawyer, succeeded in persuading the state legislature that Wright's new civic center, some sixty feet high, would block a view of the lake from the State Capitol. Another opponent gave a speech before the state legislature stating that he had a secret dossier on Wright and that, were its contents divulged, members would be induced to take action against Monona Terrace. Wright was "unfit to characterize the city of Madison," he said. The legislature subsequently passed a bill limiting the height of any new structure to twenty feet. This effectively destroyed the city's hope of building anything on Lake Monona, and certainly not Wright's project. In 1959 the law was repealed, but by then it was too late.

It was perhaps just bad luck on Wright's part that the revival of the Monona Terrace project should come just as the state supreme court was about to return its unfavorable verdict against Taliesin. He was fighting to save his reputation on yet another front. When the air force announced a competition for a new academy, to be built in Colorado Springs, Wright submitted a design. The field was narrowed down to Skidmore, Owings and Merrill, a prominent Chicago architectural firm, and himself. The final decision was about to be made when, in July 1954, the American Legion threatened to make a public protest if Wright were chosen. Wright then withdrew from the competition. None of this was known until August 1955, when *Architectural Forum* magazine stated, "The American Legion had readied a public blast at Wright, dredging up past anti-militaristic activities and associations of the architect, which, front-paged for America in its 1955 mood would have made it awkward for the Air Force to consider Wright and his group. The Legion's price for silence: elimination of Wright." Wright said, "I do not know why the American Legion puts me on its blackened page unless because I hate war and openly oppose it. I equally hate American Legion opposition to the exercise by others of the same rights it takes to itself." And, when Congress held hearings to consider the merits of the eventual academy, prepared by Skidmore, Owings and Merrill, Wright was one of the star witnesses who attacked the ultramodern, International Style design. Revenge may have been sweet, but that was yet another desirable commission lost in the cause of character assassination during the turbulent 1950s.

The FBI files reveal that Wright was once more investigated for sedition in 1955. No charges were ever brought.

Two years before he died, Wright was still fighting the same battle. By then he was the architect of choice to design an $8 million civic center for Marin County on 130 acres just north of San Rafael, California. The building, which includes a main administration building and hall of justice, as well as offices and a library, is a long, low structure designed of concrete and metal, linking two hills. Once it was learned that Wright planned to make a personal appearance before the Marin County board of supervisors and sign an actual contract, a seven-page dossier was introduced at the meeting by a local resident, who said it had been written by J. B. Matthews, former chief investigator for the House Un-American Activities Committee and former staff director of the Senate Investigations Subcommittee. (Matthews had resigned four years earlier after writing an article accusing the Protestant clergy of supporting the communist conspiracy.) The dossier began, "Frank Lloyd Wright, America's best known architect, now in his 89th year, has a record of active and intensive support of Communist views and enterprises. He belies the popular notion that youth alone is beguiled by the appeals of radicalism and subversion. . . ." At that point, Wright stood up and left the meeting. The supervisors, voting four to one, refused to listen to a full reading of the document. As one of them, Vera Schultz, said, the Marin County board did not inquire into the religious or political beliefs of any of its employees and, "It is most inappropriate that we should subject a man of Mr. Wright's caliber to the reading of unfounded and unsubstantiated charges." Two hours after that, the architect was back in a good humor, had gone on a tour of the site and signed the official contracts. He had also, in passing, delivered his last and best word on the subject: "I am what I am," he told the meeting before he left. "If you don't like it, you can lump it."

Had he not made such a statement, of course, someone would have invented it, and there was no more richly appreciative audience in those days for Wright as showman than a university campus. Yale, for instance. In the autumn of 1955, Richard P. Goldman and his roommate, Henry F. S. Cooper, organized a lecture series, inviting fifty or sixty prominent participants. Wright was one of the first to accept. Goldman said, "I was a nervous twenty-year-old dealing with this genius. In retrospect I think he was having fun at our expense." Wright arrived by train from New York to New Haven to find that, owing to a misunderstanding, no one was there to meet him. He was about to turn around when someone rushed in and coaxed him in the direction of the Taft Hotel and WYBC, the Yale Broadcasting Company's offices in Hendrie Hall. Then there was another spate of flustered apologies when he arrived for his interview half an hour early. Wright "waved his stick, swirled his cape, and marched across the Green to the Taft, kicking pigeons out of his way as he went," Cooper, who was editor, subsequently reported in the *Yale Daily News*. About twenty minutes later the reception committee attempted to coax the great man back to the studio. They were finally ready for him but he had changed his mind. He was taking the 7:10 back to New York. But sir. . . . They explained that he would be speaking to an audience of at least four hundred. There was a pause. "Well, . . ." he said.

Some moments later the elevator door opened, and Wright "sailed" into the lobby, kicking ottomans aside and unleashing criticisms of the hotel's poor design as he "stalked" back to WYBC. Arriving at the studio he caught sight of Philip Johnson, now a famous architect. He greeted him warmly, exclaiming wickedly that he thought he was dead. Cooper wrote, "Mr. Johnson sidled up and explained that he really wasn't dead at all." To think of it, said Wright, reminiscing,

" 'Little Phil, all grown up, an architect, and *actually* building his houses out in the rain.' Philip Johnson, one of America's top architects, wiggled his toes (you could see the top of his shoes moving) and sidled off."

Wright was having a wonderful time, surrounded by undergraduates eager to hear his next epithet or, as Cooper put it, "awaiting any barnacles of wisdom which might fall from the venerable craft anchored before them." It was perfectly marvelous to see the positive genius Wright had for disconcerting people, and then watch him at dinner, dumping his ice cream in his coffee, brushing sauce from his pinstriped suit and signing his name in the guest book several inches high. It was still more fun when a packed audience in Sterling Stratcona Hall, which had gathered to hear Wright lecture, listened to the courtly introduction that was being made by Mr. Johnson. Cooper wrote that Johnson was "praising him in one sentence after another —I think he even called him 'America's greatest living architect.' " And as these honeyed phrases fell from Johnson's lips, the subject of the encomiums could be heard to comment, in a stage whisper loud enough for the back of the hall, "Attaboy, Phil," and, "Try a little harder."

For Wright had never forgiven this young man, whose collaborative efforts with Hitchcock had, he felt, been so destructive to his reputation. He was, at bottom, too insecure, for, as William Short, who became clerk of the works for the Guggenheim and saw a great deal of him in those last years, observed, he was still bitter because he felt that he was being given less recognition than practitioners of the International Style. Despite his tremendous personal success, critically he was still being considered a forerunner of modernism, his best ideas forty years old. Lewis Mumford averred that the International Style, with its dogmatic assertiveness, its emphasis on mechanical function and the aesthetically puritanical, was becoming outdated. He wrote in 1947, "The modern accent is on living, not on the machine," but his conclusion was somewhat premature. Johnson, working with Mies van der Rohe, was in the midst of building the Seagram Building on Park Avenue, a skyscraper of "grand and honorific character, sober and symmetrical, clothed in elegant materials such as bronze-tinted auburn glass," Curtis observed. It was being erected opposite another symbol of the triumphant ascendance of the International Style, the Lever Building of Skidmore, Owings and Merrill, built four years before. (Wright liked to call them the "Whiskey" and "Soap" build-

Interior view of the Guggenheim Museum

Detail of the domed roof

Exterior view of the Guggenheim Museum
Detail: Wright during construction of the Guggenheim,
late 1950s

ings.) The new United Nations Headquarters overlooking the East River, designed by Harrison and Abramovitz, had clearly been adapted from an earlier idea by Le Corbusier; in short, the "glass-box boys," and their "elegant monuments of nothingness" had swept the stage clean. No wonder Wright was so ready to launch an attack on "Skiddings, Own-More and Sterile," as he childishly called them, when Congress gave him an opportunity to testify on the Air Force Academy in 1955. In his mind he was still, and would always be, the outsider.

In retrospect it is easy enough to see why Wright's design for the Guggenheim Museum, his first and only commission for that prominent showcase, Manhattan, took the form that it did. If he had never experimented with circular forms, he would still have concluded that, having only one chance to make his mark, and in light of everything that was boxy, streamlined, uniform and regimented, his must be flowing, asymmetrical, idiosyncratic and free-form, in a word, curved. However, to suggest that a desire to display his superior gifts was the main motive would be unwarranted. As has been seen, Wright had been experimenting with a particular form for decades, beginning with his urnlike design for a house for himself in the Mojave Desert. This fascination with the enclosing, enveloping shape, symbolized by the cauldron, was an enduring metaphor for his spiritual quest, the "architecture of the within." As others have pointed out, he had experimented for years with a central open space ringed with balconies, and its consistent appeal for him was shown by the Larkin Building, Unity Temple, the Johnson Wax Administration Building and others. The ziggurat design, which he had already developed for Sugarloaf Mountain but had not built, was simply a refinement of that undeviating choice, "fully expressive of the sculptural freedom possible with reinforced concrete," as William H. Jordy pointed out. It was the final expression of his search for logical movement through space. Jordy wrote, "It is not the spatial continuity characteristic of European modernism—that is, not an open box of space encouraging activity in all directions—but a molded space forcefully conditioned by the path of movement through it." It was "both monumental and ultimate." Wright set on a certain course, as has been seen, was Wright stubbornly determined to the end. But there was a special quality to this perseverance, as he drew and redrew the museum's design from the time that it was first commissioned, in 1943, until it was finally constructed in 1959, leading one to believe that this particular choice meant as much as life itself to him.

From the point of view of a museum dedicated to abstract art, his plan made superficial sense. The viewing public would be taken to the top floor in elevators and then, at its leisure, would walk down its spiraling balconies to the ground floor. It must have looked marvelously creative and original on paper, but, as has been amply demonstrated since, it was most impractical for hanging paintings. The curve of the walls was pronounced and, given the modern artist's preference for larger and larger canvases, that meant an immediate mismatch. The walls sloped outward as well, giving each painting a backward tilt, and Wright's ingenious rationalization notwithstanding—he argued that this made the picture look as if it were on an easel—it was a slant no one else liked. Standing to view the paintings on a floor sloping imperceptibly downhill was another disconcerting detail, and there were problems of lighting, rotating exhibition space and many other basic issues to contend with. These practical shortcomings were clear enough once the museum opened, but they had been foreseen beforehand, guaranteeing endless points of conflict. Of all his commissions, the Guggenheim Museum probably gave Wright the most problems.

The guiding light of the original decision to build a "temple" for the display of non-objective painting, as it was called, was a German baroness and connoisseur, Hilla Rebay, who was curator of the collection of major works by Vasily Kandinsky, Rudolph Bauer, Jean Arp, Max Ernst, Hans Richter and others amassed by her great and good friend, the multimillionaire Solomon R. Guggenheim. Hilla Rebay was enthusiastically convinced that Wright's buildings had the necessary spiritual qualities to provide a fitting background for her collection, and there was never any basic point of disagreement between the three principals. But there were endless delays. First, the right site had to be found. Then the war ended, and Guggenheim, in the mistaken belief that a building slump was imminent (Wright argued, unsuccessfully, that the reverse would be the case), wanted to wait. The years dragged by, and in 1949, just as the future looked bright, Guggenheim died, throwing the whole question of a museum in doubt. The baroness began to behave irrationally and to attack Wright, the trustees expressed profound lack of interest, and, just as all seemed lost, Solomon's nephew, Harry Guggenheim, was appointed the new president of the museum's foundation. The project was then revived,

and, as actual preparations for construction lurched forward, Hilla
Rebay was replaced as future director of the museum by James Johnson
Sweeney.

Hilla Rebay had not been easy to deal with, but she was, at least,
committed to Wright's ideas. Sweeney, whom one former Guggenheim staff member described as "large, rumpled and opinionated,"
appeared to have the professional status and diplomacy necessary to
guide the museum through the crucial building stage. But his interest
in Wright's design had to be how well it fulfilled its function, that
is, to show the art. He would be bound to see its shortcomings, and
Wright seemed to take an almost perverse pleasure in dismissing
Sweeney's valid concerns and asserting the primacy of his architecture
which, he liked to remind Hilla Rebay, was "the mother art." When
one reflects that Wright had banished paintings from the walls of his
houses at an early stage, conflict between the two seemed almost
guaranteed. The situation was certainly not improved by Wright's
fondness for going through the museum twirling his cane at a canvas,
saying, "What do you call this stuff?" as Sweeney turned redder and
redder. Such studied lack of interest did not, of course, stop him from
interjecting his opinion on matters of art, especially if Sweeney were
involved. When the latter expressed an interest in buying Picasso's
sculpture *The Bathers* and exhibiting it in the museum's garden, *Time*
magazine published a letter from Wright suggesting that this "con-
catenation lacks the quality of art and will simply disgrace the great
purpose of the Guggenheim Museum." That must have set the director's teeth on edge.

However, a year after Sweeney's appointment, there was a more
immediate issue, i.e., the resistance of New York's building authorities
to the whole idea of the museum itself. Since the trustees had made
the safe assumption that the museum's design would not be easy to
maneuver through New York's building department, Arthur Cort
Holden, a partner in the firm of Holden, McLaughlin and Associates,
was engaged to act as mediator and facilitator for the various regulatory
procedures involved. As Holden, who was engaged in January 1953,
wrote to Wright a month later, "The problem . . . is that your design
for the Guggenheim is unique in the City's construction experience."
First questions had to do with the reinforced concrete Wright planned
to use, which did not meet New York City codes, but there were
many other objections, involving the slope of the ramps, the clear
glass in the entrance doors and partitions, the construction of elevator

shafts, fire exits and other matters. Finally, the authorities objected
to the fact that, at its highest point, the museum would project four
and a half feet over Fifth Avenue. That year of 1953 was spent dealing
with objections and revisions and attempting to get a verdict from
the board of standards and appeals. The atmosphere appeared cordial,
and Holden was kept believing that permission was just about to be
granted. Finally, the issue was taken up with Robert Moses, who
liked to say that he had a "roundabout family relationship" with
Wright and who, by virtue of his positions as head of the city and
state of New York park systems and as the city's construction coor-
dinator, was a very powerful man. He immediately interceded on
Wright's behalf with the head of the city's board of standards and
appeals with the words "Damn it, get a permit for Frank. I don't care
how many laws you have to break. I want the Guggenheim built."
Holden also believed that Moses advised Wright that "if he expected
to get along in New York, he had 'to pay the tolls.' " A special
inspector was hired to expedite matters. The bill was $3,000. Peters
said, "Guggenheim grumbled, but paid."

There were some battles on other fronts that year. One of the
influential figures in the New York magazine world was Elizabeth
Gordon, editor of Hearst's *House Beautiful*. She recalled that she and
Wright became friends after she ran an article critical of the International Style and received a mysterious telegram. It read, I DIDN'T
KNOW YOU HAD IT IN YOU. I AM AT YOUR SERVICE FROM NOW
ON. It was signed THE GODFATHER. That was peculiar, but the
dateline was Spring Green so she was soon asking Wright exactly
what he meant by being at her service. She was welcome, he said, to
make use of the Taliesin staff. Eventually, she was using the services
of four of Taliesin's members (including John DeKoven Hill, who
became the magazine's editorial director and, as such, a very important
ally for Wright).

House Beautiful's attack on the International Style was published in
April 1953 and centered on a discussion of a new house Mies van der
Rohe had designed for a Chicago physician and close friend, Dr. Edith
Farnsworth. Blake has called the building "the most complete statement of glass-and-steel, skin-and-bones architecture Mies or anyone
else will ever be able to make. It is, also, the ultimate in universality,
the ultimate in precision and polish, the ultimate in the crystallization
of an idea." The house was, for Elizabeth Gordon, the detestable
symbol of a threat to the new America. She believed "that a sinister

group of International Stylists, led by Mies, Gropius, and Corbu, and supported by the Museum of Modern Art, was trying to force Americans to accept an architecture that was barren, grim, impoverished, impractical, unlivable, and destructive of individual possessions, as well as of individuals themselves." To the admirers of the International Style, the attack seemed wildly off the mark, but to Wright it must have seemed like a voice from heaven. Not only had Gordon said exactly what he believed, but she had said it at a moment when he must have been feeling particularly embattled. The New York authorities might never give permission for his Guggenheim design to be built. Monona Terrace might go down to defeat again, just as it seemed to be resurrected. All those years of struggle had taken their toll. His mood, that spring of 1953, can be inferred from a reply sent to him by Douglas Haskell, the sympathetic young critic who had become editor of *Architectural Forum*, the magazine that consistently supported Wright. Wright had submitted his own attack on the International Style, no doubt emboldened by Elizabeth Gordon's emphatic position, and he wanted Haskell to print it. But for once that editor refused, citing the tone of bitterness that lay "across the page like a murky glass." He advised Wright not to publish the article at all. Wright ignored the advice, and a somewhat revised version of the article, along with a letter from him, was published in *Architectural Record* in June. The International Style, Wright declared, was "an evil crusade" and a manifestation of "totalitarianism," fostered by the relentless publicity it had been given by the Museum of Modern Art, which had made "a sinister attempt to betray American Organic Architecture." It is interesting to find Wright using terms that sound more like those used to denounce communism than an architectural movement, suggesting that he was influenced, more or less unconsciously, by the political barbs being directed at him. The publication of the article did not help his cause at *Architectural Forum*. Haskell commented in a memo, "I'm afraid FLLW is simply displaying the complete development of his Messianic complex." That same year there was what seemed like another defection, this time by Lewis Mumford. When Wright's exhibition "Sixty Years of Living Architecture" arrived in New York, housed in a temporary building on the site of the future Guggenheim Museum, along with his exhibition house, Mumford wrote a two-part essay summing up the work of his lifetime. It was sympathetic and admiring, but by no means uncritical. Wright, displaying his usual "either all for me or against me" attitude, responded, "The International Style . . . seems to have found a friend in you." That was not what Mumford had meant. "If I had wanted only to write an encomium that would have been easy; but it seemed to me that the moment demanded something more comprehensive, more penetrating, more judicious than this; and so, in fear and trembling and admiration and love I dared write the article about your work [that] no one else, friendly or hostile, has yet dared to write."

Mumford began by calling Wright the most original architect the United States had produced and "one of the most creative architectural geniuses of all time"; at this stage, "the Fujiyama of American architecture, at once a lofty mountain and a national shrine. . . ." His radical reform of housing design, with his interiors of unadorned brick and wood, his vast fireplaces and immense roofs, brought to domestic architecture the benevolent influence of "the whole Romantic movement, which popularized the picnic, the play school, the virtues of country living. . . ." Mumford rightly observed that many of these innovations for which Wright was now claiming sole credit, the open plan, for instance, were not his inventions, but that he had grasped their significance and made unique use of their advantages. These changes had come about so gradually, and had been so widely disseminated, particularly through the modern ranch house, that they seemed almost old-fashioned. This passion for unity sometimes led to excesses, as when Wright seized upon a certain motif, such as a hexagon or triangle, and applied it relentlessly to every single aspect of his total design, and, "One's eye vainly seeks relief from this almost obsessive reiterativeness." A more basic objection, for Mumford, was that Wright's work was so deeply personal that it was difficult to separate his personality from the work, for, as Sir Herbert Read had noted, "carried to its logical conclusion, a sense of unity . . . implies that every house Mr. Wright builds is his own house and the people who live in them are not his clients but his guests."

What also seemed to rankle, for Mumford, was Wright's insistence, of recent years, that the flowering of his genius owed very little, or almost nothing, to other influences, and certainly not foreign ones, when it was perfectly clear that his ideas had been drawn from every direction under the sun, and that in fact his ability to synthesize was one of his great strengths. Another Wrightian statement that Mumford believed seriously misguided was Wright's assertion that cities ought to be abolished. Developing this theme, Mumford claimed that Wright's designs were all "solo performances." To say this required ignoring the evidence of Oak Park, although it certainly could be said for the later houses that "ideally, each building of his must stand alone . . . in a completely natural setting." That, for Mumford, showed "the limitations of Romanticism, with its rebellion against everything that demands conformity to a general social pattern."

Mumford was, perhaps, too close to his subject to see what a triumph the decade of the 1950s represented for Wright. If nothing else, this final burst of astonishing creativity put the lie to the general cultural expectation that old age brought with it a dwindling and drying up of the artist's creative powers. Mumford missed what Wright's life demonstrated, that is, that great men can delay indefinitely the process of aging. Wright, if he ever thought about it, would immediately move to demolish such an assumption. On his eightieth birthday he said, "a creative life is a young one. . . . What makes you think that eighty is old?" He also said, revealingly, "The purpose of the universe is play. The artists know that, and they know that play and art creation are different names for the same thing. . . ." As Bertrand Russell observed, "The decay of art in our time is not only due to the fact that the social function of the artist is not as important as in former days, it is due also to the fact that spontaneous delight is no longer felt as something which it is important to be able to enjoy. . . . [A]s men grew more industrialized and regimented the kind of delight that is common in children becomes impossible to adults, because they are always thinking of the next thing, and cannot let themselves be absorbed in the moment. This habit of thinking of the 'next thing' is more fatal to any kind of aesthetic excellence than any other habit of mind. . . ." Wright's lifelong refusal to cultivate in his personality what Russell called "prudence and foresight" may have stemmed from an instinctive awareness that to do so would smother in him that capacity for joyful self-expression, which was the wellspring of his art, leading him on the artist's eternal exploration, "and since self-knowledge is a never ending search, each new work is only a part-answer to the question, 'Who am I?' " What is strikingly evident is the fact that, with one or two minor exceptions, Wright's work, seemingly such a bewildering variety of styles, has an inner consistency firmly based on his vision of what architecture should be, the vision he had first formed as an adolescent reading Ruskin. He remained faithful to that inner ideal long after it had gone out of fashion and become almost an object of derision. But every instinct told him he was right. That inner knowledge proved to be his greatest strength, carrying him through bankruptcy, arrest, murder, fires, divorce, indifference, hostility and years of social ostracism—successive blows of fate that would have destroyed anyone less committed, convinced, or indomitably courageous. He had survived it all, and he had triumphed. Five years later, he would be standing on the top balcony of the almost-finished Guggenheim Museum, looking with profound satisfaction at all that his energy, will and gifts had wrought.

Wright's response to Mumford's measured words seemed almost halfhearted and certainly not the outburst of rage one might have seen in past years. For the fact is that, ageless as he might essentially be, he was beginning to hear "time's wingèd chariot" at last. His mood, if not introspective to any marked degree, was certainly elegiac. His daughter-in-law, Mrs. Robert Llewellyn Wright, thought he mellowed considerably during those last years, an opinion that was shared by other relatives and friends. He began to look backward with a certain awareness that there were aspects of his life that had been left unexamined for, as he told an old friend and collaborator, the architect Charles Morgan, it was difficult to find happiness in places where there were the ghosts of so many past failures.

After the Cheney house was sold, it passed through numerous hands and was standing empty when Mrs. Joy Corson moved there with her parents in 1941. She said, "Perhaps the house did not fare well because people thought there were ghosts. The story is that Mamah Cheney haunted the house. I never did see anything, but the floors sure creaked a lot. I used to be afraid, because they creaked exactly as if someone was walking across them." Even so, they loved living there, worked hard to restore it and lived there until 1962. Her mother, Mrs. Joseph Brody, added, "It was unusually efficient. Inside, there are dividers between the living and dining rooms, but the wall only comes up to your eye. We had plenty of shelves for books, and wonderful art glass, and plenty of light.

"It was not unusual to have people appear unannounced. They'd show up in busloads, college students studying architecture. For a time my dad kept a guest book. Well, one day this man appeared. I think I was painting. I went to the door, and he said, 'Mr. Wright is in the car. Can he come in?' 'Oh, of course!' I ran to tell my family, and they said, '*Sure* he is!' They couldn't believe it. He went around looking at everything and asking about everything. On the way out, we took a picture of him. He is gesturing with his cane and saying, 'Those gutters have to be fixed!' They were his parting words."

Norris Kelly Smith wrote, "Toward the end of his life Wright confessed rather ruefully . . . that the one area in which he felt he had failed was that of human relationships." Typically, his first impulse would be to make amends. Bill Short, who used to meet his plane at Kennedy International Airport, then called Idlewild, said, "His reaction as he got into the car was to talk about his fall, which he had two weeks ago." (This diary entry was written on February 5, 1958.) "He said, 'I thought that was the end and I am chastened. It made me think that enmity is a very petty thing and I do not want to die with any enemies, so I am going to call up Philly Johnson, Sweeney, Mies and Henry Russell Hitchcock and have them all in for dinner.' " One doubts that any such dinner ever took place, but the impulse behind it was genuine enough. When he learned that Rudolf Schindler was in the hospital and dying, Wright wrote, "No matter how ambition may lead us astray, the old bonds still hold and I am sorry my once faithful helper should suffer. My best feelings go to you to tell you I still cherish memories of your ready smile and vivacious wit. . . ." He had an appreciative response from Schindler two months before he died. Pauline Schindler wrote, "Of the salutes and guarded farewells which came to him in those final weeks, yours gave him the deepest and most special joy." That there was a similar desire to heal the breach between himself and Catherine, tearing down the old barriers, is clear.

Bill Calvert recalled that as plans were being made to erect the exhibition house on its site at the Guggenheim, along with the immense collection of photographs and models that had toured the world, his team was encountering the usual problems with unions and city officials. "Wright's response to that was, as usual, 'Come on boys, we are going to New York to finish that house and show them how it's done.' The 'Taliesin spirit.' We were to jump to and finish everything, work all night if necessary. It sounds great, but in fact they never did finish. In 'pushes' of this kind, the work was done hastily and for show, because they were working with a lot of amateurs, minor Italian royalty, who would do a flashy job. But it wasn't good work.

"Anyway, Edward Thurman, who was in charge, was a responsible person and a pretty good administrator. One day as the exhibit was almost finished, Wright told him that he wanted the whole Fellowship to go to Long Island, where he had bought up a whole nursery, and spend the day there digging up plants. At the same time he had arranged to have Mrs. Wright go out of town; she would spend the day with friends in Bethel, Connecticut. On that particular day Wright's daughter Frances, who lived on the East Coast, arrived just before noon. With her was an older woman. Mr. Wright embraced the lady, full of smiles. He said, 'See, Mother, do you remember when we did this one?' They went through the whole exhibit arm in arm.''

By then Wright might have been able to show Catherine his latest find, two small stone lions sitting on their haunches, which he had bought to grace the entrance to the exhibition. The story is that the exhibition hall and house were almost finished, and Wright, who paid to have them built, had the last installment in his pocket when something made him go on the hunt for a beautiful, exquisite object—shades of Richard Lloyd Jones! He returned, triumphant, with these two wonderful sculptures. (Holden did not think they were Chinese.) He was, of course, penniless. Holden added that employees of the museum took up a collection and raised the rest of the money. That was Wright, consistent to the last. But he may have felt that the museum could afford to assume some of his financial burden. And much as he may have wanted to settle his differences with Sweeney, there always seemed to be a new dispute. From the very start, Sweeney had disapproved of the idea of holding a Wright exhibition on the site and argued against it. He seemed deaf to Wright's often-repeated argument that Solomon Guggenheim had wanted the kind of museum he had designed. Sweeney kept reviving old objections and raising new ones when the museum's construction was far advanced. In fact, his objections seemed to become more heated as the completion date grew closer.

Bill Short said of Wright, "Yes, he was formidable, but he didn't scare me and I would ask provocative questions. I never saw him put anyone down. He was very gentle and I thought he was a very decent person as a man, with a very deep sense of his work and all the obstacles. He certainly was suspicious of people, including Sweeney's motives, and with reason. I thought of him as a man embattled and holding his own, rather than as someone looking for trouble.

"Wright certainly had no respect for paintings, and this was a continuing problem. But it is also true that Sweeney was set on creating this very pristine museum. He was trying to move beyond Hilla Rebay's original concept. His idea was to have an absolutely white interior with fluorescent lighting to display paintings that Wright didn't like. There was constant friction, and Sweeney and Wright ended up refusing to speak to each other. Both sides were at fault. I think Sweeney wanted to prove it wouldn't work. I was in the middle. . . ."

Another problem, for Short, was the one historically faced by architects Wright was supervising, i.e., that he was indignant if they made decisions that he, for one reason or another, would not make himself. In the case of the Guggenheim, Wright was annoyed because the trustees refused to pay travel expenses for Wesley Peters, and would not send him. In the fall of 1957, he complained that Short had not properly "conveyed to the owners the idea that he, Wright, had been supervising the job." Short replied that he had not meant to imply this, but there were questions that could be taken up with Peters, to spare Wright himself. Wright answered testily, "Wes is not qualified to make decisions," and "you are to report directly to me on all questions."

Things were not particularly easy for Peters either. Calvert recalled that he helped install the first telephone dial system at Taliesin. "Before this we had a magneto phone system in Wisconsin, one you crank, and no telephone at all in Scottsdale. Wright used telegrams and letters. Using the phone was so difficult in Wisconsin. The office was on a party line with ten others. Wright had a private line in the house, but it was linked to Hillside, and he used it only for bare necessities. Gene [Masselink] and Dick [Carney] pressed and pressed to have a dial phone in Scottsdale, and Mr. Wright finally agreed to let them have one in the office. But Wes wanted one in the drafting room, too, and Mr. Wright was absolutely against that. He didn't believe in too much efficiency and convenience. So Wes had one installed, secretly, at one end of the drafting room. Wes would go there with the Guggenheim drawings, and whisper over the phone to Bill Short in New York so Wright wouldn't hear his voice."

As for the color of the walls, Wright wanted ivory, the same color as the exterior, but said he would take any color but white, the only one Sweeney wanted. Then there was the matter of how the paintings should be hung. On that seemingly minor issue the two fought out their basic differences to the last. Wright wanted the paintings to rest against the slanting exterior walls, lit naturally from continuous wall skylights that were controlled by adjustable louvers, with added spotlights. Sweeney argued that the paintings would be too far from the viewer and wanted them thrust forward with a system of vertical poles. He wanted to do away with natural light altogether and bathe the exhibits in fluorescent lighting. Wright, having lost the battle of the color scheme, was even more determined not to lose this one. When Guggenheim decreed that both men present demonstration models of their own systems for the trustees to decide, Wright refused to allow Short to cooperate on Sweeney's plan or present his own in a competition. So the matter stood when he died in April 1959. Short is not at all sure Wright would have attended the museum's opening, had he lived. Louise Svendsen, a former employee of the Guggenheim, remembers seeing Mrs. Wright at the dedication, sitting on the platform, looking stern: "She is reported to have said, 'This is a sorry day. They have spoiled a great monument.'" Short confirmed that Mrs. Wright was antagonistic, and noted that Harry Guggenheim planned the dedication ceremony so that neither Sweeney nor Mrs. Wright made a speech, and invited them to separate dinners.

An indication that his last great battle was taking its toll was that Wright became subject to recurrent attacks of Ménière's syndrome. This is characterized by sometimes violent waves of dizziness, nausea and vomiting, along with a painful throbbing in the ears, thought to be an indication that the adrenals are exhausted. The acute symptoms sometimes lasted as long as a month and cast a shadow over Wright's generally robust health, because he never knew when he might fall. Peters recalled an occasion when Wright became ill in his Plaza Hotel suite in New York. Peters said, "He had no sense of balance and was crawling around the floor on his hands and knees. It was terrible. Olgivanna was also ill. She called me up and said, 'Wes, you have got to take my place.' It lasted for the better part of a month and was not entirely cured when we went home.

"When the symptoms were at their worst, the Baroness showed up. She had this doctor in Germany who applied leeches and claimed to have added years to Solomon Guggenheim's life. Anyway, she came in one day to see Mr. Wright and learned he was ill. Her conclusion was, 'He's in bad hands.' Next morning she appeared with two round-trip airline tickets to Germany to see this doctor. I couldn't see how he could travel. I talked to him and he said no, but he was overcome by her forcefulness and in no position to resist.

"So I decided to call up Mrs. Wright and ask her. She was furious at the idea that I had not made the decision myself. Of course he should not go, she said. In the end, he didn't."

During those last years he had a more or less permanent office in a second-floor suite at the Plaza, one set of windows looking out over the tops of trees in Central Park, and the others facing Fifth Avenue and Fifty-ninth Street. Loren Pope stayed there just as Conrad Hilton, the new owner, was making great changes and removing all traces of the beautiful, but old-fashioned, interior decor designed by its architect, Henry Hardenberg. So did Wright. Appearing at his suite one day, his sister Maginel found the door unlatched, but the room was empty. She called for her brother and found him sitting on a chair in the bathroom, because he could not bear the new Hilton furnishings. Wright soon redecorated the suite to his own specifications, with gold walls and deep wine-colored curtains. Among the objects in it that were listed in an inventory made after his death— along with the Hokusai prints, the details of carving from the Imperial Hotel, the vases and objets d'art—were a small portable typewriter, a wool lap robe, a drawing board, an umbrella, an electric iron and two hammers.

Maginel Wright Barney was a frequent visitor, smuggling up paper bags of baked ham and potatoes cooked in their skins in response to her brother's call, made with a kind of a roar, for "Plain food!" She remembered his walking about the room, hands clasped behind his back and head thrust forward, pacing and talking about architecture. "Now and then he would pause to rearrange an ornament. . . ." He might shift an armchair a few degrees with a swift kick and then, dissatisfied, poke it back into place. They would talk about The Valley, and their childhoods, and his first difficult days on Uncle James's farm, and the fact that he came to love the work. "After a while The Valley taught me everything," he said. Then he would talk about going back home. In August 1988, Wes Peters was in the living room of Taliesin, Spring Green, contemplating the long vistas and gesturing toward a thicket of trees in the distance through which one ought to have seen a glitter of water. "If Mr. Wright were alive right now, we'd be out clearing those trees so he could have a view of the river." As Boris Pasternak wrote, "This was real life, meaningful experience, the actual goal of all quests, this was what art aimed at—homecoming, return to one's family, to oneself, to true existence." Maginel Wright Barney thought, as she visited her brother in that elegant Fifth Avenue suite, "More than any other thing, Frank is a Lloyd-Jones."

Wright visited Wales for his first and last trip three years before he died, in 1956, to receive his honorary degree from the University of Wales. He went to Bangor and Portmeirion in the scenic and mountainous northwest, driving all over Wales, accompanied by Ol-givanna and Iovanna, in the space of a few days. Although it seems likely, there is no record of a visit to Llandysul, or the family homestead or even to the chapels founded by his distinguished ancestors, now deserted and gently decaying. He might have been expected to take a particular interest in Capel Llwynrhydowen, for instance, founded in 1726 by Jenkin Jones, and famous thereafter for the ministry of Gwilym Marles, (great-uncle of Dylan Thomas), who became such a champion of the poor and oppressed, and who was ministering to his flock in 1844 when Richard and Mallie Lloyd Jones left for the New World. But Clough Williams-Ellis, who accompanied them on part of their trip, noted that Wright had visited the tomb of Lloyd George in Llanystumdwy, North Wales, and the small garden that he had designed as a shrine. The Welsh architect wrote that the tomb, "being all boulders built amongst old trees and poised above a rushing river, gave him special satisfaction." As *An Autobiography* demonstrates, Wright was too much of a Welshman not to attach importance to the symbolism of the final resting place. In fact, he wrote a kind of fantasy about his own death, ready to laugh at himself, yet unable to let go of the idea. In his imagination it seemed to him that he was walking through the family graveyard one evening at dusk, looking at the graves of "Ein Mam" and "Ein Tad," and all those headstones of their sons and daughters. Then he sat on a low grass-covered mound in the chapel yard, and began to hear voices. Soon he saw his mother, and the ghosts of other members of his family, with a message for him: he should look at the symbol carved upon the gate.

He continued, "Wondering still and remembering I looked back at the gate. There it was in stone . . . Truth Against the World, the revered . . . symbol old Timothy had carved there on the gatepost for the Lloyd-Joneses. . . .

"Strange . . . a new meaning. . . . Why had I not seen it before? . . .

" 'The truth to set against the woes of this world is Joy!' "

The last time Herbert Fritz, who had become a successful architect, went to see his old mentor was in the autumn of 1958. He had heard about Wright's dizzy spells, and how potentially dangerous these were for a man of his advanced age, and was concerned. When he arrived with a loaf of homemade bread as a gift, he found Wright sitting in

The funeral procession of Frank Lloyd Wright, with Taliesin in the center background

UNITY TEMPLE
TALIESIN VALLEY
FRANK LLOYD WRIGHT ARCHITECT

Wright's design for Unity Temple at Spring Green, Wisconsin, which was to have been his final resting place

a screened area off the living room, overlooking the Taliesin pond and dam. He was wearing a dark suit and looked wonderful. He seemed unchanged, but it was disturbing, just the same, to think of him in less than perfect health, although the Fellowship was making elaborate plans to celebrate his ninetieth birthday, in June 1959 (actually, his ninety-second), as if nothing could go wrong.

Fritz wrote, "But early in April, soon after the Easter Breakfast, which at Taliesin was equal in importance to Christmas, we heard that Mr. Wright was in the hospital." Frances, the second of his children to die, had died in Washington that February at the age of sixty-one. The news came to him in Scottsdale where, as was his custom, he was spending the winter. A month later, Catherine Wright died, one day short of her eighty-eighth birthday. Her son David was at her side and returned to Phoenix on his mother's birthday, March 25, the day she was cremated in Santa Monica. He went straight to Taliesin West to give his father the news and was surprised to find that Wright was very upset by it. David Wright said, "He wanted to know, 'Why didn't you tell me?' and his eyes watered up. I said, 'You never showed any interest.' " On Saturday, April 4, just ten days later, Wright was admitted to the hospital. He had an operation on Monday, April 6; he died on Thursday, April 9. His death was a shock to almost everyone except those members of his family who, like Frances's daughter, Nora Natof, held to the fatalistic conviction that because Catherine's father, Samuel Clark Tobin, had succumbed soon after the death of his wife, Flora, Frank Lloyd Wright would do the same. In fact, Tobin died in December 1916, ten days after his wife.

Years later, Herb Fritz would write, "I dream of him often. This week I saw him in a dream: Mr. Wright and I were both very old and were making our way up a hill. There were a few deserted buildings on each side of the road and we were helping each other up the hill.

Beyond the buildings were bald hills covered with golden grass with large limestone outcroppings. Our progress was slow, but then we were on the ridge and suddenly we were young men dressed in buckskins and riding fine horses. Our horses began walking, then broke into an easy canter and we disappeared into the distance."

Notes

ABBREVIATIONS

A1	*An Autobiography*, by Frank Lloyd Wright, 1932, 1938
A2	*An Autobiography*, 1943
A3	*An Autobiography*, 1977
AP	*Associated Press*
AR	*An Autobiography*, by Antonin Raymond
ATL	*The Art That Is Life*
BL	*The Master Builders*, Peter Blake
BR	*The Prairie School*, by H. Allen Brooks
CD	*The Crowning Decade, 1949–1959*
CT	*Madison Capital Times*
CU	*Modern Architecture since 1900*, by William J. R. Curtis
DAV	*They Thought for Themselves*, by D. Elwyn Davies
DDM	*Darwin D. Martin Archives*
EB	*Encyclopaedia Britannica*, 1957
EW	Eric Wright Archives
EWH	Elizabeth Wright Heller memoir
FP	Franklin Wright Porter archives
GI	*Space, Time and Architectural*, by Sigfried Giedion, editions: 1941, 1967, and 1974
HA	*The Decorative Designs of Frank Lloyd Wright*, by David A. Hanks
HACat	*Frank Lloyd Wright: Architectural Drawings and Decorative Art*
HER	*Heritage: The Lloyd Jones Family*
HI	*In the Nature of Materials*, by Henry-Russell Hitchcock
HLV	*Frank Lloyd Wright: His Living Voice*
JSAH	*Journal of the Society of Architectural Historians*
LAP	*Letters to Apprentices*
LAR	*Letters to Architects*
LCL	*Letters to Clients*
LL	*Lloyd Letters & Memorial Book*
MAG	*The Valley of the God-Almighty Joneses*, by Maginel Wright Barney
MAN	*Frank Lloyd Wright to 1910*, by Grant Carpenter Manson
MJ	*Milwaukee Journal*
MM	*Many Masks*, by Brendan Gill
MOR	*The Matter of Wales*, by Jan Morris
NE	*Richard Neutra and the Search for Modern Architecture*, by Thomas S. Hines

NYT	*New York Times*
PSR	*The Prairie School Review*
RR	*The Rebecca Riots*, by David Williams
SC	*Frank Lloyd Wright*, by Vincent Scully, Jr.
SM	*Frank Lloyd Wright, A Study in Architectural Content*, by Norris Kelly Smith
SOT	*The Song of Taliesin*, by Thomas Beeby
ST	*The Architecture of Frank Lloyd Wright*, by William Allin Storrer
SW	*Frank Lloyd Wright: An Annotated Bibliography*, by Robert L. Sweeney
T	Archives at Taliesin
TAF	*Years with Frank Lloyd Wright: Apprentice to Genius*, by Edgar Tafel
TRIL	*Trilogy: Through Their Eyes*
TW	*Frank Lloyd Wright: His Life and His Architecture*, by Robert C. Twombly
WE	*The Harmonious Circle*, by James Webb
WOW	*Writings on Wright*

CHAPTER 1: BEDD TALIESIN: TALIESIN'S GRAVE

3 Fate has smashed these wonderful walls: *Poems from the Old English*, translated by Burton Raffel. (Lincoln: University of Nebraska Press; 1960).

4 A painting by René Magritte: *Le Domaine Enchanté*, 1952.

5 More Welsh in Milwaukee in the middle 1850s than Germans: *The Welsh in Wisconsin*, Phillip G. Davies, p. 4.
Similar to rude stone monuments of Celtic Britain: SOT.
"[H]e went through the moist woods . . .": A2, p. 25.
"the sacred place": *Patterns in Comparative Religion*, Mircea Eliade, p. 360.

6 Unitarian Grove meetings described: LL, p. 70.
"The near world was growing dim": LL, p. 69.

7 Wright's letter to Jenkin Lloyd Jones: August 22, 1885: LCL, p. 1.
Date of the chapel's opening: August 15, 1886.
Jenkin Lloyd Jones dedicates the chapel: *Unity* magazine, vol. XVII, August 28, 1886, pp. 356–357.

8 Weeping for joy: A2, p. 310.

9 "a characteristic hero figure of Celtic myth": *The Taliesin Tradition*, Ermy Humphreys, pp. 48–49.

10 Wright describes the building of Taliesin: in *Liberty*, March 23, 1929.

11 "I get back to it happy to be there . . .": A2, p. 368.

13 One can still see the outline marking the spot: based on interviews with John H. Howe, Robert Graves and others.

14 A memorial chapel would be built: NYT, April 19, 1959, p. 46.

16 An act of vandalism: *Inland Architect* July/August 1985, p. 3.
Provisions of Wright's will: dated April 25, 1958.

17 "uprooting Jefferson": NYT, April 19, 1985.
He still felt a part of it: A2, p. 167.
"Much more than ashes have been taken": *Inland Architect* op. cit.
"I think he would have wanted it done": NYT, April 10, 1985.
The ashes of Frank and Olgivanna Lloyd Wright have since been interred in a garden he designed at Taliesin West. Richard Carney to author, May 30, 1991.

18 "he may be laughing": NYT, op. cit.

CHAPTER 2: THE BLACK SPOT

19 Fate has opened: *Poems from the Old English*, p. 59.

A description of *hwyl: Americans from Wales*, Edward George Hartman, p. 105; Jenkin's sermons described: MAG, p. 99.

20 Early memories of Jenkin Lloyd Jones: TRIL, pp. 1–25.

"The Methodist Revival": MOR, p. 110.

21 Early history of the Welsh chapels: *Welsh Chapels*, Anthony Jones, p. 3.

Early history of preachers in the Lloyd Jones family: DAV, p. 34 ff.

22 History of Rev. Jenkin Jones: LL, p. 4.

Success of David Lloyd: *A History of Unitarianism*, David Wilbur, p. 322.

"utterly damned": DAV, p. 28.

24 Named "union churches": *Americans from Wales*, p. 103.

They associated freely: to author, letter, July 15, 1989.

"The heretical faith": TRIL, p.12.

Most Nonconformists were Calvinists: *Americans from Wales*, p. 103.

A "canker of heresy" and decision to depart voluntarily: from Jenkin Lloyd Jones's account, TRIL, pp. 12–13.

25 On the more benign Celtic laws: MOR, p. 223.

26 Recognizable Celtic roots: *The Celts*, Nora Chadwick, p. 284.

"a certain sense of the dream of things": MOR, p. 534.

"the same volatile mixture": MOR, p. 53.

"cultural nationalism": *Americans from Wales*, p. 31.

Related to a noble line: LL, p. 8.

27 Dates of birth given an asterisk in the text are based on those found in an old family Bible and cited in LL, p. 66.

30 Effect of the Enclosure Acts and the poem, "They hang the man and flog the woman . . .": from *A Social History of England*, Asa Briggs, pp. 172 and 174.

A ruling class monopolized Welsh parliamentary seats: RR, p. 8.

31 "The tolls . . .": RR, p. 397.

"the strangest series of riots": RR, p. vii.

Date of the decision to emigrate established: HER, pp. 3 and 67.

The first riots and their aftermath: RR, p. 199.

32 Hardly a gate left standing: ditto.

Llandysul even more a center of protest: Mrs. Aubrey Martin to author.

"provided their hearers": *People & Protest*, Trevor Herbert and Gareth Elwyn Jones, p. 121.

33 Swept up with revolutionary fervor: *The Search for Beulah Land*, Gwyn A. Williams, p. 11.

The New World their only hope: ditto, p. 40.

"They were building a *Kingdom*": ditto, p. 38.

The free farmer on his own land: *Welsh in Wisconsin*, Phillip G. Davies, p. 5.

34 Torments of an Atlantic crossing: ditto, p. 9.

36 Story of the Lloyd Jones family emigration drawn from an account, *Youngest Son*, written by Chester Lloyd Jones, and excerpted in HER. Her American descendants: letter from Margaret Lloyd Jones to one of her sons (not identified), July 27, 1852, made available to author by Prof. A. Douglas Jones.

36 What the immigrants found: based on contemporary accounts in *The Welsh in America: Letters from the Immigrants*, Alan Conway, pp. 69–70.

Jenkin Lloyd Jones gives a vivid account of the battle against mosquitoes and malaria, describing the forested land that adjoined the valley of the Rock River as "interlaid with marshes like jelly in a layer cake": *Wisconsin Magazine of History*, vol. 67, no. 2, Winter, 1983–84, p. 133.

Mary Jane Hamilton, foremost Wisconsin scholar on the early history of the Lloyd Jones family in America, is author of a paper, "The Lloyd Joneses in America: Their First Half Century," on which this account is based.

37 "he chose to be a builder": TRIL, p. 52.

"and by intense application"; op. cit., p. 46. In great demand: ditto.

Recollections of her uncle: MAG, p. 77–78.

Lloyd Jones departure from Ixonia and arrival in The Valley: Mary Jane Hamilton chronology.

"The Valley of the God-Almighty Joneses": MAG, p. 19.

38 Plenty of government land: ditto, p. 49.

"milk pails washed and drying . . .": ditto, p. 93.

"a lovely view of plowed fields . . .": ditto, pp. 78–79.

Feeding from your hand: ditto, p. 79.

39 Pulling up the vegetables: ditto, p. 95.

"To me they seemed . . ."; ditto, p. 77.

40 "a spectral figure . . .": ditto, p. 83.

He refused painkillers: TRIL, p. 59.

Breaking a leg on the ice: MAG, p. 47.

41 Falling from the second floor: TRIL, p. 51.

42 ". . . I would pull something down . . .": MAG, p. 147.

Tears of gratitude: HER, p. 98.

". . . immortal and invincible . . .": MAG, p. 107.

43 ". . . something not quite right; . . .": ditto, pp. 79–80.

Nell's bout with smallpox: ditto, p. 119.

Having her mother to herself: TRIL, p. 36.

44 Education of Nell and Jane: MAG, pp. 93, and pp. 113; Anna's lack of formal training: HER, p. 94.

". . . she would teach anyone . . .": MAG, p. 61.

46 Anna's hairstyle described: ditto, p. 66; A fine horsewoman: ditto, p. 62; assisted the midwife: ditto, p. 61.

Hemmed in all her life: from a letter to Frank Lloyd Wright, T, January 24, 1921.

"More like Lincoln": from a letter to Frank Lloyd Wright, T, October 20, 1918.

Using the garden as her hackneyed metaphor: from a letter to Frank Lloyd Wright, T, no date, c. 1919–20.

47 The role faith had played: from a letter to Frank Lloyd Wright, T, December 10, 1918.

The Valley as holy ground: from a letter to Frank Lloyd Wright, T, May 4, 1916.

Her mother's methods of education: from a letter to Frank Lloyd Wright, T, December 21, 1919.

Seeing The Valley in her mind's eye: from a letter to Frank Lloyd Wright, T, April 11, 1916.

The reassurance of familiar objects: from a letter to Frank Lloyd Wright, T, January 26, 1919.

Her room and her very existence were one and the same: from a letter to Frank Lloyd Wright, T, January 24, 1921.

47 Her son and her brother pursued the same goal: from a letter to Frank Lloyd Wright, T, January 18, 1921.
48 ". . . some elusive thing . . .": MAG, p. 64.
An account of the meeting between Anna Lloyd Jones and William Carey Wright, MM, p. 31.
He was superintendent of her school district: Mary Jane Hamilton.
William Carey Wright's illustrious forebears: from a genealogy prepared by Mrs. Abbie Whitaker; The family genealogist: Mrs. David Wright.
49 ". . . His friends speak very highly . . .": TW, p. 2.
". . . appropriate and eloquent . . .": ditto, pp. 4–5.
50 The move to Richland Center: TW, p. 4.

CHAPTER 3: THE SHINING BROW

51 Yet through his flight . . .: *Taliesin*, no pagination.
". . . a prophetic birth . . .": *Frank Lloyd Wright: His Life, His Work, His Words*, Olgivanna Lloyd Wright, p. 11.
She rose early: from a letter to Frank Lloyd Wright, T, June 8, 1887.
52 Sanctity of mother love: ditto, T, January 26, 1919.
The sacred places in Wales: SOT, pp. 4–5.
The legend of Taliesin: in Joseph Campbell's *The Hero with a Thousand Faces*, p. 198; "Behold a radiant brow . . .": ditto, p. 239; ". . . chief bard am I . . .": ditto, p. 241.
53 Nothing to save: AP, April 11, 1972. Patrick J. Meehan, in *The Master Architect: Conversations with Frank Lloyd Wright*, published a photograph on p. 13 of Wright's purported birthplace in Richland Center and gives its address as 774 South Park Street. Date of move to Richland Center: based on a chronology by Mrs. David Wright and EWH, p. 7.
William Carey Wright's first concert: TW, p. 5.
54 Life in McGregor, Iowa: TW, ditto.
"He is a plain speaker . . .": TW, ditto.
The move to Pawtucket: ditto, p. 6.
55 The new house described: EWH, p. 12; later, a house to themselves: ditto.
"earnest, unwearied . . .": TW, p. 6.
". . . no financial sense . . .": ditto, p. 5.
56 The virtues of extravagance: *Beau Nash*, Oliver Goldsmith, p. 16.
Her father's bad luck: EWH, p. 167.
57 She lived for years in hope: FP, November 24, 1905; Cooking was the worst: FP November 14, 1898; Snubs from the relatives: T, undated.
Her stepmother was jealous: EWH, p. 5.
58 English cathedral pictures could not have been hanging around his crib: this point is made by Edgar Kaufmann, Jr., in *Frank Lloyd Wright's Mementos of Childhood*, JSAH, vol. XLI, no. 3, October 1982, pp. 232–33.
". . . intended . . . to be an Architect.": A2, p.11
". . . nothing . . . so sacrosanct, . . .": HLV, p. 20
"And this our life, . . .": from *As You Like It*, Act 2, Scene 1.
59 Jennie had studied Froebel's methods: TRIL, p. 34.
An idealized mother: *Friedrich Froebel*, p. 11; "God's works reflect the logic of his spirit . . .": from "The Anatomy of Wright's Aesthetic," by Richard MacCormac,

published in the *Architectural Review*, February 1968, pp. 143–46, in which the author discusses the extent to which Wright's three-dimensional way of seeing had been derived from Froebel's exercises; "Education [was] the direct manifestation of God," A2, p. 9;

59 "UNITY was their watchword . . ." A2, p. 16.

61 Date of first textbook in English: MAN, pp. 5–6.
"You're a widow now!": HLV, pp. 44–45.

62 Anna nursed her: EWH, p. 12.
Graham bread, porridge and religion: A2 p. 15.
Dropped his clothes: TAF, p. 127.

63 Account of the impromptu party: A2, p. 38; ". . . mother understood . . .": ditto.
"Isaiah's awful Lord . . .": A2, p.7.

64 ". . . an escaped convict . . ." T, February 21, 1905.
". . . the impatient hand . . .": A2 p. 12; "The boy worked away . . ." ditto.

65 Saw William roll up his sleeves: EWH, p. 277; Anna would pick a fight: ditto.
Frank runs away: A2, p. 22; Uncle James would call in vain: ditto, p. 23

66 Jennie reprimanded her: EWH, p. 277.
Lizzie piped up boldly: ditto, pp. 45–46.

67 ". . . didn't seem at all formidable . . .": HLV, p. 17.
Into the stable to be "thrashed": A2, p. 49.
Wright finally "charged" them: ditto, p. 115; Authority was losing: ditto, p. 116; "the young rebel": A2, p. 49.
"All art constantly aspires . . ." *The Renaissance*, Walter Pater, p. 135.

68 "They were happy riots . . ." A1, p. 33.
". . . a kind of listening. . .": A2, p. 13.
". . . a sort of listening": *The Renaissance*, p. 151.
The sound of a meadow lark: A2, p. 121; the "world of daylight gold": ditto, p. 26; even the blackest cypress, *The Renaissance*, p. 153; "night shadows so wonderfully blue": A2, p. 26; ". . . slender metallic straight lines": ditto, p. 3; "catkins cutting circles": ditto, p. 27; "milkweed blossoming . . .": ditto, p. 26; weeds against a background of snow: ditto, p. 3 ". . .; a delight *in and for themselves* . . .": *Essays*, Ralph Waldo Emerson, p. 14; "the informing, artistic spirit": *The Renaissance*, p. 137; ". . . an end in itself . . .": ditto, p. 125; ". . . *character* to the trees": A2, p. 27; "a country of the pure reason . . .": *The Renaissance*, p. 137; transported by delight: A2, p. 12; the splash of red against a pasture: ditto: p. 27.

69 Date of the family's move to Madison has been established from the divorce testimony in the files of the Circuit Court of Dane County, Wisconsin, April 24, 1885; Interiors of the house described: MAG, p. 59; Wright's reminiscences: A2, p. 32.

70 Whether or not Wright attended the Philadelphia Centennial Exposition cannot be established: Bruce Brooks Pfeiffer, Taliesin archivist.
Innovations of the exhibition: *In Pursuit of Beauty*, Metropolitan Museum of Art, p. 111.
The then "modern" vogue: A2, p. 32.

71 Actual location of the Madison house was established by Thomas S. Hines, Jr., in "Frank Lloyd Wright—The Madison Years: Records Versus Recollections" (*Wisconsin Magazine of History*, vol. 50, no. 2, winter 1967; pp. 109–119).
An influential Unitarian: TW, p. 9.
William Wright became a Unitarian: Mrs. David Wright chronology.
An outstanding lecturer: TW, p. 10.
Opened a Conservatory of Music: A2, p. 31.

72 A fragile baby: ditto, p. 17.

72 Uncle James brings a cow: ditto, pp. 17–18.
A "startled-looking" robin: MAG, p. 75.
73 "aloneness, shyness, isolation . . .": *Acts of Will*, James D. Lieberman, p. 403.
"afraid of people": A2, p. 48.
"charge it to the Town Pump": A1, pp. 12–13.
Robie Lamp: A2, p. 32, and MAG, p. 75; his own roof garden: A2, p. 32 adolescent embarrassments recalled: A1, p. 35; "Oh, sir, I am a poor widow . . .": ditto; boys ran after him: ditto, p. 36.
75 Rev. David Wright's death: MAG, p. 63; in the autumn of 1881: the exact date is October 21; disintegration of the Wright marriage: based on testimony filed by William Carey Wright during the divorce proceedings already described (Anna Wright did not testify).
77 ". . . little French kid shoes . . .": MAG, p. 69.
". . . all the money I have . . .": ditto, p. 67.
"one more handicap": A2, p. 51.
"Tell us about your father": MAG, p. 72; "Say he's dead": ditto, p. 73.

CHAPTER 4: ALADDIN

78 Old as man's moral life . . .": A2, p. 94.
"I'll learn": Eric Wright, interview with author.
79 A person of substance: to Frank Lloyd Wright, T, undated.
Origin of "Truth Against the World": MOR, p. 155.
81 Had she been born with his advantages: to Frank Lloyd Wright, T, October 12, 1918.
To shake the foundations of his life: *Neurosis and Human Growth*, Karen Horney, p. 197.
82 His accident described: A2, p. 38.
". . . release from anguish . . .": MAG, p. 147.
Enrolled as a special student: on January 7, 1886.
Proposed himself as an architect: Thomas S. Hines, Jr.
Attempting to recoup his losses: TRIL, p. 51.
83 Published a drawing of Silsbee's completed Unity Chapel: from "The Earliest Work of Frank Lloyd Wright," by Wilbert R. Hasbrouck, A.I.A., in PSR, vol. 7, no. 4, 1970.
84 The most beautiful gift: MAG, p. 82; had sold his mother's books: ditto; had pawned Plutarch's *Lives*: A2, p. 60.
Referring to his debts: T, May 28, 1887; Confident he would make good: T, undated; He must manage money wisely: T, June 26, 1887; Begging him to settle: T, September 7, 1887.
85 Go on reading and studying: T, undated.
86 The equivalent of a bishop: Graham article, op. cit., pp. 121–122; bedding down on the depot floor: from a dissertation, *Jenkin Lloyd Jones: Lincoln's Soldier of Civic Righteousness*, by Richard Harlan Thomas, 1967, p. 3.
"Do you know who I am . . .": MAG, p. 99.
87 "We made a deep impression . . .": quoted by Robert Moses during inaugural proceedings of the Guggenheim Museum in 1960.
"I enjoyed listening": A2, p. 71.
State Capitol wing collapses, "rising high into the summer air", "clinging to the iron fence": A2, p. 56; notorious for the trouble it caused: the Midway Gardens.
88 He had bought the book: Arthur Cort Holden to author.

88 "... used them, fooled them ..." A2, p. 37.
   "... very wonderfully optimistic ...": FP, May 13, 1919.

89 A stellar year: BR, p. 34, note 27.
   A dangling gold chain: A2, p. 68; a "characteristic" pattern: ditto, p. 69.
   All Souls Unitarian: A2, p. 69, and MAN, p. 15.
   Had little to do with the reign of Queen Anne: in her essay for *In Pursuit of Beauty* (p. 66), Catherine Lynn noted, "Designs owing a debt to Tudor, Elizabethan, and later periods were sometimes called post-medieval. . . . In common and commercial parlance they usually bore the name Queen Anne, a confusing and (as Anne reigned for only twelve years, from 1702 to 1714) historically almost irrelevant label."

90 "our domestic life . . .": *The Shingle Style and the Stick Style*, Vincent Scully, Jr., p. 37.
   Silsbee's role in introducing the Shingle Style in Chicago: ditto, p. 158, note 10.

91 Uncle Jenkin did not approve: T, August 12, 1887.

92 Designing Edgewater: A2, p. 70; marvelous façades, ditto; overlooking the name of Adler and Sullivan: ditto, p. 75.
   Wright's deep sense of personal destiny: SM, p. 25.

93 "by understanding the organic and natural . . .": HA, p. 2.
   "I needed exercise . . .": A2, p. 75.
   Wright's drawings are conventional: this point is persuasively made by Eileen Michels in "The Early Drawings of Frank Lloyd Wright Reconsidered," JSAH, vol. 30, no. 4, December 1971, pp. 294–303.
   The date of the drawing Wright says he drew in 1887 or 1888: H. Allen Brooks, a noted authority on the dating of Wright's work, accepts it as correct, and so does the Taliesin achrivist, Bruce Brooks Pfeiffer (letter to author, June 24, 1989). Those supporting Eileen Michel's position have included Prof. Patrick Pinnell of the Yale School of Architecture, another authority on Wright's early work, and Henry-Russell Hitchcock, JSAH, vol. XIX, no. 3, 1960, p. 129.

94 It stretches credulity: after presumably demonstrating his mastery of the technique, Wright reverted to his early student style, as demonstrated by Eileen Michels.
   ". . . I had . . . drawn . . . little . . .": *Genius and the Mobocracy*, Frank Lloyd Wright, p. 71.
   The Aunts wore silks and satins: MAG, p. 155.

95 The Madison dancing master: MAG, p. 116.
   Boys stitching seams: MJ, January 3, 1927.
   He had already been to Hillside: Aunt Nell to Frank Lloyd Wright, T, March 9, 1887.
   Silsbee played the largest role: MAN, p. 18.
   His first attempt "amateurish": A2, p. 133.

98 Working for Adler and Sullivan by early 1888: probably by February.
   Anna was worried: MAG, p. 127.
   "gay-spirited, sunny-haired": A2, p. 77.
   "unquenchable triumphs": A2, p. 47.

100 "as if on a magic carpet . . .": *Collected Works of C. G. Jung*, vol. 9, p. 97.
    "stiffest, horridest thing . . .": sister Jane to Frank Lloyd Wright, T, April 10, 1887.
    He liked meeting girls: A2, p. 77.

101 "The ceremony of introduction . . .": *Pickwick Papers*, p. 388.
    "Often in error . . .": As quoted by Mrs. Russell Bletzer.

102 He should not trifle: the letter has no actual date.
    ". . . a true gentleman"; T, August 12, 1887.
    The first girl he felt "at home" with: A2, p. 86.

CHAPTER 5: "LIEBER MEISTER"

103 ". . . he thought of the great continent . . .": CT, June 3, 1936.
104 The great Chicago fire: *Chicago Then and Now*, p. 28.
  "wildly original": Henry-Russell Hitchcock, "Frank Lloyd Wright and the 'Academic Tradition' of the Early Eighteen-Nineties"; *Journal of the Warburg and Courtauld Institute*, vol. VII, January–June 1944, pp. 46–63; p. 58.
105 ". . . a new thing under the sun . . .": *Louis Sullivan: His Life & Work*, Robert C. Twombly, p. 285.
106 ". . . between the Infinite Spirit and the finite mind . . .": from Section XII, "Function and Form," *Kindergarten Chats and Other Writings*, Louis Sullivan, p. 45.
  ". . . they treated it as an end.": *The New Yorker*, October 11, 1947.
  A design should convey abstract qualities: *The Function of Ornament*, Wim deWit, p. 18.
  ". . . themes of central concern . . .": "American Architecture and the Aesthetic Movement," by James D. Kornwolf, *In Pursuit of Beauty*, p. 367.
  ". . . a lyric poet": *Genius and the Mobocracy*, Frank Lloyd Wright, p. 78.
107 From theaters to opera houses: *Louis Sullivan: His Life & Work*, p. 229.
  ". . . reeled at the achievement . . .": ditto, p. 161.
  Claimed to have added touches: *Genius and the Mobocracy*, pp. 63–64.
  ". . . enthusiasm now evoked was contagious . . .": ditto, p. 64.
108 ". . . reclaimed the wilderness . . .": *Halley's Pictorial*, p. 4.
  Known as "Saint's Rest": A2, p. 79.
110 Preferred a rustic barn: ditto, p. 80; neighbors were indignant: ditto.
  The highest paid draftsman: *Genius and the Mobocracy*, p. 56, and A2, p. 106.
  Sullivan's interest in Wright was sexual: MM, p. 63.
111 He fought two battles: A2, pp. 96–102; a point of pride: ditto, p. 102.
  ". . . she didn't deserve . . .": MAG, p. 130.
112 ". . . ran across the garden . . .": ditto, p. 130.
  The most important office: *Genius and the Mobocracy*, p. 62; "Get the job": ditto, p. 56.
  A feather in one's cap: ditto, p. 67; a stream of projects: ditto, p. 68.
113 "ineffable harmonies": A2, p. 147; a house must be welcoming: ditto, p. 174; "crown the exuberance of life": ditto, 170; its roof should be low: ditto, p. 174; one should rest there: ditto, p. 175; ". . . the solid white blank wall": ditto, 165; "the house of houses": ditto.
114 ". . . something church-like . . ." SM, p. 21; ". . . redefining and reaffirming the significance": ditto, p. 22.
  "lied about everything": "Recollections: United States, 1893–1920." *Architects' Journal*, vol. LXXXIV, July 16, 1936, pp. 76–78.
  "a moral, social, aesthetic excrement": *Genius and the Mobocracy*, pp. 32–33.
  "Life Is Truth!": A2, p. 106.
117 Similarities between the façades: SC, plates 4 and 5.
  Links between the tomb Sullivan designed and Wright's Winslow house: see *The Autobiography of an Idea*, Louis Sullivan, plate 13, the tomb of Charlotte Dickson Wainwright; Wright executed tracings for the design of that tomb's ornamental gate: H. Allen Brooks, *Frank Lloyd Wright and the Prairie School*, plate 4.

117 Derived from McKim, Mead and White pattern books: Pinnell to author; clear resemblances: "Frank Lloyd Wright and the 'Academic Tradition' of the Early Eighteen-Nineties", p. 16.
Wright's house resembled Spencer's: BR, p. 59.
118 Mackintosh's drawing published: in the *British Architect*, vol. XXXIV, October 30, 1890, pp. 324–325.
"I suppose I stole them": *Genius and the Mobocracy*, p. 78.
119 An architect should be expelled: *American Architect & Building News*, vol. XXIII, 1888, p. 277.
Further births of children: John was born December 12, 1892 and Catherine, January 12, 1894.
Corwin took credit: *Louis Sullivan: His Life & Work*, p. 237; ". . . had offended the one man . . .": ditto, p. 238.
120 ". . . embodied in imitated Renaissance and classical forms": "Frank Lloyd Wright and the 'Academic Tradition' of the Early Eighteen-Nineties," p. 47.
Following Norman Shaw's example: ditto, p. 49.
This "urban palazzo": HI, p. 12; almost precocious refinement: ditto.
"a personal application . . .": ditto, p. 60.
121 Could have been a great architect: ST, plate 14.
"serene horizontality . . .": HI, p. 62.
"simplicity achieved by . . .": *Journal of the Royal Society of Arts*, November 1983, p. 11.
122 Adler and Sullivan in the second five: "Frank Lloyd Wright and the 'Academic Tradition' of the Early Eighteen-Nineties," p. 56.
". . . a splendid rebirth . . .": GI, p. 316; marked his decline: ditto, p. 317.
123 ". . . pseudo 'classic' now an 'ism . . .": *The Future of Architecture*, Frank Lloyd Wright, p. 223.
"a gentleman's house . . ." A2, p. 125.
Asked for Burnham's help: "Frank Lloyd Wright and the 'Academic Tradition' of the Early Eighteen-Nineties," p. 46.

CHAPTER 6: SERMONS IN STONES

127 "honest, true to itself . . .": in a speech to the University Guild of Evanston, Illinois, 1894 (Library of Congress).
128 "Ask any Arts and Crafts man . . .": *C. R. Ashbee*, Alan Crawford, p. 207.
On a par with Scott and Dickens: p. ix; concepts of the beautiful: ditto, p. 74; ". . . a moral test": ditto, p. 91; ". . . the romantic misapprehension . . ." ditto, p.66.
". . . the absolute values . . .": *John Ruskin: The Argument of the Eye*, Robert Hewison, p. 133.
129 The Red House the prototype: *M. H. Baillie Scott and the Arts & Crafts Movement*, James D. Kornwolf, p. 11.
"seemed to breathe . . .": "Frank Lloyd Wright and the 'Academic Tradition' of the Early Eighteen-Nineties": p. 50.
130 ". . . flame as the soul . . .": *The English House 1860–1914*: Gavin Stamp, p. 32; a lack of ornamentation: ditto, p. 34; they took great pains: ditto, p. 40; ". . . peace and contentment": ditto, p. 14.
"the whole titanic struggle . . .": SC, p. 24.

131 ". . . the internal tensions . . .": *The Dynamics of Creation*, Anthony Storr, p. 252; more psychopathological traits: ditto, p. 261; ". . . inner artistic standard of excellence . . .": ditto, p. 235; endlessly curious people: ditto, p. 238; ". . . nothing but labour and diligence": ditto, p. 255.

132 Used to guide the traveler: EB, vol. 6, p. 754.
     The reconcilation of opposites: *The Dynamics of Creation*, p. 287.
     The birth of David Samuel: on September 26, 1895.

135 "his first design in straight-line pattern": *The Plan for Restoration and Adaptive Use of the Frank Lloyd Wright Home and Studio*, p. 25.
     "filled with noise . . .": MAG, p. 133; "He loved to show off . . .": ditto; "Old Kent Road" his signature: ditto.

136 ". . . an epic of wit . . .": *My Father Who Is on Earth*, John Lloyd Wright, p. 31; father would "pop" him: ditto, p. 27; "so handsome a fellow . . .": ditto, p. 36.
     ". . . a lifelong habit . . .": Robert Llewellyn Wright.
     A Welsh belief in spirits: *My Father Who Is on Earth*, p. 43.

137 "He'd take my daughter by the thumb . . ." Richard Wolford to author.
     "a childlike quality": to author.

138 "It took some skill": to author.
     ". . . she'd tell him so": to author.

139 Samuel Clark Tobin died soon after his wife: on December 5, 1916.
     A new piano for the chapel: bought in 1902.

140 Jenkin Lloyd Jones was stingy: *Jenkin Lloyd Jones: Lincoln's Soldier of Civic Righteousness*, Richard H. Thomas, p. 50.

141 ". . . a builder for men . . .": *Wisconsin Magazine of History*, vol. 67, no.2, 1983–84, p. 128.

142 "Am I to get a chance . . .": May 15, 1894, University of Chicago.
     Jenkin Lloyd Jones wanted to be his own architect: to author.
     It became just "All Souls' Church": *Wisconsin Magazine of History*, vol. 67, no. 2, 1983–84, p. 123.
     "a four-square building . . .": MAN, p. 158.
     He made Wright collaborate: BR, p. 28.

143 ". . . deliberately impertinent . . .": T, undated; "I *know* and *would stake* . . .": ditto.

144 The tower did not fall: A2, p. 138.
     He lectured frequently: H. Allen Brooks, Jr.: "The Early Work of the Prairie Architects," JSAH, vol. XIX, March 1960, p. 3.

145 ". . . reinterpreting and simplifying . . .": BR, p. 91.
     ". . . office in his hat": *Genius and the Mobocracy*, Frank Lloyd Wright, p. 87.
     ". . . Inspiring days they were . . .": *Myron Hunt, 1868–1952: The Search for a Regional Architecture*, Baxter Art Gallery, p. 10.
     From a low of two to a high of nine, in 1900: from an informal chart made by John Lloyd Wright and now at the Avery Architectural Library, Columbia University.
     Wright exhibited Mahony's renderings as his own: BR, P. 80.

146 "one of nature's noblemen": MM, p. 141.
     Proud to call him a friend: July 19, 1908, Archives of American Art.
     The year he began to show at the Chicago Architectural Club: 1894.
     Photograph of a winged cherub: *My Father Who Is on Earth*, pp. 23–24.

147 Sturgis did not "understand": White to Willcox, May 13, 1904.
     ". . . he 'has no appetite . . .' ": White to Willcox, February 13, 1905.
     Plenty of speeding tickets: *My Father Who Is on Earth*, p. 51.

147 Paid erratically: White to Willcox, March 4, 1906.

148 Nagged by his debts: A2, p. 110; ". . . how much punishment . . .": ditto.
How to avoid paying a bill: Robert Llewellyn Wright.

149 Catherine asked for a dime: A2, pp. 116–117.
". . . I was on the smoking roofs . . .": A2, p. 261.
Account of the Iroquois Theater fire derived from *My Father Who Is on Earth*, pp. 45–48, and contemporary accounts including that of the *Chicago Record-Herald*, December 31, 1903.

151 Copies of the *Studio* were pounced upon: "C.F.A. Voysey—To and From America," by David Gebhard, JSAH, vol. XXX, no. 4, December 1971, p. 307.

152 ". . . industrialism had shattered . . ." ATL, p. 103.
An ecclesiastical look: SM, p. 74.
". . . the *integral* fireplace . . ." A2, p. 141.

153 Richardson's innovations: *In Pursuit of Beauty*, Metropolitan Museum of Art, pp. 350–351.
Voysey and Baillie Scott's innovations: ATL, p. 83.

154 Did not rule out the machine: David Hanks, "The Decorative Designs of Frank Lloyd Wright," *Frank Lloyd Wright Newsletter*, vol. II, no. 3, second quarter 1979.
". . . thoroughly at one . . .": T, April 2, 1901.
His goals identical to Baillie Scott's: *M. H. Baillie Scott and the Arts and Crafts Movement*, James D. Kornwolf, p. 394, and *The Future of Architecture*, Frank Lloyd Wright, pp. 141–142.

155 A magazine would be founded: BR, p. 24, note 39, and HA, pp. 200–201.
Elizabeh Gordon, former editor of *House Beautiful*, and a friend of Wright's, believes that he was one of the ideological founders of the Chicago magazine. (Conversation, October 4, 1989.) Author was unable to verify.
". . . good to catch a glimpse . . .": T, Jan. 30, 1899.
A dismissive reference: letter to Samuel R. Morrill, September 27, 1949, Houghton Library, Harvard University.

CHAPTER 7: A HOUSE DIVIDED

156 See: this wood has come to make you remember . . . : *Poems from the Old English*, p. 22.

158 Designed to silence comment: RTL, p. 362.

159 "Modesty being egotism. . ." : *My Father Who Is on Earth*, John Lloyd Wright, pp. 32–33.
Some outstanding examples: Some of these wonderful objects are now in the collection of the Victoria and Albert Museum, London.

160 The year Ashbee and Wright met: to Linn Cowles, February 3, 1966.
"Ashbee was very vague . . .": to author, June 8, 1988.
". . . and be our guest . . .": C. R. Ashbee to Wright, April 2, 1901. Wright did not actually visit England until 1910.
". . . the ablest man . . .": written around December 8, 1900; "I want to have a good fight . . .": ditto.

161 ". . . a sad, thought-worn face . . .": December 21, 1908.
"How I have wasted . . .": "A Last Prayer," a poem by Helen Hunt Jackson, *Familiar Quotations*, by John Bartlett, p. 652.

161 "Birthdays have gotten . . .": FP, June 15, 1897.

A tree trunk has been included: *In Pursuit of Beauty*, Metropolitan Museum of Art, p. 348.

163 *Sesame and Lilies* was published in 1865.

". . . the diverse meanings . . .": *Marcel Proust, A Biography*, George Painter, vol. 2, p. 356.

164 "showing me every detail . . .": Ashbee, around December 8, 1900.

". . . a kind of 'pinwheel' rotation . . .": CU, p. 80; ". . . the same formal intelligence . . .": ditto.

168 ". . . a specifically American image . . .": SC, pp. 17–18.

Another kind of pattern: CU, p. 81.

169 Making the corners disappear: "Frank Lloyd Wright and the Destruction of the Box" by H. Allen Brooks, JSAH, March 1979, p. 5.

A cantilevered roof: *The Robie House of Frank Lloyd Wright*, Joseph Connors, p. 1.

170 An integral part of American houses: Reyner Banham in "The Well-Tempered Home," *The Architecture of the Well-Tempered Environment*, pp. 104–121.

The unwholesome basement: A2, p. 141; as if sitting on a chair: ditto, p. 140.

Wright's "grammar" of exterior design: White to Willcox, May 13, 1904.

171 "a lot of junk . . .": WOW, p. 47.

In her architect's clothes: HA, p. 25.

176 The amazing annual salary: *Frank Lloyd Wright's Larkin Building*, Jack Quinan, p. 14.

An Indian war whoop: ditto, p. 12.

"Papa remembered Mr. Martin . . .": *My Father Who Is on Earth*, p. 42.

177 A monument to himself: *Frank Lloyd Wright's Larkin Building*, p. 9; ". . . largely his creations . . .": ditto, p. 131; working side by side: ditto, p. 116.

178 "one of the seminal works . . .": CU, p. 42.

". . . a man is hiding . . .": *Kindergarten Chats and Other Writings*, Louis Sullivan, p. 25.

180 ". . . a lot of Wright details.": to author.

". . . shall lie foursquare . . .": Revelations 21, verse 16.

". . . uniquely Welsh nonconformist . . .": to author, October 17, 1988.

181 Common elements of Wright's designs: described in *Consecrated Space*, Jonathan Lipman, June 5, 1989.

". . . consecrated space . . .": A2, p. 156.

A resemblance between Unity Temple and the work of Olbrich: first pointed out by Narciso G. Menocal in "Frank Lloyd Wright and the Question of Style," *Journal of Decorative and Propaganda Arts*, summer/fall 1986, p. 11.

Influence of pre-Columbian and Mayan architectural forms: "Frank Lloyd Wright and Pre-Columbian Art—The Background for his Architecture," by Gabriel Weisberg, *The Art Quarterly*, vol. 30, spring 1967; "Exotic Influences in the Architecture of Frank Lloyd Wright" by Dimitri Tselos in the *Magazine of Art*, vol. 46, no. 4, April 1953; and "Frank Lloyd Wright and World Architecture" by Dimitri Tselos in JSAH, vol. XXVIII, no. 1, March 1969.

184 Wright's early chairs: HA, p. 9.

Known as the "Spook School": CU, p. 30.

From the pencil of Wright himself: ATL, p. 84, Figure 13.

"it can only have been in one direction . . .": *Mackintosh Furniture*, Roger Billcliffe, p. 10.

His first barrel-shaped armchair; HACat, p. 14.

185 The Darwin D. Martin Archives: at the State University of New York, Buffalo.
Owes its origins to Hiroshige: in the opinion of Dr. Ross Edman of the University of
Illinois in Chicago, an art historian specializing in oriental art, who has made a special
study of Wright's personal symbols; Taken from the seals of Japanese censors: ditto.
The first real introduction of Japanese art to the Middle West: MAN, pp. 34–35.

186 The first English language book: ATL, p. 109; ". . . the organic quality . . ." ditto.
Impossible to get Wright's attention: White to Willcox, February 14, 1905.
Confined with tonsillitis: Wright to Darwin D. Martin, no date, DDM; ". . . can lick
my weight in wild cats . . .": ditto, May 18, 1905.
Seemed to suggest Japanese models: SC, p. 17; like a Japanese shrine: ditto, plates 20
and 21.
Most influenced by the Japanese print: SM, p. 77.
Such prints prominently displayed: "Frank Lloyd Wright's Other Passion" by Julia
Meech-Pekarik, in *The Nature of Frank Lloyd Wright*, Bolon, Nelson and Seidel, editors,
showing a photograph of the octagonal library c. 1902, p. 131, plate 6.4.

187 The greatest influence on the West: ditto, p. 132; the first *ukiyo-e* exhibition: ditto;
admired for its "spirituality": ditto, p. 146.
". . . *against my very religion*": T, September 26, 1910.
In an effort to save her marriage: to author.

188 collapsed and died EWH, p. 242.

189 At a distinct distance: TW, p. 112; and MM, p. 130.
He and Lloyd came to blows: Eric Wright.
His sixth birthday: he would celebrate it on November 15, 1909.
". . . rebuffs and bumps . . .": DDM, Jan. 2, 1906.

192 She patrolled the city parks: Mrs. Robert Llewellyn Wright to author.

193 Lines of tension: December 21, 1908.
A leading light: Verna Ross Orndorff to author; ". . . a buccaneering type": ditto.

195 ". . . breaking his leg . . .": MAG, p. 110–111.
"people from all over . . .": *Home News*, October 26, 1907.

197 "called 'the foreign market' ": MAG, p. 110.
". . . wanted a Welsh feel . . .": TRIL, p. 39; "They that wait . . .": ditto.
James Lloyd Jones owed $65,000: Andrew Porter to Frank Lloyd Wright, December
21, 1919.

198 A desperate attempt: Franklin Porter to author.
". . . was the executioner": MAG, p. 111.
". . . hold-fast and hang-tight . . .": DDM, December 19, 1907.
". . . Life is not simple . . .": ditto, December 2, 1908.
". . . has grown bitter . . .": from Ashbee's *Journal*, December 1908, cited in BR,
p. 42, note 60.

199 "Because I did not know . . .": A2, p. 162.
"all architecture proposes . . .": *Ruskin Today*, Kenneth Clark, p. 201.
"I cannot make . . ." : DDM, November 1, 1910.

200 "I go to the cross . . .": ditto, February 12, 1910.
". . . awaiting the artist's conventionalization . . .": *Frank Lloyd Wright on Architecture:
Selected Writings, 1894–1940*, Frederick Gutheim, editor, p. 23.

201 ". . . a divided life . . .": FP, July 4, 1910.

CHAPTER 8: FLOWER IN THE CRANNIED WALL

202 Smoke leaps up . . .: *Poems from the Old English*, p. 82.
203 He borrowed ten thousand dollars: established from the DDM correspondence.
Her husband received a letter: *Chicago Tribune*, November 9, 1909.
She did not intend to return: ditto, August 6, 1911.
They had embarked for Europe: ditto, November 9, 1909.
"two abandoned homes . . .": ditto.
204 Amounted to self-delusion: as he expressed it in "Letters to his Children on his Childhood."
She was bartered and sold: October 12, 1910.
His indignation was still vivid: interview with author.
205 "in the drifting mists . . .": July 8, 1910.
Mamah Cheney had settled in Berlin: *Chicago Examiner*, September 8, 1911.
". . . wreathed in smiles": ditto, October 9, 1910.
"He has returned as stated. . ." MM, p. 212.
206 ". . . as a prudent man or woman . . .": "Getting Married" (1908), *Prefaces*, George Bernard Shaw, p. 1.
". . . crossing the road to avoid me . . .": DDM, October 25, 1910.
His friends had deserted him: August 11, 1912, Archives of American Art.
Asked him to send some clients: in a letter dated December 30, 1911.
207 "What I have seen and felt . . .": DDM, October 12, 1910.
"You see I am bad . . .": DDM, October 30, 1910.
208 ". . . a lurking suspicion . . .": DDM, November 20, 1910.
Besieging her hourly: DDM to Wright, November 8, 1911.
"What you term . . .": DDM to Wright, April 24, 1912.
The first boat for Europe: he returned in January 1911.
". . . a more severe and extended . . . scheme . . .": DDM, April 30, 1912.
209 Wright had a car accident: April 18, 1912.
Over in two years: DDM, December 20, 1912.
In imitation of the Villa Medici: *The Nature of Frank Lloyd Wright*, Bolon, Nelson and Seidel, editors, p. 33.
210 "I saw the hill-crown . . ." A2, pp. 169–170.
". . . he thinks directly in terms of shapes . . .": SM, p. 106.
The Tennyson poem was written in 1869.
". . . signifies a continuity . . .": *The Nature of Frank Lloyd Wright*, pp. 34–36.
211 ". . . sacred hill temples . . .": SOT.
212 A "love nest" or "love cottage": on September 8, 1911.
"a good deal of lingerie . . .": December 24, 1911; "Just say for Mr. Wright . . .": ditto.
His first statement: in the *Chicago Tribune*, December 26, 1911; "The ordinary man . . .": ditto.
213 Buy back their control: letter from C. E. Buell to Jenkin Lloyd Jones, April 20, 1912.
A bad influence: from A. J. Cole, January 6, 1912.
A notarized public statement: February 12, 1912.
About to sit in judgment: *Chicago Record-Herald*, December 28, 1911.
To have Wright arrested: *Chicago Tribune*, December 30, 1911.
Edwin Cheney's remarriage took place on August 5, 1912.

214 A hotel costing $7 million: SM, p. 298.

Garnering architect's fees: DDM, January 10, 1913.

Not formally named: SM, pp. 298–299.

The rooms were spared: the living room was put on exhibition at the Metropolitan Museum of Art, New York, the library at the Allentown (Pennsylvania) Art Museum.

He owed $25,000: established in the DDM correspondence for November 1914.

". . . put me out of business": DDM, September 9, 1913.

". . . up and doing": DDM, May 17, 1914.

The altered date a mystery: Bruce Brooks Pfeiffer to author, September 3, 1988.

215 What new disaster: July 23, 1913.

Make her its editor: SW, xxv, note 26.

217 ". . . would send him to hell . . .": *Home News*, August 20, 1914.

"black son of a bitch": Herb Fritz to author.

He had to defend himself: *Wisconsin State Journal*, August 18, 1914, and *Home News*, August 20, 1914.

Gertrude was homesick: *Home News*, August 20, 1914.

Contradicted a day later: on August 21, 1914.

"Something terrible has happened": *Wisconsin State Journal*, August 18, 1914.

218 ". . . talkin' bout killin' folks.": *Dodgeville Chronicle*, August 21, 1914.

219 ". . . until they led him away": A2, p. 185.

220 Ready to "string him up": *Dodgeville Chronicle*, August 21, 1914.

He died in jail: on October 7, 1914.

221 Help soon arrived: *Dodgeville Chronicle*, August 28, 1914.

TALIESIN BURNING . . . SEVEN SLAIN: *My Father Who Is on Earth*, John Lloyd Wright, p. 82; ". . . It couldn't be worse . . .": ditto, p. 83.

222 ". . . infinitely sad": to author.

Cheney left next day: the account of the fire and murders compiled from contemporary newspaper accounts (No state records of the preliminary trial testimony exist).

Standing in the rain: as described by Cary Caraway to author.

"All I had left . . .": A2, p. 186.

He had believed: ditto, p. 189.

A sudden rush of water: *Dodgeville Chronicle*, August 28, 1914.

CHAPTER 9: LORD OF HER WAKING DREAMS

223 . . . while I / Go struggling . . .: *Poems from the Old English*, p. 83.

". . . a hope, and a haven": MAG, p. 141.

224 Might be born again: "Having died to his personal ego, he arose again established in the Self," in *The Hero With a Thousand Faces*, Joseph Campbell, p. 243.

". . . pacing back and forth": MAG, p. 146; ". . . the faint elusive fragrance . . .": ditto, p. 145; "staunch as always . . .": ditto, p. 147; fragments of statuary: ditto.

225 He had not wanted Anna's company: A2, p. 188.

"dalliance and self-indulgence": DDM, October 29, 1914.

226 Offers of quasi solutions; October 20, 1914.

"Roaming through the Wisconsin countryside . . .": AR, no pagination.

230 ". . . imagination was the chief guide . . .": ditto; ". . . rude and insulting . . .": ditto.

231 Without unqualified praise: *Chicago Examiner*, April 13, 1907.

"no power to harm . . .": April 18, 1907; University of Chicago Libraries.

231 *A Poet's Life*: published by Macmillan, New York, in 1938.
232 ". . . slower to condemn": T, October 1911.
Cheapening his ideas: *Architectural Record*, May 1914.
". . . put me out of business": DDM, September 9, 1913.
233 ". . . concern was over ornament . . .": BR, p. 197.
Compared with those of European artists: HACat, pp. 16–17.
234 He did not understand: AR.
235 ". . . The shade will rattle . . .": DDM, March 21, 1903.
". . . extremely insignificant . . ." DDM, March 25, 1903.
Learn to have faith: LCL, p. 9.
She wanted a round table: DDM, August 30, 1905.
"gentleness of spirit": LCL, p. 16.
236 ". . . palazzo among prairie houses": MAN, p. 188.
237 She would hear from him: September 18, 1914.
". . . the old poisonous idea . . .": EW, December 10, 1914.
A commiserating letter: T, December 12, 1914.
238 Her husband having died: in 1911.
A circle of prominent friends: MJ, May 8, 1932; ". . . all treasured gifts . . .": ditto.
Attracted to spiritualism: Jane Porter to Frank Lloyd Wright, undated letter.
239 It had broken her health: A2, p. 202.
240 A morphine addict: As his letter to her reveals: MM, p. 255.
"I '. . . had fed in honeydew . . .' ": MJ, May 8, 1932.
241 "Lord of my Waking Dreams!": T, undated.
242 To wreak "vengeance": CT, September 1, 1926.
"I know how to be a lover . . .": T, December 19, 1914.
"I had not loved you much": MM, p. 255.
243 "I put on the simplest . . .": MJ, May 8, 1932.
"[a] dead woman whom you tortured . . .": *Chicago Tribune*, November 7, 1915; "I am going . . .": ditto.
244 "It cannot continue. . .": T, n.d., 1915; "It is to be a narrow . . .": ditto.
". . . its sheer *goodness* . . ." DDM, February 28, 1916.
To lay down her life: T, April 8, 1915.
245 Grumbled about the "effete" atmosphere; MJ, May 8, 1932.
Not an American: *Chicago Examiner*, November 4, 1915.
"Well might any woman . . .": *Chicago Sunday Tribune*, November 14, 1915.
246 "I am here at Taliesin to stay . . .": *Chicago Tribune*, November 8, 1915.
"O, it was really very terrible . . .": *Chicago Tribune*, November 7, 1915.
". . . continued his silence": MJ, May 22, 1932; "bubbled over with good nature . . .": ditto; ". . . just in time to board . . .": ditto; "upheavals" of polishing: ditto.
247 The quarrel in Japan: AR.

CHAPTER 10: THE CAULDRON

249 . . . I travelled / Seeking the sun . . .": *Poems from the Old English*, p. 36.
"I have that which I have given away": Gabriele D'Annunzio, the Italian poet, dramatist and World War I hero, engraved the words *Io ho quel che ho donato* at the entrance to his estate and final resting place, *Il Vittoriale*, outside Gardone Rivera.
"the creative and joyful . . ." ATL, p. 223.

250 "He would enter . . .": "Reflections of Taliesin" by John H. Howe, *Northwest Architect*, July–August 1969, p. 27; ". . . agile on his feet . . .": ditto.
251 "I am the greatest:" Jonathan Lipman.
". . . almost refused to acknowledge . . .": "Reflections of Taliesin," p. 29.
252 They were turning to Wright: SC, p. 23; "interwoven stripping . . .": ditto.
A direct outgrowth: GI, p. 426.
". . . I still remember clearly the shock . . .": JSAH, December 1983, pp. 350–359.
". . . This miracle man . . .": NE, p. 23.
"I still imagined . . .": A2, p. 193.
". . . we all seem somnambulists . . .": May 13, 1919.
253 He agreed to care for: May 10, 1915.
Thought he had a buyer: December 15, 1916.
"Vandals got into . . .": AR.
"She died there, alone": MAG, p. 123.
"The situation between her . . .": FP, n.d.; "jealousies that burn fiercely . . .": to Jane Porter, ditto, n.d.
254 Too "ornate and mannered": CU, p. 337.
A commission of 10 percent: it was known that this was the fee he charged to Aline Barnsdall.
255 ". . . an objective problem in engineering . . .": SM, p. 114.
Slither like a jelly: A2, pp. 214–215.
"floating foundation": GI, p. 381.
Supported by pilings: EB, vol. 5, p. 448.
257 The bulk of his time in Japan: Wright's period in Japan has been exhaustively studied by Kathryn Smith and is described in "Frank Lloyd Wright and the Imperial Hotel: A Postscript," *The Art Bulletin*, vol. LXVII, no. 2, June 1985, pp. 296–310.
258 Arato Endo a collaborator: John H. Howe.
"dramatic and musical": February 19, 1916.
"a modest little nook": A2, p. 203.
259 The climate was better: a letter to Aline Barnsdall, March 14, 1934.
An incident took place: on April 16, 1922.
260 He must have been limp with gratitude: MJ Magazine, April 29, 1932.
". . . victim of strange disturbances" A2, p. 204.
". . . in the palm of her hand": April 14, 1916; " 'There's one thing I cannot allow . . .' ": ditto.
He still looked like a Puritan: February 25, 1916.
264 Attacked the British position: April 29, 1916.
The FBI report: No. 100-240585.
Refused to accept his magazine: *Wisconsin Magazine of History*, vol. 67, no. 2, winter 1983–84, p. 123; his death described: ditto.
". . . the voice of 'the Lord' . . .": February 25, 1916. ". . . 'new unities' . . .": *The Nature of Frank Lloyd Wright*, Bolon, Nelson and Seidel, editors, xiv.
265 Pre-Columbian themes: the A.D. German Warehouse in Richland Center, Wisconsin.
Derived from the Temple of Three Lintels: "Exotic Influences in the Architecture of Frank Lloyd Wright" by Dimitri Tselos, *Magazine of Art*, vol. 46, no. 4, April 1953, p. 164.
". . . a monumentality even more dense . . .": SC, p. 24.
"most significant works . . .": *Art in America*, vol. 71, September 1983, p. 150.
Born in Bradford, Pennsylvania: on April 1, 1882.
266 Approached Wright at an early stage: a major source of information about this collab-

oration is Kathryn Smith's article, "Frank Lloyd Wright, Hollyhock House, and Olive Hill, 1914–1924", in JSAH, March 1979, pp. 15–33; first sketches for Olive Hill are marked "TANYDERI TALIESIN": Smith, p. 21.

266 A development boom: T, undated.

267 The venture was shortlived: Smith, p. 16, note 3. He returned to Chicago in January 1925. Commissioned forty-five buildings: ditto, p. 33.

Gave it to Los Angeles: in 1927.

"I don't want it to *look* green . . .": letter to Frank Lloyd Wright, T, January 29, 1920.

268 "arbitrary conditions": letter to Aline Barnsdall, June 27, 1921.

Artists were perfectionists: T, May 30, 1920.

They were both Celts: T, December 3, 1930.

Genuinely nice: T, May 11, 1930.

"You judge me by . . .": T, February 4, 1926.

"You will marvel then . . .": T, June 27, 1921.

". . . The damned thing will float . . .": T, November 18, 1930.

269 "Fire and water emerge . . ." *Art in America*, vol. 71, September 1983, p. 160.

He remained faithful: *The Nature of Frank Lloyd Wright*, p. 21.

"It represents an abstraction . . .": *Art in America*, vol. 71, September 1983, p. 162.

270 Levine's thesis: published in *The Nature of Frank Lloyd Wright*.

Replacing it with a tub: Levine, in *The Nature of Frank Lloyd Wright*, p. 43.

". . . a transformation of matter": *Moments of Vision*, Kenneth Clark, p. 6.

271 Total value of his Orientalia: DDM correspondence, August 20, 1922.

The Met was a steady customer: Julia Meech-Pekarik in *The Nature of Frank Lloyd Wright*, p. 141.

Were judged worthless: Smith article on the Imperial Hotel, p. 307, note 51; the date is 1921.

He would soon sell: based on Wright's letters to DDM, around May 8, 1924.

". . . I am extremely hard up . . .": LAR, p. 20. Date of the letter is November 30, 1922.

That phase of his life was over: the letter is undated but is probably November 1923. Avery Architectural Library, Columbia University.

". . . amazing dexterity . . .": AR.

"dragged out too late . . .": DDM, August 20, 1922.

272 ". . . Always the foundations . . .": A2, p. 219.

". . . I was knocked down . . .": ditto, p. 221.

Made a graceful exit: on August 1, 1922.

About 150,000 lost their lives: *Columbia Encyclopedia*.

"We had word . . .": MJ, May 29, 1932.

273 ". . . hailed as its architect": p. 310.

He had arrived: BL, p. 364.

". . . the dualism of God . . .": *Letters of an Architect*, Oskar Beyer, editor, pp. 71–74.

". . . getting into trouble": T, November 5, 1930.

Act as a restorative: undated letter to DDM.

"Cyrano you remember . . ." T, dated March 24, 1922. He liked the analogy and used it again in *An Autobiography*, p. 250.

274 ". . . my physical resources . . .": February 7, 1921, Art Institute of Chicago.

". . . I rather dread it . . .": T, February 7, 1921; "Have waded through . . .": ditto.

275 "We ride about . . .": T, May 13, 1919.

Intercepted a letter: this information was made public when the letter was sold at auction in Chicago April 21, 1990, by the Leslie Hindman Auctioneers: no. 516 in the catalogue.

275 "I loved her enough . . .": item 521, Hindman catalogue.
276 A fragmentary diary: in the possession of Franklin Porter.
   Who had become his ideal: MM, p. 256.
   ". . . mostly in the right": T, May 13, 1919.
277 The lady was Russian: the letter is undated.
   The person closest to Frank's heart: T, September 12, 1917.
   Had tried to make her welcome: T, July 1, 1918.
   "The situation between . . .": FP, September 11, 1922; ". . . dressed and snap-py . . .": ditto.
278 ". . . my drooping spirits . . . ": DDM, September 1, 1922.
   "I have no right . . .": to Jane Porter, September 11, 1922.
   Knew she was exiled: T, n.d.
   Wright's absence at his mother's funeral: his sister's memoir, *The Valley of the God-Almighty Joneses*, states he was there, but she would have been likely to want to defend her brother against possible reproaches; his letters to Sullivan indicate that by then he was in Los Angeles and could not have returned in time. To add to the obstacles, there was a heavy snowstorm.
   She felt so alone: T, January 1, 1922.
279 He married Miriam: TW, p. 183.

CHAPTER 11: THE CAUSE CONSERVATIVE

280 It's easy to smash . . .: *Poems from the Old English*, p. 64.
   an "entanglement": DDM notes; the remark was made in 1917.
281 "slip and slide and cheat": MM, pp. 254–256; "This inner chamber . . .": ditto, p. 256.
282 ". . . frequent yawning . . .": *The American Disease*, David F. Musto, p. 86; needing psychoanalytic help: the date was 1920: ditto, p. 83.
   "It seems that I have . . .": EW, date is probably February 4, 1925.
283 ". . . I came to really love you": MM, p. 255; "save you for myself": ditto.
   "That said treatment consisted . . .": extracts from testimony on file in Circuit Court, vol. 37, p. 229, drawer 574, May 19, 1927.
   Malicious and vindictive: MM, p. 255.
   "an unfortunate encounter . . .": MJ, June 5, 1932; asking for a divorce: ditto.
284 "Enough of 'crawling back' . . .": item 518 in the Hindman catalogue; "whatever was in me . . .": item 523, ditto.
285 "The aim is not to anchor . . ." GI, pp. 496–497 (1974).
   ". . . the pervasive factuality . . .": CU, p. 182.
286 ". . . elegant monuments of nothingness": *The Visual Arts, A History*, Hugh Honour and John Fleming, p. 617.
287 "He prided himself . . ." SM, p. 46.
   ". . . a cause conservative . . .": "In the Cause of Architecture," by Frank Lloyd Wright, *The Architectural Record*, vol. XXIII, no. 3, March 1908.
   "my heart is still . . .": LAR, p. 54.
288 "there he was torn . . .": NE, p. 53; "Our own tribe destroys . . .": from an unpublished essay, "Salvation by Imagination," Frank Lloyd Wright, Taliesin Archives.
   "It is a long time . . .": MM. p. 278.
289 "Real opportunity" awaited: EW, August 19, 1924.

291 Not have a drop of water: curator Jeffrey M. Chusid to author.

Eager to prove he had cured their drawbacks: in letters to his cousin Richard Lloyd Jones.

"Wright's regional sensitivities . . .": CU, p. 154.

"renew again and again . . .": ditto, p. 76.

292 "Sometimes if they are in luck . . .": T, July 24, 1929.

"My office is *me* . . .": MM, p. 323.

"I had worked extensively . . .": on July 17, 1929.

". . . there is no reflection . . .": July 24, 1929.

On the same day as his letter to Schindler: June 19, 1931.

". . . I accepted reluctantly . . ." T, August 7, 1931.

293 ". . . your honest enmity . . .": AR.

"I am reckessly open . . .": T, March 24, 1922.

"Anybody can leave . . .": *Richard Neutra: Promise and Fulfillment*, Dione Neutra, editor, p. 135.

". . . worth any sacrifice . . .": NE, p. 51; ". . . not a well-behaved one . . .": ditto, p. 52.

294 "as though I were in a Japanese temple . . .": NE, p. 52.

". . . a significant head . . .": *Richard Neutra: Promise and Fulfillment*, p. 126.

". . . a glorious day . . .", We were told . . .", "Moser had told us . . .": *Richard Neutra: Promise and Fulfillment*, p. 128; "In spite of the many . . .": ditto.

295 ". . . A happy one . . .": A3, pp. 530–531.

297 "You are 'spongy' . . .": MM, pp. 275–276; "You are quick to impute . . .": ditto, p. 276.

298 At about the same time: in 1921.

"I do not know myself . . .": T, May 13, 1919.

Destined for great things: Eric Wright, interview with author.

"lack of consideration . . .": MM, p. 276.

299 Quarreled over wages: *My Father Who Is on Earth*, John Lloyd Wright, p. 102.

To "avoid being destroyed": "In My Father's Shadow," *Esquire*, vol. XLIX, February 1958, pp. 55–57.

". . . 'How stupid can you get?' . . .": related to author.

300 Introduced to Sullivan: the diary entry is December 8, 1900.

Acknowledged Sullivan's influence: "The Early Work of Frank Lloyd Wright," Robert C. Spencer, *The Architectural Review*, vol. VII, June 1900.

"In the Cause of Architecture": published in *The Architectural Record*, vol. XXIII, no. 3, March 1908, p. 156.

301 ". . . To think I should come . . .": LAR, p. 5.

". . . I would share . . .": ditto, p. 20; ". . . yours won't go unscathed!": ditto, p. 15.

"I saw 'him' die . . .": letter, October 26, 1956, Archives of American Art.

Three weeks after Sullivan died: on April 20, 1924.

"I don't know where to turn . . .": letter undated, MM, p. 285.

Did not know the whereabouts: F. W. Kraft to DDM, January 23, 1925.

". . . entirely of a piece . . .": DDM, January 26, 1925.

302 "You gave me a good laugh": DDM, February 5, 1925.

Before he left Sullivan: in 1892.

" 'Get those things out of here!' . . .": *Still Small Voice, the Biography of Zona Gale*, August Derleth, pp. 150–151.

CHAPTER 12: A STERN CHASE

303 How gaily, how often . . . : *Poems from the Old English*, p. 36.
304 ". . . a tidy little town . . .": *The Native's Return*, Louis Adamic, pp. 136–137.
305 Launched into a denunciation: Mrs. Robert LLewellyn Wright to author.
306 ". . . an international highway . . .": *Gurdjieff: Making a New World*, J. G. Bennett, p. 21.
     "I lived some very rich years . . .": *Arizona Living*, May 1983.
307 Thwarted by the boy's father: the early life of Olgivanna recalled by Kay Rattenbury.
     Full of hothouse flowers: William Wesley Peters to author.
     The year Hinzenberg said they were married: CT, September 4, 1926.
309 "a pair of shoulders . . .": WE, p. 259.
     "Turkish and Albanian . . .": CT, April 18, 1960.
     "I wish for immortality": *Teachings of Gurdjieff*, C. S.Nott, p. 85.
     ". . . vied incessantly . . .": WE, p. 156.
     Decided upon France: he arrived there in 1922.
310 Set up a separate household: CT, September 4, 1926.
     One of Gurdjieff's six assistants: *Our Life with Mr. Gurdjieff*, Thomas and Olga de Hartmann, p. 114.
     ". . . an inner something . . .": *Teachings of Gurdjieff*, p. 85.
     "We expected to see . . .": WE, pp. 268–269.
311 An invitation from DeMille: Kay Rattenbury to author.
     "From what I could follow": *Teachings of Gurdjieff*, p. 84.
     She should go to her brother: Kay Rattenbury.
     Thoughts of forming a new center: *Arizona Living*, May 1983.
312 "I instantly liked her . . .": A2, p. 509; "They are all dead . . .": ditto; "sensitive feminine brow . . .": ditto.
     "I fell in love . . .": *Arizona Living*, May 1983.
     "none so sure as I": A2, p. 512.
313 "You see how easy . . .": T, November 18, 1930.
314 Found her safety: CD, p. 126.
315 The last Oak Park papers signed: DDM, July 21, 1925.
     A formal agreement: dated February 1, 1918.
316 ". . . That merciless wind! . . ." A2, p. 261.
     ". . . knocked me flat . . .": dated October 30, 1925.. Roberts collection.
     "Taliesin lived . . .": A2, p. 262; ". . . turned to the color of bronze . . .": ditto, p. 263.
317 "A stern chase . . .": DDM, June 9, 1919.
     ". . . harder than that": DDM, November 4, 1925.
     ". . . increasing the load . . .": about November 18, 1924. University of Chicago.
     "Life is like that!": A2,p. 272.
     "You are hereby invited . . .": to Mr. Dietrich, T, June 2, 1925.
     The steel cathedral: LAR, p. 58; ". . . a charming and graceful compliment . . .": ditto, p. 58.
318 Close by his side: introduction to *The Work of Frank Lloyd Wright*, H. Th., Wijdeveld, editor.
319 A charge of desertion: T, August 8, 1925.

319 Reporters were most attentive: November 17, 1925.

The incriminating evidence: CT, November 17, 1925.

320 ". . . the world famous architect . . .": *Home News*, December 3, 1925.

To New York on a stretcher: CT, October 22, 1926.

CHAPTER 13: TRUTH AGAINST THE WORLD

322 Alas, you glorious . . . ; 'Fate blows hardest . . .: *Poems from the Old English*, pp. 61 and 59, respectively.

". . . this low spreading shelter . . .": A1,p. 272.

Who flattered his art: *United News*, November 29, 1925.

323 ". . . Where to turn?": DDM, November 1, 1925.

"I tried to show you . . .": T, September, 7, 1925.

There were no funds: CT, November 17, 1925.

". . . obscene matter": CT, February 22, 1926.

324 ". . . the humiliation and misery . . .": A1, p. 275.

325 The case was closed: Chicago File, no. 31–479.

"These peregrinations . . .": A1, p. 276.

"All traces of . . .": DDM, May 10, 1926.

"I had no money . . .": MJ, June 5, 1932.

326 It made good copy: in the NYT, June 3, 1926.

Miriam conceded defeat: CT, June 10, 1926; "I feel that I belong . . .": ditto.

A measly $1,500: A1, p. 277.

327 "They have merely . . .": T, August 23, 1926.

". . . what the word 'Taliesin' means . . .": DDM, about July–August 1926.

328 "the ends of the earth": CT, October 28, 1926.

329 Obtained adultery warrants: on September 9, 1926.

Rumors spread: compiled sources.

". . . simple and truthful . . .": DDM, December 23, 1926.

330 ". . . drawn and haggard": CT, October 22, 1926.

Released from charges: CT, October, 28, 1926.

"immoral purposes": A2 p. 288.

331 ". . . one blunder after another . . .": published November 5, 1926.

A "moral" victory: CT, October 28, 1926.

". . . an avenging angel": Arthur D. Cloud in the CT, October 1, 1926.

Expunged from the record: TW, p. 190.

She collapsed: CT, October 26, 1926; NYT, October 30 and 31, 1926; November 2, 1926.

332 "I lived in it . . .": T, November 16, 1926.

". . . not well off . . .": interview with author.

"persecution and revenge": NYT, October 29, 1926.

". . . a hopeless romanticist": T, December 10, 1926.

333 A tart reply: T, November 5, 1926.

"the world's best . . .": DDM, May 10, 1926.

He had retired: in September 1925.

Ambitious to endow: on February 22, 1928.

". . . when the wolf came . . .": September 28, 1926.

334 "very ingenious": DDM, November 24, 1926.
Until November 1925: CT, November 17, 1925.
". . . shall be in my fifties . . .": DDM, June 8, 1934.
". . . you need me . . .": Thomas Heath to author.
"try me out": Library of Congress, n.d.
"I just can't do it!": DDM, January 4, 1927.

335 It was very rare: NYT, January 2, 1927.

336 a "technical . . . violation": NYT, March 5, 1927.
No crime had been committed: MJ, February 2, 1927.
"Alone, deserted, desolate . . .": CT, June 19, 1927.
"And there's a diploma . . .": T, April 1927.
$3,000 in damages: CT, February 23, 1927.
Totaled its losses: TW, p. 191.

337 Appeared to arrest her: A2, p. 291; "My sense of humor . . .": ditto.
". . . how the devil do you expect . . .": L. H. Bancroft, T, May 2, 1927.
Served two terms: 1931–33 and 1935–39.

338 Enjoining from entering: TW, p. 191.
Forever renounced Olga: CT, June 28, 1927.
". . . all is bright again . . .": T, July 23, 1927.
Agreed not to interfere: DDM correspondence, May 2, 1927.
"snatched a revolver . . ." A2, pp. 294–295.

339 She was arrested: CT, October 6, 1927.
If Miriam would leave: CT, October 8, 1927.
"I don't want to see her . . .": CT, October 19, 1927.
". . . a warrant for my arrest . . .": DDM, July 21, 1928.
Would not bring charges: T, July 17, 1928.

340 ". . . I wrecked the place . . .": MJ, June 5, 1932.
Heir to a throne: TW, p. 191.

341 Patient negotiating: La Follette, DDM, October 2, 1928.
They needed money: DDM, October 20, 1928.
"For sale: One romantic . . .": *Chicago Tribune*, July 31, 1928.

342 He had not "strong-armed" it: DDM, August 28, 1928.
Page was disapproving: T, November 7, 1928.
"We have made . . .": The saddle had been sent C.O.D. when the letter was written, on October 4,1928. A month later Wright had not been to claim them and the N. Porter Saddle & Harness Company sent him a telegram of reminder.

CHAPTER 14: WORK SONG

344 The funeral / Pyre . . .: *Poems from the Old English*, p. 108.
"Already the frosts and thaws . . .":" CT, July 11, 1928.

345 "The fragrance of fresh-hewn wood . . .": CT, August 8, 1928.
"battered up," but still in the ring: to Mumford, T, January 7, 1929.
Before he left: in late December 1927.

346 His first priorities: to DDM, n.d., about November 19, 1928.
". . . take pioneers' fare . . .": EW, August 19, 1924.
"Come back, Frank . . .": A1, p. 365; ". . . eternity that is now . . .": ditto.
". . . still 'as was,' ": T, n.d., c. January 1929.

347 "And if the laughter . . .": EW, n.d., c. January 1929.
Not wearing any shoes: interview with author.
"That filial promise . . .": A2, p. 387.

349 Training in use of machinery : *Design in America*, Detroit Institute of Arts, p. 145; "all
the related arts . . .": ditto, p. 24; reminiscent of Hillside: ditto, pp. 59–60.
"beyond our scope": DDM, January 7, 1929.

352 An average of fifty-six cents: EW, February 8, 1928.
Had been patented: Gibson, Dunn & Crutcher to McArthur, T, January 16, 1930.
Happy to be hired: to DDM, March 25, 1928.

353 Acted as advisor: McArthur to Wright, T, May 23, 1920.
Wright was the designer: see ST, nos. 221 and 222.

354 His major accomplishment: her letter to Wright, T, April 16, 1951.
"The whole office knew . . .": T, April 19, 1951.
Questioning him closely: Stockton & Perry, T, January 20, 1930.
Had never quite managed: Wright to ditto, T, January 21, 1930.
Destroying his chances: T, April 2, 1930.
"To Whom It May Concern": dated June 2, 1930.

355 ". . . an adequate expression . . .": HI, p. 77.
"The slope of the talus is a triangle . . ." EW, June 1, 1928.
A modified zigzag: see HI, plate 282.
Looked like a dotted line: HI, p. 78.
"These dotted-horizontals drip . . .": To Lloyd Wright, EW, June 1, 1928.
"The color of the building . . .": ditto.
"IDEAL COMMISSION SETTLED . . .": DDM, April 6, 1928.

356 He was ready to drive: by January 14, 1929; DDM correspondence, to La Follette,
January 15, 1929.
Photographs of the camp: HI, p. 280.

357 In the corporation's account: DDM, January 15, 1929.
Wright wanted this function: DDM, March 4, 1929.
An unsuccessful attempt: DDM, March 12, 1929.
"loving it too much . . .": DDM, May 18, 1929.
Jumped on the idea: DDM, May 22, 1929.

358 ". . . none too sympathetic . . .": T, August 1, 1929.
Marginally less hopeful: T, October 29, 1937.
". . . a serious crimp . . .": T, April 12, 1930.
Bank was about to foreclose: August 11, 1930.
". . . go 'flooey or phlooey' . . .": DDM, August 11, 1930.
Sending out appeals: on February 4, 1930.
"Wright didn't seem to have . . .": letter to author, May 20, 1988.

359 About four dollars: MJ, February 16, 1930.

360 Trips to North Carolina: from a chronology prepared by Mrs. David Wright.
Her lease would be up: to the Ashbees, July 16, 1930.
"playing around with a friend . . .": T, September 5, 1929.

361 She did not enjoy: David Wright, Mrs. Robert Llewellyn Wright, to author.
The strain of a fulltime job: to the Ashbees, July 16, 1930.
"Why didn't you say . . .": DDM, July 14, 1930.
Alimony for June: Wright to DDM, July 16, 1930.
"Thanks for your wire": to Wright, T, June 25, 1930.
Time to be legally married: CT, October 14, 1927.

361 Expensive and time consuming: Wright to Chandler, T, December 28, 1929.
    Proceedings had been dropped: on February 14, 1929.
364 Still needed his rail fare: Jenkin Lloyd Jones (Richard's son) in "A House for a Cousin:
    The Richard Lloyd Jones House," *Frank Lloyd Wright Newsletter*, vol. 2, no. 4, fourth
    quarter 1979, p. l.
365 "a Puritan and a publican of the worst . . .": T, November 6, 1928.
    A thunderbolt of criticism: T, November 26, 1928.
    "a screen of closely spaced piers . . .": HI, p. 78.
366 A very rough floor plan: T, November 26, 1928.
    "the full benefit . . .": T, December 14, 1928.
    Glad to send more: T, March 8, 1929.
367 His limit was $50,000: T, April 15, 1929.
    Dispensing free advice: T, April 30, 1929.
    A few Japanese prints: T, May 15, 1929.
368 He might end up in jail: T, May 25, 1929.
    At sixty miles an hour: T, May 29, 1929.
    ". . . have fought a good fight": T, December 5, 1928.
    Relations were his enemies: T, March 7, 1929.
    Muttering imprecations: T, September 16, 1929.
369 He absolutely insisted: T, October 8, 1929.
    Practicalities first: T, June 12, 1929.
    Allaying his cousin's reservations: T, October 10, 1929.
370 A ten-foot incline: T, November 12, 1929.
    "What you now say about the slope . . .": LCL, p. 58.
    Wright's new vertical plan: T, Lloyd Jones to Wright, November 21, 1929; Wright
    to Lloyd Jones, December 12, 1929.
371 Looked like a penitentiary: HI, p. 78.
    Went on absorbing water: T, March 10, 1933.
    This "slat device": T, September 19, 1930.
372 He was out of funds: "A House for a Cousin: The Richard Lloyd Jones House," *Frank
    Lloyd Wright Newsletter*, vol. 2, no. 4, fourth quarter 1979, p. 2; "A pickle factory":
    ditto; ". . . it's leaking on my desk!": ditto; ". . . this is what we get . . .": ditto.
373 "a man doesn't need any money.": T, March 10, 1933.
    "Peasant meals of potatoes . . .": from a speech, "The Frank Lloyd Wright I Knew."
    Two cardinal rules: T, December 3, 1927.
    "More and more a stranger . . .": T, December 7, 1927; he loved and admired him:
    ditto.
374 "So good a mind . . .": *The New Yorker*, July 19, 1930.
    "to apply the word 'genius' . . .": ditto.
    ". . . any damned old way . . .": T, May 27,1932..
    "There is probably something coming . . .": EW, July 7, 1931.

                CHAPTER 15: THE WORLD'S GREATEST ARCHITECT

375 Lack of interest in himself: FP, May 13, 1919.
    "Welsh ire": to Catherine Wright Baxter, T, February 7, 1921.
    A "modern Druid": William Wesley Peters to author.
    Anyone named Jones: Mrs. Ernest Meyer to author.

376 ". . . hot water of his own boiling": MAG, p. 21.

". . . their backs to the wall . . .": *The Changing Anatomy of Britain*, Anthony Sampson, p. 325.

"I was under oath . . .": MJ, April 10, 1959.

". . . five times as attractive . . .": T, April 25, 1937.

". . . what a bore . . ." T, March 23, 1932.

". . . naturally rather dumb . . .": T, April 30, 1951, to Oskar Stonorov.

"I thought I was the limit": T, September 12, 1931, to Lewis Mumford.

377 "It seems gross injustice": December 26, 1906, Roberts collection.

Had to tell him to stop: in 1931, W. Willcox papers.

". . . he will always be right where he has been . . .": April 3, 1934, Roberts collection.

"Character is fate . . .": DDM, December 6, 1935.

". . . too many people . . .": T, June 13, 1952.

"I wish I had": interview with author.

378 "I guess my talent . . .": Hindman catalogue, no. 515.

"What would you like to do for us?": interview with author.

"I've always wanted to take . . ." *The New Yorker*, June 15, 1956.

". . . kick them in the shins . . .": interview with author.

". . . lack of sensitivity . . .": interview with author.

379 Generosity and understanding: interview with author.

". . . that wonderful swift look . . .": "Our House," CT, January 1, 1959.

"There is some swelling . . .": June 2, 1953, Archives of American Art.

"dear old buxom": T, May 1, 1952; "ample fanny": T, December 8, 1951.

". . . I can't strike the blow . . .": LAR, p. 144, undated.

380 ". . . some sort of witty comment . . .": interview with author.

"I was so disappointed . . .": T, March 23, 1932.

"Here is apology . . .": October 26, 1956, Archives of American Art.

"Like all geniuses . . .": *Further Teachings of Gurdjieff*, C. S. Nott, p. 153.

"Managed" is the word they used: Eric Wright to author.

". . . it was antipathetic . . .": interview with author.

381 ". . . the higher were his expectations . . .": to author.

Thousands of insects: *The Shining Brow*, Olgivanna Lloyd Wright, p. 89.

"He had sciatica . . .": to author.

"He had to believe in himself . . .": Mrs. Russell Bletzer to author.

". . . he was a boy . . .": *Further Teachings of Gurdjieff*, p. 153.

". . . are still 'as was,' . . .": T, January 1, 1929.

A happy life: to Kay Rattenbury.

382 He dismissed what he had once built: to author.

". . . the important thing . . .": T, February 7, 1921.

". . . I'll take twelve dozen": William H. Calvert to author.

Refused to categorize him: in an interview.

". . . two hundred percent alive": interview with author.

383 "She believed in God . . .": *Abraham Lincoln, The Prairie Years*: vol. 1, Carl Sandburg, p. 13.

384 His truth seemed curved: MOR, p. 169.

Coined by someone else: BR, p. 18.

" . . . nineteenth-century themes . . .": *The Atlantic*, August 1959, p. 24.

385 A handsome new edition: published in 1977.

". . . no such spontaneous flood . . .": T, April 19, 1932.

385 ". . . a form of auto-intoxication . . .": LAR, p. 23, in a letter dated June 8, 1923.
". . . the few really great men": *Chicago Daily News*, April 7, 1932.
"irrational and organic": GI, p. 336 (1941).

386 "appealed to our emotions . . .": *The Romantic Rebellion*, Kenneth Clark, p. 19; ". . . all the healthier for being tasteless": ditto, p. 20.
The "soul" of a design: A2, p. 158; a belief in art: ditto, p. 160; the "countenance of principle": ditto, p. 161.
". . . the production of wealth": *M. H. Baillie Scott and the Arts & Crafts Movement*, James D. Kornwolf, on p. 490; a revolutionary idea: ditto; "For a short time . . .": ditto; "The mortal peril . . .": ditto, p. 508; "considerable sacrifices were demanded . . .": ditto, p. 507.

387 "Why should architecture or objects of art . . .": NYT *Book Review*, August 3, 1941.
"Wright's generation was as shocked . . .": *M. H. Baillie Scott and the Arts & Crafts Movement*, p. 488.
". . . comparative children . . .": To Stonorov, T, March 31, 1956.

388 Had just published an essay: November 26, 1928.
". . . the greatest Architect who will ever live . . .": T, March 1930.
"immediate and total": *M. H. Baillie Scott and the Arts & Crafts Movement*, p. 507; "If Humanism be not . . .": ditto.
"Like the Frenchman he admires . . .": T, July 10, 1928.

389 "Emersonian quality": T, January 24, 1931.
"Your recent work . . .": T, May 11, 1928.
". . . Nor am I a lion . . .": The comment was made in the spring of 1928.
Responded with a card: as described in his review, *New York Herald Tribune*, May 29, 1941.
". . . push a whole civilization . . .": the *Nation*, December 3, 1930.

390 ". . . the newest thing . . .": published on June 29, 1930.
"refined geometrical formalism": *In the Deco Style*, Klein, McClelland and Haslam, p. 31; the prototype for the California Deco Style: ditto, p. 162.
No longer afraid of him: T, March 1, 1930.
The day might be saved: T, November 18, 1930
They were taking notes: T, September 11, 1930.

391 No longer any ill feelings: EW, October 29, 1929.
". . . justice I am asking": T, November 7, 1929.
A prominent mention: A. Lawrence Kocher, managing editor, T, November 23, 1929.
"Don't you think . . ." T, December 9, 1931.
". . . a race to win . . .": DDM, March 18, 1929.

392 The newly founded Museum of Modern Art: it opened on November 8, 1929.
"His name was an echo . . .": *Alfred H. Barr, Jr., Missionary for the Modern,* Alice Goldfarb Marquis, p. 85; "I was the drummer . . .": ditto.
". . . greatest nineteenth century architect": NYT, April 20, 1979.
Still on his guard: to Mumford, April 7, 1931.

393 Had not met with favor: NE, p. 105.
"Frank Lloyd Wright middle . . .": in a letter to the Neutras, T, January 8, 1953.
Demanded his work be withdrawn: It was not withdrawn for the Los Angeles showing but was removed for the subsequent tour.
"All novices, in the nature of the Cuckoo . . .": letter to the Neutras, T, January 8, 1953.
". . . too much at stake . . .": T, January 19, 1932.

393 An anguished telegram: T, January 21, 1932.
    . . . nothing to show": T, January 23, 1932.
    The forerunner of a movement: NE, p. 102.
394 "a sinister attempt . . .": *Architectural Record*, September 1953, p. 12.
    ". . . out in the rain.": the remark sounds apocryphal but, according to Johnson, was
    actually made.
    "evil crusade": *Architectural Record*, September 1953, ditto.
    "summoned to leadership": *Vanity Fair*, February 1931, p. 197.

CHAPTER 16: TALIESIN

395 No colors fade . . .: *Poems from the Old English*, p. 108.
396 Elegiac terms: in 1936.
    ". . . approaching the end . . .": *Architectural Forum*, February 1936, p. 7.
    "attacked their integrity . . .": the *Atlantic*, August 1959.
    "American Institute of Appearances": *Louisville Courier Journal*, April 9, 1959.
    "old gentlemen afraid . . .": "The Frank Lloyd Wright I Knew," speech by Frederick
    Gutheim.
    "Frank Lloyd Wrong": Edgar Tafel to author.
    Eventually needed glasses: Wright to DDM, 1929.
    ". . . wouldn't remind me of my age": remark made to William H. Short.
397 "he was so afraid . . .": interview with author.
    A bottle of Bushmill's: John H. Howe to author.
    ". . . I have this": to author.
    "I have not dared to ask . . .": DDM, March 24, 1932. (Frank Lloyd Wright, Inc.
    was dissolved in 1933.)
    "vegetables, meat, laundry . . .": DDM, February 26, 1930.
    ". . . Like a drowning man . . .": DDM, March 26, 1932; ". . . kicking at the end
    of the rope . . .": ditto.
398 A last-minute appeal: T, December 30, 1931.
    Threatening to foreclose: A2, p. 31.
    "You cannot get away . . .": T, November 28, 1930.
399 ". . . the old gospel of hard work . . .": from a 1940 bulletin.
    ". . . invented slave labor": to author.
    Industry would eventually sponsor: NYT, November 6, 1932.
400 Ordering directly: Sophia Mumford to author.
    Wrote to describe their progress: to Jane Porter, March 19, 1932.
    ". . . no stopping to mourn": *Liberty*, March 23, 1929.
    "I remember the sunny day . . .": "At Taliesin," *An Uplands Reader*, April 1979, pp.
    129–148.
    ". . . had emotional problems . . .": interview with author.
    ". . . scarcely wide enough . . .": "At Taliesin," *An Uplands Reader*, April 1979.
402 On a bright sunny morning: the actual date, according to William Wesley Peters, was
    June 17, 1932.
403 "I have never received such a lecture . . .": interview with author.
405 His practical jokes: related to the author by William Wesley Peters.
    A pony in the bedroom: John H. Howe to author.
406 "I had no inkling . . .": *Frank Lloyd Wright's Fallingwater*, Donald Hoffmann, p. 11.
    ". . . lost his patience . . .": John H. Howe to author.

407 ". . . could not let him go.": Professor Lilien to author.

". . . making a show of something . . .": John H. Howe to author.

"Come up and see me . . .": Professor Lilien to author.

408 "There were amplifiers . . .": John H. Howe to author.

"They knew too much . . .": interview with author.

Anywhere they "damn pleased": interview with author.

409 "roofs leaked equally . . .": *Wisconsin Magazine of History*, autumn 1989, p. 35.

410 ". . . some of their banana cream pie.": John H. Howe to author.

To get his gun: TAF, p. 161; ". . . forever falling off horses . . .": ditto; a tablespoon of castor oil: ditto, p. 152.

411 ". . . one of my fondest memories of him": John H. Howe to author.

". . . my youngest apprentice": interview with author.

"our hopeless ship": to Mrs. Darwin D. Martin, DDM, December 6, 1935.

". . . It's so perfect . . .": to author.

412 ". . . a large part of Hillside had burned down . . .": "At Taliesin," *An Uplands Reader*, April 1979, p. 147.

"The important point to grasp . . .": interview with author.

The eye of calm: Mr. and Mrs. Howe to author.

Built in Shorewood Hills: in 1939.

413 The Christmas and birthday boxes: "At Taliesin," *An Uplands Reader*, April 1979, p. 139.

"He didn't get it": as related by his mother, Mrs. Robert Llewellyn Wright.

Plowing back the profits: T, December 2, 1934.

Influential contacts: Wright to Klumb, T, December 9, 1934.

414 Hoped he would understand: T, December 5, 1934.

"I hated to go away . . .": interview with author.

In other words, exploited: Larry Lemmon to author.

415 "He could take a theme . . .": Cary Caraway to author.

416 The master's grudging permission: in 1948.

"There in a beautiful forest . . .": *Frank Lloyd Wright's Fallingwater*, pp. 17–18.

419 ". . . was about to drive . . .": he arrived on Sunday, September 22, 1935. Established from a Wright letter in the Kaufmann correspondence, T, September 18, 1935.

". . . took two hours": interview with author.

"The warming kettle . . .": TAF, p. 7.

420 ". . . executed entirely . . .": *Frank Lloyd Wright's Fallingwater*, p. 21.

" 'Don't change a thing' ": interview with author.

CHAPTER 17: BROAD ACRES

421 First the heavens were formed . . .: *Poems from the Old English*, p. 21.

422 ". . . we are only trades people . . .": T, April 16, 1936.

"made the pilgrimage": "Frank Lloyd Wright and the Origins of Fallingwater," speech by Franklin Toker.

423 The house would be sold: TAF, p. 92.

". . . less taking and more giving . . .": DDM, December 6, 1935.

Almost a crime: T, October 3, 1927.

Let their patrons pay their bills: T, November 16, 1927.

Eventually cost $75,000: *Frank Lloyd Wright's Fallingwater*, Donald Hoffmann, p. 52; too far from the original concept: ditto.

424 ". . . made to complement . . .": CU, p. 199; "the materials of the structure . . .": ditto, p. 200.

His initials contained in the name: "Frank Lloyd Wright and the Origins of Fallingwater."

425 Essentially a pyamid: SC, pp. 26–27; "like country cross roads . . .": ditto, p. 18.

"the mysticism that has always governed . . .": BL, p. 59.

426 "again ashes and vain regrets": T, October 15, 1952.

"Romeo, as you will see . . ." A2, p. 135.

427 ". . . they became Mrs. Wright": Mrs. Ernest Meyer to author.

Continued to disclaim all knowledge: *Wisconsin Magazine of History*, autumn 1989, p. 41.

428 "something like a national treasure . . .": Loren Pope to author.

Persuaded him to abandon his artist's tie: Dr. Joseph Rorke to author.

Intercepted his letters: interview with author.

". . . as strong as steel . . .": interview with author.

Knees buckling and fingers trembling: *The Shining Brow*, Olgivanna Lloyd Wright, pp. 83–84; "Boys, she's mine!": ditto, pp. 78–79.

429 "You may be a woman . . .": CD, pp. 109–110.

"a darling sensitive soul . . .": to William R. Heath, T, 1927.

430 " 'Please come back, Daddy' . . .": CD, pp. 146–147.

431 "rather like a brilliant undergraduate . . .": *Further Teachings of Gurdjieff*, C. S. Nott, p. 139; " '. . . You are idiot,' . . .": ditto, p. 152.

". . . dumped the barrels . . .": TAF, p. 139.

Iovanna's poetic gift: Olgivanna Wright to Mrs. Jane Porter: FP, March 24, 1931.

434 ". . . an image of greatness . . .": Elizabeth Kassler to author.

Iovanna's memories of childhood: interviews with author.

435 Ideal parent figures: William Wesley Peters to author.

436 ". . . Cain and Abel": William Calvert to author.

". . . accusations and unkind words . . .": A2, p. 466; practically single-handedly: ditto.

437 ". . . 'Is there a difference?' ": A2, p. 435.

Details of the financial arrangments involving Taliesin were sent to Edward H. Kavinoky, a Buffalo attorney representing Darwin D. Martin's son, Darwin R. Martin, by James E. Doyle of La Follette, Sinykin & Doyle of Madison, Wisconsin, DDM, March 30, 1949.

Charmed him into signing: DDM, December 11, 1935.

"helpless to turn a penny . . .": DDM, June 30, 1939.

438 The mortgage was transferred: on September 26, 1936. Doyle to Kavinoky, op. cit.

"I saw no good reason . . .": DDM, June 30, 1939.

Frank Lloyd Wright Foundation: established November 29, 1940.

No enforceable rights: Doyle to Kavinoky, op. cit.

Dwindled to seventy acres: NYT, July 31, 1928.

Its first direct access: Wright to H. F. Johnson, December 30, 1939.

439 Three miles of waterfront: A2, p. 467.

He burned them down: John H. Howe to author.

The burning of Stuffy's Bar: CD, pp. 158–159.

The official post office: from 1889 to 1919.

440 ". . . would actually do it": Mr. and Mrs. Herbert Fritz to author.

Had already flushed it: Mr. and Mrs. Henry Sayles Francis to author; Henry Sayles Francis to author, December 30, 1986.

440 Got back on the train: Prof. William Morgan to author.

441 Deserved a more experienced overseer: A2, p. 448.

Laughed and paid up: anecdote from Mr. and Mrs. John H. Howe.

". . . one for my friend, too,": Mosette Broderick to author.

" . . . taking him to task . . .": Mrs. Mumford, interview with author.

442 " . . . a connecting-rod design . . .": interview with author.

"too far gone on along the lines of Lincoln . . .": *The Master Architect: Conversations with Frank Llyod Wright*, Patrick J. Meehan, p. 243; ". . . they're all preachers . . .": ditto, p. 215.

Armfuls of flowers: TAF, pp. 175–176.

". . . at each others' throats": *Frank Lloyd Wright and the Johnson Wax Buildings*, Jonathan Lipman, p. 13; ". . . he must have something": ditto.

443 ". . . seduced wax manufacturers . . .": the *Washington Post*, April 26, 1959.

". . . don't scold me . . .": LCL, p. 131.

". . . what we don't do tomorrow . . .": TAF, p. 70; at the temperamental opposite of Mies van der Rohe: ditto, p. 70.

"the machine and the hope it held . . .": *American Art Deco*, Alistair Duncan, p. 271.

444 "a sort of extended family . . ." CU, p. 201.

Built a smaller building: as pointed out in "Consecrated Space," unpublished articled by Jonathan Lipman.

"We achieved international attention . . .": *American Institute of Architects Journal*, January 1979.

445 ". . . a sensible plan for living . . .": T, February 14, 1937.

446 ". . . characteristic trait of women . . .": T, July 23, 1937.

". . . 'The young mistress will never . . .": A2, p. 477.

". . . I don't think she and Mr. Wright ever spoke seriously . . .": *American Institute of Architects Journal*.

447 ". . . a practical political economic proposition": WOW, p. 200; ". . . The city is a process . . .": ditto, p. 202.

449 ". . . captured precisely the ethos . . .": CU, p. 203.

450 Fell off the road grader: LCL, p. 120.

Contracted pneumonia: to E. Willis Jones, T, January 13, 1937.

Ran a high temperature: Masselink to Carl Sandburg, T, December 17, 1936.

". . . some speckled trout . . .": interview with author.

Phlebitis in his left leg: LCL, p. 126.

". . . the world from his chair": to E. Willis Jones, T, January 13, 1937.

"pretty ragged": T, May 28, 1937.

A second Taliesin: LAR, p. 76.

451 Had gone up in flames: T, June 3, 1930.

More than it was worth: T, June 6, 1930.

". . . such a different world . . .": *The Shining Brow*, Olgivanna Lloyd Wright, p. 92.

". . . here we constructed . . .": "Reflections of Taliesin," John H. Howe, *Northwest Architect*, July–August 1969.

Had turned him down: to Wright, T, April 25, 1936.

About eight hundred acres: TAF, p. 453; water had been found: ditto, p. 194.

452 Recollections of their trips: interviews with author.

453 ". . . We often stopped . . .": "Our House," CT, February 1, 1958.

"No blueprints . . .": "Reflections of Taliesin," *Northwest Architect*, July–August 1969, p. 141.

453 ". . . a lovely glow . . .": BL, p. 385.

". . . promising the crew a dinner out . . .": "At Taliesin," *An Uplands Reader*, April 1979, p. 142; tried jumping and missed: ditto, p. 141; ". . . under water up to my knees": A2, p. 454–455.

457 "He was soon adrift . . .": "At Taliesin," *An Uplands Reader*, April 1979, p. 144.

". . . ascetic idealization of space . . .": A2, p. 453.

458 "I'm not against capitalism": the *Washington Post*, July 2, 1935.

". . . I only wish I could see it tried . . .": "Frank Lloyd Wright in Moscow: June 1937," by Donald Leslie Johnson, JSAH, March 1987, pp. 65–79; enjoying a European revival: ditto.

459 Less than the overwhelming ovation described in his autobiography (A2, p. 544): Johnson, "Frank Lloyd Wright in Moscow" June 1937," pp. 71–72.

". . . I would kick them out . . .": A2, p. 542.

461 "glance now and then at the walls": ditto.

". . . the creation of suburban sprawl . . .": CU, p. 144.

". . . should be spread out horizontally . . .": NYT, September 18, 1938; "vainglorious skyscraper": ditto, September 15, 1938.

462 ". . . Molochs raised for commerical greatness": NYT, November 4, 1931.

Made the cover of *Time*: on January 17, 1938.

On the cover of *Life*: on September 26, 1938.

An honorary member: on February 2, 1932.

". . . when he was an active architect . . .": July 21, 1937.

463 ". . . you only serve to abuse and confuse . . .": T, September 15, 1937.

". . . a good talk . . .": T, June 15, 1938.

". . . heaping coals of fire": T, July 12, 1938.

"an intelligent adaptation . . .": CU, p. 226.

The Lubetkin-Hitchcock exchange related to author by Gavin Stamp, letter, January 4, 1988.

A photographic exhibition: *Frank Lloyd Wright's Fallingwater*, Donald Hoffmann, pp. 69–70.

464 ". . . a man who can dance circles . . .": *The New Yorker*, February 12, 1938.

Offered to pay all expenses: T, November 23, 1940.

Jumped at the chance: T, November 27, 1940.

"purely archaeological": T, March 26, 1941.

465 "young academic whiskers": T, June 7, 1941.

He should get three-fourths: T, June 13, 1941.

Could not afford it: T, June 16, 1941.

"a good job": T, May 28, 1942.

"bring his autobiography up to date . . .": Frederick Gutheim to author; Hitchcock's contribution: ditto.

466 Mechanization had reached a crisis: CU, p. 144.

Offered to John Ruskin: Ruskin caused consternation by refusing to accept the Royal Gold Medal, in protest against what he felt to be the neglect and destruction of historic buildings in England (May 20, 1874).

The year Wright and Ashbee met: T, May 9, 1939.

Delighted to have met Lutyens and Voysey: T, May 11, 1939.

467 ". . . we would see that the radical is the actual conservative": "Dinner Talk at Hull House: November 8, 1939," Frank Lloyd Wright; "unashamed preference . . .": Peter Fuller, *Modern Painters*, spring 1989, p. 31.

CHAPTER 18: THE REVOLUTIONIST AS ARCHITECT

468 Because I never forget . . .: *Poems from the Old English*, p. 65.
    "a rich and poetic . . .": SM, p. 157.
469 A windless mooring shelter: *Building with Frank Lloyd Wright*, Herbert Jacobs, p. 83;
    "sought his help": ditto, p. 97.
473 Wright fired him: A2, p. 496.
    Yodeling songs: Georgiana Hansen to author.
    ". . . in this incredible room": LCL, p. 197.
    A few months later: on February 23, 1940, LCL, p. 204.
474 ". . . pretty damn near jail . . .": T, December 12, 1939.
    ". . . more money than they have . . .": T, March 5, 1940.
    Lewis was insistent: August 29, 1940.
    Instructed Edgar Tafel , who had been sent: August 31, 1940.
    Expense he would like to avoid: Lewis, T, September 1, 1940.
    Balcony heights "ridiculous": T, September 2, 1940.
    Wright was insulted: T, September 3, 1940.
    ". . . You misread the letter . . .": September 3, 1940, LCL, PP. 205–206.
475 Solving the kitchen problem: LCL, p. 207.
    The problem of insulation: to Wright, March 4 and 8, 1940.
    As Tafel acknowledged: to author, March 17, 1990.
476 Fireplace refused to draw: T, February 17, 1941.
    "not intended to coddle . . .": T, March 8, 1941.
    ". . . a haze of heat waves": T, March 10, 1941.
    "a passing petty epidemic . . .": T, August 3, 1941.
477 ". . . uplifts the heart . . .": to Wright, April 29, 1942, LCL, p. 211.
    In such close contact: T, n.d., 1949.
    ". . . it takes all kinds!": T, July 2, 1957.
479 ". . . utterly changed our ideas . . .": BL, p. 401.
480 That was a pity: Geoffrey Baker in the NYT, November 24, 1940.
481 A Mediterranean villa: *Progressive Architecture*, November 1987, p. 129.
482 No furniture at all: "The Organic Ideal: Frank Lloyd Wright's Robie House," by William
    H. Jordy, *Progressive and Academic Ideals at the Turn of the Twentieth Century: American
    Buildings and Their Architects*, p. 211.
483 ". . . the hard job for an original mind . . .": T, June 28, 1951.
    "For whether or not you belong . . .": May 4, 1941.
    "one of the most challenging . . .": *Oakland Post-Enquirer*, June 7, 1941.
484 ". . . virtues of architecture . . .": NYT *Book Review*, August 3, 1941.
    "It is difficult to find . . .": April 8, 1941.
    For old time's sake: T, September 29, 1940.
    ". . . ideas appeared almost simultaneously . . .": R. L. Duffus, NYT *Book Review*,
    August 3, 1941.
485 "no really critical . . .": BL, p. 389.
    The two to battle it out: T, April 4, 1941.
    "Democracy's real enemy . . .": T, December 22, 1942.
    "Nature's organic law": unpublished essay, "The New Discretion."
    Son of a Jewish lawyer: *Lewis Mumford, A Life*, Donald L. Miller, p. 10.
486 His "Chamberlain" period: T, April 20, 1941.

486 ". . . we have no quarrel . . .": T, April 20, 1941, and LAR, p. 146.

"In this strange tirade . . .": *Lewis Mumford*, pp. 398–399.

His reply a few days later: on June 3, 1941.

He should examine his heart: LAR, pp. 146–148.

". . . the wide range of his mind . . .": *The New Yorker*, pp. 60–61.

487 Like his plan for Broadacre: in the *News Chronicle*, January 17, 1841.

488 "I was startled . . .": *News Chronicle*, January 21, 1941.

Continued his journey: CT, November 13, 1933.

". . . no place for a gentleman . . .": T, March 7, 1941.

489 ". . . Wright's projects first": TAF, p. 205; some in tears: ditto, pp. 206–207.

Signed the document: dated March 28, 1941.

490 ". . . poisoning your minds": CT, December 10, 1942.

Whether the investigation should be continued: March 24, 1943.

Did not warrant prosecution: April 22, 1943.

". . . the common pattern. . .": review dated June 6, 1943.

491 Personally critized President Roosevelt: March 21, 1941.

Japanese were really nice people: FBI files, October 18, 1941.

Wright's opposition to the entry of the United States into World War II continued unabated, and accounts for his slighting references to the decisions of presidents Roosevelt and Truman.

A new surge of loyalty for Wright: on June 10, 1940.

492 Whether . . . statutes had been violated: July 17, 1943.

Send more evidence: September 2, 1943.

"American customs or citizens": June 6, 1943.

"on the only front . . .": to Burt Goodrich, November 30, 1942, LAP, p. 148, and to Edgar Tafel, T, November 30, 1942.

"I was on the staff . . .": interview with author.

A new method of building defense housing: *Buffalo Courier*, September 27, 1942.

493 The deal collapsed: *Building with Frank Lloyd Wright*, p. 73.

" . . . a highly nervous state . . .": EW, November 1943; a state that continued: Lloyd Wright to his father, EW, September 6, 1944.

"we are hard to take . . .": T, January 12, 1942.

494 The hardest worker there: EW, September 6, 1944.

"Once when I was digging . . .": to author.

" . . . responsibility of the individual": A2, p. 560.

495 "Heroic Materialism": in *Civilisation*, Kenneth Clark, p. 326.

" . . . a heroic being . . .": *The Passion of Ayn Rand*, Barbara Branden, p. 52.

"Certain philosophers . . .: *Civilisation*, p. 330.

Only asked for the chance: T, December 12, 1937.

496 Had left for Arizona: T, December 31, 1937.

"I spent three hundred . . .": *The Passion of Ayn Rand*, p. 189.

He was not impressed: T, November 18, 1937.

497 As repelled as delighted: *The Passion of Ayn Rand*, pp. 190–91.

CHAPTER 19: THAT STRANGE DISEASE, HUMILITY

499 The Phoenix's breast . . .: *Poems from the Old English*, p. 116.

Babette Eddleston's impressions of Taliesin: from an unpublished account.

500 An invitation to spend the weekend: November 1945.

500 Carter H. Manny, Jr.'s impressions of Taliesin: from a letter to William Marlin. n.d.
503 " 'Take that thing away . . .' ": Peter Matthews, interview with author.
Some thirty-two commissions: LAP, p. 159.
" . . . my flanks tremble . . .": EW, July 11, 1944.
"I keep nothing for myself . . .": on August 21, 1946, LAP, p. 44.
A single ten-dollar note: Sherry Lewis, letter to author, September 24, 1987.
505 Hopelessly crumpled: Carter H. Manny, Jr.
To buy timber: interview with author.
"We need Money . . .": T, November 12, 1949.
"Can I help you?": Bruce Brooks Pfeiffer, interview with author.
". . . wanted her own nest": interview with author.
506 ". . . if that was Catherine": interview with author.
". . . Frank Lloyd Wright letters": interview with author.
Richard Carney's impressions of Taliesin: interviews with author.
508 ". . . agreed to let me stay": ditto.
"loved to quote himself . . .": interview with author.
509 ". . . who *is* this woman?": Rupert Pole to author.
510 "the general cook . . .": T, August 6, 1934.
Theirs was a special menu: *The Passion of Ayn Rand*, Barbara Branden, p. 190.
" '. . . bend like the grass . . .' ": to author.
". . . sometimes had to crack heads open . . .": Eloise Fritz to author.
". . . to hear the song of fools": "Our House," CT, January 14, 1957.
"In the first six months . . .": to author.
511 ". . . He had no weaknesses": to author.
". . . I saw through her . . .": to author.
"I was very poor . . .": reminiscences of Taliesin in interview with author.
512 Had wired her room: Iovanna Wright to author.
"I pretty much accepted . . .": Reminiscences of Taliesin in interview with author.
513 Never received a letter: interview with author.
". . . no successful apprentice families . . .": interview with author.
515 Jealousy was the explanation: *Frank Lloyd Wright in the Realm of Ideas*, Bruce Brooks Pfeiffer, p. 170.
517 Made himself thoroughly unpleasant: CD, p. 114; ". . . a pair of trousers . . .": ditto, p. 116.
As good as his word: *Frank Lloyd Wright in the Realm of Ideas*, p. 175.
He cut off his pants: William Calvert, interview with author.
518 Her husband's life in his hands: "How Frank Lloyd Wright Got His Gold Medal," *Harper's*, May 1958.
Took care of the relatives: Mrs. Robert Llewellyn Wright to author.
Svetlana's death: from contemporary accounts and CT, September 30, 1946.
519 "I remember I was working . . .": interview with author.
" 'It can't be that bad,'. . .": interview with author.
". . . put her in the garden room": Kay Rattenbury to author.
521 "She's in the car crying": anecdote related by Jonathan Lipman.
522 ". . . Anything he wanted, they did": interview with author.
Account of the awarding of the gold medal, from letters of Arthur Cort Holden to author, September 19, 1988, and June 19, 1990; A.I.A. banquet description, in *Architectural Record*, May 1949, pp. 87–88; speech, *Journal of the American Institute of Architects*, vol. XI, no. 5, May 1949, pp. 199–207.

524 " 'One is never too old'. . . ": interview with author.
". . . 'Put it on!'. . .": interview with author.
Wearing a black tie and a white linen suit: CD, p. 34.

CHAPTER 20: THE SHINING LAND

525 So the blesséd one . . . *Poems from the Old English*, p. 117.
". . . the two most interesting people . . .": July 1, 1954.
"the universally acknowledged architectural genius . . .": on April 23, 1955.
526 In lieu of payment: "Our House," CT, June 5, 1961.
". . . all eyes followed": Mrs. Ernest L. Meyer to author.
". . . pianissimo raillery . . .": the *Washington Post*, April 26, 1959.
". . . malleable as an aging cat": the *Washington Post*, April 26, 1959.
"about ninety-five years old": to Steichen, T, December 9, 1931.
"a blueness and intensity . . .": interview with author.
"looked like an old hag,": EW, July 11, 1944.
528 ". . . like an old woman": CT, February 27, 1956.
". . . the bust was never finished": "Our House," CT, August 3, 1961.
529 Suggested by Gutheim: as related in his lecture, "The Frank Lloyd Wright I Knew."
531 It was abandoned: LAP, p. 181.
The narrowness of artists: to William H. Short, in an interview August 21, 1954, Princeton University Archives.
". . . structural, spatial, and formal abstraction . . .": SC, p. 26.
532 Much-watered-down: SC, p. 26.
Perfectly disgusted: Sophia Mumford to author.
Five trips overseas: Prof. Jack Quinan.
533 "solve the small house . . .": TW, p. 337.
Any child could play: *Frank Lloyd Wright's Usonian Houses*, John Sergeant, p. 145; ". . . an incremental error . . .": ditto, p. 134; a new answer to prefabrication: ditto, p. 145; the price jumped again: ditto, p. 146.
536 ". . . The appraisers didn't like . . .": the *Washington Post*, June 2, 1974.
He never had a father: interviews with author.
537 Had brought about World War II: from FBI files, October 25, 1943. "Roosevelt has sold . . .": LAP, p. 100.
538 NOTED ARCHITECT APES . . .: October 30, 1953.
"Go home and make . . .": *Architectural Forum*, July 1949, p. 14.
". . . did not promise . . .": NYT, May 26, 1949.
Ought to be abolished: NYT, March 7, 1947.
". . . all we have called progress . . .": NYT, ditto.
539 "Communist front": on April 26, 1950.
A list of Americans: UPI and INS, April 5, 1951.
"We have nothing to fear . . .": NYT, June 9, 1950.
A Christmas appeal: the *Daily Worker*, December 21, 1950.
540 "the fear and suspicion . . .": to Wright, T, February 28, 1953.
". . . The judicial mind . . .": November 15, 1954.
541 Taliesin's architectural function: CT, November 9, 1954.
Would burn Taliesin down: CT, November 11, 1954.
"I was born in Wisconsin . . .": CT, February 11, 1955.

542 ". . . sold for five thousand dollars": to author.

Induced to take action: MJ, memo, May 20, 1957.

"unfit to characterize . . .": Jackson's speech was reported to Douglas Haskell by Robert L. Wright, May 13, 1957.

543 ". . . elimination of Wright": AP, August 11, 1955; "I do not know why . . .": ditto. One of the star witnesses: May 28, 1955.

". . . active and intensive support . . .": *San Francisco Chronicle and Examiner*, NYT, August 3, 1957.

544 ". . . fun at our expense": interview with author.

Wright's visit to Yale: as described by Henry S. F. Cooper, Jr., in a column, "Sound and Fury," written for the *Yale Daily News*, September 22, 1955.

545 "Attaboy, Phil . . ." to author.

His best ideas forty years old: Prof. Jack Quinan.

"The modern accent is on living . . .": *The New Yorker*, October 11, 1947.

". . . honorific character . . .": CU, p. 266.

548 ". . . the sculptural freedom . . ." *The Impact of European Modernism in the Mid-Twentieth Century*, William H. Jordy, p. 280; ". . . a molded space . . .": ditto.

549 Guggenheim died: March 11, 1949.

550 "What do you call this . . .": Doris Murray Kuhns to author.

". . . will simply disgrace . . .": *Time*, March 26, 1959.

". . . your design for the Guggenheim is unique . . .": Arthur Cort Holden to Wright, February 26, 1953.

551 "Damn it, get a permit for Frank . . .": NYT, May 11, 1987.

" 'to pay the tolls' ": from a memoir by Arthur Cort Holden, Princeton University Archives.

". . . grumbled, but paid": William Wesley Peters to author.

". . . ultimate in precision and polish . . .": BL, pp. 242–243; "that a sinsister group . . .": ditto, p. 246.

552 ". . . like a murky glass": April 3, 1953, Avery Architectural Library, Columbia University.

"an evil crusade": *Architectural Record*, September 1953, p. 12.

". . . Messianic complex": July 13, 1953: Avery Architectural Library, Columbia University.

553 ". . . found a friend in you.": T, December 18, 1953.

". . . I dared write . . .": T, November 23, 1953.

"one of the most creative . . .": quotations are from two columns in *The New Yorker*, November 28 and December 12, 1953.

554 "a creative life . . .": *Architectural Forum*, July 1949, p. 14.

"The purpose of the universe . . .": CD, p. 31.

"The decay of art . . .": *Authority and the Individual*, Bertrand Russell, p. 27.

". . . 'Who am I?' ": *The Dynamics of Creativity*, Anthony Storr, p. 289.

Wright's visit to the Cheney house: interviews with Mrs. Joy Corson and Mrs. Joseph Brody.

556 ". . . human relationships.": SM, p. 29.

". . . I am going to call up . . .": William Short papers, Princeton University Archives.

". . . I still cherish memories . . .": T, June 12, 1953.

". . . most special joy": T, September 28, 1953.

Catherine Wright's visit to the exhibition: interview with author.

558 Is not sure Wright would have attended: to author.

559 Adrenals are exhausted: Adelle Davis in *Let's Get Well*, p. 290.
". . . call up Mrs. Wright . . .": Peters to author.
560 The Hilton furnishings: Elizabeth McKee Purdy to author, December 9, 1987.
The inventory of objects in the Plaza Hotel suite was made by William Short, April
24, 1959; Princeton University Archives.
"Plain food!": MAG, p. 10; "After a while . . .": ditto, p. 13.
"If Mr. Wright were alive . . .": to author.
"This was real life . . .": Boris Paskernak, *Dr. Zhivago*, New York: Pantheon, 1958,
p. 164.
". . . Frank is a Lloyd-Jones": MAG, p. 13.
He went to Bangor: CD, p. 31; "special satisfaction": ditto.
561 ". . . I looked back at the gate . . .": A2, p. 441.
562 ". . . 'You never showed . . .": to author.
"I dream of him often . . .": "At Taliesin," *An Uplands Reader*, April 1979, p. 148.

Selected Bibliography

Adamic, Louis: *The Native's Return*. New York: Harper, 1934.

Alliluyeva, Svetlana: *The Faraway Music*. New Delhi: Lancer International, 1984.

Barney, Maginel Wright: *The Valley of the God-Almighty Joneses*. Spring Green: Unity Chapel Publications, 1986.

Baxter Art Gallery: *Myron Hunt, 1868–1952: The Search for a Regional Architecture*. Santa Monica: Hennessey & Ingalls, 1984.

Beeby, Thomas: "The Song of Taliesin." Charlottesville: "Modulus," *University of Virginia Journal of Architecture Review*, 1980, pp. 2–11.

Bennett, J. G.: *Gurdjieff: Making a New World*. New York: Harper, 1973.

Beyer, Oskar (editor): *Eric Mendelsohn: Letters of an Architect*. London: Abelard Schuman, 1967.

Billcliffe, Roger: *Mackintosh Furniture*. New York: Dutton, 1985.

Blake, Peter: *The Master Builders: Le Corbusier, Mies van der Rohe, Frank Lloyd Wright*. New York: W. W. Norton, 1976.

Bolon, Carol R., Nelson, Robert S. and Seidel, Linda (editors): *The Nature of Frank Lloyd Wright*. Chicago: University of Chicago Press, 1988.

Branden, Barbara: *The Passion of Ayn Rand*. New York: Doubleday, 1987.

Briggs, Asa: *A Social History of England*. London: Penguin, 1985.

Brooks, H. Allen: *The Prairie School: Frank Lloyd Wright and His Midwest Contemporaries*. New York: W. W. Norton, 1976.

——— *Frank Lloyd Wright and the Prairie School*. New York: George Braziller, 1984.

——— "Frank Lloyd Wright—Towards a Maturity of Style (1887–1893)." London: AA Files, Architectural Association School of Architecture; no. 2.

——— "Frank Lloyd Wright and the Destruction of the Box." Louisville: *Journal of the Society of Architectural Historians*, March 1979.

——— "Chicago Architecture: Its Debt to the Arts and Crafts." Louisville: *Journal of the Society of Architectural Historians*, December 1971.

——— "The Early Work of the Prairie Architects." Louisville: *Journal of the Society of Architectural Historians*, March 1960.

Brooks, H. Allen (editor): *Writings on Wright*. Cambridge: MIT Press, 1985.

Campbell, Joseph: *The Hero with a Thousand Faces*. Princeton: Princeton University Press, 1949.

Chadwick, Nora: *The Celts*. London: Penguin, 1979.

Clark, Kenneth: *Landscape into Art*. New York: Harper, 1976.

——— *Moments of Vision*. London: John Murray, 1981.

——— *Ruskin Today*. London: Penguin, 1967.

——— *The Romantic Rebellion*. New York: Harper, 1973.

——— *Civilisation*. New York: Harper, 1969.

Connors, Joseph: *The Robie House of Frank Lloyd Wright*. Chicago: University of Chicago Press, 1984.

Conway, Alan: *The Welsh in America: Letters from the Immigrants*. Minneapolis: University of Minnesota Press, 1961.

Cooper, Jackie (editor): *Mackintosh Architecture*. London: St. Martin's Press, 1984.

Crawford, Alan C. R.: *Ashbee: Architect, Designer & Romantic Socialist*. New Haven: Yale University Press, 1985.

Curtis, William J. R.: *Modern Architecture since 1900*. Englewood Cliffs: Prentice-Hall, 1987.

Davies, D. Elwyn: *They Thought for Themselves*. Llandysul: Gomer Press, 1982.

Davies, Phillip G.: *Welsh in Wisconsin*. Madison: The State Historical Society of Wisconsin, 1982.

Derleth, August: *Still Small Voice, the Biography of Zona Gale*. New York: D. Appleton-Century, 1940.

Detroit Institute of Arts: *Design in America, The Cranbrook Vision, 1925–1950*. New York: Harry N. Abrams, 1983.

Dodd, A. H.: *A Short History of Wales*. London: B.T. Batsford, 1987.

Duncan, Alistair: *American Art Deco*. New York: Harry N. Abrams, 1986.

Eaton, Leonard K.: *Two Chicago Architects and Their Clients*. Cambridge: MIT Press, 1969.

Emerson, Ralph Waldo: *Essays and Lectures*. New York: The Library of America, 1983.

Farr, Finis: *Frank Lloyd Wright, A Biography*. New York: Charles Scribner's & Sons, 1961.

Fritz, Herbert: "At Taliesin." Blanchardville: *An Uplands Reader*, April 1979.

Gebhard, David: *Romanza, the California Architecture of Frank Lloyd Wright*. San Francisco: Chronicle Books, 1988.

———— *Lloyd Wright, Architect*. Santa Barbara: University of California, 1971.

———— "C. F. A. Voysey—To and From America." Louisville, *Journal of the Society of Architectural Historians*, December 1971.

Giedion, Sigfried: *Space, Time and Architecture*. Cambridge: Harvard University Press, 1941, 1962, 1967 and 1974.

Gill, Brendan: *Many Masks: A Life of Frank Lloyd Wright*. New York: G.P. Putnam's Sons, 1987.

Graham, Thomas: *Trilogy: Through Their Eyes*. Spring Green: Unity Chapel Publications; 1986.

———— "Jenkin Lloyd Jones and 'The Gospel of the Farm.' " Madison: *The Wisconsin Magazine of History*, winter 1983–1984.

Gutheim, Frederick (editor): *In the Cause of Architecture: Frank Lloyd Wright*. New York: Architectural Record Books, 1975.

———— *Frank Lloyd Wright on Architecture: Selected Writings, 1894–1940*. New York: Duell, Sloan & Pearce, 1941.

Hamilton, Mary Jane: *The Lloyd Joneses in America: Their First Half Century*. Privately circulated.

Hanks, David A.: *The Decorative Designs of Frank Lloyd Wright*. New York: Dutton, 1979.

———— *Frank Lloyd Wright: Architectural Drawings and Decorative Art*. Middlesex: The Hillingdon Press, 1985.

———— "The Decorative Designs of Frank Lloyd Wright." Chicago: *Frank Lloyd Wright Newsletter*, second quarter 1979.

Hanna, Paul R. and Jean S.: *Frank Lloyd Wright's Hanna House*. Carbondale: Southern Illinois University Press, 1987.

De Hartmann, Thomas and Olga: *Our Life with Mr. Gurdjieff*. New York: Harper, 1964.

Hartmann, Edward George: *Americans From Wales*. Boston, Christopher Publishing House, 1967.

Harris, Leslie: *Robert Adam and Kedleston*. London: The National Trust, 1987.

Heinz, Thomas A.: *Frank Lloyd Wright*. New York: St. Martin's Press, 1982.

Herbert, Trevor and Jones, Gareth Elwyn: *People & Protest: Wales, 1815–1880*. Cardiff: University of Wales Press, 1988.

Hewison, Robert: *John Ruskin: the Argument of the Eye*. Princeton: Princeton University Press, 1976.

Hines, Thomas S.: *Richard Neutra & the Search for Modern Architecture*. New York: OUP, 1982.

Hitchcock, Henry-Russell: *In the Nature of Materials: The Buildings of Frank Lloyd Wright, 1887–1941*. New York: Da Capo, 1986.

―――― *The Architecture of H. H. Richardson and His Times*. Cambridge: MIT Press, 1966.

―――― "Frank Lloyd Wright and the 'Academic Tradition' of the Early Eighteen-Nineties." London: *Journal of the Warburg & Courtauld Institutes*, January–June 1944.

Hoffmann, Donald: *Frank Lloyd Wright's Fallingwater*. New York: Dover, 1978.

―――― *Frank Lloyd Wright's Robie House*. New York: Dover, 1984.

―――― *Frank Lloyd Wright: Architecture and Nature*. New York: Dover, 1986.

Honour, Hugh and Fleming, John: *The Visual Arts: A History*. Englewood Cliffs: Prentice-Hall, 1982.

Howe, John H.: "Reflections of Taliesin." *Northwest Architect*, July–August 1969.

Hubert, Henri: *The Rise of the Celts; The Greatness and Decline of the Celts*. London: Constable, 1987.

Hughes, Robert: *The Shock of the New*. New York: Alfred A. Knopf, 1981.

Humphreys, Emyr: *The Taliesin Tradition*. London: Black Raven Press, 1983.

Jacobs, Herbert, with Jacobs, Katherine: *Building with Frank Lloyd Wright*. Carbondale: Southern Illinois University Press, 1986.

Jones, Anthony: *Welsh Chapels*. Cardiff: National Museum of Wales, 1984.

Jordy, William H.: *The Impact of European Modernism in the Mid-Twentieth Century*. New York: Oxford University Press, 1986.

Jung, Carl G.: *Man and His Symbols*. New York: Doubleday, 1964.

Kaplan, Wendy: *'The Art that Is Life': The Arts & Crafts Movement in America*. Boston: Museum of Fine Arts, 1987.

Kaufmann, Edgar, and Raeburn, Ben: *Frank Lloyd Wright: Writings and Buildings*. Cleveland: The World Publishing Company, 1969

Kiser, Heidi, (editor): *Lloyd Letters & Memorial Book*. Privately printed, 1986.

Klein, Dan, McClelland, Nancy A., and Haslam, Malcolm: *In the Deco Style*. London: Thames and Hudson, 1987.

Kornwolf, James D.: *M. H. Baillie Scott and the Arts & Crafts Movement*. Baltimore: Johns Hopkins Press, 1972.

Lipman, Jonathan: *Frank Lloyd Wright and the Johnson Wax Buildings*. New York: Rizzoli, 1986.

Lukach, Joan M.: *Hilla Rebay: In Search of the Spirit in Art*. New York: George Braziller, 1983.

Makinson, Randell L.: *Greene & Greene. Architecture as a Fine Art*. Salt Lake City: Peregrine Smith, 1977.

Manson, Grant Carpenter: *Frank Lloyd Wright to 1910. The First Golden Age*. New York: Van Nostrand Reinhold, 1958.

Marquis, Alice Goldfarb: *Alfred H. Barr Jr., Missionary for the Modern*. Chicago: Contemporary Books, 1989.

McCormick, Donald: *The Mask of Merlin. A Critical Biography of David Lloyd George*. New York: Holt, Rinehart & Winston, 1963.

Meehan, Patrick J. (editor): *The Master Architect. Conversations with Frank Lloyd Wright*. New York: John Wiley, 1984.

The Metropolitan Museum of Art: *In Pursuit of Beauty: Americans and the Aesthetic Movement*. New York: Rizzoli, 1986.

Meudt, Edna: *The Rose Jar, The Autobiography of Edna Meudt*. Madison: North Country Press, 1990.

Miller, Donald L.: *Lewis Mumford, A Life*. New York: Weidenfeld & Nicolson, 1989.

Morris, Jan: *The Matter of Wales*. New York: Oxford University Press, 1984.

Muschamp, Herbert: *Man About Town: Frank Lloyd Wright in New York City*. Cambridge: MIT Press, 1983.

Musto, David F.: *The American Disease. Origins of Narcotics Control*. New Haven: Yale University Press, 1973.

Neutra, Dione (editor): *Richard Neutra: Promise and Fulfillment, 1919–1932*. Carbondale: Southern Illinois University Press, 1986.

Nott, C. S.: *Teachings of Gurdjieff*. York Beach: Samuel Weiser, 1982.

——— *Further Teachings of Gurdjieff*. York Beach: Samuel Weiser, 1984.

Pappas, Bette Koprivica: *No Passing Fancy*. St. Louis: privately printed, 1985.

Pater, Walter: *The Renaissance*. London: Fontana/Collins, 1975.

Pevsner, Nikolaus: *Pioneers of Modern Design*. London: Penguin, 1986.

Pfeiffer, Bruce Brooks (editor): *Frank Lloyd Wright: The Crowning Decade, 1949–1959*. Fresno: The Press at California State University, 1989.

——— *Frank Lloyd Wright: His Living Voice*. Fresno: The Press at California State University, 1987.

——— *Frank Lloyd Wright: Letters to Apprentices*. Fresno: The Press at California State University, 1982.

——— *Frank Lloyd Wright: Letters to Architects*. Fresno: The Press at California State University, 1984.

——— *Frank Lloyd Wright: Letters to Clients*. Fresno: The Press at California State University, 1986.

——— *Frank Lloyd Wright: The Guggenheim Correspondence*. Carbondale: Southern Illinois University Press, 1986.

——— *Frank Lloyd Wright in the Realm of Ideas*. Carbondale: Southern Illinois University Press, 1988.

Porter, Franklin and Mary (editors): *Heritage: The Lloyd Jones Family*. Spring Green: Unity Chapel Publications, 1986.

Powell, T. G. E.: *The Celts*. London: Thames and Hudson, 1980.

Quinan, Jack: *Frank Lloyd Wright's Larkin Building*. Cambridge: MIT Press, 1987.

Rand, Ayn: *The Fountainhead*. New York: New American Library, 1971.

Raymond, Antonin: *Antonin Raymond: An Autobiography*. Rutland: Charles E. Tuttle, 1973.

Reed, Henry Hope: *The Golden City*. New York, W. W. Norton, 1971.

Rybczynski, Witold: *Home: A Short History of an Idea*. New York: Penguin, 1987.

Schapiro, Meyer: *Modern Art: 19th and 20th Centuries*. New York: Braziller, 1978.

Scott, Geoffrey: *The Architecture of Humanism*. London: The Architectural Press, 1980.

Scully, Vincent, Jr.: *Frank Lloyd Wright*. New York: Braziller, 1985.

——— *The Shingle Style and the Stick Style*. New Haven: Yale University Press, 1971.

Sergeant, John: *Frank Lloyd Wright's Usonian Houses*. New York: Watson-Guptill, 1984.

Smith, Norris Kelly: *Frank Lloyd Wright: A Study in Architectural Content*. Englewood Cliffs: Prentice-Hall, 1966.

Soleri, Paolo: *Matter Becoming Spirit*. New York: Doubleday, 1973.

Spencer, Brian A. (editor): *The Prairie School Tradition*. New York: Watson-Guptill, 1985.

Sprague, Paul E.: *Guide to Frank Lloyd Wright & Prairie School Architecture in Oak Park*. Oak Park Bicentennial Commission, 1986.

Stamp, Gavin, and Goulancourt, Andre: *The English House, 1860–1914*. London: Faber and Faber, 1986.

Stein, Roger B.: *John Ruskin and Aesthetic Thought in America, 1840–1900*. Cambridge: Harvard University Press, 1967.

Stickley, Gustav: *Craftsman Homes*. New York: Dover, 1979.

Storr, Anthony: *The Dynamics of Creation*. London: Penguin, 1986.

Storrer, William Allin: *The Architecture of Frank Lloyd Wright*. Cambridge: MIT Press, 1986.

Sullivan, Louis H.: *The Autobiography of an Idea*. New York: Dover, 1956.

———— *Kindergarten Chats and Other Writings*. New York: Dover, 1979.

Sweeney, Robert L.: *Frank Lloyd Wright: An Annotated Bibliography*. Los Angeles: Hennessey & Ingalls, 1978.

Tafel, Edgar: *Years with Frank Lloyd Wright: Apprentice to Genius*. New York: Dover, 1979.

Thomas, Richard H.: *Jenkin Lloyd Jones: Lincoln's Soldier of Civic Righteousness*. Ann Arbor: University Microfilms, 1967.

Tolstoy, Nikolai: *The Quest for Merlin*. Boston: Little, Brown, 1985.

Twombly, Robert C.: *Frank Lloyd Wright: His Life and His Architecture*. New York: John Wiley, 1979.

———— *Louis Sullivan: His Life & Work*. Chicago: University of Chicago Press, 1986.

———— *Frank Lloyd Wright in Spring Green, 1911–1932*. Madison: State Historical Society of Wisconsin, 1980.

Von Holst, Hermann Valentin: *Country and Suburban Homes of the Prairie School Period*. New York: Dover, 1982.

Webb, James: *The Harmonious Circle*. Boston: Shambhala, 1987.

Williams, David: *The Rebecca Riots*. Cardiff: University of Wales Press, 1955.

Williams, Gwyn A.: *The Search for Beulah Land*. New York: Homes and Meier, 1980.

Williams-Ellis, Clough: *Portmeirion*. London: Faber and Faber, 1963.

Winter, Robert: *The California Bungalow*. Los Angeles: Hennessey & Ingalls, 1980.

De Wit, Wim: *Louis Sullivan: The Function of Ornament*. New York: W. W. Norton, 1986.

Wright, Frank Lloyd: *An Autobiography*. New York: Longmans, Green, 1932; Duell, Sloan and Pearce, 1943; Horizon Press, 1977.

———— *The Early Work of Frank Lloyd Wright: The 'Ausgefuhrte Bauten' of 1911*. New York: Dover, 1982.

———— *The Living City*. New York: New American Library, 1958.

———— *The Natural House*. New York: Horizon Press, 1954.

———— *Genius and the Mobocracy*. New York: Horizon Press, 1971.

———— *An American Architecture*. New York: Bramhall House, 1955.

———— *The Future of Architecture*. New York: Horizon Press, 1953.

———— *A Testament*. New York: Horizon Press, 1957.

Wright, John Lloyd: *My Father Who Is on Earth*. New York: Putnam's, 1946.

Wright, Olgivanna Lloyd: *The Shining Brow*. New York: Horizon Press, 1960.

———— *Frank Lloyd Wright: His Life, His Work, His Words*. New York: Horizon Press, 1966.

———— *The Struggle Within*. New York: Horizon Press, 1955.

———— *Our House*. New York: Horizon Press, 1959.

Index

Numerals in italics indicate illustrations.

PICTURE CREDITS

David Jones: 23 above, 23 below, 27 below, 28 below, 134 below. Meadville/Lombard Theological School Library: 27 above. State Historical Society of Wisconsin: 28 above, 45 above, 45 below, 60, 80, 97 below, 98 above, 98 below, 141, 143, 157 above, 183 above, 196 below, 227 above, 228 above and below, 256 below, 279, 290 above, 362 above, 432 below, 433 below, 534 above and below. Meryle Secrest: 97 above. Oak Park Home and Studio: 99 above, 192, 126 above. Mrs. Robert L. Wright: 99 below, 191, 509, 547 inset. Historic American Buildings Survey: 109 below, 115 top left, 115 top right, 126 below, 133, 165 below, 173 above, 173 below left, 262 below, 263. Richard Nickel: 115 below. Avery Architectural Library: 125 above and below, 418. Oak Park Public Library: 139, 196 above. Ausgefuhrte Bauten und Entwurfe von Frank Lloyd Wright: 166, 173 below right. © 1979 Frank Lloyd Wright Foundation: 167 above and below. Northwest University Library: 174 above, 229 above, 229 below, 455 above, 471 center, 471 below, 478. State University of New York: 175, 176 above and below. Art Institute of Chicago, Ryerson and Burnham Libraries: 184 below, 256 above, 227 below, 527, 562 below. © 1991 Frank Lloyd Wright Foundation: 183 below, 227 below, 527. Jerry A. McCoy, © 1990: 257. Virginia Ernst Kazor: 262 above. Library of Congress: 321 above. Stanford University Libraries: 321 below. Arizona Biltmore: 351 above and below, 352 above and below. Tulsa Tribune: 362 below, 362 inset. John H. Howe: 404, 504. Harold Corsini: 417 above. Madison Capital Times: 54, 455 below, 516 above and below, 546 above. Johnson Wax: 456 above and below, 457 above. Wisconsin State Journal: 520 above. District of Columbia Public Library: 546. William H. Short, FAIA: 546 below, 547 above. © 1992 Frank Lloyd Wright Foundation: 562 below. Milwaukee Journal: 562–3.

A NOTE ON THE TYPE

The text of this book is set in Garamond No. 3. It is not a true copy
of any of the designs of Claude Garamond (1480–1561), but an
adaptation of his types, which set the European standard for two
centuries. It probably owes as much to the designs of Jean Jannon,
a Protestant printer working in Sedan in the early seventeenth century,
who had worked with Garamond's romans earlier, in Paris, and who
was denied their use because of the Catholic censorship. Jannon's
matrices came into the possession of the Imprimerie Nationale, where
they were thought to be by Garamond himself, and so described when
the Imprimerie revived the type in 1900. This particular version is
based on an adaptation by Morris Fuller Benton.

Composed by PennSet, Inc., Bloomsburg, Pennsylvania
Printed and bound by Halliday Lithographers,
West Hanover, Massachusetts